HOMILIES OF ÆLFRIC

A Supplementary Collection

EARLY ENGLISH TEXT SOCIETY

No. 259

1967

PRICE 84s.

British Museum MS. Cotton Vitellius C. v, f. 17ᵛ. The beginning of homily I in interpolator's hand on erasure following *CH* I, II in the original hand.

for hir lufon · rehte leofað ·] mixað abucan eno

DOMINICA · III · IN QUADRAGESIMA   Erat ihc eici

On þære mænan tide þære mild heorta hæleno þ
num onroðþe mennisc nytte punopa þ ymcen
ge broht to rum þit reoc man punooplice geop
lice be næmeð hir ge rihð] ppæc ·] he rpa ð
deoplice þeooe; þæt þa re mild heorta cryrt
oan mihte þone mann ge hælðe] ðone hæela
ffram aðpæfoe þehine opehte oððæ ·] heþa
] ge hyroe ·] eall reo meniu micclum þær puno
þa inoeircan þ uþe opuhten rceolðe þa punopa j
deopler mihte þemen hataþ beel Zebub achi
Sume hi poloon eac þ he rum fyllic racen opl
eopoe · ac he cþæþ himto þaða hege reah heoþi
ge þohtar; Ælc cyne þice þebið onhim fylfum
lice to porþen] ne þunaþ na onribbe] hir þæ
hir pæ oene; Gifre rceocca poðlice ir onhim þj
hu mæg þonne ranoan hir þice rtaþolfært; (

Corpus Christi College, Cambridge, MS. 188, p. 123. The beginning of homily IV
in the main hand, following *CH* I, XI.

HOMILIES OF ÆLFRIC

A Supplementary Collection

BEING TWENTY-ONE FULL HOMILIES OF
HIS MIDDLE AND LATER CAREER
FOR THE MOST PART
NOT PREVIOUSLY EDITED

WITH SOME SHORTER PIECES

MAINLY PASSAGES ADDED TO THE
SECOND AND THIRD SERIES

Edited from all the known manuscripts
With Introduction, Notes, Latin Sources
and a Glossary by

JOHN C. POPE

VOLUME I

Published for
THE EARLY ENGLISH TEXT SOCIETY
by the
OXFORD UNIVERSITY PRESS
LONDON   NEW YORK   TORONTO
1967

PRINTED IN GREAT BRITAIN
AT THE UNIVERSITY PRESS, OXFORD
BY VIVIAN RIDLER
PRINTER TO THE UNIVERSITY

PREFACE

THIS edition, of which I have sketched the background in the introduction, is the outgrowth of a study of some of the Ælfric manuscripts which I first undertook in 1927 as a doctoral dissertation under the supervision of the late Robert J. Menner. His impressive learning and wise counsel were ever at the service of his pupils and colleagues as long as he lived, and my debt to him is far greater than can well be evident in the ensuing pages. In 1931 I had the further good fortune to enlist the friendly interest and encouragement of Dr. Kenneth Sisam, whose familiarity with the Ælfric manuscripts long antedated my tentative explorations. A few years afterwards the late Max Förster gave me helpful advice out of his vast store of pertinent learning. These three scholars were my earliest guides, and they helped me to persist in spite of many unforeseen interruptions.

I wish to thank the owners and custodians of the manuscripts to which I have had access in London, Cambridge, and Oxford for their many good offices, including the permission to assemble a large collection of photostats and to print the relevant texts. I remember with particular gratitude the late Sir Edwyn Hoskyns of Corpus Christi College, Cambridge, whose kindness never failed despite my frequent demands upon it—once for months on end—between 1927 and 1933. To the authorities at the British Museum, the Bodleian, and two of the Cambridge colleges, Corpus Christi and Trinity, I owe additional thanks for permission to include the seven illustrations. My obligation to the librarian of the Bibliothèque Publique at Boulogne-sur-Mer is separately acknowledged on page 409 below.

It is with great regret that I mention here, rather than on the title-page, the contribution of Professor Edna R. Williams of Smith College. Between 1948 and 1951 she was actively engaged, as my collaborator, in translating the homilies. The translations had been projected as a part of the edition; but in 1951, when Miss Williams had already made great progress, a change of policy on the part of the Society forced us to abandon the translations and Miss Williams decided to withdraw rather than transfer her attention to other parts of the edition. Although her work has thus borne no visible fruit, my own understanding of the homilies has been sharpened at many points by her erudite and sensitive interpretations.

In preparing the edition for the press I have had expert assistance from three of my former pupils, Dr. Edgar S. Cahn, Dr. Frances Randall Lipp, and Mr. Robert K. Diebold. All three helped with the more difficult parts of the typing and made valuable contributions as readers. Mr. Diebold, who typed a large part of the glossary, assisted also in its compilation.

I owe much to the efforts of all those who have been concerned with the last stages of publication: to the skill and care of the printer and his staff, and to the members of the Council of the Society, several of whom have kept a watchful eye on the proofs. The honorary secretary, Mr. R. W. Burchfield, has been unfailingly attentive to every detail, and I have been saved from several errors and omissions by Professor Norman Davis, Professor Dorothy Whitelock, and especially Mr. N. R. Ker.

In the introduction I have acknowledged the very large debt I owe to Dr. Peter Clemoes for his invaluable analysis of the textual relationships of the manuscripts. The debt has been increased by his extremely careful scrutiny of the proofs of the introduction. I have incorporated nearly all his suggested revisions, to the great advantage in clarity and accuracy of many passages.

Particular mention will be found in the pages below of the generous help I have had from Professor J. E. Cross, Professor Stephan Kuttner, and Mme Jacqueline Rambaud of the Bibliothèque Nationale in Paris. Miss Celia Sisam most kindly verified some readings about which I was in doubt in MS. Hatton 115.

It is beyond my power to give adequate thanks to those nearest to me for their practical assistance, their comfort, and their forbearance. I must mention in particular my friend and colleague, Professor E. T. Donaldson, on whom I have imposed dozens of petty problems of the sort that plague an editor from day to day, and from whose learning and discretion I have profited at every turn.

J. C. P.

New Haven, Connecticut
June 1966

CONTENTS

VOLUME ONE

VOLUME TWO

THE HOMILIES FOR THE PROPER OF THE SEASON (*cont.*)

THE HOMILIES FOR UNSPECIFIED OCCASIONS

ILLUSTRATIONS

VOLUME I

VOLUME II

ABBREVIATIONS AND SHORT TITLES

Admonitio ad Filium Spiritualem Ælfric's version, in rhythmic prose, imperfectly preserved in MS. Hatton 76 and printed in *The Anglo-Saxon Version of the Hexameron of St. Basil ... and the Saxon Remains of St. Basil's Admonitio ad Filium Spiritualem*, ed. by Henry W. Norman (London, 1848), pp. 31–55.

Assmann *Angelsächsische Homilien und Heiligenleben*, hrsg. von Bruno Assmann. Kassel, 1889. (Bibliothek der angelsächsischen Prosa, III.) Reprinted, with supplementary introduction by Peter Clemoes, Darmstadt, 1964. Articles I–IX are by Ælfric; X–XIX by other writers. Cited by number of article and line.

Belfour *Twelfth Century Homilies in MS. Bodley 343*, ed. by A. O. Belfour. EETS, o.s. 137. London, 1909. Cited by number of article.

Bethurum *The Homilies of Wulfstan*, ed. by Dorothy Bethurum (Mrs. Roger Loomis). Oxford, 1957. Cited by number of article and line.

Bosworth–Toller *An Anglo-Saxon Dictionary*, by J. Bosworth and T. N. Toller. Oxford, 1898. *Supplement* by T. N. Toller. Oxford, 1921.

Brotanek *Texte und Untersuchungen zur altenglischen Literatur und Kirchengeschichte*, von Rudolf Brotanek. Halle, 1913. The two homilies printed on pp. 3–27 and numbered I. 1 and 2, are cited as Brotanek I and II respectively.

BT, BTS The Bosworth–Toller *Dictionary* and *Supplement*, as above. BT includes both unless there is explicit mention of BTS also.

Campbell *Old English Grammar*, by A. Campbell. Oxford, 1959. Corrected reprint, 1962. Cited by paragraph.

CCSL Corpus Christianorum, Series Latina.

CH = Catholic Homilies *The Homilies of the Anglo-Saxon Church. The First Part, Containing the Sermones Catholici, or Homilies of Ælfric*, ed. by Benjamin Thorpe. 2 vols. London, 1844, 1846. Cited by volume (I, II) and number of article (roman, small caps.) or page and line. If there is reason to distinguish between Ælfric's two series of homilies (*CH* I, *CH* II) and the edition, or to refer to extra matter at the end (II. 596 sqq.) Thorpe I and II, with page (and line) are used.

Cleasby–Vigfusson *An Icelandic–English Dictionary*, by R. Cleasby and G. Vigfusson. 2nd ed. with a Supplement by Sir William A. Craigie, Oxford, 1957.

Clemoes, *Chronology* 'The Chronology of Ælfric's Works', by P. A. M. Clemoes, in *The Anglo-Saxons. Studies in Some Aspects of their History and Culture presented to Bruce Dickins*, ed. by Peter Clemoes (London, 1959), pp. 212–47.

Colloquy Ælfric's Colloquy, ed. by G. N. Garmonsway. Methuen's Old English Library. 2nd ed. London, 1947.

Cpb = Campbell, as above.

Crawford See *Hexameron* and *Old English Heptateuch.*

CSEL   Corpus Scriptorum Ecclesiasticorum Latinorum.

De Cogitatione A detached paragraph by Ælfric published by A. S. Napier, *Anglia*, X(1888), 155. The first 8 lines are collated for homily VI and the remainder is printed in the note on VI. 284.

De Duodecim Abusivis Ælfric's version, in rhythmical prose, of a Latin tract falsely attributed to Cyprian and others. The best printed text is in Morris, *Old English Homilies*, pp. 299/1–304, as the second part of an unauthorized compilation, *De Octo Vitiis et de Duodecim Abusivis*, found in MS. R and elsewhere. For the Latin original see S. Hellmann, *Pseudo-Cyprianus de xii abusivis saeculi*, in *Texte und Untersuchungen zur Geschichte der altchristlichen Literatur*, Reihe 3, Bd. 4, Hft. 1 (Leipzig, 1909), pp. 1–62.

De Infantibus An Old English admonition published by A. S. Napier, *Anglia*, X(1888), 154 sq. Attributed to Ælfric below, pp. 55–56.

De Sanguine Part of an Old English letter published by F. Kluge, *Englische Studien*, VIII (1885), 62 sq. Attributed to Ælfric below, pp. 56–57.

De Septiformi Spiritu Brief tract by Ælfric in Latin (Napier VII) and Old English (Napier VIII). An Old English adaptation by Wulfstan fills the remainder of Napier VII.

De Temporibus Anni Ælfric's *De Temporibus Anni*, ed. by H. Henel. EETS 213. London, 1942.

Dietrich 'Abt Aelfrik: Zur Literatur-Geschichte der angelsächsischen Kirche', von Eduard Dietrich. Niedner's *Zeitschrift für historische Theologie*, XXV (1855), 487–594; XXVI (1856), 163–256.

Dubois *Ælfric: Sermonnaire, docteur et grammairien*, par Marguerite-Marie Dubois. Paris, 1942.

EETS Early English Text Society.

Fehr *Die Hirtenbriefe Ælfrics*, hrsg. von Bernhard Fehr. Hamburg, 1914. (Bibliothek der angelsächsischen Prosa, IX.) Reprinted, with supplement by Peter Clemoes, Darmstadt, 1966. The volume is cited as *Hirtenbriefe*; individual letters, in the order printed, as *Brief* I (for Wulfsige); *Brief* 2, 3 (Latin letters for Wulfstan); *Brief* II, III (OE letters for Wulfstan); *Brief* 2a (Latin letter to Wulfstan).

Förster, Max 'Über die Quellen von Ælfrics exegetischen Homiliae Catholicae', *Anglia*, XVI (1894), 1–61. Cited by page unless paragraphs are specified. A sequel to Förster's dissertation, *Über die Quellen von Ælfric's Homiliae Catholicae. I. Legenden*. Berlin, 1892. This contains §§ 1–38; the sequel begins with § 39.

Grammar Ælfrics Grammatik und Glossar, hrsg. von J. Zupitza. Berlin, 1880.

Hall-Meritt *A Concise Anglo-Saxon Dictionary*, by J. R. Clark Hall. 4th ed. with a Supplement by Herbert D. Meritt. Cambridge, 1960.

Hexameron Ælfric's Exameron Anglice, or The Old English Hexameron, ed. by S. J. Crawford. Hamburg, 1921. (Bibliothek der angelsächsischen Prosa, X.)

Holthausen *Altenglisches etymologisches Wörterbuch*, von F. Holthausen. Heidelberg, 1934. 2nd ed., 1963, unaltered except for bibliographical supplement.

Interrogationes Sigewulfi G. E. MacLean, 'Ælfric's Version of Alcuini Interrogationes Sigeuulfi in Genesin', *Anglia*, VI (1883), 425–73 (introduction) and VII (1884), 1–59 (text). Also separately printed, Halle, 1883.

JEGP Journal of English and Germanic Philology.

Jost, Karl (a) *Polity* = *Die 'Institutes of Polity, Civil and Ecclesiastical', ein Werk Erzbischof Wulfstans von York*. Bern, 1959. (Schweizer anglistische Arbeiten, 47.) (b) *Wulfstanstudien*. Bern, 1950. (Schweizer anglistische Arbeiten, 23.)

Judges Ælfric's homiletic version of the O.T. *Judges*, in Crawford's *Old English Heptateuch*, pp. 401–17.

Kemble, *Salomon and Saturn* The Dialogue of Salomon and Saturnus, by John M. Kemble. London, 1848.

Ker, *Catalogue* Catalogue of Manuscripts Containing Anglo-Saxon, by N. R. Ker. Oxford, 1957. Normally cited by catalogue number.

Leechdoms T. O. Cockayne, *Leechdoms, Wortcunning, and Starcraft of Early England* (Rolls Series, 35). 3 vols., London, 1864–6.

Letter to the Monks of Eynsham 'Excerpta ex Institutionibus Monasticis Æthelwoldi Episcopi Wintoniensis Compilata in Usum Fratrum Egneshamnensium per Ælfricum Abbatem', transcribed and edited by Mary Bateson. In G. W. Kitchin, *Compotus Rolls of the Obedientiaries of St. Swithun's Priory, Winchester* (London, 1892), pp. 171–98.

Letter to Sigefyrth By Ælfric. Assmann II.

Letter to Sigeweard By Ælfric. See *Old and New Testament*.

Letter to Wulfgeat By Ælfric. Assmann I.

Letter for Wulfsige By Ælfric. See Fehr.

Letters to and *for Wulfstan* By Ælfric. See Fehr.

Liebermann, *Gesetze* Die Gesetze der Angelsachsen, hrsg. von F. Liebermann. 3 vols. Halle, 1903–16. Unveränderter Neudruck, Scientia Aalen, 1960.

LS = *Lives of Saints* Ælfric's Lives of Saints, ed. by W. W. Skeat. EETS, o.s. 76, 82, 94, 114. 2 vols., London, 1881–1900. Reprinted, as 2 vols., 1966. (The word *Metrical* has always been included in the title as listed by the Society but Skeat seems to have left it out before Part I was published, doubtless because some of the lives he included are in ordinary prose.) Usually cited by number of article and line. Vol. I has I–XXIII; vol. II has XXIII B–XXXVII.

Luick, Karl *Historische Grammatik der englischen Sprache*. Erster Band. Leipzig, 1914–21 (I. Abteilung), 1929–40 (II. Abteilung, completed after Luick's death by Friedrich Wild and Herbert Koziol). Reprinted, with an index by Richard Hamer, Oxford and Stuttgart, 1964.

McIntosh, Angus *Wulfstan's Prose*. Sir Israel Gollancz Memorial Lecture, British Academy 1948 (*read* 11 May 1949). *Proceedings of the British Academy*, XXXV (1949), 109–42. References are to the separate printing, London: G. Cumberlege, n.d., pp. 3–36.

MED Middle English Dictionary, ed. by H. Kurath, S. M. Kuhn, and others. Michigan, 1952– (in progress).

Migne, *PL, PG Patrologia Latina* and *Graeca* respectively, ed. by J. P. Migne. Paris, various years.

MLR *Modern Language Review.*

Morris *Old English Homilies,* ed. by Richard Morris. First Series. EETS, o.s. 29, 34. London, 1867–8.

Napier (*a*) *Wulfstan: Sammlung der ihm zugeschriebenen Homilien nebst Untersuchungen über ihre Echtheit,* hrsg. von Arthur Napier. Erste Abteilung: Text und Varianten. Berlin, 1883. (No more published.) Cited by number of article. (*b*) *COEL* = 'Contributions to Old English Lexicography' by A. S. Napier in *Transactions of the Philological Society,* *1903–6,* pp. 265–352.

OE Old English.

OED Oxford English Dictionary.

O.E. Hept. or *Old English Heptateuch* *The Old English Version of the Heptateuch, Ælfric's Treatise on the Old and New Testament and his Preface to Genesis,* ed. by S. J. Crawford. EETS, o.s. 160. London, 1922.

Old and New Testament (*ONT*) Ælfric's *Letter to Sigeweard, On the Old and New Testament,* in *O.E. Hept.,* pp. 15–80.

Old English Bede *The Old English Version of Bede's Ecclesiastical History of the English People,* ed. by Thomas Miller. EETS, o.s. 95, 96. London, 1890–1 (reprinted 1959).

Old English Homilies See Morris.

ON Old Norse.

ONT See *Old and New Testament.*

Paris Psalter The Metrical Psalms of the Paris Psalter, in *The Paris Psalter and the Meters of Boethius,* ed. by G. P. Krapp. New York, 1932. (The Anglo-Saxon Poetic Records, V.)

PL See Migne.

RES *Review of English Studies.*

Riddles The riddles of the Exeter Book, in *The Exeter Book,* ed. by G. P. Krapp and E. V. K. Dobbie. New York, 1936. (The Anglo-Saxon Poetic Records, III.)

S-B = Sievers-Brunner *Altenglische Grammatik nach der angelsächsischen Grammatik von Eduard Sievers,* neugearbeitet von Karl Brunner. 3rd ed., Tübingen, 1965. Cited by paragraph.

Sermo ad Anglos *Sermo Lupi ad Anglos,* ed. by Dorothy Whitelock. 2nd ed., revised. Methuen's Old English Library. London, 1963. Also in Bethurum, *Homilies of Wulfstan,* xx (three versions).

Sisam, *Studies* *Studies in the History of Old English Literature,* by Kenneth Sisam. Oxford, 1953.

Skeat See *LS.*

Solomon and Saturn *The Poetical Dialogues of Solomon and Saturn,* ed. by Robert J. Menner. New York, 1941. (Modern Language Association of America, Monograph Series, XIII.) Not the same as Kemble, above.

Thorpe See *CH.*

Vita S. Æthelwoldi Ælfric's Latin life of Bishop Æthelwold I of Winchester, in *Chronicon Monasterii de Abingdon,* ed. by Joseph Stevenson (Rolls Series 2), London, 1858, II. 253–66.

Walde-Pokorny Alois Walde, *Vergleichendes Wörterbuch der indoger-*

manischen Sprachen, hrsg. und bearbeitet von Julius Pokorny. 3 vols. Berlin and Leipzig, 1927, etc.

Wanley, *Catalogus Humphredi Wanleii Librorum Vett. Septentrionalium . . . Catalogus*, the *Liber Alter* in vol. III of *Linguarum Vett. Septentrionalium Thesaurus*, by George Hickes, Oxford, 1705.

Warner *Early English Homilies from the Twelfth Century MS. Vesp. D. xiv*, ed. by Rubie D–N. Warner. EETS, o.s. 152. London, 1917.

West Saxon Gospels   *The Gospels in West-Saxon*, ed. by J. W. Bright. 4 vols. Belles-Lettres Series, Boston, 1904–6. Also in *The Holy Gospels in Anglo-Saxon, Northumbrian, and Old Mercian Versions*, ed. by W. W. Skeat. Cambridge, 1871–87.

Wordsworth and White   *Nouum Testamentum . . . Latine*, ed. by J. Wordsworth and H. I. White. Pars prior—Quattuor Euangelia. Oxford, 1889–98.

SIGLA OF THE MANUSCRIPTS

B Bodleian MS. Bodley 343.
C Corpus Christi College, Cambridge, MS. 303.
D Bodleian MS. Bodley 342.
E Corpus Christi College, Cambridge, MS. 198.
F Corpus Christi College, Cambridge, MS. 162.
G British Museum, MS. Cotton Vespasian D. xiv.
H British Museum, MS. Cotton Vitellius C. v.
J British Museum, MS. Cotton Cleopatra B. xiii.
K University Library, Cambridge, MS. Gg. 3. 28.
L University Library, Cambridge, MS. Ii. 1. 33.
M University Library, Cambridge, MS. Ii. 4. 6.
N British Museum, MS. Cotton Faustina A. ix.
O Corpus Christi College, Cambridge, MS. 302.
P Bodleian MS. Hatton 115.
Q Corpus Christi College, Cambridge, MS. 188.
R Corpus Christi College, Cambridge, MS. 178.
S Bodleian MS. Hatton 116.
T (Junius 121) Bodleian MS. Junius 121.
T (113) Bodleian MS. Hatton 113.
T (114) Bodleian MS. Hatton 114.
U Trinity College, Cambridge, MS. B. 15. 34.
V (419) Corpus Christi College, Cambridge, MS. 419.
V (421) Corpus Christi College, Cambridge, MS. 421.
W British Museum, MS. Cotton Julius E. vii.
Z Bodleian MS. Laud Misc. 509.
X^d British Museum, MS. Cotton Otho C. i, vol. 2.
X^k Bibliothèque Nationale, Paris, MS. Lat. 7585.
f^b Jesus College, Cambridge, MS. 15.

INTRODUCTION

1. BACKGROUND AND AIM OF THIS EDITION: SELECTION OF TEXTS

THE principal aim of this edition, though imperfectly realized, has been to make available all the previously unedited homiletic work that can justly be attributed to Ælfric. A good many of the Old English homilies still extant in manuscripts of the eleventh and twelfth centuries have remained unprinted, and it has long been known or supposed that some of these were by Ælfric. Certainly this part of his literary output was by no means limited to the three imposing series which have been preserved more or less faithfully as such, with attesting prefaces: namely, the two series of *Sermones Catholici* edited from the most complete of the surviving manuscripts by Thorpe,[1] now generally called, as here, the *Catholic Homilies*; and the *Lives of Saints*, represented less accurately by the manuscript on which Skeat based his edition.[2] Some additional homilies, homiletic letters, and tracts have found their way into print at various times from the seventeenth century to the twentieth. These, still inconveniently scattered and unevenly edited, are enumerated below in section 6.[3] A few of them were first identified by Dietrich when he surveyed the Ælfric manuscripts as part of his fundamental study of Ælfric's life and writings.[4] But Dietrich did not attempt a thorough examination of the unprinted materials, and much remained in manuscript, largely unregarded.

[1] For bibliographical details here and elsewhere, see the preliminary table of Abbreviations and Short Titles.

[2] Skeat, following his manuscript (Cotton Julius E. vii, here called W), included, besides the freshly interpolated piece he numbered XXIII B, three other prose lives that should not be attributed to Ælfric (XXIII, XXX, XXXIII). See below, pp. 83–84.   [3] 'The Ælfric Canon', pp. 136 sqq.

[4] Eduard Dietrich, 'Abt Ælfric: Zur Literaturgeschichte der angelsächsischen Kirche', *Zeitschrift für historische Theologie*, XXV (1855), 487–594; XXVI (1856), 163–256. In XXV. 511–16, he classified the chief manuscripts of the *Catholic Homilies* (mainly from Wanley's catalogue, partly from his own observation), commented on the likelihood that Ælfric wrote a good many extra-serial homilies, and listed a few that seemed most certainly his. Those that he singled out, if not already in print, were published by Assmann in his *Homilien und Heiligenleben*, 1889. Some parts of Dietrich's study are incorporated in C. L. White's *Ælfric, a New Study of his Life and Writings*, Yale Studies in English, Boston, 1898.

So far as I know the first attempt to sort out from the manuscripts all the unprinted Ælfric homilies was made by A. S. Napier in the course of a project he did not live to complete. As early as 1891 he was proposing to edit for the Early English Text Society 'all the Anglo-Saxon Homilies and Lives of Saints not accessible in English editions'.[1] The Society continued to announce the project until Napier's death in 1916, but it remained unfulfilled. Already, however, before the turn of the century, Napier had gathered transcripts of a number of the homilies, some of them done by his own hand, and had begun the work of collation. In 1931, when I had completed a preliminary study of the manuscripts of the *Catholic Homilies*[2] (a nearly inclusive group) and had made arrangements to bring out the unedited Ælfric homilies, the Napier transcripts were turned over to me by S. J. Crawford, to whom they had earlier been entrusted.[3] They did not take the place of photostats, but I have found some of the all too rare marginalia helpful and have taken comfort from Napier's occasionally explicit recognition of Ælfric's authorship.

During the long period over which, though with many interruptions, I have been preparing this edition, the Ælfric manuscripts have been re-examined by two different scholars with consequences of great value for this project among others. I refer first of all to N. R. Ker's *Catalogue of Manuscripts Containing Anglo-Saxon*, Oxford, 1957, the now indispensable guide to all the vernacular manuscripts of the Anglo-Saxon period, which in most respects, except for manuscripts that have since been lost or burnt, has taken the place of Wanley's great *Catalogus* of 1705. Besides the wealth

---

[1] The quoted words appear in the Society's reports from 1892 on. The project was first announced in a different form in the report of 1891, p. 8. (I have seen a copy issued with O.S. 97.)

[2] A Yale doctoral dissertation, 1931. It has been superseded in part by the articles of Kenneth Sisam in the *Review of English Studies*, 1931–3, to which I refer more explicitly at the beginning of section 2, partly by Ker's *Catalogue*, as indicated below. Anything left over, if it has seemed of any value, has been incorporated in this edition.

[3] I owe this kindness to the friendly mediation of Dr. Sisam. The transcripts that I received corresponded to the following homilies here edited, and were taken from the manuscripts indicated, according to the sigla of the present edition: II, III, V, VI (all from MS. F); IV (from M and T); VII, IX, X (from N and U); VIII (from U collated with M, from N, and—a paragraph only—from J); XI (from U with notes on readings of M and T; separately from T); XII (from U); XIII (from U, partly collated with H); XIV–XVI (from U); XVIII (from P, R); XIX (from C, P); XX, XXII (from P); XXI (from R); XXIII (from T). The transcripts have now been returned to the Early English Text Society.

of accurate palaeographical description, which has not only en-
lightened me but has relieved me of the burden of less competent
technical description of my own, Ker has analysed with great skill
the contents of the manuscripts. He has appended to the catalogue
a table of the two series of *Catholic Homilies* as these occur in the
many manuscripts (pp. 511 sqq.), and the following index contains
(pp. 527 sqq.) a comprehensive list of the surviving Old English
homilies, published and unpublished. In listing the unpublished
homilies he has refrained from stating his opinion of their authorship, but in the body of the catalogue the frequently recurring
statement that an unpublished item is 'in rhythmical prose' nearly
always points, as he is well aware, to something by Ælfric. My own
list of the unpublished Ælfric material has been enlarged here and
there as a result of his careful comparison of texts and his tabulations.

Secondly, there is the ground-breaking and illuminating study
of the whole range of Ælfric's work, derived to a great degree from
a penetrating analysis of the manuscripts, to which I refer again
and again as Clemoes, *Chronology*.[1] A few pages of this study (213-
19) are devoted to a comprehensive list of Ælfric's works, including
all the unpublished material except additions to earlier compositions, and therefore all the contents of the present edition
except nos. XXIII–XXIX, to most of which reference is made in the
course of the discussion. In drawing up his list of the unpublished
material Dr. Clemoes took into account, as he says, a list I had
drawn up previously for the Early English Text Society, but the
material was already well known to him and the decisions were his
own, so that the very close correspondence between his judgements
of Ælfric's authorship and mine—we differ mainly with respect to
Ælfric's responsibility for certain compilations made from his
writings—is a source of encouragement to me.

For practical reasons I have not included quite all the unedited
homiletic material. Among the omissions are, first, the various
additions, two of them extensive, to homilies in Ælfric's First
Series. This series (represented by Thorpe's first volume) is being
edited afresh from all the manuscripts by Dr. Clemoes, and it is
obviously right that he should include the additions.[2] Secondly,

---

[1] P. A. M. Clemoes, 'The Chronology of Ælfric's Works', in *The Anglo-
Saxons: Studies . . . presented to Bruce Dickins*, edited by Peter Clemoes, London,
Bowes & Bowes, 1959, pp. 212–47.

[2] I have included, however, as nos. XXIII–XXIX, similar additions to homilies

I have omitted two pieces that are treated as consecutive homilies, though they look like parts of a single composition, perhaps a homiletic letter, in MS. Cotton Otho C. i, vol. 2, one called *De Creatore et Creatura*, the other *De Sex Ætatibus Huius Sæculi*. A more detailed account of these pieces, of which the first is a compilation from Ælfric's earlier writings with some added passages in his style, the second a fresh treatment of a familiar theme, will be found under the description of the manuscript below.[1] Dr. Clemoes, who was the first to identify in *De Creatore* a passage corresponding to Belfour IX and to list the two pieces among Ælfric's writings, plans to edit them separately.

I believe these are the only unprinted vernacular pieces that might have been included, but there is one unprinted Latin homily that should be mentioned, since it has been tentatively ascribed to Ælfric. It has survived in a manuscript that has close associations with him and it is remarkably similar to the Christmas homily in the *Lives of Saints*.[2] Whether it is actually a piece of Ælfric's composition, as indeed it appears to be, can hardly be satisfactorily determined without a thorough study of its relation, not only to the Christmas homily just mentioned, but also to the partially rewritten version of that homily in Belfour IX.[3] It seemed best to leave this interesting but problematical and tangential document for separate study and publication.

On the other hand I have included four pieces that are not strictly to be classed as unedited, though they are available only in texts that are in various degrees unsatisfactory. Three of them (IV, VIII, and XII) have been edited before from complete though inferior manuscripts; and important sections of another (XXI) have been edited from seriously incomplete manuscripts. No. IV was edited by Müller in 1835 and again by Stephens in 1853, but only from Grundtvig's transcript of MS. N (Cotton Faustina A. ix), a relatively inferior copy, though sufficiently faithful to the forms of Ælfric's language to allow his authorship to be recognized. The

---

of the Second Series and to one piece, *De Auguriis*, among the *Lives of Saints*, because it is a question how soon these sets will be re-edited.

[1] pp. 86–87.

[2] See Enid M. Raynes, 'MS. Boulogne-sur-Mer 63 and Ælfric', *Medium Ævum*, XXVI (1957), 65–73. This important article is described in the introduction to XI, pp. 407–8 below, where I have pointed out that both Miss Raynes and Mr. Neil Ker have thought the homily might be Ælfric's.

[3] I owe this cautionary advice to a conversation with Dr. Clemoes, who has made some preliminary study of the relations of the three pieces.

decision here was particularly delicate, but since these two editions
are neither satisfactory nor easy to obtain I thought it proper to
re-edit the homily from all eight of the extant manuscripts, basing
the text on one that is decidedly superior to N. Nos. VIII and XII
seemed more clearly in need of an improved text. They were
printed from MS. B (Bodley 343) by Belfour as nos. I and II of
his *Twelfth Century Homilies*; but this manuscript is so late that
many features of Ælfric's language are obscured. Manuscripts
much closer to the original have enabled me to supply a text that
harmonizes with the main body of his writings.[1] The fourth
piece, XXI, *De Falsis Diis*, though long familiar in part, has never
been printed in its entirety. A complete edition was therefore
overdue.[2]

A few other pieces, though largely unfamiliar, contain passages
that have already appeared in print. No. VI, besides a few lines that
correspond to a passage in Ælfric's brief *De Cogitatione*, has extended parallels with Belfour XIV, which is an excerpt from the
revised version of the homily with a partially rewritten passage that
serves as an introduction. Everything except this brief introduction
has been collated for the homily. No. XIa, a compilation for which,
in my opinion, Ælfric was not responsible, includes excerpts from
the *Letter to Wulfgeat* (Assmann I) and the *Interrogationes Sigewulfi*, besides our own XI. No. XVII incorporates an account of some
of Jesus's miracles that had first appeared as a loosely attached
pendant in *Catholic Homilies* II; and no. XXIX, an addition to *De*

---

[1] Belfour's volume, in spite of its title, contains nothing but pre-Conquest
material with a heavy sprinkling of twelfth-century spellings and a few changes
in syntax and vocabulary. Some pieces are earlier than Ælfric, others perhaps
a bit later, and several besides Belfour's I and II are by Ælfric: namely III, IV,
VII, VIII, IX, XIII, and most if not all of XIV. But the first four of these are unique
and so cannot be supplied with more Ælfrician texts. Belfour IX is partly a revised form of *LS* I, mainly unique though a little of it is in the *De Creatore et
Creatura* mentioned above, and partly a second copy of *LS* I. The textual
advantage of a new edition would be slight. What is wanted is a study of the
relations between *LS* I, Belfour IX, *De Creatore et Creatura*, and the Latin
Christmas homily mentioned above. Belfour XIII is a mere excerpt from the
Catholic Homilies. Belfour XIV is discussed in the next paragraph. For further
details see the description of MS. B, pp. 15–17 below.

[2] After the present edition had gone to press, there appeared an edition of
De Doctrina Apostolica, no. XIX below, by W. Braekman, based on all the manuscripts. Since in several respects, however, the editor has not duplicated my
work, and the textual relations of the piece make its inclusion desirable, there
seems no reason to withdraw it. An account of Braekman's edition will be found
in the introduction to no. XIX in the second volume.

Auguriis, begins with a little story once attached to *Lives of Saints* XXI.

The date and range of the texts here edited are considered in relation to the hitherto known body of Ælfric's work in section 7 below.

2. THE MANUSCRIPTS

The following description of manuscripts depends heavily on an analysis by Dr. Clemoes which he will set forth in full, with the supporting evidence, in his forthcoming edition of the *Catholic Homilies*, Series I, for the Early English Text Society.[1] Since the manuscripts of the First Series are basic to the study of Ælfric's homiletic work and the same codices supply most of the texts for both editions, it seemed best that we should use the same sigla. Indeed, for good measure, as will presently appear, we have adopted a set of sigla somewhat more extensive than either of us requires, in order to allow for future editions of Ælfric's related writings. Our main concern, however, was with the principal manuscripts of the First Series, for which Dr. Clemoes had already devised a set of sigla that would keep in view the successive states of the revision which, as the manuscripts reveal, Ælfric gave his text. Both Dr. Clemoes and I felt that these sigla supplied too valuable an outline of the complicated textual history of the First Series, as he has come to understand it, to be abandoned in favour of a neutral and therefore random set. Consequently I have adopted them, and in so doing have assumed the responsibility for explaining some of the more basic aspects of Dr. Clemoes's analysis. I shall not attempt to deal with any of the details except as they are relevant to the present edition, and shall leave the bulk of the exposition, along with most of the evidence, to Dr. Clemoes, who alone has complete collations of the texts of the First Series.

Three crucially revealing manuscripts of the First Series, among the many that survive, bear witness with remarkable clarity to certain states through which the text of the series passed under Ælfric's supervision, from a time shortly before publication to a much later period when it had received some additions. Although

---

[1] His main conclusions about the order of publication of Ælfric's works are on view in his *Chronology*, but since writing that piece he has reviewed the manuscript evidence, completing his collations and making some minor alterations.

Thorpe had made use of two of these manuscripts and Dietrich had singled out all three as primary authorities, their full textual significance, separately and collectively, was first apprehended by Kenneth Sisam, who set forth the main facts about them in the course of a series of articles aimed partly at the related volumes named in his title, 'MSS. Bodley 340 and 342 and Ælfric's Catholic Homilies'.[1]

The earliest of the three, MS. Royal 7 C. xii in the British Museum, contains a text of Series I alone, without prefaces, of which the original state is still visible in spite of a large number of revisions indicated by directions for excision, interlinear substitutions, and additions supplied in the margins or on extra pieces of parchment carefully sewn into place. The original text represents the earliest known state of the homilies, containing certain readings that were evidently suppressed or altered before publication, others that achieved a limited circulation. The various revisions, some of them executed in a hand that is almost certainly Ælfric's, the others in contemporary hands, have brought the text closer to the state represented by the second of the three manuscripts, Gg. 3. 28 in the University Library, Cambridge.

Gg. 3. 28 is the manuscript used by Thorpe as the basis for his edition. It is the only one that contains the First and Second Series in their original order—in fact also the only one that gives us a complete record of the Second Series. Unique are the prefatory matter, Latin and English, for both series, the closing prayer at the end of the second, and some of the Latin notes that appear here and there throughout, usually as part of the text, rarely in the margins. Since the manuscript contains additional writings by Ælfric at its close, copied continuously by the same scribe, it is evidently a copy, made a few years after the publication of Series II, of a manuscript that had remained in Ælfric's possession long enough to receive these additional pieces as they were composed. The text of Series I embodies minor revisions that do not appear in Royal 7 C. xii or in the surviving descendants of certain intermediate copies, now lost, one of which was presumably the copy sent to Archbishop Sigeric. The writing and revision of the Royal manuscript probably took place in 990, the sending of Series I to Sigeric in

[1] *Review of English Studies* for 1931, 1932, and 1933. Now reprinted, with additional notes, in his *Studies in the History of Old English Literature*, pp. 148–98.

the first half of 991. The state of this series in Gg. 3. 28 was
probably reached at some time within the next two or three years.[1]

The third manuscript, no. 188 at Corpus Christi College, Cambridge, is likewise a good (though not necessarily direct) copy of
one that had been in Ælfric's possession. It contains Series I with
a few additional homilies and some extra passages—a substantially
revised and expanded version—and, at the end, the extra homily for
a confessor printed by Assmann as no. IV, with a prefatory note in
Latin indicating that it was composed for Bishop Æthelwold II of
Winchester and added to the volume containing Series I in order
that Ælfric might retain a copy. Thus the original volume must have
been in Ælfric's possession until some time after the ordination of
Æthelwold, which took place in 1006, a year or so after Ælfric
himself had become abbot of Eynsham. It seems probable that the
expanded First Series, though some of the extra material was composed several years earlier, belongs as a whole to the period of his
abbacy. This manuscript is fully described below under the letter
Q, since it serves as the basis for the texts of homilies IV and XI.

With these manuscripts as chief points of reference, and with
further testimony from several others, Dr. Clemoes has assessed
the textual states of all the manuscripts of the First Series, and has
arranged the most important of them in a corresponding order
expressed by the alphabetical order of the sigla, A–H, J–V.[2] It
must be emphasized that this order is based on the successively
altered readings of Ælfric's original as attested by the most reliable
manuscripts, not at all on the relative dates of the manuscripts
themselves. When there is more than one witness to a particular
state of Ælfric's text sigla are assigned according to relative importance: for instance, K and L represent the same state, but K
is more important than L. Within the order thus established,
however, there are complications to be explained.

The manuscripts A–H and J–L represent the early dissemination

[1] See Sisam, *Studies*, p. 160, note 1, and pp. 180–4; Clemoes, *Chronology*,
p. 243, note 2, and especially Clemoes's introduction to the facsimile of the
Royal manuscript, *Early English Manuscripts in Facsimile*, XIII, Copenhagen,
1966, which he has kindly allowed me to see in proof. Sisam may be right in
thinking that certain grammatical changes were made after Ælfric had sent
Series II to Sigeric (*c.* 992), but they need not be associated with Ælfric's work
on his *Grammar*, for changes of the same sort occur in the Royal manuscript.

[2] By assigning a single letter to companion volumes (sometimes widely
separated in modern libraries) he includes twenty-six volumes under twenty-one
sigla.

of copies of Series I. The three or four distinct states detected by Dr. Clemoes need not be particularized here. Some of these manuscripts, however, contain texts of more than one state even for the First Series, the assigned letter referring only to the earliest. Most of them include additional homilies that may be derived from considerably later originals. It must not be assumed that the state or states revealed by collation of homilies of Series I will be a reliable index for the states of homilies outside the set, whether those of Series II or others. Except for A, the Royal manuscript, even the earliest as judged by its handwriting may be late enough to include texts that were not in existence at the time when its ancestral version of Series I left Ælfric's possession.

The most extreme examples of divergence are furnished by the manuscripts called B and C. These belong to the twelfth century and contain rich collections of diverse origin, some of the Ælfrician texts having a surprisingly early character, some a late. B in particular (MS. Bodley 343), though it is full of altered forms and spellings, has readings in certain homilies of the First Series that place its text of these items next after A's; but it also has a number of Ælfric's latest compositions, not to mention pieces by Wulfstan that may not have been written until after Ælfric's death. Hence, although for a part of Series I Bodley 343 is correctly designated by B, for the pieces here edited its place is with or after U and V. Similarly MS. H (Cotton Vitellius C. v), a volume exhibiting three distinguishable strata, is properly called H for the earliest of these, but should probably come just after K for its second stratum and close to U and V for its third.

Each of the manuscripts B, C, E–H, J, and L contains at least one text later than Series II and thus becomes a legitimate contributor to the present edition, whereas A is altogether excluded and D and K have only the Series II version of a passage that Ælfric long afterwards incorporated in an otherwise new homily.

After K and L and before the third of our chief guides, Q, Dr. Clemoes has found reason to place only four manuscripts, though the interval between the states of K (L) and Q is presumably much greater, as measured by years, than that between the states of A and K, and includes the composition of the *Lives of Saints*, the *Grammar*, the various translations of, and certain homilies on, portions of the Old Testament, and a number of miscellaneous pieces including a good many of the homilies in the present collection. Dr.

Clemoes has placed here the group M–N–O, to the combined evidence of which he has already pointed as the basis for his theory that Ælfric issued part of a Temporale, made up of homilies from the first three series and a few additional homilies for the period between Christmas and the first Sunday after Pentecost.[1] This theory is discussed at length under M and some questions are raised about it, but the position assigned to M, N, and O seems to me in itself unassailable. P appears to have been freshly compiled by its scribe from more than one exemplar and to represent more than one textual state, although its content is such that comparisons are limited. Some of its items seem to be textually earlier than Q, but at least one item is not. A stray leaf now in Kansas shows that it once contained the whole of Ælfric's second homily for a confessor, Assmann IV, which Ælfric did not issue till after it had been entered, with the revealing note I have already mentioned, in the archetype of Q.[2]

The five manuscript collections that Dr. Clemoes has placed after Q make eight volumes, since T designates a set of three and V a pair. R, S, and T are rather closely related and show signs of a close connexion with Q for some of their content. U and V are again closely related, and U, one of the most valuable of all our manuscripts, marks what appears to be another stage in the evolution of Ælfric's homiletic work. It has lost some leaves at the end, but it preserves a portion of a very systematic, purely Ælfrician Temporale, resembling the set that seems to lie behind M–N–O but overlapping it only at the beginning, and where the two correspond showing genuinely Ælfrician additions.[3] Thus we have a state certainly later than M–N–O, probably later than Q and its partially related R–S–T. Certainly where Q and U overlap, U incorporates all the new features of Q. Thus the only manuscripts that might challenge U–V as representatives of the last state of the First Series, and indeed of Ælfric's homilies as a whole, are some mixed volumes that belong early on account of a portion of their content:

---

[1] *Chronology*, pp. 227 sqq. He refers to this incomplete set of temporal homilies as TH I.

[2] See the description of P below, pp. 53 sqq., especially p. 58.

[3] Dr. Clemoes has argued that U represents a second, possibly complete edition of a Temporale by Ælfric. Accordingly he refers to this edition as TH II. See his *Chronology*, pp. 230 sqq. Although I question some features of the argument, the case for Ælfric's responsibility seems to me stronger here than for TH I.

above all the two already mentioned, B and H. The interpolated stratum of H tends to confirm and supplement the testimony of U, and the latest discernible stratum of the Ælfric homilies in B may be slightly more advanced.

Such, in crude outline, is the pattern of development in accordance with which Dr. Clemoes has assigned the twenty-one sigla, A–H, J–V. Confirmation of the finer points of his scheme must await the publication of his edition of Series I, with the full collations on which his decisions are based.[1] Meanwhile, in spite of some doubts I have expressed concerning what might be called hypothetical adjuncts of the scheme, I am persuaded of its essential validity and usefulness. The main points are established, not by fine-spun decisions regarding small verbal variants, but by conspicuous differences, such as whole passages cancelled or added, new homilies inserted. One or two letters of the alphabet may turn out to be incorrectly assigned or uncertain, but future adjustments, if they should prove advisable, will hardly be numerous enough to destroy the outline so conveniently provided.

As I have already said, however, the letters, being assigned on the basis of texts belonging to the First Series, do not apply consistently to the material here edited—hardly at all if they fall within the sequence from A to K, not invariably if they come after K. I have tried, therefore, in describing the several manuscripts, to supply what chronological evidence I can for the texts under consideration. Only a few (VI, VII, XXI) show clearly more than one state that can be attributed to revision on the part of the author, though of course all the passages added to earlier homilies, if we hold Ælfric responsible for adding them (as I do with confidence for XXII–XXVI and XXVIII, and with some hesitation for the central part of XXVII and most of XXIX), bear witness to revision of the earlier homilies in which they appear. Not nearly as much evidence is available as for the First Series, but such as there is tends, when we make the proper allowances, to confirm the Clemoes analysis; and that analysis in its turn points to sequences and relationships that would otherwise hardly be guessed. Both the sequence of sigla and the acutely divined, complex order they partially reveal have helped to put the small, often mutually unrelated textual problems of the present edition in a clearer light.

[1] I have complete collations for the First Series in A, H, K, Q, and for the Second Series in K, besides scattered collations elsewhere, but this is not enough.

Beyond the letter V, for a few major and a great many lesser manuscripts, the sigla have no textual significance, being assigned arbitrarily within certain broadly defined categories. As already stated, Dr. Clemoes and I have gone somewhat beyond our immediate needs in order to allow for editions of related portions of Ælfric's writings. Previous editors of Ælfric's homilies, MacLean, Assmann, Skeat, and Crawford, operating on a relatively small scale, have suited their own convenience in the use of sigla, so that some frequently used codices have received a varied assortment of letters. The confusion is increased by the sigla chosen by Napier for his *Wulfstan*, since a number of the Wulfstan manuscripts contain Ælfric homilies as well.[1] We have not attempted to reconcile the Wulfstan and Ælfric editions, nor to provide for such easily separable works of Ælfric himself as the *Grammar* or the *De Temporibus Anni*. We have also set aside the pastoral letters, Latin and English, for Wulfsige and Wulfstan (since these are already elaborately edited by Fehr and some inconsistency in sigla will not be disturbing), and the miscellaneous pieces, such as the translation of Basil's *Admonitio ad Filium Spiritualem* and the separate Latin compositions, that occur in only one manuscript. Many of the excluded works occur, to be sure, in the manuscripts we have listed, but we have not enlarged the list on their account. Our main concern has been to allow for future editions of the Second Series, the *Lives of Saints*, and the miscellaneous homilies and letters to laymen now scattered in editions by MacLean, Morris, Assmann, Napier, Belfour, and Crawford. We have also included the partially Ælfrician translation of the Heptateuch, because of its close connexion with Ælfric's numerous homilies on various parts of the Old Testament.

Our complete list of sigla is arranged in three main categories, as follows:

1. The principal manuscripts, as judged by the quantity of relevant material they contain, are lettered A to Z, omitting I and X. After the carefully ordered manuscripts containing members of the First Series come three others of importance in an arbitrary order: W stands for the chief representative of the *Lives of Saints*, Y and Z for the chief representatives of the Old English Heptateuch

[1] In the descriptions below I have noted the sigla used by Skeat and Napier, since these are perhaps better established than the rest and are attached to a good many of the important manuscripts.

(part of which is by Ælfric) and the letters to Wulfgeat and Sige-weard. All these manuscripts are listed, though not quite all contain texts here edited, in the descriptions that follow.

2. Eleven manuscripts of secondary importance for Ælfric's homiletic work, as containing no more than a few homilies or letters, sometimes only brief excerpts, amid other work not his or not of the same character,[1] are designated by the letter X, each with a distinguishing superscript letter in lower case: X^a to X^k. The order is simply that of Ker's *Catalogue*, two manuscripts omitted by Ker because of their late date (Cotton Vespasian A. xxii and Lambeth 487) being put in the appropriate places. Of the eleven only two, X^d and X^k, are described below. The others, being irrelevant to the present edition, are merely listed.

3. Mere fragments, ranging from meagre remnants of volumes largely destroyed by fire to binding strips, are placed in a third category (except for a fragment now in Kansas, which once belonged to Hatton 115 and is therefore listed with it under P in the first category). To each of these leaves or groups of leaves we have given the lower-case f with a distinguishing superscript letter, also in lower case. We have listed seventeen such fragments, f^a to f^q, following once more Ker's *Catalogue* for the order. Since others are likely to turn up, and only one fragmentary group of leaves, f^b, is relevant here, I have left the list to Dr. Clemoes to publish in his edition of Series I.

Although I had made my own examination of the physical characteristics of the manuscripts, size, gatherings, script, &c., mainly in the years 1927–33, all this has been superseded by Ker's *Catalogue*. I have therefore limited the physical description to a minimum, merely enough to supply a reader with what he may wish to know in a hurry. The summary statements at the beginning of the descriptions, including the dates,[2] are, unless otherwise stated, mere digests of Ker, to whose work the reader must turn for details. Once or twice I have corrected something that went wrong in the printing of the *Catalogue*. My main concern in the descriptions is to show the significance, for Ælfric, of the content

---

[1] e.g. Faustina A. x, which contains, besides the *Grammar* in section A, only the short excerpts from Ælfric's homily on St. Gregory described by Ker under section B, 4.

[2] For the degree of precision intended by Ker's dates, see his *Catalogue*, pp. xx sq. His dates are usually in accord with, though often more precise than, Wanley's in his *Catalogus* of 1705. I have rarely seen any reason to question them.

of the volumes and thus to provide a context for the pieces I am
editing. In considering the content I have tried to keep in view the
Clemoes analysis of the textual sequence. When such matters as
the date and diversity of script, constitution of gatherings, dialectal
colouring, and provenance have seemed to call for particular comment I have said what I could.

DESCRIPTION OF THE MANUSCRIPTS

CLASS I: THE PRINCIPAL COLLECTIONS OF ÆLFRIC'S LITERARY
WORKS: MSS. A–H, J–V, in which the *Catholic Homilies* are represented; MSS. W, Y, Z, limited to other writings.

A

[*London, British Museum, Royal 7 C. xii*, ff. 4–218. Ker 257. sæc.
x ex. (*c.* 990). The earliest authority for Series I, to which it is
limited. Not used in this edition.]

B

Oxford, Bodleian Library, Bodley 343.[1] Ker 310. sæc. XII². 205
original leaves, *c.* 308 × 200 mm., foliated vi–xxxix, 1–167, 169–72,
and two medieval fly-leaves, iii and 173.

Collated for VI, VIII, and XII.

The English parts of this large, unsystematic collection of homilies and related pieces were all assembled from pre-Conquest
materials. The volume falls into two divisions according to the
work of two nearly contemporary scribes, the first of whom has the
more archaic script. If we disregard some later additions in
originally blank spaces (Ker's articles 76 and 85 in OE, 86–90 in
Latin), the contents of the two sections (fully described by Ker)
may be summarized as follows:

The first section, ff. vi–xxxix, has parts of four homilies of *CH* I
and II on imperfect quires, followed by sixty-five short homilies
in Latin on the Gospels for the year (Ker's articles 1–5).

The second, much larger section, ff. 1–170 (omitting 168), has
seventy-eight articles (Ker 6–75, 77–84) of which the majority are
by Ælfric. Forty-seven are from *CH* I and II; three from *LS*

---

[1] Formerly NE. F. IV. 12. Napier's H; Skeat's B.

(Ker 18, 22, 31); one is the extra sermon for a confessor, Assmann IV (Ker 84); one *De Septiformi Spiritu*, Napier VII (Latin) and VIII (Ker 69); one (Ker 65) an adaptation of the *Letter to Sigeweard on the Old and New Testament*, printed by Assmann (VII) and Crawford (*O.E. Hept.*); two are Old English letters for Wulfstan, Fehr, *Brief* II and *Brief* III (Ker 67, 68). In addition to these fifty-five, there are nine others, including the three collated for this edition, which should be attributed to Ælfric. These nine are identified below in the account of Belfour's edition, in which they have all been printed.

There are fourteen articles not by Ælfric which remain to be mentioned. Four of these are by Wulfstan (Ker 66, 70–72; Bethurum VIIIc, V–Ib–IV, XX (BH), and VI respectively; Napier V, XIII–XII–XVI, XXXIII, and II). The rest are anonymous: Ker 12, on the Rood, printed in Napier's *History of the Holy Rood-tree*; Ker 16, on the Virgin (part of the *Gospel of pseudo-Matthew*), Assmann X; Ker 37, on confession, Napier LVI; Ker 64, here called *De doctrina sancti Gregorii*, Napier XLVI; Ker 81, dialogues in Latin expounding the Lord's Prayer and Creed; and five of the articles printed by Belfour, as indicated in the list below.

The fourteen articles in Belfour's *Twelfth Century Homilies* (EETS 1909) are taken from this manuscript alone and include all the vernacular material that had not already been printed from this or some allied manuscript. One of these pieces is actually part of one of the *Catholic Homilies* with two short prefatory sentences; eight others have clear marks of Ælfric's authorship, and are duly listed as his in Clemoes, *Chronology*, pp. 214 sqq. I have re-edited three of them because they occur in other, earlier, and more accurate manuscripts. The nine by Ælfric and the other five are as follows according to Belfour's numbering:

I.   Ker 7, homily XII in this edition, also in M and U.

II. Ker 8, homily VIII in this edition, also in M, N, U, and partly in J.

III. Ker 9, homily on *John* iv. 46 sqq., the pericope for the 22nd Sunday after Pentecost. Occurs nowhere else, but the style is Ælfric's.

IV. Ker 10, homily on *Matth.* xviii. 23 sqq., the pericope for the 23rd Sunday after Pentecost. Again unique and Ælfrician.

[v. Ker 28, for the first Sunday in Lent. Not by Ælfric. Appears in Vercelli Book III, Bodley 340 (D), &c.]

[vi. Ker 29, for the second Sunday in Lent. Not by Ælfric. In Bodley 340 (D), CCCC 198 (E).]

vii. Ker 54, homily on *John* ix. 1, the pericope for Wednesday in the fourth week of Lent. Unique and Ælfrician. A characteristic back-reference, 'swa swa we sædon hwilon ær', is evidently to our II, 212–75, esp. 256 sqq.

viii. Ker 61, a homily on *John* XII. 24, for a martyr, who is identified as St. Vincent at Belfour, p. 76/12. Unique and Ælfrician. This, then, as Dr. Clemoes has pointed out (*Chronology*, p. 236), is meant to accompany Ælfric's account of St. Vincent's passion (*LS* XXXVII), printed by Skeat from the unique copy in ULC Ii. 1. 33, our L. St. Vincent's day is Jan. 22.

ix. Ker 77, a unique second version of Ælfric's Christmas homily, *LS* I. The beginning, almost a half, is rewritten in Ælfric's characteristic rhythmic prose. The remainder corresponds to Skeat's text from Julius E. vii, our W, a version that as a whole is likewise unique. A part of the revised beginning occurs also in *De Creatore et Creatura* in Otho C. i, vol. 2, our X^d.

[x. Ker 78, an untitled Lenten homily, perhaps derived from the same source as *CH* I. XI, *Dom. I in Quad.*, but not by Ælfric.]

[xi. Ker 79, an untitled homily on the transfiguration. Not by Ælfric.]

[xii. Ker 80, an untitled homily against worldliness, called by Belfour 'A Message from the Tomb'. Not by Ælfric. The beginning has a common source with Vercelli XIII; the end, from Belfour, p. 128/29, corresponds to Napier XLIX, p. 261/15 on.]

xiii. Ker 82, a paragraph on avarice excerpted from *CH* II. XXX (Thorpe, p. 410/2–28), with two introductory sentences that may or may not be by Ælfric. The same paragraph occurs in MS. R, and a large part of it in f^b (Jesus College 15). It has not hitherto been identified in print, though Dr. Clemoes recognized it independently.

xiv. Ker 83, an excerpt from the longer version of homily VI in this edition. The first nineteen lines in Belfour, though mainly rhythmic, may not be Ælfric's. They are a re-ordering of materials in homily VI. See the introduction to that homily.

Eight of the nine Ælfrician pieces in Belfour—that is, all but the trivial XIII—are important witnesses to Ælfric's homiletic output beyond the limits of the first three series. Five of them, Belfour's III, IV, VII, VIII, and IX in its rewritten portion, add otherwise unknown homilies to the canon. The other three (I, II, and XIV) are valuable though subordinate contributors to our XII, VIII, and VI respectively.

Clearly the Ælfrician pieces in B have been derived from several different sources, for it includes not only copies of homilies in *CH* I that derive from almost the earliest ascertainable state of the text—hence Dr. Clemoes's decision to call it B—but a good many of Ælfric's later compositions, including not only the Belfour homilies, which are probably not all of the same period and cannot easily be dated, but also the letters for Wulfstan, the adaptation of *On the Old and New Testament*, and the homily for a confessor, Assmann IV, all of which belong to the years of Ælfric's abbacy. This is such a compilation as might have been made from half a dozen old exemplars in a monastic library a little removed from the big centres, one that had received Ælfric's writings (and eventually some of Wulfstan's) intermittently from the very beginning of his literary career to the end, but without keeping track of his numerous revisions. The three pieces included in the present edition seem to belong to as late a textual stratum as we have in any manuscript. In VI B's text is a revision (by Ælfric or another) of the augmented text witnessed by H. In VIII and XII B agrees in error with U against M (and N). And the texts added to H by the interpolator, like the texts of U, are uniformly late.

The peculiarities of the language of B as written by the second scribe (the only one we are concerned with here) are fully represented in Belfour's text. They are analysed by Napier, *History of the Holy Rood-tree*, pp. xlvii–lix. Napier came to the conclusion that the scribe was writing the normal early Middle English descendant of the West Saxon dialect, the few forms that were originally Anglian, such as *isegen* for WS *gesawon* or *gesewen*, having become common in the south by the middle of the twelfth century. He believed, however, that the language had a much more archaic cast than was proper to its period, as was to be expected from the fact that in every instance where there was evidence, the scribe was copying works that had been composed before the Conquest. Napier's analysis is directed chiefly, of course, to article 12, the anonymous history of the Rood, but he rightly maintains that it applies to the great bulk of the volume—more precisely, as has been said, to the work of the second scribe. Ker, in agreement with the *Summary Catalogue* of the Bodleian, suggests the West Midlands as the place of origin, largely because on f. iii there is a rhymed antiphon commemorating St. Wulfhad (chiefly honoured, says the *Catalogue*, at Stone in Staffordshire) and because a sketch of a bishop with a mitre on f. 173 has an unexplained inscription in which the name 'Wolstane' occurs—possibly referring to Bishop Wulfstan II of Worcester. Since there is no evidence of a connexion with Worcester itself, some other west midland library is likely as the original home of the manuscript; but to judge by the language, it was sent there after having been written in the south.[1] Certain textual associations with MSS. U and V may point even to the south-east. (See the description of V.)

C

Cambridge, Corpus Christi College 303.[2] Ker 57. sæc. XII[1]. 182 original leaves, *c.* 260 × 196 mm., paginated on rectos 1–141, 141–361, leaves missing at beginning (forty-four according to medieval foliation) and end, otherwise intact.

Collated for IV, VI (original version), XI, XIX, XXI, and the passage from *CH* II in XVII.

Ker lists seventy-three articles in this large collection, of which sixty-one are by Ælfric and twelve by other, anonymous writers of the tenth and eleventh centuries. Articles 1–61, with two sequences of temporal homilies in an incomplete annual cycle separated by an incomplete series for saints and the common of saints, is dominated by selections from the *Catholic Homilies*, I and II, from which forty-five articles are derived. Five other homilies by Ælfric are interspersed: *De Auguriis*, *LS* XVII (Ker 47); *De Nativitate S. Mariæ*, Assmann III (Ker 27), and homilies IV, VI,

---

[1] So, it seems, K was sent to Durham, and W to Bury St. Edmunds, both probably from southern centres.

[2] Formerly S. 17. Skeat's D.

and XI in the present edition (Ker 9, 11, 41 resp.). The other eleven articles are all anonymous (Ker 15, 17, 18, 23, 26, 34, 39, 40, 43–45), including some that appear in the Vercelli Book (15, 43, 44) and three unique lives of saints (23, 26, 34).

The end of the volume, articles 62–73, is dominated by selections from the *Lives of Saints*, including the appendix partly preserved by Skeat's manuscript, Cotton Julius E. vii (our W). Ker's articles 62, 67, 68, 70–72 are all represented in Skeat's edition. Articles 63, *De Duodecim Abusivis*; 65, *De Falsis Diis* (our XXI); and 66, *Interrogationes Sigewulfi*, are all listed in the table of contents of Julius E. vii, though only the *Interrogationes* and part of *De Falsis Diis* remain and Skeat did not include any of them. Two other articles, readily associated with these, are by Ælfric: his homily on Judith, Assmann IX (Ker 73), and *De Doctrina Apostolica*, our XIX (Ker 64). The remaining article, not by Ælfric and different in kind from the rest, consists of Latin and OE forms of excommunication (Ker 69).

Like B, this manuscript is obviously of mixed lineage. Dr. Clemoes has called it C in virtue of what he finds to be the earliest strain in the homilies of *CH* I, but there seem to be at least two other strains. There are seven homilies of *CH* I among the eighteen homilies (35–38, 48–61) that Ker designates as copies of D (Bodley 342, arts. 64–67, 42–47, 54–56, 58–62); and at least one other homily of *CH* I (Ker 33, *CH* I. XXXVIII, on St. Andrew) has a passage not in K that is found in the revised version of *CH* I represented by Q. In general C shows little acquaintance with the range of Ælfric's later work. It is more limited in this respect than B. Both are witnesses to our homily VI, but C to its first form, B to its second or third. I think it is probable that our IV, VI as first written, XIX, and XXI, besides the *Judith* homily, Assmann IX, all belong roughly to the years when Ælfric was at work on the *Lives of Saints*, and come well before the revision of *CH* I marked by Q. Somewhat later, probably, are Assmann III and our XI. Q gives these a place in *CH* I as it does our IV, and there is no reason with them, as there is with IV, to suppose that they were in circulation much before the time when Q's original was put together.

Ker discerns the hands of three different scribes in this codex. The first, to whom he attributes pp. 1–50 and all but a few of pp. 203–362, must then be credited with having copied all the homilies here collated. In spite of the up-to-date, twelfth-century character of his script, his spelling is markedly though inconsistently archaic. He is obviously inclined to preserve the spelling of his exemplars. When he departs from it, he sometimes gives us the levelled endings we expect, sometimes sheer chaos. Either his attention wandered from time to time or he scarcely understood what he was writing. In contrast to the scribe of B, he preserves many words and even passages in their earlier form with great fidelity, yet shows far less grasp of the whole. A number of his extraordinary lapses are illustrated in the apparatus, though it has seemed advisable not to report all his small deviations of spelling in every homily.

I cannot point to anything that distinguishes his dialect from late West Saxon as it underwent the modifications of the early twelfth century in the south. Ker notes that the third scribe regularly substitutes *e* or *a* for WS *æ* and occasionally *u* for WS *y*.[1] This in itself does not seem to narrow the choice very much. It does not include any distinctively Kentish feature. Yet Ker is probably right in suggesting, on the basis of the script and the dependence on MS. D, that Rochester was the place of origin.

D

Oxford, Bodleian Library, Bodley 340, 342. Ker 309. sæc. XI in.–XI med. This two-volume homiliary has great importance for the text of the *Catholic Homilies* but does not contain any of Ælfric's later work. It is included here only because article 46 in the second volume, Bodley 342, ff. 71ᵛ–73, has been collated for *CH* II. XXVII, *Alia Narratio de Evangelii Textu*, which is incorporated in our otherwise unique homily XVII. The two volumes are discussed at length in relation to the *Catholic Homilies* by Dr. Sisam in his *Studies in the History of Old English Literature*, pp. 148–98.

E

Cambridge, Corpus Christi College 198.[2] Ker 48. sæc. XI¹, XI². 395 original leaves, *c.* 271 × 187 mm., foliated iii, 1–394, probably lacks only one written leaf, that which followed f. 247.

Collated for IV and for the passage from *CH* II in XVII.

---

[1] This scribe's work appears on pp. 226/27–231/28 and 251/10–254/5 as Ker notes, and also on the whole of p. 233. For characteristic spellings, see Skeat's list of variants from D in *LS* XVII, 1–18 and 77–133 (from pp. 231 and 233 in the manuscript).

[2] Formerly S. 8. Skeat's C.

Ker describes this as 'a thick volume of homilies, consisting of an orderly collection written in the early eleventh century (I) and of additions in nearly contemporary hands (II) and in hands of s. xi² (III)', and lists the contents in accordance with the three strata of texts thus designated.

Ker's I (ff. iii, 1–149, 160–217, 248–91) consists of forty-three homilies arranged in series from Christmas to the end of June. It is derived, as Dr. Sisam pointed out in 1931 (see *Studies*, pp. 154 sqq.), from the same homiliary as D (Bodley 340 and 342), having a closely similar sequence in which homilies from *CH* I and II are interspersed with non-Ælfrician homilies. This collection, not a copy of D itself, includes one piece from *CH* II where D has one not by Ælfric, omits several pieces that D includes, and does not, like D, complete the annual cycle. Ker gives the details, which are not here relevant, since this part of E, like D, contains nothing of Ælfric's beyond the *Catholic Homilies* and has been used, like D, only as a witness for the original text of *CH* II. xxvii, *Alia Narratio de Evangelii Textu*, which is incorporated in our otherwise unique homily xvii. This text is Ker's 37, ff. 266–7ᵛ.

Ker's II (nearly contemporary additions in several hands, ff. 150–9, 218–47, 291–321, 328–66, 378–94), has twenty-one articles, 44–64 (not counting 63*a*, a later insertion not relevant here). Two of these articles and part of a third are not by Ælfric, but the others are his, three from *CH* I, eleven from *CH* II, the first part of another the *De Penitentia* following *CH* II in Thorpe's manuscript (our K), and printed by him at II. 602 sqq., three from the *Lives of Saints* (v, xv, and xxv), and, as Ker's article 63, ff. 316–21, our homily iv.

Ker's III (additions of the second half of the eleventh century on ff. 321–7, 367–77) has only three homilies, two of which are from *CH* I, the third not by Ælfric.

It appears, then, that the original compilers of the volume and those who added to it in the first half of the eleventh century (for the later interpolations are too few to support a generalization) had at their disposal very little of Ælfric's work beyond the *Catholic Homilies*. Besides the three pieces from the *Lives of Saints*, which they may or may not have had access to in a complete set, they include only (i) *De Penitentia*, a piece earlier than *LS* xii, which embodies a part of it, and (ii) our iv, which refers back at line 75 to an earlier composition, either *LS* xviii or *De Falsis Diis*, but may nevertheless have been issued, as Dr. Clemoes has suggested, before the publication of the *Lives* as a set.

This volume contains glosses and annotations by the famous Worcester scribe with the 'tremulous' hand, showing that it was at Worcester by the beginning of the thirteenth century. Its earliest connexions (although these are not direct) are with the Rochester volumes, our D, and there is a chance that it originated in or near Kent,[1] but Ker finds western traces in the dialect of the three pieces added last (his group III). The one thing that seems probable about its early history is that it was not at Worcester itself in the eleventh century. For the scribes of Worcester, in that century, had access to a greater range of Ælfric's work, not to mention Wulfstan's; and even their known styles of writing do not seem to resemble those of the very numerous hands here.

F

Cambridge, Corpus Christi College 162, pp. 1–138, 161–564.[2] Ker 38. sæc. xi in. 271 original leaves, *c.* 297 × 203 mm., paginated on rectos, 1–135, 161–257, 257*, 259–563, probably complete except for loss of three leaves after p. 136 and one leaf after p. 382. Facsimile of p. 275 in this volume, facing p. 312.

The basis of the text of III, V, VI (first version); collated for II, and for the passage from *CH* II in xvii. Has rubric and Latin text of IV.

Like D and E, this manuscript shows a very limited acquaintance with Ælfric's later work and acquaintance with a good many non-Ælfrician homilies. Some of the non-Ælfrician homilies are the same in all three, but some are peculiar to F. What distinguishes F sharply from E is the fact that it is a very orderly book executed by one main hand; and unlike both E and D, which in orderliness it resembles, it excludes the saints, the one exception being the first few sentences of a homily for St. Augustine of England, which are added in another hand at the end. The book begins with eight pieces intended for any occasion and then gives a series for Sun-

---

[1] Sisam, *Studies*, pp. 154 sq. I find nothing revealing in E's text of homily IV; but see further below, section 9, p. 180.

[2] Formerly S. 5. Skeat's F. Omitted here are pp. 139–160, since they were inserted by Parker out of CCCC 178 (our R), to which Ker restores them in his description.

days and festivals, other than Saints' days, from the second Sunday after Epiphany to the second Sunday in Advent.

Thirty-four of Ker's fifty-five articles are from *CH* I and II, and another (32), though mainly not by Ælfric, incorporates passages from *CH* II. xv, *Sermo de Sacrificio in die Pascæ*. Two others are from the *Lives of Saints*, the Mid-lent homily on the prayer of Moses (*LS* XIII) and the homily for Ash Wednesday (*LS* XII), with a short non-Ælfrician beginning that includes the substance of lines 289–92, explaining why the homily is read on the preceding Sunday. Beyond this the only other Ælfrician pieces are those for the five Fridays in Lent, of which the fifth is Assmann v (Ker 26) and the others are in the present edition, II, III, V, VI (Ker 17, 20, 22, 24). The rubric and Latin text of our IV appear, but not the homily.[1] This leaves twelve articles that are not by Ælfric (Ker 4, 19, 28–31, 35–38, 52, and 55, the fragment on Augustine of England) besides one already mentioned (Ker 32) that is mainly not by Ælfric. Several of these articles, which include some that appear in the Vercelli Book and in D and E, are older than Ælfric.

On the whole then this manuscript shows almost the same limitation with respect to Ælfric's later work as E. Its different selections from the *Lives of Saints* reflect mainly, I think, its different principle of organization, its exclusion of homilies or reading-pieces on the saints.[2] Its failure to include homily IV after writing out the heading may mean no more than that its exemplar was defective at this point. Its inclusion of the five homilies for Fridays in Lent is one of the reasons for thinking that these were issued by Ælfric very close to the time when he was at work on the *Lives of Saints*. That E does not include them may mean only that its compilers did not wish to provide for more than the Sundays during Lent. (Both E and F resemble D in supplying a non-Ælfrician block of homilies for Palm Sunday and the Thursday, Friday, and Saturday of Holy Week, three days on which Ælfric said no sermon ought to be preached.)

F, like other manuscripts of the early eleventh century, is written in a fairly pure Late West Saxon. I have observed no local peculiarities[3] in the Ælfrician portions, though Napier, in his edition of

---

[1] Clemoes (*Chronology*, p. 221, n. 1) has reported an erased *N*, perhaps the second letter of *On*, the first word of the homily.

[2] But for evidence that these selections are textually earlier than the corresponding articles in W (Skeat's MS.), see Clemoes, *Chronology*, p. 221, n. 2.

[3] An Anglian *in* for *on* has found its way from this manuscript into Thorpe's

article 4, *English Misc. in Honour of Dr. Furnivall*, p. 361, n. 3,
points to a Late Kentish *Geornost* for WS *Eornost*; and Ker has
pointed out several conspicuously south-eastern spellings that
occur in the additions and corrections made by later eleventh-
century hands. He also finds resemblances in script and ornamental
initials to both D (early at Rochester but possibly written at
Canterbury) and MS. Royal 6 C. i, 'a later eleventh-century manuscript from St. Augustine's, Canterbury'. These observations, supported by article 55, point to the south-east for both the origin and
the early preservation of the book.

G

London, British Museum, Cotton Vespasian D. xiv, ff. 4–169. Ker
209. sæc. XII med. 166 original leaves, *c.* 191 × 122 mm., foliated
as above. Seven leaves missing after f. 6 (though they were present
in the sixteenth century), and the last piece ends imperfectly. Ker
detects, besides one main hand, two others of the same period.

Collated for IV. 41–55 (in Ker's second hand) and XXI. 300–496
(in the main hand).

This collection has been published completely by Warner, *Early
English Homilies*, and described in detail by Max Förster, *Englische
Studien*, LIV (1920), 46 sqq. It consists of a miscellany of theological pieces, some given at full length, others mere excerpts. Of
the fifty-three articles listed by Ker, twenty-seven are from *CH* I
and II, seven others and part of one already counted are from later
writings of Ælfric. The remaining nineteen, all anonymous and for
the most part not associated in other manuscripts with the Ælfric
homilies, seem to derive mainly from the eleventh century, but
include a few translations of twelfth-century Latin writings. Of the
eight articles from Ælfric's later compositions, four are associated
with the *Lives of Saints*. Ker's 7 and 8 are the passages on the eight
chief sins and the corresponding virtues which occur consecutively

---

edition of the *Catholic Homilies*, I. 618/35. The last three lines of Ælfric's
homily for the second Sunday in Advent were missing from Thorpe's basic
manuscript, Gg. 3. 28 (our K) and the missing words were supplied at the top
of f. 134 from F, p. 563, in the hand of Abraham Wheloc, whence they were
printed by Thorpe. The Anglian *in* is too widespread to be classed as a local
feature, and might have been copied from an exemplar almost anywhere; but
there is reason to believe that it was more likely to be *substituted* for *on* in the
south-east than in strictly West Saxon territory. See the description of V below,
and the note on XXX. III.

in *LS.* XVI. 267–312, 312–81. Ker's 6 is the *De Duodecim Abusivis* once included in the appendix to Skeat's manuscript (our W). A combination of these pieces, called *De Octo Vitiis et de Duodecim Abusivis*, appears in MSS. R and S and was printed from the former by Morris, *Old English Homilies*, pp. 296 sqq. Ker's 15, though it begins with *CH* II. XXXIII, for the twelfth Sunday after Pentecost, substitutes for the concluding lines the story of Daniel as Ælfric had given it in *De Falsis Diis*, our XXI. 300–493. Now *De Falsis Diis* stood just before *De Duodecim Abusivis* in the appendix to MS. W, and the beginning of it is still there. A small part of one other Ælfrician homily is represented. Ker's 20, which he describes as 'an addition in a blank space [on f. 67^v] and perhaps in another hand', contains an excerpt from our homily IV, lines 41–55 (a consecutive excerpt, not a series of excerpts as Ker reports), followed by a detached sentence that is not Ælfric's. The other three articles represent Ælfric's letters. Ker's 2, now consisting of only a few lines on f. 6^v, was evidently a complete copy of the letter to Sigefyrth on chastity, Assmann II, when Archbishop Parker's secretary, Joscelyn, made a copy of it in Cotton Vitellius D. vii, ff. 10–12. An old foliation shows that seven leaves are now missing after f. 6^v. The few lines now remaining at the beginning are our only ancient witness to the prefatory address to Sigefyrth. Ker's articles 5 and 25 are excerpts from the two OE letters for Wulfstan, Fehr's *Brief* III and *Brief* II respectively.

Förster's analysis of the dialect of the manuscript[1] caused him to believe that it was written in the south-east and Ker suggests Rochester or Canterbury, partly from the script and partly from the fact that article 44 translates a Latin sermon by Ralph d'Escures, bishop of Rochester 1108–14, archbishop of Canterbury 1114–22. There is also a Latin prayer mentioning St. Thomas of Canterbury on f. 4, in a hand that Ker dates at the end of the twelfth century. Another prayer in the same hand just above this is written to be spoken by a woman and probably indicates the sex of an early owner. In the sixteenth century the book came into the possession of Laurence Nowell and contains annotations in his hand.

Like D, E, and F, and to a greater degree than C, this book shows limited acquaintance with Ælfric's later work. Its textual associations within *CH* I are comparatively early, and beyond the

---

[1] Based partly on the careful study by Karl Glaeser, *Lautlehre der Ælfricschen Homilien in der Handschrift Cotton Vesp. D. xiv*, Leipzig, 1916.

Lives of Saints it shows knowledge of only the not very late homily IV and the letters. These letters, to be sure, belong to the period of Ælfric's abbacy. They may well have reached the south-east in a special group.

H

London, British Museum, Cotton Vitellius C. v. Ker 220. sæc. x/xi, xi¹. 254 parchment leaves, estimated by Ker at 235 × 160 mm., but shrunk at the top and variously damaged by the Cottonian fire of 1731, set separately in modern paper. No leaf has been entirely lost since Wanley described the manuscript before the fire (*Catalogus*, p. 208). The 252 leaves now foliated 1, 4–254 were together by the middle of the eleventh century. Their proper order is 1 (reversed), 4–13, 15, 14, 16–114, 116, 115, 117–235, 237, 238, 236, 239–254. Already in Wanley's time single leaves were missing after ff. 30, 149, 158, and several leaves after f. 254. Ff. 2 and 3 contain a late copy (fifteenth or sixteenth century?) of part of the first article, our xi*a*. Its peculiarities and date are discussed in the introduction to xi*a*, for which it has been collated. On the original make-up of the volume and the various hands see the description below. Facsimiles of ff. 17ᵛ and 236ᵛ in this volume, frontispiece and facing p. 230.

The basis of the text of I, II, VI (209–91), xi*a*, XVII, and XXVII; collated for III, IV, V, VI (1–208, 292–357), XIII, XIV, XV, XVI, and XXVI.

This, the richest of all manuscripts in the homilies here edited, contains three distinct groups of Ælfrician texts belonging to three clearly defined stages in the growth of the volume. For much of what follows I select details, as above, from Ker's admirably thorough description.

1. In its earliest stage, traceable by the script and the distinctive ruling of the leaves, the volume was the work mainly of one scribe[1] whose handwriting points to a date in the neighbourhood of 1000. The volume in this earliest form contained, presumably, a complete text of Ælfric's First Series. Not quite all of this survives. Besides the fire-damage and the three missing leaves mentioned

---

[1] Ker notes that two other, contemporary hands appear briefly on f. 191/13–16 and on ff. 191ᵛ–192ᵛ. The first of these appears also, I believe, for a few lines near the top of f. 186ᵛ; the second, on ff. 168ᵛ (three lines at the top) and 185 (a few lines near the bottom). A third auxiliary hand of the same type appears on ff. 161ᵛ (bottom), 162 (bottom), 163ᵛ (top), 164 (middle); and possibly a fourth at the bottom of 192ᵛ.

above, certain parts of the original text, a few of them amounting
to full homilies, have been replaced by the interpolator at stage 3,
as described below.[1] What remains of Series I in the original
hand, together with whatever is merely a copy made from that
hand by the interpolator at stage 3, represents a homogeneous
early state of the text of the series. It is because of this text that the
manuscript is designated H in Clemoes's classification, not because
of the portions of the volume that figure in the present edition,
those that were introduced in the next two stages of growth.

2. At the second stage an appendix was added to the volume
by a hand nearly contemporary with the main hand of the first
stage. This appendix, as described in the table on f. 1, contained
six pieces: Ælfric's five homilies for Fridays in Lent (our II, III,
V, VI, and Assmann's V) and another unidentified piece of which
the title can no longer be read in full. Ker has made out *Sermo
episcopi* [. . . . .] *ezechiele propheta*, and I cannot see any more.
Apparently, however, this was a bishop's sermon and not one of
Ælfric's. Perhaps it was added by the interpolator at stage 3 or by
yet another hand rather than by the original scribe of the appendix.
There is no good way to tell, because, as already mentioned, the
appendix has lost several leaves at the end, containing part of our VI,
all of Assmann's V, and the mysterious last article of the table.

Except for the addition to VI described below, the surviving part
of the appendix is the work of a single scribe. He seems to have
made a slightly more accurate copy of Ælfric's text than the scribe
of F, the only volume in which all five of the Friday homilies are
now to be found. The fact that the five homilies were placed
together as an appendix to so early a copy of *CH* I suggests that
Ælfric may have sent them out as a set; their occurrence here at
stage 2, and the fact that they are included within the temporal
order of F, a manuscript that shows very little acquaintance with
Ælfric's later work, suggest that they were issued not long after
Ælfric had completed his Second Series—possibly even before the
Lives of Saints had been issued as a complete set. That only two
of the five appear at all in other surviving manuscripts may mean
no more than that sermons for the Lenten Fridays were not much
in demand.

3. At the third stage, which by the character of the script may

---

[1] If the Latin and English prefaces were present at first (as we cannot safely
assume), they were discarded when the volume was enlarged at stage 3.

have been twenty or thirty years later, a scribe made systematic interpolations throughout the original volume, including the appendix. Whether on his own initiative or by the direction of someone else, he inserted seventeen extra homilies at their proper places in the church year and made substantial additions to two homilies already present; and in order that the volume might not be disfigured by visible cancellations at the points of insertion, he excised some of the original leaves, erased short passages to make way for new matter, and made fresh copies of whatever was thus removed at the appropriate places on added leaves. Thus we find short passages of Series I written in his hand on ff. 5ᵛ, 21ᵛ, 33, 69, 75ᵛ, 95, 131, and 184ᵛ, all these being extra leaves; and on f. 168ᵛ, an original leaf, he added the last two letters of AMEN at the close of the homily on St. Lawrence, starting an extra homily on the added leaf that follows. On three occasions he found it convenient to remove all or most of a homily and copy it afresh. Hence his added leaves contain, on ff. 69–71ᵛ, the whole of *CH* I. xi, for the first Sunday in Lent; on ff. 145–148ᵛ (the first two leaves copied by an assistant whose hand I have not noticed elsewhere) all but the last few lines of *CH* I. xxv, for the Nativity of John the Baptist; and on ff. 177ᵛ–181, the whole of *CH* I. xxx, for the Assumption of the Virgin. Perhaps because of some blemish or defect in the original text, the interpolator also supplied, on an erasure, the first three lines of *CH* I. xvii, for the second Sunday after Easter, at the bottom of f. 96, an original leaf; and almost certainly to repair the loss of leaves he supplied three freshly written leaves, ff. 229–31ᵛ, to *CH* I. xxxviii, containing the end of the first part of the homily on St. Andrew and almost the whole of the second part, on his passion. Altogether nearly a third of the fifty-two leaves he added to the volume contain parts of Series I; on the others, and over the erasures on the original leaves, are the interpolations that were his main concern.

The two passages and the seventeen full homilies constituting the interpolations may conveniently be classified as follows (I have silently normalized several titles):

(*a*) Passages added to homilies already present:

    1. To art. 21, *Dom. I Post Pascha*, *CH* I. xvi: a passage by Ælfric on immortality, which appears also as an addition to

this homily in MSS. N, Q, R, T (Hatton 114), and U. To be edited by Clemoes.

2. To art. 66, *Feria VI in IV. Ebd. Quad.*, our VI: lines 209–91. Most of this passage is also contained in Belfour XIV, printed from MS. B.

(*b*) Homilies of Ælfric's Second Series, standard versions:

1. Art. 15, *Dom. II in Quad.*, *CH* II. VIII, p. 110.
2. Art. 30, *Dom. III Post Pent.* (here *Dom. II*), *CH* II. XXVI, p. 370.
3. Art. 34, *Dom. VIII Post Pent.*, *CH* II. XXIX, p. 394 (in Thorpe's manuscript VIII is altered to V).
4. Art. 35, *Dom. IX Post Pent.*, *CH* II. XXX, p. 404.
5. Art. 48, *De Assumptione S. Mariæ, Evangelium*, *CH* II. XXXIV, p. 438. The original opening, all that precedes *Hælend*, Thorpe 438/7, is replaced by the following: 'Ðis dægðerlice godspell þæt man gewunelice ræt æt þissere halgan mæssan on þysum healican freolsdæge geond ealle godes cyrcean segð þæt ure'. This rather clumsily anticipates Thorpe line 11, which is nevertheless allowed to stand. The substitution is clearly not Ælfric's.

(*c*) Homilies of Ælfric's Second Series with additions:

1. Art. 44, *Dom. XII Post Pent.*, *CH* II. XXXIII, p. 426. Our XXVI is added. Also in MS. R.
2. Art. 46, *Dom. XVI Post Pent.*, *CH* II. XXXVI, p. 460. Our XXVII is added. Unique, not entirely Ælfric's. See below.

(*d*) Other homilies:

1. Art. 1, *De Sancta Trinitate et de Festis Diebus per Annum*. Our XIa, a unique compilation from several of Ælfric's writings.
2. Art. 4, *Nativitas Domini*. Unique, by Ælfric. Our I.
3. Art. 7, *Item de S. Iohanne Apostolo*. The story of John and the young robber from Eusebius, published by Crawford from MS. Z alone as a part of Ælfric's letter to Sigeweard, *Old and New Test.*, 1017–1153, for which it was surely designed by Ælfric. (See Clemoes, *Chronology*, p. 238, n. 3.) Also as a separate homily in MS. Harley 3271 (X^h), Ker 239, art. 22.

4. Art. 16, *Dom. III in Quad.* By Ælfric. Also in MSS. C, E, M, N, O, Q, T (Hatton 114), and an excerpt in G. Our IV, previously edited from N alone by Müller and, later, Stephens.

5. Art. 31, *Dom. V Post Pent.* By Ælfric. Also in MS. U. Our XIII.

6. Art. 32, *Dom. VI Post Pent.* By Ælfric. Also in MS. U. Our XIV.

7. Art. 33, *Dom. VII Post Pent.* By Ælfric. Also in MS. U. Our XV.

8. Art. 36, *Dom. X Post Pent.* By Ælfric. Also in MS. U. Our XVI.

9. Art. 45, *Dom. XIII Post Pent.* A unique homily by Ælfric incorporating *CH* II. XXVII. Our XVII.

10. Art. 49, *De Sancta Virginitate, vel de tribus ordinibus castitatis.* A composite piece: Assmann II without the address to Sigefyrth and with Ælfrician expansions included by Assmann in his text, plus Assmann III, 505–97. See the discussion below.

It will be seen from this list that nearly everything in it is to be attributed to Ælfric, whether by long-standing agreement or by the evidence furnished in the present edition. But at two points the compiler may have allowed himself to combine pieces of Ælfric's that had previously been separate; and at another, perhaps unwittingly, he introduced a couple of paragraphs that are almost certainly the work of another writer.

The paragraphs that I consider non-Ælfrician are to be found in article 46, the augmented homily for the 16th Sunday after Pentecost listed above under *c*, 2. The addition here made to the homily as it was issued in Ælfric's Second Series is printed in its entirety as our XXVII, but although the middle portion is clearly Ælfrician, the non-rhythmical portions at beginning and end, as I try to show in the introduction to the piece, appear to be another man's work. Hence it is unlikely that Ælfric was responsible for adding even the part that is his to the original sermon. Whether the compiler found this sermon already augmented by someone else or concocted the addition himself must probably remain uncertain.

It seems to me likely, however, that the compiler was indeed responsible at least once, perhaps twice, for combining materials that in themselves are genuinely Ælfric's. The clearest instance is article 1, *De Sancta Trinitate et de Festis Diebus per Annum*, listed above under *d*, 1, and edited as XI*a*. In the introduction to the piece I have tried to show how ingeniously, though by devices that Ælfric as an original author would scarcely have resorted to, someone has amalgamated at least three, probably four separate compositions of Ælfric's, making the whole into a remarkably apt introduction for a temporally organized series of homilies that starts with the Christmas season. If Ælfric himself did not compile it, then who more likely to do so than the compiler of this very rich volume of Ælfric's homilies?

I feel less certain about the responsibility for the other rather questionable combination. This is article 49, *De Sancta Virginitate*, which stands last in the list above. There is no sign of ingenuity here, only a simple joining of two originally separate passages, a joining that Assmann partially rejects by including the first, major passage in his edition of the *Letter to Sigefyrth*, his no. II, and the conclusion in his edition of the long homily for the nativity of the Virgin, no. III. There can be little doubt that Ælfric adapted the letter to service as a homily and added certain passages internally that now appear only in H and in another compilation, called *De Virginitate*, in V.[1] The only question is whether he also transferred the passage on the beatitudes at the conclusion of Assmann III (admittedly a very long homily) to this shorter piece, as Dr. Clemoes has not unnaturally supposed that he did.[2] My reasons for hesitation are chiefly that the transferred conclusion seems to me less effectively related to what precedes in its new position than in its old, and the preacher's address to *eow mædenum* (Assmann III. 573), which is allowed to remain, seems inappropriate after Assmann II. I also wonder why Ælfric, having on hand two appropriate sermons for the feast of the Assumption, should have put together such a makeshift as this for a third; but if he did actually piece out the short Assmann II with the beatitudes he may have issued the combination with a *quando volueris* rather than specifically for the occasion indicated by its position in MS. H.

In spite of these doubtful points, the material added to H at its third stage has exceptional value as a witness to Ælfric's later

---

[1] On *De Virginitate* see the introduction to XXX, which exhibits as much of it as has not been printed elsewhere.

[2] *Chronology*, pp. 217, 245, 247.

homiletic output. Of the seven full and clearly genuine Ælfric homilies for which it supplies readings to the present edition (I, IV, XIII–XVII), the first and last are preserved nowhere else, and four others (XIII–XVI) are preserved in only one other manuscript. The passage added to our VI is only partially represented elsewhere by the late MS. B. One augmented homily, of which the added part is our XXVI, occurs in only one other manuscript; the other is unique, and the bulk of the passage added, our XXVII, is clearly Ælfric's though the enclosing paragraphs are not. Even the introductory compilation, XIa, has been assembled from wholly Ælfrician materials, some of which are not to be found elsewhere.

The material of the third stage includes some that was written during Ælfric's abbacy: that is, in 1005 or later. The clearest examples are the excerpt from the *Letter to Wulfgeat* in XIa, the expanded form of the *Letter to Sigefyrth* in *De Sancta Virginitate*, and the homily on St. John the Evangelist extracted from the *Letter to Sigeweard*. In general we may suppose that the interpolator of the volume had at his disposal both a number of Ælfric's latest homilies and comparatively late additions to earlier homilies (as witnessed by the passages added to *CH* I. XVI and to our VI, and by the genuinely augmented *CH* II. XXXIII, containing our XXVI). Hence we may suppose that even early homilies added by the interpolator (the substantially unmodified group from *CH* II and the slightly later IV) stem from a textually late tradition and should reflect Ælfric's late revisions in so far as he made any. Further, the homilies that are uniquely preserved here at stage 3 or appear elsewhere only in the textually comparable U (I, XIII–XVII) are likely to be late compositions.

The combined materials of stage 2 (II, III, V, and the early form of VI) and stage 3, and the chronological implications of the stages themselves, are thus of great importance for this edition.

According to Wanley, H once belonged to Lord Francis Russell, earl of Bedford, and may have been the volume referred to in the note on f. 1 of MS. M, which reads: 'Hunc codicem cum altero consimili reperit R. Ferro' seruus comitis Bedfordie in Domo quondam cenobio de Tavestocke in Devinshire, Aᵒ 1566.'[1] The spellings at all three stages of H are normal Late West Saxon. A distinctive feature of the spelling of the interpolating scribe at the third stage is *heom*, sometimes *hiom*, in the dative plural; and

---

[1] See M below, and Ker's *Catalogue*, pp. 35 and 291.

M has *heom* regularly. These are spellings that are foreign to
Ælfric himself but begin to appear with some frequency in the
course of the eleventh century, though within how restricted an
area I cannot say. Of course even if it could be proved that both H
and M were at Tavistock in the eleventh century, we should have
no right to assume that either of them was written there.

J

*London, British Museum, Cotton Cleopatra B. xiii and London,
Lambeth Palace 489.*[1] Ker 144 and 283. Both sæc. XI (third quarter).[2]
Cleopatra B. xiii has fifty-eight original leaves, *c.* 184×125 mm.,
foliated 2–55, 55*, 56–58. Lambeth 489 has fifty-eight original
leaves, *c.* 189×121 mm., foliated 1–58. Most of the first manuscript
and ff. 1–21 of the second are ruled for nineteen long lines to the
page and have nearly the same written space (*c.* 170×80 and 167×
85–80 mm. respectively by Ker's measurement). Ker dates the
numerous hands at the same period, thinks they represent the
same scriptorium at Exeter, that one of the hands in the first may
be identical with one in the second, and that the two may have been
bound together before the sixteenth century. Hence, since the contents do not overlap, Dr. Clemoes has found it convenient to
use a single letter for both and to treat them tentatively as a single
collection.

Cleopatra B. xiii has been collated for the opening paragraph of
VIII. Otherwise these two volumes contain none of the texts in the
present edition.

Cleopatra B. xiii has eight articles, five of which are full sermons
in substantially the same form we find elsewhere: three in the
group published by Napier (including one by Wulfstan), two from
CH I. A sixth homily is one of the Vercelli set with a number of
short passages from a *CH* I homily worked in. The last three folios
have miscellaneous short items. One, clearly incomplete, is the
end of Napier XXVII, another a coronation oath. From Ælfric are
the Paternoster and Creed which are included at the end of Thorpe's
manuscript, K (printed by him *CH* II. 596/1–23), and the first
few sentences of our homily VIII, probably intended only as an
excerpt dealing with the meaning of *godspell*.

[1] Napier's N and Z respectively.
[2] Ker must have intended to give this date to both manuscripts, though
Lambeth 489 is marked 'xi quarter'.

Lambeth 489 has eight homilies, the first four and the last two being straightforward copies of homilies that appear in substantially the same form elsewhere. The first three, for Christmas, Easter, and All Saints, are from *CH* I (II, XV, and the first part of XXXVI), the fourth is the anonymous Napier LVII (one of the versions of the 'Sunday letter'),[1] and the last two are the homilies for the dedication of a church found also in MS. Lat. 943 of the Bibliothèque Nationale in Paris and published by Brotanek in his *Texte und Untersuchungen*. Though Brotanek tried to prove that both these homilies are by Ælfric, only no. 1, which stands last, as Ker's article 8, in the Lambeth manuscript, can properly be attributed to him.[2] The other two homilies (Ker's 5 and 6) start like *CH* I. XIX and II. XLV respectively, but they are shortened and supplemented with passages culled from elsewhere in *CH* I and II, from *LS* XIII and XIX, from some of Wulfstan's homilies and others printed by Napier, and even from the non-Ælfrician Brotanek II which appears as a whole as the very next article in the volume. Ker gives a complete analysis of all these pieces.

Evidently the miscellaneous selections in these two volumes were drawn from older manuscripts of diverse origin. Clemoes has assigned to the *CH* I homilies a position indicating a textual state just earlier than that of Thorpe's manuscript, K. One or more exemplars representing a later state must account for the other Ælfrician items, at least for Brotanek I, the excerpts from the *Lives of Saints*, and the first paragraph of VIII, which was probably the last to be composed, though it may not be later than the turn of the century. The bits from Wulfstan must belong to a still later stratum.

K

Cambridge, University Library Gg. 3. 28. Ker 15. sæc. X/XI. 260 original leaves, *c.* 275×218 mm., foliated 1–266 with gaps to indicate six missing leaves. Leaves missing at end.

This volume, like D above, contains none of the new material in the present edition and is represented in it only because it has been collated for the original text of *CH* II. XXVII, *Alia Narratio de Evangelii Textu*, which is incorporated in our homily XVII, an otherwise unique member of the collection in MS. H.

---

[1] See especially Jost, *Wulfstanstudien*, pp. 222 sqq.
[2] See below, p. 141, n. 1.

The manuscript is of great importance, however, as a point of reference for all matters pertaining to the textual history of Ælfric's homilies, and as such is referred to frequently in this edition. It is the manuscript on which Thorpe based his edition of the *Catholic Homilies*. Hence a very large part of its contents, its nearly complete copy of the two series of homilies in two books, is well known. Written in the neighbourhood of the year 1000, it is the only manuscript that contains the prefaces, Latin and English, by which each of the two books is preceded, or the final prayer, and the only one that presents the homilies of the second series in their original order. A careful estimate of its significance will be found in Sisam, *Studies in the History of Old English Literature*, pp. 165–71 (first published in *RES*, 1932).

Besides the *Catholic Homilies* and the closing prayer there are included at the end of the volume several other writings of Ælfric's, in the following order: (1) *De Temporibus Anni*; (2) the Paternoster, Creeds, and Prayers printed in Thorpe II. 596–600; (3) the Lenten piece, *De Penitentia* (Thorpe II. 602–8); (4) the paragraph on abstinence at holy times and times of fasting (Thorpe II. 608); (5) the *Letter for Wulfsige* (Fehr, *Brief* I), ending imperfectly at the bottom of the last surviving leaf.

Since the whole volume is written continuously and in one main hand it must be a copy, not the original, of a manuscript in Ælfric's possession containing at first, probably, the two series of homilies alone, but receiving a few other pieces from time to time at the end. The latest of these is probably the *Letter for Wulfsige*, to which various dates have been assigned within the span of Wulfsige's term as bishop of Sherborne (992–1002). The effort to reform Wulfsige's secular clergy may well have preceded rather than, as Dietrich argued, coincided with Wulfsige's introduction of Benedictine monks into Sherborne in 998. Dr. Clemoes associates the letter, in style and matter, with work done soon after the completion of the Second Series,[1] so that a date as early as 993–5 seems probable.

L

Cambridge, University Library Ii. 1. 33.[2] Ker 18. sæc. XII². 226

[1] Clemoes, *Chronology*, pp. 222 and 223, n. 7; also his supplement to Fehr's introduction in the reprint of the *Hirtenbriefe*.
[2] Skeat's U; Crawford's C in the *O.E. Hept.*

original leaves, *c.* 220 × 158 mm., foliated 2–227. Leaves missing after f. 52 and a quire after f. 184.

Collated for XXI, of which it has a generous portion (1–140, 150–508, 510–44).

Of the forty-four articles enumerated by Ker, 1–7, 9–39, and 43 are by Ælfric. As Ker points out, the collection is mainly a passional, and most of the articles are drawn from the supply of homilies for saints' days in the *Catholic Homilies* and the *Lives of Saints*. Chief among the exceptions is the first article, a translation of *Genesis* i–xxiv. 22 'god heriende', mainly if not entirely by Ælfric[1] and headed by his preface to Æthelweard. All the other articles in the volume are homiletic in character, and most, as already indicated, have narratives of the lives and passions of saints.

From the *Catholic Homilies* come twenty of Ker's articles. All those dealing with the passions of the apostles (but not the expositions of gospel-texts accompanying some of these) have been included, and likewise the homilies on St. Stephen, the Holy Innocents, and SS. Gregory, Benedict, Lawrence, and Clement. The homily on Job (*CH* II. xxxv) makes a not unsuitable companion to these. At the head of the collection, just after the translation of *Genesis*, are two homilies pertaining to Christ: *CH* II. xiii, for the fifth Sunday in Lent, which begins with the announcement that the next two weeks are set apart in the services of the church as the Saviour's passiontide; and *CH* I. ii, Ælfric's first and most basic treatment of the Lord's Nativity. (It may seem strange that the Palm Sunday homilies, *CH* I. xiv, and II. xiv, dealing directly with the Lord's passion, are not here also, but as Ker points out, the collection seems to have been put together over a period of years, and is not completely systematic.) Article 43, set among articles not by Ælfric, is the Rogationtide account of Drihthelm's vision, *CH* II. xxiii.

From the *Lives of Saints* come sixteen of Ker's articles, including those on SS. George, Mark, Alban, Æthelthryth, Abdon and

---

[1] K. Jost, 'Unechte Ælfrictexte', *Anglia*, LI (1927), 177–219, argued that the version in our L contains just the portion of *Genesis* that Ælfric told Æthelweard he had translated and is more consistently Ælfrician in style than the sometimes divergent version in MSS. Claudius B. iv (Y) and Laud Misc. 509 (Z). But some of Jost's conclusions are questioned by J. Raith, 'Ælfric's Share in the Old English Pentateuch', *RES*, N.S. III (1952), 305–14. It is probably wise, in view of Raith's argument, to question the authenticity of both of the extant versions of *Genesis* iv, v, x, and xi. Both versions of *Genesis* i–xxiv are printed in Crawford's *O.E. Hept.*

Sennes, Oswald, Denis, Edmund, Thomas the Apostle, and Vincent. With these are associated the homilies on St. Peter's chair, on the memory of the Saints, on the Maccabees (including the appended piece, Ker's 36, on beadsmen, labourers, and soldiers), and on the exaltation of the Cross; and with less obvious relevance, *De Auguriis* (*LS* xvii). The St. Vincent homily, though printed by Skeat at the end of the *Lives of Saints*, no. xxxvii, is not included in Skeat's basic manuscript (Cotton Julius E. vii, our W) and is indeed found here only. It was probably composed after the series had been issued. Very likely the companion piece, Belfour viii, on *John* xii. 24–26, which occurs uniquely in MS. B with assignment to a martyr's day, but with explicit mention of St. Vincent, was composed by Ælfric at the same time as the passion and was meant to accompany it, but has been deliberately excluded from L like the similar expositions of gospel-texts for the apostles.

The St. Vincent homily is probably the latest of Ælfric's compositions to appear in this manuscript, for the translation of *Genesis* was probably finished before the completion of the *Lives of Saints*. The only other Ælfrician piece not yet mentioned is *De Falsis Diis*, our xxi. This lacks the little passage, 141–9, that appears in R and S and partially in the Wulfstan revision in T; hence it belongs with W (Skeat's basis for the *Lives*) and C as a representative of the original version. It is incomplete at the end because of loss of a quire. In W, *De Falsis Diis* occurs as an appendix to the *Lives of Saints*, though it may have been composed, as Dr. Clemoes has suggested (*Chronology*, 221, 224, and 244) before the set was complete. It probably owes its presence here to association with the *Lives*, for, like *De Auguriis*, it is not obviously to be expected in the midst of the passions of saints.

In spite of the specialization in this manuscript, Ælfric's homilies and reading pieces on the saints are by no means fully represented. There is nothing here, for instance, on John the Baptist, though there are some marginal quotations about evil women extracted from Ælfric's homily on his Decollation, *CH* I. xxxii (for which see Ker's art. 44). Among others passed over are SS. Cuthbert, Swithun, and Martin. More conspicuous is the absence of any homily on the Virgin, and the general exclusion of women. St. Æthelthryth alone is represented, and her position (Ker 4) next after Christ and before St. Benedict makes me suspect some local reason for her presence.

The non-Ælfrician pieces, except for a few lines inserted on a half-empty page (Ker's 8) are at the end, articles 40–42 and 44. For details of these, see Ker. With 43, Ælfric's account of the vision of Dryhthelm, already mentioned, the end-pieces constitute a kind of moralizing and admonitory appendix to the passions. Article 44 is a crudely versified set of apothegms.[1]

Among early marginalia in the volume are, as Ker notes, two short metrical passages in Old French, one on St. Andrew (f. 70ᵛ), the other three rhymed proverbs (f. 120). These three proverbs occur (though very likely not for the first time) in Guillaume de Berneville, *La Vie de Saint Gilles*, ed. G. Paris et A. Bos (*Soc. des Anc. Textes*, 1881) at lines 89–90, 305–8, and 547–8. I do not know whether anything can be made of this as a clue to the provenance of the manuscript.

The dialect of the manuscript awaits a comprehensive study. Crawford's analysis of the translation of *Genesis* (*O.E. Hept.*, App. II) reveals a mixture of dialectal spellings that caused him to suggest, very tentatively, Berkshire as the scribe's home. But the markedly south-eastern, normally Kentish spellings, such as *ia*, *ya* for WS *ea*, short and long, do not appear at all in *De Falsis Diis*, nor in any of the variant readings supplied by Skeat for his x, XIV–XVI, XIX, XX, XXIV–XXVII, XXIX, XXXII, and XXXVI, nor in the text of his XXXVII, which is printed from this manuscript alone. Now, according to Ker there are probably only two main hands in the volume (the first, ff. 2–36ᵛ, 120ᵛ–227ᵛ; the second, ff. 37–120ᵛ) and the one that is responsible for *Genesis* copied also *De Falsis Diis* and all the Skeat homilies mentioned except x, xv, xvi, and xxxvi. What distinguishes the work of both scribes in the Skeat homilies, as in *De Falsis Diis*, is their extraordinary faithfulness to the Late West Saxon spellings of the eleventh century. Ker's second scribe, who was responsible for *LS* x, xv, xvi, and xxxvi, was especially conservative, so that examples of late or dialectal spellings in his section are exceedingly rare. Only once does Skeat record the substitution of *þ* for *s* in *se*, *seo* (*LS* XVI. 280, *ðeo* for *seo*) and I have noticed only one instance of *u* for WS *y* (the unstable *y* in *nytenu*, *LS* x. 86, where L has *nutene*). Ker's first scribe, with whose work we are especially concerned, admits a somewhat greater number of twelfth-century spellings, though inconsistently enough to suggest

---

[1] Now edited by J. L. Rosier, '"Instructions for Christians"; A Poem in Old English', *Anglia*, LXXXII (1964), 4–22.

a difference in the exemplar (itself, then, of the twelfth century) or the presence of a third scribe. What seems most inconsistent is the absence or comparative infrequency of *ðe*, *ðeo* for *se*, *seo* in *LS* XXXVII, XIV, XIX, XXXII, and XXVI (which fall within ff. 128ᵛ–166) as opposed to the predominance of these forms in *Genesis* and *LS* xx (ff. 2–36ᵛ) and in *LS* XXIX, *De Falsis Diis*, *LS* XXV, XXIV, XVII, and XXVII (ff. 166–206ᵛ). In certain respects, however, the work of the 'first scribe' shows recurrent characteristics. The pieces from the *Lives of Saints* share with *Genesis* the occasional substitution of *u* for WS *y*, whether the i-umlaut of *u* or the unstable *y*. Characteristic of both scribes is the use of *andwerdan* for *andwyrdan*, and perhaps (though this is less consistent) the occasional substitution of *e* for WS *æ*. It is rash, however, without a full and systematic study, to generalize much further. As already said, the peculiarly south-eastern spellings do not appear in any of the pieces mentioned except *Genesis*, though Ker has called attention to some comparable spellings in the non-Ælfrician *Apothegms* (in the hand of the 'first scribe') at the end of the volume. I am driven to suppose that these spellings are due to the exemplars used for *Genesis* and the *Apothegms*, not to the scribes of L. I suspect that the instances of unrounded *y* to which Crawford points as suggesting a region north of the Thames (spellings very rare indeed in the homilies I have examined) should also be attributed to predecessors. No doubt further light will be shed on the problem by the collations that Dr. Clemoes will supply for the homilies in *CH* I. Meanwhile it seems unwise to say more than that the language of the scribes, in so far as it is revealed in spite of their conservatism, has a prevailingly southern look.

M

Cambridge, University Library Ii. 4. 6.[1] Ker 21. sæc. XI med. 299 original leaves, *c*. 261 × 150 mm., foliated 7, 9–303, 306, 308, leaves missing at beginning, within last quire, and at end.

The basis for the text of VII (original version), VIII, IX, X, and XII. Collated for IV, XI (an excerpt), and the passage from *CH* II in XVII.

This homiliary, drawn almost entirely from Ælfric, is of great value to the present edition, not only because it contains six of our homilies and part of another in a remarkably correct text, but because it seems to mark a new stage in the growth of Ælfric's

---

[1] Skeat's W.

homiletic writings. To grasp its character and its probable significance requires a careful analysis of its organization and contents
and a comparison with two manuscripts, N and O, that are
strikingly similar at certain points.

The volume resembles F and parts of C in being designed as
a Temporale as opposed to a Sanctorale. That is, it is limited to
homilies for Sundays and fasts or feasts other than saints' days, and
these are placed in a temporal order according to the annual cycle.
As it stands now, having lost an undeterminable number of leaves
at the beginning, it covers the period between the second Sunday
after Epiphany and the octave of Pentecost, with an incomplete
appendix that adds to the stock of homilies for Rogationtide, a
period already recognized within the temporal sequence. In view
of the character of the appendix we may safely assume that the
sequence did not continue beyond the first Sunday after Pentecost,
but where it began must remain conjectural. The volume now
begins with the closing paragraphs of Ælfric's homily for the
second Sunday after Epiphany, written at the head of a perfect
quire of eight leaves. The missing portion of the homily must have
been contained on some eleven leaves, too many for one quire, too
few for two. Hence this homily could hardly have been the first
article in the volume. Since there is no extant Ælfrician homily
for the first Sunday after Epiphany, we may suppose that whatever
preceded was either proper to the Christmas season, as suggested
by MS. O, or unassigned, as suggested by the 'quando volueris'
category at the beginning of MS. F. (C and N present the same problem, since they also begin imperfectly with Ælfric's homily for the
second Sunday after Epiphany.) Fortunately a decision is not vital,
for the extent of the volume when complete is of much less consequence for us than a clearly delimited sequence within it that has
survived without loss of a single leaf.

Ker, in calling attention to this sequence, has also indicated its
basic importance by deducing the stages in which the volume was
put together. A blank half page at f. 21ᵛ after the conclusion of
article 3, the excision of the last two leaves of the same quire
immediately after, and the different hand that starts article 4 on
the next full quire are among the bits of evidence that have led Ker
to his conclusion. He distinguishes two hands of which the first in
order of time[1] began on f. 22 with article 4, Ælfric's homily for

[1] Ker does not say 'in order of time' but he regards articles 1–3 as 'additions'

Septuagesima Sunday, and continued to the end of the Palm Sunday homilies (f. 148). The second then completed the temporal series to the octave of Pentecost (ending on f. 289ᵛ), after which he added an undeterminable number of pieces at beginning and end of the volume. The two now remaining at the end (the second imperfect) are, as already stated, an appendix or supplement that serves to increase the supply of homilies for Rogationtide. The three at the beginning (the first imperfect) extend the temporal sequence by placing in proper order three pieces for Sundays after Epiphany. The first two of these are Ælfric's only extant homilies for the period (*CH* II. iv for the second Sunday, *CH* I. viii for the third Sunday). The third is the short *Alia Narratio de Evangelii Textu* (*CH* II. xxvii) that Ælfric at first appended to his homily for the third Sunday after Pentecost and eventually incorporated in a new homily for the thirteenth Sunday (our xvii). Clearly it was not designed as a complete sermon, but its position in M is understandable when we observe that the first of the two gospel-texts it sets forth (*Matthew* viii. 23–27 and *Mark* v. 1–20) is normally the pericope for the fourth Sunday after Epiphany. Probably the scribe himself or his supervisor made the assignment in an effort to supply a gap in the series without admitting non-Ælfrician material.

In the two appended pieces for Rogationtide the scribe likewise sticks to Ælfric. The first of these, containing all but the beginning of *CH* I. xviii, clearly supplements one of the articles (Ker's 29) in the main series, which contains the first two paragraphs only. The second, now lacking leaves in the middle and at the end, is the next homily in Ælfric's series, *CH* I. xix, for Rogation Tuesday, on the Lord's Prayer. Very possibly the scribe went on to add *CH* I. xx, for Wednesday, on the Catholic Faith, but of course there is no trace of this now.

Thus the contents of the volume fall into two distinguishable groups: the methodically arranged series from Septuagesima to the octave of Pentecost, which seems to have constituted the whole scope of the volume as originally planned, and the expansions at either end. These expansions, of which those still extant belong exclusively to the *Catholic Homilies*, may fairly be supposed to have

by the 'second' scribe (*Catalogue*, p. 31), and this seems to me probable in view of the content, though it is conceivable that the two scribes were at work concurrently.

been selected by the scribe himself or his supervisor from a collection entirely distinct from the one that served as exemplar for the main series.[1] That this main series had behind it a single similarly ordered exemplar (with or without supplementary material) is rendered almost certain by the corroborative evidence of the two manuscripts next to be described, N and O. These two are considerably later than M (O at least fifty years, N nearly a hundred), both contain several non-Ælfrician pieces, and each has its own peculiarities. Nevertheless, it appears that M on the one hand and N–O as a subordinately related pair on the other are descended, though by separate intermediate steps, from a common ancestor consisting wholly of Ælfrician homilies in a temporal series from Septuagesima to the octave of Pentecost. The three manuscripts, when their relevant portions are put side by side, offer us an opportunity to reconstruct this ancestral set of homilies with a fair degree of probability. They are most conspicuously in accord within the limits that have just been deduced for the main series of M. Beginning with Septuagesima, M and N show extraordinary similarity as far as Pentecost, where N stops; and O, which has subordinate correspondences with N, agrees with them almost perfectly for part of the series. Gradually it becomes more selective, and finally stops at the end of Rogationtide.

Rogationtide itself, however, constitutes a period of disagreement among the three manuscripts. M, with four articles altogether (besides the two appended), has two that are unique compilations, partly from Ælfric, partly from other writers.[2] O, with five articles, has two that are entirely non-Ælfrician and do not occur in the other manuscripts. Even the Ælfrician selections in M and O are out of accord. O has the three Rogation homilies of *CH* I; M had only the two paragraphs of the first until the rest of it and the second were appended; but it has *CH* II. xxv, which N and O lack. N has only the third homily of *CH* I, which it shares with O. The special vagaries of M and O and the general disagreement of the two main branches, M and N–O, are most easily explained if

---

[1] It is notable that one of the homilies added by the second scribe, *CH* I. viii, lacks the addition we find in Q, though this addition is in ordinary prose and should have been made before the period represented by the main series in M. The same is true of one of M's Rogationtide pieces, as explained on p. 43, n. 1.

[2] The contents of these two are analysed by Ker, arts. 27 and 29. The first has been collated for its long extract from the *Sermo in Octavis Pentecosten*, no. xi. M's readings here are intelligent but less faithful to Ælfric than usual.

we assume that the common ancestor did not contain anything at all for Rogationtide.[1]

The points of significant resemblance between the two branches are indicated in the following table, which lists the contents of M, N, and O between Septuagesima and the octave of Pentecost, omitting only the homilies for the three days of Rogation. The numbers attached to the sigla are those of the articles according to Ker's analysis. When all three manuscripts agree, or M and one other (usually N, but once O where N has lost a quire), I conclude that the common ancestor of the two main branches, M and N–O, contained that article, and place an asterisk at the left of the relevant entry. If only one manuscript, or only N and O, have an article it is necessarily doubtful whether it has been inherited from the common ancestor, and its claims must be weighed separately.

*Septuagesima Sunday (with pendant)	CH II. v	M 4	N 7, 8	O 13, 14
*Sexagesima Sunday	CH II. vi	M 5	N 9	O 15
*Quinquagesima Sunday	CH I. x	M 6	N 10 imp.	O 16
*The same, for Ash Wednesday	LS xii	M 7	[N lost]	O 17
*First Sunday in Lent	CH I. xi	M 8	N 11 imp.	O 18
*The same	CH II. vii	M 9	N 12	O 19
*Second Sunday in Lent	CH II. viii	M 10	N 13	O 20
*Third Sunday in Lent	Pope iv	M 11	N 14	O 21
*Fourth Sunday in Lent (Mid-Lent)	CH I. xii	M 12	N 15	O 22
*The same	CH II. xii–a	M 13	N 16	
*The same	CH II. xii–b	M 14	N 17	
*The same	LS xiii	M 15	N 18	
*Fifth Sunday in Lent	CH II. xiii	M 16	N 19	O 23
Friday in the Fifth Week of Lent	Assmann v		N 20	O 24

[1] Alternatively, by accepting as a genuine part of the Rogationtide set in the ancestor every complete homily by Ælfric assigned to Rogationtide in N, O, and the ordered part of M, we should have the following list:

Monday: CH I. xviii (O 30).
Tuesday: CH I. xix (O 32).
Wednesday: CH I. xx (N 34 O 34).
Wednesday (as Vigil of the Ascension): CH II. xxv (M 30).

There is something to be said for this, because (1) the first three homilies are the ones chosen in the later, very orderly set in U; and (2) it is surprising that the homily for the Vigil of the Ascension, which has the gospel-text for that day, should not have been included. But if M inherited its text of CH II. xxv from the otherwise textually advanced ancestor, why do we not find the additions that occur in R's text and are printed as no. xxv below? These are plain prose and should have been inserted in Ælfric's copies long before the time this Temporale was put together.

*Palm Sunday	*CH* II. xiv	M 17	N 22	O 26
*The same	*CH* I. xiv	M 18	N 21	O 25
The same, or Tuesday	Not Ælfric		N 23	
Maundy Thursday	Not Ælfric		N 24	O 27
*Easter Sunday	*CH* I. xv	M 19	N 25	
*The same	*CH* II. xv	M 20	N 26	O 28
*The same	*CH* II. xvi	M 21	N 27	
*Wednesday in Easter week	*CH* II. xvii	M 22	N 28	
*First Sunday after Easter (Which version was in ancestor?)	*CH* I. xvi	M 23 (unexpanded)	N 29 (expanded)	
*Second Sunday after Easter (expanded)	*CH* I. xvii	M 24	N 30 imp.	O 29
Third Sunday after Easter	Napier viii plus part of Pope xix		N 31 imp.	
*Fourth Sunday after Easter (unexpanded)	Pope vii	M 25	N 32	
*Fifth Sunday after Easter	Pope viii	M 26	N 33	
[Rogationtide variously recognized here, after which O ends.]				
*Ascension Day	*CH* I. xxi	M 31	N 35	
*Sunday after Ascension	Pope ix	M 32	N 36	
*Pentecost	*CH* I. xxii	M 33	N 37	
*The same	Pope x	M 34	N 38 (end of N)	
First Sunday after Pentecost	Pope xii	M 35		

If we examine the items in the list that are marked with an asterisk as being surely in the common ancestor, we find that the list is confined to Ælfric and contains twenty-three homilies for Sundays, three others that are proper to weekdays (Ash Wednesday, Monday and Wednesday in Easter Week), but, as their texts show, were written to be read on the preceding Sundays, and a homily for the Lord's Ascension, the one great weekday festival in the period covered by the series. I think it probable, therefore, that the man who designed the ancestral copy intended to restrict it to Sundays and Ascension Day. If so he probably included the first Sunday after Pentecost, since that Sunday (not yet generally designated as Trinity Sunday) marks the close of the Pentecostal festival, as indicated in Ælfric's review of the chief festivals in our xi. The most trustworthy of the three manuscripts includes it, and since it comes last its absence from the others may be due to no more than a decision to stop at an earlier point.

The effort to restrict the collection to Sundays would explain the omission from the ancestral copy of Ælfric's Rogation homilies, of which there are three in *CH* I, three in *CH* II (the second, for Tuesday, in three parts, Thorpe XXII–XXIV), and one in *LS* (XVII, *De Auguriis*). The same restriction would explain the omission of the homilies for the five Fridays in Lent (our II, III, V, VI, and Assmann's V), which had pretty surely been written in time to be included, as pointed out in the descriptions of F and the appendix of H. Actually the fifth *is* included in N and O and may possibly have constituted an exception to the Sunday rule in the ancestral copy; but N and O have obviously intrusive homilies for Tuesday and Thursday of Holy Week, and I am therefore inclined to believe that this genuine piece of Ælfric's has also been added somewhere along the line of transmission that is common to both manuscripts but not to M. For Sundays the plan is comprehensive. Hence, if the designer of the archetype had seen fit to include one of the Friday homilies, I should think he would have included them all. If Belfour VII on *John* ix. 1–39, which as Clemoes points out is the pericope for Wednesday in the fourth week of Lent, was already on hand when the original set was put together, it would naturally have been excluded along with the Friday homilies. But it is later than the Friday homilies, to one of which it refers, and may not have been available.

If we take the restriction to Sunday seriously (though with the qualifications that have been stated and with the exception of Ascension Day) we see that the putative original set contains nearly all the appropriate homilies that, so far as we know, Ælfric ever wrote. Within its limits it has whatever is in the *Catholic Homilies* and the *Lives of Saints*, and several additional homilies: our IV for the third Sunday in Lent, our VII–IX for the fourth, fifth, and sixth Sundays after Easter, our X for Pentecost and our XII for the octave of Pentecost. There are only two omissions: the homily for the third Sunday after Easter that occurs uniquely in MS. U and is printed by Assmann as no. VI, and the long *Sermo ad Populum in Octavis Pentecosten*, our XI. It is reasonable to suppose that they had not yet been written when the set was assembled. It is true that an excerpt from *In Octavis Pentecosten* does occur in M, but not in the series we are concerned with. It is part of a compilation that includes non-Ælfrician material in one of the Rogation homilies (Ker 27) and we have seen that these homilies are most easily regarded as an interpolation made in some manuscript of the line of M after it had separated from that of N–O.

Nothing has yet been said about the homily for the third Sunday in Easter that occurs uniquely in N. Unfortunately the beginning is lost because of a missing leaf, but it seems to have consisted of Ælfric's *De Septiformi Spiritu*, of which the latter portion is still extant (Napier VIII, pp. 58/1 to the end, 60/4), followed by one of the two *exempla* that occur in *De Doctrina Apostolica*, our XIX, and a refashioned form of the conclusion to the same piece with a plainly non-Ælfrician closing sentence. As I have explained in the introductory comment on XIX, there are several reasons for thinking that Ælfric was not responsible for this compilation. Its absence from O, however, as the chart shows, is quite likely not a sign that it was absent from the ancestor of N–O, for O at this point in the series is leaving out a great deal. It may well have entered the N–O line at the same time as the Friday homily and the non-Ælfrician material.

One curious inconsistency in the evidence for the make-up of the original set remains to be discussed. For the first Sunday after Easter, M has the simple prose version that occurs in A, D, E, F, H as originally written, and K; whereas N has the expanded version, with a considerable addition in Ælfric's rhythmic prose, that appears also in H as interpolated at the third stage of its growth, and in Q, R, T, and U. Which version was in the common ancestor, and how are we to account for the divergence of the two branches of descent?

In general, certainly, the ancestral set marks a stage in Ælfric's literary career when he had produced several homilies in addition to those of the first three series: let us say at least the five for Fridays in Lent besides the six in the set itself. He had also produced a greatly enlarged version of his homily for the second Sunday after Easter. The short version appears in A, B, D, E, F, H (untouched by the interpolator), J, and K; the long, in M, N, O and also in Q and U. One naturally assumes, therefore, that the addition to the homily for the first Sunday after Easter had also been composed; but it is equally possible that it had not, and that the set was issued without it, just as M indicates.

If M is to be trusted in this respect, then we must explain the presence of the expanded version in N. I do not think it is safe to suppose that Ælfric issued two similar sets at different times, one without the addition becoming the ancestor of M, the other, with it, the ancestor of N–O. For there is clear evidence in the various readings of homily IX that M and N, in contrast to U, are descended from a common faulty ancestor. (See the introductory comment preceding homily VII). It is conceivable, to be sure, that mistakes in Ælfric's own copy of IX were allowed to remain uncorrected long enough to be transmitted to M and N by way of two distinct sets made from Ælfric's originals at different times; but it does not seem probable. I prefer to suppose that M and N–O had a common ancestor already at some remove from Ælfric himself.

In that case, if M has inherited the short version properly, we must suppose that N has acquired the expanded version by the activity of an interpolating editor. This is likely enough when we recognize that the N–O line has other signs of such a person, not merely in the non-Ælfrician additions it received, but also, as I have suggested, in certain Ælfrician ones: the homily for Friday in the fifth week of Lent, and the curiously compiled homily for the third Sunday after Easter.

There is, however, another possibility. Perhaps N, though generally less reliable than M, truly inherits the expanded version from the common ancestor, and M has reverted by some mechanical accident to the short version. This could have happened if M's immediate exemplar had lost leaves at the crucial point and the scribe had tried to repair the loss from a manuscript of earlier descent. Consequently, unless further textual evidence can be adduced, I do not think a firm decision can be reached.

My presentation of the case for an ancestral set behind M, N, and O has been strongly influenced by Ker's analysis of M as well as by the very pregnant suggestions of Clemoes in *Chronology*, pp. 227–9. In working out the details I have found reason to differ from Clemoes here and there, especially by limiting the archetypal set to the period from Septuagesima to the octave of Pentecost. It is true that Ælfric himself began the year with Christmas in both series of *Catholic Homilies* and the *Lives of Saints*; but he or anyone else would have found it convenient, in planning a Temporale for a portion of the year only, to limit it to festivals of which the date is governed by Easter. The Sundays in Advent and after Epiphany depend on Christmas; all the rest, except the saints' days, on Easter. Hence Septuagesima is the beginning of a system of festivals that is entirely consistent for the greater part of the year. I hesitate to pronounce judgement on Clemoes's theory that the original set implied by M and N–O was a more or less formal publication by Ælfric himself. It is a plausible and in many ways attractive theory. Whoever made the set would seem to have been close enough to the author to include everything that was available in its then latest form. I do not feel able, however, to draw the line between a set somewhat casually authorized to satisfy a particular demand, and a set sent out into the world in several copies as a more or less formal publication. In any event it seems that M, with the help afforded by comparison with N–O, gives us an opportunity to estimate Ælfric's store of homilies for an important part of the church year at a stage only a few years later than the completion of the *Lives of Saints*.

There is no direct indication in MS. M as to where it was written, but, as Ker explains, a note on f. 1 says that it was found at Tavistock in 1566. It reached the University Library in 1574 by way of the earl of Bedford and Archbishop Parker.[1] The texts it has supplied to this edition (apart from the excerpt from our XI in the Rogationtide section) are seldom in error, and its spellings are as close to a standard Late West Saxon as any that our manuscripts provide. The only notable deviation from the forms of the earliest Ælfric manuscripts is the dative plural *heom*. Compare what is said above on the dialect and provenance of H.

N

London, British Museum, Cotton Faustina A. ix. Ker 153. sæc. XII[1]. 195 original leaves, *c.* 230 × 150 mm., foliated 2–196. Probably in one hand only. Leaves are missing at the beginning, probably nine leaves after f. 50, one after f. 102, one after f. 159, probably none containing writings at the end.

Collated for IV, VII (original version), VIII, IX, X, and XIX (136–207, 242–5, 250–4).

This is a somewhat fuller collection of the same type as M, starting imperfectly like M with the second Sunday after Epiphany and extending to Pentecost instead of the octave of Pentecost. As already explained, it is related to M, but more closely related to O, and is the latest in date of the three.

The table that has been given above under M shows the contents of N from Septuagesima Sunday onwards, except for Rogation-

[1] Valuable information on Parker's use of the manuscript for the publication of *A Testimonie of Antiquitie* will be found in John Bromwich's article, 'The First Book Printed in Anglo-Saxon Types', *Trans. of the Cambridge Bibliographical Society*, III (1962), 265–91.

tide: that is, it includes Ker's articles 7–33, 35–38 (ff. 31^v–169^v, 176^v–196^v) with allowance for an extra article, *LS* XII, in the gap caused by loss of one quire and the first leaf of another between the now imperfect articles 10 and 11. This part of N includes all the articles that are collated for the present edition. A glance at the table will show that the entire section is close in content to M but has four extra articles: Ælfric's homily for Friday in the fifth week of Lent (Assmann V); a compilation made from two of Ælfric's writings (Napier VIII and our XIX), now imperfect at the beginning, for the third Sunday after Easter; and two non-Ælfrician pieces assigned to Tuesday and Thursday of Holy Week (part of Blickling Homily VI for Palm Sunday and Assmann XIII). The first of these (art. 20) corresponds to O, 24, the last (art. 24) to O, 27. Although O lacks the other two, one cannot be sure that they were absent from the common ancestor of N and O, for O is selective and leaves out other homilies that are shown by the combined testimony of M and N to have belonged to the still more distant ancestor of the three manuscripts. One further difference between M and N has been discussed under M: the expanded version of *CH* I. XVI, for the first Sunday after Easter, which occurs in N but not in M.

Not included in the table are article 34, the one homily for Rogationtide, *CH* I. XX, on the Catholic Faith (which is also one of O's five Rogation homilies), and articles 1–6, for successive Sundays after Epiphany. These fall into two groups. Articles 3–6, here assigned to the fourth, fifth, sixth, and seventh Sundays after Epiphany (but absurdly, since there are never more than six of these Sundays before Septuagesima) correspond exactly to articles 9–12 in O, where they are the only pieces for the Sundays after Epiphany and are assigned to the second, third, fourth, and fifth. Evidently these homilies belonged to the common ancestor of N–O, and represent something there prefixed to the sequence common to M and N–O. The first of the four is Ælfric's letter to Sigefyrth, Assmann II, presented as a homily by the omission of the opening address. The other three are not Ælfric's at all. The letter to Sigefyrth, which may never have been used as a homily in this form by Ælfric himself, was sent out as a letter after he had become abbot (1005) and is therefore later than the presumptive date of any of the homilies in the M–N–O ancestor. Its assignment to the Second Sunday after Epiphany, as in O, makes some sense, in that its theme of chastity and its discussion of the three estates, marriage, widowhood, and virginity, are appropriate to the pericope for the second Sunday, *John* ii. 1–11, on the miracle performed by Jesus at the wedding at Cana in Galilee. Ælfric's regular homily for the day mentions these matters, though it is taken up mostly with a review of the six ages of the world as symbolized by the six water-vessels. Even so the assignment may well be merely a part of the N–O compiler's makeshift effort to supply homilies for Sundays before Septuagesima.

But it appears that the compiler of N, or some very near predecessor after the lines of N and O had separated, was not satisfied with the inherited set for Sundays after Epiphany. The first two articles in N, which do not appear in O, are Ælfric's standard homilies for the second and third Sundays, *CH* II. iv and *CH* I. viii, the first lacking a few lines at the beginning which have been supplied in a sixteenth-century hand on f. 1. Now it is true that these are the very homilies that appear just before Septuagesima at what is now the beginning of M, and at first sight one might be disposed to think that the M–N–O ancestor had contained them. But there are three objections to this view: first, that M's inclusion of these homilies appears to be an afterthought on the part of its second scribe; second, that there are signs of their being equally an afterthought on the part of someone responsible for the make-up of N—for if they had been present in the N–O line, it is unlikely that four more pieces for Sundays after Epiphany would have been sought out; and third, that N's version of *CH* I. viii, unlike M's, has the addition that appears also in Q. Even the numbering of the Sundays up to the seventh in N looks like someone's thoughtless device for accommodating an extra pair at the beginning. And one can readily understand the desire to add Ælfric's pair to the rest, not because a larger supply was urgently required, but simply on the score of their weight and merit. Consequently I think the correspondence of M and N at this point is a mere coincidence. So far as we know Ælfric offered no wider choice for the Sundays after Epiphany.

For its late date N is remarkably conservative, reproducing the forms of Late West Saxon pretty consistently, though with occasional slight deviations and a few sheer blunders.[1] For the homilies

---

[1] N and O share a few spellings that may point to the south-east. See below, pp. 52 and 181.

here presented it is often helpful though only in a secondary capacity. I do not know where it came from—but see Ker for its sixteenth-century connexions.

O

Cambridge, Corpus Christi College 302.[1] Ker 56. sæc. XI/XII. 111 original leaves, *c.* 253×168 mm., paginated on rectos 11–232, lacking only one leaf after p. 188 and an undeterminable number at the end. All but eight lines on p. 29 in one hand.

Collated for IV.

This manuscript, written about 1100, and textually less reliable than the somewhat later N, has little importance for this edition except for its close relation to N and their combined relation to M, as pointed out in the two previous descriptions. The text of IV shows, as we should expect, agreement in error with N against all other manuscripts.

The thirty-four articles are placed in temporal series after the first (Ælfric's *Hexameron*), from the first Sunday in Advent to the end of Rogationtide. I shall describe the contents in four groups in order to keep in view what has already been said under M and N.

Articles 1–8 may or may not have had counterparts in N, which now begins imperfectly at a later point in the annual cycle. The same is true of M, but it is most unlikely, because of the way in which M is put together, that there were significant correspondences between it and N–O in this part of the year. After the *Hexameron* (art. 1), O has four pieces for successive Sundays in Advent, the first two being Ælfric's familiar homilies, *CH* I. XXXIX and XL, the next *De Auguriis*, *LS* XVII, the fourth a piece on baptism by Wulfstan, printed by Bethurum, *Homilies of Wulfstan*, VIIIb. Articles 6–8 are three consecutive homilies from *CH* I (II, III, IV), for Christmas, St. Stephen, and St. John. There is precedent for including the saints' days of Christmastide in a Temporale and also (though not in other Old English manuscripts) for beginning with Advent, but the series is lamely filled in for Advent and has only a few of Ælfric's homilies for the Christmas season. Certainly this part of O cannot be trusted to indicate what once stood at the beginning of N, much less anything that N and O might have shared with M. There are signs also that the texts of

[1] Formerly S. 9. Napier's D. Skeat's E.

Ælfric's Advent homilies are differently derived from most of the *CH* I texts in the volume. (Clemoes, *Chronology*, p. 228, n. 1. My own incomplete collations are in accord.)

Articles 9–12 are the four pieces for Sundays after Epiphany already described under N: Assmann II as a homily and three non-Ælfrician pieces. These all belong to the N–O ancestor but have no counterpart in M.

Articles 13–29 are the series from Septuagesima to the second Sunday after Easter that is included in the table under M and is there discussed. In this part O has nothing that was not originally in N also, but leaves out several of N's articles.

Articles 30–34 are the five pieces for Rogationtide already mentioned under M. The three Rogation homilies in *CH* I (xviii, xix, xx) are separated from one another by two pieces not by Ælfric, the first unique though similar to part of a composite homily in T (Hatton 114, art. 52, ff. 100/12–102^v/17), the second also in V (CCCC 421) and imperfectly in the Blickling Homilies. It is Napier's XLIX. The third homily by Ælfric (*CH* I. xx, *De Fide Catholica*) is the last article in the volume and a great part of it is missing, though this part has been supplied in a hand of the sixteenth century. In consequence of the loss one cannot tell whether or not the volume originally contained other homilies at the end.

The spellings of the manuscript so rarely depart from orthodox Late West Saxon that it is difficult to make a case for any locality other than southern. Crawford's phonological analysis of O's text of the *Hexameron* is faintly supported by the variant readings of IV with respect to omission of *h* (IV. 182, 189) and unorthodox gemination (IV. 253), and there are confusions of *ð* and *d* at IV. 139, 141, and 143. Crawford's supposedly Mercian or Kentish *æ* for the i-umlaut of *ā* before *n* and a consonant[1] is represented only by *blænd* for *ablende* at IV. 6. Since this spelling is shared by N, which has *ablænde* again at IV. 62, where O has *ablende*, it is likely enough that these spellings are not characteristic of O but rather of one or more ancestors. The same may be said of the spelling *mæniu* (IV. 11, 51, 63, 270). Of the provenance of the volume before it came into the hands of Archbishop Parker nothing has so far been discovered.

[1] See the description of U (p. 79) and the comment on this feature in section 9 (p. 181).

P

Oxford, Bodleian Library, Hatton 115,[1] Ker 332; and *Kansas, University Library, Y 104*, described by Bertram Colgrave and Ann Hyde, *Speculum*, XXXVII (1962), 60–78, esp. 67–75 and facs. Plates III and IV. Facsimile of f. 63 in second volume, facing p. 728.

The 156 medieval leaves of Hatton 115 (*c.* 248×160 mm.) include 139 from a volume written in a single hand of saec. XI[2]. These are foliated 1–64, 66–139, 139*a* (blank). To them were added ff. 65 and 140–7 (of about the same date) and ff. 148–55 (saec. XII). Between ff. 82 and 83 six leaves of the original volume (not two as was once supposed) are missing, and one of these (evidently the third), which turned up as a binding leaf in a seventeenth-century book, is now MS. Y 104 at the University of Kansas and has been duly identified by Colgrave in consultation with Ker.

Hatton 115 provides the basis for the text of XIX, XX, XXII, XXIV, and XXVIII. It has been collated for XVIII, for eight lines of VI, and for the extract from Ælfric's *Letter to Wulfgeat* in XIa.

This volume is an important witness for several of Ælfric's later compositions. As originally constituted it had thirty-two articles, Ker's 1–17, 20–33 in Hatton 115 and one more represented by the Kansas leaf. All thirty-two, as I believe, are by Ælfric, although there are two short articles (14 and 15) that have not previously been credited to him. Nevertheless the volume does not look like a set authorized by Ælfric.

It is a miscellany of sermons and shorter bits of instruction and admonition, in which the principle of selection appears to be simply that no piece shall be limited to a specific occasion. From the two series of *Catholic Homilies* all the eligible Rogationtide homilies are included: *De Dominica Oratione* (XIX, originally for Tuesday) and *De Fide Catholica* (XX, for Wednesday) from the First Series, and from the Second Series the homilies for Monday (XXI) and Tuesday (XXII–XXIV). All these, in spite of their original assignment to particular days, are not restricted to these days by their content and are presented here, plausibly enough, as for any occasion. The Monday homily in the First Series (XVIII, *In Letania Maiore*) and the Wednesday homily in the Second Series (XXV, properly for the Vigil of the Ascension) are restricted internally,

---

[1] Formerly Junius 23. Napier's R (collated only for Ælfric's *De Septiformi Spiritu*). Skeat's J.

by their gospel-texts and by explicit statements, to the designated days, and so not eligible. Also included are the last six pieces of the Second Series, five for the common of the saints and one for the dedication of a church. In Ælfric's first two series as printed by Thorpe there is only one obviously eligible homily that has been omitted: the first, *De Initio Creaturæ*.[1]

The *Lives of Saints* as printed by Skeat provides only two full homilies: XVII, *De Auguriis*, and XVIII, *Sermo excerptus de Libro Regum*, besides some shorter pieces to be considered later. No. XVI, *De Memoria Sanctorum*, which is expressly labelled *quando volueris* in Skeat's manuscript, W, is not included, nor is XIII, *De Oratione Moysi*, which may have seemed too closely attached to Lent by the passage on fasting at lines 93 sqq., but specifies no particular occasion except in the title. The appendix to the *Lives*, now incomplete in Skeat's manuscript, is represented by two of its three pieces: *De Duodecim Abusivis* and *Interrogationes Sigewulfi*; not, however, by *De Falsis Diis*, our XXI.

There are six other full homilies still present in Hatton 115: article 1, Ælfric's *Hexameron*; article 27, the letter to Wulfgeat (Assmann 1) converted into a homily by omitting the first six lines in Assmann and altering the seventh; article 30, *Sermo excerptus de Libro Iudicum* (*O.E. Hept.*); and three homilies of the present edition: article 4, our XVIII, *De Die Iudicii*; article 6, our XIX, *De Doctrina Apostolica*; and article 29, our XX, *De Populo Israhel*. To these six must be added one other, now preserved only fractionally in Kansas Y 104 but once complete. This is Ælfric's second homily for a confessor, written for Æthelwold II of Winchester (as we are told in MS. Q) and printed by Assmann as no. IV. It was included in the set of homilies for the common of the saints, of which the other five are from the Second Series, and it followed directly after the *first* homily for a confessor, Ker's article 24.

Not quite a full homily but occurring between full homilies with the heading *Alia*, article 28, is an adaptation of Ælfric's Old English preface to the First Series, Thorpe I. 2/28–6/34. This is the part of the preface dealing with Antichrist and the last days, and the excerpt stands here without significant change except that the first

---

[1] Also eligible, and omitted, is the *Alia Narratio de Evangelii Textu*, *CH* II. XXVII, but this, which was originally a pendant to the homily for the third Sunday after Pentecost, was later incorporated in our homily XVII for the thirteenth Sunday after Pentecost. Perhaps it had already lost its semi-independent status before the date of P's basic authority for *CH* II.

word, 'menn', is preceded by 'Læwede' and the last words of the excerpt, 'For swylcum bebodum', are followed by a conclusion: 'we secgað eow þas láre. þæt ge æfre gelyfon on þone ælmihtigan god seþe ealle gesceafta gesceop þurh his mihte. þam sy wuldor 7 lóf á to worulde. AMEN.' This little conclusion is in Ælfric's characteristic rhythmic prose and seems to indicate that he was responsible for the adaptation. A similar adaptation, but without 'Læwede' and with two short additions, occurs in Q, R, and T. Hence we must recognize two revised forms of the excerpt, of which the simpler is represented by P alone.

Twenty-four articles in the original volume (Ker 1–10 and 21–33 plus Kansas Y 104) have now been mentioned. Eight others occur together in the midst, articles 11–17 and 20 (18 and 19 being on the inserted f. 65). These are all short and decidedly miscellaneous, and several of them are found also in MSS. R and S. Two of them appear as pendants to longer pieces in the *Lives of Saints*: article 11 is the passage on *Oratores, Laboratores, Bellatores* appended to *LS* xxv on the Maccabees; article 20 is the discussion of the suffering of criminals, including an account of Absalom and Achitophel, appended to *LS* xix on St. Alban. Article 13 is the paragraph of admonition regarding continence addressed to laymen printed by Thorpe (II. 608) from among the various pieces appended to the *Catholic Homilies* in MS. K. Article 16 is *De Septiformi Spiritu*, the Latin as in Napier VII, the Old English as in Napier VIII. So far we are unquestionably dealing with Ælfric's compositions; and hardly less certainly when we come to two other short pieces in his characteristic rhythmic prose. One of these, article 12, *De Cogitatione*, was printed long ago by Napier (*Anglia*, X. 155) from MS. S. It consists of twenty-nine metrical lines, of which the first eight correspond to lines 284–91 in our homily VI. The rest develop further, and uniquely, the theme of good and bad intentions.[1] The other conspicuously Ælfrician piece, article 17, occurs only in this manuscript and is here printed for the first time as XXII. It appears to be (as Dr. Clemoes has already surmised— *Chronology*, p. 241) an excerpt from one of Ælfric's admonitory letters.

The remaining pieces, articles 14 and 15, are at first sight something of a puzzle. Article 14, which occurs also in R and S, is called *De infantibus* in S and has to do with the precautions that must be

---

[1] These lines are printed for convenience in the note on VI. 284–91.

taken, both before and after birth, to prevent infants from dying unbaptized. This was published by Napier from S, *Anglia*, X (1888), 154 sq. There is nothing very distinctive about its prose and it has never been credited to any author, but it is well within the range of Ælfric's normal expression, the sentiment is characteristic of him, and its presence in wholly Ælfrician surroundings both here and in MS. R strongly suggests that he was the author.[1]

Article 15, *De Sanguine*, is partly in R and S also, but the latter part of it, addressed as a letter to 'broðor eadweard', is curtailed in R and absent from S, though the scribe of R started to copy the final section from his exemplar and then changed his mind, erasing its opening words. The whole has been printed by Kluge, *Englische Studien*, VIII (1885), 62 sq. The first part, common to all three manuscripts, warns against eating the blood of animals, giving the substance of *Genesis* ix. 2–6, *Leviticus* xvii. 10–14, and certain unidentified canons. This is in plain prose and is introduced by the statement, 'Her geswutelað on ðysum gewrite hu god ælmihtig forbead mancynne ælces cynnes blod to etenne', as if what follows were being quoted from a tract or, more likely, a letter. The second part is plainly from a letter and is written in Ælfric's characteristic rhythmic prose, though it begins uncertainly, as may be seen in the first four lines of the following passage in my arrangement:

> Ic secge eac ðe, broðor eadweard,
> nu ðu me þyses bæde, þæt ge doð unrihtlice
> þæt ge ða engliscan þeawas forlætað þe eowre fæderas heoldon,
> and hæðenra manna þeawas lufiað þe eow ðæs lifes ne unnon,
> and mid ðam geswuteliað þæt ge forseoð eower cynn,
> and eowre yldran mid þam unþeawum,
> þonne ge him on teonan tysliað eow on denisc,
> ableredum hneccan and ablendum eagum.
> Ne secge ic na[2] mare embe ða sceandlican tyslunge
> buton þæt us secgað béc þæt se beo amansumod
> þe hæðenra manna þeawas hylt on his life,
> and his agen cynn unwurþað mid þam.

This part of the letter is included in R also, but R omits what follows, in which the writer asks brother Edward to try to put a stop to the shocking habits of certain country women at feasts.

[1] For other comments of Ælfric on the baptism of infants see *CH* II. 50, 52; Fehr, *Brief 2a*, x (*Hirtenbriefe*, p. 224).
[2] I think it is a later hand that converts *na* to *nan*. R has *na*.

Kluge printed the two sections clearly addressed to Edward as an independent letter and relegated the first section, the warning against eating blood, to a footnote. But I think there is no doubt that all three sections are Ælfric's, and it is conceivable that they are derived from a single pastoral letter in which Ælfric shifted from plain prose to his rhythmic style as he turned to matters that strongly affected his feelings. The introductory sentence, however, is surely that of an excerptor, who thus acknowledges that he is selecting from, and perhaps at first abridging, a longer composition. The style of the last two sections seems to guarantee Ælfric's authorship, and the plain prose of the first section seems well within his range of syntax and expression. A strong indication that he wrote the first part is its substantial correspondence to a passage in the Latin letter to Wulfstan printed by Fehr from MS. Boulogne-sur-Mer 63 as *Brief 2a* (*Hirtenbriefe*, p. 223/12–19).

The group of short pieces just described corresponds in part to similar though smaller groups in R and S. S merely repeats what the others have, but R has two articles not in P, so that there are altogether ten different short pieces in the three manuscripts, not counting the adapted preface to *CH* I. It looks as if someone had made a miscellany of Ælfric's pronouncements on a variety of themes and these manuscripts had drawn upon it. P's article 15, the letter to Edward, and 17, our XXII with its advice to kings, are plainly excerpts, probably from more or less private letters. Thus it appears that the compiler of the miscellany was able to quarry some of Ælfric's literary remains. Conceivably Ælfric himself had done most of the work for him by keeping a book in which short themes, *obiter dicta*, and letters were put on record from time to time as they were composed. Several of these may have been composed and recorded before being attached to or incorporated in homilies; others may have remained unpublished until quarried for the miscellany.

With respect to the full homilies of the collection several things are still to be noted. The two groups of homilies from the Second Series (arts. 7–10 and 21–26) seem to represent collectively an advanced state of the text, since one homily in each group (art. 7, *CH* II. XXI, and art. 25, *CH* II. XLIV) contains an addition in Ælfric's rhythmic prose: our XXIV and XXVIII respectively. The first passage appears also in f^b (Jesus College 15), the second also in V. One cannot tell much about the date of these additions, however, since there are no other extant copies of the two homilies that could be expected to represent a state later than K.

The discovery that the second homily for a confessor, Assmann IV, was included in the volume shows that some part of its content is later than the state represented by Q, since, as explained below under Q, Assmann IV was added to Q's exemplar when it was first composed. On the other hand, the adaptation of the preface to *CH* I shows, perhaps, a state earlier than Q,[1] and the *Interrogationes Sigewulfi* does not contain the rhythmic conclusion attached to it in R and S.[2] It would seem, therefore, that the group of texts in P is of mixed origin.[3]

Although P was at Worcester early enough to receive the glosses of the 'tremulous' hand towards the beginning of the thirteenth century, it was probably written elsewhere. Ker has noted the striking resemblance in script and ornament between the original part of P and the copy of Ælfric's *Grammar* in MS. Cotton Faustina A. x (our X[b]), which has no trace of having been at Worcester. Almost certainly the same scribe was responsible. Considering the fact that he seems to have been writing several years after the Conquest, he has been remarkably faithful to the forms of his originals. There are blunders here and there, but in the main he gives us the spellings of Ælfric's day unaltered. The neat, rather delicately graceful script accords well with the conservatism of the text.

The leaves early added to P are of less interest here. The extra leaf, f. 65, which is inserted appropriately enough in the midst of the short articles, is written in two hands roughly contemporary with the hand of the original volume. The first hand wrote Ker's article 18, a series of admonitions which seems to have been garnered from several sources. At the beginning it resembles the closing lines of Ælfric's addition to the homily for the second Sunday after Easter (*CH* I. XVII); in the middle it corresponds roughly

[1] See the remarks under Q, p. 60 below.

[2] It is not certain that Ælfric meant the passage to be attached to the *Interrogationes*, but the immediate ancestor of R and S was probably not responsible. P's unenlarged text of *De Auguriis* and *De Duodecim Abusivis* is another matter, for the author of the colophon in R takes credit for the enlarged versions that appear in R and S.

[3] Textual diversity is all the more to be expected in that, as Dr. Clemoes has recently pointed out (Assmann reprint, p. xii), the scribe of P copied the Ælfric material in three separate blocks, of which the middle one contained articles 21–24, Assmann IV, and articles 25–26. Evidently he was making a fresh compilation, perhaps at intervals, from several different exemplars.

to a part of *De Auguriis* (*LS* XVII. 129–35 and 148–50), but as a whole it is plainly not Ælfric's composition. Article 19, written in the second hand, consists of five manuscript lines in Wulfstan's style printed by Napier at the end of XLI (p. 190/20–23), from MS. CCCC 201. It appears also, with a minor variation, at the beginning of a Wulfstan homily in Hatton 113 (our T), as printed by Napier in the footnote to XXXVII, p. 177. It is not included in Bethurum's *Homilies of Wulfstan.*

The quires added at the end, ff. 140–55, articles 34–37, contain non-Ælfrician matter for the most part. Article 34, on one quire in a hand earlier than the main hand, has a sermon that corresponds roughly with Vercelli IX. Article 35, filling one and a half short quires, ff. 148–53^v, in a hand of the early twelfth century, has eleven short memoranda, chiefly on the significance of dreams and various natural phenomena, for which see Ker's list. The only item relevant to Ælfric is article 36, an extract from *CH* II. 528/1–4 on what it means to pray in the name of Jesus. This was evidently copied from article 21 in the main volume and linguistically modified to accord with the language of the early thirteenth century. The writer was the Worcester scribe with the 'tremulous' hand.

Q

Cambridge, Corpus Christi College 188.[1] Ker 43. sæc. XI[1]. 221 original leaves, *c.* 278 × 175 mm., incorrectly paginated on rectos, in twenty-eight quires of eight, of which the twentieth has lost the first three leaves. See Ker for pagination, the misbinding of two quires, loss of one quire at the beginning, two in the middle, one or more at the end. Written in a single hand[2] of about the second quarter of the eleventh century. Facsimile of p. 123 in this volume, frontispiece.

The basis of the text of IV and XI.

This manuscript belongs with A and K as a major witness to the development of the First Series of *Catholic Homilies.* Hence it has been carefully described by Sisam (*Studies*, pp. 175 sqq., from *RES*, 1932), and further aspects of its significance have been brought out by Clemoes (*Chronology*, pp. 234 sq.).

[1] Formerly S. 7.

[2] This is Ker's opinion, which I think must be right. M. R. James, in his catalogue of the Corpus manuscripts, stated that there were at least two hands, with a change at p. 199 that is not evident to me. On p. 392 there appears a new form of *y* and the script seems gradually to become a little heavier, but I have not been able to detect a point of change.

The volume must once have contained all the homilies of the First Series as represented by A, H, and K. It now lacks only the first (*De Initio Creaturæ*) which would have filled the greater part of the missing quire at the beginning, and the twenty-first (*In Ascensione Domini*), which would have stood, together with the missing portions of xx and xxii, in the two missing quires after the thirteenth. But it contains additional matter. In its new version of the series several homilies are augmented and four extra homilies are inserted at their proper places. Following the series is one full homily prefaced by a Latin note, and a second homily, though it has lost all but the rubric and two almost completely erased lines at the bottom of the last page, may once have been complete.

Among the augmented homilies the most conspicuously altered are those for the first two Sundays after Easter (*CH* I. xvi and xvii), which have received long additions in Ælfric's rhythmic prose. Next comes the homily for the first Sunday in Advent (*CH* I. xxxix), to which is attached, at the end, the section on Antichrist and the last days in Ælfric's preface to the First Series (Thorpe I. 2/28–6/34), with a brief conclusion quoted by Ker and, as Ker has noted, two short additions (the first actually a substitution) at pp. 4/15 and 6/18 in Thorpe.[1] The adaptation of the preface shows clearly that Ælfric had not retained it in its original form, as witnessed by K, at the head of his First Series.

A minor addition in plain prose occurs in the homily for the third Sunday after Epiphany (*CH* I. viii) after the sentence ending at Thorpe 130/27. It fills almost nine lines in the manuscript, pp. 60/21–61/4, and develops the idea of God's kingly estate and the great multitude of mankind that he will receive into his heavenly retinue. This passage is found also in N (f. 15), but not in the nine other copies, A, B, C, D, E, F, H, K, M. Another short passage in plain prose connects the two parts of the homily on St. Andrew

---

[1] These two additions (the first on the parentage of Antichrist, replacing the contrast to Christ, the second a loose paraphrase of II *Thessalonians* ii. 9–11) are in ordinary prose, whereas the conclusion is rhythmic. Since Ælfric normally inserts rhythmic additions into his early plain prose, I should suppose that the additions had been made at an early date, before the preface had been adapted to another use by omitting the personal beginning and substituting the new conclusion. If so, Ælfric did not insert the additions into all his copies when he made the adaptation. MS. P, as indicated above, has the new conclusion without the additions; R and T (Junius 121) have additions and conclusion as in Q, though they treat the passage as an independent piece, not as an addition to the Advent homily.

(*CH* I. xxxviii). This passage, quoted by Ker, occurs also in C
(p. 167) and S (p. 251), not in A, D, H, K, which are the only others
containing both parts.

The homilies added within the series are the *Hexameron* (art. 1,
now lacking a leaf at the beginning), which, as Ker and Clemoes
have made clear, probably followed rather than replaced the missing
De Initio Creaturæ; our homily IV for the third Sunday in Lent
(art. 12); our XI for the octave of Pentecost (art. 23); and Assmann
III for the nativity of the Virgin (art. 35).

The first homily appended is Assmann IV, for the nativity of a
confessor; the second, of which, as has been stated, only a trace
remains, was apparently *De Die Iudicii*, our XVIII.

An important clue to the volume is given by the often quoted
Latin note that precedes the appended homily for a confessor:

Hunc sermonem nuper rogatu uenerandi episcopi athelwoldi scilicet
iunioris anglice transtulimus quem huius libelli calci inscribi fecimus, ne
nobis desit cum ipse habeat.

The note takes us into Ælfric's own library or scriptorium at
Eynsham at the time when he was sending his newly completed
sermon to Bishop Æthelwold II of Winchester (*c.* 1006–12 or
1014). Probably, as Sisam has suggested, he composed his sermon
on wax tablets, made (or had someone make?) a fair copy, and
directed a scribe to add a second copy to the end of the augmented
version of Series I that had just been completed.[1]

We can hardly suppose that Q is that copy, for it shows no sign
of an author's revisions or corrections, and the script itself is not
likely to have been produced during Ælfric's lifetime. It is pretty
surely a descendant, though a very faithful one, of the volume to
which the revealing note and the homily for a confessor were first
attached. Up to and including that homily there is no reason to
believe that there was any significant departure from the archetype,
but whether that archetype included *De Die Iudicii* or anything
else after it cannot well be determined.

Equally uncertain is the question whether Ælfric regarded the
archetype of Q as the model for a new edition of the First Series,

[1] Clemoes suggests that Ælfric should logically have added the Assmann
homily to the group for the common of the saints at the end of *CH* II (where in
fact it was placed in P) and that his failure to do so may indicate that he had not
made a revision of *CH* II. Perhaps it means only that, for the moment, he had
no copy of *CH* II in a state to receive an additional homily.

to be circulated widely in just that form, or merely as a somewhat casual representative of one stage in a gradual process of revision, to serve as an exemplar on demand until some further change occurred to him. Q's value as evidence for an advanced state of revision and for his composition of several new homilies is in any case very great. We cannot attach a precise date to the completion of Q's archetype, but we know that it cannot be earlier than Æthelwold's ordination as bishop in 1006.

Q itself is certainly one of the most reliable of the Ælfric manuscripts, with few discoverable errors and a general fidelity to Late West Saxon forms. A few very small oddities of spelling and some thoroughly erratic uses of accents will be observed in the texts of homilies IV and XI,[1] the only ones here edited that this remarkable volume contains. Where it was found by Archbishop Parker is not known.

R

Cambridge, Corpus Christi College 178, pp. 1–270, plus *Corpus Christi College 162*, pp. 139–60.[2] Ker 41A. sæc. XI[1]. 144 original leaves, *c.* 287 × 195 mm., eighteen quires of eight still extant, but eleven of the leaves were transferred from 178 to 162, apparently in Parker's time. The leaves of both codices are paginated on the rectos, not quite accurately, and their proper sequence is MS. 178, pp. 1–30; MS. 162, pp. 139–60; MS. 178, pp. 33–270. Within the eighteen quires nothing is lost, but a quire is missing at the end. In two hands, one writing to the bottom of p. 169 in MS. 178, the other 170–270. Both, in my opinion, may be dated only a little before the middle of the century.   Facsimile of p. 156 in second volume, frontispiece.

The basis of the text of XVIII, XXI, XXV, XXVI, and XXIX. Collated for XI, the passage from the *Interrogationes* in XIa, and the second part of XXX.

This manuscript, like Q, is a descendant, substantially unchanged, of a lost volume of some importance, though not of one that was put together under Ælfric's supervision. The extant volume is arranged in two books, each containing twelve full

---

[1] See the introductions to these two homilies.

[2] Formerly S. 6, with eleven leaves from S. 5. Skeat's H. We are concerned here with only Part A of MS. 178, Part B being an originally distinct copy of the Benedictine Rule, though the two were both at Worcester in the eleventh century and may have been bound together then.

homilies, but the first contains six short pieces in addition, some of which we have encountered in P, and the second had originally two or more pendants, one of which remains. The first book has homilies for unspecified occasions (resembling P in this respect also); the second for important festivals; and the design of the whole is confirmed by a colophon in Old English and Latin that separates the two books.

The Old English part of the colophon (quoted in full by Ker, art. 19) makes the following points: 1. There are twelve sermons in each book. 2. Those in the first book may be delivered whenever one pleases; those in the second, only on the appointed days. 3. Twenty-two sermons are set down entirely as they were in the old exemplar ('on þære ealdan æ-bysne'). 4. Two sermons, one on the capital sins and another on auguries, are augmented from other sermons.

The Latin part, referring to the second book only, says it contains twelve sermons in English, which have been taken from the books that Abbot Ælfric translated. It then lists the twelve, which are still to be found—though certain qualifications must be made.

Let us examine first the sermons that the author of the colophon says he has augmented. Both are in the first book, articles 7 and 8. The first carries the title, *De octo uitiis et de duodecim abusiuis gradus*, and in fact we find that the part dealing with the *octo vitiis* or eight capital sins has been augmented, the only question being how much. The whole homily has been printed from this manuscript by Morris, *Old English Homilies*, I. 296 sqq., so that it has become a familiar member of the Ælfric canon. The essential parts are undoubtedly his, but at least some credit for the combination must belong to the author of the colophon. Perhaps he did no more than add to a piece on the capital sins the little treatise *De Duodecim Abusivis*, which was once the last item (according to the table) in Skeat's manuscript (W) of the *Lives of Saints*. It actually appears as an independent article in C, G, and P, and was once, according to the Parkerian table, in V (CCCC 421). But the part on the capital sins, though most of it corresponds to *LS* XVI. 267–381, has a few introductory sentences that do not appear together anywhere else except in the two other copies of the combined homily, those in S and in the thirteenth-century Lambeth 487 (also printed by Morris). The opening quotation appears, with the same translation, in Ælfric's third Christmas Homily, *LS* I. 162 sq., and Ker has noted three lines that are in Ælfric's Mid-lent homily, *LS* XIII.

98–101. But since these introductory lines (the first thirteen in Morris) are not as a whole in Ælfric's rhythmic prose, I think the author of the colophon was responsible for them as well as for the addition of *De Duodecim Abusivis*.[1]

The second homily, *De Auguriis, LS* XVII, poses a similar question. There is no doubt that it is augmented, for it contains at the end both the short piece on Macarius that forms a pendant, in Skeat's manuscript of the *Lives*, to XXI, on St. Swithun (lines 464–98), and also a longer piece on Saul and the Witch of Endor. The whole addition has been printed below as our XXIX. I am uncertain whether the author of the colophon put these three pieces together or merely inserted the Macarius passage near the beginning of an addition that Ælfric had already made. The matter is discussed in the introductory comment on XXIX.

In spite of these doubts it is clear that each of the two homilies as they stand in R was augmented by the author of the colophon from another source. If they appear elsewhere in exactly the same form the same man must be responsible. Now they do appear elsewhere in the same form—both of them in S, and one, as we have seen, also in the late manuscript, Lambeth 487, which is not otherwise of interest to us here. But since S, though several of its homilies show a close relation to R, cannot be derived from R, we must conclude that these two augmented homilies were already present in a manuscript older than R, from which both R and (in part) S are descended. The colophon of R must have been present in that earlier manuscript, which must therefore have contained all twenty-four of the full homilies in R.

The twelve full homilies in the first book are articles 1–11 and 18 in Ker's list. Articles 1, 4, 5, and 10 are from the *Catholic Homilies* (I. 1, XXIV, XX; II. XXXIII); article 8 is the expanded *De Auguriis* (*LS* XVII); article 7 is the compounded *De Octo Vitiis et de Duodecim Abusivis*, partly corresponding to *LS* XVI, partly to the appendix to the *Lives* in W. To this same appendix belong articles 3 and 18, the *Interrogationes Sigewulfi* and *De Falsis Diis* (our XXI). The other four are among Ælfric's later homilies, composed at various times, as we may assume, after the *Lives*. Article 2 is the *Hexameron*; article 6 is our XI, for the octave of Pentecost; article 9 is our XVIII, on the Day of Judgement; article 11 is Assmann IV, for

---

[1] The authenticity of the combined homily, and of the opening lines, is questioned by Clemoes also, *Chronology*, p. 239, n. 3.

a confessor. The last of these was entered in the archetype of Q before any copy had left Ælfric's possession, and the author of the colophon could have found all four, with the possible exception of our XVIII, in that archetype or a descendant of it.[1]

More interesting in some ways, however, is the evidence that the author of the colophon had access to augmented copies of some of the older homilies. Since he so positively insists that all the homilies except the two he names are reproduced as he found them, there is a strong presumption that any additions we find in the other homilies were already present in the old exemplar ('on þære ealdan æ-bysne'), and are to be attributed to Ælfric himself. Now article 10 contains a version of the homily for the twelfth Sunday after Pentecost (*CH* II. xxxiii) to which two separate additions, both of some extent, have been made. One of these, on tithes, is in plain prose and was, I think, added first. All but the introductory sentence occurs also at the close of *De Virginitate* in V (CCCC 419), from which it is printed as the second half of our xxx. The other, added at a slightly earlier point in the original homily, is our xxvi, an *exemplum* in rhythmic prose on Ambrose and Theodosius.[2] Again, both the *Interrogationes* (art. 3) and *De Falsis Diis* (art. 18) have additional passages that appear also in the related S but not in other copies. The *Interrogationes* concludes in R and S, but not in C, P, or W, with the rhythmic passage on the Trinity that appears also as a conclusion to our xia. In spite of the colophon its attachment to the *Interrogationes* has been understandably questioned by Clemoes, a matter that is discussed in the introduction to xia. *De Falsis Diis* contains in R and S, but not in C, L, or W, the passage printed below, xxi, 141–9, for which there is evidence also in the Wulfstan revision of the homily in T (Hatton 113).[3] If Ælfric added the passage on the Witch of Endor (though not that on Macarius) to *De Auguriis*, we have a further instance.

The twelve full homilies in the second book are all from the *Catholic Homilies* (I. ii, vi, ix, xiii, xv, xvi, xxi, xxii; II. iii, vii,

[1] It may be expedient to allow for an intermediary containing deviations common to R and T (cf. Clemoes, Assmann reprint, pp. xxi and xxiv), but see below, pp. 75–76.

[2] This passage, without the one on tithes, occurs also in the copy of the homily that has been added to H by the interpolator. I think Ælfric must have issued a version in which the earlier addition on tithes was cancelled and the original ending restored. For details see the introductory comment on xxx.

[3] Already pointed out by Clemoes in a review of Bethurum's *Wulfstan*, *MLR*, LIV (1959), 81 sq.

xiv, xxv). They are arranged in the normal order from Christmas to Pentecost, except that the homily on the Annunciation (*CH* I. xiii), in deference to historical time, precedes that on the Nativity. Two of these homilies are expanded: that for the first Sunday after Easter, *CH* I. xvi, as we expect from the presence of the same addition in H (interp.), N, Q, T, and U; and that for the vigil of the Ascension (*CH* II. xxv). This has the three additional passages printed below, no. xxv. They appear nowhere else in full, but the third can still be identified in f^b (Jesus College 15, f. 4^v). The fact that they are plain prose suggests that Ælfric added them very soon after the completion of *CH* II. There is indeed no obviously conflicting evidence, for it seems possible that all the unexpanded copies of the homily (in C, D, K, and the irregular Rogationtide section of M) represent early states of the Second Series.

In addition to the full homilies in the second book there is a pendant to the Palm Sunday homily: article 27, a mere paragraph excerpted from *CH* I. xiv, and followed by Ælfric's injunction against preaching on the three still days before Easter (as Thorpe I. 218; more briefly at II. 262). There was also a pendant to the homily for Pentecost, which now ends imperfectly at the bottom of p. 270, after which the Parkerian pagination indicates that there was another quire of eight leaves, now missing. About two of these leaves would have been required for the conclusion of the homily on Pentecost, and rather less than two for *De Septiformi Spiritu*, with its Latin summary (Napier vii) and English expansion (Napier viii). That this piece followed the homily for Pentecost is shown by the early-thirteenth-century table on p. (vii), which listed other items after it in writing that has been erased.

The two pendants do not constitute a significant deviation from the announcement of the colophon, but other matter contained at the end of the lost quire might have done so, and the six items mentioned above in the first book certainly do. These six, articles 12–17, are of the same character as the short pieces we have met in P, and four of them are actually in P: Ælfric's preface to *CH* I adapted to homiletic use (art. 12, P 28)—though R has the little additions that appear in Q and not in P, and the apparent correspondence is probably accidental; the passage on beadsmen, labourers, and soldiers from *LS* xxv. 812–62 (art. 14, P 11); the piece on the baptism of children printed by Napier, *Anglia*, X. 154–5 (art. 15, P 14); and the piece here called *De Sanguine Pro-*

hibito, which was printed by Kluge (*Englische Studien*, VIII. 62 sq.) from the fuller form in P (art. 13, P 15). The other two pieces are excerpts from *CH* II, each with a small addendum: article 16 from the homily on virgins, *CH* II. XLIV (Thorpe II. 572/16–31), with an appended quotation (*Matth*. xiii. 45) in Latin and Old English; and article 17, called *De Avaritia*, from the homily for the ninth Sunday after Pentecost, *CH* II. xxx (Thorpe II. 410/2–28) with two introductory sentences translating and defining *avarus* and *avaritia*. The same piece occurs in B and is printed as Belfour XIII.[1] Thus, except for these trifling additions, the two pieces are certainly by Ælfric; and so is everything else if the argument on behalf of *De Infantibus* and *De Sanguine*, presented under P, is valid.

What is chiefly of interest about this group of short pieces is its origin. Was it included by the author of the colophon in the older volume of which R is a copy? If so, why did he not mention it? We must allow for the possibility that it was introduced by the compiler of R; but the derivation of certain articles in S is involved in the problem, which is discussed further under that manuscript.

Where R was written is not known, but it was at Worcester shortly after the middle of the eleventh century if it was one of T's exemplars, as I argue below (pp. 76–77), and it was certainly there in time to receive a marginal note with the signature of Coleman, probably the monk of Worcester who wrote the life of St. Wulfstan. He is said to have left Worcester to become prior of Westbury in 1093, and died in 1113 (see Ker, art. 27, and his Introduction, p. lvi, as well as his article, *Medium Ævum*, XVIII [1949], 29 sqq.). During the first half of the thirteenth century the manuscript received the characteristic marks and glosses of the Worcester monk with the 'tremulous' hand.

A few of R's spellings (which are displayed in XVIII, XXI, XXV, XXVI, and XXIX) are unlike those that prevail in the other manuscripts of the first half of the eleventh century, but there is nothing, so far as I am aware, that can be regarded as a deviation from West Saxon. See further below, section 9, p. 178.

S

Oxford, Bodleian Library, Hatton 116.[2] Ker 333. sæc. XII[1]. 201

[1] See also MS. f[b] (Jesus College 15), below.
[2] Formerly Junius 24. Napier's S (collated for Ælfric's *De Septiformi Spiritu* only).

original leaves, *c.* 260 × 170 mm., in eighteen quires variously constituted, but with no apparent losses of written material. For a misplaced quire and the irregular pagination see Ker. Written in one large hand of a type recognized by Ker as characteristic of the west of England in the first half of the twelfth century.

Collated for xxi, xxix, and the closing passage, from the *Interrogationes*, in xia.

Of the twenty-six original articles listed by Ker, the first (a homily on St. Chad) and the last (a homily for Rogationtide) are older than Ælfric and markedly different in language and style. The rest are all, as I believe, by Ælfric.

Articles 2–15, following the homily on St. Chad, present in order all the homilies for saints' days in the revised version of *CH* I represented by Q, from the nativity of John the Baptist on June 24 (*CH* I. xxv) to the end of the year. What distinguishes the series as Q's is the presence of the homily for the Nativity of the Virgin, Assmann III, and the link between the two parts of the homily on St. Andrew.

The very next article, 16, is the sermon for a confessor, Assmann IV, which stands at the end of Q and would therefore have been copied next if an exemplar like Q had in fact been used.

Articles 17 to 21 are, in order, the *Hexameron*, the *Interrogationes Sigewulfi*, *De Octo Vitiis et de Duodecim Abusivis*, *De Auguriis*, and *De Falsis Diis*. All these occur in precisely this order (though with other pieces between), and the last four occur with precisely the same increments, in R, under which all are described. Article 16 is also in R as one of the articles between *De Auguriis* and *De Falsis Diis*, but its position in S suggests that it was taken rather from the exemplar of type Q.[1] The text of *De Falsis Diis* is defective, apparently because a whole quire had disappeared from the immediate exemplar of S.

Now articles 18 and 19 (*De Octo Vitiis* and *De Auguriis*) must be descended from the compilations first made by the author of the colophon in R, as already explained under R. They cannot be descended by way of R, because R introduces little deviations that do not appear in S. Consequently articles 19 and 20—and presumably also 17, 18, and 21—must be descended from a volume earlier than R with the same colophon. The textual relations of the

---

[1] Assmann's collations for the homily show merely that R and T share errors not present in B, Q, and S. This proves nothing about the relations here in doubt.

five homilies, wherever I have been able to test them, bear out this conclusion.[1]

Articles 22–25 pose a problem. They are four short pieces, of which all occur in P, two only in R as it now stands. Certainly Ælfric's are article 22, *De Septiformi Spiritu* (among the miscellaneous short pieces in P, appended to the Pentecost homily in R and now lost), and article 25, *De Cogitatione* (in P, not now in R). Probably Ælfric's are article 23, *De Sanguine* (in P at full length; lacking the last part in R, the last two parts here), and article 24, *De infantibus* (in P and R). The case for regarding these as Ælfric's is presented under P.

We have seen that R and S shared an ancestor closely resembling R, one that contained the same colophon and must therefore have contained the same twenty-four full homilies. And we have seen that several of the full homilies in the first book of R are represented also in P, but three of these in unexpanded versions (the *Interrogationes*, *De Auguriis*, and *De Duodecim Abusivis*). Further, if we can trust the author of the colophon, the expanded version of the *Interrogationes* was in his exemplar, since he admits having made additions to the other two only. It follows that P and the ancestor of R–S drew on different authorities for the text of the homilies that both include.

What, then, of the remarkable correspondences among the short pieces in P, R, and S? If we are to assume that R and S derived these also from their common ancestor, we must suppose that the author of the colophon regarded them as too small to need mention. We must also suppose that *De Cogitatione*, not now in R, was nevertheless in the common ancestor. All this seems possible, and indeed we cannot be sure that *De Cogitatione* was not once in the lost quire of R, following *De Septiformi Spiritu*. But the position of *De Septiformi Spiritu* in R suggests that it appeared in the R–S ancestor in a different context. And the colophon itself suggests that the other short pieces in R were added as a group by some inter-

---

[1] The *Hexameron* shows agreement of R and S against O, P, Q (or, according to Crawford's sigla, B and A against D, X, C respectively) in two trifling errors —*cræftum* for *cræfte* at 189, *swa* for *swa swa* at 195. Otherwise nothing helpful is revealed by the variants. A conspicuous agreement between O and S (Crawford's D and A) at 247, where both omit a line and a half, must be treated with suspicion. The mistake is due to eye-skip and may well have been made independently by two scribes. A close relation of O and S does not seem probable on other grounds.

polator who succeeded the author of the colophon—possibly, of course, the scribe of R himself. In that case all three manuscripts, P, R, and S, may have drawn independently on one or more representatives of the same all-inclusive collection of short pieces, a collection entirely distinct from the collection of full homilies in the common ancestor of R and S. Unless further evidence can be brought to bear on the problem I fear it must remain unsolved.[1]

S is written very conscientiously according to the spellings of its exemplars, as shown by the great dialectal difference between the non-Ælfrician life of St. Chad (edited by Napier, *Anglia*, X, and later by R. Vleeskruyer, *The Life of St. Chad*, Amsterdam, 1953) and the Ælfrician articles. Vleeskruyer (p. 9) has observed differences in spelling between articles 2–16 and 17–26 (2–18 and 19–28 in his numbering), indicating that the exemplar of 2–16 had acquired some mildly dialectal features not present in the exemplar (or exemplars) of 17–26. In the pieces here edited (from the latter group) there is little deviation from standard LWS except for an occasional *e* for *æ* and *u* for *y*. Ker observes that the style of the handwriting is characteristic of certain western manuscripts in the first half of the twelfth century. By the beginning of the thirteenth century it was at Worcester, as shown by the marks and glosses in the 'tremulous' hand of the Worcester scribe. Its relation to R suggests that it was written in the neighbourhood of Worcester, but not necessarily at Worcester itself. Its grossly imperfect text of *De Falsis Düs* might not have been left uncorrected if R had been present in the same library when it was written.

T

Oxford, Bodleian Library, Junius 121 and Hatton 113, 114.[2] Ker 338 (Junius 121) and 331 (Hatton 113, 114). sæc. XI (3rd quarter). Companion volumes, products of the Worcester scriptorium, largely the work of one scribe. Junius 121 has 161 original leaves, *c.* 263 × 153 mm.; Hatton 113 has 154 original leaves, *c.* 255 × 158 mm.; Hatton 114 has 248 original leaves, *c.* 268 × 160 mm.; all

---

[1] The fact that R and S have shortened forms of *De Sanguine* probably means nothing, for in R the scribe started to write the next section and then erased what he had written, showing that the whole piece was before him in his exemplar. S stops earlier and has no sign of erasure, but the scribe may equally well have had the whole piece before him.

[2] Hatton 113 was formerly called Junius 99, Napier's E; Hatton 114, Junius 22, Napier's F. Junius 121 is Napier's G.

three have the same written space, 200 × 95 mm., twenty-three long lines to the page. Further details are given below, but see Ker for foliation, quires, and the many complications of the script.

Junius 121 is collated for IX; Hatton 113 for XI and for the Wulfstan revision of XXI. Hatton 114 has the unique copy of XXIII and is collated for IV.

These three volumes are associated by their major content with both Archbishop Wulfstan and Ælfric, though they also contain the work of other writers. By the time and place of writing, as by the calendar and other matter prefixed to Hatton 113, they are associated with St. Wulfstan, bishop of Worcester, 1062–95. Although Junius 121 was early detached, the three seem to have been written consecutively at first, and with trifling exceptions, presumably accidental, their contents do not overlap.[1] Hence it is convenient to refer to them as a set with the same letter, T. When necessary, the individual volume is specified, as T (Junius 121), etc.

As originally constituted, Junius 121 was, as Ker says: 'a collection of ecclesiastical institutes, etc.' The first twenty-five articles, ff. 9–101, are mostly associated with Archbishop Wulfstan, being the so-called 'Institutes of Polity', 'Canons of Edgar', the 'Benedictine Office', and two penitentials.[2] At the end of article 25 is a colophon naming *wulfgeatus scriptor wigornensis*, and this has led to the assumption that the very handsome main hand of this and the other two volumes is that of a scribe named Wulfgeat. But Ker is probably right in thinking that the colophon has been copied from the exemplar. There is no break in the text where the colophon occurs, and the same scribe continues without noticeable interruption to copy the next article, which is at last something of Ælfric's, his pastoral letter for Wulfsige (Fehr, *Brief* I). Only when this is finished, on f. 110ᵛ, one leaf short of the end of a quire, is there any sign that the scribe thought he had reached an end of one portion of his task.

At first, apparently, the scribe left blank the last leaf of the quire just mentioned and began a new quire with the first of the large

[1] Arts. 70 and 71 in Hatton 114 repeat a small part of art. 23 in Junius 121; and a paragraph in a composite homily, Junius 121, art. 33, corresponds to most of the excerpt from Ælfric in Hatton 114, art. 49.

[2] But on f. 34 are a few rhythmical lines by Ælfric describing the punishment of priests and deacons for breach of chastity. Printed for the first time by Jost, *Institutes of Polity*, pp. 217 sq. (XXIII. 1–5), and attributed by him to Ælfric, pp. 26 sq.

collection of homilies in Hatton 113 and 114. This is deduced from several bits of evidence, all pointing in the same direction. 1. The quires of Junius 121, ff. 9–111, are lettered on first rectos, at the bottom, a–n, whereas the later quires are not marked in any way. 2. The original table of contents, ff. 5–8, covered only items 1–26, ff. 9–110ᵛ. 3. The sequence of lettered quires continues in Hatton 113 for 14 quires, ff. 1–112. What is now the second quire, beginning with the series of homilies on f. 1, has no clear trace of o, but f. 9 has a clear p and the series continues to z and four extra signs beyond, as noted by Ker. Later quires in Hatton 113 and those in Hatton 114 are without signatures. Evidently, the original plan was to put institutes and homilies into a single volume until the scope of the homiliary became too great and Junius 121 was detached. 4. There is a change in the character of the handwriting in Junius 121 at f. 111 (the last leaf of quire n). Ker believes that the scribe is the same because the letters are formed individually in the same style as before, but he admits the difference in appearance (chiefly that the letters seem slightly higher and narrower). This difference is readily explained by the assumption that the scribe did not write the series of pieces that begin on f. 111 until he had written a large part of the collection in Hatton 113 and 114.

If we take ff. 9–110ᵛ as constituting the whole of Junius 121 when it was first detached and given its own table of contents, we must look upon the remaining leaves, ff. 111–60, as containing two nearly contemporary sets of additions. The first set, ff. 111–37ᵛ, is written in the slightly modified script of the main volume, apparently by the same scribe after an interval of time. Of the four articles the first three are (at least mainly) by Ælfric. The first is the second Old English letter for Wulfstan (Fehr, *Brief* III). It is followed by two homilies about which something must be said. One of these, article 28, is an adaptation of Ælfric's letter to Wulfgeat, Assmann 1.90 sqq. This portion of the letter is in fact a self-contained homily, but Ælfric's five-line introduction to it in the letter (Assmann 85–89) has been replaced by an eight-line introduction (printed by Assmann at the foot of the page, under line 90) that I do not consider genuine.[1] The other Ælfrician homily is our IX for the Sunday

---

[1] There is a ninth line of Latin introducing the gospel with a common formula, 'In illo tempore dixit Iesus discipulis suis'. Ælfric does not use this formula, partly, no doubt, because he has usually given an equivalent substitute for it in English. It is entirely out of place here, but one could argue that it was a separate scribal intrusion, the presence of which did not invalidate the rest of

after Ascension. On the whole this is a correct copy as shown by its substantial agreement with other manuscripts, but (like other homilies in this collection) it has here and there little additions and other changes, all incorporated into the carefully written text, as if it were descended from some copy that a reader or preacher had modified in small ways. The most interesting of its additions is, before line 52, a line suggestive of Wulfstan's style.[1] Following this homily, with again a slight change, as Ker thinks, in the appearance of the hand, is a short piece of Wulfstan's, *De Anticristo*, Napier XII and Bethurum 1b.

The second set of additions comes next, on two final quires, ff. 138–60. Here several fresh hands are in evidence, and it is likely that their work was done a few years later. One scribe adds Ælfric's two homilies for Advent (*CH* I. XXXIX and XL). Three others collaborate in writing a homily (art. 33) on the harrowing of hell, mainly not by Ælfric[2] but containing one paragraph from his Palm Sunday homily, *CH* I. XIV (Thorpe 216/4–17).[3] Another scribe now adds the adaptation of Ælfric's preface to *CH* I that appears in Q and R, and in a slightly different form in P. Finally, still another adds Ælfric's second homily on the Assumption of the Virgin (*CH* II. XXXIV), without the introductory sentences.

The homiliary as first compiled in Hatton 113 and 114 had Ker's articles 1–75 when the first table of contents was written on f. xi^v, the last leaf of a preliminary quire at the beginning of Hatton 113, containing also a calendar and computus besides other pieces in

---

the introduction. The eight lines of Old English are rhythmically acceptable and full of characteristic Ælfrician phrases, some being similar to those in the rejected lines, some made familiar by other passages. But I cannot find anywhere among Ælfric's accredited introductions so poorly organized a sequence of phrases. After the first four lines, which are plausible enough, the passage becomes almost ludicrous by its grammatically and logically uncontrolled inclusiveness, and the alliterative pattern (not always regular, to be sure, in Ælfric) lapses for three of the four lines. The fourth, where it returns, is almost embarrassingly otiose. I must suppose that the whole passage is a mere imitation, and that in spite of what one would expect from so thrifty an author, neither of the surviving adaptations of the letter as a homily (here and in P) can safely be credited to Ælfric. Both, however, have good texts of the letter from the two points at which, respectively, they begin to copy it.

[1] See the introductory comment on IX.

[2] A considerable section, extending in the manuscript from f. 150^v to the bottom of f. 153, is an adaptation of one of the *Blickling Homilies*, pp. 85–89 in Morris's edition.

[3] The same paragraph, with three more lines, occurs as a pendant to Ælfric's other Palm Sunday homily in R and in Hatton 113, art. 49.

Latin, for which Ker may be consulted (arts. 79–81). Articles 76–78 were added at the end, apparently not long after, since their titles are inserted in the table by a more or less contemporary hand. Eventually, when Hatton 113 and 114 were split apart as two volumes (the division coming in the midst of art. 36), a quire containing further additions was attached to the beginning of Hatton 114 (arts. 82–84) and one more leaf was put at the end (art. 85). The greater part of the collection, articles 1–71, seems to have been written by the main scribe of Junius 121, and possibly (for Ker is doubtful of a change) articles 72–75, 77, 79, and 82. Other hands in the additional pieces are still early enough to be dated in the second half of the eleventh century.

The first part of the homiliary, articles 1–30, was printed almost consecutively from Hatton 113 in Napier's *Wulfstan*, and all but articles 1, 2 (Napier I, LXII), 22–24 (Napier XXIX–XXXI), and 29 (Napier XXXV) are accepted as Wulfstan's by Dr. Bethurum, who nevertheless omits part of article 20 and all of 21 (Napier XXIV and XXV) as not being homilies. One of the pieces not by Wulfstan, article 24 (Napier XXXI), has been recognized as Ælfric's.[1]

The remainder of the homiliary is mostly by Ælfric. Exceptions include several anonymous pieces, articles 44, 53–55, 70–72, 78 (with a concluding paragraph like that of Napier LIV), and 82 (Napier XL), and the largely anonymous article 56 (Napier XLII) containing a translation of Adso's treatise on Antichrist, with a conclusion attributed to Wulfstan by Dr. Bethurum and edited separately as her no. VII. There are two homilies that combine Ælfric's work with that of other writers: article 43 (Napier LV), which begins with a passage by Wulfstan and later includes extensive passages from Ælfric, mainly from *CH* II. VII, for the first Sunday in Lent;[2] and article 52, a Rogationtide homily including,

---

[1] See A. McIntosh, *Wulfstan's Prose*, p. 23, n. 9; and K. Jost, *Wulfstan-studien*, pp. 210 sq., where F. Kluge is credited with being the first to suggest Ælfric as the author, in *Englische Studien*, VII. 481.

[2] Jost's account of this homily in *Wulfstanstudien*, 261 sq., if modified by one or two details in Ker's *Catalogue*, will harmonize with the following: Napier 282/22–283/18 corresponds to Napier 6/2–7/14 (Bethurum VI. 3–24). Napier 284/18–27 and 285/15–289/14 (the end) correspond to *CH* II. VII (Thorpe, pp. 98–108), but a long passage, Thorpe 100/28–104/13 *swa*, is omitted and there is one clause, Napier 286/2–4, that does not appear in Thorpe's text of the homily. As Jost has observed, it occurs in the admonition printed in Thorpe II. 608/17–19. It also occurs less exactly in Ælfric's earlier homily for the first Sunday in Lent, *CH* I. 178/34–35. Another passage in this same homily (Thorpe 178/16–26) may have contributed the substance, but not the style, of several lines in

with much else, parts of *CH* I. xviii and II. xxi. Professor Whitelock has recently presented evidence to show that parts of this
homily, including the Ælfric passages, which are slightly revised,
are the work of Wulfstan; but since there are other passages not
by Ælfric or Wulfstan she concludes that the whole is put together
by a compiler.[1]

The other forty articles enumerated by Ker (not counting 79–81,
those in the first quire of Hatton 113) are all by Ælfric. Twenty-
four full homilies and an excerpt are from *CH* I. Among these is
CH I. xvi, for the first Sunday after Easter, which has the same
addition as H (interp.), N, Q, R, and U. Seven full homilies and an
excerpt are from *CH* II, including xx, on Alexander, Eventius, and
Theodolus, which appears in its usual form as article 63 in the
original collection but receives an otherwise unknown introductory
narrative (our xxiii) in one of the later additions, article 84. Article
85 is Ælfric's version of the Mass Creed (Thorpe II. 596). There
is one homily (no. xiii) from the *Lives of Saints*, and a marginal
quotation from the *Interrogationes Sigewulfi*, listed by Ker as a part
of article 38.

The only other homilies by Ælfric in the original set (1–75) are
our iv (art. 45) and xi (art. 32). Among the additions are article 76,
Assmann iv (the homily for a confessor, imperfect at the end) and
article 77, Brotanek i (for the dedication of a church, imperfect at
the beginning—the manuscript has lost two leaves). To these we
must add the pieces already listed under Junius 121: the adapted
letter to Wulfgeat (Assmann i), our ix, and the adapted preface
to *CH* I.

There is some order in the main collection of Hatton 113, 114.
After the first thirty articles, mainly by Wulfstan and uncontrolled
by the calendar, the dominantly Ælfrician part starts with the
homily on the Lord's Prayer and the homily for the octave of
Pentecost (our xi). These are evidently meant to be treated as
'quando volueris', as in the first book of R, where they occur in the
same order. Then comes a sequence (arts. 33–40) starting at Christmas and including the fixed festivals of the Christmas season, the

---

an anonymous passage (Napier 283/18–284/17). Jost notes, besides the possible
borrowing from Ælfric, a resemblance to Blickling Homily iii, and Dr. Clemoes
has pointed out to me that the passage recurs, slightly varied, in Belfour x.
104/32–106/2 and 106/8–24. A second anonymous passage (Napier 284/28–
285/14) recurs, as Ker says, in article 52 of the same manuscript.

[1] *Sermo Lupi ad Anglos*, ed. D. Whitelock, 3rd ed., Methuen, 1963, pp. 22 sq.

Purification (2 Feb.), and the Annunciation (25 Mar.). Articles 41–58 now give us a Temporale series from Quinquagesima to Pentecost. This is followed by a Sanctorale series (arts. 59–69, 72–75) from St. Gregory (12 Mar.) to All Saints (1 Nov.). Here we must observe that although the scribe has followed sequences as they occur, first in *CH* II (arts. 59–63), then in *CH* I (arts. 64–69, 73–75), he usually gives no dates in his titles and gives wrong dates twice (arts. 59 and 68).

There is reason to believe that one of the exemplars of T was R. Ker points out that Ælfric's homily for Ascension Day, *CH* I. xxi, appears in R (art. 31) with two marginal additions that make it suitable for reading on the Sunday after Ascension; and that these same additions are incorporated in the text of Hatton 114, article 57. Again, article 26 in R, Ælfric's second sermon for Palm Sunday, *CH* II. xiv, is followed (art. 27) by a brief excerpt from the first sermon for that day (*CH* I. xiv), and this in turn by Ælfric's little warning against preaching on the three still days before Easter. It is not likely that two persons selecting a set of sermons from the *Catholic Homilies* would hit on exactly this sequence; but we find it also in Hatton 114, articles 48 and 49. Indeed articles 48–51 are exactly the same as R's 26–29, and the last piece in the series is the expanded *CH* I. xvi, for the first Sunday after Easter. My collations of the expanded passage show a very close agreement between R and T, such as would suggest that T was a copy of R. This relationship is confirmed at two other points where the evidence is available to me. One of these is Assmann iv, which is article 11 in R and article 76 in Hatton 114. Assmann's collations not only show close agreement between R and T in contrast to the other manuscripts at numerous points (e.g. lines 23, 36, 154, 169, 171, 198, 202, 216, 237, 240, and especially 213–16, an erratic rearrangement of clauses), but at 143 the substitution in R of *woruld*, written above the line, for *land*, the original reading and that of all the other manuscripts except T, which has simply *woruld* as a normal part of its text. The same phenomena are plain to be seen in the table of variants in our xi, where R and T stand very close together in contrast to all the other manuscripts, and at lines 72 and 240 R has early additions above the line that are incorporated in the text of T.[1]

---

[1] For instances of agreement where various departures from the authoritative text are indicated, see lines 6, 31, 66, 102, 120, 125, 168, 169, 176, 180, 188,

There are altogether thirteen articles in T that are also in R: Junius 121, article 34 (R 12); Hatton 113, 114, articles 31–32 (R 5–6), 37 (R 22), 39 (R 24), 40 (R 20), 48–51 (R 26–29), 57–58 (R 31–32), and 76 (R 11). I am unable to say how many of these pieces may actually have been copied from R. Dr. Clemoes tells me that article 37 is differently derived, and this may be true of others.[1]

The principal scribe of T and most of the others adhere to very orthodox Late West Saxon spellings. Where, as I think, T has copied R it does not follow R in doubling the *o* of the adjective *good*. The dative plural of the pronoun is often *heom* instead of *him* or, as often in R, *hym*, but there are very few other deviations from spellings that are found in the best Ælfric manuscripts. In contrast the scribe of Hatton 114, article 24, our XXIII, introduces a number of Anglian spellings. These are pointed out in the introductory comment on XXIII.

Like other Worcester manuscripts, T has the marks and glosses made during the first half of the thirteenth century by the Worcester scribe with the 'tremulous' hand.

U

Cambridge, Trinity College B. 15.34.[2] Ker 86. sæc. XI med. 216 original leaves, *c.* 248×161 mm., paginated on rectos 1–431; twenty-seven quires of eight, no losses except at end.

The basis of the text of XIII, XIV, XV, XVI, and the addition in VII; collated for the rest of VII and for VIII, IX, X, XI, and XII. Facsimile of p. 358 in second volume, frontispiece.

For careful arrangement and faithfulness to Ælfric this manuscript has no rivals except A, K, and Q. Unlike them, it is exclusively a Temporale. It begins with Easter and gives at least one homily for every Sunday as far as the eleventh after Pentecost. There are two for Easter Sunday, another for Wednesday in Easter Week, one each for the three Rogation Days and for Ascension Day, two for Pentecost and two for the octave of Pentecost. The

241, 265, 274, 284, 297, 318, 363, 396, 407, 413, 431, 475, 494–5, 515, 535, 537, 560, 564. Agreements at 159, 370, and 420 are complicated by the agreement of M; and the reading at 159 is not quite certainly an error.

[1] See further Clemoes, Assmann reprint, pp. xxii (on the make-up of T) and xxiv (on his view, more cautious than mine, of its relation to R).

[2] Napier's T, used by him only for Ælfric's *De Septiformi Spiritu*, VII (Latin) and VIII.

last homily, for the eleventh Sunday after Pentecost, ends imperfectly with what is now the last quire. Probably, since there
seems no reason for stopping with the eleventh Sunday, not just
a leaf or two but several quires have been lost at the end.

In making this set the compiler limited himself strictly to Ælfric
and included all eligible homilies of which we now have any record
except a few in the Second Series and one in the *Lives*. He included
the eleven homilies from the First Series (xv–xxiv and xxvii) and
five from the Second Series (xvi, xvii, xxvi, xxix, and xxx),
omitting one for Easter (xv), all five for Rogationtide (xxi–xxv),
and xxvii, the *Alia Narratio* appended in K to xxvi for the third
Sunday after Pentecost, but later, as witnessed by the interpolator
of H, incorporated in a new homily for the thirteenth Sunday, our
xvii. This last omission (*CH* II. xxvii) and the presence of the
expanded forms of *CH* I. xvi and xvii (the only older homilies in
this set that are known to have been expanded) point to the compiler's access to revised texts for the members of the first two series.[1]
The Third Series, the *Lives of Saints*, is not represented, the only
eligible member, *De Auguriis* (xvii), which is sometimes assigned
to Rogationtide, being omitted.

The compiler included without exception all the later pieces of
which we have any record: a homily for the third Sunday after
Easter (Assmann vi), which appears only here; a uniquely expanded version of our vii (otherwise in M and N) for the fourth
Sunday after Easter; our viii–x for the next Sundays up to and
including Pentecost (all in M and N, two in other manuscripts);
our xi for the octave of Pentecost (in Q, R, T, V, etc.); our xii for
the same day (also in M and the variously derived B); and our
xiii–xvi for otherwise unrepresented Sundays after Pentecost
(homilies of which the interpolator of the now damaged H supplied
our only other copies). In addition we find, appended to the Pentecost homilies (*CH* I. xxii and our x), where it fits most naturally,
the short *De Septiformi Spiritu* (Napier vii, Latin, and viii).

By comparison with the hypothetical ancestor of M and N–O,
which overlaps U between Easter and the octave of Pentecost, U
offers less for Easter (omitting *CH* II. xv) and more elsewhere: it

---

[1] There is an alternative ending in the margin of p. 135 beside the regular
conclusion of the first Rogation homily, *CH* I. xviii, written, as Ker says, by a
nearly contemporary scribe. It imitates Ælfric for a few clauses but is plainly
not his work.

has Assmann VI for the third Sunday after Easter, *De Septiformi Spiritu* as a pendant for Pentecost, and the weighty XI as well as XII for the octave of Pentecost. It also has Ælfric's addition to the homily for the first Sunday after Easter, which is in N but not in M and may not have been in their ancestor. Whether this ancestor had nothing at Rogationtide, as I am inclined to believe, or the same selection as U (*CH* I. XVIII–XX), or some other combination, is doubtful.[1]

There can be no doubt that, for the portion of the year it covers, U gives us a significantly inclusive Temporale set. Perhaps Ælfric himself made up and distributed copies of a Temporale for the whole year, revising and extending the Temporale behind M and N–O.[2] Perhaps others who had access to his work as it grew, or even as he left it when he died, were responsible for putting it together. The evidence does not seem decisive, though certainly Clemoes is right in pointing out that Ælfric's major literary achievement in his last years was the enlargement of the Temporale, chiefly by fresh homilies on gospel-texts. It would have been natural for him to compile and issue the series. If he did so, he may have made it fuller even than U indicates. I cannot quite believe that he would have omitted any of the eligible homilies in *CH* II, especially since two of those omitted (XXI and XXV) occur with additions in P and R respectively (and imperfectly in fᵇ) and the second, on a gospel-text for the vigil of the Ascension, cannot be assigned to any other place or category. Someone else, either as compiler or copyist, might have been content with less than all where there seemed to be enough.

The text of U is on the whole very accurate, though here and there it has been marred by the erasures of a reviser of the twelfth or thirteenth century, who has also made substitutions and inter-linear additions. Among occasional deviations of spelling from most of the early Ælfric manuscripts are *æ* for *e* (as *i*-umlaut of Gmc. *a*) in the present stem of *secgan* (a widespread variant) and also before nasals (e.g. *sændan*, *wændan*, *stæmne*). The last feature, which appears only at odd moments (not at all, for instance, in XI) is usually associated with the south-east.[3] Meanwhile Ker has given

---

[1] See above under M.   [2] Clemoes, *Chronology*, pp. 230 sqq.

[3] On this peculiarity (found also in the later manuscripts, N and O) see below, section 9, p. 181. See also the introduction to homily VIII, on unsyncopated forms in the present third singular, which occur frequently enough in U to impart a mildly non-West-Saxon flavour.

strong reason (on the basis of the script and ornamentation) for believing that the volume was written at Canterbury. If so it may not have remained there, for, as Ker again points out, the twelfth-century additions show no trace of a south-eastern dialect.[1]

V

Cambridge, Corpus Christi College 419 and *421*.[2] Ker 68 and 69. sæc. XI[1], XI (3rd quarter). Companion volumes, 183 original folios in 419 (*c.* 210×125 mm.)[3] and 176 in 421 (*c.* 200×125 mm.), paginated on rectos. Ker points out that the first leaf of 421 was originally the first in 419, so that 421, pp. 1–2+419, pp. 1–366 form twenty-three quires of eight; and 421, pp. 3–354 form twenty-four irregular quires (see Ker), some lacking leaves, but the text appears to have lost nothing except at the end.

419 provides the basis for the text of xxx and the same composite homily is collated for a part of xix. 421 is collated for xi and xxviii.

These volumes contain fifteen homilies each and a short prayer (419, art. 16). All the homilies in 419 and eight of those in 421 are written in one hand which seems to belong near, perhaps just before, the middle of the eleventh century. The rest of 421 is written, according to Ker, in three other, slightly later hands, which he regards as characteristic of Exeter. It is important to keep the work of these Exeter hands distinct from the other, because there is reason to believe that this other hand is to be associated with a very different region, perhaps Canterbury.

The homilies of 419 and the eight copied by the same hand in 421 consist of seven by Ælfric, six by Wulfstan, two partly by Wulfstan, and eight by unknown writers. All but two of those not by Ælfric (419, arts. 1–11; 421, arts. 7–9) are published in Napier's *Wulfstan*, and the six by Wulfstan (419, arts. 4–7, 9, 10) are also in Bethurum, *Homilies of Wulfstan* (xx [BH], VIIIc, VI, VII, xc, and XIII). The other two (419, arts. 13, 14) are Belfour VI and Assmann XI respectively.

There are two Ælfric homilies in 419, article 12 being the Roga-tiontide homily elsewhere called *De Auguriis* (*LS* XVII), and article 15 a unique compilation, *De Virginitate*, part of which corresponds to Assmann II, part to *De Doctrina Apostolica* (our XIX), for which

[1] See also the description of V, last paragraph, for apparent interrelations among B, U, and V.
[2] Formerly S. 14 and S. 13 respectively, Napier's B and A.
[3] Ker has a misprint here.

this portion is collated. The remainder is edited below as our XXX, where the whole is discussed. I am not at all sure that Ælfric is responsible for the compilation, though the parts are his.

There are five more Ælfric homilies copied by the same hand in 421. Article 6 is *In Octavis Pentecosten*, our XI. Articles 12–15 are four homilies that occur in sequence in Ælfric's First Series and also in the temporal series of MS. U: they are the three Rogationtide homilies and the homily for the Lord's Ascension (*CH* I. XVIII–XXI). The last homily lacks a few lines at the end, and a number of leaves have probably been lost, some at least since Parker's time, for as Ker points out the sixteenth-century table of contents lists another of Ælfric's sermons, *De Duodecim Abusivis*, as beginning on p. 356, the verso of the leaf on which the Ascension homily should have ended. Whether the group of sermons (arts. 6–9) beginning with *In Octavis Pentecosten* was originally intended to follow the other group of Ælfric homilies is uncertain, but clearly the present order of the volume is not original. Ker reports the observation of Miss Enid Raynes that p. 98 has an offset of the writing on p. 209, and this shows that the homilies written by the 'Exeter' hands were once in sequence (arts. 1–5 being followed directly by arts. 10 and 11).

The first group of homilies added by the 'Exeter' hands (arts. 1–5) is by Ælfric, the second (arts. 10, 11) at least partially by Wulfstan (Napier L and XV; the latter also in Bethurum, III). The five by Ælfric are headed by his first homily for Pentecost (*CH* I. XXII), as if to fill the gap in the earlier scribe's series between Ascension and the octave of Pentecost. The next four are from the common of the saints at the end of the Second Series: *CH* II. XL, XLII–XLIV. The same set is more fully represented in the slightly later manuscript, Hatton 115 (though it is now defective), and these two manuscripts share an Ælfrician addition to *CH* II. XLIV that appears nowhere else and is edited below as no. XXVIII.

The relation between this little group of homilies (arts. 2–5) and the corresponding group in P, though it need not be very close, seems to be confirmed by the fact that P is the only extant manuscript after D and K (which represent earlier states of the text) in which all four of V's homilies are to be found. Now P, which eventually came to Worcester, seems to have been written in some scriptorium in the south-west, and a link between a near ancestor and a group of sermons copied at Exeter is not surprising.

A very different link seems to exist for five of the Ælfric sermons copied by the earlier hand. These are all in 421: articles 12–15 for Rogationtide and Ascension, and article 6, *In Octavis Pentecosten*. My table of variants for the latter (XI) shows that the text of the homily in 421 is related to that in Q and U, especially U, from which it might even have been copied, though it is safer to suppose that it was copied from a near ancestor of U, very likely its exemplar. Dr. Clemoes has kindly informed me that the other four homilies, articles 12–15, show exactly the same close relationship to U.

Now U, as Ker has shown, was almost certainly written at Canterbury and may have been copied from a Canterbury exemplar. There are reasons of another sort for supposing that the earlier portion of V—that is, all of 419 and the eight articles of 421 in the same hand—was produced either at Canterbury or some near-by scriptorium and only later sent to Exeter. There is a radical difference in dialectal colouring between what I will call for convenience the early portion of V and the Exeter portion. This shows itself but faintly in the Ælfric homilies, because these are all reasonably accurate texts and Ælfric's own spelling, or that of his earliest exemplars, still prevails. Yet in at least two instances, in Ælfric homilies in the early portion, we encounter non-West-Saxon forms: in our XI. 78, V has *gelefað* for *gelyfað*; and in XXX. 111 it has the preposition *in* for *on*. This is the only instance of *in* for *on* in all the homilies here edited; but it is by no means the only instance in the early portion of V; nor is the Anglian *gelefað* alone. Napier's XLIII (419, art. 2) has several examples of *gelefan* (p. 206/4, 15, 16, 31; p. 207/21; p. 214/20) along with a very Anglian-looking *wexes* (p. 208/7), and an example of *in* (p. 215/13). Another text, Napier's XL (419, art. 8) has *in* for *on* regularly not only in V but in other manuscripts (including T) in which it is not normally to be expected. Similar instances, with other Anglian forms not illustrated, occur in Napier's XLV (419, art 3). The phrase *a in ecnesse* occurs here twice (p. 229/27; p. 232/10). Napier's XLIX (421, art. 9) has two more examples of *in* (p. 263/18; p. 265/19). Thus the very lonely Anglianisms of the same scribe in the Ælfric homilies are probably an indication not of the scribe's own dialect nor of oddities that had crept into his exemplars, but merely of the unsettling effect of recognizing the rival claims of two widespread systems of spelling. It will be observed that the dialectal colouring in these texts is not specifically Kentish or south-eastern. Rather it is

Anglian. But Canterbury, quite apart from its ancient political connexions, as the seat of the Archbishop had Anglian as well as West Saxon literary connexions. MS. U is a good illustration of the skill with which Canterbury could preserve the main features of West Saxon orthography in a homogeneous collection of West Saxon sermons. The early part of V shows a nearly but not quite successful effort on the part of a single scribe to be faithful to the Anglian character of one group of texts and the West Saxon character of another. We have a conflict of literary conventions, not an intrusion of local dialect; but I think Canterbury or its neighbourhood is a more likely setting for such a conflict than Exeter. Certainly the Exeter hands, in copying Ælfric and Wulfstan, show no vestige of Anglian forms. And if several of the Ælfric texts copied by the early scribe are closely connected with U or U's exemplar, Canterbury is indicated.[1]

W

London, British Museum, Cotton Julius E. vii. Ker 162. sæc. XI in. 238 original leaves, *c.* 273 × 185 mm., foliated 3–240; prefaces and table of contents on two leaves, then quires of eight except ff. 133–6, an incompletely filled quire of four with conclusion of Skeat XXIII B, a piece added too late to be included in the table. No losses except at end.

Collated for XXI and XXIX. 4–35.

This is Skeat's basic manuscript of the *Lives of Saints*, of great value for Ælfric's prefaces, for its comparatively early date, and for the general accuracy of its text and arrangement. Skeat printed from it consecutively to the end of the last life, Ker's 47, which in his numbering is XXXVI, at f. 230. Skeat was aware that one of the lives, that of St. Mary of Egypt (XXIII B), was not by Ælfric, since it differed conspicuously in style and had been added to the volume at the last minute, as indicated above. It has since become apparent

---

[1] According to Dr. Bethurum, the Wulfstan homilies of 419 show affinity with Bodley 343 (our B) in opposition to Hatton 113 (our T) and CCCC 201. She also finds that the text of her III in 421 (an Exeter hand) stands apart from Hatton 113 and CCCC 201, but this does not mean that the Exeter text is derived from the same source as the texts of 419. What is interesting is the link in the Wulfstan part of 419 with our B; for B elsewhere (in our VIII and XII) shows close relationship with U. It looks as if U, B, and the pre-Exeter part of V were textually interrelated, and all at least partly derived from south-eastern exemplars.

to students of Ælfric that three other lives cannot safely be attributed to him: XXIII, on the Seven Sleepers; XXX, on St. Eustace; XXXIII, on St. Eufrasia.[1]

Skeat did not include the last pieces in the manuscript, which are not lives and have no place in the temporal scheme. There were originally three, as the table of contents shows, but only the first and part of the second remain. The first is the *Interrogationes Sigewulfi*, edited by MacLean in *Anglia*, VI and VII; the second, *De Falsis Diis*, our XXI. 1–140, 150–91, where the text breaks off abruptly at the end of the last remaining quire. The text of this manuscript only was first published by Unger (as below under XXI) in 1846. The third piece was *De Duodecim Abusivis*, published by Morris, *Old English Homilies*, pp. 299 sqq., as part of the unauthorized compilation, *De Octo Vitiis et de Duodecim Abusivis*, in R and S, but occurring alone, as here, in C, G (followed by the genuine part of *De Octo Vitiis*), and P, and formerly in V.

Except for the four lives excluded above, W seems to represent the text of Ælfric's Third Series (mainly lives) as first issued, though certainly individual members of the set may have been sent out earlier.[2] The *Interrogationes*, as in C and P, lacks the passage on the Trinity at the end of R and S; and the *De Auguriis*, expanded without authority (at least in part) in R and S, has its normal form as in C, L, O, P, and V.[3] *De Falsis Diis*, as in C and L, lacks lines 141–9, probably a later addition which appears in R and S and partially in Wulfstan's revision in T.

---

[1] Sisam, *Studies*, p. 185, n. 1 (reprinted from *RES*, 1932), rejects, besides XXIII B, XXXIII (which, like XXIII B, is out of place by the calendar), and points out rhymes of a non-Ælfrician character in XXIII. Even earlier, Jost had set aside these and XXX as under suspicion ('Unechte Ælfrictexte', *Anglia*, LI [1927], 85); and in 1955 Miss E. M. Liggins, then preparing a dissertation on *The Expression of Causal Relationship in OE Prose* at the University of London, wrote to tell me that she had independently found syntactical reasons for rejecting all these pieces. Ker points out that XXIII, XXIII B, and XXXIII are not genuine, and Clemoes (*Chronology*, p. 219) eliminates these and XXX also from the canon, saying rightly that they differ from the rest of the *Lives* in 'intention, style and linguistic usage'. All are in prose which is conspicuously unlike both the rhythmic prose of all the other saints' lives in the set and Ælfric's ordinary prose as well. They are not all alike, but they are equally uncharacteristic of Ælfric. When these are rejected, we find Ælfric writing ordinary prose only in the Christmas homily and in parts of the homilies for Ash Wednesday (*LS* XII), the Memory of Saints (*LS* XVI) and Rogationtide (*LS* XVII, *De Auguriis*).

[2] Cf. Clemoes, *Chronology*, p. 222, where it is also suggested that *LS* XVI may once have been placed at the beginning of the series.

[3] The passage on Macarius, which is part of the addition to *De Auguriis* in

According to the thirteenth-century inscription on f. 3, the manuscript belonged to Bury St. Edmunds. It was probably written in the south.[1]

Y

[*London, British Museum, Cotton Claudius B. iv.* Ker 142. sæc. XI^1. One of the two chief witnesses to the translation, partly by Ælfric, of the first six books of the Bible. It contains no homilies and has not been used in the present edition. It is printed in Crawford's *Old English Heptateuch*.]

Z

Oxford, Bodleian Library, Laud Misc. 509.[2] Ker 344.[3] sæc. XI^2. 141 ff., 211×138 mm., mainly in one hand. One leaf missing after f. 5; three-quarters of quire 18 in the portion now in Cotton Vespasian D. xxi.

Collated for the excerpts from the *Letter to Wulfgeat* in xi*a*.

This manuscript runs parallel to Y for Ælfric's Preface to his translation of *Genesis* (here complete, there imperfect) and for the partly Ælfrician *Pentateuch* and *Joshua*.[4] Then follow Ælfric's homily on *Judges*, the *Letter to Wulfgeat* (Assmann 1), and the *Letter to Sigeweard: On the Old and New Testament*. The homily is also in P; the letters are preserved as such here only; the first is adapted as a homily in two different ways in P and T; parts of the second appear as homilies in B, H, and X^h (Harley 3271). All the texts in Z except Assmann 1 are printed or collated in Crawford's *Old English Heptateuch*.

Ker has traced the manuscript to the old Royal Library in 1542, but its earlier history is unknown.

CLASS II: SECONDARY MANUSCRIPTS[5]

X^d

London, British Museum, Cotton Otho C. i, vol. 2. Ker 182. sæc.

R and S (hence included in our XXIX. 4–35), is appended to the life of St. Swithun, where Skeat prints it (*LS* XXI. 464–98).

[1] Dr. Clemoes has pointed out to me that if Ker's estimate of the date of the manuscript is correct, it was probably written before 1020, when the Benedictine abbey at Bury was founded.   [2] Formerly Laud E. 19.

[3] Ker includes, as properly a part of the same manuscript, Cotton Vespasian D. xxi, ff. 18–40, containing a non-Ælfrician life of St. Guthlac. It is omitted here as not relevant to the present edition.

[4] On the problem of the authorship see below, section 6, p. 143.

[5] In this class are manuscripts containing only a few Ælfric homilies or mere excerpts. They are arranged according to their position in Ker's *Catalogue*. Those

XI in., XI med. 155 leaves damaged by fire and mounted separately, much of the writing still legible. The best preserved leaves *c.* 260 × 165 mm. A leaf missing after f. 97 and other leaves at the end. Folios 1–61 in a hand of the beginning of sæc. XI, the rest in three other hands (beginning at 62, 139ᵛ/5, and 149) dated by Ker about forty years later. The Ælfric material is in the last of these hands, ff. 149–55.

A thorough description of this manuscript (and of the unrelated vol. I formerly bound up with it) is given by Sisam, 'An Old English Translation of a Letter from Wynfrith to Eadburga', *Studies*, pp. 199–224 (originally *MLR*, XVIII [1923], 253 sqq.). The matter of ff. 1–148 has no connexion with Ælfric. The bulk of it (1–137) is an incomplete copy of the Alfredian translation of Gregory's *Dialogues*, to which have been added three translations from the *Vitæ Patrum* (Assmann XVIII), an Old English translation of a letter from Boniface (Wynfrith) to Eadburga (printed by Sisam), and a homily now almost destroyed that Sisam calls 'Evil Tongues' from its opening text (*Ps.* cxix. 2).

Folios 149–55 belonged originally, it appears, to a different volume, for they are in a different hand, are ruled for thirty-one instead of thirty lines, and begin imperfectly. The three articles in this section are all by Ælfric and contain some unpublished material, not all of which is accounted for in the present edition. The last article is our XX, lines 1–268, breaking off at the bottom of the last page. The first two are to be published separately by Dr. Clemoes. They are small homiletic treatises; the second, though separated by an *Amen* and a blank space in the manuscript, is really a continuation of the first. According to the running titles still partially visible at the tops of the pages, they are called *De Creatore et Creatura* and *De Sex Etatibus Huius Seculi*.[1] The first begins imperfectly with a passage on the Trinity. Its first page was badly rubbed and then partially retouched, often incorrectly. Fortunately most of it can be made out with the aid of Ælfric's revision of *LS* I, the Christmas homily printed by Belfour as no. IX.

not used for the present edition are Xᵃ, CCCC 190; Xᵇ, CCCC 320; Xᶜ, Cott. Faustina A. x; Xᵉ, Cott. Tiberius A. iii; Xᶠ, Cott. Tiberius C. VI; Xᵍ, Cott. Vespasian A. xxii (not included by Ker because of its late date); Xʰ, Harley 3271; Xⁱ, Lambeth 487 (not included by Ker because of its late date); Xʲ, Paris, Bibl. Nat. Lat. 943.

[1] The words *Huius Seculi*, still partly visible, are correctly given by Wanley and Sisam. Ker has *Mundi* by mistake.

F. 149ʳ and the first line of 149ᵛ correspond to Belfour, 80/27–82/29. After this, ff. 149ᵛ–151ᵛ contain extensive excerpts from the *Hexameron*, rearranged and interspersed with new matter in Ælfric's rhythmic style, as Sisam and Ker have shown.[1]

This piece ends with Adam's expulsion from Paradise and the next, ff. 151ᵛ–2ᵛ, 154ʳᵛ, takes up the story of mankind at that point and surveys the history of the world in each of its six ages, mentioning the highlights and including a brief account of the ten commandments. The six ages are a familiar theme in Ælfric, being treated elaborately in *CH* II. iv, for the second Sunday after Epiphany, and again in the letter to Sigeweard *On the Old and New Testament*. This account, in Ælfric's rhythmic prose, partially echoes *De Initio Creaturæ* at first, and later sometimes resembles the letter, but is nevertheless an independent composition. The account of the ten commandments is similarly independent though again reminiscent of Ælfric's other expositions, especially that in the second Old English letter to Wulfstan (Fehr, *Brief* III). Apparently, as Clemoes has said, we have in these two pieces a further sign of Ælfric's reworking of themes fundamental to his conception of the universe and the history of the world. They may have formed the body of an instructive letter of the sort that Ælfric wrote for Wulfgeat and for Sigeweard.

The manuscript was certainly at Worcester at the beginning of the thirteenth century, since it is glossed throughout by the 'tremulous' hand. Sisam and Ker have given strong reasons for believing that both parts of it were already there in the second half of the eleventh century. The work of the first hand, ff. 1–61ᵛ, was probably written elsewhere, but Ker regards the hands of ff. 62–148 as characteristic of the Worcester scriptorium in the middle of the century. The running titles discernible here and there in that section (ff. 64, 90, 94, and less clearly elsewhere) and in the Ælfrician section, ff. 149–55, resemble those of the three-volume T, which was certainly written at Worcester at about the same time.

Xᵏ

Paris, Bibliothèque Nationale, Lat. 7585, f. 238ᵛ. Ker 366, article *a*. I can do no better than quote Ker's description:

A brief account of the gods of Roman mythology in eleven lines on the

---

[1] Ker had noticed the general resemblance of the matter on f. 149 to *LS* i, and Clemoes (*Chronology*, p. 242, n. 1) pointed to Belfour ix for the actual passage.

originally blank last leaf of the last quire of a copy of Isidore's Etymologies, some quires of which are written in continental caroline minuscule, s. ix/x, and others—together with the outside sheets of quires 14, 21, 24—in English caroline minuscule, s. x ex., the former being decorated with initials in the 'Franco-Saxon' style and the latter with typically English zoomorphic initials. . . . An imperfect continental manuscript which is likely to have been completed in England in the tenth century and to have been in England in s. xi when the OE was added.

The eleven lines are excerpted, with a few modifications, from Ælfric's *De Falsis Diis*, and have therefore been collated for xxi. They were first printed by Müllenhoff in 1886 (see xxi, apparatus) and later by Dubois, *Ælfric*, p. 363. I have relied on the facsimile of f. 238^{v} in Dubois, pl. 2, which, though reduced, shows very clearly a hand of the first half of the eleventh century.

Class III: Fragments[1]

f^{b}

Cambridge, Jesus College 15, binding leaves. Ker 74. sæc. xi^{1}. 20 folios, *c.* 279 × 195 mm., ten before (ff. i–x) and ten after (ff. 1–10) the main text as described below.

Collated for xi (the last lines, 526–74) and xxiv; has a few words of xxv.

The discernible content and the main features of these troublesome leaves are summed up as follows by Ker:

> Fragments of homilies by Ælfric. The leaves were employed in the medieval binding of a thirteenth-century copy of the Sentences of Peter Lombard which belonged to Durham Cathedral Priory (*Catt. Vett. Dunelm.*, p. 22 P). All the text has been erased except the recto and verso of f. i and the last six lines of f. vi^{v}: a table to the Sentences, the verses beg. 'Peniteas cito', and other texts have been written in part of the space thus procured, s. xiii/xiv. Enough OE is legible on ff. ii–vi, 5 for purposes of identification and words and letters are legible also on ff. x, 1–4, 6, 9. The upper half of f. x and the outer margins of all the leaves have been cut off. Ff. vii–x, 1, 10 are upside down. The insides of the boards show traces of offset writing in OE and some letters can be read on the back board.

Ker has identified parts of five Ælfric homilies. In what follows

[1] Dr. Clemoes and I have drawn up a list of seventeen, lettered from f^{a} to f^{q} according to their order in Ker's *Catalogue*. Since only one of these contains anything in the present edition, and new fragments are likely to turn up, it seems advisable not to print the list here.

I have added only certain distinguishing features of the best-preserved homily, on ff. i^v–vi^v, and an identification of a few words on f. 4^v that were partly discerned by Ker. These additional details make it apparent that two of the homilies in the collection had additions by Ælfric. Very likely, then, this collection was drawn from textually late copies of Ælfric's homilies, but it may not have been uniform. The order of the homilies as indicated by the first three, which are in their original sequence, was non-temporal, and the variation in the number of lines to a page (27, 23, 24, as reported by Ker) suggests intermittent copying, especially if, as all reasonably clear traces of the script seem to indicate, there was only one scribe. His firm upright hand, with ascenders and descenders of only moderate length, which Ker assigns to the first half of the eleventh century, may be as late as the third or fourth decade.

Ff. i–vi are a consecutive portion of the original volume on three bifolia, evidently, as Ker says, the central three of a single quire. F. i, entirely legible on both sides, has the concluding lines of our homily XI (526–74), ending on the first line of f. i^v. The remainder of that page has the beginning of Ælfric's second homily for Rogation Monday, *Letania Maiore* (*CH* II. XXI), which extends all the way to f. vi^v. Very little can be read on ff. ii–iv^v because they are overwritten, but enough can be seen at tops and bottoms of pages to indicate that this part of the homily was substantially the same as in Thorpe's edition. Both ff. v and vi are still legible for the most part in spite of erasure, since they are not overwritten, and these folios contain notable alterations of the text as given by Thorpe. On f. v^r/23–v^v/6 is the short addition by Ælfric that appears also in MS. P and is edited below as no. XXIV. On f. vi^r/7–vi^v/1, as a substitute for the sentences printed by Thorpe at 330/9–23, we have a passage that belonged originally to Ælfric's homily for the ninth Sunday after Pentecost, *CH* II. 410/5–28, preceded by a unique introductory sentence: *Augustinus se wisa and se wurpfulla biscop manede us ealle on sumum trahte ðus cweðende.*[1] The same passage, but with a few more lines of the original homily at the beginning and a different introductory sentence, appears as a separate paragraph in MSS. B and R, entitled *De avaritia* in R and printed from B by Belfour as no. XIII. I do not know whether

---

[1] Cf. I. 55: *Augustinus se wisa and se wordsnotera biscop*; and *On the Old and New Testament*, 1017 sq.: *Hieronimus se wurpfulla and se wisa bocere.* The present sentence may be an editor's imitation. After the characterization of Augustinus it is not alliterative.

the attribution to Augustine here made is correct (even to the extent of being a traditional medieval ascription), but I doubt if Ælfric was responsible for substituting the passage in the Rogation-tide homily. The substitution is not especially apt, it does not occur in the other copies, even in P, and I do not see why Ælfric should have wanted to remove the passage from the *CH* II homily. Following the substitution in the present manuscript, the ending of the homily is shortened by the omission of two sentences, Thorpe 330/29–332/2.

Following the end of the Rogationtide homily on f. vi^v/8 there is an illegible title, then the beginning of Ælfric's homily for the twelfth Sunday after Pentecost (*CH* II. xxxiii), of which the first eleven manuscript lines are partially erased, the last seven intact. The last words on the page, 7 *þet heþet* [*sic*] *hæþene folc*, corre-spond inexactly to Thorpe II. 428/10. No more of this homily has been found on the other surviving leaves.

The next four leaves (ff. vii–x), bound upside down, have, as Ker says, a few legible OE letters and an occasional legible word (especially on f. x), but I have not been able to read enough con-secutively to identify anything.

The ten leaves following Peter Lombard's Sentences (ff. 1–10) have yielded no identifications except on ff. 4 and 5, which are not consecutive.[1] At the bottom of f. 4^v, as Ker has said, the words *godes þearfum on godes naman* are fairly easy to read. Now these words occur in the addition that Ælfric made to his homily for the vigil of the Ascension, *CH* II. xxv, after the last line of Thorpe 368. It is the third addition (*c*) edited below under no. xxv, and the words are in lines 9–10. With the help of the printed text, taken from MS. R, the last two lines of f. 4^v can be reconstructed as follows, the words in italics being altogether invisible or so faint that they are beyond recognition:

> me etan; *Him hingrað on his ðearfum.* 7 *swa hwæt swa we doþ* godes þearfum on godes naman. ðæt we doð *gode sylfum;*

There may have been room for *Eac*, beginning the next sentence, at the end of the last line.

---

[1] As Ker says, 1 and 10 (upside down), 4 and 9, 6 and 7 are bifolia, not neces-sarily of the same original quire, whereas 2, 3, 5, and 8 are single leaves, and 5 at least, if not the others, is out of place. The overwriting on these leaves makes identification of the erased OE original almost impossible except here and there at the tops and bottoms of pages.

In partial confirmation of this identification, I think there are
traces, at the bottom of the previous page, f. 4ʳ, of the following
sequence in Thorpe 368/20–23, except that there is space for 4–6
letters at the point marked by square brackets. The italicized letters
are very doubtful or invisible:

cume
to ðe; *Sumne* dæl [*space*] ðisses and*gite*s we trahnodon hwe*ne*
ær. *þæt ealle* ðing *synd gemæne þam fæde*r 7 *hi*s su*na* 7 heora

The interval between the bottom of f. 4ʳ and the bottom of 4ᵛ
is about right if we assume that the second as well as the third
addition represented in MS. R was included.

The traces on the unrelated f. 5 are much clearer and Ker has
already identified the two homilies represented there. At the top
of f. 5ʳ we have the conclusion of Ælfric's first homily for Rogation
Monday, *In Letania Maiore*, CH I. xviii, beginning at Thorpe
256/21 -*sunge*. This proceeded, probably, to the end as in Thorpe.
The last eight lines on the same page, and all of the verso, are given
over to the beginning of the next homily in Series I, on the Lord's
Prayer, CH I. xix, here entitled FERIA III. ON OÐER GANGDAGA DÆG,
the lettering still visible between lines of the superimposed text.
At the bottom of f. 5ʳ are the words *he him tæhte . . . hælende*,
Thorpe 258/13–15, and the next words, *Leof . . . gebiddan*, can be
seen at the top of the verso. Two lines at the bottom of the verso
correspond to Thorpe 260/9–12, *þæt we ne sceolon . . . Witodlice*.

There is some likelihood that a few other passages on other
leaves could be identified by the use of ultraviolet light or even by
the help of some shrewd guessing; but I have not succeeded in
going further. Ker has read part of an unidentified title on f. 6ᵛ,
Eft be cristes . . . 7 be . . . a . . ., and a red initial *M*.

Ker has likewise called attention to the main oddity in the
spelling, the frequent, but not invariable, substitution of *e* for *æ*,
long and short. This is illustrated in the variant readings of xi
(last lines) and xxiv. Similar spellings occur in MS. S, written
about a century later.

3. TABLES SHOWING THE DISTRIBUTION OF TEXTS IN THE MANUSCRIPTS

TABLE I

Manuscript sigla:

- B = Bodley 343
- C = CCCC 303
- D = Bodley 342
- E = CCCC 198
- F = CCCC 162
- G = Cotton Vespasian D. xiv
- H = Cotton Vitellius C. v, Appendix
- H = (Interpol.)
- J = Cotton Cleopatra B. xiii
- K = ULC Gg. 3. 28
- L = ULC Ii. i. 33
- M = ULC Ii. 4. 6
- N = Cotton Faustina A. ix
- O = CCCC 302
- P = Hatton 115
- Q = CCCC 188
- R = CCCC 178
- S = Hatton 116
- T = Junius 121
- T = Hatton 113
- T = Hatton 114
- U = Trinity B. 15. 34
- V = CCCC 419
- V = CCCC 421
- W = Cotton Julius E. vii
- Z = Laud Misc. 509
- X^4 = Cotton Otho C. i, vol. 2
- X^k = Paris, Bibl. Nat., Lat. 7585
- f^b = Jesus College, Cambridge, 15

	B	C	D	E	F	G	H(App)	H(Int)	J	K	L	M	N	O	P	Q	R	S	T(Jun)	T(113)	T(114)	U	V(419)	V(421)	W	Z	X^4	X^k	f^b
I. Nativitas Domini								4																					
II. Fr. vi in I Ebd. Quadragesimae					17		63																						
III. Fr. vi in II Ebd. Quadragesimae					20		64																						
IV. Dominica III in Quadragesima		9		63	(21)	20		16				11	14	21		12					45								
V. Fr. vi in III Ebd. Quadragesimae					22													25											
VI. Fr. vi in IV Ebd. Quadragesima	83	11			24		65+66	66+66							12														
VII. Dominica IV Post Pascha												25	32									7							
VIII. Dominica V Post Pascha	8								8			26	33									8							
IX. Dominica Post Ascensionem Domini												32	36						29			13							
X. Dominica Pentecosten												34	38									15							
XI. Sermo . . . in Octavis Pentecosten								1				27				23	6			32		17		6					
XIa. De Sancta Trinitate, etc.															27		3									3			1
XII. Dominica I Post Pentecosten	7																	18				18							
XIII. Dominica V Post Pentecosten								31				35										22							
XIV. Dominica VI Post Pentecosten								32														23							
XV. Dominica VII Post Pentecosten								33														24							
XVI. Dominica X Post Pentecosten																													
XVII. Dominica XIII Post Pentecosten		52	46	37	42			45		71		3										27							

TABLE II

Legend of manuscripts (sigla):

- B = Bodley 343
- C = CCCC 303
- D = Bodley 342
- E = CCCC 198
- F = CCCC 162
- G = Cotton Vespasian D. xiv
- H = Cotton Vitellius C. v, Appendix
- H = " " " Interpol.
- J = Cotton Cleopatra B. xiii
- K = ULC Gg. 3. 28
- L = ULC Ii. 1. 33
- M = ULC Ii. 4. 6
- N = Cotton Faustina A. ix
- O = CCCC 302
- P = Hatton 115
- Q = CCCC 188
- R = CCCC 178
- S = Hatton 116
- T = Junius 121
- T = Hatton 113
- T = Hatton 114
- U = Trinity B. 15. 34
- V = CCCC 419
- V = CCCC 421
- W = Cotton Julius E. vii
- Z = Laud Misc. 509
- Xd = Cotton Otho C. i, vol. 2
- Xk = Paris, Bibl. Nat., Lat. 7585
- Fb = Jesus College, Cambridge, 15

Item	B	C	D	E	F	G	H(App.)	H(Interpol.)	J	K	L	M	N	O	P	Q	R	S	T(Jun.121)	T(Hat.113)	T(Hat.114)	U	V(419)	V(421)	W	Z	Xd	Xk	Fb
XVIII. Sermo de Die Iudicii		64													4		9								49				
XIX. De Doctrina Apostolica													31		6	(46)											7		
XX. De Populo Israhel																	18												
XXI. De Falsis Diis		65				15					34				29			21		16*			15						
XXII. 'Wyrdwriteras . . .'—An Excerpt															17						84								
XXIII. Addition to CH II. xx																	30												
XXIV. Addition to CH II. xxi																													
XXV. Three Additions to CH II. xxv															7														x
XXVI. Addition to CH II. xxxiii								44									10												
XXVII. Addition to CH II. xxxvi								46									8												
XXVIII. Addition to CH II. xliv															25			20					15		28				
XXIX. Addition to LS xvii																	10							5					
XXX. Passages from De Virginitate																												a	2

The numbers under the manuscripts correspond to those in Ker's *Catalogue*. Italicized items have only a portion of the edited text. The two bracketed items have rubrics only.

* Revised and abridged by Wulfstan.

4. EVIDENCE OF ÆLFRIC'S AUTHORSHIP

FOR the authenticity of the pieces here attributed to Ælfric we lack some of the most obvious kinds of evidence, such as the prefaces and the epistolary salutations with their 'Ego Ælfricus' or 'Ic Ælfric'. We are thus heavily dependent on style; but before taking up this central, complex, and sometimes delicate criterion I shall mention a few ancillary guides.

The manuscripts themselves bear witness both directly and indirectly, and with varying force. All of them by date, language, and general content, establish a basic possibility; some go a good deal further. Thus the colophon of R assures us that the twenty-four full homilies it contains are Ælfric's, though two have been augmented with passages from his other writings. This testimony is not to be trusted without due examination, since, first, the colophon appears to be a copy; secondly, even the original must have been composed after Ælfric's death; and thirdly, some short pieces actually present in the volume are not mentioned; but in fact many of the full homilies and some of the short pieces have long since been established as Ælfric's on other grounds, and I cannot find reason to doubt his authorship of anything, long or short, except a few introductory lines to one of the admittedly augmented pieces, *De Octo Vitiis et de Duodecim Abusivis*. Hence I count R as a good witness for as much of the material here edited as it contains: XI, XVIII, XXI, XXV, XXVI, XXIX (though the colophon admits that this addition to *De Auguriis* was not authorized by Ælfric, at least not the whole of it), and the passage on tithes in XXX.

In spite of the lack of any inclusive statement, Q, with its copy of Ælfric's Latin note at the head of the appended homily for a confessor, is a stronger witness than R. As the preceding description shows, it is an early and apparently faithful copy of a volume that was in Ælfric's possession towards the end of his life. It contains only two of the homilies here edited (IV, already accepted as Ælfric's, and XI), but for these it speaks firmly.

Less powerful but still persuasive is the testimony of H and U, then M. We are not directly concerned with the first stage of H, when it was a contemporary and straightforward copy of Ælfric's First Series in a state prior to that of K; but what remains of the slightly later appendix and the additions made a few decades afterwards by the interpolator show rather an effort to enlarge the representation of Ælfric than to mix his work with another's. I think the interpolator introduced a compilation made from genuine works of Ælfric's at the head of his reconstructed volume (our xia) and perhaps inadvertently slipped in two non-Ælfrician paragraphs enclosing the Ælfrician part of our xxvii, but in spite of this he remains a fairly persuasive witness for i, xiii–xvii (though he was probably responsible for omitting a passage in xiv), xxvi, and the interpolated passage in vi, not to mention the much-witnessed iv. The appendix as originally written supports ii, iii, v, and the first state of vi.

U is a slightly stronger witness. Its methodical completeness in the part of the year it covers suggests an arrangement sanctioned if not designed by Ælfric himself, and it contains nothing that shows signs of different authorship. Hence it gives good support to vii (second version), viii–x, xii–xvi, besides the still better witnessed xi.

M is almost equally reliable if we set aside certain isolable sections as explained in the description. Its central core seems to be purely Ælfrician, representing a temporal set put together earlier than the archetype of U and giving us an earlier state of certain homilies. Thus it supports vii (first version), viii–x, and xii. Its excerpt from xi belongs to an unreliable section.

Besides the manuscripts thus far mentioned, four others are used as the basis for certain texts: F, P, T, and V. The first of these, though it contains material earlier than Ælfric, is very nearly contemporary and gives good support to ii, iii, v, and vi (first version). P, sole witness for xxii, sole complete witness for xx, basis for xix, xxiv, and xxviii, is not to be despised in spite of its comparatively late date, its occasional blunders, and its tendency to abridge. As first written it contained nothing, I believe, that is not to be attributed to Ælfric, and the fact that the same scribe seems to have made the copy of the *Grammar* in MS. Cotton Faustina A. x may add somewhat to its credit. The three volumes of T and the two of V, on the other hand, draw freely on non-Ælfrician material. The texts they offer to this edition derive most of their credit from their content alone, or from other manuscripts. The third volume of T (Hatton 114) gives us the unique copy of xxiii as a mere addition to the volume, and the first volume of V (CCCC 419) has the compilation called *De Virginitate*, which includes a passage from xix and the two passages (one unique) printed as xxx.

Otherwise T gives us secondary copies of IV, IX, XI, and the Wulfstan revision of part of XXI (needless as testimony to the authorship of the original but useful here and there as a guide to Ælfric's text). V has secondary copies of XXVIII (helpfully corroborative of P) and once more XI.

A second type of evidence approaches outright declaration. Eight of the thirty pieces contain references to the author's previous writings. In each case the reference itself is of a type that can be matched elsewhere in Ælfric,[1] and the passage referred to can be satisfactorily identified among his established works. There is a reference at IV. 75 to a previous treatment of Beelzebub, called Beel or Baal by the heathen. This is probably either XXI. 354 sqq.[2] or LS XVIII. 85 sqq. At VIII. 103 there is a clear reference to XXI. 575 sqq. At IX. 72 there is a reference to CH I. XXVI, pp. 364 sqq., and at 144 to CH I. XXII, esp. p. 326. At X. 106 the reference is to another part of the same homily, esp. p. 314; and at XI. 69 once more to the end of this homily, pp. 322–6.[3] At XII. 224, there is reference to two homilies, CH II. XIII, pp. 238, 240 and our XX. 304–52, which in turn refers at 335 to CH II. XIII. Homily XX also refers in its second line to CH II. XII, pp. 194, 196. Finally, there are two references in XXII. The first, at 58, refers to LS VII. 296 sqq.; the second, at 79, to the epilogue to the homily on *Judges*, 45–77.

Familiar themes or ideas, especially if introduced as elaborations of something stated in Ælfric's immediate source and not directly suggested by it, can help to confirm his authorship. Here, however, it is very difficult to separate the thought itself from the mode of expression. Many instances where familiar ideas and familiar phrases work together will be found mentioned in the notes, and many others will occur to readers who are well acquainted with Ælfric. I will content myself here with mentioning a few instances. One of the shortest and clearest is the reference to John the Evangelist as the son of Christ's maternal aunt. As explained in the note on I. 5, this is an established notion of Ælfric's, introduced in much the same language at many places in his work where he has occasion to mention John or his brother James, and always, so far

---

[1] See especially *Old and New Testament*, ed. Crawford, lines 48, 163, 229, 381, 405, 443, 507, 660, 744, 770, 776, 836, 922, 1,006.

[2] Enough of XXI, *De Falsis Diis*, has been long accepted as Ælfric's to allow it to be regarded as an established work rather than one of those on trial.

[3] The references at IX. 144 and XI. 69 are not, I think, to *De Septiformi Spiritu*, Napier VII (Latin) and VIII.

as I can ascertain, without warrant from his immediate source. Thus, although he certainly had a source of some kind in the first place, the association is his own. This curious little piece of lore, not accepted by Ælfric's main authorities, appears in I. 5, II. 6, and XIV. 212. In its small way it helps to confirm Ælfric's authorship of these pieces. Again, in homily VI, where lines 209–91 constitute an addition based on a source distinct from that of the original homily, Ælfric's responsibility for both the original and the addition is confirmed when we find that exactly the same collocation of themes occurs in his early homily, *CH* I. XXXIII, pp. 490 sqq. In no. XI*a*, where three unique passages (54*b*–74, 81–85, 102–27) occur among passages culled from well-known works of Ælfric's, I have taken the trouble to assemble a number of parallels to the unique lines, since Ælfric's authorship of these in the midst of a compilation that looks like an editor's might be seriously questioned. The evidence of the parallels, which seems to me to remove all doubt, is mainly a matter of style, but the thematic material, broadly dictated by tradition but freely selected and arranged, is as familiar as the expressions. When Ælfric turns to contemporary problems there is an obviously personal slant to his thought no matter how much it may be bolstered by his reading. What he says about kings and counsellors in IX and about the need for a king to delegate authority in XXII cannot be duplicated in his established work, but can easily be seen to grow out of such a passage as we find in his homily on the prayer of Moses, *LS* XIII. 116–77, a passage starting with precepts from *De Duodecim Abusivis* and developing into a contrast between Edgar's reign and the present. And the rebuke to the laity for failing to defend the realm is a natural forerunner of the bitter outburst against traitors in XIV.

As we approach the problem of style we may notice first the general construction of the homilies, the selection of sources, and the author's competence and method in handling them. Most of the homilies here edited conform to well-established Ælfrician types. Among the first seventeen, all except XI and XI*a* are exegetical and display Ælfric's characteristic adaptations of such models as were provided for him by Augustine, Gregory the Great, and above all Bede and Haymo.[1] Similar homilies are well represented in the first two series and in Assmann IV, V, VI, and a

---

[1] Some characteristic features of these homilies are specified below, pp. 150 sq.

portion of I. They are rare in the other Old English homiletic literature. Perhaps the closest approach to Ælfric's characteristic form among earlier homilies is to be found in Blickling II and III, though in details of structure, still more in language and expression, they are conspicuously different.

No. XVIII, *De Die Iudicii*, falls half-way between the exegetical homilies and those that expound, in logical sequence, some aspect or feature of the divine order. It presents two complementary gospel-texts as a means of shedding light on the topic, the day of judgement, treating each of them in turn, though selectively, in exegetical form. Free from the control of scriptural texts, which they nevertheless incorporate, are XXI, *De Falsis Diis*, already a part of the Ælfric canon, and XI, the *Sermo ad Populum in Octavis Pentecosten Dicendus*. This begins with a seasonal prelude, a half-lyrical exposition of the high events celebrated in the liturgy between Christmas and the Octave of Pentecost. Similar but more limited expositions of the liturgy are found in the *Catholic Homilies*, and the themes themselves are naturally among the most familiar in Ælfric. Following this comes a grandly inclusive treatment, modelled on Julian of Toledo's *Prognosticon*, of death, the life after death, and the judgement. In spite of the many thematic echoes and characteristic passages of this homily it can hardly be said to belong to a well-defined Ælfrician class, but it can be loosely associated with such broad-gauged discourses as *De Initio Creaturæ*, *De Fide Catholica*, *De Falsis Diis*, and the philosophically discursive Christmas homily in the *Lives*. The partly related compilation, XIa, is not considered here, since I do not think the compiler was Ælfric.

There are only two other full homilies: XX, *De Populo Israhel*, with its obvious resemblance to the early homilies on *Exodus* and *Joshua* (the two parts of *CH* II. XII) and the later homily on *Judges*; and XIX, *De Doctrina Apostolica*. This, as I have explained more fully in the separate introduction preceding the text, belongs generally with Ælfric's rather small group of pieces giving detailed moral instruction. Typically its first part provides a compendium based on authority, this time St. Paul's, and thus reminds us most directly of another Pauline piece, the first part of *De Auguriis*, *LS* XVII. Like some other admonitory sermons by Ælfric, it is very loosely organized, and the *exempla* at the end, in themselves typical of him, illustrate a theme that may seem rather casually attached to the other themes in the expository portion.

The selection of sources and the treatment of them are discussed below in section 8. Not only are the Latin authors consulted for these homilies largely those whom Ælfric is already known to have used, but their writings are treated in characteristic ways, as can be seen throughout this edition by comparison of the text with the Latin passages at the foot of the page. Whether in close translation or in loose paraphrase and epitome we find the ease and clarity that speak for the author's command of Latin and his thorough assimilation of the materials he is using. Equally characteristic are the deliberate simplification and the discriminating choice, whether a single authority has been abridged or elements from two or more are combined.

Without the confirmation of style in the narrower verbal sense none of the kinds of evidence I have mentioned would be acceptable. Within this area one must consider such matters as vocabulary, syntax, rhetoric, rhythm, and various sound-effects. Ælfric had such a rich vocabulary that each fresh homily is likely to contain something new, but there is a core of familiar words that recur again and again, not only for everyday matters but also for the basic doctrinal ideas and themes. The best proof that the vocabulary of the texts here attributed to Ælfric lies within the range one would expect from his established writings is the glossary. I had at one time considered affixing a sign to each word or meaning in the list that was already illustrated from Ælfric in Bosworth–Toller, but refrained because, in spite of Bosworth–Toller's incompleteness, the sign would have been attached to all but a handful of rare words. If the reader will test for himself any portion of the glossary he will find, I am sure, that the correspondence with the Bosworth–Toller citations is remarkably exact and frequent.

Normally Ælfric welcomes synonyms for variety and sometimes for exactness, but in some instances he uses one word or form in preference to another, or even to the exclusion of another. Some of these peculiarities have been noticed by Dietrich[1] and Jost.[2] Among them, the following can be illustrated in the present texts: Ælfric uses *gefredan* in the sense 'to feel', not *felan*; *gearcian* in the sense 'to prepare', not *gearwian*; *ælfremed* and *ælþeodig* for 'foreign', not *fremde*;[3] *hreppan* (*hrepian*) for 'to touch', not *onhrinan*; *cwear-*

---

[1] *Zeitschrift für hist. Theologie*, XXV. 544, n. 140.
[2] See especially *Wulfstanstudien*, pp. 159–76.
[3] The one occurrence of *fremde* thus far recorded for Ælfric is in the Cuthbert

tern for 'prison', not *carcern*; *hogian* and *forhogian* for 'to consider, take care for' and 'to despise', not *hycgan, forhycgan*.[1] He uses *þearf* sparingly, altogether avoiding the common introductory formula, frequent in Wulfstan and other preachers, *us* (*him, cristenum mannum*) *is þearf* (*swiðe micel þearf*) with dependent *þæt*-clause. He does not use the phrase *manna gehwylc* (the appearance of which in XXVII. 108 is therefore one of the minor indications that the paragraph is not Ælfric's), or a combination of which Wulfstan was fond, *æfre ænig*. Like most West Saxon writers, including King Alfred and Wulfstan, he avoids the negative *nænig*, using *nan* instead.[2] A rarity is *æghwilc*, for which Jost could find only three examples in Ælfric. There are none here. In its place we find *gehwa, gehwilc*, and most frequently *ælc*.[3] Almost entirely foreign to Ælfric are compounds with *med-*, such as *medmicel* 'not large' and *mettrum* 'weak, sick', for which Ælfric's normal word is *untrum*.[4]

One or two other peculiarities have emerged from the present study. Ælfric normally uses *lybbende* as the present participle of *lybban* (*libban*)[5] 'to live', and applies it to God or man when the ordinary verbal sense is operative. The alternative form *lifi(g)ende*, which some writers use instead of or beside *lybbende*, is used by Ælfric exclusively as an honorific adjective applied to the divinity or to some pretender to divinity. It would be strange, considering the caprices of scribes, if there were not somewhere an exception to this rule, but so far I have been unable to find one, and examples of *lifiende* in the specialized use are very numerous. At *CH* I.

homily, *CH* II. 142/26, where it governs the genitive (*lofes*) and means 'a stranger to, deprived of'.

[1] Jost, op. cit., p. 174, cites a few examples of *hycgan* in the sense 'to strive'.

[2] Jost gives some statistics for *nænig*, chiefly an Anglian form, pp. 159 sqq. There are rare occurrences of the word in the *Chronicle* (e.g. 755), one in the account of Wulfstan's report in the *Orosius* (Sweet, p. 20/18), none in Alfred's versions of the *Cura Pastoralis*, the *Soliloquies*, or Boethius, two in texts assumed to be Archbishop Wulfstan's (but only by error in the *Sermo ad Anglos* as it appears in Sweet's *Reader*, 14th ed., l. 80), none whatever, so far as I know, in Ælfric, from whose works its absence was first noted, according to Jost, by B. Schrader, *Studien zur Ælfricschen Syntax*, Göttingen, 1887, p. 58.

[3] Jost, pp. 162–5.

[4] BT cites one example of *mettrum* from the homily on St. Martin, *CH* II. 512/7, where it alliterates. Otherwise Ælfric seems to have used only the disyllabic *medum* and its compounds (all told about half a dozen instances cited in BT, BTS).

[5] Originally Class III, with preterite *lifde*, but partially assimilated to Class II, with infinitive *lifian* and preterite *lifode* or *leofode*. Ælfric uses this Class II preterite exclusively, but infinitive *libban* or *lybban*.

366/33, after several occurrences of *lifigende* in an exposition of Peter's words, 'Ðu eart Crist, þæs lifigendan Godes Sunu', we have a sentence beginning, *Se is lybbende God þe . . .*; as if to say, This honorific epithet *lifigende* is no empty formula; it is applied to God because he is truly *lybbende*.

Another peculiarity is the nearly complete fusion of the strong verb *faran* 'to make one's way, travel, go' and its weak derivative *fēran*, anciently perhaps with a stronger sense of the journey (*fōr*) that is being made, but for Ælfric apparently a scarcely distinguishable synonym. Ælfric uses *faran* in the present and in the past participle, *fēran* in the preterite, thus making a single verb. Modern English was to inherit this composite verb, as is recognized in the *OED*, which nevertheless dates its establishment as a regular form several centuries after Ælfric's time. In Ælfric's works I have found only two instances of *fēran* with the present stem: the dative infinitive *ferenne*, Assmann VI. 10, and the participle *ferende* in the Cuthbert homily, *CH* II. 136/4.[1] Examples of the preterite *fōr* are very rare, but I have noted three in the *Lives of Saints*, at XXXI. 351, XV. 1 (*gefor*, with *ferde*, line 4), and XXV. 721 (*gefor*, with *geferde*, line 730), besides a clear instance of variation in the Epilogue to *Judges*, line 67: *sume foran ongean, sume ferdon hindan*. The distinction was not general in Ælfric's time. Wulfstan uses *misfor* rather than *misferde* at the beginning of his adaptation of *De Falsis Diis*, and there are examples of *gefor* in the non-Ælfrician *LS* XXIII and XXIII B as well as in the doubtful parts of the Pentateuch.[2] In the texts here edited, as the glossary indicates, *faran* and *fēran* are abundantly represented and the distinction between them is absolute: *faran* is used for all forms built on the present stem and for the past participle in the compound *forþfaren* 'dead'; *fēran* appears only in the preterite, where it entirely supplants *fōr*, even in the compound *forþferde* 'died'. An interesting juxtaposition of *ferde* and *fare* occurs at VIII. 42 sq.

Another peculiarity is too rare to be of much use as a test of authorship. This is what appears to be Ælfric's use of *syndon* not only as an indicative but also as a subjunctive form, corresponding to the singular *sy*. The proof of this is the absence of a plural form *syn*

---

[1] I have verified the manuscript readings for Assmann (MS. U) and for Thorpe (MS. K) but not for the other two copies (D and E) of the Cuthbert homily. Thorpe has *ferende* also in the Cuthbert text he printed from D in *Analecta Anglo-Saxonica*.

[2] See BTS, *gefaran*.

and the appearance of *syndon* instead on the few occasions when the plural subjunctive is called for.[1] It is a natural development in view of the analogy of *-on* as the regular plural ending of the present subjunctive of other verbs in the Ælfric manuscripts and generally in Late West Saxon.[2]

Syntactically Ælfric's style varies widely in complexity as he passes from exposition or argument to narrative, but wherever he resorts to hypotactic sentences we find careful articulation, showing itself especially in the systematic use of a large number of subordinating conjunctions and relative pronouns. He tends also, in paratactic sequences, to ease transitions by an assortment of introductory adverbs, ranging from the local *þær* and temporal *þa* to the more or less logical *eornostlice* 'therefore, accordingly', the adversative *þeah-hwæðere*, and the vaguely asseverative *soþlice* and *witodlice*. These last, corresponding more or less to Latin *vero*, are used more sparingly in the early prose than in the later, rhythmical variety, where they are sometimes almost meaningless fillers.

Jost has called attention to Ælfric's characteristic use of the modal conjunctions *swa* (*swa*) and *swylce* and the temporal conjunction *þa* (*þa*).[3] Ælfric almost invariably uses *swa swa* rather than *swa* unless an adverbial *swa* has preceded in the main clause; and he very rarely admits *eall swa* (*ealswa*) as a substitute for *swa swa*,[4] whereas some writers, including Wulfstan, use an unemphatic *ealswa* very freely. When *swylce* introduces a clause of manner, it regularly means 'as if' and the verb is in the subjunctive.[5] When it

[1] See the glossary and the note on l. 162.

[2] Conversely, Wulfstan uses *syn* as an indicative: e.g. *Sermo Lupi ad Anglos*, ed. Whitelock, 1963, lines 72, 73, 109, 147.

[3] 'Unechte Ælfrictexte', *Anglia*, LI (1927), 81–103.

[4] Jost could find only two examples of *eall swa* as subordinating conjunction in Ælfric: one in *Hexameron* 377, where *eall* alliterates and emphasizes the exactness of the comparison, 'just as'; and once in the *Letter for Wulfsige*, Fehr, *Brief* I. 20, where *eal* does not alliterate and there is no reason for emphasis. But Jost misread Fehr's apparatus, which indicates that he inserted the *eal* from the not very reliable Junius 121, our T, whereas the other two manuscripts, one of which is the highly authoritative Gg. 3. 28, our K, have merely *swa*. (On the manuscripts see Clemoes, Fehr reprint, pp. cxxiv sq.) Two examples of a properly emphatic *eall swa*, with *eall* alliterating, will be found at XIII. 9 (repeated in 38) and XVI. 132.

[5] What Jost thought was an exception at *LS* xxv. 312 is really an instance of what is noticed just above, Ælfric's use of *syndon* instead of *syn* for the present plural of the subjunctive. At *ONT* 496, *na swilce ge secgað*, the *swilce* seems to me adjectival in an elliptical construction, standing for *swilce swa* 'such [proverbs] as'.

introduces an adverbial phrase the meaning is still 'as if'; and even when it introduces a noun there is usually a stronger sense than with *swa swa* that the likeness is fanciful or inexact. Ælfric's fondness for *swa swa* instead of the single *swa* is paralleled by his fondness for *þa þa* rather than *þa* as a subordinating temporal conjunction, unless of course adverbial *þa* has preceded in the main clause. These peculiarities of Ælfric's are sometimes useful in distinguishing his work from that of contemporary writers, as Jost has shown. They are all to be seen in the texts here credited to Ælfric, and there would be cause for suspicion if they were not. Yet their presence is scarcely, in itself, decisive, since they may have been habitual with one or more of Ælfric's contemporaries also. Moreover, single *swa* for *swa swa* and *þa* for *þa þa* do appear in Ælfric, so that one must judge by the tendency of considerable passages, not by isolated instances, even if there is no reason to suspect scribal modifications. A paragraph that I consider non-Ælfrician at the beginning of XXVII has single *swa* in a construction in which Ælfric generally uses *swa swa*, but several examples would be needed to establish this as a significantly non-Ælfrician feature.

Very nearly all the pieces in this edition are written in the so-called rhythmical prose that appears first intermittently in Ælfric's Second Series and becomes habitual in his later work. This form is so distinctive that it is a strong indication of Ælfric's authorship wherever it appears. I have devoted the next section of this introduction to a description of it. But there are a few passages of ordinary prose—ordinary in the sense that its rhythms are freely varied. For these we must rely in the main on such criteria as I have already mentioned. Since the passages are so few, I shall enumerate them here and indicate briefly the main reasons why I do (or in one instance do not) attribute them to Ælfric. The list includes, all told, a small part of XVII, the first half of XIX, the first paragraph of XXI, the three paragraphs of XXV, the beginning and end (two paragraphs) of XXVII, and the end of XXX.

The ordinary prose in XVII, since it comes from a regular member of the Second Series, here made part of an otherwise fresh composition, needs no special proof of Ælfric's authorship. It tells two stories of miracles from the gospels with a minimum of interpretation. Although Ælfric follows the gospel stories closely, his narrative art is apparent in the vigorous diction and the carefully controlled though varied movement. Alliteration links important words and sometimes pervades sentences without forming a set pattern. The opening paragraph of xxi is equally well established as Ælfric's, since this part of *De Falsis Diis* has long been known. Ælfric may have cast it in ordinary prose, in contrast to the rest of the homily, because it translates rather closely the preceding Latin exordium, mainly quoted from St. Paul, and seems to gain authority by keeping close to the Latin sentence-rhythms, which depend largely on balanced phrases arranged in threes instead of the pairs favoured by Ælfric's rhythmical prose.

The three paragraphs of xxv, being additions to a homily of the Second Series (*CH* II. xxv) that extend and qualify what was said at first, are based on certain passages from Augustine, an author frequently consulted by Ælfric, and seem thoroughly consistent with Ælfric's vocabulary and syntax as well as his sentiment. All are well ordered rhythmically, and the first, like a good many of the 'ordinary prose' passages, as I explain in the next section, is on the verge of being 'rhythmical'.

The admonition on tithes at the end of xxx, which perhaps has better standing as an addition to *CH* II. xxxiii in MS. R than as the conclusion of the composite *De Virginitate* in MS. V, includes a good deal of homely instruction on a practical matter but seeks authority from the words of God himself, as Ælfric is prone to do whenever he can, and shows his customary familiarity with the Old Law and his readiness to explain how it is to be modified as an element in the New. Here we find once more Ælfric's vocabulary and syntax, his clear and concise exposition, his firmness in prescription combined with emotional restraint. Direct exhortation, as a personal appeal from the preacher to his congregation, such as we find in Wulfstan and in a good many of the anonymous sermons, is very rare in Ælfric.

The prose beginning of xix, *De Doctrina Apostolica*, is once more well within the normal limits of Ælfric's vocabulary and expression. At the start it develops with characteristic freedom St. Paul's own comparison of milk and strong meat as a preparation for the severity of the counsel on sexual matters. The propitiatory opening is as characteristic as the firm insistence on the apostolic doctrine that follows. A similar use of another part of St. Paul's teaching occurs in the first section of *De Auguriis*, as I have already remarked; and Ælfric's frequent concern for sexual continence needs no reminder.

There is even an addition, out of Cæsarius, to St. Paul's advice, urging young men to be chaste before marriage—a plea that occurs elsewhere in Ælfric.[1]

All these passages, then, seem readily acceptable as members of the Ælfric canon if they have not already been securely established there. The two prose paragraphs in XXVII, on the other hand, seem to me definitely unacceptable. I have given my reasons in the separate introduction to XXVII. Here I will say only that the chief ground for suspicion is not the ideas, most of which are to be found in Ælfric and may have been borrowed from him, nor the vocabulary, nor even the presence of one passage in an anonymous member of Napier's collection, but the emotionally overcharged, intellectually undernourished rhetoric.

For all the other texts in this edition the strongest and most pervasive evidence of Ælfric's authorship is the distinctively organized rhythmical prose. Familiar and easily recognized though it is, its evolution as a form in Ælfric's writings and its characteristics have not been very fully described, and some disagreements have emerged. Hence it is treated at some length in the separate section that follows.

5. ÆLFRIC'S RHYTHMICAL PROSE

THE term 'rhythmical prose' as applied to Ælfric's compositions must be understood to refer to a loosely metrical form resembling in basic structural principles the alliterative verse of the Old English poets, but differing markedly in the character and range of its rhythms as in strictness of alliterative practice, and altogether distinct in diction, rhetoric, and tone. It is better regarded as a mildly ornamental, rhythmically ordered prose than as a debased, pedestrian poetry. It is different enough from the ordinary, rhythmically varied prose of Ælfric and other writers to be printed in lines like verse—a procedure on which I shall comment at the end of this section—but the controls are weak enough to permit relatively easy transitions to and from passages of an irregular sort. So far as we know Ælfric invented the form, and none of his contemporaries, except perhaps certain compilers who may have had reason to imitate him for a few sentences, followed his example.[2] Hence any

[1] Assmann II. 147 sqq. See the note on XIX. 102–4.
[2] I agree with McIntosh, *Wulfstan's Prose*, pp. 7 and 22 sq., that the English version of the Ely charter dated 970 but preserved in a manuscript of the latter

considerable passage in this form, unless there is clear evidence to the contrary, has a strong claim to be regarded as his.

The distinctive features of this prose have been recognized with varying degrees of accuracy since as long ago as 1834, when Thorpe, prompted by Joseph Stevenson, drew attention to the 'alliterative' character of the homilies on St. Cuthbert and St. Edmund in his *Analecta Anglo-Saxonica*.[1] Not long after, and several decades before the large editions of Skeat (1881–1900) and Assmann (1889), metrical printings of a few texts, in single verses (half-lines) or pairs of verses (long lines) began to appear.[2] Concurrently there were attempts to describe and classify this disconcertingly mixed form. Its general character and some of its particular features were well set forth by Dietrich in the second instalment of his study of Ælfric in 1856.[3] He included a list of homilies and parts of homilies where this form appears. The list is not quite accurate with respect to the *Catholic Homilies*, and of

half of the eleventh century (Birch 1267, edited by A. J. Robertson, *Anglo-Saxon Charters*, pp. 98–102) is written so entirely in Ælfric's manner that it must in fact be his. Its relation to Edgar, Æthelwold I of Winchester, and the cause of the monasteries can furnish a plausible motive for the translation, which may be of Ælfric's time even if the Latin version is earlier. This is the only extended passage in a rhythmical prose closely resembling Ælfric's that has even a superficial claim to be the work of a predecessor. See further below, p. 145. On the likelihood that Ælfric's rhythmical prose influenced the author of the 'Katherine Group' in the late twelfth or early thirteenth century, see the article by Dorothy Bethurum, *JEGP*, XXXIV (1935), 553–63. In spite of the resemblance I agree with those who hesitate to call the Katherine Group metrical, even in the loose Ælfrician sense.

[1] Preface, p. v. Thorpe printed the texts as ordinary prose, and repeated this treatment for the Cuthbert homily in his edition of the Second Series in 1846, merely remarking in a note, p. 611, 'This homily, like some others in the volume, is alliterative.'

[2] For Unger's and Kemble's texts of *De Falsis Diis* (1846 and 1848), see the introduction to xxi. For Stephens's text of two other homilies (1853), see the introduction to iv. Grein's metrical arrangement of *Judges* (in long lines without a space in the middle) was published after his death by Wülker, *Anglia*, II (1879), 141–52; and Assmann printed *Esther* and *Judith* separately in *Anglia*, IX and X before they appeared as numbers VIII and IX in his collection. Ettmüller had printed considerable excerpts from the Cuthbert homily in long lines (*Engla and Seaxna Scopas and Boceras*, 1850, pp. 85–92); but since he thought these passages had been lifted by Ælfric from another man's poem and altered in the process, he undertook to restore the original readings, rewriting a number of lines that seemed unmetrical as judged by poetic practice.

[3] *Zeitschrift für hist. Theologie*, XXVI, 180 sqq. Dietrich printed a few passages metrically, pp. 182 sq., though in the first of these the half-lines have been thrown into hopeless confusion by the printer. In XXV. 496 sq. he had printed a close metrical translation of the beginning and end of the homily on *Judges*.

course not complete, but it established the main appearances of
the form in the works as Dietrich knew them. Later, as the features
of the orthodox alliterative verse were coming to be more exactly
defined by German scholars, including Max Rieger and Eduard
Sievers, there were attempts to describe Ælfric's practice more
narrowly and to determine its relation to that of the traditional
poets. Jakob Schipper's first study, in 1881, antedates Sievers's five-
type analysis of the *Beowulf* metre in 1885 and has little to say of
Ælfric's rhythms, but indicates his principal departures from the
alliterative practice of the poets.[1] Schipper's analysis was based on
Grein's arrangement of *Judges* in *Anglia*, II, with occasional reference to two of the homilies of the Second Series, those on the
Lord's passion and on St. Martin. Schipper's conclusions were
extended and given wider statistical support by his pupil, Arthur
Brandeis, whose Vienna dissertation of 1891 was published in part
six years later under the title, *Die Alliteration in Aelfric's metrischen
Homilien*.[2] Brandeis analysed the alliterative practice in seven of
the rhythmical homilies: *Judges, St. Eugenia* (*LS* II), and five
of the Assmann homilies (I, IV, VI, VIII, IX). His statistics have not
been duplicated and are still helpful, though some qualification is
needed. His preliminary comments on the rhythms properly set
aside some abortive attempts to associate Ælfric's form with that
of Otfried but exaggerate the resemblance of Ælfric's patterns to
the five types of the poets as defined by Sievers. The same tendency
is observable in Schipper's second description of Ælfric's form in
1895,[3] which was written in the light of Brandeis's dissertation.
Even though Schipper was aware of the essentially prosaic character of Ælfric's performance, he lent some colour to the notion that it
represented a late Old English decline in poetical standards, a more
extreme example of the trend observable in the *Battle of Maldon*,
rather than a development within the domain of prose. In this
respect Skeat's description of the form in his edition of the *Lives*[4]
comes closer to the mark, for Skeat emphasized the very loose and
prosaic character of the rhythms. His account is essentially right,
but it does not furnish the detail needed to deal with the questions
that have been raised in the present century.

---

[1] *Altenglische Metrik (Englische Metrik* I), pp. 60–66.
[2] Vienna, 1897. The 32 pages were included as a part of the *Jahresbericht der
K. K. Staatsrealschule . . . im VII. Bezirke in Wien für das Studienjahr 1896–97*.
[3] *Grundriss der englischen Metrik*, pp. 39–43.
[4] Vol. II, pp. l–liii. This introduction appeared with the fourth part in 1900.

An influential protest against treating Ælfric as a poetaster was made by G. H. Gerould in his article, 'Abbot Ælfric's Rhythmic Prose'.[1] Gerould pointed to Latin 'rhymed prose' as a source of inspiration for Ælfric's invention and suggested that it furnished examples of his principal devices, citing not only its use of alliteration as well as inflectional rhyme but especially its fondness for the rhythmically ordered clause endings classified as *cursus planus*, *tardus*, *velox*, and the like. Now it is true that a great deal of the Latin prose with which Ælfric was familiar, from Cyprian, Ambrose, and Augustine to Bede, not to mention a good many authors of saints' lives, including Sulpicius Severus and Abbo of Fleury, was highly artificial and employed various rhythmical devices, including not only the *cursus* but parallel clauses of similar rhythm, and some partly structural, partly ornamental features such as alliteration and various types of rhyme.[2] It is therefore more than probable that Ælfric was conscious of these devices, at least in conspicuous instances, and that they encouraged him to develop a prose that sounds to our modern ears too much like verse. But Gerould's notion that Ælfric's form sprang somehow from a carefully considered adaptation of Latin devices will hardly stand scrutiny. In the first place, such direct imitation of Latin devices as we find in Ælfric can be seen quite as well in his 'ordinary' as in his 'rhythmical' prose. In the second place, imitation of anything as peculiarly Latin as the *cursus* is rare in Ælfric and likely to be purely accidental unless it occurs at a point where he is echoing several features of his immediate source. In the third place, the distinctive pairing of two-stress phrases by alliteration, which is carried out by Ælfric much too often to be accidental, is a device fundamental to Old English poetry and foreign to Latin. The general debt of Ælfric's style to Latin is very great though often half concealed by his sensitive respect for English idiom, but there is nothing to show that the rhythmical form as such was directly inspired by Latin. What is valuable in Gerould's essay is simply,

[1] *Modern Philology*, XXII (1925), 353–66.
[2] See especially Eduard Norden, *Die antike Kunstprosa*, Leipzig, 1898, II. 573–656 and (for the history of the *cursus*), 909 sqq., and Karl Polheim, *Die lateinische Reimprosa*, Berlin, 1925, esp. ix–xx, 55–87, 201–325. I am indebted at this point to an unpublished paper by a former pupil, Frances Randall Lipp, though I have not included any of the particulars of her study. Mrs. Lipp examined with some thoroughness Gerould's claims with respect to the *cursus* in Ælfric's rhythmical prose.

I think, the notion that Ælfric, in developing a semi-metrical form, may well have felt that he was acting in harmony with the spirit of the Latin prose-writers. The form itself is unique, but essentially native.

Gerould's exaggerated claims were ably qualified by Dorothy Bethurum in her article, 'The Form of Ælfric's Lives of Saints'.[1] Particularly valuable is her demonstration that, in the life of St. Agnes (*LS* VII), where Ælfric is making use of a highly artificial Latin life by Ambrose, he does allow himself at one or two points to imitate the rhetorical structure of the original, but in so doing *deviates* from his normal metrical procedures. More recently Angus McIntosh, in his lecture on *Wulfstan's Prose*,[2] has brought us back from speculations about the sources of Ælfric's inspiration and his intent to a sharper awareness of the form itself. His description, though brief, is accurate, and brings out the metrical features. The description that follows hardly differs except in elaboration.

There has never been a careful study of Ælfric's earliest experiments with the rhythmical form, nor of its relation to his ordinary prose. Yet one of the sources of confusion for critics and editors has been that the ordinary prose, in its most carefully elaborated paragraphs, is marked by rhythmic balance and by several other devices, including abundant alliteration, that sharpen our awareness of the logical or rhetorical structure or promote coherence and euphony. Sometimes its rhythms are strikingly different from those of the metrical form, but at other times the resemblance is strong enough to be deceptive. Two of the more brilliant passages will show some of its striking features. In addition to rhythm and alliteration, on which I shall comment presently, these passages repeat elements of meaning, words and parts of words, sometimes with inflectional variation, as with the element *miht*, which corresponds to the preterite form *mihte* but may easily be associated with the present *mæg*. I have called attention to these repetitions by the use of italics:

An angin is *ealra þinga*, þæt is *God Ælmiht*ig. He is ordfruma and *ende*, forði þe he wæs *æfre*; he is *ende* butan ælcere ge*end*unge, forðan þe he bið *æfre* unge*end*od. He is *ealra cyninga Cyning*, and *ealra hlaforda Hlaford*. He hylt mid his *mihte* heofonas and *eorðan*, and *ealle gesceafta* butan geswince, and he besceawað þa niwelnyssa þe under þyssere

¹ *Studies in Philology*, XXIX (1932), 515–33.
² Sir Israel Gollancz Memorial Lecture, *Proceedings of the British Academy*, XXXV (1949), 111 sqq. Separate printing, pp. 5 sqq.

eorðan sind. He awecð *ealle* duna mid *a*nre handa, and *ne mæg nan þing* his *willan* wiðstandan. *Ne mæg nan gesceaft fulfremedlice* smeagan ne *understandan ymbe God.* Maran cyððe habbað englas to *God*e þonne men, and þeah-hwæðere hi *ne magon fulfremedlice understandan ymbe God.* He *gesceop gesceafta* þa ða he wolde; *þurh his* wisdom he geworhte *ealle þing,* and *þurh his willan* he hi *ealle* geliffæste.

De Initio Creaturæ, CH I. 8, 10.

We sprecað embe *ærist.* Nu sind sume men þe habbað twynunge be *æris*te, and ðonne hi *geseoð dead*ra manna *ban,* þonne *cweðað* hi, Hu *magon* ðas *ban* beon ge-edcucode? Swilce hi wislice sprecon! Ac we *cweðað* þær-togeanes, þæt *God* is *Ælmihti*g, and *mæg eal* þæt he wile. He *geworhte* heofonas and eorðan and *ealle gesceafta* butan antimbre. Nu is geðuht þæt him sy sumera ðing*a eað*elicor to *aræren*ne ðone *dead*an *of ðam duste,* þonne him wære to *wyrcenne ealle gesceafta* of nahte: ac soð*lice* him sind *ealle ðing* ge*lice eað*e, and nan *ðing* earfoðe. He *worhte* Adam of *lame.* Nu ne *mage* we asmeagan hu he of ðam *lame flæsc worhte,* and blod *ban* and fell, *fex* and næglas. Men *geseoð* oft þæt of anum lytlum *cyrnele* cymð micel *treow,* ac we ne *magon geseon* on þam *cyrnele* naðor ne wyrtruman, ne rinde, ne bogas, ne *leaf:* ac se *God* þe forðtihð of ðam *cyrnele treow,* and wæstmas, and *leaf,* se ylca *mæg of duste aræran flæsc* and *ban,* sina and *fex,* swa swa he cwæð on his *god*spelle, 'Ne sceal eow beon forloren an hær of eowrum heafde.'

Dominica Prima Post Pasca, CH I. 236.

The device of repetition as used in these passages is mainly a means of promoting coherence and securing emphasis, though occasionally we find a familiar play on words such as the juxtaposition of verb and noun in *gesceop gesceafta,* or the deliberate etymologizing of *Ælmihtig* in *mæg eal.* Whether the first element in *godspelle* would have been understood as *God* or *gōd* may be left to Ælfric himself and what I take to be his deliberately ambiguous etymologizing of *godspell* in the opening paragraph of homily VIII. The first passage has no direct source, so far as is known, but the second is a free adaptation of a passage in Gregory the Great,[1] who repeats thematically important words and syllables quite as frequently as Ælfric. The device is so common among the Latin writers whom Ælfric consulted that he probably learned it from them. I mention it here because, although it so clearly antedates the

---

[1] *Hom. in Evang.* XXVI, cap. 12, *PL* LXXVI. 1203 sq., as pointed out by Max Förster, *Anglia,* XVI. 5. Ælfric is merely abridging and paraphrasing Gregory for the most part, but he qualifies Gregory by the reminder that all things are equally easy to God, and nothing is hard.

rhythmical prose, it appears there also with comparable frequency and sometimes supplements alliteration as a means of linking pairs of phrases.

Almost equally conspicuous in the first passage is the alliteration, which is by no means limited to the repeated syllables.[1] Notice the almost constant vocalic alliteration in the first three sentences, and later the frequent use of initial *w* and *s* (including, as is legitimate in Ælfric, *sc* and *st*). The situation is almost the same as with the full repetitions: the alliteration makes us feel that the sounds themselves, apart from the meaning, are forming a coherent pattern; but it is not yet, as it will become, a metrical device, since it does not yet, in any consistent fashion, link pairs of phrases. In the second passage the alliteration is more subdued.

When we look at the rhythms we find a contrast between the first and the second. The first, asserting grand truths in a solemn and half incantatory manner, tends to fall into evenly balanced phrases and clauses, and these are frequently paired. When there is also alliteration we can isolate what would pass for metrical lines. The following are perhaps the most obviously acceptable combinations of two-stress members:

> He is órdfruma and énde, forði þe he wæs æfre. . . .
>
> He hýlt mid his mihte heofonas and eorðan,
> and ealle gesceafta butan geswince. . . .
>
> He awecð ealle duna mid anre handa. . . .

As the passage stands it has just enough unruly members to keep us from taking the two-stress pairs as the norm. But one may see, here and in many another passage of 'ordinary' prose, how strong is Ælfric's tendency toward the rhythms he later selects as metrical controls. Such rhythms and such alliterative combinations are in fact present in the homiletic prose of an earlier day, as has recently been pointed out.[2] Ælfric was regularizing something already indigenous in sermons, unless it was something so nearly universal in eloquent speech as to resist so narrow a classification.

[1] Identical rhyme, when the meaning is identical, differs from both end-rhyme and alliteration in that sound and sense are working in unison instead of in opposition; but physically, identical rhymes include alliteration and end-rhyme, and when Ælfric uses them as binders their function is to that extent the same.

[2] See Otto Funke, 'Studien zur alliterierenden und rhythmischen Prosa in der älteren altenglischen Homiletic', *Anglia*, LXXX (1962), 9–36.

In the second passage the rhythmic variety is greater and there are conspicuous rhythmic sequences that are altogether unlike those of the rhythmical prose. The tone is argumentative, with shifting pace and mood. The enumerations toward the end form patterns of varying shape, culminating in the three-part movement of *treow, and wæstmas, and leaf* and its four-part sequel, *flæsc and ban, sina and fex*. These enumerations were already present in Gregory's Latin, but Ælfric has adapted them to his own logical and rhythmic designs.[1]

Thus, although a good deal of Ælfric's 'ordinary' prose is much more pedestrian than these two passages, we must recognize that, from the beginning, he dealt in alliteration, verbal repetition, rhythmic balances and contrasts. Undoubtedly his grammatical studies as well as his familiarity with the Bible and the Latin fathers were of great importance to his success in developing a style so articulate and rhetorically so resourceful. In spite of his concern for an essential simplicity of effect and his sensitiveness to English idiom, his Latin training is everywhere discernible and he frequently helps himself to devices that will serve his turn. But whatever there may have been in the Latin prose tradition to encourage him to take the next step, that step in itself moves toward the native verse tradition. The crucial difference is the introduction of metrical controls similar to, though much looser than, those of the alliterative poets: the linking of roughly equivalent, normally two-stress phrases in pairs by a nearly constant use of phonetic correspondences, chiefly alliteration. Such pairs have been present along with other rhythmic combinations in Ælfric's ordinary prose, and in that of some of his predecessors. They have now become the rule. In this methodical pairing Ælfric goes further than Wulfstan, whose equally artificial rhythmical prose is not equally metrical. Wulfstan's fundamental units of rhythm and syntax, his two-stress phrases, are on the whole less varied and more dynamic than Ælfric's, but he allows them to form larger patterns in an irregular

---

[1] Gregory's passage includes the following: 'Ecce in uno grano parvissimi seminis latet tota quæ nascitura est arboris moles. . . . Consideremus nunc ubi in illo parvo grano seminis latet fortitudo ligni, asperitas corticis, saporis odorisque magnitudo, ubertas fructuum, viriditas foliorum. . . . Ex semine quippe producitur radix, ex radice prodit virgultum, ex virgulto oritur fructus, in fructu etiam producitur semen. . . . Quid igitur mirum, si ossa, nervos, carnem, capillosque reducat ex pulvere, qui lignum, fructus, folia, in magna mole arboris ex parvo quotidie semine restaurat?'

fashion instead of binding them systematically in pairs. His alliteration more often links the main syllables within a single phrase than
those of two or more phrases, and it is intermittent, appearing most
conspicuously at moments of heightened emotion. Ælfric's form,
in comparison, is metrically complex, much nearer to verse.[1]

The form emerges first in certain homilies of Ælfric's Second
Series.[2] In six of these pieces it is used continuously throughout
with only the minor exceptions noted: XIV, *Dominica Palmarum,
De Passione Domini* (except for a few scattered sentences); XVIII,
Apostolorum Philippi et Jacobi (both parts except for the first paragraph); XIX, *Inventio S. Crucis* (except for the first sentence); XX,
SS. Alexandri, Eventii, et Theodoli (except for the first sentence,
which adjusts itself to the rhythm but does not alliterate regularly);
XXI, *Feria Secunda, Litania Majore* (except for a few scattered sentences); and XXXIX, *Depositio S. Martini Episcopi* (except for the
first paragraph). The form appears intermittently, though pre-
dominantly, in X, *Depositio S. Cuthberhti Episcopi*, and consecutively toward the end of the short XXVII, *Alia Narratio de
Evangelii Textu* (incorporated in our homily XVII, where the
metrically consistent portion is printed accordingly). It is intermittent also in the second part of the Mid-lent homily, XII: the
Secunda Sententia on Joshua. There are brief passages of it in two
other homilies: in most of the last paragraph of XI, *S. Benedicti
Abbatis* (Thorpe II. 188/10–23), and in the closing doxology of
XXXV, *Dominica I in Mense Septembris*, on Job (Thorpe II. 460/18–
20).

We may suppose that all the rhythmical passages in the Second
Series were composed at nearly the same time and represent a
somewhat experimental stage. The Cuthbert homily, which occurs
first in the set, may be among the earliest in date of composition
and certainly exhibits an interesting mixture. In Thorpe's edition (II. 132–54) there are twenty-one paragraphs, of which the
first seven, the fourteenth, and the fifteenth contain irregularities,
though several of these (especially 5, 6, 7, 15) contain a good many
sentences that are strictly rhythmical. Paragraphs 8–13 and 16–21

---

[1] McIntosh, op. cit., brings out this difference clearly with emphasis on
Wulfstan.

[2] Dietrich listed, in the First Series, the homily on St. Clement and a few
short passages elsewhere, but I agree with Skeat that he was mistaken. The list
here given for the Second Series differs intentionally from the lists of Dietrich,
Skeat, and Bethurum, though for the most part all agree.

are rhythmical throughout, although 16 verges on irregularity by contrasts of long and short lines. In Thorpe's manuscript, paragraphs 9–13 and 18–21 are further remarkable for their almost continuous half-line pointing. Paragraph 13, pointed as in the manuscript but arranged in metrical lines, will serve as an example.[1] At the beginning the scribe reverted for a moment to syntactical punctuation and omitted the first three metrical points, which I have supplied within brackets. Another is omitted near the end:

> Eft ða siððan [·] oðre twegen [·]
> swearte hremmas [·] siðlice comon·
> and his hús tæron· mid heardum bile·
> and to neste bæron· heora briddum to hleowðe;
> Þas eac se eadiga· mid ealle aflígde·
> of ðam eðele· mid anum worde;
> Ac an ðæra fugela· eft fleogende com·
> ymbe ðry dagas· þearle dreorig·
> fleah to his foton· friðes[2] biddende·
> þæt he on ðam lande· lybban moste·
> symle unscæððig· and his gefera samod;
> Hwæt ða se halga him·[3] þæs geuðe·
> and hí lustbære· þæt land gesohton·[4]
> and brohton ðam lareowe· lác to medes·
> swines rysl [·] his scon to gedreoge·
> and hi ðær siððan· unscæððige wunedon;

A notable feature of this passage is the comparative brevity of the half-lines. McIntosh has reported that in Ælfric's life of St. Oswald (*LS* xxvi) there are, on the average, almost seven syllables to the half-line, and no half-line has fewer than five syllables.[5] Here, in thirty-two half-lines, there are seven with only four syllables, none with more than seven, and an average of 5·25.[6] To be sure, Ælfric's

---

[1] MS. K (ULC Gg. 3. 28), f. 162ᵛ sq. The scribe has used the simple point, placed somewhat above the line, for all genuine pauses except the full stop and for metrical limits also. His full stop resembles a semicolon, the sign by which I have represented it.

[2] So in the manuscript. Thorpe has *swiðe*, thus spoiling the alliteration, though his earlier text in *Analecta Anglo-Saxonica* has *friðes* (p. 80/8, from MS. D).

[3] One would expect the point to precede *him*. Perhaps the alliteration of *ða* with *þæs* seemed as important as that of *Hwæt* and *halga* with *him*.

[4] MS. *gesohten*.

[5] *Wulfstan's Prose*, p. 14. His average for the phrases of the *Sermo ad Anglos* is just over six.

[6] I have counted *rysl* as two syllables.

average varies from passage to passage in most of his rhythmical homilies, and many of them have four-syllable half-lines, though at rare intervals. There is considerable fluctuation also within the Cuthbert homily, many passages having a higher average; but both here and in the Palm Sunday homily, *De Passione Domini*, the general average for all the acceptable half-lines seems to be lower than in the later homilies, just over six rather than just less than seven. I have tested McIntosh's figure in a good many passages and found it, for the *Lives of Saints* and later pieces, just about right. And I cannot recall any passage in a later homily where the syllabic count is as low as it is here, whereas there are several other passages in this same homily that can match it.

If we look at the passage itself we see that it is rather cramped and bare. Most of the four-syllable lines resemble type A in the Sievers classification and start abruptly without anacrusis. In the later homilies these abrupt openings are more sparingly used, lightly accented preludes of one or more syllables being very common even for the second half-line. It is hard to escape the feeling that Ælfric is here imitating the poetical verse a little more closely with respect to number of syllables and even stress-patterns, though the distance between the two forms is great even here. His rhythms seem slightly awkward, less in accord with the rhythms of his un-regulated prose than those that prevail later.

Two of the inconsistent paragraphs in the Cuthbert homily have a sprinkling of deviations that look like an effort to try out other formal possibilities. Thus end-rhyme figures twice in the fifth paragraph:

(1) on lilian beorhtnysse scinende, and on rosan[1] bræðe stymende.[2]

(2) se ðe ðone heofenlican fodan him brohte, and ðæs eorðlican ne rohte.[3]

The phrases in the first example balance, but are ampler than usual and have three main stresses apiece; the clauses of the second are far out of balance and suggest the irregularities of ordinary prose.[4]

---

[1] MS. *hrosan*.　　　　[2] Thorpe II. 136/29.　　　　[3] Ibid. 138/1.

[4] In this homily Ælfric is guided alternately by the prose and the metrical lives of Cuthbert written by Bede. Here he seems to be influenced by the rhyme and the antithetic balance in the prose life: 'Nam et lilia candore, et rosas odore, et mella præcellunt sapore. Unde constat quia non densa tellure orti, sed de

In the sixth paragraph there are two alliterative sequences, the second a variation upon the first, in which we have three two-stress phrases instead of two, or, according to the punctuation of the manuscript, one four-stress group followed by a two-stress:

(1) and standan on ðam sealtan brymme oð his swyran· syngende his gebedu·[1]

(2) sang his gebedu on sælicere yðe· standende oð þone swyran·[2]

Such quasi-triplets as these are too rare in Ælfric to be of much account, but there are plausible instances in much later and otherwise regular compositions, as is pointed out below.[3]

Most of the deviations in the Cuthbert homily are more easily regarded as lapses into ordinary prose than as momentary exploitations of some alternative pattern. Such irregularities occur with some frequency in the Second Series and even in certain passages in the Third Series, both the interspersed homilies and the *Lives* proper; and there are passages of an intermediate sort that are hard to classify. Skeat confessed that he had sometimes, for convenience, arranged in lines what was best regarded as ordinary prose.[4] Gradually the rhythmical style seems to have become so habitual with Ælfric that he used it for nearly everything he wrote, and in the later compositions that have survived, including most of the pieces here edited, irregularities are much less extensive, being confined to an occasional unruly or incomplete line or (as we learn to expect in late as well as early compositions) a failure of alliteration for a line or two. Yet at no time after the invention of the rhythmical form does Ælfric seem to have hesitated to insert a

paradiso voluptatis allati sunt. Nec mirum quod epulas in terris sumere respuerit humanas, qui æterno vitæ pane fruitur in cælis' (*PL* xciv. 744). The stylistic imitation, however, if such it is, is as free as the paraphrase of Bede's meaning.

[1] Thorpe II. 138/4–5. [2] Ibid. 138/8–9. [3] pp. 120 sq.

[4] *LS*, II. li. Except for the non-Ælfrician lives (xxiii, xxiii B, xxx, xxxiii) Skeat prints as ordinary prose only i (entire), xii (141–80), xvii (1–48) and xxxii (the twelve-line preface). To these might have been added, as at least too loosely metrical for assurance, xii. 1–15, 33–140, 254–67, 289–94; xvi. 1–35; xviii. 1–11 (gradually becoming regular); xxxv. 1–5, and xxxvi. 13–17 (the first five lines after the Latin preface). Another homily of the intermediate sort, with only one passage (the greater part of the pericope) in rhythmical prose, is Brotanek i. The fact that some of the *Lives* are rhythmically more regular than others may depend in part on date of composition, but can hardly be used as a test of date. Ælfric may simply have taken greater pains with some of them.

freshly composed rhythmical passage into an early homily written
in ordinary prose (as he inserted our XXVIII), to attach a rhythmical
exemplum to an ordinary prose admonition (XIX), or to include an
early piece, partly ordinary, partly rhythmical, in an otherwise
consistently rhythmical homily (XVII).

In spite of the intermediate passages with which early examples
of the rhythmical form may be accompanied and the momentary
lapses that may occur at any time, really doubtful passages are of
very slight extent in comparison to the unmistakable examples of
the form, and it is possible to describe its main characteristics,
allowing, at least in a general way and often precisely, for the most
likely exceptions. The following description, guided by the findings of others and supplemented by my own observations, may be
helpful in this limited way. Its statistical generalizations are based
on samplings amounting to a very small proportion of the huge
body of Ælfric's rhythmical prose.

In comparison with the verses of classical Old English poetry,
the paired rhythmical phrases of Ælfric's prose (the half-lines, as
I shall call them for convenience) are loosely regulated. There are
ordinarily two main stresses in each member of the pair, but
secondary stresses are freely introduced, and three full stresses may
appear. The relatively firm patterns of the Sievers types, where
secondary stresses have fixed positions and their presence limits
the number and position of other syllables, are replaced by the more
casual undulations of ordinary speech, in which the syllabic content of the lightly stressed portions varies unpredictably and is little
regarded. In the passage quoted above from the Cuthbert homily
there is an unusually close approach to conventional verses. Several
half-lines fit exactly the requirements of the Sievers types A, B,
and C, and the line *fleah to his foton, friðes biddende* is a perfect
combination of types A and D, alliteration and all.[1] But even here
we find a looser structure, with several examples of disyllabic
anacrusis before what would otherwise pass for type A. The more
characteristic passages show much greater freedom along with a
preference for a larger number of syllables. A passage from the

---

[1] This combination seems to have stuck in Ælfric's head and become almost
formulaic, to judge by the later *and feoll to his fotum, fulluhtes biddende*, which
appears once at XXI. 634 and again at XXIII. 36. But although the syntactical
pattern, the alliteration, and the gesture of supplication are the same (allowing
for the difference between birds and men), *fulluhtes* destroys the resemblance
to type D and brings us closer to Ælfric's normal manner.

introduction to the epistolary treatise *On the Old and New Testament*, a late composition, is fairly representative:

> Se ælmihtiga Scippend geswutelode hine sylfne
> þurh þa micclan weorc ðe he geworhte æt fruman,
> and wolde þæt ða gesceafta gesawon his mærða
> and on wuldre mid him wunodon on ecnisse
> on his underþeodnisse him æfre gehirsume,
> for ðam þe hit ys swiðe wolic þæt ða geworhtan gesceafta
> þam ne beon gehirsume þe hi gesceop and geworhte.[1]

Here we may see vague resemblances to types A and B at least, but I think it is a mistake to look for any significant resemblance. In the experimental stage Ælfric may sometimes have tried to approximate the rhythms of the poets, but in the great bulk of his work he is selecting and only mildly readjusting the rhythmic sequences of his ordinary prose. Especially noteworthy in the passage above is the reduced importance in the rhythmic scheme of such poly-syllables as *ælmihtiga* (which Ælfric alliterates vocalically or with *m* and may have accented on the first or second syllable according to the rhythm of his sentence), *geswutelode*, *ecnisse* (of which the last two syllables had still, no doubt, some weight, but hardly as much as in an orthodox verse of type C or D), *underþeodnisse*, and *gehirnisse*. In short, the syllabic weight and distinct rhythmic organization of the poetry are approached but rarely, and chiefly at moments of heightened feeling.[2] Distinctions between long and short syllables, though probably perceptible, could hardly have metrical significance in so relaxed a scheme; and certainly no one who accepts my theory of initial rests in the poetry will be tempted to introduce any here.

In mere number of syllables Ælfric's half-lines differ from those of the poets not only in range but more importantly, as has already been intimated, in his preference for the middle rather than the

---

[1] Ed. Crawford, lines 24–29 (*O.E. Hept.*, pp. 16 sq.).

[2] Thus the pompous opening of the life of St. Edmund, *Eadmund se eadiga, East-Engla cyning*, may remind us of royal panegyric and more specifically of the *Chronicle* poems, and could be classified according to the Sievers types (A*, E). Again, the climactic *onsorh deaðes* in our homily II. 114 has both the form (type A2a) and the elevation of feeling to remind us of the poets. A more original example of rhythmic control is to be found at VII. 38, where, as pointed out in the note on the line, Ælfric gives us a dative absolute phrase and then echoes its rhythm in a six-syllable adverb. Exact and approximate rhythmic repetitions within and between lines are indeed fairly common.

lower range. After the short half-lines of certain early passages, such as those I have quoted from the Cuthbert homily, the majority of Ælfric's half-lines fluctuate between five and nine syllables, with an average a little under seven, whereas the average in *Beowulf* is not quite five and even in *Maldon* only a little more than five.[1] Ælfric's limits, however, are wider than five to nine. Half-lines of four syllables appear rather frequently in the earliest pieces and occasionally in some of the later. Once or twice the number is reduced to three.[2] At the other extreme we find half-lines of nine or ten syllables rather frequently, and on rare occasions eleven or twelve.[3]

When more than two stresses are present, the extra ones are usually subordinate, but now and then there is reason to admit three equal stresses, not only in the otherwise exceptional three-syllable half-line, *Her, her, her,* just mentioned in a footnote, but in several of the half-lines that have many syllables. A somewhat surprising juxtaposition of extremes (3–10 syllables) occurs in the Cuthbert homily, paragraph 16 at the end:

swa swa hit gefyrn ær [·] gesæd wæs [·]

ðurh ðæs cildes muð· and þæs mæran biscopes Boisiles·

ðe him mid soðre witegunge [·] his lifes endebyrdnysse sæde;[4]

Here one may feel that the uneven movement approaches ordinary prose, but in *On the Old and New Testament* there are two instances of three-stress pairs that are easily accepted for their added emphasis:

God lufað þa godan weorc, and he wyle hig habban æt us.[5]

[1] See above, p. 114, where I have referred to McIntosh's estimates. Heavily hypermetric poems, such as *The Dream of the Rood*, show a higher average, but the hypermetric form has no special relevance for Ælfric.

[2] In the life of St. Edmund, *LS* XXXII. 151, Ælfric reproduces exactly the cry, *Her, her, her,* from the Latin life by Abbo of Fleury. I am not sure of the authenticity of the one-stress phrase, *of deofle,* at XIA. 56.

[3] Half-lines of eleven syllables occur at *LS* VIII. 76b; XVIII. 229a; our v. 48a, repeated at 166a (though the lineation is doubtful); and v. 95b, which Ælfric has treated as a whole line in a modified repetition at 286. A very awkward sequence of twelve syllables occurs at *LS* XI. 108b, where Ælfric is translating a single verse from a Psalm and takes what amounts to a line and a half. At *LS* VII. 405, where another grotesquely long line appears, the fault is with Skeat's division. Lines 404 and 405 should be arranged as three lines, with half-lines of 5/7, 5/6, and 6/6 syllables respectively. For the thirteen-syllable sequence at I. 41b and other problematical rhythmic divisions see below, pp. 121 sq.

[4] Thorpe II. 148/11–14.   [5] Crawford, line 18.

The second is followed by a line that could be treated as a three-stress pair or a two-stress with strong secondary stress, before we return to the normal two-stress pattern:

Her is seo halige þrinnis on þisum þrim mannum:

se ælmihtiga Fæder of nanum oðrum gecumen,

and se micla Wisdom of þam wisan Fæder.[1]

Long after Ælfric has ceased to vacillate between metrical and non-metrical passages we encounter occasional irregularities in lineation that go beyond the substitution of three stresses for two. We find left-over half-lines now and then, or three half-lines that alliterate on the same stave and might be considered a triplet, or a two-stress half-line joined by alliteration to a seemingly inseparable four-stress unit. Brandeis noticed a number of left-over half-lines in the homily on *Judges*. Finding that they coincided with the ends of Biblical verses, he concluded that Ælfric generally translated from the Bible verse by verse, and was likely to leave his own lines incomplete at the point of transition.[2] This may well be so; certainly there are times, as will be shown presently, when Ælfric makes concessions to Biblical verses; but we cannot hold his reverence for the Bible wholly responsible, for there are comparable irregularities now and then in passages where he is composing rather freely. For example, near the beginning of Assmann I, where Ælfric is writing freely on the familiar theme of the Trinity, there is a left-over half-line or (since the alliteration persists) a triplet consisting of a four-stress phrase with light cæsura and a two-stress phrase. Assmann's lineation, which goes wrong a few lines earlier, obscures this phenomenon, but it may be clearly seen in the lineation of our XIa. 11–12, since the beginning of XIa is an excerpt from Assmann I:

Se is soðlice lufu ðæs soðfæstan Fæder,
and his Suna lufu.[3]

There is a chance that a half-line has been lost, or that Ælfric lost count here, but it seems equally possible that the irregularity is deliberate: that Ælfric wanted to keep the thought of these lines together as a unit, and found that it required three half-lines instead

---

[1] Lines 36–38.   [2] Op. cit., p. 11.
[3] Assmann I. 17b–18.

of two or four. If so we probably ought to treat the combination as a triplet. The structure is similar to that of the triplets in the Cuthbert homily to which I have called attention above.[1]

There is a somewhat similar combination at the beginning of *On the Old and New Testament*, just after the salutation to Sigeweard, which I take as either one loosely rhythmical line or a bit of un-regulated prose:

> Ælfric abbod gret freondlice Sigwerd æt Eastheolon.
> Ic secge þe to soðan
> þæt se bið swiðe wis se þe mid weorcum spricð,
> and se hæfð forðgang for Gode and for worulde
> se ðe mid godum weorcum hine sylfne geglengð.

Here the third line alliterates doubly, with both *s* and *w*, and con-tains within itself the same balance that reappears in expanded form in the next two lines; but the half-line that precedes might be treated as either an unattached prelude or the first member of a triplet, since the alliterating *s* is one of the staves in the next line.[2] Our doubt may be somewhat increased by the fact that, a few lines later, after a Latin quotation from the *Psalms* that has been metrically introduced (*swa swa se sealmwyrhta þus sang be him*), we find two unattached half-line clauses separated by two lines of metrical translation: *ðæt ys on Engliscre spræce* and *þus cwæþ se witega*. Both are characteristic formulas of Ælfric's, but since neither is required at this point we may wonder whether they are scribal additions. With these exceptions the first hundred lines proceed regularly.

On the whole the metrical irregularities in the texts here edited are remarkably few, but in homily I there are some that resemble those now under consideration. They occur, this time, in the midst of the translation from the gospel and appear to have arisen because of Ælfric's desire to preserve something of the structure as well as the meaning of the original. The three combinations resembling triplets are all discussed in the note on I. 28. Another

---

[1] p. 116.
[2] If we dispense with normal alliteration in the first line we can arrange as follows:

> Ælfric abbod gret freondlice
> Sigwerd æt Eastheolon. Ic secge þe to soðan,

but this seems at least equally questionable.

irregular passage occurs at v. 44–49, likewise in a translation from the gospel. There, however, alliteration is weak and I hardly think any triplets are to be discovered. The mateless half-line at 47 and the overcrowded line that follows it are a rather desperate solution. This is a comparatively early homily and it may be that Ælfric, finding the translation hard to manage, has simply lapsed for a moment into ordinary prose.

A form so loosely governed as Ælfric's must depend upon syntax even more heavily than the traditional verse. As in the verse, the majority of Ælfric's half-lines are established by the syntactical phrasing even when no actual pause is in order. So far as half-lines go the syntactical indications are about the same in both forms; but syntax establishes the full line more firmly in Ælfric than in most of the poems. That is, Ælfric's lines are prevailingly end-stopped, with only light stops or none at all in the middle. Full stops in mid-line do indeed occur, but much less frequently than in most of the verse, and enjambment is correspondingly restrained. That is the main reason why irregularities in syllabic number, in stresses, and, as we shall see, in alliteration, do not more seriously interfere with the clarity of the form once it has become habitual with Ælfric.[1]

Close imitation of the poetic metre would hardly have been possible for Ælfric, even if he had thought it desirable, without a resort to many of the locutions and formulaic combinations of the poets; and here his independence is almost absolute. His diction, though it ranges widely and includes a dash of the poetical at times, is notably prosaic as a whole. The few formulas he shares with the poets are of the most pedestrian order, such as *æfter þisum wordum*, which is probably to be classed with formulas common to narrative, poetic or not.[2] Such everyday expressions, and some formulaic

---

[1] The half-lines are indicated by regular pointing in some of the most important manuscripts: intermittently in K (Thorpe's basic manuscript) as already indicated, and in W (Skeat's); and generally in two of the manuscripts on which I have based texts in the present edition: U and the interpolated sections of H. Syntactical pointing, which is the rule in most manuscripts, differs chiefly in leaving out points where the sense runs on, for the main syntactical pauses coincide with metrical divisions.

[2] A hasty survey reveals thirteen instances of this expression at the beginning of sentences in Ælfric's narratives: *CH* II. 148/1 (Cuthbert); *LS* II. 233, 369; III. 228 (*worde*); V. 299 (*worde*); VI. 37, 336, 343; VII. 259; XXVIII. 113; XXXII. 83; XXXVI. 151; and our XX. 194. In the poetry *æfter þam wordum* occurs at *Beow.* 1492, 2669; *Exod.* 299, 565; *Andreas* 1219; and *æfter þyssum wordum* at *Andreas*

combinations of Ælfric's own invention may be observed.[1] Compounds of the poetic sort, especially kennings, are not to be found.[2] The device of variation, so closely associated with these expressions, is likewise absent, though perhaps Ælfric's familiarity with it stimulated his search for variety in his diction and led him from time to time into variations of the 'elegant' sort. These differences keep all Ælfric's writings firmly within the domain of prose, and accord with the metrical disparities, among which those involving the use of alliteration have yet to be mentioned.

Ælfric's alliterative practice, while in phonetic conventions it differs only a little from that of the poets, differs markedly in the rules governing position. The main departures here were indicated briefly by Schipper and have been substantiated by Brandeis on the basis of some 2,500 rhythmical lines of varying subject-matter and date of composition.[3] Brandeis found that, whereas about two-thirds of the lines alliterated in accordance with standard poetic practice ($aa:ax$, $ax:ay$, $xa:ay$, or, with two different staves, $ab:ab$, $ab:ba$), the commonest pattern being $xa:ay$, the rest showed deviations of several kinds.[4] In about ten per cent. of the lines the second stress of the second half is allowed to participate. This is contrary to poetical practice unless there are two different staves. In Ælfric, when there is but one stave and it occurs on the final stress, the preceding stress (normally the bearer of the chief stave) is usually neutral ($ax:ya$ or, oftener, $xa:ya$), but sometimes it alliterates also ($ax:aa$ or $xa:aa$, very rarely $aa:aa$). Once, with

88. In the non-Ælfrician *LS* XXXIII. 56 a sentence begins, *Hi þa æfter þissum wordum,* and in the non-Ælfrician XXIII. 278, we find *Æfter swilcum wordum.*

[1] Cf. the parallel passages printed by Crawford in his edition of the *Hexameron* and by me in conjunction with the unique parts of XIa.

[2] A recent article on the OE *Exodus* credits Ælfric parenthetically with having used the expression *lyftes weard* to describe God (*Anglia,* LXXX. 372), but this is a double error. The passage referred to (Assmann XVIII. 85, p. 197) is not by Ælfric, and the anonymous author is not describing God but using the phrase *up wið þæs lyftes weard* to mean simply 'up into the sky', *weard* being part of the compound preposition *wið . . . weard.* On the other hand Ælfric is occasionally led by his Latin sources into coining metaphorical or elaborately descriptive epithets unrelated to those of the Old English poets. In the life of St. Agnes he borrows from Ambrose some abusive expressions for the saint's worldly suitor and some honorific descriptive titles for God (*LS* VII. 25 sq. and 225–32).

[3] The list of homilies is given above, p. 107.

[4] Even the lines with 'standard' alliteration include some irregularities, since the main stresses are not placed in accordance with the same rhythmic patterns as those of the poets, and when there are six or eight syllables there can be differences of opinion about where the main stresses should fall.

extra (though secondary) stresses and full repetition, Brandeis finds *aaa : aax*.[1]

There are also a few lines in which one half alliterates without the other, or even each half by itself. Brandeis counted forty-five examples of *aa : xy*, twenty-two of *xy : aa*, and three of *aa : bb*. The number in the first two groups will be greatly reduced if we reckon with minor syllables according to the principles set forth below,[2] but a few instances remain, and also a few of the last group, which can be similarly reduced but must receive one or two extra examples in compensation.[3] Alliteration of this type distinguishes the half-lines but fails to unite them, leaving this function to the sometimes indecisive syntax and the general expectation created by preceding lines. If these patterns were not so rare they would seriously weaken the form.

The same may be said more emphatically with respect to lines altogether lacking in alliteration. Brandeis estimated that about ten per cent. of the lines should be placed in this category, and gave a list for his seven texts. Upon examination, however, I have concluded that the list should be reduced by at least two-thirds, giving us about three per cent. instead of ten. The reason for this is chiefly a phenomenon that Brandeis admitted as a possibility and accepted as significant on some occasions but discounted or overlooked on many others: what I have already mentioned as the alliteration of minor syllables. This is exceedingly common, occurring sometimes in conjunction with normal alliteration, sometimes alone, and it is hard to deal with because it may often be accidental; but I think there is good reason to believe that Ælfric relied upon it when the main stresses were recalcitrant and welcomed it whenever it

[1] Assmann I. 209: *lybbe we leng her on life, libbe we læssan hwile*. (If we decide to discount the correlative *lybbe we*, we have an orthodox *aa : ax*.)

[2] e.g. *bi∂ witodlice awænd eow eall to blisse* (Assmann VI. 25), where *bi∂ : blisse* might be counted; or *eft þonne heo hæf∂ hyre cild acænned* (ibid. 27), where *heo hæf∂* might be linked with *hyre*.

[3] I count here at least one of Brandeis's examples, *hyre fæx forcurfon on wæpmonna wysan* (*LS* II. 50), though *for-* is unstressed; and I add one that he misplaced, *and nan man ne mæg eowre blisse eow ætbredan* (Assmann VI. 32), though *man* is secondary; and three he did not consider: *swa swa olfend and assa, hors and hry∂eru* (*Hexameron* 280, 281a, which I take as one line); *Ælfric abbod gret Sigefyr∂ freondlice* (Assmann II. 1), though *-fyr∂* is secondary and one might say luck had played into Ælfric's hands; and *Gif ic on Godes gaste deofla adræfe* (our IV. 138). On a line of this type that I think is not by Ælfric, see the note on IX. 52. The two other examples in Brandeis, Assmann I. 123 and VI. 173, have minor links between halves if we count pronouns beginning with *h*.

occurred. With the uncertainly graded stresses of his relaxed rhythms he could hardly be expected to be as precise about the position of the staves as were the poets, and as we study his lines we find that small concessions lead to greater, until, unable to draw a firm line, we must accept as staves what the poets would have utterly disregarded.

The problem can be illustrated from one of the most carefully composed of the *Lives*, that of St. Edmund. Among its 262 lines in Skeat's arrangement (no. XXXII) there are 246 that alliterate on what we may take to be the principal stressed syllables and show the patterns that Brandeis has observed, the only difference being that a slightly higher proportion than usual can be called orthodox according to poetic usage. The remaining sixteen, a little more than six per cent., though some of them are very obviously alliterative, are odd enough to require comment. Thus the following line, if we consider only the four main stresses, can certainly be classified as an example of *ax:ya*:

84 þe Inguar[1] him to sende, and sæde him unforht.

But *sende*, though probably subordinate in stress to the postpositive *to*, seems to be linked with *sæde*, so that we have an irregular instance of *ab:ba*.

Again, the following line could be classified as *xa:ya*:

90 Far nu swiðe hraðe, and sege þinum reþan hlaforde.

But does *hraðe* alliterate with *hlaforde* or with *reþan*, or with both? As shown below, Ælfric often disregards *h* before *r* and *l* but sometimes treats it as a stave. And must we not also recognize *swiðe* and *sege*, though only the second has full stress? The following line might be classified, though roughly, as *ax:ay*, with vocalic alliteration only:

150 Hwær eart þu nu, gefera? and him andwyrde þæt heafod.

But, as I have indicated by the accents, four syllables in the first half-line are competing for recognition, so that *eart* is not very prominent, and the alliteration of *Hwær:him:heafod* seems equally noticeable. In another line we go a step further: there is double alliteration on the two main stresses of the first half, but this is

---

[1] The manuscripts spell the name *hinguar*, but this is clearly a conventional *h*, familiar in the spelling of many proper names in Latin manuscripts, for the name is regularly treated as if it began with a vowel.

picked up in the second by a syllable that bears only secondary stress:

189 Sum wudewe wunode Oswyn gehaten.

Still other lines would have no alliteration at all if we attended to the four main stresses alone, but minor syllables provide a more or less noticeable link, here artificially emphasized by the bold-face type:

213 and ælc on his weorce wæs fæste gebunden.

247 Fela wundra we gehyrdon on folclicre spræce.

273 ac Crist geswutelað mannum hwær se soða geleafa is.[1]

38 se þe West-Sexena cyning siþþan wearð mære.[2]

54 and þu beon his under-kyning, gif ðu cucu beon wylt.[3]

176 þa wæs micel wundor þæt he wæs eall swa gehal.[3]

167 and cyrcan arærdon sona him onuppon.[4]

143 secende gehwær geond þyfelas and bremelas.

With the last two lines we approach, if we have not already passed, a limit beyond which we must say there is no alliteration at all. In the last the unstressed *ge-* and *geond* might not be noticed. Certainly our attention is caught mainly by the rhythmic similarity and the rhymed endings of *þyfelas* and *bremelas*, unless we accept the dubious hypothesis discussed below, that Ælfric alliterated *s* with *þ*, hence *secende* with *þyfelas*. One other line,

49 on sæ and on lande, hæfð fela þeoda gewyld,

would be made regular by the same hypothesis (*sæ: þeoda*), or by substitution of *leoda* for *þeoda* in accordance with the reading of one manuscript, our none too reliable L. Otherwise there is only the parallelism, with repeated *on*, within the first half-line, and

[1] Alternatively one could count six equal stresses in this line.

[2] Such departures from normal prose word-order occur just often enough to call attention to the rhythmical form, which in turn can give support to the meaning. Here *mære* receives an emphasis that makes us take it more seriously than we should if Ælfric had written, *se þe siþþan wearð mære West-Sexena cyning.*

[3] The repeated words (identical rhymes) in the first of these two lines have logical force; in the second the repeated *wæs* seems fortuitous.

[4] It is very doubtful whether *and* would ever be felt to alliterate, but the prefix *a-*, anciently at least a long vowel, may have been prominent enough to attract some attention, and there are a number of lines where it can supply needed alliteration. Here the endings *-an, -on, -on* might also be noticed.

no link between halves. Even the syntax is loose, for the first half modifies *sigefæst* in the preceding line. In two other lines—the only ones not yet accounted for—there is absolutely no link between halves, though one of the halves in each has internal alliteration or full repetition:

> 193 and his næglas ceorfan syferlice mid lufe.
> 151 Her, her, her; and swa gelome clypode.

The last line especially looks deliberate. The three-times-sounded *her* (on which I have already commented above, p. 119) sets up an unexpected rhythm of three equal beats and only three syllables, thus calling attention to the miraculous cries heard in the wood; and the balancing clause, *and swa gelome clypode*, can well be read as an echo, with three stresses. Thus it seems that Ælfric has sacrificed alliteration and modified rhythm for a mimetic effect.

As I have said, the life of St. Edmund is among Ælfric's most regular compositions. Other rhythmical homilies, early and late, show a higher proportion of irregularities, but those just exhibited are representative in kind. Everywhere we find Ælfric admitting weakly-stressed syllables into the alliterative scheme often enough to make the practice seem intentional. From the examples already given it is clear that I am disposed to include, as Schipper suggested, not only pronouns, demonstratives, conjunctions (except, perhaps, *and* and *ac*), and prepositions, but unstressed prefixes, sometimes *ge-, a-, on-, ymb-*, as well as *be-, for-, to-,* and *þurh-*, with their easily heard initial consonants. Ælfric seems particularly inclined to include *for-* and *be-* in his pattern. Nor do I agree with the implication of Brandeis, who referred to such putative alliteration as 'Augenreim', that Ælfric was thinking of the appearance of the written words, though he may sometimes have overestimated the ability of the listener to detect such barely audible concords. When nothing in the line corresponds except the initial sounds of two insignificant syllables we may prefer to say there is no alliteration, but frequently a minor syllable in one half has the same initial as a major one in the other, and the correspondence is easily noticed. Moreover, both in the life of St. Edmund and elsewhere, we encounter lines that show, in addition to normal alliteration on main syllables, the same or supplementary alliteration on subordinate syllables, and it is often hard to maintain that the effect is not intensified. For example:

swilce igles byrsta, swa swa Sebastianus wæs. *LS* XXXII. 118.

ælces yfeles orsorge on ecere blysse. *LS* V. 85.

Crist clypode þa to ðam clænan cnihte. *LS* IV. 56.

We might well refuse, in the presence of all those prominent *c*-staves in the last example, to pay attention to the minor alliteration of *þa* and *ðam*, and indeed an author has so little choice in the use of the undignified parts of speech that we are bound to attribute their alliteration as much to chance as to good management on his part. Nevertheless, since Ælfric sometimes appears to take advantage of their presence by matching them with important words or even, in default of better, with each other, we cannot, as in the poetry, say that their alliterative correspondence is of no structural significance unless the syntax of the line admits them to full stress. Ælfric seems to welcome as many correspondences as chance and his own choice will allow, and on the other hand to rest content with few or occasionally none. The impression of regularity is due in part to the comparative stability in the number of main stresses, in part to the heavy preponderance of lines that alliterate on two or three of these, and in part to the predominance of end-stopped lines.

Although Ælfric's use of alliteration differs from that of the poets mainly with respect to position, in the ways just described, some deviations in quality must also be admitted. Dietrich, Schipper, and Brandeis all observed certain clear differences between Ælfric's phonetic conventions and those of classical Old English poetry, and suggested a few others of a more doubtful sort as a means of adding to the number of lines that could be said to alliterate. In this respect I am inclined to be more conservative than they, though at some points in full agreement.

First, then, Ælfric allows *sc*, *sp*, and *st* to alliterate with one another and with *s* followed by a vowel or any other consonant,[1] though with *st* especially he seems to prefer exact correspondence.[2]

[1] I add a few instances to those given by Schipper and Brandeis. For *sc-s* see *LS* II. 81, 83, 172; *LS* III. 220, 231, 348, 375, 398, 528, 577, 665; our II. 59, 141, 150, 189, 220–35 *passim*, etc. For *sp-s* see *LS* II. 66; III. 481; XVI. 137; *Hex.* 296; and our I. 132; VIII. 45. For *st-s* see *LS* II. 16; V. 282; XVI. 283; *Hex.* 295; and our II. 22; IV. 36, 185. And for various combinations of *sc*, *sp*, *st*, with each other (sometimes including *s*) see *LS* III. 613; IV. 268, 347; V. 389; XV. 164; and our IV. 188.

[2] Separate alliteration of *st* is fairly common, of *sp* rare, but there is a cluster of instances in which *st* and *sp* alternate in *LS* IX. 102, 106, 110, 118. Now and

The alliteration of *sc* and *s* has been observed in the metrical psalms, and Ælfric may be reflecting, or exaggerating, a tendency of late Old English poetry.

Another peculiarity arises, we may suppose, from the gradually weakening aspiration of *h* before certain consonants. Already in *Beowulf* the word *hraðe* alternates with *raðe*: that is, it may alliterate with *h* or with *r* at the poet's discretion. In Ælfric the tendency has gone far enough to involve most if not all words beginning with *hr* or *hl*, and it may sometimes, though very rarely, extend to *hw*. This peculiarity has been properly observed by the earlier investigators, and is easily illustrated.[1]

Beyond this point it is hard to proceed with any certainty. Dietrich early suggested that Ælfric might alliterate *h* plus vowel with a vowel, *w* with a vowel, and *s* with *þ*.[2] The alliteration of *w* with a vowel was based on improbable examples and has won no support, so far as I know, but Schipper was inclined to accept the other two combinations and was hesitantly followed by Brandeis. The alliteration of *h* plus vowel with another vowel seems plausible enough and may sometimes occur, but I am not persuaded by the examples supplied by Schipper and Brandeis except for proper names, where there is no doubt that the *h* may be purely scribal.[3]

then *sc* alliterates by itself: e.g. *LS* III. 73, 365; our XXI. 28, 34. But we also find, on occasion, *sm-sm* (*LS* II. 113) and *sw-sw* (ibid. 165). There is no longer a separate category for *sc* or *sp* or *st*.

[1] Thus *hl* alliterates with *l* at *LS* II. 405; III. 157; VII. 208, 290; IX. 1, 46; X. 70; XI. 244; XIII. 121; XV. 160; and at our III. 12; IX. 76; X. 97; XIII. 164, 168; XX. 312; XXI. 276, 417. But it alliterates with *h* at *LS* II. 47; XI. 181; our I. 453; IV. 105; V. 32; VI. 91; and sometimes with both *h* and *l* in the same line: *LS* III. 346; VIII. 70 (?); XVII. 80; and our V. 22; XIA. 36; XIV. 39; XVII. 115. *Hraðe* alliterates with *r* in *LS* VII. 178, 209; XVIII. 306 (a line that should begin with *swa hraðe*); and XXII. 36; but in the first example it may also alliterate with a preceding *h*. In our IV. 104 it alliterates with *r*, as does *hraðor* in our XI. 340; but *hraðe* alliterates with *h* in *LS* XVIII. 168; XIX. 57; and in our VI. 91 and XI. 300. Other words with *hr* alliterate with *r* in *LS* XVIII. 307; XX. 78, 115; XXI. 171, 420; and in our III. 79; XI. 267; and XXI. 248; but with *h* in *LS* XVIII. 310, and in our XVII. 27, 31, 82, 130, 151; XVIII. 239, 309; XXI. 272. There is a clear example of *hw-w* in *LS* XI. 90 (*gehwylce* : *wæfer*); but *gehwilce* alliterates with *gehælede* in *LS* IV. 125. Equally plausible is our XXI. 530 (*beworht* : *hwitum*). Brandeis musters four examples of *hw-w* but rightly considers them indecisive, since the words with *hw* are not required to complete the alliterative link (Assmann I. 142, 143; IV. 258; *Judges* 317 in Grein's metrical arrangement, Crawford 412/22 sq., *wif*: *hwam*: *wæs*).

[2] *Zeitschrift für hist. Theologie*, XXVI. 185.

[3] Ælfric's alleged inconsistency in the treatment of *Hester* in Assmann VIII. 81 and 250, and, in Assmann IX, of *Holofernis* in 50 and 79 as opposed to 46, and of *Hierusalem* in 386 and 390 as opposed to 136, seems to me doubtful,

There is really some plausibility in the notion that Ælfric sometimes matched þ and s (as if to avail himself of a lisping pronunciation of s), since it can rescue several lines from alliterative poverty.
Dietrich, Schipper, and Brandeis mustered altogether eleven instances in some 3,000 lines, two others have been mentioned above,
and one or two more can be added without a thorough search.[1] It
must be admitted, however, that some of these lines have minor
alliteration on other syllables and that even if all are accepted the
proportion cannot be above one in two or three hundred. I am disposed to agree with Brandeis in reserving judgement. Neither this
nor other even more questionable alliterations adduced by Schipper
and Brandeis[2] can make much difference to the general effect of
Ælfric's practice, which remains irregular and uncertain enough
to perplex the analyst or editor but is nevertheless, for the reader,
prevailingly obvious. Ælfric's original auditors, being accustomed
to alliteration, were perhaps not far behind.

Ælfric's treatment of palatal and guttural g tends, I think,
toward the separation of the two sounds that has been observed
in *Maldon*.[3] Nearly always the guttural sound alliterates with itself
only,[4] and the palatal, which is much rarer as a stave in most homilies, may be similarly set apart.[5] But there are sometimes mixtures

because it is not always clear how, or whether, the names are alliterating. In
Assmann IX. 50 there is certainly alliteration on f and probably on o: *Ða ferde
(H)olofernis mid ormætre fyrde*; and in 46, certainly on f, not necessarily on h:
Holofernem gehaten, mid mycelre fyrdinge. Ælfric may always have said *Olofernis*.
(The examples are from Brandeis, p. 24.)

[1] From the Palm Sunday homily, *CH* II. XIV, *ðrowian : sylfwilles* (Thorpe
246/31); *ðegen : gesette* (250/2); *soðlice : þeoda* (254/12); *ðrowunge : soðum* (258/21).
From *Judges, geþafunge : Samueles* (Grein's metrical arrangement 23, Crawford
401/15); *þeode : ofsloh* (G 53, C 402/19); *þeowodon : geswince* (G 55, C 402/20);
also Assmann I, *þusend : soðan* (106); VIII, *þuhte : forsewennysse* (49); IX, *secgað :
þisum* (1); *þeode : swiðlicum* (84). The two examples cited above (p. 126) are *LS*
XXXII. 49 and 143. There is a plausible instance in our I. 454 (*sume : þunor*), and
another, perhaps, in IV. 47 (*þonne : seofan*, repeated 246). In a good many lines s
and þ are both present without being required to alliterate with each other. Thus,
at I. 1, we need not count *þisum : symbel* since we have *Drihten : dæge*; and at III.
54, 55, as explained below, we may be dealing with a two-line pattern in which
þ and s figure separately.

[2] These involve the second consonant in a cluster when the first is not h:
gewann : twenti (*Judges*, G 232, C 409/16); *gegladode : liþegode* (Assmann VIII.
107); *blissiende : alysednysse* (Assmann IX. 330); *hraðe : drihten* (Assmann IV. 190).
Cited by Brandeis, p. 24.

[3] See E. V. Gordon's edition (Methuen, 1937), p. 40, note on line 32.

[4] e.g. Assmann I. 2, 8, 40, 131, 141; IV. 1, 46, 72, 134, 138, 159, 173, 227, 278; &c.

[5] e.g. Assmann IV. 14, 219; VI. 178; VIII. 103, 204; *CH* II. 242/12 (*Iudeiscan :
geornlice*); 246/32 (*gyt : gingrena*); *ONT* 48 (*gifa : gifð : git*). The palatal, of

of the two, and I think it is probable that Ælfric was familiar with
the older convention and sometimes availed himself of it.[1] The
matter has not been carefully studied, and conclusions are hard to
reach because of the rarity of examples.

More important than the infrequent and therefore debatable
oddities of alliteration are several other linking devices that re-
inforce alliteration or take its place. These include the repetition
of whole words or significant parts of words, the partial repetition
involved in word-play, and end-rhyme, both of stems and of mere
inflexional terminations.

Repetition has already been illustrated in the ordinary prose.
Since it can help to enforce logic and emphasize themes, it figures
more heavily in expositions than in narratives, whether the prose
is rhythmical or not. But in the rhythmical prose, though it often
runs through a whole passage as before, Ælfric sometimes achieves
new effects with it by making it serve the rhythmic structure in the
same way as alliteration. Physically it includes alliteration and
therefore does not swell the total of phonetically linked half-lines,
but it creates a different effect because sound and sense are more
nearly in accord, and the sense-correspondence tends to over-
shadow the similarity of sound. Here are some examples from
Assmann IV, the homily for a confessor:

Matheus se godspellere us sæde on ðysum godspelle. (1)
for þan ðe we rædaþ ðas rædinge foroft. (26)
mid halgum lofsangum to lofe þam hælende,
þe hine gewurðode mid heofenlicum wurðmynte. (29, 30)
and þæt ðæt he to him cwæð, þæt he cwæþ eac to us. (32)
for þan ðe he ana is anes mannes sunu. (119)
gif we swa gesælige beoð, þæt we swa doþ geornlice. (158)
ac swa man mare swincð, swa man maran mede hæfð. (162)
Heo spræc ongean God and ongean Moysen. (176)

These examples range from the simple parallelism and logical
explicitness of 32 and 176 to the mild verbal play of most of the

course, is phonetically the same as consonantal *i*, but although Ælfric sometimes,
as above, treats Hebrew names beginning with *i* and a vowel as having this consonantal *i*, there are times when he seems to treat the *i* as a vowel: e.g. Assmann
IX. 209 (*Iudith*: *ofaxode* : *Ozias*); 385 (*Ioachim*: *yldesta*); 386 ([*H*]*ierusalem*: *eallum*).
  [1] e.g. *LS* VII. 112 (*gearum* : *glæwum* : *andgitum*), 252 (*geglengede* : *gyldenum
gyrlum*); *LS* VIII. 196 (*ageaf* : *gast* : *Gode*); *Judges*, Grein 4, Crawford 3 (*Iosue* :
Godes). Two additional examples cited by Brandeis, p. 25 (Assmann VIII. 146
and IX. 74) have other possible staves.

others, where the repeated elements do not have strictly parallel functions. They are carefully placed so as to help balance the two halves of the line as well as hold them together. Almost any of the expository homilies in this edition can supply similar examples,[1] and the account of the liturgical year at the beginning of XI achieves its incantatory effect partly by the same means.

The word-play is more conspicuous when there are slight differences of sound, sometimes involving the same stem with different vowels, related by mutation or gradation. The examples are still from Assmann IV:

> wið ðone swicolan deofol, þe hine beswican wyle. (49)
> him to become, gif hit his cyme wiste. (104)
> and nam þa storcyllan and sterde æt þam weofode. (185)
> for þære dyrstignysse, þæt he dorste onginnan. (188)
> Cain, se broðorslaga, þe Abel ofsloh. (221)

Or we may have the same root, same vowel, with a non-significant difference in meaning, so as to produce a mere jingle, here used in a narrative passage:

> þæt eal hire lic egeslice tobærst. (178)

A particular favourite is the play on *God* and *gōd*, the similarity of sound, though imperfect, seeming to enforce an affinity in meaning:

> Good is þæs lichaman wæcce, þe for Gode bið gefremod. (46)[2]

A much less frequent device is end-rhyme, either of unstressed inflexional syllables or of stems. Inflexional rhymes are the commoner of the two. Sometimes they accompany alliteration:

> mid mislicum leahtrum and manfullum dædum. (Assmann IV. 50)
> þæt hi hyne ofslogon and swiðe þæs cepton. (Ibid. V. 21)

In the following examples normal alliteration is lacking, but we find, in addition to a repeated preposition and parallel construction, rhymed endings at corresponding positions in each half-line:

---

[1] The Latin gospel of homily I is full of repetition, mainly of the type strictly called anaphora, which Ælfric usually preserves, but it balances lines only now and then. Note, however, the exposition, lines 63, 65, 98, 207, 257, 258, 345, 360, 398, 399, 401, 408, 450, 451, 458; besides some lines that belong to the categories about to be mentioned.

[2] Similarly I. 192, 198, 206. The play figures, to the confusion of etymology, in the introductory definition of *godspell* in homily VIII.

of Iudeiscre þeode and of hæþenum folce. (Assmann v. 117)[1]
cildlic on gearum and ealdlic on mode. (*LS* VII. 9)[2]

In the following example an antithetical balance is enforced by the rhymed endings of opposite verbs at beginning and end of the line, alliteration being limited to the hardly noticeable *ealle*: *and*:

lufian ealle menn, and nænne hatian. (Assmann I. 280)

The rhyming of stems, apart from the sort of repetition already discussed, is very rare. I have pointed out already two examples in the Cuthbert homily where the rhythm is irregular. There is another in the same homily a few lines later where the rhythm is carefully measured and pointed accordingly in Thorpe's manuscript:

þe hire gerihta· gedon mihte· (*CH* II. 142/9)

Still another instance, in the *Hexameron*, reinforces alliteration on both *g* and *s*, with play on *God* : *gōd*, and the next line has both alliteration and rhymed endings:

God sylf geseah ða ðæt hit gód wæs swa
and het ða eorðan ardlice spryttan. (186, 187)

Doubtless several other examples of rhymed stems can be found,[3] but the phenomenon is so infrequent that it cannot be ranked as characteristic of the style, and rhymed endings are likely to be both accidental and unnoticed. The most one can say, perhaps, is that Ælfric appears to tolerate both rhymed endings and rhymed stems if they occur to him, and may have recognized rhyme among possible substitutes for alliteration when this, his normal linking device, was not readily available. I know of no passage where rhymed stems are used consecutively, as, for example, in some of Cynewulf's poems.[4]

[1] Admittedly the inflexional -*e* produces the weakest possible rhyme, and perhaps ought not to be counted even with strictly parallel constructions.

[2] Cf. our XXIII. 7, *iunglic on gearum, and aldlic on geleafan*, where there is alliteration on palatal *g* and on *l* in addition to rhyme, repetition, and parallel construction.

[3] Note -*rice* : *lice* in IV. 33 (repeated 134, varied 174). Also the half-line, *Wif, gelif þu me*, v. 44.

[4] Sisam, *Studies*, p. 185, n. 1, calls attention to *LS* XXIII, *The Seven Sleepers*, as being 'remarkable for a number of rhymes of the type *Mycel is me unbliss minra dyrlinga miss* (ed. Skeat, i, p. 504)', casting doubt on Ælfric's authorship of this piece. To me also the frequent rhymes seem unlike Ælfric and stand among the several reasons why I agree with Clemoes in rejecting *LS* XXIII from the canon.

Brandeis, following the lead of Schipper, devoted a section of his study to what he called 'Reimverkettung', the linking of consecutive lines by alliteration. He demonstrated that such concatenated alliteration is abundant, and that it appears frequently in lines that lack internal alliteration, so that at least they are bound to their neighbours. Nevertheless I am disposed to accept such alliteration as a metrical device only in the rare instances when two lines appear to be carefully balanced, one against the other, and to complete together a clearly organized pattern by means of repetitions or simple alliteration. A particularly good example of this occurs in homily v. 54 and 55:

> God soðlice is gast, and þam ðe him to gebiddað
> gedafenað to gebiddanne on gaste and on soðfæstnysse.

Here neither line alliterates satisfactorily by itself, but when we put them together we find a chiastic arrangement, the first half of 54 being matched by the second half of 55, with the halves in the middle answering one another to complete the design. A somewhat less persuasive pair of lines occurs in homily III. 53 and 54:

> þa Iudeiscan þeode on þam selestan earde
> þysre worulde middan, and sette him ǽ.

Here, unless we follow Dietrich's notion and take both lines as examples of the alliteration of þ and s, we have þ as a dominant stave in the first half of 53 and a very minor stave in the second half and its run-on sequel (*þam* and *þysre*), but the initials of *selestan earde* are repeated in the same order in *sette him ǽ*, so that the second half of 54, less closely attached in syntax than the other three halves, seems to complete the pattern. Possibly, as I suggested earlier, we should grant that *Iudeiscan* alliterates with *earde*, but the really conspicuous correspondence seems to be that of the second halves. Still another pair of lines may be mentioned in the same homily, III. 38 and 39:

> and se ðe on þone stan fylþ, he byþ tobrocen,
> and se ðe se stan offylþ, se byþ tocwysed.

Here, if we grant that Ælfric probably wrote *se* for *he* in the first line, the *s* alliteration helps to bind each line in turn, but it is the close parallelism of the second that confirms the rhythmic structure of both and brings *f*, *b*, and *t* into the pattern.

But such combinations do not occur often enough to establish concatenated alliteration as a pervasive metrical device. In general it belongs, I think, in the same class as the repetitions of significant words in Ælfric's paragraphs when these are not used to link the two halves of a line. Such alliteration and such repetition characterize Ælfric's earliest prose as well as the rhythmical variety. They serve logic, coherence, and euphony, bind sentences and paragraphs, but do not ordinarily help to define the rhythmic organization.

In the foregoing description of the rhythmical prose I have taken the principal examples from writings already established as Ælfric's, drawing on the texts here edited for occasional confirmation or extension rather than for proof. Neither these present texts nor the many specimens of Ælfric's rhythmical prose already in print have been subjected to exhaustive analysis, and I have no doubt that a more thorough study would amplify and correct some of the suggestions here made. But I have perhaps said enough to guide the reader to a basic understanding of the form. I am confident that those already familiar with it, whether they agree with my analysis or not, will find on every page of rhythmical prose in the texts that follow Ælfric's characteristic mode of composition.

Not everyone, I am sure, will be pleased with my decision to print this prose in metrical lines. Since the days of Assmann and Skeat the current has been flowing the other way. Crawford, having arranged the *Hexameron* metrically, reverted to the justified lines of ordinary prose for all the pieces in his *Old English Heptateuch*, regardless of the fact that some are rhythmical; and most editors of Ælfric's rhythmical prose in readers have done the same. There is something to be said for their decision, not only because a prose arrangement relieves the editor from having to worry about occasional unruly passages, especially in some of the earlier homilies and the translation of *Genesis*, where the form is intermittent, but because the main spirit and style of Ælfric's work is truly much closer to prose than to poetry. Nevertheless I find a prose printing of the rhythmical form disturbing. The form is too insistently regular to be disregarded and yet not quite clear enough to make its structure apparent at a glance without further guidance. A reader is likely to miss the pairing of phrases somewhere and start floundering. If he misses Ælfric's basic rhythm he does not respond to the word-order and puts the emphasis in the wrong place. The half-line pointing sometimes used in the manuscripts does not establish the pairs and interferes with normal punctuation, which a modern reader badly needs if he is to read Ælfric rapidly with full understanding. Wulfstan's style is another matter. I agree fully with Professor Whitelock's protest in her revised edition of the *Sermo Lupi ad Anglos*[1] against a metrical printing of his prose, for although both McIntosh and Jost have shown that it can be arranged in 'Hudibrastic' lines, its two-stress phrases are not consistently paired like Ælfric's and should be grouped freely according to the overriding—and varied—syntax of the whole sentence or paragraph. For purposes of analysis or demonstration the Hudibrastic arrangement is obviously useful, but for full appreciation of the style the justified line is much better. I think it is not so with Ælfric. The structure of his rhythmical prose has the higher complexity that comes from regular pairing, and the lines are a true guide to the fundamental movement of his sentences, though certainly we must be prepared, as with the poets, to attend to the sentence-pattern as well as the line. A metrical arrangement is indispensable, in my opinion, to anyone who is preparing a text of this prose, as a means of keeping track of what Ælfric is doing and being alert to the implications of variant readings. I cannot help believing that it will be serviceable to the reader also.

Like Skeat, I have printed the metrical line continuously without inserting an extra space for the cæsura unless there is call for punctuation at that spot; though unlike Skeat I have substituted modern punctuation. The undivided line not only improves the looks of the page but better expresses, I believe, the prevailing character of Ælfric's rhythm, which runs without pause throughout the line so frequently as to make us wonder whether the basic unit is the half or the whole. There is almost always a midway point where the syntactical tension is slack enough to convey the feeling of cæsura, but sometimes a minor word could go with either half and there is no need to decide. Such uncertainties between lines are much less common.

6. THE ÆLFRIC CANON

AN analytical list of Ælfric's works, arranged in seven categories, has been published by Dr. Clemoes in his *Chronology*, pp. 214–19. It includes all the material here edited (identified by manuscripts or previous editions) except the passages added to earlier homilies

---

[1] Methuen, 1963, p. 19, n. 2.

(XXIII–XXIX). The list as a whole is so useful and at certain points so directly relevant to this edition that I have repeated some parts of it in full and summarized the rest, suggesting here and there such modifications as my work has led me to recommend. I have retained the Clemoes categories throughout, and most of the references to editions are the same, but I have substituted *LS* (*Lives of Saints*) for *Skeat*, and used my own name for the contents of the present edition, most of which will be found itemized in section 1(*a*). A few pieces are scattered about in 1(*b*), (*c*), (*d*), 2, 4, and 7. Where the homilies are itemized I have followed Dr. Clemoes's example in marking with a P those that are expositions of pericopes, the portions of the Gospels appointed to be read in the Mass, since it is clear, as he was the first to point out, that a large proportion of the homilies that Ælfric produced after the first three series are expositions of pericopes he had not yet treated, and that by the end of his life, if we consider only the direct testimony of the extant manuscripts, he had expounded nearly all the pericopes for Sundays throughout the year, and several for other important occasions.

1. *Liturgical homilies*

(*a*) The Proper of the Season

Christmas	*CH* I. ii; II. i; *LS* i, partly rewritten as Belfour ix;[1] Pope i (P).
St. Stephen	*CH* I. iii; II. ii.
St. John the Evangelist	*CH* I. iv.[2]
Holy Innocents	*CH* I. v (P).
Circumcision	*CH* I. vi (P).
Epiphany	*CH* I. vii (P); II. iii.
Second Sunday after Epiphany	*CH* II. iv (P).
Third Sunday after Epiphany	*CH* I. viii (P); addition in MS. Q.[3]

[1] Here we may add tentatively the Latin homily in MS. Boulogne-sur-Mer 63, ff. 13–18, which corresponds to *LS* i and has some of the extra features of Belfour ix. See above, p. 4, and the introduction to xi below.

[2] The story of St. John and the young robber, *Old and New Testament* 1017–1153, stands as an excerpt in MS. Harley 3271 and is treated as a supplement to *CH* I. iv in MS. H. On the unlikelihood that this was Ælfric's intention see Clemoes, *Chronology*, p. 238, n. 3.

[3] I use this formula for some additions to *CH* I that will be included in Dr. Clemoes's edition, without specifying other manuscripts in which they appear.

Septuagesima Sunday	*CH* II. v (P).
Sexagesima Sunday	*CH* II. vi (P).
Quinquagesima Sunday	*CH* I. x (P); *LS* xii.[1]
First Sunday in Lent	*CH* I. xi (P); II. vii.
Friday in the First Week of Lent[2]	Pope ii (P).
Second Sunday in Lent	*CH* II. viii (P).
Friday in the Second Week of Lent	Pope iii (P).
Third Sunday in Lent	Pope iv (P)—first edited by Müller.
Friday in the Third Week of Lent	Pope v (P).
Fourth Sunday in Lent (Midlent)	*CH* I. xii (P); II. xii (1) and (2); *LS* xiii.
Wednesday in the Fourth Week of Lent	Belfour vii (P).
Friday in the Fourth Week of Lent	Pope vi (P), in two versions; an extract from the second forms most of Belfour xiv.
Fifth Sunday in Lent	*CH* II. xiii (P).
Friday in the Fifth Week of Lent	Assmann v (P).
Palm Sunday	*CH* I. xiv (P); II. xiv.
Easter Sunday	*CH* I. xv (P); II. xv; II xvi. (P for Easter Monday); II. xxvii (P for Wednesday in Easter Week).
First Sunday after Easter	*CH* I. xvi (P); addition in MS. Q.
Second Sunday after Easter	*CH* I. xvii (P); addition in MS. Q.
Third Sunday after Easter	Assmann vi (P).[3]
Fourth Sunday after Easter	Pope vii (P), in two versions.
Fifth Sunday after Easter	Pope viii (P); late copy printed as Belfour ii.

[1] For Ash Wednesday, but intended for delivery on the preceding Sunday.

[2] I have substituted the manuscript formula for the more exact 'Friday after the First Sunday in Lent' in Dr. Clemoes's list, and so on for the other weekdays in Lent.

[3] Clemoes adds here a compilation in MS. N, made up of Napier viii (imperfect at the beginning) and excerpts from Pope xix. See description of N and introduction to xix.

The Greater Litany, day un-   *LS* XVII.[1]
  specified

The Greater Litany, Monday   *CH* I. XVIII (P);[2] *CH* II. XXI,
                                   with addition, Pope XXIV.

The Greater Litany, Tuesday   *CH* I. XIX; II. XXII, XXIII, XXIV.

The Greater Litany, Wednesday   *CH* I. XX; II. XXV (P for the
                                   Vigil of the Ascension), with
                                   additions, Pope XXV.

Ascension Day   *CH* I. XXI (P).

Sunday after the Ascension   Pope IX (P).

Pentecost   *CH* I. XXII; Pope X (P).

Sunday after Pentecost   Pope XI; Pope XII (P); late copy of
                                   the second printed as Belfour I.

Second Sunday after Pentecost   *CH* I. XXIII (P).

Third Sunday after Pentecost   *CH* II. XXVI (P); II. XXVII
                                   (originally a pendant to the
                                   preceding; see below, thir-
                                   teenth Sunday after Pente-
                                   cost).[3]

Fourth Sunday after Pentecost   *CH* I. XXIV (P).

Fifth Sunday after Pentecost   Pope XIII (P).

Sixth Sunday after Pentecost   Pope XIV (P).

Seventh Sunday after Pentecost   Pope XV (P).

Eighth Sunday after Pentecost   *CH* II. XXIX (P).

Ninth Sunday after Pentecost   *CH* II. XXX (P).

Tenth Sunday after Pentecost   Pope XVI (P).

Eleventh Sunday after Pentecost   *CH* I. XXVIII (P).

Twelfth Sunday after Pentecost   *CH* II. XXXIII (P), with addition,
                                   Pope XXVI.[4]

Thirteenth Sunday after Pente-   Pope XVII (P), incorporating *CH*
  cost   II. XXVII: see above, third
                                   Sunday after Pentecost.

[1] So assigned in MSS. W (Skeat's), C and V. Sometimes *quando volueris*. The Greater Litany is now generally called Rogationtide.

[2] Not specifically assigned to Monday in the manuscripts (except the late C), but it begins by explaining the significance of the three days, has the pericope for Monday (as in Haymo's homiliary), and is followed in *CH* I by homilies assigned to Tuesday and Wednesday.

[3] The first of two miracles in this pendant is the pericope for the fourth Sunday in Epiphany, but there is only the briefest exposition, and the second miracle receives equal attention.

[4] A second addition, occurring in MS. R, is included in Pope XXX.

First Sunday in September	*CH* II. xxxv.
Sixteenth Sunday after Pentecost	*CH* II. xxxvi (P), with addition, Pope xxvii.[1]
Seventeenth Sunday after Pentecost	*CH* I. xxxiii (P).
Twenty-first Sunday after Pentecost	*CH.* I. xxxv (P).
Twenty-second Sunday after Pentecost	Belfour iii (P).
Twenty-third Sunday after Pentecost	Belfour iv (P).
First Sunday of Advent	*CH* I. xxxix, to which an adaptation of Ælfric's preface is added in MS. Q.
Second Sunday of Advent	*CH* I. xl (P).

(b) The Proper of the Saints[2]

Here belong twenty-six of the *Catholic Homilies* and two others: Assmann III, for the Nativity of the Virgin, and a homily for St. Vincent in two parts, one on his passion, *LS* xxxvii (published by Skeat as an appendix to the *Lives*, from the unique copy in MS. L), the other a brief exposition of *John* xii. 24–26, the pericope for a martyr out of Paschaltide, mentioning St. Vincent's name, published as Belfour viii (from the unique copy in MS. B). Of the total of twenty-eight, fourteen consist of, or contain as complementary parts, expositions of gospel-texts.

Pope xxiii belongs in this category as an addition to the homily on Saints Alexander, Eventius, and Theodolus, *CH* II. xx.

Clemoes adds here a homily assigned to the Assumption of the

---

[1] The core of this addition is by Ælfric but the surrounding paragraphs are probably not his. Hence he may not have intended what he wrote as an addition to this homily.

[2] Clemoes limits this category to homilies designed for delivery from the pulpit on the saints' days (other than those listed above as a part of the Christmas season). Hence he excludes, as reading-pieces, the lives published by Skeat, with the exception noted. A general test for the liturgical pieces is that they refer in the text to *this day*, but there are some exceptions: e.g. the Decollation of St. John the Baptist (*CH* I. xxxii) and St. Andrew as in Thorpe (*CH* I. xxxviii), but Ælfric later supplied a transitional passage between the two parts (as in MS. Q) in which the day is mentioned. A further exception is St. Vincent, which would pass for a reading-piece like the other lives published by Skeat if it were not for the complementary Belfour viii.

Virgin in MS. H, ff. 182ᵛ–4ᵛ, but although the parts are certainly
Ælfric's, I question whether the compilation is his. It has been published in full by Assmann as an expanded version of his II (*Letter
to Sigefyrth*) minus the epistolary address, followed by the end of
his III (on the Nativity of the Virgin). See the description of MS. H.

(c) The Common of the Saints

An apostle	*CH* II. xl (P).
Apostles	*CH* II. xli (P).
Martyrs	*CH* II. xlii (P); on Belfour viii, with P for a martyr out of Paschaltide, see 1(*b*).
A confessor	*CH* II. xliii (P); Assmann iv (P for a confessor bishop).
Virgins	*CH* II. xliv (P), with addition, Pope xxviii.
Dedication of a church	*CH* II. xlv; Brotanek 1 (P).[1]

(d) Unspecified occasions (*Quando volueris*)[2]

De Initio Creaturæ	*CH* I. 1.
De Memoria Sanctorum	*LS* xvi.
Hexameron	ed. Crawford; added to *CH* I in MS. Q.
Sermo de Die Iudicii	Pope xviii.

[1] The authenticity of this homily has sometimes been questioned, notably
by Max Förster in *Englische Studien*, LXII (1927–8), 119–30, but I agree with
Clemoes that it is surely Ælfric's, and this is Jost's opinion, *Anglia*, LI (1927)
and *Wulfstanstudien* (1950), p. 173. Its mainly non-rhythmical form points to its
having been composed soon after the completion of Series II; a little earlier,
therefore, than the date implied by Clemoes (*Chronology*, p. 242). The rhythmical style seems here and there on the verge of breaking out, and the greater
part of the pericope (*Luke* xix. 1–10) is fully rhythmical—perhaps by last-minute
revision, for when portions of the text are repeated later, all but one of the portions is verbally different and non-rhythmical. The one that corresponds, moreover, belongs to a not fully rhythmical section. There is further casual support
for the genuineness of this homily in my notes on vi. 301 and xvi. 174 and 176.
As for Brotanek ii, Jost has shown (*Wulfstanstudien*, pp. 172–82) that it cannot
well be by either Ælfric or Wulfstan and has a strikingly clear resemblance in
style to Assmann xi and xii.

[2] This category is here limited to homilies for which no occasion is specified
even in the best manuscripts. Some of the manuscripts place here a number of
the homilies assigned by Ælfric to the proper of the season (section 1*a*) and some
of the material considered by Clemoes to be non-liturgical and listed in sections 2,
3, and 4.

De Doctrina Apostolica[1]   Pope XIX.[2]
De Populo Israhel   Pope XX.
De Sancta Trinitate et de Festis Pope XIa.
   Diebus per Annum[3]
De Virginitate[3]   Pope XXX (unpublished portion
                         only).

Clemoes adds here the homily without rubric in MS. Junius 121 (T), ff. 124–30ᵛ. This is the homily that forms the second part of Ælfric's *Letter to Wulfgeat*, Assmann I, with a few lines of introduction that I think are not Ælfric's, as I have explained in the description of MS. T, p. 72 above. Assmann has printed the introduction at the foot of p. 4 in his edition of the letter, and has collated the rest.

2. *Separate Works*

(*a*) Tracts allied to the homilies and treated as such in certain manuscripts:

   Interrogationes Sigewulfi in ed. MacLean.
     Genesin[4]
   De Falsis Diis   Pope XXI (previous editions in-
                         complete).
   De Duodecim Abusivis   ed. Morris.[5]
   De Septiformi Spiritu[6]   Napier VII (Latin) and VIII
                         (OE).

[1] Clemoes lists this piece in section 4 because he thinks it may have been extracted from a letter, but since this seems to me doubtful and in its present form it is a homily I have put it here.

[2] On the edition by W. Braekman, which appeared after the present edition had gone to press, see the introduction to XIX, Vol. II, pp. 616–21 below.

[3] I think Ælfric did not compile these two pieces, but since they contain some uniquely preserved passages of his composition I have allowed them to stand in the list. See the introductions to XIa and XXX.

[4] The first three tracts were all at one time appended to the *Lives of Saints* in MS. W, though only the first and part of the second now remain there. The first has an added conclusion in MSS. R and S, the second an interpolation (lines 141–9) in the same manuscripts.

[5] Morris's text, *Old English Homilies*, pp. 299/1–304, is taken from MS. R, which is the closest to Ælfric among the extant manuscripts although it has treated the piece as the second part of an unauthorized compilation. See further the description of MS. R. The piece occurs independently in C, G (printed by Warner), and P.

[6] Too narrow and brief for a homily. Probably written for Wulfstan, who revised it (Napier VII, Bethurum IX, excluding the Latin), but it is treated as a pendant to the homilies for Pentecost in the carefully arranged MS. U.

De Creatore et Creatura and   MS. Cotton Otho C. i, vol. 2
De Sex Ætatibus Huius   (X^d).
Sæculi¹

(b) *Admonitio ad Filium Spiri-*   ed. Norman.
     *tualem*²

(c) *De Temporibus Anni*   ed. Henel.

(d) *Grammar* and *Glossary*   ed. Zupitza.

(e) *Colloquy* (Latin only)   ed. Garmonsway.

3. *Non-liturgical narrative pieces*

(a) Old Testament³

The following portions of the *O.E. Hept.* (ed. Crawford): *Genesis*, chs. I–III, VI–IX, and XII–XXIV, 22;⁴ *Numbers*, chs. XIII–XXXI; *Joshua* (except chs. I, 1–10, and XII);⁵ and *Judges*. *Kings* (*LS* XVIII); *Esther* (Assmann VIII); *Judith* (Assmann IX); *Maccabees* (*LS* XXV).

(b) Others

All the saints' lives by Ælfric contained in MS. W: *LS* II–XI; XIV; XV; XIX (I), XX–XXII, XXIV, XXVI–XXIX, XXXI, XXXII, XXXIV–XXXVI.⁶
Vita S. Æthelwoldi (Latin), ed. Stevenson.

---

¹ To be edited by Dr. Clemoes. See the description of MS. X^d, p. 86.

² This translation from St. Basil is an independent treatise giving moral instruction for monks and nuns.

³ Clemoes admits that the line between reading-pieces and homilies cannot easily be drawn for several of these, but they are mainly narrative, though *Judges* and *Judith* have instructive epilogues. There are important treatments of Old Testament narrative in the double Mid-lent homily, *CH.* XII (I) and (2), and the homily for the first Sunday in September, *CH.* II. XXXV (*Job*), which are listed in section 1a; in *De Populo Israhel* (Pope XX, section 1c); and in *De Falsis Diis* (Pope XXI, section 2), besides smaller passages elsewhere. See further the introduction to XX.

⁴ Clemoes's decisions here are partly based, especially with respect to *Genesis*, on K. Jost, 'Unechte Ælfrictexte', *Anglia*, LI (1927), 177 sqq., and J. Raith, 'Ælfric's Share in the Old English Pentateuch', *RES*, N.S. III (1952), 305 sqq. I accept his conclusions as a working basis (his own expression) without wishing to make pronouncements of my own.

⁵ On Clemoes's reservations with respect to *Joshua* (and certain verses in *Numbers*, ch. XIII), see *Chronology*, p. 241, n. 1.

⁶ I agree with Clemoes that *LS* XXIII, XXIII B, XXX, and XXXIII are not by Ælfric. For *LS* XXXVII, St. Vincent, from MS. L, see section 1b.

4. *Letters*

(*a*) *Letter for Wulfsige* (Fehr, *Hirtenbriefe,* 1); *Latin Letter to Wulfstan* (Fehr 2a); *First Latin Letter for Wulfstan* (Fehr 2); *Second Latin Letter for Wulfstan* (Fehr 3); *First OE Letter for Wulfstan* (Fehr 11); *Second OE Letter for Wulfstan* (Fehr 111).

(*b*) *Letter to the Monks of Eynsham* (Latin), ed. Bateson.

(*c*) Letters to laymen: *Letter to Sigeweard* ('On the Old and New Testament', ed. Crawford); *Letter to Sigefyrth* (Assmann 11); *Letter to Wulfgeat* (Assmann 1).

(*d*) Passages that may have been excerpted or adapted from letters:[1]

Wyrdwriteras, etc.	Pope XXII.
In Quadragesima, de Penitentia	Thorpe II. 602–8.
Lenten Admonition to Laymen	Thorpe II. 608.
On Achitophel and other Reprobates	*LS* XIX. 155–258, *Item Alia.*

To this category I am disposed to add the excerpt *De Sanguine* published by Kluge from MS. P and occurring partially in MSS. R and S. This is discussed in the description of P, pp. 56–57 above.

5. *Prefaces*

To: *CH* I (Latin and OE); *CH* II (Latin and OE); *Letter for Wulfsige* (Latin); *Grammar* (Latin and OE); Crawford *Genesis*; *Lives* (Latin and OE); *LS* XXXII (St. Edmund—OE); *LS* XXXVI (St. Thomas—Latin); *Admonitio* (OE); *Vita S. Æthelwoldi* (Latin); *Letter to the Monks of Eynsham* (Latin); Fehr II and III (Latin).

6. *Miscellanea*

(*a*) *Ammonitio* (Latin), *De Sancta Maria, Excusatio Dictantis* and *Oratio* in *CH* II (Thorpe, pp. 4, 466, 520, 594 respectively).

[1] Clemoes tentatively assigned to this category, besides the pieces I have listed, *De Doctrina Apostolica*, which I have put in 1*d* above. I think his conjecture is almost certainly correct with respect to my XXII, but rather doubtful with respect to the other three. The second part of *LS* XIX is not wholly uncalled for as a pendant to the briefly related passion of St. Alban, since it points to the vast difference between the sufferings of martyrs and those of the wicked. It may have been composed with its present position in mind. For *De Penitentia* a former existence as a letter is perhaps a little more likely. A large part of it is incorporated in *LS* XII (above, section 1*a*, Quinquagesima Sunday). Perhaps it should be placed, together with the brief admonition that follows it, in section 6 among the miscellaneous pieces.

(b) *Pater noster*, Creeds, prayers, and blessings (Thorpe II. 596 sqq.).

(c) *De Cogitatione*, printed by Napier in *Anglia*, X (1888), 155; reprinted below: see homily VI. 284–91 and the note on 284.

(d) A detached *exemplum*, Napier's *Wulfstan* XXXI, recognized as Ælfric's by McIntosh, *Wulfstan's Prose*, p. 23.

To this category I should add, besides perhaps the pieces questioned under section 4, the following:

(e) A paragraph in MS. T (Junius 121), f. 34, describing the punishment of licentious priests and deacons, printed by Jost, *Polity* XXIII. 1–5, pp. 217–18, and attributed by him to Ælfric, pp. 26 sq. Clemoes assents in *Anglia*, LXXVIII. 282 n.

(f) The Old English version of the Ely charter (Birch 1267) discussed by McIntosh, *Wulfstan's Prose*, p. 7 and p. 22, n. 8.[1]

(g) The paragraph *De Infantibus* published by Napier in *Anglia*, X (1888), 154 sq. I have given my reasons on pp. 55–56 above.

(h) Two small Latin compilations printed in Fehr's *Hirtenbriefe*: the *Decalogus Moysi* (pp. 190–203, below the text of Brief III) and *De Septem Gradibus Aecclesiasticis* (pp. 256–7). Clemoes confirms these attributions (and rejects others suggested by Fehr) in *Anglia*, LXXVIII. 265–83.

7. Notes

In this category Clemoes has listed citations of authority and other learned explanations in Latin, besides a few directives and marginal explanations in OE, none of them being intended as part of the main text, though sometimes copied as such by the scribes. A large number of Latin notes were so copied in MS. K and thence printed by Thorpe. Another such note is printed below as a part of XXVIII, and in the introduction to it I have mentioned a few extra notes in Thorpe that should be added to Clemoes's list.

---

[1] See above, p. 105, n. 2. This attribution has been questioned by Dr. Clemoes (*Chronology*, p. 219, n. 1) and by Professor Whitelock, whose objections are set forth in E. O. Blake's edition of the *Liber Eliensis*, London, 1962, p. 415; but Professor McIntosh's note does not bring out the full strength of the stylistic evidence, which I hope soon to present in a separate study.

7. DATE AND RANGE OF THE TEXTS
HERE EDITED

A GLANCE at the lists in the preceding section will show that the
material of this edition plays a substantial part in advancing and
rounding out Ælfric's work as an expositor of Christian faith and
learning; yet it will also show that the individual items, being dis-
connected parts of the whole, have little direct relation to one
another. In date of composition, to which no heed is paid in the
present arrangement, they span a considerable period, perhaps
fifteen or twenty years. Our evidence for their date is varied in
kind and by no means always clear. A general guide is furnished
by evidence of successive stages of publication, as this has been
wrested from the manuscripts by Dr. Clemoes and partially set
forth in his *Chronology*. Some additional features of his scheme
have been mentioned at the head of section 2 above, and further
light is to be expected from his forthcoming edition of Ælfric's
First Series. But although something can be deduced about the
successive stages, dates can seldom be assigned with any precision,
and the very meaning of publication in an age of manuscripts is
hard to delimit. Moreover, the first issue of a work may be much
later than the date of composition of some of its parts. Certain
sequences can be firmly established by Ælfric's references to earlier
homilies in which he has treated the same themes, or by the
preservation of certain homilies in successive versions, but such
help is not always vouchsafed where it is most needed. Beyond
this we must deduce what we can from style, though it is at best an
uncertain guide for chronology. I am inclined to date early all the
passages in ordinary prose, including the prose parts of XIX and
XXX, even though we have no manuscript evidence that either of
these prose passages got into circulation until rather late. Detailed
comment on the dates of individual pieces will be found in the
separate introductions as occasion arises. Here I attempt a few
generalizations as a frame for these isolated bits of conjecture.

We may assume that little if anything was written before Ælfric
had completed his Second Series, probably toward the middle of
992;[1] but there is no reason why he should not have begun the work
of enlargement almost immediately afterwards. The English preface to the *Lives* implies that they were written over a considerable

---

[1] Sisam, *Studies*, p. 160.

period of time.[1] Hence it seems probable that Ælfric was at work at them intermittently while he was producing other compositions, such as his *Letter for Wulfsige*, his *Grammar*, the *De Temporibus Anni*, his translation of the first half of *Genesis* and perhaps other Old Testament pieces. For the *Lives* as a complete set, with its general Latin preface and its English preface addressed to Æthelweard, the latter's death, now held to have occurred no earlier than 1002, is the only obvious terminus, though 998, formerly accepted as the terminus, may in fact be late enough.[2] Six years is a fairly generous span for a writer who could produce the *Catholic Homilies* in not much more than three. We may reasonably suppose, then, that during the period from 992 to 998 or so Ælfric produced, besides the works already named, a certain number of homilies that he did not wish to include among the *Lives*.[3]

Among the relatively early pieces I should place, first, the non-rhythmical passages in XIX, XXV, and XXX; and at nearly the same time *De Falsis Diis* (later revised by the addition of lines 141–9), the four homilies for Fridays in Lent (II, III, V, VI, the last revised at least once at a later time), and the homily for the third Sunday in Lent (IV). For *De Falsis Diis* and nos. II–VI the manuscript evidence clearly points to their issue with or before the *Lives* set, and thus the date of composition is shown to be relatively early. No. IV may be among the last of these, since it refers back to an earlier discussion of the god-devil Beel or Baal; but it is uncertain whether this is a reference to *LS* XVIII on *Kings* or to *De Falsis Diis*. I am half inclined to nominate the former.

Between the completion of the *Lives* and the period of Ælfric's

---

[1] Clemoes makes this point, *Chronology*, p. 222. The relevant passage occurs in Skeat's edition, I. 4/36 sqq.: 'ic hæbbe nu gegaderod on þyssere bec þæra halgena þrowunga þe me to onhagode on Englisc to awendene, for þan þe ðu leof swiðost and Æðelmær swylcera gewrita me bædon, and of handum gelæhton. . . .' According to the last clause Ælfric may have supplied Æthelweard and his son with copies of single lives before issuing the set.

[2] Clemoes, *Chronology*, p. 243. Æthelweard last signed charters in 998, but a manumission printed by Kemble, *Codex Diplomaticus*, no. 981, seems to show that he was still alive in 1002. Professor Whitelock was the first to draw this conclusion. See her *Anglo-Saxon Wills*, Cambridge, 1930, pp. 144 sq.; and further, *Anglo-Saxon Charters*, ed. A. J. Robertson, Cambridge, 1939, pp. 386 sq.

[3] This general proposition is suggested by Clemoes, *Chronology*, p. 221, and his various comments on the *Lives*, pp. 219–27, should be considered. He thinks that Ælfric deliberately included with the lives the general homilies we find in MS. W, and that except for the four lives not by Ælfric it represents the content of the set as originally issued. But he gives reason to believe that *De Memoria Sanctorum* (*LS* XVI) has lost its rightful place at the head of the set.

abbacy, say 998 to 1005, I should place a fairly large company: the complete XIX (*De Doctrina Apostolica*), XX (*De Populo Israhel*), and the exegetical series running from the fourth Sunday after Easter to the first after Pentecost (VII, later expanded, VIII–X, and XII). The last of these is shown by a back reference to be later than *CH* II. XIII. The manuscripts suggest that XI (*In Octavis Pentecosten*) and XVIII (*De Die Iudicii*) are a bit later than those I have just mentioned. The fragmentary XXII, probably part of a letter, is shown by its back references to be later than *LS* VII and the epilogue to *Judges*. Hence it cannot have been written earlier than the period under discussion. On the other hand I cannot tell how late it may be.

It is perhaps idle to speculate on most of the additions to homilies of *CH* II or *De Auguriis*, or on those to VI, VII, XXI. Such a piece as XXIII, giving a narrative to precede the passion of Saints Alexander, Eventius, and Theodolus, could have been written rather early in spite of its solitary appearance as an addendum to a textually late manuscript, for there is no record of a reissue of *CH* II as a revised set, so that additions made early may have remained out of circulation, sometimes until after Ælfric's death. The three added passages of XXV, by their non-rhythmical character, look very early, as I have said, but they too appear first in a textually late manuscript. The same general argument applies to the additions to XXI (141–9) and *De Auguriis* (XXIX), though in this last instance we cannot be sure whether or not Ælfric, who certainly wrote the two passages composing the addition, attached either of them to *De Auguriis*.

Likewise doubtful are the hitherto unprinted parts of compilations. If XI*a* is a compilation from several of Ælfric's works made by someone else, the fact that one passage is drawn from a letter written during Ælfric's abbacy (Assmann I) tells us nothing about the date of composition of any other passage. The same reservation applies to the passages from the homily *De Virginitate* composing no. XXX, of which I have already mentioned the second passage since it is in ordinary prose. A passage not included comes from the revised form of the *Letter to Sigefyrth* (Assmann II), written even in its first form by Ælfric as abbot; but this tells us nothing about the date of the other passages. A somewhat similar doubt applies to the Ælfrician kernel of XXVII, since its surrounding passages look like the work of another writer. The kernel itself may not have been destined for the homily to which it is attached.

Somewhat stronger grounds for composition after 1005 (when Ælfric became abbot of Eynsham) may be assigned to the full homilies not yet mentioned: no. I and nos. XIII–XVII. They are contained only in manuscripts that have texts of a late type, and some of them at least have other signs of late composition. I have discussed XIII–XVI in the introduction to XIII, calling attention to the possibility that XIV, with its protests against religious slackness and political treachery, was written as late as 1009 or 1010. Stylistically those homilies accord well enough with a late date, though it would be hard to defend a date based on style alone. The least datable, perhaps, is no. XVII with its series of miracles, those in the middle having first appeared as a separate piece in *CH* II. I find it satisfactory to regard no. I as relatively late because of its easy mastery of a wealth of learning. It is one of the most varied yet most skilfully organized of the homilies. But certainly it is not so late as to have suffered any diminution of energy. Its imperfect preservation is much to be regretted.

If now we recall that the homilies in this edition are but a portion of Ælfric's homiletic output during the middle and later years of his literary career, we shall recognize that the stream was far from dry when he finished the *Lives of Saints*. Partly overlapping the *Lives*, but mainly following them, we must recall especially the *Interrogationes*, the *De Duodecim Abusivis*, the *Hexameron*, such Old Testament pieces as *Judges*, *Esther*, and *Judith*, the letters and homilies in Assmann I–VI, the unique Belfour pieces (III, IV, VII, VIII, and part of IX), and the *Letter to Sigeweard* (*On the Old and New Testament*)—all these in addition to other less relevant compositions.

In spite of the singleness of Ælfric's purpose in all this work, there is considerable variety of subject, tone, and treatment in the present collection. Merely in narrative we range from the miracles of the gospel, the longest being that of the raising of Lazarus, to the chastisement of the Israelites in the wilderness, and then, among the shorter pieces, in comparatively rapid succession, to a melodramatic tale of saints, the intensely moral conflict of Ambrose and Theodosius, and the simple-minded visions from the *Vitæ Patrum*. There is a vast difference in both tone and treatment if we move from the celebration of God's victories over his incompetent rivals in *De Falsis Diis* to counsels of mercy in homily XV or to the solemn prognostications of XI. Lyrical touches in I, the first part of XI, and the passage on the fall in *De Falsis Diis* are offset by the

moral admonitions of XIX and the political counsels of IX and XXII.
A fair proportion of the collection will hold its own, I think, both
in excellence of expression and in spirit, with the best of Ælfric's
hitherto known work.

8. THE SOURCES

IN his prefaces to the *Catholic Homilies* and the *Lives of Saints*
Ælfric repeatedly speaks of his work as translation, though he says
he has not always translated word for word, but sometimes sense
for sense.[1] In fact he sometimes treats his authorities with such
freedom that, quite apart from personal comments and topical
applications, his work approaches original composition, not merely
in style, as we tend to expect, but even in substance. His dis-
claimers of originality and his occasional references to authorities
are by no means sufficient to guide us to a just estimate of his
accomplishment. Under their influence we are quite as likely to
exaggerate as to underestimate his indebtedness to the Latin
expositors. Those who study the sources of the homilies discover
how little in them beyond the Biblical passages is closely translated,
how often Ælfric omits, condenses, expands, rearranges, synthe-
sizes two or more interpretations, rejects one in favour of another,
imports examples or parallel texts, reminds us of something he has
dealt with more extensively elsewhere. The very intensity of his
effort to be faithful to his role as interpreter has made him take
full responsibility for what he says. The thought is scrupulously
traditional yet fully digested and feelingly his own.

The exegetical homilies regularly differ in one obvious but
important respect from their Latin models, in that they begin with
a straightforward translation of the gospel for the day. For the
contemporary congregations these translations must have had the
advantage of novelty to add to their normal interest, for the corresponding lessons were read in Latin. Their presence alters the
proportions and the emphasis of the homilies, not only making it
desirable to shorten the exegesis but giving some encouragement
to simplified interpretations of which the chief function is to
emphasize the direct meaning of the gospel itself. Ælfric varies
greatly, under the influence of different pericopes and different
expositors, in the degree to which he follows the routine of a

[1] 'Nec ubique transtulimus verbum ex verbo, sed sensum ex sensu.' *CH.* I. I.

verse-by-verse exposition. One of the richest of the homilies, our
no. I, expounds each of the verses of *John* i. 1–14 in turn with some
care in spite of a wealth of elaborations and digressions; but our
no. VI, on the raising of Lazarus, after a pericope much longer than
usual, devotes a good deal of space to a general topic treated by
Augustine, follows this (in the augmented revision) with a second
topic from a different sermon by Augustine, and then, returning
to the pericope, selects only a few of its verses for a rather hasty
exposition. In no. VIII the routine is broken by an introduction on
the meaning of 'godspell' and by three striking *exempla* imported
from two different sources; in no. IX, by animadversions on kings
and counsellors; in no. XIV, by attacks on the English for religious
laxity and on some among them for treason. The interweaving of
sources is conspicuous in several homilies, including I, II, XIII,
XV, XVI.

Ælfric's treatment of his sources can be studied in some detail
in the present edition. I have identified as many sources as I could,
putting the directly relevant passages at the foot of the page below
the corresponding passages of Ælfric's text. A comprehensive list
of the non-Biblical sources thus quoted will be found at the end of
this section of the introduction.[1] Certain limitations of this list, and
the character of the texts, non-Biblical and Biblical, chosen for
quotation should be understood at the outset.

The list of non-Biblical sources, though large, is far from complete, and besides other imperfections that are discussed in a later
paragraph, it includes here and there some vaguely similar passages,
quoted in default of better, that may not be sources at all. Moreover, even when the correspondence with Ælfric is persuasively
clear, it must not be unquestioningly assumed that the Latin as
quoted is precisely what Ælfric had before him. Except for the
source of XI, considered separately below, I have depended for the
Latin text on the modern editions, which are often based on manuscripts remote from Ælfric in time and place if not in their sub-
stantive readings. A search among the extant manuscripts for the
closest possible readings must be left to some hardy explorer of the
future; nor will he find it easy to reach conclusions. In the best
modern editions, such as Hurst's of Bede's homilies and commentaries, there are variant readings from which to choose, but Ælfric's

---

[1] The list is supplemented by a list of the few non-Biblical Latin quotations in
Ælfric's text, and by an index of his quotations and translations from the Bible.

characteristically free rendering seldom affords any basis for a choice. In the freer passages the most we can expect is correspondence with the source in idea and in a few significant words, and for such correspondence the printed text will usually serve as well as another.

For Ælfric's Biblical translations the Latin version cannot always be determined, but the possibilities are considerably reduced, partly because he tends to be scrupulously faithful to the sense if not to the verbal sequences of the original. We must distinguish between the extended translations, for which Ælfric presumably turned to his own copy of the Latin Bible, and brief citations, often quoted in Latin and then translated. Frequently such a citation is borrowed from a commentator, and Ælfric may quote it in the commentator's form. Hence we find a few bits of Old Latin interspersed with the prevailing Vulgate readings. Once Ælfric quotes, from a commentary by Jerome, a version of *Matthew* xxiii. 24 that is closer to the Old Latin than to Jerome's own Vulgate.[1] Ælfric's pericopes and other extended translations from the gospels clearly follow the Vulgate, though one cannot always choose among the minor variants. I have normally quoted the Clementine recension, as for the rest of the Bible, since it is generally satisfactory, but have compared the recension of Wordsworth and White, and on very rare occasions have found reason to cite it for punctuation or a likely variant.

Ælfric's translations from the *Psalms* are neither long nor numerous and are always accompanied by at least a portion of the Latin text, so that it is easy to identify the version he is following. Six of his quotations are common to the 'Roman'[2] and 'Gallican'[3] psalters; three are Gallican rather than Roman; one, evidently borrowed from Bede, is Roman rather than Gallican.[4] There is no

---

[1] Hom. XIII. 163.

[2] According to the text of R. Weber, *Le Psautier Romain*, etc., *Collectanea Biblica*, X, Rome, 1953.

[3] According to the Clementine Vulgate and the recension authorized by Pius XII, *Biblia Sacra iuxta Latinam Vulgatam Versionem*, X, *Liber Psalmorum*, Rome, 1953, which is not always quite the same, as indicated in the next note.

[4] The six common quotations are at I. 81 and 357; VII. 97 (where Ælfric rejects Augustine's *infantium* for *paruulorum* if indeed he has Augustine's commentary before him); XIII. 73; XV. 181; and XVI. 58. Gallican rather than Roman are those at I. 99 and 376 (where, however, Ælfric has *deos* with the Clementine Vulgate and many of the Gallican manuscripts rather than the *Deus* chosen by the editors in 1953); and VII. 113, reading *infirmate* for the scribe's merely erroneous *infirmitate(s)*. The one Roman reading is *laborant* for the Gallican *laboraverunt* at XIV. 120, where Bede's commentary has *laborant* also.

trace of the 'Hebrew' version.[1] These findings are what we might expect, for the Hebrew version was never much in use and the Gallican, later adopted for modern editions of the Vulgate, began to displace the Roman in England a few decades before the start of Ælfric's literary career, as a consequence of the Benedictine reform.[2]

Although the detailed presentation of Ælfric's sources is designed chiefly to illuminate his learning, his methods as a homilist, and his style, it sometimes has further, very practical uses. For example, the sources have helped to determine, and help now to justify, the choice of readings at VI. 10; XII. 156–8 (where there is nevertheless an interesting *difference* from the source); XIV. 88; and XXI. 314 (where the erroneous but plausible-looking reading of MS. C might otherwise cause speculation). At two points in Ælfric's translation of a part of *Daniel* (XXI. 352 and 446) the source helps to define otherwise unrecorded words, though on the second occasion it cannot shed light on the puzzling form. At XXI. 115 the source supports the *Minerua* of the manuscripts against Kemble's emendation, *Diana*. At V. 108–9, where one manuscript omits some words that were present in the other until they were partially destroyed by fire, two sentences in the source establish the true reading beyond reasonable doubt. At VI. 363, where both manuscripts have a confused reading, the source guides us to an easy emendation. At VIII. 96, where all four manuscripts are metrically defective, the source (this time a gospel-text quoted in Latin by Ælfric himself) shows that an element of meaning not quite indispensable has been lost. And at II. 196–7, though I cannot reconstruct the proper reading from the differing but equally corrupt readings of the two manuscripts, the source gives us an idea of the basic meaning. Many times, too, I have found the sources reassuring as well as enlightening at points where the manuscript readings, though correct, were at first sight cryptic or ambiguous. At III. 147–54, for instance, Ælfric's interpretation is given without a hint of the reasoning behind it, so that we may wonder what to make of it, and whether the text is correct, unless we consult the much fuller interpretation in Haymo. I need hardly add that where the text depends solely on the damaged MS. H (in I, XVII, XXVII)

---

[1] As given by H. de Sainte-Marie, *Sancti Hieronymi Psalterium iuxta Hebraeos*. *Collectanea Biblica Latina*, XI, Rome, 1954.

[2] See the discussion and the list of extant psalters of the Anglo-Saxon period in C. Sisam and K. Sisam, *The Salisbury Psalter* (EETS, 1959), pp. 47 sqq.

our chief guides to what is missing in the larger lacunae are the Latin sources.

The study of Ælfric's sources has, however, much wider implications, and if these are to be apprehended the findings of the present edition must be seen in relation to those already made with respect to the main body of the homilies. The pioneering study, and the most comprehensive, was made by Max Förster on the sources of the *Catholic Homilies*.[1] Here the exegetical homilies (among which Förster included several that are better classified as topical or as mere expansions of a scriptural narrative) are of particular interest. Ælfric himself in his Latin preface to the First Series named as his sources for these homilies Augustine, Jerome, Bede, Gregory the Great, Smaragdus, and Haymo. Förster's investigation showed that Ælfric had made particularly heavy use of Gregory the Great's *Homiliæ in Evangelia*, and secondarily of certain homilies and commentaries of Bede and Augustine. After these major sources Förster placed a large number of minor ones, including Gregory's *Dialogues*, Bede's writings on natural science, the homilies collected by Smaragdus (whose regularly unoriginal excerpts from other writers nevertheless contain occasional small additions, with a few of which Ælfric reveals his acquaintance), a few passages from Jerome, Haymo's homilies, the anonymous chapters (27–34) appended to Alcuin's *Liber de Virtutibus et Vitiis*, one or two of Cassian's *Collationes*, the *De Ecclesiasticis Officiis* of Amalarius, an unidentified comment on *James* ii. 19, quoted by Ælfric and tentatively attributed by him to a St. Hilarius (*CH* I. 304), an interpretation of the Sacrifice of the Mass by Ratramnus, the *Historia Ecclesiastica* of Rufinus (credited by Ælfric, as Förster reminds us, to Jerome), and the *Vitæ Patrum*.[2]

Later studies, as will presently appear, have modified Förster's conclusions in some respects and added a few more names to the list of authorities, but his study establishes the most important

---

[1] The main study was published in two parts, the first, on the saints' lives, as a doctoral dissertation: *Über die Quellen von Ælfric's Homiliae Catholicae. I. Legenden*, Berlin, 1892. The second part appeared as an article, 'Über die Quellen von Ælfrics exegetischen Homiliae Catholicae', *Anglia*, XVI (1894), 1–61, which contains on p. 59 a summary of the findings of both parts and on pp. 60–61 an index to the treatment of the individual homilies. Förster added a further source in *Englische Studien*, XXVIII (1900), 423.

[2] Förster named as sources of the saints' lives not only a legendary of a familiar type but also passages from Bede's *Historia Ecclesiastica* and Gregory of Tours's *Historia Francorum*, Sulpicius Severus on St. Martin, and again Rufinus.

sources and draws the same general conclusion about Ælfric's treatment of them that has been expressed above. That is, he stresses the independence and freedom with which Ælfric handles his sources, the fact that he often takes over only the substance of an idea, clothing it for himself, and he surmises, having pointed to a number of passages for which he has found no specific sources, that Ælfric must be credited with having supported the learned tradition with his own additions and elaborations.[1] The list of sources given at the end of this section for the homilies here edited contains a few more names, but accords with Förster's general picture except in certain understandable shifts of emphasis. Bede holds his ground as a major authority, but Gregory, whose homilies on the gospels took first place among the sources of the *Catholic Homilies*, is here much less prominent, whereas Augustine has grown very considerably. Haymo also looks a good deal more important than before, but this is partly, as we shall see, because his influence was underestimated by Förster.

Like Förster, I have been guided in the first instance by the degree of verbal correspondence between Ælfric's text and such conceivably eligible Latin writings as I could find, and when the closest of these have been determined I have named them according to modern notions of their authorship and their occurrence in modern editions without trying (unless some unusual piece of evidence made the task easy) to decide in what form or under what author's name a particular piece of writing had reached Ælfric. The miscellaneous list that results is far from satisfactory even if we discount its undoubted errors and omissions. If we are to answer even tentatively certain questions it must be subjected to two different kinds of analysis.

For the history of ideas what matters most is the originator of the idea and secondarily the extent of its dissemination and its persistence. From this point of view the list, taken uncritically, is seriously misleading. The authors are all borrowers, and some are little else. Ælfric probably consulted Haymo's homiliary (apparently an interpolated version much like the one printed by Migne)[2] for every one of the sixteen exegetical homilies here edited, but even the twelve relevant homilies actually by Haymo are

---

[1] *Anglia*, XVI. 59. A number of additional sources have been found, but Förster's generalization holds.
[2] See below, pp. 157, n. 2, and 160.

largely rewritings of Bede, Augustine, Gregory, or Jerome. Augustine, on the other hand, though of course a borrower himself, was by far the most original thinker of the group, and communicated both ideas and expressions to most of his successors; as, to a somewhat lesser extent, did Jerome and Gregory. Bede helped himself very freely to the work of these predecessors, as he took pains to declare, but he also contributed far more of his own than Haymo. A careful reckoning of indebtedness is beyond the scope of this edition, but it may be confidently asserted that, among the authors to whom Ælfric turned most frequently (Bede, Haymo, and Augustine being, for the present collection, in the lead, then Gregory and Jerome), Augustine exerted, directly or indirectly, much the greatest influence, Haymo the least.

Another kind of analysis is required if we seek to determine the particular books and collections that Ælfric used. How, we may ask, in such a remote place as Cerne Abbas or even later at Eynsham, did he gain access to the large number of works, by a great variety of authors, that he seems to have known and used? Were there collections rich enough to serve him and limited enough to be kept at hand in a small library? Did even the principal English libraries of his day supply the complete works of a large number of authors, or did these too depend heavily on selective compilations? These are far-reaching questions, unanswerable in the main without further investigation, but so far as Ælfric is concerned some illuminating though partial answers have been given in two recent studies by the Revd. Cyril L. Smetana, O.S.A.

In an article entitled 'Ælfric and the Early Medieval Homiliary', *Traditio*, XV (1959), 163–204, Father Smetana has shown that nearly all the material that Ælfric drew from Gregory, Bede, and Augustine for the *Catholic Homilies* is to be found in one or other of the surviving versions of the comprehensive homiliary first compiled for Charlemagne by Paul the Deacon and long reproduced, with variations, for Western Christendom.[1] What makes Ælfric's

---

[1] The table of contents of the original collection was reconstructed by F. Wiegand, *Das Homiliarium Karls des Grossen auf seine ursprüngliche Gestalt hin untersucht* (Studien zur Geschichte der Theologie und der Kirche, I. 2, Leipzig, 1897). His schedule was reproduced by Father J. Leclercq in *Scriptoruim*, II (1948), 205–14, in skeletal form but with extra identifications supplied by Dom G. Morin. Finally, the full schedule, as thus improved and with modernized references to patristic works, is printed by Father Smetana on pp. 165–80. A much later version of the homiliary is published by Migne in *PL* xcv. The

use of some form of the collection virtually certain is that where, as is usual for the greater feasts, the collection provides more than one sermon for an occasion, we are likely to find Ælfric drawing, not on one alone, but on all or most of them. Indeed, Father Smetana has discovered a good many additional sources, including some attributed to authors not listed by Förster (Fulgentius, Severianus [now identified as Peter Chrysologus], Origen, Chrysostom), simply by studying the collection.

In a second article, 'Aelfric and the Homiliary of Haymo of Halberstadt', *Traditio*, XVII (1961), 457–69, Father Smetana shows that Ælfric must have had at hand, besides the big homiliary of Paul the Deacon, a copy of Haymo's.[1] The interpolated version of this homiliary published by Migne, containing a very full Temporale and a smaller Sanctorale, but limited to one homily for each occasion, includes pieces by Bede, Alcuin, and others,[2] and, as I

contents of these two versions, being generally accessible, are referred to in my list below. Father Smetana mentions variant versions in certain manuscripts, but I have not consulted them. No version yet investigated by Father Smetana has precisely the content one would expect to find in Ælfric's copy.

[1] Most of the works attributed to Haymo, bishop of Halberstadt (840–53) in *PL* CXVI–CXVIII, including the homilies, the commentaries on St. Paul's *Epistles*, the *Epistle to the Hebrews*, the *Apocalypse*, and the *Song of Songs*, and also the *Epitome Historiæ Sacræ*, now appear to be the works of his contemporary, a simple monk named Haymo who wrote and taught at the abbey of St. Germain in Auxerre. The case for this Haymo, named as author of a similar list of works by a twelfth-century chronicler of Melk, was elaborately presented by E. Riggenbach, *Die ältesten lateinischen Kommentare zum Hebräerbrief* (Forschungen zur Geschichte des neutestamentlichen Kanons, hrsg. von Theodor Zahn, VIII. 1), Leipzig, 1907. Riggenbach, having found internal evidence in some of the commentaries that they were written in France between 840 and 860, accepts the suggestion already made by L. Traube in his edition of the poems of Hericus (Heiric or Héric) of Auxerre, who died in 876, that this is the Haymo to whom Hericus refers as his master in some poems prefixed to excerpts from Haymo's teachings (*Poetae Latini Aevi Carolini*, III [1892], 422, n. 4). Riggenbach's view has gradually gained approval. G. Mathou, in the article 'Haymon d'Auxerre', *Catholicisme*, V (1962), 538 sq., gives a good summary of the external evidence. Recently a very important advance has been made by Henri Barré, C.S.Sp., in *Les Homéliaires Carolingiens de l'École d'Auxerre*, Studi e Testi 225, 1962, to which Mr. N. R. Ker has kindly directed me. In this study Haymo's identity as a monk of Auxerre is confirmed and his authentic homiliary (along with that of Hericus) is established. See especially pp. 33–70 and the inventory of Haymo's genuine homilies, pp. 145–60.

[2] Barré, op. cit., p. 51, lists seventy-two interpolations in the Temporale of the Migne version, and points to a manuscript of the tenth century that already contains all those within its span (Easter to the twenty-fifth Sunday after Pentecost). That Ælfric's copy was interpolated is indicated by his use of at least three of the homilies from an unedited Carolingian commentary on *Matthew* (Barré,

have already remarked, the part actually by Haymo draws upon earlier writers, mainly Bede, Augustine, Jerome, and Gregory. Hence it often restates what is contained in one or more of the homilies of Paul's collection. Ælfric, as Förster ascertained, used Haymo as chief source for only two of the *Catholic Homilies*, but Father Smetana shows that he consulted Haymo for many other homilies and took enough from him to modify slightly what he derived from other authors.

These two homiliaries do not by any means account for all the sources that have been established, chiefly by Förster, for the *Catholic Homilies*.[1] Nevertheless they account for so many of the exegetical homilies that they must be regarded as Ælfric's chief quarries and as important guides to the organization of his own selective sets. The assignment of pericopes in Haymo's Temporale corresponds very regularly with Ælfric's, and there may have been a similar correspondence in his copy of Paul's homiliary, though the original collection differed at several points.

There is enough evidence of Ælfric's continued use of these two collections to warrant the assumption that they were with him not only at Cerne but at Eynsham also, but he seems to have found Paul's collection less consistently helpful after the completion of the first two series. In the list below I have noted the presence of an item in the original homiliary by the letters PD; in the Migne version by PDM. It will be seen that PD (supported most of the

p. 50 and n. 6); *PL* cxviii, nos. xl (chief source of our iii), lxiii and xciii (minor sources of *CH* I. xiv and xviii according to Smetana, pp. 459, 466). See further below, p. 160.

[1] One additional source, together with one previously noted by Förster, was discovered by C. R. Davis, *JEGP*, XLI (1942), 510–13; and several others are now being turned up by J. E. Cross. See his article, 'A Source for one of Ælfric's "Catholic Homilies"', *English Studies*, XXXIX. 6 (Dec. 1958), pp. 1–3 (a source independently noted by Father Smetana); and 'Ælfric and the Mediæval Homiliary—Objection and Contribution', Kungliga Humanistiska Vetenskapssamfundet i Lund, *Scripta Minora 1961–2*, no. 4 (Lund, 1963). Father Smetana, in the articles cited, has added many more. Sources of the *Lives of Saints* have been explored chiefly by J. H. Ott, *Über die Quellen der Heiligenleben in Ælfric's Lives of Saints I*, Halle, 1892, and Grant Loomis, 'Further Sources of Ælfric's Saints' Lives', *Harvard Studies and Notes in Philology and Literature*, XIII (1931), 1–8. See also G. H. Gerould, 'Ælfric's Lives of St. Martin of Tours', *JEGP*, XXIV (1925), 206–10. Among the miscellaneous homilies those most thoroughly studied for sources are the *Interrogationes* (in MacLean's edition) and the *Hexameron* (in Crawford's).

time by PDM) had almost all the Bede homilies listed[1] and all three of Gregory's, besides a few other pieces: three from Augustine (13, 19, and 20), three from Bede's commentary on *Luke* (Bede 11, 13, 14), a passage from Jerome (6), and a homily by Origen that Ælfric did not certainly use. Nearly all of these were probably available in Ælfric's version of the homiliary, and perhaps some of the pieces that are in PDM but were not in PD: a sermon by Cæsarius (item 2) and the homilies by Hericus of Auxerre.[2]

This list need not be regarded as unimpressive if we recognize that the homiliary may have been consulted by Ælfric for at least some passage in each of thirteen of the twenty-one full homilies here edited (I, IV, VII–X, XII–XVIII), but it does not compare with the record for the exegetical homilies of the First and Second Series. It leaves us to wonder where Ælfric went for most of what he took from Augustine and pseudo-Augustine, besides a great deal else. Unless his copy of Paul's homiliary was much richer in selections from Augustine than PD or PDM, we must suppose that he used some other collection of Augustine or went directly to such works as the tractates on *John* and the *Enarrationes* on the *Psalms*. In the *Letter to Wulfgeat*, Assmann 1. 103 sqq., Ælfric credits Augustine with having written *an pusend boca* and says that of these *sume becomon to us*. On the whole it seems probable that, sooner or later, he had succeeded in reading, if he did not own, a good many of Augustine's works; but it may be said that the gaps in his reading of Augustine are conspicuous too. It looks as if he had had to depend on incomplete collections or perhaps on short visits to distant libraries. His acquaintance with Gregory the Great has been demonstrated for a few works only. He made extensive use of the homilies on the gospels, nearly all of which were in Paul's homiliary. Beyond these Förster showed that he made some use of the *Dialogues*, and in two of the present homilies he seems to have consulted two books of the *Moralia*. For Bede, though he used, first and last, nearly everything in PD, he clearly had access to additional works: to the *Ecclesiastical History*, to the commentaries on *Luke* and *Mark* (beyond what had been excerpted for

---

[1] The two homilies not included (items 4 and 5) may not have been directly known to Ælfric. He may have known only Alcuin's excerpts from the first and Haymo's repetition of the relevant passage from the second.

[2] Thirty-nine of these are identified in PDM by Barré (op. cit., supra, p. 157, n. 1) in his inventory of Héric's homiliary, pp. 160 sqq. Five are listed below, p. 169.

PD) and the Pentateuch, to the *De Natura Rerum* and *De Temporum Ratione*.[1] There are, besides, a considerable number of scattered items in the list that cannot well have been in any version of Paul's homiliary. Father Smetana has questioned Ælfric's acquaintance at first hand with the *Ecclesiastical History* of Rufinus, but Förster's evidence was considerable and is strongly supported by VIII and XXI here, while XXI, XXII, and XXVI show that we must add to the list the *Historia Ecclesiastica Tripartita* ascribed to Cassiodorus.[2]

Although in his later homilies Ælfric seems to have gone beyond Paul's and Haymo's homiliaries more frequently than for the First and Second Series, even for exegesis, the evidence for his habit of consulting Haymo's is stronger than ever. I think he consulted it (though seldom accepting it as his primary authority) for every one of the exegetical homilies, I–X, XII–XVII, though there is no direct proof for homilies II, V, and VI. These are three of the four homilies for Fridays in Lent, which make a set of five if we add Assmann V for the fifth Friday. Now homilies for these Fridays are very rare. The only two Latin sets that I have encountered among collections that might have been known to Ælfric are in Haymo's (nos. 33, 40, 47, 54, 61) and in the Migne version of Paulus Diaconus (nos. 77, 86, 95, 102, 110). The Migne homilies, which have now been persuasively attributed to Hericus (Héric) of Auxerre,[3] may have been available to Ælfric, but I can find only a few inconclusive resemblances to suggest that he had consulted them. The corresponding group in Haymo's homiliary, on the other hand, could have been the starting-point for Ælfric's composition of the series, though the fact that all five pieces in Haymo are interpolations makes it impossible to prove that this was so. For the second Friday the interpolated homiliary has a mildly original elaboration of Jerome's commentary on *Matthew* and this was undoubtedly Ælfric's chief source for homily III.[4] For the other Fridays, which have gospel-texts drawn from various chapters of *John*, the homiliary provides the relevant sections of Alcuin's commentary on *John*. This commentary itself is derivative, being largely a compilation from Augustine, Bede, and

---

[1] For the *Catholic Homilies* Förster detected some signs that Ælfric had consulted Bede's commentary on the *Acts* (*Anglia*, XVI, §§ 54, 102), and J. E. Cross has added to the evidence, as explained below, p. 394.

[2] On Father Smetana's partly justified but seemingly exaggerated claim for Haymo as intermediary between Ælfric and the historians, see below, p. 394, n. 2.

[3] See above, p. 159, n. 2.   [4] See above, p. 157, n. 2.

Gregory, with a good deal of abridgement and a few more or less original passages. Alcuin's work is distinctive enough to be recognized as one of Ælfric's sources for homilies II and V, and it is probable from what has just been said that Ælfric found this source already adapted to homiletic use in his copy of Haymo. For the fourth and fifth Fridays, however, corresponding to our VI and Assmann's V, Alcuin's commentary is drawn exclusively from Augustine's Tractate XLIX. 1–25 and 26–28 respectively. Although the part used for the fourth Friday is abridged, neither part can be distinguished verbally in any significant way from Augustine's original. Consequently the correspondences between Alcuin and Ælfric's two homilies, our VI and Assmann's V, do not establish Alcuin rather than Augustine as a source, and for VI we know that Augustine was directly consulted because Ælfric uses passages from his tractate that Alcuin omits. Nevertheless I think it probable that the five Friday homilies in the interpolated version of Haymo's homiliary, excerpted from Alcuin and the unidentified commentator on *Matthew*, were the foundation on which, after further exploration, Ælfric constructed his own set.

What has just been said shows how questionable it is whether Ælfric ever encountered, as a separate work, Alcuin's *Commentaria in Ioannis Evangelium*, or the pseudo-Bede *Expositio* on the same gospel, which is merely a copy of Alcuin's for the first twelve chapters of *John*, and after that almost entirely a mere abridgement of Augustine's tractates.[1] Max Förster names the *Expositio* among Ælfric's sources and I have named the *Commentaria*, but there is no evidence at all that Ælfric had seen the *Expositio* as distinct from the *Commentaria*, and very little that he had seen the *Commentaria*. In my own list below, the first item is identical with a passage in Bede, the third with an entire homily of Bede's, and both, as Bede's, were in Paul's homiliary. The fourth and fifth are two of the interpolations in Haymo. The sixth, a source for VII, occurs as a homily in Smaragdus, whom Ælfric himself named as an authority in his Latin preface to the First Series and whose col-

[1] The authenticity of the *Commentaria* was established by Frobenius (Froben Forster) in the introduction to his edition of Alcuin's work. This introduction is reprinted by Migne in *PL* C. 736. Froben Forster was surely mistaken in thinking that the *Expositio*, from *John* xiii onward, was a second, more fully digested version by Alcuin. The impression of digestion and homogeneity is due to its being almost pure though slightly abridged Augustine, at least at several points where I have examined it.

lection he appears, though not nearly as often as Haymo's or Paul's, to have consulted. This leaves only the second item unaccounted for, the little passage cited for I. 65–69. This is indeed closer to what Ælfric says than anything else I can find, but the same words, or something sufficiently similar, may have escaped my attention in some other place, and certainly the passage is not distinctive enough to be depended on as evidence that Ælfric consulted Alcuin's commentary directly.

Max Förster cites the *Expositio* of pseudo-Bede twice (*Anglia*, XVI, §§ 58, 65) where it is not only identical with Alcuin's *Commentaria* but with two homilies by Bede (II. 1 and II. 18 in Hurst's edition). The first of these homilies is in Haymo, verbatim, as no. 50; the second was in the original homiliary of Paul the Deacon, II. 16, and is also in the Migne version, no 157. Förster cites the *Expositio* once more (*Anglia*, XVI, § 61) where it differs from Alcuin's *Commentaria* but corresponds, with some abridgement, to Augustine's Tractates LXXXIII–LXXXV, for which Ælfric's immediate source was probably Paul's homiliary, II. 102.[1]

I am equally dubious about Ælfric's acquaintance with or use of the pseudo-Bede commentary on *Matthew*, which Förster occasionally cites (*Anglia*, XVI, §§ 60, 86, 89–91, 112). This derivative and meagre work, so far as I have been able to tell, can always be matched or surpassed by other sources that Ælfric is much more likely to have consulted: Bede's homilies, his commentaries on parallel texts in *Luke* or *Mark*, Jerome's commentary on *Matthew*, sermons or tracts by Augustine. As for the pseudo-Bede commentary on the *Psalms*, I have cited it once but without conviction that it was Ælfric's source.

One way by which Ælfric may sometimes have obtained working copies of material in distant libraries is suggested by Miss Enid M. Raynes's discovery of the excerpts that served as the immediate source of homily XI. These excerpts, apparently made by Ælfric himself from the *Prognosticon* of Julian of Toledo, are described

---

[1] Because Ælfric's second source for his homily (*CH* II. XL) was Gregory's twenty-seventh, which directly preceded the Augustine in Paul's homiliary. So argues Father Smetana in *Traditio*, XV. 201; but with respect to Augustine his argument needs correction. PD II. 102, according to the first and last words as quoted by Wiegand (op. cit., p. 58), comprised Tractates LXXXIII. 2–LXXXVI, not, as Leclercq and Smetana say, LXXXIII only. This is important because Ælfric draws slightly (ll. 26–46) on Tract. LXXXIII. 3 and heavily (ll. 47–53) on Tract. LXXXV. 2 and 3.

in the introduction to XI. They constitute a single instance, but the fact that they survive in a unique copy made rather surprisingly by someone who had access to Ælfric's personal records suggests that there may have been similar records now utterly lost. It would have been natural for Ælfric, if he came upon interesting material in some library not his own, to copy it outright or excerpt what he most wanted. The excerpts from Julian are partly rearranged and interpolated with comments, so as to produce a connected discourse somewhat beyond a mere digest, but we need not insist on such modifications as a regular procedure in order to understand how Ælfric was able to draw rather exactly, though often for brief passages only, on so many different works that seem not to have been available in collections. Some of these he probably had at hand even at Cerne, but hardly all.

I have said enough, I trust, to show how tentative and incomplete is the list that follows, and how much interpretation it must undergo before anyone can hope to say exactly what authors and works Ælfric used directly and to what extent he gained access to them by means of selective compilations. What is presented below must be looked upon as altogether provisional. It is intended chiefly for the very practical end of supplying the reader with a guide to the citations at the foot of the page and with the essential bibliographical references. A comprehensive study of the sources of Ælfric's homilies, if anyone should care to undertake it, will require wider and deeper investigation.

NON-BIBLICAL LATIN WORKS QUOTED AS SOURCES[1]

No. of article
where quoted

Acta Alexandri Papæ. (a) In Acta Sanctorum, XXIII
ed. Henschenius, XIV (Maii Tom. I), 375–
80. (b) In Surius, Historiæ seu Vitæ Sanctorum, V (Maius),Turin, 1876, pp. 73–81. (A

[1] Line-numbers follow the number of the article when it seems desirable to indicate that a source has been used for limited passages only. As explained in the preceding discussion, I have included references to two versions of the homiliary of Paulus Diaconus. PD means the original homiliary as reconstructed by Wiegand and listed by Smetana. I is for Pars Hiemalis, II for Pars Æstiva, each being followed by the number of the homily. PDM means the late version of the same homiliary published in skeletal form by Migne, *PL* xcv, where the numbering is consecutive throughout the Temporale, then separate for the saints. Not included in this list are certain sources mentioned in the notes at points where Ælfric is summarizing what he has said in some earlier work.

slightly different version usually less close to
Ælfric than the first but cited for line 65.
A third version in Mombritius, *Sanctuarium*,
Paris, 1910, I. 44–49, is still less close and has
not been cited.)

Adso, *De Ortu et Tempore Antichristi*, ed. E.   XVIII (303–5, 369, 388,
Sackur, *Sibyllinische Texte und Forschungen*,   403)
Halle, 1898.

Alcuin, *Commentaria in S. Ioannis Evangelium*.
PL c. 733 sqq. The commentary on *Ioan.* i–
xii is reproduced exactly in the pseudo-Bede
Expositio (*PL* XCII), which thereafter diverges
and is largely a mere abridgement of Augustine's tractates on *John*. Our VII is definitely
from the complete Alcuin, not the pseudo-
Bede, but nearly everything in the list, as
indicated within brackets below, could have
reached Ælfric by way of a collection familiar
to him. See further the preceding discussion.

[1] Prefatory epistle. *PL* 741. [= Bede 3, in   I (20–26)
PD and PDM.]
[2] In cap. i. 1. *PL* 745.   I (65–69)
[3] In cap. iii. 1–15. *PL* 778–82. [= Bede 10,   XII
in PD and PDM.]
[4] In cap. iv. 5–42, esp. 7 and 13. *PL* 792–   V (118–29, 141*b*–7)
800. [Excerpted by Haymo as Hom.
XLVII.]
[5] In cap. v. 1–15. *PL* 803–7. [Excerpted by   II
Haymo as Hom. XXXIII.]
[6] In cap. xvi. 5–14. *PL* 950–4. [Excerpted   VII
by Smaragdus, *PL* CII. 296–9.]

Ambrosiaster. See pseudo-Augustine, *Quæstiones Veteris et Novi Testamenti*.

Augustine, [1] *De Bono Coniugali*. *PL* XL. 373–   XIX (106–8)
96. (Quoted at 378.)

——, [2] *De Diversis Quæstionibus ad Simpli-*   XXIX (101)
cianum, Lib. II, Quæst. iii, 'Samuel per
pythonissam evocari quomodo potuerit.' *PL*
XL. 142–4.

——, *Enarrationes in Psalmos*. *PL* XXXVI–XXXVII.
Also *CCSL* XXXVIII–XL, ed. Dekkers and
Fraipont, Turnholti, 1956.

[3] In Psal. lvi. *PL* xxxvi. 669; *CCSL* xxxix.   VII (103–12)
703.

[4] In Psal. lxiii. *PL* xxxvi. 767 sq.; *CCSL*   VII (94–126)
xxxix. 815 sq.

[5] In Psal. c. *PL* xxxvii. 1282–93; *CCSL*   XIII (76–81)
xxxix. 1405–17. (§§ 1 and 13 quoted, *PL*
1282 and 1293.)

Augustine, *In Ioannis Evangelium Tractatus
CXXIV*. *PL* xxxv. 1369 sqq. Also *CCSL*
xxxvi, ed. Willems, Turnholti, 1954.

[6] Tractatus I, II, III.   I
[7]   „   XII. 5.   XII (156–8)
[8]   „   xv. 6 sqq.   V
[9]   „   XVII.   II
[10]   „   XX. 3; XXXVI. 8, 9; XXXVII. 6, 7.   VIII (190–202)
[11]   „   XXI. 7.   XXV (*c.* 1–10)
[12]   „   XLIX.   VI
[13]   „   LI. 11–13. [LI. 9–13, not 13   XXV (*a.* 3–9, 15–16)
only, in PD II. 68; PDM, De Sanctis 42].
[14] Tractatus LVII. 1.   XXV (*c.* 1–4)
[15]   „   LXXVIII, LXXIX.   X (151–8, 190–8)
[16]   „   XCV. 4.   VII (177–80)

——, *Quæstiones in Evangelium sec. Lucam*. *PL*
xxxv. 1333 sq. No proof that Ælfric consulted
this work directly. The following passages
probably reached him by way of Bede's commentary on *Luke*, though he probably had
no. 19 in his copy of PD.

[17] In Luc. v. 3–11. *PL* 1333 sq.   XIV (111–84, 199–206)
[18] In Luc. xvi. 1–9. *PL* 1348 sq.   XVI (146–58, 207–9)
[19] In Luc. xvii. 34–35. *PL* 1357. [PD I. 7;   XVIII (89–125)
PDM 6.]

——, *De Sermone Domini in Monte*. *PL* xxxiv.
1229 sqq.

[20] In Matth. v. 20–24. *PL* 1241–3. [PD II.   XV (134–77, 203–13)
58; PDM 165.]
[21] In Matth. vi. 3, 4. *PL* 1273–4.   XXX (56–74)

——, *Sermones*. *PL* xxxviii, xxxix. The first
fifty also in *CCSL* xli, ed. Lambot, Turnholti, 1961.

[22] *Sermo* I. 2. Cited as source or analogue.   I (70–76)
[23] *Sermo* LXIV, in Matth. x. 16.   XVI (235–57)

No. of article
where quoted

[5] Hom. I. 25, lines 46–50 in Hurst, 179;   XIII (208–11)
    PL 107.

[6] Hom. II. 6. Hurst, 220–4; *PL* 234–7.   XVII
    [PD II. 69; PDM 172.]

[7] Hom. II. 11. Hurst, 253–9; *PL* 158–63.   VII
    Perhaps used only by way of the exten-
    sive excerpts in Alcuin 6. [PD II. 22;
    PDM 139.]

[8] Hom. II. 12. Hurst, 260–6; *PL* 163–8.   VIII
    [PD II. 24; PDM 140.]

[9] Hom. II. 16. Hurst, 290–300; *PL* 181–   IX
    9. [PD II. 29; PDM 145.]

[10] Hom. II. 18. Hurst, 311–17; *PL* 197–   XII
    202. Same as Alcuin 3. [PD II. 16;
    PDM 157.]

Bede, *In Lucæ Evangelium Expositio*, ed. D.
Hurst, *CCSL* cxx, Turnholti, 1960. Also *PL*
XCII. 301 sqq.

[11] In cap. v. 1–11. [PD II. 57, not PDM.]   XIV
[12] In cap. vi. 10.   II (84–90)
[13] In cap. vi. 37–42. [PD II. 37, not PDM.]   XIII
[14] In cap. xi. 14–28. [PD I. 90; PDM 89.]   IV
[15] In cap. xvi. 1–9.   XVI
[16] In cap. xvii. 20–37.   XVIII (first half)

——, *In Marci Evangelium Expositio*, ed. D.
Hurst, as above. Also *PL* XCII. 131 sqq.

[17] In cap. iv. 35, 40.   XVII (213, 215–19)
[18] In cap. v. 6–7, 11–13.   XVII (252–71, from *CH*)
[19] In cap. vii. 31.   XVII (78–81)
[20] In cap. xi. 23.   VIII (99 sqq.)
[21] In cap. xiii. 14, 18, 19, 20.   XVIII (281–306 [?], 328–
                                                44, 347–65, 369)

——, [22] *De Natura Rerum*, cap. xii. *PL* XC.   XXI (181–6)
208 sqq.

——, [23] *De Temporum Ratione*, cap. viii, in   XXI (181–6)
Bedae Opera de Temporibus, ed. C. W. Jones,
Cambridge, Mass., 1943, p. 196/25–30.

——, [24] *In Pentateuchum*, Gen. i. 2. *PL* XCI. XII (98–105)
193.

pseudo-Bede, [1] *In Ioannis Evangelium Expositio. PL* XCII. See above under Alcuin.

No. of article
where quoted

pseudo-Bede, [2] *In Matthæi Evangelium Expositio. PL* xcii. Corresponds only where
other sources are as close or closer.

pseudo-Bede, [3] *In Psalmorum Librum Exe-*   I (84–97)
gesis. PL xciii. 477 sqq. In Psal. xxxii. 6. *PL*
647 sq.

Boulogne Excerpts. MS. Boulogne-sur-Mer 63,   xi
ff. 1–10ʳ. Chief source of xi (94 to the end),
discovered by Enid M. Raynes. (See introduction to xi.) Mainly from Julian, archbishop of Toledo, *Prognosticon Futuri Sæculi,*
q.v.

Cæsarius of Arles, [1] *Homilia* xvi, *De Decimis.*   xxx (85–90, 99–103,
PL lxvii. 1078 sq. A short and altered ver-   note on 75–81)
sion of *Sermo* xxxiii in Morin's ed.

———, *Sermones*, ed. G. Morin, Editio Altera,
CCSL ciii, civ, Turnholti, 1953.

  [2] *Sermo* xliii, *Ammonitio ut iugalis castitas*   xix (102–4)
      conservetur, CCSL ciii. 190.
  [3] *Sermo* cxlviii, in Matth. vii. 1–5. *CCSL*   xiii (88–97, 186); xv
      civ. 605–8. [PDM 162; not PD.]   (170)
  [4] *Sermo* cliv. 3, in Matth. xxiv. 19. *CCSL*   xviii (320–5)
      civ. 630.

Cassiodorus, see *Historia Ecclesiastica Tripartita.*

pseudo-Cyprian, *De Duodecim Abusivis Sæculi,*
    ed. S. Hellmann, *Texte und Untersuchungen
    zur Geschichte der altchristlichen Literatur,*
    Reihe 3, Band 4, Heft 1, Leipzig, 1909, 1–62.
  [Cap. ix,] 'Nonus abusionis gradus est, rex   ix (46–54)
    iniquus.' Hellmann, 51–53. Also in *PL* iv.
    956 sq.

Gregory the Great, *Homiliæ in Evangelia. PL*
lxxvi.
  [1] Hom. xxiv, passage at *PL* 1185. [PD II.   xiv (127b–31, 147–71)
      11; PDM 129.]
  [2] Hom. xxvii. 6, 7. *PL* 1208 sq. [PD II.   viii (59–72)
      101; PDM, De Sanctis 72.]
  [3] Hom. xxx. *PL* 1219–27. [PD II. 33;   x (31–126)
      PDM 147.]
———, *Moralia in Iob. PL* lxxvi.
  [4] Lib. xxxi, cap. 47. *PL* 625.   I (10–16)
  [5] Lib. xxxii, cap. 24. *PL* 650.   xviii (347–65)

Haymo, *Homiliæ de Tempore. PL* cxviii. (See
also Alcuin 4, 5.)

[1] Hom. ix. *PL* 54–64.	i (with Bede)
[2] Hom. xx. *PL* 147–54, esp. 148, 150.	xvii (213, 215–19)
[3] Hom. xlii. *PL* 253–63.	iv (with Bede)
[4] Hom. lxxxvii. *PL* 516–20, esp. 516 sq.	vii (32–38)
[5] Hom. lxxxix. *PL* 522–7.	viii (with Bede)
[6] Hom. xcviii. *PL* 550–3.	ix (with Bede)
[7] Hom. c. *PL* 556–62.	x
[8] Hom. cviii. *PL* 578–84.	xii (with Bede)
[9] Hom. cxv. *PL* 615–22.	xiii (with Bede)
[10] Hom. cxvii. *PL* 624–9.	xiv (with Bede)
[11] Hom. cxviii, *PL* 629–34.	xv
[12] Hom. cxxi. *PL* 646–53.	xvi (with Bede)
[13] Hom. cxxiv. *PL* 664–9.	xvii (with Bede)

pseudo-Haymo, a Carolingian commentary on
Matthew interpolated as homilies in Haymo's
homiliary. *PL* cxviii. See above, p. 157, n. 2.

   Hom. xl. *PL* 244–7.   iii

Hericus of Auxerre, in homiliary of Paulus Diaconus. *PL* xcv. 1159 sqq. (= PDM). See
above, p. 159, n. 2.

   [1] *Feria VI Post Invocavit. Ioan.* v. 1–15.
   [PDM 77.] No evidence that Ælfric used
   this for ii.
   [2] *Feria VI Post Reminiscere. Matth.* xxi.   iii (176–87)?
   33–46. [PDM 86.]
   [3] *Feria VI Post Oculi. Ioan.* iv. 5–42.
   [PDM 95.] No evidence that Ælfric used
   this for v, but see below, p. 286.
   [4] *Feria VI Post Lætare. Ioan.* xi. 1–45.   vi (346–8)?
   [PDM 102.]
   [5] *Dominica V Post Pentecosten. Luc.* vi.   xiii (113–16, 175–7)?
   36–42. [PDM 163.]

Historia Ecclesiastica Tripartita, traditionally
ascribed to Cassiodorus, but largely the work
of his pupil Epiphanius. *CSEL* lxxi. Also
PL lxix. 879 sqq.

   [1] Lib. ix, cap. 27–28. *CSEL* 536–9.   xxi (516–64)
   [2] Lib. ix, cap. 2, 4 (*CSEL* 494–501) and   xxii
   xi, cap. 9, 15, 17–18 (*CSEL* 638–56).
   [3] Lib. ix, cap. 30. *CSEL* 541–6.   xxvi

No. of article
where quoted

Isidore, *Etymologiæ*. *PL* LXXXII.

  [1] Lib. VIII, cap. xi. *PL* 314.   XXI (197–201; notes on
                                                99–112); XXIX(102-4)

  [2] Lib. XII, cap. viii. 2. *PL* 470.   I (269–72)

——, *Chronicon*. *PL* LXXXIII.

  [3] Cap. 113, death of Olympius. *PL* 1053.   X (170–6)

Jerome, *In Matthæum*. *PL* XXVI.

  [1] 'Prologus.' *PL* 18 sq.   I (20–26)
  [2] In cap. vii. 3–5. *PL* 46 sq.   XIII (163–71)
  [3] In cap. viii. 27. *PL* 53.   XVII (213)?
  [4] In cap. xii. 22–30, 43–45. *PL* 79 sqq.   IV (with Bede)
  [5] In cap. xxiv. 15, 20. *PL* 177 sq.   XVIII (281–306, 328–44)

——, *Epistula* CXXI, *ad Algasiam*. *CSEL* LVI.
1–55. Also in *PL* XXII. 1006–38.

  [6] Cap. vi, in Luc. xvi. 9. *CSEL* 21–27, esp.   XVI (269–92)
      24. [PD II. 62; not PDM.]

  [7] Cap. xi, in II Thess. ii. 3 sqq. *CSEL* 50–   XXVIII (8–14)
      55, esp. 54.

Julian, archbishop of Toledo (680–90), *Prog-*   XI
nosticon Futuri Sæculi. *PL* XCVI. 461–524.
Chief source of the *Boulogne Excerpts*, q.v.,
and quoted independently at XI. 94–102,
184–94, 229–31, and 360.

Martin, bishop of Braga (d. 579), *De Correc-*   XXI (28–196)
tione Rusticorum, in C. P. Caspari, *Martin*
von Bracara's Schrift De Correctione Rusti-
corum, Christiania, 1883. Also in *Martini*
Episcopi Bracarensis Opera Omnia, ed. C. W.
Barlow, Yale Univ. Press, 1950.

Origen, Latin translation of a homily on Matth.   XVII (213, 215–19)?
viii. 23–27, attributed to Origen and included
in *Origenes Werke*, ed. Benz and Klostermann,
Leipzig, 1941, XII. 256–62. [Dom. IV Post
Epiphaniam, PD I. 64; PDM 55.] Possibly a
source of the passage indicated, beside Bede
and Haymo.

Quodvultdeus, bishop of Carthage *c*. 437–9. See
pseudo-Augustine, *Adversus Quinque Hæreses*.

Rabanus Maurus, [1] *Commentaria in Librum*   XIV (172–5)
Iudicum, in cap. iii. 15. *PL* CVIII. 1129.

——, [2] Hom. XII, passage on masters and   XIII (56–61)
servants. *PL* CX. 26.

*No. of article
where quoted*

Rufinus, *Historia Ecclesiastica*, ed. T. Momm-
sen in *Eusebius Werke*, ed. E. Klostermann,
II. ii, Leipzig, 1908.
  [1] On Gregory Thaumaturgist, added to   VIII (106–31); XXI (577–
      Eccl. Hist. vii. 28; Mommsen, pp. 953–5.   644)
  [2] On Serapis. Lib. XI, cap. 23–24, pp.   XXI (521–71)
      1026–30.

——, [3] *Historia Monachorum. PL* XXI. Cap.   XXIX (13–34)
xxviii, 'De Macario Ægypto,' *PL* 451.

Sedulius Scottus, *De Rectoribus Christianis*, ed.
S. Hellmann, *Quellen und Untersuchungen zur
lateinischen Philologie des Mittelalters*, I. 1,
München, 1906, 21–91. Also in *PL* CIII. 291
sqq.
  Cap. xix, Hellmann, p. 86; *PL* 328–30.   IX (48–50)

Smaragdus, *Commentarius sive Collectio in
Evangelia et Epistolas. PL* CII. 13–552. This
collection includes (col. 135 sqq.) Ælfric's
principal source for IV, listed above as Bede
14, and (col. 141 sqq.) an abridgement of his
principal source for V, Augustine 8; but Bede
14 is also in PD and PDM, and Ælfric apparently used the complete text of Augustine 8.
There may be other excerpts in Smaragdus
that could have served Ælfric, but I have
noted only the following as probably used.
The second is a possible source for a passage
originally included in the *Catholic Homilies*,
for several of which Ælfric seems to have consulted Smaragdus.
  [1] *Dom. IV Post Pascha. Ioan.* xvi. 5–14. *PL*   VII
      296–9. [= Alcuin 6.]
  [2] Definition of *legio*, *PL* 182 (Förster,   XVII (249)
      Anglia, XVI. 42).

Surius, see *Acta Alexandri Papæ.*

Vitæ Patrum. PL LXXIII.
  [1] Lib. V, cap. xv. 88, of two excommuni-   XIX (62–65)
      cated monks. *PL* 968 sq.
  [2] Lib. VI, cap. ii. 12, discomfiture of Julian   VIII (139–52)
      the Apostate. *PL* 1003.
  [3] Lib. VI, cap. iii. 13–14, how good and bad   XXVII
      men die. *PL* 1011 sq.

NON-BIBLICAL LATIN QUOTATIONS

EXCEPT for some introductory words in XVIII. 227, XXI. 1, and XXVIII. 1, all the Latin passages in these texts are quotations. Only the three following are non-Biblical:

1. A passage attributed to Hermes [Trismegistus], alleged author of the book, *Verbum Perfectum*: 1. 122–8; OE translation 129–37 (both imperfectly preserved).

2. *Nemo inobediens parentibus saluus erit*, cited with OE translation in XIX. 58–60, as if from the Bible. I am unable to identify it; but cf. *Exod.* xx. 12; *Deut.* xxvii. 16; *Ephes.* vi. 1–2.

3. An unidentified malediction concerning tithes, XXX. 82–83.

BIBLICAL QUOTATIONS IN LATIN AND OLD ENGLISH

THIS index is restricted for the most part to direct quotations from the Latin Bible (labelled L) and reasonably close translations of it into Old English (labelled OE), but occasionally it has seemed desirable to mention loose paraphrases, summaries, adaptations, or verbally reminiscent allusions. These are designated accordingly. Merely general references to Biblical persons, stories, and themes are excluded, as are slight verbal reminiscences, such as often occur when Ælfric absorbs the substance of scriptural quotations from commentaries without calling attention to them as authorities or giving them distinctive expression. Such reminiscences are best studied by way of the sources quoted beneath the text. No notice is taken of the Latin incipits in the superscriptions of the exegetical homilies, but the substantial passages from the gospels that constitute the pericopes of these homilies are preceded by the letter P. Other passages that Ælfric treats at length as central to his discourse are preceded by asterisks. On the occasional departures of Latin quotations from the readings of the Vulgate, see above, p. 152, and the notes on individual passages.

Genesis	Ælfric	Exodus	Ælfric
i. 1	I. 71, 72 (L, OE)	xii–xx	XX. 2–40 (OE summary)
i. 2	XII. 100–1 (OE)		
i. 28	XIX. 33–34 (OE)	xvii. 8–16	XXII. 87–90 (OE summary)
xviii, xix	XVIII. 65–74 (OE summary)	xxiv. 18	XX. 41–42 (OE summary)
Exodus		*xxxii. 1–8, 15, 19, 26–28 plus part of 20	XX. 42–67 (OE)
vii. 1	I. 365–9 (L, OE)		
viii. 19	I. 263 (L); IV. 144 (L, OE)		

Numeri	*Ælfric*
*xi. 1–2, 4–6, 10, 16, 19–20, 31–34	xx. 68–77, 83–103 (OE)
*xiii. 2—xiv. 11, 29–32, 36–45	xx. 140–213 (OE)
*xvi. 1–7, 12–21, 31–35, 41–49	xx. 217–28, 231–73 (OE)
xx. 29	xx. 367 (OE allusion)
*xxi. 4–9	xx. 304–32 (OE); XII. 227–32 (OE summary)
xxvi. 63–65	xx. 359–60 (OE allusion)
xxvii. 22–23	xx. 368–9 (OE allusion)

Deuteronomium	
viii. 2	xx. 353–6 (OE allusion)
xi. 13–14, 23	xx. 376–81 (OE allusion)
xxxiv. 5, 7	xx. 365–6 (OE allusion)

Iudicum	
iii. 15	XIV. 174–5 (OE allusion)

I Regum (*I Samuelis*)	
iv. 10–11	XXI. 214–16 (OE summary)
*v. 1–9, 12; vi. 2–5, 7–12; vii. 4, 13–14	XXI. 221–85
xv. esp. 1–9, 32–33	XXII. 91–94 (OE summary)
xv. 22, 23	xxx. 20–28 (L for v. 22a, OE)
*xxviii. 4–25, xxxi. 1–4	XXIX. 36–96 (OE summary with comment and some direct quotation)

II Regum (*II Samuelis*)	
x. 7–14	XXII. 17–20 (L for v. 7, OE summary)

II Regum (*II Samuelis*)	*Ælfric*
xi. 1	XXII. 21–23 (L)
xi. 1 and xii. 26	XXII. 24–27 (OE summary)
xx. 6	XXII. 28–29 (L)
xx. 1–22	XXII. 30–36 (OE summary)
xxi. 15–17	XXII. 37–49 (L for v. 15, OE free translation)

Iob	
xxvii. 3–4	XVII. 164–7 (OE adaptation)
xl. 16	IV. 221–3 (L, OE)

Psalmi	
v. 7	XXII. 101, 103 (L, OE)
xxxii. 6	I. 81–83 (L, OE)
xlviii. 13	XVI. 58–61 (L, OE)
lviii. 18	xv. 223–6 (L, OE)
lxiii. 8	VII. 97–102 (L, OE)
lxiii. 9	VII. 113–15 (L, OE)
lxxxi. 1	I. 376–9 (L, OE)
lxxxi. 6	I. 357–9 (L, OE); XXI. 670, 671 (L, OE)
c. 1	XIII. 73–75 (L, OE)
ciii. 24	I. 99–105 (L, OE)
cxxvi. 1	XIV. 120–2 (L, OE)
cxl. 3	xv. 181–3 (L, OE)

Proverbia	
xx. 4	XVI. 117–18 (OE)

Sapientia	
i. 13	XI. 107–8 (OE)
ii. 24	XI. 109, 110 (L, OE)
xi. 21	I. 178–81 (L, OE)

Ecclesiasticus	
i. 1	I. 334 (OE)
xx. 32	IX. 42–45 (L, OE)
xxxii. 24	IX. 37–39 (L, OE)

Isaias	
*v. 4–7	III. 65–79 (OE)
xi. 1–3	v. 210–13 (OE allusion)
xi. 2	IX. 139–43 (OE)

Matthæus	_Ælfric_	_Lucas_	_Ælfric_
xxiv. 13	XVIII. 391-2 (OE, same as _Marc._ xiii. 13)	*iv. 31-37	XVII. 281-305 (OE)
		P-v. 1-11	XIV. 1-40 (OE)
xxiv. 15	XVIII. 228 (L)	vi. 6-10	II. 84-90 (OE summary)
*xxiv. 15-25, 29-31	XVIII. 233-69 (OE, suppl. by _Marc._ xiii. 14-27)	vi. 35	XIII. 40-45 (OE, modifies _Matth._ v. 44-45)
xxiv. 27	XVIII. 8-9 (OE, supplements _Luc._ xvii. 24)	P-vi. 36-42	XIII. 9-33 (OE, part of v. 36 in L, line 8)
xxiv. 29	XI. 285, 288 (OE adaptation)	vii. 21-22	XI_a_. 104-7, 113-14 (OE paraphrase)
xxiv. 31	XI. 343-4 (OE)	vii. 37-38, 47	VI. 302-9, 311-12 (OE)
xxv. 1-12	XVI. 110-15 (OE summary)	x. 16	XX. 283-6 (L, OE)
xxv. 21, 23	XVI. 210-14 (L, OE)	x. 17-19	VII. 183-6 (OE adaptation)
xxv. 31	XI. 347-8 (OE paraphrase)	x. 20	XXV (_c_). 13-15 (L, OE)
xxv. 33	XI. 345-6 (OE paraphrase)	P-xi. 14-28	IV. 3-55 (OE; part of v. 19, L and OE, at 124 sq.; vv. 20, 23 in L at 173, 197)
*xxv. 34-40	XI. 405-29 (OE, part of v. 34 in L at 408)		
xxv. 35	XXV (_c_). 7-8 (L, OE)	xii. 37	XXV (_a_). 10-13 (L, OE)
*xxv. 41-46	XI. 435-54		
xxvii. 40	VII. 118 (OE)	xiv. 2-6	II. 266-75 (OE)
xxviii. 19	IX. 98-103 (L, OE)	xiv. 13-14	XVI. 168-71 (OE)
xxviii. 20	VIII. 225-7 (OE adaptation)	P-xvi. 1-9	XVI. 1, 4-38 (OE)
		xvi. 10	XVI. 280-3 (OE)
Marcus		xvi. 15	XV. 72-75 (L, OE)
iv. 38	XVII. 208 (OE, supplements _Matth._ viii. 24)	*xvii. 20, 21, 24, 26-37	XVIII. 2-39 (OE)
		xvii. 21	IV. 176, 177 (L, OE)
iv. 39	XVII. 211 (OE, supplements _Matth._ viii. 26)	xvii. 26-30	XI. 280-3 (OE paraphrase)
		xix. 8-9	XVI. 175-80 (OE)
*v. 1-20	XVII. 220-48 (OE)	xx. 38	VI. 363a (OE, supplements _Matth._ xxii. 32)
P-vii. 31-37	XVII. 21-45 (OE)		
xi. 23	VIII. 88-96 (L, OE)		
xi. 25-26	XV. 198-202 (OE)	xxi. 18	VII. 160-1 (OE)
xii. 42-44	XVI. 187-93 (OE summary)	xxiii. 40-43	XIX. 246-9 (OE summary)
xiii. 13	XVIII. 391-2 (OE, same as _Matth._ xxiv. 13)	xxiv. 16-46	VII. 127-44 (OE, free summary)
*xiii. 14-27	see _Matth._ xxiv. 15-25, 29-31	_Ioannes_	
xiii. 32	XI. 273-5 (OE paraphrase)	P-i. 1-14	I. 28-54 (OE, part of v. 1 in L at 27)
		i. 17	I. 464-6 (OE paraphrase)
Lucas		ii. 1-11	XI_a_. 112 (OE allusion)
i. 38	XI_a_. 67-68 (OE)		

Hebr.	Ælfric	II Petr.	Ælfric
ix. 4	XXI. 217–20 (OE adaptation)	ii. 22	XVI. 67–68 (OE reminiscence)
Iac.		I Ioan.	
ii. 13	XIII. 101–2 (OE)	ii. 1	VIII. 212 (OE paraphrase)
v. 17–18	VIII. 79–84 (OE, free)	iii. 2	XI. 537 (OE)
II Petr.		Apoc.	
		ii. 24	XXIX. 111, 112 (L, OE: adaptation)
ii. 20, 22	XIII. 230–4 (OE adaptation)		
ii. 21	IV. 255–7 (OE adaptation via Bede)	iii. 5	XXV (c). 15–16 (L, OE)
		xx. 13–14	XI. 460–2 (OE)
		xx. 15	XI. 467–9 (OE)
ii. 21–22	XVII. 262–6 (OE elaboration)	xxi. 1	XI. 508–10 (OE paraphrase)

9. THE LANGUAGE OF THE MANUSCRIPTS

In general the language of these homilies needs no comment, being very close to the standard by which Late West Saxon has been judged. Among the various manuscripts there is indeed some deviation, but what is remarkable is the degree to which, in the course of the eleventh century, the conventions of spelling remained constant. Even manuscripts of the twelfth century, thanks in part to the conservatism of the scribes, show fewer departures from the earlier standard than might be expected. Since I have been able to choose as the basis for most of the texts manuscripts written within the first five or six decades of the eleventh century with strong adherence to the West Saxon standard (F, H, M, Q, R, U, V), the majority of the spellings are just what readers of the *Catholic Homilies* are accustomed to. Even the slightly later manuscript, P, on which I have based the text of XIX, XX, XXII, XXIV, and XXVIII, is extremely conservative. It has pure blunders now and then but nothing that looks dialectal and little if any levelling beyond what may occur in the manuscripts of Ælfric's time. The one text with frequent departures from the prevailing forms is that of XXIII, preserved uniquely in a quire added to T (Hatton 114) and written in a hand of the Worcester type, probably in the last decades of the eleventh century. Both levelled endings (chiefly -*en* for the infinitive -*an*) and the substitution of *a* for *ea* before *l* or *r* plus consonant (normally an Anglian feature) are conspicuous, whereas the main hand of the manuscript, likewise of the Worcester type but some decades earlier, spells according to the Late West Saxon standard.[1]

The usual spellings, together with the exceptions that occur in the basic manuscripts, are recorded in the glossary. Characteristic are, for example, *y* and *i* for EWS *ie*, interchanges of *i* and *y* (including the complete standardization of *drihten* for the etymologically correct *dryhten*), *sylf* and *syllan* for *self* and *sellan*, *hwylc* or *hwilc* rather than *hwelc*, *ur* for *eor* in *wurðan*, *wurpan*. The suffix *-nes(s)*, *-nis(s)*, *-nys(s)* appears in all three forms, but in most of the manuscripts *-nys(s)* prevails. MS. R tends to prefer *þar*, *hwar* to *þær*, *hwær*, and to substitute *a* for *o* in the verbal endings *-on* and *-ode*. These features appear now and then elsewhere, as in the interpolated parts of H. A purely orthographic feature of R is its fondness for doubling the *o* in *good* to distinguish it from *God*.

Deviations in certain manuscripts of the twelfth century are of course much more numerous, as the apparatus shows in spite of the selectiveness with which variants from the latest ones are treated. The un-Ælfrician spellings of two of them, B (Bodley 343) and G (Cotton Vespasian D. xiv), are fully displayed in the editions of Belfour and Warner respectively, which include these manuscripts' versions of the texts here printed; and the spellings in several parts of the inconsistent L (ULC Ii. 1. 33) are recorded in Crawford's *Old English Heptateuch* and Skeat's *Lives of Saints*. For these and other manuscripts I have been able to refer in my descriptions to earlier studies.

For the establishment of Ælfric's text the slight inconsistencies of the best manuscripts are of small importance; but there is a larger problem on which I have touched with respect to several of the manuscripts described in section 2, each time near the end of the description. This is the tantalizing relation between the place where a manuscript is known or supposed to have been written and the dialectal colouring of its texts. The complicated problems that emerge here and there from the apparent lack of agreement between the two cannot well be solved without investigating all the texts of a number of manuscripts, not just a selection of texts by one author. The present study affords only a few preliminary generalizations.

---

[1] See the description of T (end) and the introduction to XXIII, where there is a more detailed account of this scribe's peculiarities.

In the first place, then, we must reckon with the political and cultural dominance of Wessex between King Alfred's time and the Conquest. In Ælfric's day and after, the spelling conventions of the West Saxon scribes were widespread. These conventions were offset in some degree by the habit of faithful copying, so that we find not only the poetical manuscripts of this period but certain prose texts also retaining traces of earlier spellings, often non-West-Saxon. But with Ælfric, schooled at Winchester, whose homilies represented the Late West Saxon dialect at its literary best and purest, faithfulness to the letter and regard for the conventions worked together to promote uniformity. Thus, on the one hand, we must expect scribes in centres outside of Wessex to preserve the West Saxon forms almost if not quite intact; and on the other hand, we must look upon occasional deviations, proportionately slight though they may be, as doubly significant.

In the second place, we must look sharply at statements concerning the provenance of the manuscripts. Little enough is known of this matter, but, thanks to a number of palaeographers from Wanley onwards, among whom the late M. R. James and Mr. Neil Ker deserve particular mention, it is possible to connect several of the Ælfric manuscripts with particular localities. Whatever has been thus far discovered in this matter is set forth in Ker's *Catalogue*. At the beginning, however, we must draw a sharp distinction between the place where a manuscript was *stored* and the scriptorium where it was *written*. When we learn that Thorpe's manuscript, K, was found in Durham we must not assume that it was written there. Neither ought we to assume that Skeat's manuscript, W, was written at Bury St. Edmunds, or that the late twelfth-century B, prevailingly southern in its forms, was written somewhere in the west midlands. In all probability these manuscripts were written in southern scriptoria, where their exemplars were at hand, and then sent forth to their respective libraries.[1] In such manuscripts it is idle to look for traces of the local dialect unless in additions made after they had reached their destinations. Even within Wessex we must be wary of the distinction. There is a chance that H and M were found at Tavistock, but if so it does not follow that they were written there. Again, though Ker associates the script of J and a part of V with Exeter, he makes no such claim for the earliest part of V, on which there is more to be said below.

[1] Not necessarily at once or directly. On W. see above, p. 85, n. 1.

Several of the Ælfric manuscripts are known to have been at Worcester in the first half of the thirteenth century if not before, since at about that time they received a large number of glosses and marks of alteration, on which I have commented separately in the section that follows. But the Worcester manuscripts, as thus identified, seem to have had diverse origins. Among the six here represented (E, P, R, S, the three volumes of T, and X^d), only T and a portion of X^d can with any assurance be said to have been written at Worcester. They show, in the Ælfric texts copied by their main scribes, a standard West Saxon orthography, though one of T's additions, our xxiii, has been remarked upon already as dialectal. It is possible that R, slightly earlier than T and almost certainly present at Worcester when T was being compiled, was also written there, but it does not show the same characteristics as T and the Worcester section of X^d. Its language is standard West Saxon, though a few of its spellings are not those preferred by some of the best Ælfric manuscripts. E was probably written elsewhere. Its numerous hands are not of the Worcester type, only some late additions have, according to Ker, a Western colouring, and its earliest textual stratum is closely allied with D, a manuscript probably written in the south-east and certainly stored at Rochester during the eleventh century.[1] Neither P, already mentioned for its conservatism, nor the twelfth-century S with differences in its forms depending on differing textual inheritance, can safely be associated with the Worcester scriptorium.

Another group of manuscripts is associated with the south-east. Besides D, already mentioned but of slight importance for the present edition, and possibly E, this group includes C, F, G, U, and perhaps the early stratum of V. Ker shows reason to connect both F, of the early eleventh century, and U, of the middle of the century, with scriptoria in Canterbury, to which, or to Rochester, the twelfth-century G is also to be assigned. He associates the other twelfth-century manuscript of the group, C, with Rochester. In my description of V I have given my reasons, based on spelling-conventions and textual relations rather than script, for the conjecture that the earliest scribe did his work in the south-east.[2]

---

[1] The close textual relationship of D and E was first pointed out by Dr. Sisam. See his *Studies*, pp. 154 sq. He finds 'certain signs of Kentish dialect' in E, but is not sure whether it was written in the south-east or merely had a south-eastern book (not D) in its pedigree.   [2] Above, pp. 82–83.

Now the eleventh-century manuscripts in this group have very few if any specifically Kentish traits in the Ælfrician portions of their main texts. F (as pointed out in section 2)[1] seems to have at least one such trait in a homily not by Ælfric, and there are traces of south-eastern dialect in later additions. D has additions made in the course of the eleventh century with markedly Kentish features.[2] But F, U, and V are not quite absolute in their adherence to West Saxon. U has several examples, not necessarily original with its scribe, of *æ* as the mutation of *á* before nasals in such words as *sendan, wendan*. This trait has been associated with the south-east on evidence from Middle English, though it has been observed in late Old English manuscripts connected with other parts of the south.[3] In F I have noted one instance of Anglian *in*, and in the early stratum of V I have called attention to this and other Anglianisms, exceedingly rare in the Ælfric texts but plentiful in others, for which the same scribe was responsible. What we seem to have here is rather the confusion of two literary standards than the intrusion of anything local, but a south-eastern centre might be a likelier setting for such confusion than the heart of Wessex. Certainly the early stratum of V is very different from the later, for which there is no reason to doubt Ker's assignment to Exeter.[4]

As I have already intimated, however, one has to consider not only the conventions and the local dialects that may be represented in a given scriptorium, but also the strong tendency of scribes to copy what they see. In some manuscripts this tendency shows itself in the markedly different colouring of successive sections, even when there is no change of scribe. The early stratum of V and the twelfth-century S, already mentioned, are among the examples. The most complicated of all, perhaps, is another twelfth-century

---

[1] Above, pp. 23–24.   [2] Sisam, *Studies*, p. 153.

[3] The south-east, especially Essex and Middlesex north of the Thames, is favoured by Luick, *Historische Grammatik*, §§ 186 and 363.2; and Campbell, § 193 (*d*), includes Kent; but these limitations are challenged in *The Salisbury Psalter*, ed. Celia Sisam and Kenneth Sisam, EETS 1959, pp. 13 sq. See further D. Whitelock, *Sermo Lupi ad Anglos*, 3rd ed., Methuen, 1963, pp. 39–43. MSS. N and O share a few similar spellings, perhaps from an exemplar. Above, p. 52.

[4] It is to the Exeter portion of V that Miss Pamela Gradon refers in her 'Studies in Late West-Saxon Labialization and Delabialization', *English and Medieval Studies presented to J. R. R. Tolkien*, London, 1962, pp. 63 sqq. (esp. p. 66).

manuscript, L, on which enough has been said in the description
in section 2.[1]

I turn now to certain features of the declensions and conjuga-
tions as they appear in these texts. A few have already been mentioned in section 4 among characteristics of Ælfric's usage: the
specialized sense he reserves for the form *lifiende*, the form *syndon*
as a present subjunctive, and the combined verb *faran*, *fērde*,
faren.[2] The features listed below may sometimes reflect his idio-
syncrasy but most of them are probably to be regarded as typical
of Late West Saxon usage in and after Ælfric's time. They have
been brought to my attention chiefly by my work on the glossary.
As we might expect, some of them show a partial loss of older
distinctions that results in confusion of forms, some a complete
loss that results in a new standard, one or two the emergence, from
earlier confusion, of new distinctions. These features can be observed in texts that have long been available, and most of them are
mentioned as alternatives in the grammars of Sievers-Brunner and
Campbell, but the more constant of them do not receive the attention they deserve as the firmly established, hardly varying forms of
a new standard, in so far as this can be judged by the rather considerable range of the Ælfric manuscripts of the eleventh century.

1. Among the rare declensions of nouns we find varying degrees
of assimilation to the common declensions. The feminine *niht*,
originally athematic with genitive and dative singular *niht*, retains
the old form in the phrase *on niht* but has ds. *nihte* in other constructions.[3] The analogy of *on dæg*, which, as indicated below,
requires a different explanation, may have had something to do
with the survival of *on niht*. Another survival is ds. *-a* in *wintra*
(XVIII. 246, 326 in both manuscripts, R and P) and *sumera* (XVI. 118
in both manuscripts, U and H).[4] The declension of *sunu* and *wudu*
still shows the regular ending *-a* in the genitive, dative, and accusative singular. Occasionally *-a* replaces *-u* in the nominative
singular of *sunu*. The nominative and accusative plural of this word
is regularly *suna*; only in one or two late manuscripts do we find,
rarely, *sunas*.[5]

[1] Above, pp. 38–39.
[2] Above, pp. 100–2.
[3] Cf. S–B 284, Anm. 4; Cpb 628, 3.
[4] Cf. S–B 273, Anm. 2; Cpb 614.
[5] e.g. in MS. C at IV. 121. Cf. S–B 270, 271 Anm. 1; Cpb 611, 613.

In the following group of words, on the other hand, there are signs of a change that may have become firmly established, though examples are infrequent. This is the group of feminine abstracts ending prehistorically in *-iþu (Gmc. *-iþō). Those that occur in the present texts are entered in the glossary as cȳþþ, mǣrþ, myrhþ, strengþ, geþincþ, yrhþ, and yrmþ, although only mǣrþ actually occurs here in the nominative singular, and in earlier texts we generally find the ending -þu or -þo. But nominative singulars with simple -þ are recorded by BT and BTS from other works of Ælfric for myrhþ, gesǣlþ, strengþ, and yrmþ, and from a contemporary work for cȳþþ. This leaves only geþincþ and yrhþ without evidence. Since I can find no conflicting examples, these two words and all the rest are entered without -u or -o.[1]

Nouns in -end show an intrusive r in the nominative and accusative plural, -endras: e.g. biddendras, v. 51, etc.; bepæcendras, XXI. 289.[2]

2. In the dominant a-declension of masculines and neuters, there are survivals of the so-called endingless locative in a few set phrases, æt ham, ælce dæg, sume dæg, on dæg, and in phrases with wic 'village': to Bethania(n)-wic.[3] Whether on dæg was felt to be dative or locative seems doubtful in view of the fact that on takes the accusative in the phrase on þone seofoðan [dæg] at II. 216, 221, though it takes the dative in on þam Sunnan-dæge, II. 251.

3. In neuters of the a-declension we find a modified standard for the nominative and accusative plural. Monosyllables remain without ending as before, but the intermediate wundor and tac(e)n end regularly in -a, or occasionally -u, thus agreeing with the anciently trisyllabic deoflu or deofla[4] and the neuter ja-stem wite, nap. wita. The ending -a, which prevails, is thus the same as that of feminines of the o-declension.

4. The old instrumental singular has lost most of its distinctive forms. The ending -e of strong adjectives (masculine and neuter) has been superseded entirely by the dative -um except in the set phrases cited above: ælce dæg, sume dæg. Similarly the demon-

---

[1] Cf. S–B 255, 3; Cpb 589, 6. The word wurþmynt, originally of this group, is regularly without -u. The word fyrhtu, on the contrary, of the in-declension, appears as fyrhtu in Ælfric's Grammar, ed. Zupitza, 217/1.

[2] Cf. S–B 286, Anm. 3; Cpb 633.

[3] See the glossary for examples. Cf. S–B 237, Anm. 2 ('Endungslose Dat. Sg.'); Cpb 571.

[4] Cf. S–B 243, 3; Cpb 574, 3 and 4.

stratives, when used with masculine and neuter nouns, have dative singular *þam* and *þisum* for older *þȳ* and *þȳs*. The instrumental *þys* does not appear at all, but *þy* is preserved as a pronoun in *forþy* (*-þi, -þig*) 'therefore', in *to þy þæt* 'in order that', in *þy læs þe* 'lest' (often weakened to *þe læs þe* or *þelæste*), and with comparatives, *þe anrædran* 'the more constant', etc. The instrumental *þon* survives only in *for þon þe, for þan þe*, where it is freely interchanged with the dative *þam*. *Hwi* (*hwȳ*), the instrumental of *hwæt*, survives as the independent interrogative adverb and in the alternative phrase, *to hwi* 'for what reason, why'.

5. In the declension of the strong adjective, the nominative singular and the nominative-accusative plural have become uniform for all genders. The nominative singular is without ending in the feminine as well as the masculine and neuter, even with short-stemmed monosyllables and polysyllables. For example, *sum earm wudewe* (not *sumu*).[1] The nominative and accusative plural end uniformly in *-e* for all genders. An exception is *manega*, nap., linked in these manuscripts with the mutated singular *menig*, *mænig*, which occurs much less frequently than the plural forms (*manega, -ra, -um*). Like *manega* is nap. *feawa*, and both bear a superficial resemblance to the indeclinable *fela* when it modifies nouns in the nominative or accusative plural.

6. The past participle with *habban* is normally uninflected, the only exception in these homilies being at XXI. 466 *abedene*, where it follows the object and seems to be felt as an adjective. With *beon-wesan* or *wurðan* it agrees with the subject as usual, so that it is always nominative, either singular (uninflected) or plural, ending in *-e*. There is no distinction of genders in these participial forms, which obey the rule stated above for the strong adjectives. As an adjective modifying a noun, the participle is declined strong or weak like other adjectives.

7. In the dative singular of the adjective, masculine or neuter, strong *-um* rather frequently replaces weak *-an* after a demonstrative or possessive. This occurs in the earliest Ælfric manuscripts and may be attributable to the author. Conversely, *-an* sometimes replaces *-um* in the dative plural of weak nouns. An indiscriminate replacement of *-um* by *-an*, *-on* cannot be said to occur, unless in rare instances, much before the twelfth century.

8. A curious consistency prevails in the spelling of the various

[1] See XVI. 187 and the note on 163.

forms of *halig*, and since the pattern is different from that indicated in the grammars (on the basis of earlier usage) I have drawn attention to it in the glossary. The word regularly loses the medial *i* in inflected forms when the ending begins with *a* or *u*: *halga*, *halgan*, *halgum*, but retains it when the ending begins with a consonant or *e*: *haligre*, *haligne*, *haligra*, and *halige*, *haliges*. It is in these last two forms that we notice a departure from the prescription of the grammars. Perhaps the *i* in these two forms is a mere indication of the palatal pronunciation of *g* (which is occasionally omitted altogether in the later manuscripts), but it may represent a perceptible syllable.

10. GLOSSES IN THE WORCESTER AND OTHER MANUSCRIPTS

IN the preceding section I mentioned that six of the manuscripts of this edition[1] had received marks of alteration and glosses at Worcester during the first half of the thirteenth century or thereabouts. The chief glossator, whose 'tremulous' hand appears in several other Worcester books besides these, has long been recognized and valued, both for his service in helping to identify so many of the Old English books of the Worcester library and for the fruit of his patient industry.[2] A facsimile of the Nicene Creed, written in his hand in the English of his own day on f. vi of MS. Junius 121 (T), was published by S. J. Crawford in his valuable article, 'The Worcester Marks and Glosses'.[3] The hand appears most extensively as the text hand of a fragmentary copy of Ælfric's *Grammar* in the library of Worcester Cathedral.[4] In most of the manuscripts, however, it appears primarily in a multitude of glosses, chiefly in Latin, but sometimes in the vernacular, written between the lines and in the margins.

The earlier investigators, Keller and Crawford, were inclined to believe that the owner of this hand had done his work toward the

---

[1] MSS. E, P, R, S, the three volumes of T, and X^d.

[2] Wolfgang Keller was the first to print a list of the manuscripts glossed by this scribe, in his Strassburg dissertation of 1897, later published in expanded form as *Die litterarischen Bestrebungen von Worcester in angelsächsische Zeit*, Strassburg, 1900 (*Quellen und Forschungen*, LXXXIV). The list is on p. 20. It was enlarged by Crawford in the article mentioned below and again by Ker in his *Catalogue*, p. lvii.   [3] *Anglia*, LII (1928), pp. 1–25.

[4] MS. F. 174 (Zupitza's W), Ker's *Catalogue*, p. 466.

end of the twelfth century, but Mr. Ker has given us strong reason
to accept a later date, probably within the second quarter of the
thirteenth century, though he would admit that the duct of the
script might have been formed before 1200. The argument depends
on the discovery that the scribe entered a correction in a marginal
table on f. 10 of MS. Hatton 114 (T), the table itself being written
in a set hand that Ker is confident of dating close to the middle of
the thirteenth century and certainly not earlier than 1225.[1] There
is no difficulty in accepting the revised date, especially if the owner
of the tremulous hand was an old man, as has generally been supposed; but it makes a difference. On the one hand it extends the
period during which we know that Old English prose was understood and valued at Worcester. On the other hand it causes us to
regard the vernacular glosses and the altered spellings in these
manuscripts as specimens of a slightly more advanced state of
Middle English than we had supposed. Many of the vernacular
glosses and some of the Latin are written in other, firmer hands,
but most of them appear to be of approximately the same date.

   In his ubiquitous Latin glosses the scribe with the trembling
hand shows both his sound training in that language and his
familiarity with Old English. He rarely makes mistakes and often
glosses words of some difficulty. We may notice, however, that he
tends to gloss the same words on page after page, and sometimes
words that look hard, at least to a modern eye, are passed over.
In some passages, too, a great part of his energy is spent in clearing
up possible ambiguities in the little words: glossing the pronoun
ge as *vos* to make sure it is not mistaken for the prefix, sorting
out the relatives, distinguishing the adverb *þa* from the demonstrative, and the like. He was doing his best, apparently, to make
Old English writings—chiefly the translations of King Alfred's day
and the homilies of Ælfric and Wulfstan—available to his contemporaries, perhaps his pupils, at Worcester.

   The vernacular glosses, much less frequent than the Latin and
often written in hands that do not tremble, are of varied character
and interest. Sometimes they are mere modernized spellings of the
original words, but more often they are substitutions, suggesting
the obsolescence of the Old English. Some of the replacements
look like scarcely naturalized borrowings from Anglo-Norman;

---

[1] N. R. Ker, 'The Date of the "Tremulous" Worcester Hand', *Leeds Studies
in English*, VI (1937), 28–29, with facsimile of the crucial page.

others, whether French or English in origin, are already, we may assume, staples of everyday speech.

In addition to the glosses, the Old English texts in these manuscripts have been subjected to another type of editing. Crawford was not certain whether it was carried out by the owner of the tremulous hand, nor am I, though I am inclined to think that some of the work at least is his. At any rate it seems to belong to the same era and to express the same fundamental desire to keep these old writings alive. Someone went through all these manuscripts, word by word, and without destroying the original readings entered alterations of spelling that would bring the pronunciation up to date. This work is systematic, and invaluable for its demonstration of the literary standard if not the local dialect of Worcester soon after 1200. For the most part the changes are effected by small superscript letters, comma-like carets, and underdottings for deletion. The vowels receive a great deal of attention, but certain consonants (especially c and g) are not far behind. An excellent classification of these changes, which are much too complicated for a summary, will be found in Crawford's article. A full exposition of their significance is still to seek.

No attempt is made in this edition to take account of these marks of alteration, since they leave the original readings intact and constitute a separate subject of inquiry. The glosses, on the other hand, both Latin and vernacular, are reported at the foot of the page. They too can be treated as a separate subject, but they have a bearing, usually slight yet occasionally important, on the interpretation of Ælfric's text, and the interest they have in their own right depends in part on their being seen as glosses upon that text. The Latin glosses have not been printed before. Crawford, in the article already mentioned, printed some of those in the vernacular; but his list, much larger than mine in one direction (since it included everything in a given volume), is smaller in another, in that he limited it to the manuscripts at Oxford, thus excluding the rather numerous glosses in R and a few in E and X^d. Where our lists overlap they are in substantial agreement, though here and there I have added something and once have differed.[1]

The Worcester manuscripts are the only ones glossed in Latin, but two others have, now and then, some vernacular glosses. MS. C

[1] At XI. 478, where in T (Hatton 113, f. 113), *smeagað* is glossed *þencð* rather than *weneð*.

contributes four to homily IV, two to XI, and there are a number of both glosses and alterations at intervals in MS. U. See, for example, homilies VII, XI, and XIV, in the first and last of which the few glosses (sometimes intended as substitutions) are included with variants in the apparatus. I am at a loss to date these glosses precisely. Most of them appear to belong to either the twelfth or the thirteenth century.

I must warn the reader that my reports of the glosses, having been based mainly on photostats, are limited to what is readily visible. At some points the manuscripts are rubbed, and glosses originally faint have virtually disappeared. Mr. John Bromwich, who has in preparation a comprehensive study of all the vernacular glosses of Old English manuscripts made during the Middle English period, has obtained a number of additional readings by the use of ultra-violet light. To his study, which alone can do full justice to the glosses as an index to the development of the English language, we must look for a definitive list.

11. EDITORIAL SIGNS AND PROCEDURES

(a) In the main text

The spelling is that of the basic manuscript except for passages enclosed in brackets and for expanded abbreviations. In most of the texts the abbreviations are expanded without notice, but in four (I, XIa, XVII, XXVII), where the text depends on the damaged H alone (except for the passages in XIa and XVII excerpted from other compositions) all expansions are indicated by *italics* and the ampersand (7) is retained.

The metrical lineation is editorial and the punctuation has been modernized throughout. Sentences, however, accord with the capitals and punctuation of the basic manuscript unless otherwise stated. In texts based on MS. U, which points with some regularity by metrical phrases or half-lines, erratic pointing as judged by my own lineation is noted in the apparatus. The capitals of proper and sacred names are modern: no manuscript normally uses capitals for this purpose, though there are rare instances of the capitalization of proper names. Accent-marks in the basic manuscript are reproduced unless they appear to be unoriginal.

Interlinear or marginal insertions are enclosed in slanting lines, ` ´. Unless otherwise stated in the apparatus, they are the work of the original scribe or a contemporary corrector. They are normally relegated to the apparatus if they do not appear to be authentic readings.

Round brackets call attention to lacunae, whether caused by damage to the parchment or by erasure, and whether or not some trace of the letters remains. The letters, if any, enclosed in these brackets are conjectural, being supplied from imperfect traces, from the parallel readings of other manuscripts, or from the implications of the context, always with consideration of the space available in the manuscript. When no strongly persuasive reading has been found, the approximate number of missing letters is indicated by colons, one for each letter, regardless of differences in width. Few scribes write with such uniformity that the number of missing letters in a lacuna can be determined with precision, and the lacunae in a burnt manuscript, such as H, are especially hard to measure because of the uneven shrinking of the parchment. Conjectural readings that seem unduly hazardous, if proposed, are put in the apparatus.

Square brackets indicate departure from the reading of the basic manuscript, whether by omission, addition, substitution, or transposition. When anything is *omitted* from the text as it stands in the manuscript, a letter adjacent to the point of omission is bracketed. See, for example, v. 30. All readings in square brackets are explained on the spot in the apparatus.

Quotation marks are not used for direct discourse. They are reserved for parts of the gospel-texts when these are repeated verbatim in the course of the exposition.

Latin quotations are italicized. In some manuscripts there is a comparable distinction: the scribes use Caroline minuscule for Latin, insular for Old English; but this is not universal.

(b) *In the apparatus*

The same signs are used as in the main text, but capitals are used only when they occur in the manuscripts, and accent marks are not reported unless on special occasions. Lemmata are given before the variant readings only when their omission might lead to uncertainty. When given the lemma is followed by a bracket (]). The lemmata and variant readings are in roman, all else in italic type.

When glosses are separately reported the lemma is regularly

given and followed by a colon. Since the interpretation of abbreviations in these glosses is sometimes hazardous, all expansions are indicated by italics.

(c) In the quotations of Latin sources

Since the quotations are drawn from a great variety of texts, each of which has been normalized by its editor according to a system not shared by more than a few others, it has seemed advisable to modify their spellings in the direction of a common standard. That which I have adopted is a compromise between the late medieval spellings that prevail in most of the Migne texts and the more nearly classical spellings of several modern editors, many of which are actually closer to the spellings in the manuscripts of Ælfric's time. I have rejected *j* for consonantal *i* but used *v* for consonantal *u*, retained somewhat regretfully the *Ioannes* of Migne and most editions of the Vulgate for the *Iohannes* of Ælfric's time and the best modern editions, and wavered hopelessly, I fear, between *spiritualis* and *spiritalis*, *intelligo* and the more classical *intellego*. My procedure for the excerpts from the Boulogne manuscript in XI is different, as explained in the separate introduction to that homily.

In order to distinguish the quoted sources sharply from editorial notes and bibliographical insertions, I have enclosed all such added matter in brackets and printed it in italics. Square brackets are the rule except for identifications of scriptural quotations or allusions within quotations, which are in round brackets, the scriptural quotations themselves, if exact, being italicized.

I

NATIVITAS DOMINI

Ioan. I. 1–14

WE owe the preservation of this homily to the interpolator of MS. H. The absence of other copies need not be taken to indicate a lack of interest in its theme if we remember that it was probably composed rather late in Ælfric's life, when many libraries were already stocked with his earlier sermons, and also that among the surviving witnesses to his later work the Christmas season is for some reason very weakly represented. The homily may have been composed about the same time as our XIII–XVI, which survive in two copies rather than one merely because MS. U is at hand to support the interpolator of H for the period after Pentecost to which these homilies are assigned. U does not include the Christmas season, and there is no other extant codex, among those that draw on Ælfric's later work, that can match, for this season, its methodical inclusiveness. Actually Ælfric composed three other Christmas homilies, one for each of the two series of *Catholic Homilies*, one for the *Lives of Saints*; and he partially rewrote the last, as Belfour IX attests; but only the first of them is well represented among the surviving manuscripts. All these are rather weighty sermons, dealing with important themes. The first, as is to be expected, begins with the simple story of the nativity according to Luke before taking up doctrinal matters, but only this fourth homily on the opening verses of John deals methodically with a text. It survives in sadly mutilated form in consequence of the Cotton fire; yet in spite of this its careful workmanship, its warm and lucid treatment of a difficult theme, and its scope give it a high place. It is clear that Ælfric gathered materials for his exposition from many different sources, and put them together with skill.

Two sources stand out with particular prominence. One is the beginning of Augustine's commentary on John, *In Ioannis Evangelium Tractatus CXXIV*. Augustine devotes two tractates or sermons to the first fourteen verses of the gospel and recapitulates at the beginning of the third tractate, adding further comments on the fourteenth verse. The other source is a Christmas homily on the same text by Bede, numbered I. 8 in D. Hurst's recent edition of the fifty genuine homilies.[1] Like most of the later expositors of the Gospel according to John, including Bede, Ælfric has consulted Augustine directly and drawn from him not only a general understanding of the whole but a number of particulars that do not appear at all, or not so explicitly, in other writers. But the tractates are often both closely reasoned and repetitious in their concentration on a few ideas. Ælfric usually prefers a concise statement to slow persuasion. He simplifies argument (sometimes even obscuring the point) while he increases variety by adding informative details to a list of authorities or developing the human interest of some scriptural illustration. For the general outline of his homily, and for a number of specific interpretations, Ælfric relies rather upon the concise and more variously informative Bede. Sometimes, to be sure, Bede comes so close to repeating Augustine, and Ælfric's treatment of the common idea is so free, that it is hard to tell which author has influenced him more; but there are enough decisive passages to assure us that he had studied the interpretations of both authors with some care.[2]

In comparison the other sources seem of minor importance, but taken together they suggest Ælfric's zealous search for interpretation and illustration, and some of them are not without interest. Two works that stand very close to Bede's homily may be mentioned first. One is Alcuin's *Commentaria in Ioannis Evangelium*, which draws, for the first fourteen verses of *John*, almost exclusively upon Bede's homily, and includes other gleanings from Bede in the prefatory epistle, where the character of the evangelist and the circumstances of the writing of the fourth Gospel are treated. Nearly everything I have quoted as Bede's can be found again in the same or nearly the same words in Alcuin's commentary; but not quite everything. Toward the beginning of Bede's homily are

---

[1] For bibliographical details concerning these sources, see the list in the Introduction, pp. 163–71 above.

[2] Several other sermons of Augustine's dealing with one or more of the first fourteen verses of *John* have survived, but although they often repeat certain ideas in the connected sermons of the Commentary I have found no evidence that Ælfric made use of them. As I have indicated in the Introduction, pp. 159 and 166 (the list of sources), Ælfric probably had Bede's homily at hand in his copy of Paul the Deacon's homiliary, but for Augustine's tractates he may have had to consult the complete Commentary.

some passages that Alcuin skips and Ælfric uses. Conversely,
toward the beginning of Alcuin's commentary there is one brief
passage not from Bede that Ælfric appears to be following. I think
it possible, therefore, that Ælfric consulted both, but certainly the
design of the whole was largely inspired by the clear, firm, and
inclusive outlines of the homily by Bede.[1] The other work to be
mentioned at this point is a Christmas homily by Haymo on the
same text (Hom. ix in Migne's edition). Like several of Haymo's
homilies, it is little more than a rewriting of Bede. Haymo is more
explicit and more long-winded than Bede, sometimes clearer but
usually duller. When Ælfric has his choice he seems almost always
to pay greater attention to Bede. But sometimes Haymo supplies
an interesting phrase, such as the 'irreverberatis oculis' that he or
some predecessor devised,[2] and sometimes he supplies a reference
to some Biblical text that Ælfric finds helpful, as at lines 81 and
461. What is remarkable is not that Ælfric should have consulted
Haymo, for it appears that Haymo was constantly at his elbow,[3]
but that having found so much of Haymo less useful to him than
Bede or Augustine, he should nevertheless have been alert to the
worth of these scattered trifles.

The most notable difference between Ælfric's homily and the
homilies of Bede and Haymo, which have similar outlines, is the
number of bulges in Ælfric's. Occasionally these are created by
Ælfric's addition of something in Augustine (rarely Alcuin or
Haymo) to what is given by Bede, but more often by his inclusion
of material from other sources, for which there is no hint in his
basic authorities, or at most only a bare suggestion. Several of these
expansions consist largely of scriptural elaborations: testimonies
concerning the Word and Wisdom from the Psalms and from St.
Paul in lines 77–109; details concerning Moses and the plagues of
Egypt, elaborating a brief allusion by Augustine, in lines 222–46;
a passage on the Egyptian magicians in illustration of the limits of
human magical powers and of human arts in general by contrast
with divine wonders, in lines 247–74 (where Isidore proves helpful); and a further treatment of Moses in elaboration of the promise
to men that they might be God's sons, in lines 364–85. Another

---

[1] But see what is said about Alcuin's *Commentaria* in the Introduction, pp.
161–2.
[2] See the sources quoted for lines 10–16 and the note on 16.
[3] Introduction, p. 160.

passage, lines 195–221, merely reviews the familiar outline of man's fall in order to emphasize, on general scriptural authority, that God gives gifts in abundance even to fallen man.

Two striking passages are taken from a work which passed for Augustine's until modern times and is now attributed to his friend and pupil, Quodvultdeus, Bishop of Carthage, who was driven out of his see by the Vandals in 439 and, escaping to Campania, died there about 453.[1] His treatise, *Adversus Quinque Hæreses*, provided Ælfric with the alleged prophecy of Hermes Trismegistus and the essentials of its interpretation (lines 110–47), and likewise with the diatribe against the Manichaeans for their slander of the Virgin Mary (lines 410–26). Ælfric's manuscript of this treatise evidently differed a little from the text published in the Benedictine edition of Augustine (Vol. VIII, App. I) and reprinted in Migne, *PL* XLII. 1101 sqq., for the prophecy of Hermes as Ælfric gives it contains several interesting variants toward the end. Nevertheless the printed version is much closer to Ælfric than any other Hermetic text I have been able to find. It has something in common with a passage in Lactantius's *Divine Institutes* and is quoted by the editor of that work by way of illustration.[2] Whether Ælfric had read Lactantius also, or some work derived from Lactantius, I am not sure. In any event Ælfric has introduced these two passages with no more than the vaguest hint from his chief authorities. In telling about Hermes he may have tried to give substance to Augustine's comment (given at line 110) on the heathen philosophers who knew that all things were made by the Word of God, and that God had an only-begotten Son, through whom are all things. In denouncing the Manichaean heresy Ælfric was substituting a sensational passage for much tamer references to heresies at approximately the same place in the homilies of Bede and Haymo.

The homily stands first in the present collection because of its place in the church year. Ælfric himself, when he arranged the *Catholic Homilies* and the *Lives of Saints*, started each of the three volumes with Christmas, though the first volume has an introductory survey of doctrine, *De Initio Creaturæ*, before the homily on the Nativity. There is a further propriety to be observed: Ælfric

---

[1] See Otto Bardenhewer, *Geschichte der altkirchlichen Literatur*, IV. 522 sqq.
[2] Divinarum Institutionum Lib. IV. 6, 7, ed. S. Brandt, *CSEL* XIX. 286 and 292 and notes. The passage from the treatise *Adversus Quinque Hæreses* is only partially represented in W. Scott, *Hermetica*, I. 298 sq.

here treats the challenging opening of that Gospel which he
had treated rather sparingly in his earlier series and now, in
the scattered homilies of his later career, treats more frequently
than any other. And he begins his own exegesis of the gospel with
explicit mention of Augustine, 'se wisa and se wordsnotera bisceop',
the expositor of John *par excellence* by whom, directly or indirectly,
he is more profoundly affected in these homilies than by any other,
even Bede.

Because of the unusually large number of sources cited for this
homily I append a list, in which the abbreviations used for those
frequently referred to are indicated:

Bede = Hom. I. 8, ed. Hurst, on *Ioan.* i. 1–14; and for 20–26,
   Hom. I. 9.
Haymo = Hom. IX, on *Ioan.* i. 1–14.
Augustine = *In Ioan. Ev. Tract.* I, II, III as indicated; and for 70–76,
   Sermo de Principio Genesis; and less directly, for 267–74, *De
   Trinitate*, quoted in note on these lines.
See line 10 for Gregory, *Moralia in Iob*; 65 for Alcuin, *Com. in Ioan.*
   i. 1; 88 for ps.-Bede, *In Psalm.* xxxii. 6; 113 and 410 for ps.-
   Augustine (Quodvultdeus), *Adversus Quinque Hæreses*; 269 for
   Isidore, *Etymologiæ*.

For bibliographical details see the master list above, pp. 163–71.

[VIII. KL̄ IANUARII. NATIVITAS DOMINI]

Euangelium. *In principio erat Verbu*m.

(We ræda)ð on þisum Drihtenlican symbeldæge
þæt (halige) godspell be þæs Hælendes acennednysse,
æg(ðer ge be) his godcundnysse ge be his menniscnysse,
(swa swa) Iohannes awrát þe her on life mid him
on (: : : : : : : : :) wunode, his modrian suna,   5
7 Crist hine (: : : : : : : : : : :) clænan mægðháde,
7 he lede his hea(fod on þæs Hæle)ndes breost,
on þam þe wunode þæs (: : : : : : : : : : : : : :
: : : : : : : :)hte cyðan be Cristes god(cundnysse.   9
: : : : : : : : : : : : : : : : : :) on þære gastlican *gesihðe,   *f. 18

Text based on the unique copy in H (Cotton Vitellius C. v), ff. 17ᵛ–21ᵛ.
Round brackets indicate lacunae, most of which have resulted from the fire of
1731. As far as line 4, *awrat*, and in the concluding lines, these lacunae have been
filled from Wanley, *Catalogus*, p. 208. Otherwise their content is conjectural.
Unless, therefore, there seems no reasonable doubt as to the missing letters, colons
are placed within the brackets to indicate merely their approximate number, and
suggested readings, if any, are placed at the foot of the page.

Sup.: Title from previous homily, f. 12ᵛ (CH I.28 sqq.). Here MS. has (IN)
EODEM DIE.

2 godspell] *sic MS.*; Godspel *Wanley.*   3 godcundnysse ge be his] *om.*
Wanley.   5 on (his hirede)? *Cf. XV. 2; but perhaps not quite enough space.*
6 (lufode for his)?   8 (wisdomes : : : : : :)?   9 (þæt he swa mi)hte?
10 (Be him God geswutelode)?

SOURCES. 1–26 [*These introductory lines contain much that Ælfric had already
stated elsewhere, as pointed out in the Commentary; but he probably made fresh use
of some of the material below.*]

1–9 [*Bede, Hom. I. 8, begins with the same sequence of themes:*] Quia temporalem
mediatoris Dei et hominum hominis Iesu Christi nativitatem quæ hodierna
die facta est sanctorum verbis evangelistarum, Matthæi videlicet et Lucæ,
manifestatam cognovimus, libet etiam de Verbi, id est de divinitatus eius
æternitate, in qua Patri manet semper æqualis, beati Ioannis evangelistæ dicta
scrutari, qui singularis privilegio meruit castitatis ut ceteris altius divinitatis
ipsius caperet simul et patefaceret archanum. Neque enim frustra in cæna supra
pectus Domini Iesu recubuisse perhibetur (*Ioan. xiii. 25*), sed per hoc typice
docetur quia cælestis haustum sapientiæ ceteris excellentius de sanctissimo eiusdem pectoris fonte potaverit. [*Haymo's Hom. IX has nearly the same material
but in a different order and it leaves out the theme of chastity. On 'his modrian
suna', line 5, see note.*]

10–16 [*Bede*] Unde et merito in figura quattuor animalium aquilæ volanti

ærest þurh Ezechiel 7 eft on Apocaly(psi,)
on earnes gelicnysse mid þam oðrum godspellerum,
þæt he mihte scea(wia)n mid scearpum eagum
on earnes gelicnysse be þæs Hælendes god(cundny)sse,
swa swa se earn sceawað þære sunnan leoman   15
unateorig(: : : : : : :) ofer eallum nytenum.
Ða þry oðre godspelleras awriton (heora gods)pell
be Cristes menniscnysse, hu he to mannum com,
7 eac be þam wun(drum) þe he geworhte on life.
Ða bædon þa bisceopas binnan Asian (land)e   20
þone halgan Iohannem þæt he him awrite
sume gewissunge be þæs Hælendes godcundnysse.
And he him béad þa þreora daga fæsten,
7 æfter þa(m) fæstene he wearð swa afylled
mid þam Halgan Gaste þæt he ongann to writenne   25
þa halgan Cristes bóc swa swa we her secgað:

---

16 unateorig (endum eagum)?   23 him] *alt. to* hiom *MS.*

---

comparatur. Cunctis quippe avibus aquila celsius volare cunctisque animantibus clarius solis radiis infigere consuevit obtutus. [*Haymo*] Quia sicut aquila . . . præ cunctis animantibus iubar solis irreverberatis oculis contemplatur, ita Ioannes præ cunctis hominibus subtilius ex divinitate sensit. [*These passages stem from Gregory's Moralia in Iob, Lib. XXXI, Cap. 47, PL LXXVI. 625. Gregory mentions the two visions, of Ezechiel and the Apocalypse, and in the following sentence his 'acies' may have suggested Ælfric's 'scearpum eagum':*] Cunctarum quippe avium visum acies aquilæ superat, ita ut solis radius fixos in se eius oculos nulla lucis suæ coruscatione reverberans claudat.

17–19 [*Bede*] Alii evangelistæ Christum ex tempore natum describunt, . . . inter homines eum subito apparuisse commemorant, . . . magnalia quæ in homine gessit perhibent. [*Similarly Haymo.*]

20–26 [*Not in Bede's homily. Elaborately, in another order, in Haymo's; but Ælfric seems rather to follow Bede's homily I. 9, on St. John the Evangelist,* ed. Hurst, lines 227 sqq.:] Sed dum ipse . . . rediret Ephesum, compulsus est ab omnibus pæne tunc Asiæ episcopis . . de coæterna Patri divinitate Christi altius facere sermonem, eo quod in trium evangelistarum scriptis . . . de humanitate eius ac de his quæ per hominem gessit sufficiens sibi viderentur habere testimonium. Quod ille se non aliter facturum respondit nisi indicto ieiunio omnes in commune Dominum precarentur ut ille digna scribere posset. Et hoc ita patrato, instructus revelatione ac Sancti Spiritus gratia debriatus, omnes hereticorum tenebras patefactæ subito veritatis luce dispulit, *In principio*, inquiens, *erat Verbum, et Verbum erat apud Deum, et Deus erat Verbum.* [*Alcuin quotes this passage verbatim in the prefatory epistle to his Commentaria in Ioan. Ev., Migne, PL C. 741. The essentials and much of the language are in Jerome's Prologus to his commentary on Matthew, PL XXVI. 18 sq., which was used as a preface to the Latin Gospels.*]

In principio erat Verbum, ET RELIQVA:
þæt is on Engliscre spræce, On angynne wæs Word,
⁊ þæt Word wæs mid Gode, ⁊ þæt Word wæs God.
Ðis wæs on anginne mid þam ælmihtigan Gode.　　　　　　30
Ealle þing syndon gesceapene þurh þæt Word,
⁊ butan þam Worde nis geworht nan þing.
Ðæt geworht is wæs lif on him sylfum,
⁊ þæt lif witodlice wæs manna leoht.
And þæt leoht scean on ðeostrum, ⁊ þa ðe(ostru ne) underfengon
þæt foresæde leoht.　　　　　　　　　　　　　　　　36
Sum man wæs asend fram (God)e sylfum to us,
⁊ his nama wæs witodlice Iohannes.
Ðes com on gecyðnysse þæt (he c)ydde be ðam leohte
soðe gecyðnysse, þæt ealle gelyfdon þurh hine.　　　　40
Næs he (na) him sylf leoht, ac þæt he cydde 'gecyðnesse' be þam
leohte.
Ðæt soðe leoht (wæs þe on)liht ælcne mannan
þe on þisne middaneard becymð to menn gebor(en).
On middanearde he wæs, ⁊ þes middaneard wæs geworht

---

35 ðeostru ne] *confirmed by line 292.* 　　37 Gode] *confirmed by 299.* 　　39 he
cydde] *confirmed by 304.* 　　41 na] *confirmed by 310.* 　　42 wæs þe onliht]
confirmed by 328. 　　43 geboren] *confirmed by 329.* 　　44–45 geworht eall]
transposed at 336–7.

27–54 [*Ioan. i. 1*] In principio erat Verbum, et Verbum erat apud Deum, et
Deus erat Verbum.
[2] Hoc erat in principio apud Deum.
[3] Omnia per ipsum facta sunt, et sine ipso factum est nihil. Quod factum
est,
[4] in ipso vita erat, et vita erat lux hominum.
[5] Et lux in tenebris lucet, et tenebræ eam non comprehenderunt.
[6] Fuit homo missus a Deo, cui nomen est Ioannes.
[7] Hic venit in testimonium, ut testimonium perhiberet de lumine, ut omnes
crederent per illum.
[8] Non erat ille lux, sed ut testimonium perhiberet de lumine.
[9] Erat lux vera, quæ illuminat omnem hominem venientem in hunc
mundum.
[10] In mundo erat, et mundus per ipsum factus est, et mundus eum non
cognovit.
[11] In propria venit, et sui eum non receperunt.
[12] Quotquot autem receperunt eum, dedit eis potestatem filios Dei fieri,
his qui credunt in nomine eius:
[13] qui non ex sanguinibus, neque ex voluntate carnis, neque ex voluntate
viri, sed ex Deo nati sunt.
[14] Et Verbum caro factum est, et habitavit in nobis; et vidimus gloriam eius,
gloriam quasi Unigeniti a Patre plenum gratiæ et veritatis.

eall þurh (hi)ne, 7 middaneard ne oncneow hine.   45
On his agenum he com, 7 his age(ne) ne underfengon hine.
Swa fela swa hine underfengon, þam (he for)geaf anweald
Godes bearn to beonne, þam þe on his naman gel(yfað;
þa) þe na of blodum, ne of þæs flæsces willan,
ne of þæs weres (willan, ac ða) þæ of Gode synd acennede.   50
And þæt Word is geworht flæsc (7 hit wunode) on ús.
And we sylfe gesawon soðlice his wuldor,
swylc w(uldor swa geda)fenað Godes ancennedan Suna,
eall fulne mid gy(fe 7 mid soðfæstnysse.)

    Augustinus se wisa 7 se wordsnotera bisceop   55
sæde þæt h(: : : : : : : : : : : : : : : :) gehyran
þonne he him sylf wæs embe þæt halig(: : : : : : : : :
: : : : : : : : : : : : :) deopnysse þæs diglan andgites.
Ac he 'a's(me :)nunge
þurh Godes sylfes fultum þæs (: : : : : : : : : : : : : : : : :   60
: : : : : : : : : :)genysse we hit awritað
on e(: :)

   *Se soðfæsta (godspe)llere us sæde þurh God   *f. 18ᵛ
þæt þæt Word wæs on anginne mid þam ælmihtigan (Gode:
O)n anginne wæs þæt Word: 7 þæt angin is se Fæder,   65

---

45 hine] *confirmed by 337.*   46 agene] *confirmed by 344.*   47 he for-
geaf] *confirmed by 350.*   48 gelyfað] *confirmed by 351.*   49 þa þe]
confirmed by 391.   50 willan, ac ða] *confirmed by 392.*   51 7 hit
wunode] *confirmed by 403.*   53 wuldor swa gedafenað] *confirmed by 428.*
54 eall] Eall *MS.*   gyfe 7 mid soðfæstnysse] *confirmed by 456.*   56 h(e ne
mihte : : : : : : : : :)?   57 þæt halig(e godspell)?   58 (for þære micclan)?
59 as(meade þeah hwæðre sume þa getac)nunge?   61 (7 be his onwri)-
genysse?   62 on E(ngliscre spræce :)? *After the
indicated lacuna, another ruled line at the bottom of the page in the MS. may have
contained writing* (55 *or* 60 *letters*), *but nothing is clearly legible and the line may
have been blank.*   64 Gode] *confirmed by 78.*   66 wunigen(de æfre)?
67 word] *here the MS. has* w, *not the runic* wynn.

55–60 [*The editor has not found this statement in Augustine, but cf.* In Evang.
Ioan. Tract. I:] Postremo aderit misericordia Dei, fortasse ut omnibus satis
fiat, et capiat quisque quod potest: quia et qui loquitur, dicit quod potest. Nam
dicere ut est, quis potest? Audeo dicere, fratres mei, forsitan nec ipse Ioannes
dixit ut est, sed et ipse ut potuit; quia de Deo homo dixit et quidem inspiratus
a Deo, sed tamen homo. Quia inspiratus, dixit aliquid; si non inspiratus esset,
dixisset nihil: quia vero homo inspiratus, non totum quod est dixit; sed quod
potuit homo, dixit.

65–69 [*Alcuin,* In Evang. Ioan. Commentaria] Nam Pater principium est. . . .
In Patre est Filius, quem Verbum nominavit iste evangelista. Nec nos movere
debet quod in sequentibus huius Evangelii, Iudæis interrogantibus quis esset
ipse Deus, Dei Filius respondit: *Principium, qui et loquor vobis* (Ioan. viii. 25).

mid þam wæs þæt Word wunigen(: : : : : :);
7 þæt Word is anginn, swa swa he eft sæde,
Ego principium qui et loquo(r uobis):
Ic sylf eom anginn, ic ðe to eow sprece.

Be þam awrat Moyses se (mæra her)etoga, 70
In principio fecit Deus celum et terram:
God geworhte on anginn(e heo)fonan 7 eorðan,
7 þæt anginn is his a`n´cenneda Sunu,
þurh þone he gesc(e)op ealle gesceafta
7 hi ealle geliffæste þurh þone lyfiendan Gast: 75
hi þry syndon an anginn 7 an ælmihtig God.

We cweðað eft gyt be þam ylcan anginne
(þæt) þæt Word wæs on anginne mid þam ælmihtigan Gode.
7 se sealmwyrhta sang be þam Worde
swa swa we her secgað eow to swutelunge: 80
*Uerbo Domini cæli firmati sunt et spiritu oris ei*us *omnis uirt*us
*eor*um.

78 *þæt þæt*] confirmed by 64.   79 A corrector has indicated a new sentence in
the MS by converting a point to a full stop and enlarging the abbreviation 7.

70–76 [*Probably an independent elaboration, but Augustine brings Ioan. i. 1 and
viii. 25 to bear on Gen. i. 1 in Sermo I, PL XXXVIII. 24, and also in the following
passage from his Sermo de Principio Genesis, in Miscellanea Agostiniana, ed. G.
Morin, I. 12*:] Denique narrator operum famulus Dei Moyses: *In principio*,
inquit, *fecit Deus cælum et terram*. Fecit in principio cælum et terram. Per quid
fecit? Per Verbum. Numquid et Verbum fecit? Non: sed quid? In principio
erat Verbum. . . . Possumus intellegere, et recte intellegimus, in ipso unigenito
Verbo factum esse cælum et terram. . . . Ipsum enim Verbum est et Sapientia
Dei, cui dicitur: *Omnia in Sapientia fecisti (Psal. ciii. 24)*. Si in sapientia Deus fecit
omnia, et unigenitus eius Filius procul dubio est Dei Sapientia, non dubitemus
in Filio facta esse, quæ per Filium facta esse didicimus. Nam ipse Filius est profecto principium. Interrogantibus quippe Iudæis et dicentibus, *Tu quis est?*
respondit, *Principium*. Ecce *In principio fecit Deus cælum et terram*. . . . *Spiritus
Dei superferebatur super aquas (Gen. i. 2)*, et ipse opifex, nec a Patre et unigenito
Verbo seiunctus. Nam ecce, si diligentur adtendamus, Trinitas nobis insinuatur.
Ubi enim dicitur, *In principio fecit*, usia intellegitur Patris et Filii: in principio
Filio, Deus Pater. Restat Spiritus, ut Trinitas impleatur: *Spiritus Dei superfere-
batur super aquas*.

77–147 [*No earlier passage has been found in which the two passages from the
Psalms are brought together or associated with the testimony of Hermes, but
Augustine and Haymo together may have prompted this elaboration.*]

81 [*Psal. xxxii. 6, as given. Haymo quotes this verse and links it with the testimony of St. Paul as in Ælfric's line 109*:] Sicut nos interiorem cordis nostri
voluntatem per verbum patefacimus [*cf. Ælfric's line 87*], ita Deus Pater per
Filium cuncta quæ videntur operatus est, teste Psalmista, qui dicit: *Verbo Dei*,
etc. [*as above*]. Sive Verbum Patris Filius dicitur, quia, ut ait Apostolus, *Virtus
et sapientia est Patris (I Cor. i. 24)*.

Heofonas synd gefæstnode þurh þæt halige Godes word,
7 þurh his muðes gast heora miht is getrymmed.

Her (is nu beloce)n on þysum lytlan ferse
eall seo halige Ðrynnys þe is þrymwealdend God: 85
se Fæder 7 his Word, þæt is his agen Wisdom,
for ðan þe word is wisdomes geswutelung,
7 se Halga Gast, þe hylt ealle þing.

(: : : : : : : : : :)glas þe on heofonum wuniað
syndon gestaþelfæste 7 gestrangod(e : : : : :) 90
þurh þæt halige Word þæs heofonlican Fæder,
7 þurh þone Halgan G(ast : : : : : :) gegladode
to heora Scyppendes lufe, þe hi gesceop on wuldre;
7 (þæra) manna heortan þe on middanearde gelyfað
on þone soðan God symble beoð on (lus)te 95
þurh þone sylfan Gast, 7 he sylð us eallum
ure synna forgyfennysse swiþe mihtiglice.

Eft sang se sealmwyrhta on sumum oðrum sealme:
Quam magnificata sunt opera tua, Domine:
omnia in sapientia fecisti; 100
impleta est (terra possess)ione tua:
Eala þu soþa Drihten, swiðe synd gemærsode
þine (: : : : : : : we)orc; 7 þu geworhtest ealle þing
on þinum wisdome; 7 witodlice is ge(: : : : : :)

84 is nu belocen] *partially visible.* 88 þing] *followed by erasure of about seven letters at end of line in MS. Beginning of next line may have been filled out in margin.* 89 (Ða halgan en)glas? 90 gestrangod(e swiðe)? 92 G(ast hi synd)? 94 gelyfað] y *alt. to* v MS. 95 luste] *partially visible.* 96 sylð] y *alt. to* v MS. 102 gemærsode] æ *alt. to* e MS. 103 (micelan we)orc *or* (mihtigan we)orc? 104 ge(fylled)?

84–97 [*Cf. ps.-Bede, In Psalmorum Librum Exegesis, PL XCIII. 647 sq.:*] *Cæli firmati sunt Verbo Domini.* id est, hoc quod cælestis exercitus, ut cherubin et seraphin, prævaricante diabolo, perstiterunt, non ex se, sed a Domino Patre et Verbo eius habuerunt. Et non pars virtutis, sed *omnis virtus eorum* est a *Spiritu oris eius,* id est Domini, id est, a Spiritu sancto. Nota sanctæ Trinitatis ordinem. Prius enim posuit Dominum Patrem et Verbum, nunc ponit Spiritum sanctum. . . . Dominus misit . . . apostolos per totum orbem terrarum, qui ubique seminarent et spargerent misericordiam eius. Nulla enim misericordia maior est quam peccatorum remissio, quam remissionem ipsi in Trinitatis nomine per totum orbem prædicaverunt. . . . Et per hoc maxime *firmati sunt,* quia *omnis virtus eorum* est a Spiritu sancto, quo de cælis misso super eos, ita corda eorum confirmata sunt, ut nequaquam inter sævientes lupos trepidarent.

99–101 [*Psal. ciii. 24, as given. Cf. the passage from Augustine quoted above at 70–76. Augustine also cites the verse in his commentary on this gospel, though a little later, with reference to verse 4, PL XXXV. 1387.*]

eall eorðan ymhwyrft mid þinre æhte.   105

Ær he sang be þam Worde, (: : : : : : : : : : : W)isdome.

Paulus se apostol 'eac' on his pistole awrat
be urum Hæ(lende : : : : : : :) cwæð þæt he wære
þæs halgan Fæder wisdom 7 his wundorlice miht.

(: : : : : : : : : : : : : : :)ne on heora gesetnessum   110
þæt we sceolon gelyfan on þone so(: : : : : :
: : : : : : : : : : :)nas 7 geworhte ealle þing.

An hæðen mann wæs iú (: : : : : : : : : : : : : : : :
: : : Cri)stes acennednysse, 7 he cydde be Criste,
Hermes ge(: :)   115
hine to gewitnysse for his micclan wisdome.

(: :) Leden:
Uerbum Perfectum, þæt is, Fulfremed (Word.

: :)s word
þæt ge magon gehyran hu se (: : : : : : : : : : : : : : : : : :   120
: : : : : : : : : : : : : : : :) soðlice oncneow:

*Filius bene(dicti Dei atque bonæ uoluntatis,
cuius nomen non potest hum)ano ore narrari.*
Est autem inenarrabilis sermo sapientiæ,   *f. 19

---

105 æhte] æ alt. to e MS.   106 (7 æfter be þam W)isdome?   108 hæ-]
alt. to he- MS.   Hæ(lende Criste 7)?   wære] æ alt. to e MS.   109 fæder]
æ alt. to a MS.   110 (Eac sædon sume hæð)ne?   111 gelyfan] y alt. to v MS.
so(þan God)?   112 (þe wylt þa heofo)nas?   113 hæðen] æ alt. to e MS.
wæs] æ alt. to a MS.   (on Egypta lande)?   114 (ær Cri)stes?   115 ge(haten,
7 se Hælend geceas)?   117 (He awrat ane boc, þe hatte þuss on) Leden?

---

109 [I Cor. i. 24] . . . Christum Dei virtutem, et Dei sapientiam.
110–44 [Perhaps a hint for this passage in Augustine's commentary, Tract. II,
PL XXXV. 1390, speaking of the philosophers attacked by St. Paul, Rom. i. 20–
22:] Hi ergo de quibus dixit, Qui cum cognovissent Deum, viderunt hoc quod
dicit Ioannes, quia per Verbum Dei facta sunt omnia. Nam inveniuntur et ista
in libris philosophorum: et quia unigenitum Filium habet Deus, per quem sunt
omnia.
113–44 [Pseudo-Augustine, Adversus Quinque Hæreses, cap. III] Hermes, qui
latine Mercurius dicitur, scripsit librum qui Λόγος τέλειος appellatur, id est,
Verbum perfectum. . . . Audiamus quid loquatur Mercurius de Verbo perfecto:
. . . Filius benedicti Dei atque bonæ voluntatis, cuius nomen non potest humano ore
narrari . . . . Quid tu, Mercuri, ab hominibus dicis nomen Dei Filii narrari non
posse? A te narretur, qui non homo, sed deus ab hominibus æstimaris. Loquitur
autem ad Filium suum dicens: Est autem. Quis? Filii inenarrabilis sermo sapientiæ
Sanctus sanctus. Nonne hoc est, In principio erat Verbum? Dic, Hermes, sermo iste
sapientiæ habet matrem? Sequitur: De solo Deo Domino est, omnibus dominante
Deo mortalibus. Et quia ab hominibus indagari non potest, addit et dicit: Super
homines est. [Ælfric's text evidently differed in detail.]

sanctus sanctis, de solo Deo: 125
Dominus est omnium, dominante Deo mortalibus,
et qui ab hominibus indagari non potest,
super omnes est.
He cwæð be urum Hælende: He is sunu witodlice
þæs gebletsodan Godes (7) þæs godan willan,   130
7 mannes muð ne mæg his nama'n' fullcyðan.
He is wisdomes sp(ræ)c us unasecgendlic,
7 halig his halgum of Gode anum;
he is ure ealra Drihten,
of þam wealdendan Gode þe gewylt þa deadlican,   135
7 se 'þe' ne mæg nateshwon fr(am) mannum beon asmea(d),
for þan ðe he is ofer ealle menn.
Ðus wrat se Herm(es) on his gesetnysse
be þam ælmihtigan Fæder 7 his ancennedan Suna,
7 het hine Wisdomes Spræc, 7 se godspellere Word;   140
7 he cwæð þæt he wære of Gode sylfum anum,
for ðan þe he næfde nane modor þa gyt
on þære godcundnysse, ac he is of Gode anum,
mannum unasecgendlic, swa swa Hermes awrat.
Fela we mihton secgan swylcera gewi(tn)yssa   145
þurh hæðene witegan be þam heofonlican Gode,
gyf us to lang ne þu(hte) hit her to logienne.
   'On anginne wæs Word,
7 þæt Word wæs mid Gode, and þæt Word wæs God.
Ðis wæs on anginne mid þam ælmihtigan Gode.'   150
Sume gedwolmen dweledon on geleafan

---

130 þæs, 131 mæg] æ *alt. to* a *MS.*   135 *space for another letter or two before*
of *but nothing seems to be missing.*   138 Hermes] her(:)m(es) *MS., letter erased*
after her.   139 fæder] æ *alt. to* a *MS.*   141 wære] æ *alt. to* e *MS.*   sylfum]
y *alt. to* v *MS.*   142 næfde] æ *alt. to* a *MS.*   gyt] y *alt. to* v *MS.*   143 þære]
æ *alt. to* a *MS.*   146 hæðene] æ *alt. to* e; *a letter erased after* n *MS.*   147
þuhte] *partially legible.*

151–60 [*Bede's homily*] Fuere namque hæretici, qui dicerent: Si ergo natus
est Christus, erat tempus quando ille non erat: quos primo sermone redarguit
[Ioannes], cum ait: *In principio erat Verbum.* .... Item fuere hæretici, qui tres
Sanctæ Trinitatis personas esse negantes, dicerent: Idem Deus quando vult,
Pater est: quando vult, Filius est: quando vult, Spiritus Sanctus est: ipse tamen
unus est. Quorum destruens errorem, subiungit: *Et verbum erat apud Deum.*
Si enim alius apud alium erat, duo sunt profecto Pater et Filius, et non unus
(ipse modo Pater, modo Filius, modo etiam Spiritus Sanctus) est: quasi
mutabilis sit divinæ substantiæ natura. .... Item fuere quidam pravi dogmatis

7 noldon gelyfan þæt þæs lyfigendan Godes Sunu
wære æ(f)re mid him butan anginne;
ac se godspellere oferdrifð þyllice gedwolan
þus awritende: 'On anginne wæs Word,   155
7 þæt Word wæs mid Gode, 7 þæt Word wæs God.'
Her ge magon gehyran on þisum halgan godspelle
þæt oðer is se F(æder), oðer is se Sunu,
7 oðer is se Halga Gast, þeah ðe hi(m) eallum si
an godcundnys æfre, 7 an mægenðrymnys 'gemæne'.   160
Seo án godcundnyss þe hi(m) eallu(m) is gemæne
nele na geþafian þæt hi þry godas syndon,
ne þæt heora ænig beo unmihtig(ra) þonne oðer;
7 þeos godcundnyss ne ongan'n' næfre,
ac heo wæs æfre wunigende (on) ðrymnysse [sic]   165
7 on soðre annysse a butan ende.
   'Ealle þing syndon gescea(pene) þurh þæt Word,
7 butan þam Worde nis geworht nan þing.'
Nis he na gesc(eapen), ne he nis na gesceaft,
þurh þone ðe syndon ealle þing gesceapene.   170
Eal(le þa) gesceafta gesewenlice on worulde
7 þa ungesewenlican on þam upp (: : : : : : : :)
þe ænige wununge habbað, ge furðon þa wurmas,
ealle hi synd gesc(eapene) þurh þone soðan Wisdom,
þe is Word gehaten on þisum godspelle;   175
'(7 butan þam) Worde nis nan þing geworht.'

159 him] m *erased to produce* hiom MS.   si] *perhaps alt. from* sy *or* sie *by
erasure.*   161 him] hiom MS., *as above.*   167 word] *preceded by* godcunde
over line; but cf. 31.   172 upp(heofone)? upp(lican eðle)?

auctores, qui Christum hominem tantum confitentes, Deum prorsus esse non
crederent: quos consequenter opprimit cum ait: *Et Deus erat Verbum.* [*Similarly*
Haymo. *Ælfric applies all three clauses to the first heresy and then, without mentioning the others, gives his own generalization of the true doctrine.*]
   169–70 [*Bede*] Item fuere veritatis inimici qui Christum . . . factum a Patre
et ideo minorem Patre quia creaturam crederent. . . . Patet profecto quia ipse
creatura non est per quam omnis creatura facta est. [*Similarly Haymo*].
   171–82 [*Augustine, In Ioan. Ev. Tract. I*] Omnia omnino quæ fixa in cælo
sunt, quæ fulgent desuper, quæ volitant sub cælo, et quæ moventur in universa
natura rerum . . ., ab angelo usque ad vermiculum, [per Verbum facta sunt].
. . . Per ipsum facta sunt supera, infera; spiritualis, corporalis, per ipsum facta
sunt. Nulla enim forma . . ., nulla qualiscumque substantia, quæ potest habere
pondus, numerum, mensuram, nisi per illud Verbum est, et ab illo Verbo
creatore, cui dictum est, *Omnia in mensura, et numero, et pondere disposuisti*
(*Sap. xi. 21*).

Ða gesceafta syndon gesette on (: : : : : : : : : :)
In mensura et *numero* et *pondere.*
þæt is on Engliscere sp(ræce, : : : : : : : : : : : : :)
hu miccle hi beoð 7 hwylce mihte hi habbað,   180
7 hi habbað (: : : : : : : : : : : : : : :) hylt
se ðe ana is unametendlic.
Næs næfre nan sy(: : : : : : : : : : : : : : : : :)
ne nan unrihtwisnyss ne yfel þurh hin(e)
(: :) þurh (: : : : : : : : : : : : : : : : : : :) Godes willan   185
þe ða englas forgægdon, w(: : : : : : : : : : : : : :
: : : : : : : : : : : : : :) forleton to deoflum awend(:
: :)
*7 eft þurh Adam on his forgægednysse.   *f. 19ᵛ
Næfð yfel nane wununge þæt hit wesan mæge   190
ahwær buton on gesceaftum þe góde wæron gesceapene.
Gode wæron þa englas fram Gode gesceapene
7 þæt yfel næs þa gyt nahwær wunigende,
ac hi hit afundon, 7 forferdon þurh þæt,
7 þæt yfel wunað gyt on þam earmum gastum,   195
7 eac on þam mannum þe heora mód awendað
to unrihtwisnysse, 7 yfeles ne geswicað,
7 þa godan menn dreccað Gode to forsewenysse,
7 geswencað gehú mid ofsetnyssum.
God gesceop heofonas, him sylfum to wununge   200
7 his halgum englum þe him gehyrsumedon,
7 eac he geuþe þære ylcan wununge
Adames ofspringe gyf hi hit geearnodon.
Ac æfter Adames gylte us wæs seo eorðe betæht
on to wunigenne on þissere worulde,   205

---

177 (þrim þingum,)?   179 (him is ær gesett)?   181 (gemet, 7 he hi
ealle ge)hylt?   183 sy(nn þurh God gesceapen)?   185 (ac) þurh?   205
before the first on] *erasure of two letters MS.*

183–94 [*Augustine, ibid.*] Videte ne sic cogitetis, quia nihil aliquid est.
Solent enim multi male intelligentes, *sine ipso factum est nihil,* putare aliquid
esse nihil. Peccatum quidem non per ipsum factum est, et manifestum est, quia
peccatum nihil est, et nihil fiunt homines cum peccant. [*Haymo*] *Omnia per
ipsum facta sunt,* etc. . . . Non quædam bona, quædam mala . . . sed omnia valde
bona, sicut scriptum est: *Vidit cuncta quæ fecit, et erant valde bona (Gen. i. 31).*
. . . Nam peccatum, quia subsistendi naturam non habet, non est a Deo creatum,
sed a diabolo inventum, et ideo nihil est.
195–221 [*Not in Ælfric's immediate sources.*]

7 God ús þeah geuðe for (his g)odnesse
þære sunnan leoht to leohtfate [*sic*] on dæge
7 mo(nan 7 s)teorran us mannu(*m*) on niht
7 menigfealde bricas to uru*m* bigleofan:
(fixa)s 7 fugelas þe on flodu*m* wuniað,　　　　　　　210
7 þa wildan deor þe on wudu*m* eardiað,
þa þe clæne syndon, mid his micclan cyste
he forgeaf [us] gemænelice eallu*m*,
(r)icu*m* 7 heanu*m*, þe heora hentan magon.
Nytenu 7 orfcynn he forgeaf us (to) fultume,　　　215
7 wyrta to læcedome 7 to wlite þære eorþan,
7 orfe to flæsce (mid) oðru*m* wæstmu*m*
þæra we moton brucan be ures lifes neode;
7 we magon (geea)rnian on uru*m* wræcsiðe gyt
þæt ece lif mid him 7 þa uplican wununga　　　　220
(gyf) we forlætað unriht 7 lufiað urne Scyppend.
Manega gesceafta mis(lice) ús dreccað
eall for uru*m* synnu*m*, þæt we swa tocnawon
hwæs we wyrðe (syn)don, 7 ge(wil)nian þæs beteran.
Ðin gelica þe cwyð to sum teonfullic (w)ord;　　　225
ðu modegast ongean, 7 ne miht ðe bewerian
wið flean on slæpe (þæt hi) ðe ne awreccon.
Swa wæs iú Pharao, þe wann ongean God,
se Egip(ti)sca cyning, swa swa us cydde Moyses,
þæt God hyne gewylde mid gnættu*m* (7) fleogu*m*,　　230
þæt he oft abæd áre æt Gode
þurh Moyses þingunge 7 ne mihte (: : : : :)n

207 dæge] æ *alt. to* e *MS.*　　213 us] *MS. has erasure wide enough for this word.*
216 læce-] æ *alt. to* e *MS.*　　217 orfe] *sic MS., probably for* yrfe. *See note.*
230 gewylde] y *alt. to* v *MS.*　　gnættum] æ *alt. to* a *MS.*　　231, 236 abæd] æ *alt.*
to a *MS.*　　231 are] a *alt. to* o *MS.*　　æt] æ *alt. to* a *MS.*　　232 (na fleo)n?

222–46 [*Augustine, In Ioan. Ev. Tract. I*] De poena tua peccatum tuum
accusa, non iudicem. Nam propter superbiam instituit Deus istam creaturam
minimam et abiectissimam, ut ipsa nos torqueret: ut cum superbus fuerit homo,
et se iactaverit adversus Deum; et, cum sit mortalis, mortalem terruerit, et, cum
sit homo, proximum hominem non agnoverit; cum se erexerit, pulicibus sub-
datur. Quid est quod te inflas humana superbia? Homo tibi dixit convicium, et
tumuisti, et iratus es; pulicibus resiste ut dormias: cognosce qui sis. Nam ut
noveritis, fratres, propter superbiam nostram domandam creata ista, quæ
molesta nobis essent: populum Pharaonis superbum potuit Deus domare de
ursis, de leonibus, de serpentibus; muscas et ranas illis immisit (*Exod. viii. 6,*
24), ut rebus vilissimis superbia domaretur.

þa mæðleasan hundes lys þe him on þone muð flugon
ne þæra (: : : : :)ena meniu þe his mete besæton,
ne þæra gærstapena þe gnogon (: : : : : : : : :)   235
Moyses him abæd oft miltsunge
7 Pharaó awægde his (: : : : : : : : :) wið God
oðþæt he sylf adranc mid ealre his dugoðe
on þære (: :).
Eaðe mihte God, gyf he swa wolde,   240
sendan (: : : : : : : : : : : : : : : : :) bréman cyninge,
dracan eac 7 næddran, 7 hine swa (: : : : : : :
: : : : : : : : : : : : :)sceafta sceoldon gewyldan
his modignysse, þæt he (: : : : : : : : : : : : : :
: : : : : :)wa ne (: :) flót, þæt he ne forferde   245
gyf he swa g(: :
: : : :)an wyrcð nu isen of eorðan
gold 7 seol(for :
: : : : ne mi)hte nan mann macian to wecgum
*gyf God ne geworhte þa oran to þam.   *f. 20
Ne furðon ænne sticcan ne ænne stæf we næfdon   251
ne ane oflætan to urum mæssan gode
gyf he us ne foresceawode him sylf þæt on ær;
7 we magon swaþeah mid his agenum þingum
hine us gegladian   255
7 hine eac gremian gyf we him ætbredað
his agene cyste his cystigan modes.
Ða deoplican drymen mid heora drycræftu(m)
on Egypta lande þe forlærdon Faraó
worhton manega tacna ongean Moysen   260
of þam ylcan antimbre þe God ær gesceop,
oðþæt hi sylfe sædon, o(fersw)yðede æt nextan,

---

233 mæð-] æ *alt. to* e *MS.*   234, 235 þæra] æ *alt. to* a *MS.*   234 (fleog)ena?
besæton] æ *alt. to* e *MS.*   235 gærstapena] æ *alt. to* a *MS.*   (his wæstmas)?
236 abæd] æ *alt. to* a *MS.*   237 awægde] æ *alt. to* e *MS.*   (folces mod)?
239 (Readan Sæ : : : : : : : : swicdomum)?   241 (beran 7 leon ongean þam)?
242 næddran] æ *alt. to* a *MS.*   (dreccan)?   243 (ac þa eaðelican ge)sceafta?
See note.   245 (on) flot?   247 (Oft m)an?   249 (ac hi ne mi)hte?   251
ænne] æ *alt. to* a *MS.* (*twice*).   stæf] æ *alt. to* a *MS.*   næfdon] æ *alt. to* a *MS.*
252 oflætan] æ *alt. to* a *MS.*   mæssan] æ *alt. to* a *MS.*   253 ær] *alt. to* er *MS.*
256 aet-] *alt. to* at- *MS.*

247–74 [*Not in Ælfric's immediate sources.*]

*Digit*us *Dei* est *hoc*,
þæt Godes finger wære Moysen on fultume
7 hi ne mihton na leng Moyse wiðstandan   265
for þam strangan fingre þe hi gefreddan hio*m* ongean.

Ge ne magon na swiðor, þeah ðe we eow secgon,
heora (: : : : : : : :) tocnawan, ac us secgað lareowas
þæt of fearres flæsce, fule stincendu*m*,
beoð beon acende, þæt hi cuce swa fleoð,   270
7 of assan flæsce cumað (wæpsas)
(7) of h(orses flæsce) cumað eac hyrnetta,
7 on ælcu*m* wæstme, gyf hit miswent on geare
cumað (: : :)drige wurmas, swa swa we gesawon oft.

We secgað nu forð on embe þis soð(e) godspell: 275
'Ðæt þæt geworht is wæs lif on him sylfu*m*.'
Ðeos eorðe is geworht, ac heo nis na hyre sylf lif,
ac on þam wisdome þe geworhte þa eorþan
is þæt l(i)flice gescead þe gesceop ða eorðan.

Ðu sceawast þa heofonan 7 sunnan 7 monan;   280
hi synd on þam cræfte, we cweðað nu swutelicor,
on þam Godes wisdome, þe is witodlice lif,
7 cann wyrcan his weorc be his dihte,
7 he is ure lif on þam we lybbað 7 styriað,
7 on þam we syndon, swa swa us sæde Paulus.   285

---

265 Moyse] *another letter erased in MS., probably* n.   266 hiom] *probably
altered from* him, *but MS. obscure.*   268 (scincræft)?   271 wæpsas]
partially legible in MS.   272 7 of horses flæsce] *a few traces in MS. but very
obscure.*   274 (syn)drige?

---

263 [*Ex. viii.* 19, *Old Latin as in Augustine, De Trinitate, PL XLII.* 875. *See
note on 267–74.*]

269–72 [*Isidore, Etymologiarum Lib. XII, Cap. viii. 2*] Has [apes] plerique
experti sunt nasci de boum cadaveribus. Nam pro his creandis, vitulorum
occisorum carnes verberantur, ut ex putrefacto cruore vermes creentur, qui
postea efficiuntur apes. Proprie autem apes vocantur ortæ de bobus, sicut
crabrones de equis, . . . vespæ de asinis.

277–83 [*Augustine, In Ioan. Ev. Tract. I*] Facta est terra, sed ipsa terra quæ
facta est, non est vita: est autem in ipsa Sapientia spiritualiter ratio quædam qua
terra facta est; hæc vita est. . . . Faber facit arcam. Primo in arte habet arcam.
. . . Arca in opere non est vita, arca in arte vita est; quia vivit anima artificis, ubi
sunt ista omnia antequam proferantur. . . . Terram vides; est in arte terra:
cælum vides; est in arte cælum: solem et lunam vides; sunt et ista in arte: sed
foris corpora sunt, in arte vita sunt. [*Bede, Alcuin, and Haymo say much the same
but Ælfric seems to follow Augustine except for Bede's phrase,* 'vitalis ratio', *corresponding to Ælfric's* 'þæt liflice gescead'.]

284 sq. [*Act. xvii. 28*] In ipso enim vivimus, et movemur, et sumus.

'And þæt lif witodlice wæs manna leoht.'
Ðæra manna leoht he is þe gelyfað on hine,
swa swa he sylf cwæð on sumon godspelle:
Ego sum lux mundi, et cetera:
Ic eom (mid)daneardes leoht, 7 se ðe me fyligð,   290
ne gæð he na on þeostrum, ac hæfð lifes le(oht).
'And þæt leoht scean on þystrum, 7 þa ðeostru ne under-
    fengon
þæt foresæd(e leoht).'
Swa swa þære sunnan leoht bescinð þæne blindan,
7 se blinda ne gesihð (: : : :) scinendan leoman,   295
swa eac þ[a] unrihtwisan 7 þa ungeleaffullan
mid able(n)dum modum ne mihton geseon
þæs Hælendes leoht þe onliht þas (: : : : : : :).
'Sum mann wæs asend fram Gode sylfum to us,
7 his nama wæs (witodlice Iohannes).'   300
He wæs fram Gode asend þæt he secgan mihte
soðe gecyðnysse,
swa sw(a : : : : : : : :) segð on þisum godspelle:
'Ðes com on gecyðnysse þæt he cyd(de be ðam leohte)
soðe gecyðnysse, þæt ealle gelyfdon þurh hine.'   305
Swa swa (: : : : : : : : : : : : : : :)gered up gæð
ætforan þære sunnan, swa scean Iohann(es
: : : : : : : : : : : : : : : : :) cyme, 7 he hine fullode,
7 wæs eac his bydel to þær(: : : : : : : : : : : : :
'Næs he) na him sylf leoht, ac þæt he cydde gecyð(nysse be þam
    leohte.'   310

---

295 (þone) or (þæne)?   296 first þa] þan MS.   298 (woruld)?
300 witodlice Iohannes] as in 38.   303 swa sw(a her æfter) segð?   304
completed from 39.   306 Swa swa (se dægsteorra on dæ)gered?   308
(ætforan Cristes to)cyme?   309 þær(e halgan bodunge.)?   310 completed from 41.

289–91 [Ioan. viii. 12] Ego sum lux mundi; qui sequitur me non ambulat in
tenebris, sed habebit lumen vitæ. [Quoted by Bede and Alcuin in connexion with
verse 7 below.]
294–8 [Augustine, In Ioan. Ev. Tract. I] Quomodo homo positus in sole
cæcus, præsens est illi sol, sed ipse soli absens est; sic omnis stultus, omnis
iniquus, omnis impius, cæcus est corde. [Bede] Lux quippe est hominum
Christus. . . . ; tenebræ autem stulti sunt et iniqui quorum cæca præcordia lux
. . . cognoscit quamvis ipsi radios eiusdem lucis nequaquam capere per intelli-
gentiam possint, veluti si quilibet cæcus iubare solis obfundatur nec tamen ipse
solem cuius lumine perfunditur aspiciat. [Similarly Haymo.]

: : : : : : : : : : : :) him on sumere stowe
þæt he leo(: :
: : : : : : : : : :) *bodode bealdlice be Criste,　　　　　*f. 20ᵛ.
7 se godspellere segð þæt he nære him sylf leoht
for þan þe Cristes leoht þe us ealle onliht　　　　　　　315
onlihte eac Iohannem þæt he leoht wære.

Se Hælend sæde eac to his halgum apostolum,
Vos estis lux mundi: Ge syndon middaneardes leoht,
for þan ðe hi onlihton manncynn to geleafan
mid heora halgan lare, swa swa Crist (: : : :)rde.　　　320
Paulus cwæð eac to þam geleaffullum:
Hwilon ge wæron þeostru, nu ge syndon leoht on Gode;
for þan þe hi ða gelyfdon on þone lyfiendan God.
Æc [sic] ure eagan synd(o)n gehatene leoht,
ac hi naht ne geseoð butan hi sum leoht habbon,　　　325
oððe (þæs) dæges leoht, oððe lihtinge on niht.

Nu segð se godspellere be þam soðan leohte,
'Ðæt soðe leoht wæs þe onliht ælcne mannan
þe on þisne middaneard becymð to men geboren.'
Ðæt soðe leoht is ure leofa Hælend,　　　　　　　　330
þe is him sylf leoht 7 onliht ælcne mann
þe his geleafan leoht on his life gehylt,
oððe on (: : :)um gecynde oððe on godcundum wisdome,
for þan þe ælc wisdom is of Gode syl(fum

311 (Se Hælend sæde be)?　　　312 leo(htfæt wære beorhte lixende)??
313 (for þan þe he)?　　320 (him læ)rde?　　333 (god)um? The third letter is
either d or ð, probably d.

311–23 [Bede, whose order Ælfric reverses] Et sancti quidem homines lux sunt
recte vocati, dicente ad eos Domino: Vos estis lux mundi (Matth. v. 14), et
apostolo Paulo: Fuistis aliquando tenebræ, nunc autem lux in Domino (Ephes. v. 8).
Sed multum distat inter lucem quæ illuminatur, et lucem quæ illuminat. . . .
[Iohannes] enim, ut scriptum est, erat lucerna ardens et lucens (Ioan. v. 35). . . .
Gratiam vero lucis pectoribus infundere solius est eius de quo dicitur: Erat lux
vera, quæ illuminat omnem hominem venientem in mundum.
324–6 [Augustine, In Ioan. Ev. Tract. II, in a passage which includes the
essentials of the preceding quotation from Bede] Nam et oculi nostri dicuntur lumina;
et tamen nisi aut per noctem lucerna accendatur, aut per diem sol exeat, lumina
ista sine causa patent.
331–5 [Bede] Erat lux vera quæ illuminat omnem hominem venientem in mundum; omnem videlicet qui illuminatur sive naturali ingenio seu etiam sapientia
divina. Sicut enim nemo a se ipso esse, ita etiam nemo a se ipso sapiens esse
potest, sed illo illustrante de quo scriptum est: Omnis sapientia a domino Deo est
(Eccli. i. 1).

7 we nan) god nabbað buton of Godes gyfe.   335
'On middanearde he wæs, 7 þes middaneard wæs
eall geworht þurh hine, 7 middaneard ne oncneow hine.'
He wæs on middanearde þurh his godcundnysse,
7 he com to middanearde þurh his menniscnysse,
7 þes middaneard, þæt syndon þa menn   340
þe lufiað to swiðe þas lænan woruld,
noldon oncnawan Cristes tocyme,
swa swa se godspellere gyt segð her bæftan:
'On his agenum he com, 7 his agene ne underfengon hine.'
Ðæt syndon þa ungeleaffullan men ðe his geleafan forsawon. 345
Ðis is swa gesæd be sumum mannum her,
ac (m)anega gelyfdon of þisum middanearde,
ge of Iudeiscum cynne ge of hæðenum þeodum,
(o)n þone soðan Hæle[n]d, þeah þe hi sume noldon.
'Swa fela swa hine underfengon, eal(lum) hiom he forgeaf
anweald   350
Godes bearn to beonne, þam þe on his naman gelyfað.'
(H)er ge magon gehyran þæs Hælendes cystignysse
7 his micclan godnysse ofer (manna) bearnum
þæt he gyfð us anweald, gif we on hine gelyfað,
Godes bearn to beon(ne), swa swa þis godspell segð   355
7 swa swa he sylf sæde to sumum his gecorenum:
Ego dixi (dii esti)s, et filii Excelsi omnes:

335 7 we nan] *lower half of letters still visible.*   343 bæftan] beæftan, *with
dot under* e *for deletion, MS.*   349 hæled *MS.*   350 eallum hiom] *merely*
þam *at line 47.*   353 manna] *last three letters partially visible.*

338–49 [*Bede*] In mundo erat per divinitatem, in mundum venit per incarnationem. Venire quippe vel abire humanitatis est, manere et esse divinitatis. . . .
[*Earlier*] Et mundus eum non cognovit. . . . Mundum namque hoc loco dicit
homines mundi amore deceptos, atque inhærendo creaturæ ab agnoscenda
creatoris sui maiestate reflexos. . . . [*Ælfric's abridgement obscures Bede's distinction
between the world's not recognizing God in the creation and its not receiving him
when he came into it in the flesh.*] In propria venit, et sui eum non receperunt. Quem
enim in potentia deitatis cuncta creantem regentemque non cognoverant, ipsum
in carnis infirmitate miraculis coruscantem recipere noluerunt. . . . Neque enim
omnes recusarunt, alioquin nullus esset salvus. . . . Nunc autem multi eum ex
utroque populo credendo receperunt. [*Similarly Haymo.*]
352–63 [*Bede*] Consideremus . . . quanta gratia Redemptoris nostri, *quam magna
sit multitudo dulcedinis* eius (*Psal. xxx. 20*). . . . Consideremus quanta virtus est
fidei, cuius merito potestas datur hominibus filios Dei fieri. [*Similarly Haymo.*]
357–9 [*Psal. lxxxi. 6, as given. Cited Ioan. x. 34. Cited by Augustine near the
beginning of Tract. I.*]

Ic sæde to soðan, ge sylfe syndon godas,
7 suna þæs Hex(tan þe heo)fonas gewylt.

Micel mærð is þis, 7 miccle geþingðu,   360
þæt se ælmihtiga God (: : : : : : : : : :)nysse
het us menn godas, 7 his agene bearn,
gyf we þone anweald æt(: : : : : : : : : :)að.

Be þam ylcan cwæð iú God sylf to Moysen:
Ecce constitui te deum Pha(raonis;   365
et Aaron frater tu)us erit propheta tuus.

Nu ic þe sette, cwæð God sylf to him,
þæt þu beo (: : : : : : : : : : : : : : : : : :) god,
7 þin broðor Ááron 'sceal' beon þin witega.

Swa micelne (: :) Moyse   370
þæt he hine gesette swylcum cyninge to gode,
þe (: :)ann wið God sylfne,
ac him comon þa to tyn cynna (: : : :
: :) Readan Sæ.

Be þisum sang eac se sealmwyrh(ta þus: 375
Deus stetit in synagoga deorum:
in medio) autem deos diiudicat.

He cwæð, God *sylf gestod on þæra go(da) gesamnunge,   *f. 21
7 he on middeweardan þa godas toscæt,
for þan þe God sylf deð sy(n)derlice ge'h'wylcum,   380
þam þe he g[o]das gewyrcð, synderlic'n'e wurðmynt,
ælcum heora anum be þam þe him gewy(rð)
7 be þam þe hi lufiað þone lyfiendan God
se þe ana is ælmihtig Scyppend
þurh hine sylfne (: : : : : : : : : :) á.   385

Crist is ancenned Sunu of þam ælmihtigan Fæder;

---

361 (þurh his god)nysse?   363 æt (him geearni)að?   368 (: : : : : : : : : : : :
Pharaones) god?   370 Moyse] *a final letter* (n?) *erased MS.*   373 tyn
cynna] *the y's converted to v's MS.*   (wita)?   375 *There would be room
for the conjectured* þus *if* Deus *and* deorum *were abbreviated.*   381 godas]
second letter apparently corrected but illegible.

364–85 [*Not in Ælfric's immediate sources.*]
365–9 [*Ex. vii. 1, as given.*]
375–9 [*Psal. lxxxi. 1, as given.*]
386–90 [*Bede, restating Augustine, Tract. II*] Unicus ex Patre [Redemptor
noster] natus est, et noluit remanere unus; descendit ad terram, ubi fratres sibi,
quibus regnum Patris sui dare posset, acquireret. [*Haymo has the idea but his
passage is much less close to Ælfric's.*]

nu nolde he (: : : : : : : : : : :)n he gebroðra hæfde,
ferde þa to middanearde 7 fette him gebroðra
(swa þæt he) mihte cyþan his micclan cysti'g'nysse
7 his rice him forgyfan mid him to rixienne.   390
    'Ða þe [na] of blodum ne of þæs flæsces willan
ne of weres willan, ac ða þe of Gode synd acennede.'
Ne bið na of þam blode þes halga bearnteam,
ne of weres gestreone, ne of wifes cenninge,
ac of Godes geleafan, swa swa God sylf sæde: 395
Buton gehwylc mann beo acenned of wætere
7 of þam Halgan Gaste, næfð he na Godes rice.
Ðæt þe of flæsce bið acenned, þæt bið flæsc witodlice,
7 þæt 'þe' bið acenned of gaste, þæt bið eac swylce gast:
þæt synd þa gastlican bearn þe on Godes gelaþunge   400
þurh þæt halige fulluht 7 þurh þone Halgan Gast
Gode beoð acennede, gyf hi on gode þurhwuniað.
    'And þæt Word is geworht flæsc, 7 hit wunode on ús.'
Nis þæt halige Word awend to flæsce,
ac se heofonlica Æþeling her on þas woruld com   405
7 þa menniscnysse genam of Marian innoðe,
soð man acenned on sawle and on lichaman,
7 wunode swaþeah God on þære godcundnysse,
an ælmihtig Hælend, us to alysende [sic].
Nu cwædon þa Mann(ichei), þa manfullan gedwolan,   410

---

387 (ana beon buta)n?   390 *first* him] *alt. to* hiom MS.   391 na] *not
in MS. Cf. 49.*   392 weres] ðæs weres, ðæs *crossed out, MS.*   396 mann]
mann(:), *perhaps* mann(a).

391–402 [*Bede, freely restated by Ælfric*] Carnalis quippe nostra singulorum
generatio ex sanguinibus, id est ex natura maris et feminæ, ac complexu coniugii
duxit originem: at vero spiritalis Spiritus sancti gratia ministratur, quam a
carnali distinguens Dominus ait: *Nisi quis renatus fuerit ex aqua et spiritu, non
potest introire in regnum Dei. Quod natum est ex carne, caro est; quod natum est de
spiritu, spiritus est* (*Ioan. iii.* 5, 6).
404–9 [*Bede gives the logical ground for Ælfric's simplified interpretation:*]
Solet . . . Scriptura modo animæ, modo carnis vocabulo, totum designare
hominem. . . . Sic ergo hoc in loco quod dicitur: *Et Verbum caro factum est,* nihil
aliud debet intelligi quam si diceretur: Et Deus homo factus est, carnem videlicet induendo et animam; ut sicut quisque nostrum unus homo ex carne constat
et anima, ita unus ab incarnationis tempore Christus ex divinitate, carne, et
anima constet: Deus ab æterno in æternum existens verus ut erat, hominem ex
tempore assumens in unitatem suæ personæ verum, quem non habuerat.
410–26 [*Pseudo-Augustine, Contra Quinque Hæreses, Cap. I, V*] Manichæi
dicunt phantasma esse, quod dicitur Dominum Christum femineo potuisse

þæt Gode wære unwurð on his mægenþrymnysse
(þæt he) wurde acenned of wifmannes gecynde.

Ac gehyre se dysega 7 se gedwola (: : : : : :)
þæt þæt halige mæden, þæs Hælendes modor,
næfde nane fulnysse, ne furðon (g : : : : : : :),   415
ne weres gemánan, ac þurhwunode mæden,
7 heo butan sarnysse hyre c(: : : : : : : :),
7 hyre gedafenode, þa þa heo urne Drihten gebær,
þæt heo mæden wære (: : : : : : : : :)licum wurðmynte.

Gyf seo sunne scinð, swa swa we geseoð oft,   420
on fulum adela (: : : : : : :)fyled ne bið,
micele swiðor mihte se ælmihtiga Godes Sunu
butan eallum fy(: : :) beon of hyre acenned,
7 heo mihte beon micclum geclænsod
þurh his halg(: : : : : :); 7 he næs befyled   425
7 hyre mægðhad is ansund, þonne heo butan hæmede (: : :
'And) we sylfe gesawon soðlice his wuldor,
swylc wuldor swa gedafenað Go(des ancen)nedan Suna.'
Ða apostoli gesawon þe siðedon mid him
þa wu(: : : : : : : :) worhte, 7 hu he wearð hwilon   430

413 (secgan)?   415 (galnysse)?   417 c(ild acende)?   419 (æfre on
mær)licum?   421 adela(n 7 heo be)fyled?   423 fy(lðum)?   425 halg(an
mihte)?   426 (bær)?   427–8 *completed from 52–53.*   430 wu(ndra
þe he)?

nasci ex utero. Non enim dignum est, inquiunt, ut tanta maiestas per sordes et
squalores feminæ transisse credatur. . . . [*Cap. V*] Qui libenter amplectitur
Deum natum, non horreat virginis partum. Dicit tibi Deus creator hominis,
filius hominis: Quid est quod te permovet in mea nativitate? Non sum libidinis
conceptus cupiditate. Ego matrem, de qua nascerer, feci; ego viam meo itineri
præparavi atque mundavi. Hanc quam despicis, Manichæe, mater est mea; sed
manu fabricata est mea. . . . Sicut transitu meo illius non est corrupta virginitas,
sic mea ibi non est maculata maiestas. Si solis radius cloacarum sordes desiccare
novit, eis inquinari non novit; quanto magis splendor lucis æternæ, in quo nihil
inquinamenti incurrit, quocumque radiaverit, mundare potest, ipse pollui non
potest? Stulte, unde sordes in virgine matre, ubi non est concubitus cum
homine patre? Unde sordes in ea, quæ nec concipiendo libidinem, nec pariendo
est passa dolorem?

429–36 [*Bede*] Gloriam Christi . . . homines post incarnationem viderunt,
aspicientes humanitatem miraculis refulgentem, et intelligentes divinitatem intus
latitantem, illi maxime qui et eius claritatem ante passionem transfigurati in
monte sancto contemplari meruerunt, *voce delapsa ad eum huiuscemodi a magni-
fica gloria: Hic est Filius meus dilectus, in quo mihi complacui* (*II Petr. i. 17*; *cf.
Matth. xvii. 5*); et post passionem resurrectionis ascensionisque ipsius gloria
conspecta, Spiritus eius sunt dono mirifice refecti.

uppan anre dune æt(: : : : : : : : : : : : : :),
þæt his nebbwlite scean swylce sunbeam,
7 his (: : : : : : : : : : : : : : :) þonne snaw.
Eft hi hine gesáwon syððan he of (: : : : : : : : :
: : : : : : : : :) lichaman, 7 hu he astah to heofonum,   435
7 (: : : : : : : : : : : : : : : : : : :) micelre wundrunge.
Iohannes se fullu(htere : Ior)danen,
7 Crist þa up eod*(e : : : : : : : : : : : : :   *last letter
: :) *to: visible f. 21
                                                                   *f. 21ᵛ
þes is min leofa Sunu, þe me wel licað.   440
Eft syððan on þam munte, þa þe him mid wæron
þa þa he swa beorhte scean, swa swa we sædon ær,
gehyrdo(n o)f heofonum þone halgan Fæder
þus (cweðende) him to mid cuðlicere lufe:
Ðes is min leofa Sunu, (on þam me) wel licað: 445
gehyrsumiað him. Ðus sæde Matheus.
(: : : : : þ)riddan siðe, ær Cristes þrowunge,
clypode se ylca Fæder cuðlice him to,
þæt eall þæt folc gehyrde þe þam Hælende folgode,
cwæð þæt he hine mersode, 7 hine mærsian wolde.   450

431 æt (eowed : : : : : : : : :)?   432 sun-] *preceded by* sum, *crossed out,* MS.
433 7 his *gewæda* seinon hwitre)?   434 of (deaðe aras)?   435 (on ansundum)?
Cf. hom. vii. 144.   436 (cwædon hit to mannum mid)?   (cw *partially visible but
not certain*).   437 fullu(htere hine gefullode on þære ea Ior)danen?   438
eod(e ut of þam wætere)? (*if enough room one might prefer* ardlice *to* ut *because of
Latin* confestim).   439 (7 Godes stefn of heofonum sæde him) to?   441, 442
rift in parchment after Eft *and in* beor-hte *but nothing missing.*   444 cweðende]
clypiende (*cf. 448*) *seems less probable.*   445 on þam] *The spacing favours this
variant rather than* þe *as in* 440. *See note.*   447 (Eft on þ)riddan?

432, 433 [*Matth. xvii. 2*] Et resplenduit facies eius sicut sol: vestimenta autem
eius facta sunt alba sicut nix.
437–54 [*Apparently Ælfric's own elaboration of the idea in Bede's quotation
from II Petr. i. 17 as given above. The gospel texts are given below.*]
437–40 [*Matth. iii. 13 sqq.*] Tunc venit Iesus a Galilæa in Iordanem ad
Ioannem, ut baptizaretur ab eo. . . . [*16*] Baptizatus autem Iesus, confestim
ascendit de aqua. . . . [*17*] Et ecce vox de cælis dicens: Hic est Filius meus
dilectus, in quo mihi complacui.
441–6 [*Matth. xvii. 1–5*; esp. 2, *as above, and 5:*] Ecce nubes lucida obum-
bravit eos. Et ecce vox de nube, dicens: Hic est Filius meus dilectus, in quo
mihi bene complacui: ipsum audite.
447–54 [*Ioan. xii. 23 sqq.*] Iesus autem respondit eis, dicens: Venit hora ut
clarificetur Filius hominis. . . . [*28*] Pater, clarifica nomen tuum. Venit ergo vox
de cælo: Et clarificavi, et iterum clarificabo. [*29*] Turba ergo quæ stabat et
audierat, dicebat tonitruum esse factum. Alii dicebant: Angelus ei locutus est.

Nu wæs þis micel wuldor 7 micel gewitnyss þam Suna,
þæt se Fæder swa þriwa þuss clypode him to
hlude of heofonum, þæt menn hit gehyran mihton;
7 sume eac cwædon þæt (hit) þunor wære.

Ðæt godspell geendað nú on þisum wordum þuss: 455
'Eall fulne mid gyfe 7 mid soðfæstnysse.'

On þæ(r)e (m)enniscnysse he hæfde swa micele gyfe
þæt he wæs (soð God 7 soð) mann geboren,
Dauides cynnes, of þam clænan mædene,
an Crist wuniende on twam edwistum.   460

Soðfæstnysse he hæfð, swa he sylf sæde:
Ego sum uia, & ueritas, & uita:
Ic sylf eom se weg, 7 soðfæstnyss, 7 lif.

Ðurh Moy(sen wæs ge)sett þam ealdum mannum iú ǽ,
7 open lagu, 7 se (le)ofa Hælend   465
gebrohte ús niwum mannum gife 7 soðfæstnys(se),
7 he þa þin(g) gefylde þe gefyrn wæron
be him gewitegode (þurh) Moysen 7 witegan;
7 eall his fær wæs beðoht fram frym(ðe þi)ssere worulde.

Ðam is wuldor 7 lof 7 wyrðmynt on ecnysse   470
(mid þam) heofonlican Fæder 7 þam Halgan Gaste
on anre god(cund)nysse: we cweðað, AMEN.

---

458 soð God 7 soð] *lower half of letters still visible.*

457–60 [*Bede*] Gratia plenus erat idem homo Christus Iesus, cui singulari
munere præ ceteris mortalibus datum est, ut statim ex quo in utero virginis
concipi et homo fieri inciperet, verus esset et Deus. . . . Idem veritate plenus erat
et est, ipsa videlicet Verbi divinitate, quæ hominem illum singulariter electum,
cum quo una Christi persona esset, assumere dignata est, non aliquid suæ divinæ
substantiæ, ut heretici volunt, in faciendam hominis naturam commutans, sed
ipsa apud Patrem manens totum quod erat, totam de semine David naturam veri
hominis, quam non habebat, suscipiens.
461–3 [*Haymo*] Veritate quoque plenus fuit, sicut ipse in Evangelio dicit:
Ego sum via, veritas et vita (*Ioan. xiv. 6*).
464–6 [*Ioan. i. 17*] Quia lex per Moysen data est, gratia et veritas per Iesum
Christum facta est. [*Augustine expounds this verse in Tract. III and brings it
together with verse 14. Ælfric takes only so much from Augustine as the juxtaposition itself suggests.*]
467–9 [*Augustine, Tract. III*] Sed hoc et promiserat Deus per Prophetas:
itaque cum venit dare quod promiserat, non solum gratiam dedit, sed et veritatem. Quomodo exhibita est veritas? Quia factum est quod promissum est.

NOTES

1–26. This introductory passage, though prompted by Bede and indebted, directly or indirectly, to a number of earlier treatments of John
the Evangelist and the writing of the Fourth Gospel, rehearses matter
with which Ælfric himself had already dealt at least twice, first in the
homily on the Assumption of St. John (*CH* I. 58 sqq.), and then in the
'Item Alia' on the four evangelists in the *Lives of Saints*, xv. 104 sqq.
He returns to the theme, probably after having composed the present
homily, in *On the Old and New Testament*, lines 876–90, 933–5, 991–3,
1010–17, not to mention the long story of St. John and the young robber,
1017–1153, which stands as a separate homily in MS. H. Particular
parallels are cited below.

5 b. *his modrian sunu.* That the mother of James and John, the sons of
Zebedee, was the Virgin Mary's sister is a notion that recurs several times
in Ælfric's writings, always, so far as I have observed, without warrant
from whatever Latin author Ælfric is following for the surrounding
details. See, for example, *CH* I. 58; II. 256 and 412; *LS* xv. 159; Fehr,
Brief II, sec. 15; *Old and New Testament*, 1020; and in the present
collection, II. 6 and xIV. 211, where there is vague reference to the authority
of books dealing with the lineage of James and John.

This notion, in the form in which it has been favoured by certain
modern protestant divines, rests on inferences drawn from a comparison
of three gospel texts listing the women present at the crucifixion. It is
possible to take the list of *John* xix. 25 (Vulg., *Stabant autem iuxta crucem
Iesu mater eius, et soror matris eius, Maria Cleophæ, et Maria Magdalene*)
as comprising four women instead of three, provided that *Maria Cleophæ*
(A.V. Mary of Clopas) is not the same person as the *soror matris eius.* If she
is distinct from the *soror*, her own relationship to the Virgin is undeter-
mined, and the name of the *soror* is left open. It now becomes possible
to identify this *soror* with the Salome (by later tradition, Mary Salome)
who is named in *Mark* xv. 40 and xvi. 1. If now Salome is identified with
the 'mother of Zebedee's children' who is listed in the corresponding
position in *Matthew* xxvii. 56, it appears that James and John were the
sons of Salome, the Virgin's sister. This series of inferences is mentioned
with approval in Hastings's *Dictionary of the Bible*, under *John the Apostle.*

But Ælfric's most distinguished authorities—Augustine, Gregory, and
Bede—followed Jerome in supposing that the *soror matris eius* was *Maria
Cleophæ*, and in identifying her further with the *Maria Iacobi minoris et
Ioseph mater* of *Mark* xv. 40 and (without the *minoris*) of *Matthew* xxvii.
56. Jerome had drawn these inferences in his tract *Adversus Helvidium*
(*PL* xxIII. 183 sqq.), in which he had defended his belief in the perpetual
virginity of Mary against the supposed implications of the Biblical references to brothers of Jesus (*Matth.* xiii. 55; *Mark* vi. 3), chief among whom
was 'James the Lord's brother' (*Galat.* i. 19). Maintaining that 'brother'
was used loosely for any close relative, Jerome identified this James with
the *Iacobus minor* of *Mark* xv. 40 and the *Iacobus Alphæi* of *Matthew* x. 3,

and showed, by way of *Maria Cleophæ* and the *soror*, that he was in fact the cousin of Jesus. This argument, which is still the accredited doctrine of the Roman Catholic Church, left no ground for supposing that Salome, mother of the sons of Zebedee, was the Virgin's sister.

Nevertheless the supposition appears in a work well known to Ælfric, the interpolated homily of Haymo, with reference to *Matth.* xx. 20, *Tunc accessit ad eum mater filiorum Zebedæi*, PL cxviii. 238. The homily, no. xxxviii, is one of those drawn from an anonymous commentary on *Matthew* in a ninth-century manuscript at Lyon. (See H. Barré, *Les Homéliaires de l'École d'Auxerre*, pp. 50–51, and above, p. 157, esp. notes 1 and 2.) Although the commentator elsewhere accepts Jerome's argument (*PL* cxviii. 211 A, where *Joannes* mistakenly replaces *Joseph*, and 379 C), here he says simply, 'Mater filiorum Zebedæi, matertera fuit Salvatoris, mater videlicet Jacobi et Joannis.'

This one passage is probably enough to account for Ælfric's repeated assertion of the relationship, but it seems to be part of a larger complex of notions which had been developing in western Europe, in which Jerome's view became associated with others for which there was no comparable basis. Max Förster has documented these notions from writings of a later period in his study, 'Die Legende vom Trinubium der hl. Anna', in the Hoops Festschrift, *Probleme der englischen Sprache und Kultur*, Heidelberg, 1925, pp. 105–30; and this is supplemented for twelfth-century England by M. R. James, 'The Salomites', *Journal of Theological Studies*, XXXV (1934), 287–97. (I am indebted to Mr. N. R. Ker for calling my attention to both these articles.) Förster finds no evidence for the heterodox notions he cites prior to the eleventh century, but all these notions existed, if we can trust our texts, as early as the middle of the ninth century.

One of Förster's documents comes from the *Vocabularium* or dictionary of Papias, allegedly a Lombard, which was compiled about 1053, has survived in numerous manuscripts of the twelfth and later centuries, and was printed four times, first at Milan, then Venice, before 1500. (See G. Goetz, *Corpus glossariorum latinorum*, I, Leipzig, 1923, pp. 172–84, and on the editions, Hain-Copinger, *Repertorium bibliographicum*, nos. 12378–81). The relevant passage is best represented for my purpose in the second edition, Venice, 1485, sign. o. iiii^r. Professor S. G. Kuttner has kindly allowed me to quote from his microfilm of a copy in the Vatican, STAMP. Barb. A.A.A. 1–2. I preserve the paragraphing, not the lineation, expand abbreviations, and add superscript numbers for reference:

[1]Maria mater domini.

Maria cleophe siue alphei uxor: quæ est mater iacobi episcopi et apostoli: et simonis et tadie: et cuiusdam iosep. Maria solome [*sic*] uxor Zebedei mater ioannis euangelistæ et iacobi. Maria magdalene. iste quattuor in euangelio reperiuntur. [2]Aimo Iacobus et Iudas et Ioseph filii materteræ domini fuerunt. Iacobus quoque et Ioannes alterius materteræ domini.

[3]Maria iacobi minoris et ioseph mater uxor alphei soror mariæ matris domini quam cleophe Ioannes nominat: uel a patre uel a gentilitatis

familia uel alia causa. [4]Maria salome a uiro uel a uico dicitur: hanc eandem quidam cleophe dicunt: quia duos uiros habuerit.

The four passages indicated by superscript numbers are derived from different sources. Passage 1 may be the compiler's own summary, with features borrowed from 3 and 4. Passage 3 comes, directly or indirectly, from Jerome, *Adversus Helvidium*, PL XXIII. 196. Passage 2 is inferred, probably, from the passages in Haymo's homiliary to which I have already referred. Papias's preface names *Aimo* among the sources he will cite, and the unpunctuated *Aimo*, which probably ought to have stood in the margin, refers to Haymo, as is confirmed by passage 4. This is from one of Haymo's genuine homilies, PL CXVIII. 446 (Hom. LXX, numbered II. 1 by Father Barré in his inventory, p. 152). Haymo is commenting on *Mark* xvi. 1, concerning the three women at the sepulchre:

> Et pulchre mulieres uno nomine censentur. . . . Quarum nominum distinctionem evangelica lectio ostendit, per adjectiva nomina, cum ait: 'Magdalene, Jacobi, et Salome.' Maria Magdalene a Magdalo dicta est castello. . . . Maria Jacobi a filio suo Jacob dicta est, quæ matertera fuit Domini, id est soror matris, et mater Jacobi et Joseph. Maria Salome, vel a vico, vel a viro dicta est. Tradunt enim eam habuisse duos viros, Cleopham scilicet et Salomem: ipsam volunt esse, quæ alibi Maria Cleophæ appellatur.

Papias was evidently struck by the last two sentences. The treatment of *Salome* as a genitive like *Cleophæ* shows, as Max Förster points out, that whoever invented it was judging by Latin usage, not Greek or Hebrew.

This passage is old and almost certainly original, for it is substantially the same in three tenth-century manuscripts at the Bibliothèque Nationale in Paris: Lat. 619, f. 107[r-v]; Lat. 12305, f. 183[v]; and Lat. 16819, f. 143. They were most kindly collated for me by Mme Jacqueline Rambaud, Conservateur in the Département des Manuscrits, at the instance of Professor Kuttner. The first two are Father Barré's A and B, two of the primary witnesses to Haymo's original homiliary.

Still more surprising is the following passage from another work currently attributed to Haymo of Auxerre, the *Sacræ Historiæ Epitome*, Lib. II, cap. iii, PL CXVIII, 823 sq., which outlines the whole story of the three marriages of St. Anne, the main theme of Förster's article. It purports to be Haymo's own comment on the puzzling relationship of the two Jameses to the holy family, but I am uncertain of its authenticity, for I do not know the manuscript history of this work. Ælfric's acquaintance with the passage, if it is genuine, is very probable. (See below, p. 394, n. 2.)

> Maria mater Domini, et Maria mater Jacobi, fratris Domini, et Maria [mater Jacobi] fratris Joannis evangelistæ, sorores fuerent, de diversis patribus genitæ, sed de eodem matre, scilicet Anna. Quæ Anna primo nupsit Joachim, et de eo genuit Mariam matrem Domini. Mortuo Joachim, nupsit Cleophæ, et de eo habuit alteram Mariam, quæ dicitur

in Evangeliis Maria Cleophæ. Porro Cleophas habebat fratrem Joseph, cui filiastram suam beatam Mariam desponsavit, suam vero filiam dedit Alpheo, de qua natus est Jacobus minor, qui et Justus dicitur, frater Domini, et Joseph alius. Mortuo itaque Cleopha, Anna tertio marito nupsit, scilicet Salome, et habuit de eo tertiam Mariam, de qua, desponsata Zebedæo, nati sunt Jacobus major, et Joannes evangelista.

6. *Crist hine (lufode for his) clænan mægðhade.* Cf. *CH* I. 58: '[Crist] hine lufode synderlice; na swa micclum for ðære mæglican sibbe swa for ðære clænnysse his ansundan mægðhades.'

7–9. Cf. *LS* xv. 160–1: 'Se wæs Criste swa leof þæt he hlynode uppan his breoste, / on ðam wæs behydd [eall] se heofonlica wisdom.' Cf. also *Old and New Testament*, 876 sqq.: 'Iohannes . . . began þa feorðan boc be Cristes godcundnysse, . . . and be ðære deopnysse þe him Drihten awreah / þa þa he hlinode on his luflicum breoste, / on þam ðe wæs behydd se heofonlica goldhord.'

8–9. *þæs (wisdomes : : : : : : / þæt he swa mi)hte.* Following *wisdomes*, which seems probable after *þæs*, one expects a word for fountain, source (the most frequent figure in the Latin authors), or possibly a word for treasure such as the *goldhord* above (*in quo sunt omnes thesauri sapientiæ et scientiæ absconditi, Col.* ii. 3). If there is indeed room for only five or six letters, perhaps *æ-wylm* may be considered a likely candidate, but by leaving out the conjectured *swa* at the beginning of the next line one could make room for *goldhord*, or even *wyl-spring*. Alliteration, though allowable, is not here needed to complete the line.

10–16. The following parallels may help to confirm the sense and some of the words:

and ðas feower godspelleras God geswutelode gefyrn
on ðære ealdan áe Ezechihele þam witegan.
He geseah on his gesihðe swylce feower nytenu. . . .
þæs earnes gelicnys belimpð to Iohanne
forðan þe se earn flyhð ealra fugela ufemest
and mæg swyðost starian on þære sunnan leoman.
Swa dyde Iohannes se driht-wurðe writere:
he fleah feor upp, swylce mid earnes fyðerum,
and beheold gleawlice hu he be Gode mihte mærlicost writan. . . .
Nu we habbað gesæd on ðisre sceortnysse
hu God geswutelode þa soðfæstan godspelleras
on þære ealdan áe and eac on þære niwan.

LS xv. 178–80, 197–202, 219–21.

Cf. also *Old and New Testament*, 882 sqq.:

and þas feower godspelleras wæron gefyrn getacnode,
swa Ezechiel hi geseah. . . .
Iohannes, swa swa earn, þa upplican digolnisse
mid his scearpum eagum sceawode georne,
and be Cristes godcundnysse his godspell gesette.

16. *unateorig(endum eagum)*. There seems little doubt of the proper reading here, or that Ælfric's phrase was prompted by Haymo's *irreverberatis oculis*; for the underlying notion of the Latin, that the rays of sight sent forth by the eagle's eyes are not beaten back or blunted by the rays of the sun, is substantially though more vaguely expressed by the *unateorigendum*, 'unwearying, unfailing', in Ælfric. The participle *unateorigende* is recorded by Bosworth–Toller from an Aldhelm-gloss only, but *unateorigendlic* is cited three times from Ælfric's *Catholic Homilies*.

It is always hazardous to credit a particular Latin expositor with the invention of a phrase, but I do not know of an intermediary between Gregory's use of *reverberans* in the passage cited from the *Moralia* and Haymo's *irreverberatis oculis*. The *Præfatio* to Augustine's commentary on John has, indeed, the following sentence: *Unde merito in figura quatuor animalium, aquilæ volanti comparatur: quæ volat altius cæteris avibus, et solis radios irreverberatis aspicit luminibus*. But this *Præfatio*, as the Benedictine editors pointed out, does not occur in the manuscripts of Augustine's work nor in the earliest printed editions. It first appears in print after Erasmus, and seems to be an early modern synthesis of passages from Augustine himself and several other authors. The sentence quoted starts out like Bede and continues with a variation, seemingly, upon Gregory and Haymo. Or did Gregory himself use the ablative absolute in some other passage dealing with the eagle as a type of John? However this may be, Ælfric seems to have had before him not only *irreverberatis oculis* but precisely the surrounding clause that appears in Haymo, for *swa swa se earn sceawað þære sunnan leoman* exactly translates *sicut aquila . . . iubar solis . . . contemplatur*, and *ofer eallum nytenum* renders *præ cunctis animantibus*.

17–26. The contrast between the fourth gospel and the others, the petition of the bishops of Asia, and the three-day fast are presented in *CH* I. 68–70, That passage draws, as does this, upon Bede's homily I. 9, including some details in Bede which are here omitted. It also imitates several passages in Augustine's commentary by prefacing the opening words of John's Gospel, themselves used as climax by Jerome, Augustine, Bede, and Ælfric, with an elaboration concerning the heights to which the evangelist was carried: 'and he æfter ðam fæstene wearð swa miclum mid Godes gaste afylled, þæt he ealle Godes englas, and ealle gesceafta, mid healicum mode oferstah, and mid ðysum wordum þa godspellican gesetnysse ongan.' (Cf. Aug., *In Ioannis Ev.*, *Tract.* I. 5, and especially *Tract.* XXXVI. I.)

28–29, 35–36, 41. At these points in his translation of the gospel Ælfric binds three half-line phrases into a kind of triplet which he himself seems to regard alternatively as a line and a half, to be rendered symmetrical by a fourth half-line, or as a single extra-long line. Thus at lines 28–29 and the repetition at 155–6 he prefixes an introductory half-line, whereas he allows the repetition at 147–8 to stand as a triplet. Similarly, the three phrases at 35–36 and their repetition at 293–4 form a triplet, or, as printed for convenience, a line and a half. The first two phrases are bound by the

repeated *ðeostrum–ðeostru*, the second and third by the alliterating *f*, the
first and third by the repeated *leoht*. I have treated the less obviously
tripletic 41 and its repetition at 310 (which seems to confirm the authenticity of *gecyðnysse*) as a single extra long line. One might regard *ac þæt
he cydde* (which does not alliterate with the preceding half-line) as an
extrametric introduction to the more heavily stressed words that follow,
or one might take the first half-line as an asymmetrical unit poised against
the two closely bound halves that follow. Another conspicuously tripletic
sequence occurs at 39–40 and 304–5, but Ælfric has added another half-
line to complete the gospel verse and restore the usual balance. At lines
301–2, however, he paraphrases the earlier part of the same verse in three
half-lines alliterating on *s* and does not add a fourth half-line. Such variations as these, though comparatively rare, are not without precedent in
Ælfric. Here they seem to have been prompted by Ælfric's desire to do
justice to the original, either by imitating its structure, as in the first verse,
or by finding an economical substitute when some change of structure
was required.

43. *þe on þisne middaneard becymð to menn geboren*. A frequent expression of Ælfric's for being born in the ordinary sense is *cuman to mannum*.
This he applies to the assumption of humanity by Christ himself, as at
XI. 8, *hu he to mannum com on soðre menniscnysse*, and also to the Virgin,
whose birth he regards as entirely normal, at Assmann III. 20: *And heo
wearð acenned, þæt heo com to mannum on ðysum andweardan dæge*. A little
later in the same homily (line 44) he speaks of the birth of saints in general
in the same way, *hu hi to mannum comon*; and in our homily XX. 114, he so
refers to the birth of Hebrews in Egypt. In the present passage, however,
the gospel has led him to use *becymð* with *on þisne middaneard* in order to
translate *venientem in hunc mundum*. In order to make more specific the
notion of being born he adds now a variant expression, *to menn geboren*,
'born as a human being'. This second idiom, with singular *menn* and *to*
in a different sense, is likewise illustrated by itself in Assmann III. 61,
describing how the Saviour, in the sixth age of this world, *wearð to men
geboren*.

56–62. The general sense, probably, was that Augustine had not been
able to learn about anyone who was more at a loss than he himself had
been concerning this holy gospel, on account of the great profundity of
its hidden meaning. But he had nevertheless worked out some of its
meaning by the assistance of God himself (the source of all understanding?), and according to Augustine's revelation Ælfric will write it down
in English (for the benefit of his people?). In the lacuna at 56 one would
expect something like 'h(e ne mihte nanne stuntran)', but there seems to
be too little space, and 'stuntran' may not be altogether appropriate. In
addition to the parallel quoted under *Sources*, from Augustine's Commentary on *John*, Tract. I, there are passages of similar purport in other parts
of the same work, notably in Tract. XXXVI. 5, 6.

162. *syndon*. Here and at two other places (VIII. 197 and XIa. 218)

Ælfric uses this form as an optative (or subjunctive). The singular sȳ or sī is frequent, but there is no example of the traditional plural sȳn. Evidently Ælfric has substituted syndon. It is a natural development, since the optative plural of most verbs in LWS ends in -on in both present and preterite tenses. The same usage occurs in Ælfric's early homily on the Catholic Faith, CH I. 284/15: 'Ne bepæce nan mann hine sylfne, swa þæt he secge oððe gelyfe þæt ðry Godas syndon; oððe ænig had on þære Halgan þrynnysse sy unmihtigra þonne oðer.' The parallel singular sy confirms the subjunctive force of syndon. Both verbs state a supposition contrary to fact. There is another probable example at LS xxv. 312: swylce hi cenran syndon; but the form is not common. (Jost, Anglia LI. 91 n. 1, thought the form in the passage just cited was indicative and constituted an inexplicable exception to the rule that Ælfric's swylce meaning 'as if' governs the subjunctive.) The optatives bēo and bēon have a somewhat wider use and are commoner than sȳ and syndon.

177–82. Ælfric elsewhere quotes the same text: cf. CH I. 286/12–15: 'He is butan hefe, forðon þe he hylt ealle gesceafta butan geswince; and he hi ealle gelogode on þam ðrim ðingum, þæt is on gemete, and on getele, and on hefe.' Also CH II. 586/29–32: 'He getimbrode ða healican heofenan and ealne middaneard, and ealle gesceafta gesette on ðrim ðingum: in mensura, et pondere, et numero; þæt is, on gemete, and on hefe, and on getele.' The English explanation of the Latin in the present passage was evidently much freer and cannot easily be reconstructed from what is given above. Line 177, however, probably agreed in reading 'þrim þingum' at the end.

217. orfe. Since orf is normally a neuter noun, this accusative form is irregular. Probably Ælfric wrote yrfe, the closely related neuter ja-stem, and the scribe substituted orfe because of the orfcynn just preceding. The variant yrfe is stylistically better anyway, since orfcynn is used in connexion with the fultum performed by domestic animals, and the orfe or yrfe applies rather to those that are bred to be eaten.

230, 233. gnættum 7 fleogum . . . hundes lys. According to the Vulgate the third and fourth plagues of Egypt (Ex. viii. 16–24) consisted of some kind of stinging insect called sciniphes (ciniphes, cinifex) and various kinds of flies, muscæ. The Authorized Version has lice and flies respectively, but this was not the interpretation in Ælfric's time. Bede's commentary on Exodus interprets cinifex as a small winged insect that stings, and adds, by way of supplement to the muscæ of the fourth plague, the cinomia or dog-fly, saying: 'Septuaginta Interpretes cinomiam, id est, muscam caninam posuerunt.' (Migne, PL xci. 302.) In fact the Septuagint has κυνόμυιαν, and Bede took his information directly from Isidore's Quæstiones in Vet. Test., In Exod. viii (Migne, PL lxxxiii. 292 sq.). Ælfric seems to follow these authorities here and elsewhere. Here his gnættum and fleogum correspond to the Vulgate's sciniphes and muscæ respectively, and the hundes lys to the cinomiæ of the Septuagint. In the passage from the Catholic Homilies quoted in the note on lines 240–4 below, he mentions only the *gnættas* and the *hundes lys*. On the other hand the translation of *Exodus* in *The Old English Heptateuch* (which is probably not by Ælfric) very naturally follows the Vulgate only, having *gnættas* for the third plague, *fleogena cynn* for the fourth, and no mention of dog-lice.

233. *mæðleasum*. For *mæðlēas*, 'lacking measure', hence 'greedy, rapacious', see the two quotations from Ælfric in BT and BTS.

240-4. Cf. *CH* II. 192/19-25: 'Moyses, ðurh Godes mihte, awende eal heora wæter to readum blode, and hé afylde eal heora land mid froggon, and siððan mid gnættum, eft mid hundes lusum, ða flugon into heora muðe and heora næsðyrlum; and se Ælmihtiga ðone módigan cyning mid þam eaðelicum gesceaftum swa geswencte, seðe mihte hine mid wildum berum and leonum gewyldan, gif he swa wolde.'

267-74. This excursion into the miracles wrought by nature without human interference seems to be intended to put the Egyptian magicians in their place as masters of a limited and purely natural magic. In homily IV. 142, Ælfric says that the magicians were trying to make *gnættas* when they were thwarted by the finger of God. (As explained in the note on line 230 above, he takes the *sciniphes* of *Exodus* viii. 16 as *gnættas*, so that he is properly alluding to the third plague.) Hence the miraculous generation of bees, wasps, and hornets out of decaying flesh (as reported by Isidore) and of worms out of spoiled fruit has an obvious relevance. Behind Ælfric's abrupt comment may well be the long discussion of the Egyptian magicians in Augustine's *De Trinitate*, Lib. III, cap. vii–ix. In chapter viii Augustine says, *Solus Deus creat etiam illa quæ magicis artibus trans-formantur* (Migne, *PL* XLII. 875), and in chapter ix we read,

Hoc est videre, quam multi homines noverunt, ex quibus herbis, aut carnibus, aut quarumcumque rerum quibuslibet succis aut humoribus, . . . quæ animalia nasci soleant: quorum se quis tam demens audeat dicere creatorem? Quid ergo mirum, si quemadmodum potest nosse quilibet nequissimus homo, unde illi vel illi vermes muscæque nas-cantur; ita mali angeli pro subtilitate sui sensus in occultioribus ele-mentorum seminibus norunt, unde ranæ serpentesque nascantur, et hæc per certas et notas temperationum opportunitates occultis motibus adhibendo faciunt creari, non creant? (Ibid. 878.)

270. *acende*. The standard form for the past participle, nom. pl., in the Ælfric manuscripts is *acennede*.

281. *hi synd on þam cræfte*, 'they exist in the artist's conception'. This odd use of *cræft*, which is not exactly paralleled in any of the citations of BT, is obviously prompted by Augustine's use of *in arte* as opposed to *in opere* in the passage quoted as a source. Augustine's use seems to be a slight extension of the ordinary meaning of *ars*, 'theory', to something a little closer to a mental image or idea. (For a recent succinct statement of Augustine's debt to Plotinus and his use of the Platonic Ideas, see David Knowles, *The Evolution of Medieval Thought*, Longmans, London, 1962, p. 39.)

367–9. Cf. the translation of the same verse (*Exod.* vii. 1) in *O.E. Hept.*, p. 228: 'and Drihten cwæð to Moyse: Nu ic gesette þe Pharaone to Gode, and Aaron þin broðor byð ðin witega.' The language is almost exactly the same, especially if we include the partial repetition in line 371, though the dative *Pharaone*, which is standard in the translation of *Exodus*, is at variance with the dative *Pharao* (*Farao*) in *CH* II. 192/9, 11, and our homily IV. 140. Jost, in *Anglia*, LI (1927), 12 sqq., gave strong reasons for not accepting *Exodus* as Ælfric's translation. It is not clear, however, whether Ælfric was consistent in his declension of *Pharao*, for in his un-doubted compositions the scribes give the genitive in two forms: *Pharaoes* (*Faraoes*) in xx. 3, 109 (MSS. P and X^d); *Pharaones* in *CH* I. 346/3, in the homily on *Judges*, Prol., 2 (*O.E. Hept.*, 400, according to both MSS., our P and Z), and *Old and New Testament*, 322, 356 (according to both MSS., our P and Z).

386–90. The same idea is stated a little differently in Ælfric's second Christmas homily, *CH* II. 6/24–27:

He wæs ancenned mid his Fæder on heofonum; ða nolde he
ana beon, ac wolde habban gebroðru, and com to us, forði
þæt he wolde us to his rice gebringan, þær we to gesceapene
wæron.

The lyrical and rhetorical heightening of the second version is obvious.

430–3. Ælfric's account of the transfiguration at *CH* II. 242/4–7 is somewhat similar in expression:

Moyses and Elias eac swilce sædon his ðrowunge on ær uppon anre
dune ðe se Hælend astah mid ðrim leorningcnihtum, and his ansyn
ætforan him eal scean swa swa sunne, and his gewæda scinon on snawes
hwitnysse.

445. This line, with the conjectured *on þam me*, gives the speech in precisely the same form as *CH* II. 242/9–10, whereas at *CH* I. 104/23 we find simply *ðe me*, the form that Ælfric chooses for the parallel speech at *Matth.* iii. 17, both here in line 440 and at *CH* II. 42 and 62. The *on þam* is probably influenced by the Latin *in quo*.

II

FERIA VI IN PRIMA EBDOMADA
QUADRAGESIMÆ

Ioan. v. 1–15

I

THIS homily, on the miracle at the pool of Bethesda, is the first
of a series of five for Fridays in Lent which was once to be found
in two of the surviving manuscripts, F and H. The series is still
intact in F (CCCC 162), where, however, its character is not evident, since it has been interspersed with homilies for the inter-
vening Sundays. In H (Cotton Vitellius C. v) it was kept together,
constituting the first five items in a section appended to the main
volume soon after its completion. There were formerly six of these
appended items, according to the table of contents made a few
years afterwards and still partially legible, but at some period
before Wanley examined the volume it had lost some leaves at the
end. The text now ends abruptly just before the conclusion of
the fourth item. The unidentfied sixth, a bishop's *Sermo* according to the fragmentary title in the table (above, p. 27), was certainly not a part of the series and very likely not by Ælfric. The
four Friday homilies that remain have been severely damaged by
the Cottonian fire of 1731.

All five of the Friday homilies are in Ælfric's alliterative style,
and there is no reason to question his authorship. The fifth, indeed,
was attributed to him long ago somewhat tentatively by Dietrich
and then firmly by Assmann, who edited it from its three surviving
manuscripts (our F, N, and O) as homily v in his collection.

The other four homilies are here presented as numbers II, III,
V, and VI. Except for a part of VI that turns up in the twelfth-
century MS. B and was printed by Belfour, these four have not
previously been edited. Their occurrence, along with Assmann v,
as a set in the appendix of H, and their presence in F suggest that
Ælfric issued them together at a fairly early date, perhaps, as

Clemoes has suggested (*Chronology*, p. 221), even before he had completed the *Lives of Saints*. The interpolation in VI belongs, of course, to a later period.[1]

By the term 'series' I mean only a group set apart by its assignment to a particular set of days, the five consecutive Fridays of Lent that precede Good Friday. Ælfric accepted the gospel texts assigned to these days and consulted the best authorities he could find for each of them. I am not aware that he was attempting to develop a carefully related set of themes. Since, however, each homily has some relevance to the season, there are recurrent themes and some sense of progression. The first brings out several aspects of Lent and refers here and there explicitly to the central themes, as an introductory homily should do. The second deals with a parable that points directly to the passion and casts reproach on the unbelieving Jews. The third, on the Samaritan woman, broadens the themes of salvation and of the coming passion besides introducing the Gentiles. In the fourth, on Lazarus, and the fifth (Assmann's V) on the Pharisees, besides all else there is the imminence of the passion in the stress laid on the plots that the Jews are forming against Jesus.

Of the two codices in which all four of the Friday homilies here edited are represented, H had originally a somewhat better text than F. But H has lost the conclusion of the fourth, homily VI, and all its remaining leaves in this section (the appendix) have been more severely damaged by the fire than elsewhere. In order to represent its worth and condition as fairly as possible yet not encumber the text of every homily with editorial signs I have hit upon the compromise described in the headnotes to the apparatus of homilies II and III. The composite text of homily II, where H is used as the basis and most of the bracketed portions are from F, results in a conflict of two systems of spelling, but it is a very minor one, for the two manuscripts are nearly contemporary and dialectally similar. In the interpolation of homily VI, for most of which H has only the partial support of the late twelfth-century MS. B, serious conflicts have been avoided by normalizing the bracketed insertions from B.

There is very little evidence for the textual relations of the manuscripts of these homilies. The first three have survived only in F and H, and we must assume that this part of H, the appendix, has

---

[1] See the descriptions of F and H in the Introduction.

a different textual history from the rest of the volume, except where, as in a part of homily VI, we are dealing with the work of the interpolator. In homily II. 196–7, and V. 29, 40, 88, as pointed out in the notes and the introduction to V, both manuscripts seem to be united in error; yet the relationship may not have been very close. In homily VI as originally written, where a third manuscript, C, can be compared, C and F appear to be closer to each other than to H. The slender evidence for this is discussed in the introduction to VI.

II

In homily II Ælfric's chief guide for the interpretation of the gospel is Augustine, to whom he refers in line 61: specifically, the commentary *In Ioannis Evangelium, Tractatus* XVII, on *John* V. 1–15. He does not seem to have made use of either of two additional sermons by Augustine on the same text (Migne, *PL* XXXVIII. 686 sqq. and 688 sqq.). But many of Ælfric's phrases and a few ideas that do not occur in Augustine are to be found in Alcuin's exposition of the text in his *Commentaria in S. Ioannis Evangelium.*[1] Ælfric may have turned, not to the complete commentary, but to Haymo's homiliary, in which the homily for Friday in the first week of Lent is precisely the portion of Alcuin's commentary that deals with *John* V. 1–15.[2]

Ælfric may have been familiar with the main source behind Alcuin, whose commentary as a whole is largely a compilation from the writings of Augustine, Gregory, and Bede. In the portion here under consideration he incorporated verbatim about two-thirds of Bede's homily on *John* V. 1–18, numbered I. 23 in Hurst's edition, and summarized other parts of it. But if Ælfric recognized Bede in Alcuin he did not turn to him directly, or at least left no sign of having done so. At no point does he make precise use of anything that Alcuin has omitted, whereas at two points (220–31 and 276–86) he seems indebted to passages in Alcuin that are free abridgements of Bede in distinctly different language. For this reason the *Commentaria* is cited throughout in preference to the homily, but

---

[1] On this work and its relation to the pseudo-Bede *Expositio* of the fourth gospel see the discussion of the sources in the Introduction, p. 161.

[2] *Hom. XXXIII de Tempore, PL* CXVIII. I think it probable that Ælfric's starting-point for the series of homilies for Fridays in Lent was Haymo's homiliary, but all five are interpolations, four from Alcuin's commentary, one from an anonymous commentary on *Matthew*. See Introduction, p. 157, notes 1 and 2, and pp. 160–1.

where the two are in exact or substantial verbal agreement the heading is 'Alcuin (Bede)' rather than simply 'Alcuin'.

There is also an anonymous homily for the same Friday, on the the same gospel-text, in Migne's edition of the homiliary of Paulus Diaconus.[1] This is a free rewriting of Alcuin, with several additional passages and some omissions. It corresponds at several points to passages that are quoted below from Alcuin; but its *additional* matter has left no trace in Ælfric, and it *omits* certain passages in Alcuin that Ælfric uses. Hence I have not included it as a source. Indeed, there is reason to doubt whether Ælfric had seen any of the homilies for the first four Fridays in Lent that appear in the Migne edition, since they were not a part of the original collection of Paulus, and it has not yet been ascertained at what time, or how generally, they were added to the collection.[2]

A sentence from Bede's commentary on *Luke* is quoted for lines 84–90.

[1] *Hom. LXXVII, PL* xcv. 1228–33. Now attributed to Hericus of Auxerre. See above, p. 159, n. 2.

[2] On the importance of the homiliary for Ælfric and its original contents, see Introduction, pp. 156–61. Some very slight correspondences with Ælfric in the homilies for the second and fourth Fridays, at points where the other sources cited are blank, are mentioned in the introductions to III and VI below.

(FERIA VI IN PRIMA EBDOMADA
QUADRAGESIMÆ

Ðis spel gebyra ð on Frige-dæg on þære forman Lenctenwucan

EVVANGELIUM: *Erat dies festus Iudæorum, et reliqua*

Men þa leofostan, us lyst) nu eow secgan
be þam halg(a)n godspelle (þe ge gehyrdon nu ræd)an,
þæt ge beon þe geleaffulran þu(r)h þa boc(lican lare,
and þe a)nrædran on eowrum Drihtne.
Se godspellere (Iohannes, þe w)æs Godes dyrling,   5
Cristes moddrian sunu, sæde on (þære Crist)es bec
þæt ure Hælend Crist, þá þá hé her on life wæs
lic(hamlice wu)nigende, þa wolde hé faran
on sumne symbeldæg soþli(ce to Hie)rusalem.
On þære byrig wæs gehæfd, gehende þam temple,   10
(an wundo)rlic wæterscipe, Bethsaida gehaten;
þone wæterscipe be(worhte s)e wisa cyning Salomon
mid fif porticon fæstum weorc(stanum,
and) man on þa ealdan wisan þa offrunga þær þwoh
þe (man offr)ode symle on Salomones temple,   15

Text based on H (Cotton Vitellius C. v), ff. 236ᵛ, 239–42ᵛ. (Ff. 237–8 are mis-
bound.) Collated with F (CCCC 162), pp. 227–37. H has been given precedence
because it had originally a slightly fuller and better text than F, but it has suffered
serious loss from the fire of 1731. Round brackets enclose portions of the text
which are altogether missing in it or no longer legible. These portions have been
supplied, at beginning and end, from Wanley's *Catalogus* (p. 210), which antedates the fire; everywhere else, from F.

---

*Sup.: all three lines as in H according to Wanley; second line om. F; third line
merely* Erat dies festus *F.*
1–4 *entire sentence om. F; gaps in H supplied from Wanley.*
6 modrian *F*   7 þæt ure hælend crist] *om. F.*   8 wuniende *F.*
9 sumne symbeldæg] *sic both MSS. originally; alt. to* sumum symbeldæge *H.*
12 kyning *F.*   13 porticum *F.*   14 *first* þa] *om. F*   15 symble *F.*

SOURCES. 7–13 [*Ioan. v. 1*] Post hæc erat dies festus Iudæorum, et ascendit
Iesus Ierosolymam.
[*2*] Est autem Ierosolymis probatica piscina quæ cognominatur Hebraice
Bethsaida, quinque porticus habens.
14–16 [*Alcuin's Commentaria (from Bede's hom.)*] Vulgo autem *probatica*, id
est, pecualis piscina fertur appellata, quod in ea sacerdotes hostias lavare con-
sueverint.

British Museum MS. Cotton Vitellius C. v, f. 236v. The imperfect beginning of homily II in the main hand of the appendix.

Gode to wyrþmynte, on (þære Iudei)scra wisan.

On þam wæterscipe wurdon wundra gelo(me
þurh þone) ælmihtigan God, swa þæt hé his engel asende
of heofon(licum þrymme, and he) þæt wæter styrode
binnan þam porticum be Godes (dihte gelome,   20
and swa hwilc) untrum man swá cóme into þam wætere
(æfter þæs engles styrun)ge, se wearþ sona hal
fram swa hwilcere (untrumnysse swa he wæ)re gehæfd.

þær lagon þa forþi on þam fore(sædum porticum
fela) untrumra manna mislice gebrocode,   25
blin(dra and healtra, and on ha)ndum alefode,
andbidigende þære styrunge (þurh þæs engles toc)yme.

þær læg þa sum beddryda andbidigende (þæs ylcan,
eahta and þ)rittig wintra on his untrumnysse.

Ða þa se (Hælend þider com, swa) swa we ær sædon,   30
and wiste be þam men þæt he wæs (lange untrum,

16 wurðmynte *F.*   þære] *sic F.*   23 hwilcre *F.*   26 alefode] *alt. to*
alæmode *F.*   27, 28 anbidigende *F.*   28 bedryda *F.*   30 þa ðe *F.*
31 menn *F.*

17-58 [*Ioan. v. 4*] Angelus autem Domini descendebat secundum tempus in
piscinam: et movebatur aqua [*v. l.* movebat aquam]. Et qui prior descendisset
[*v. l.* quicumque prius descenderet] in piscinam post motionem aquæ, sanus
fiebat a quacumque detinebatur infirmitate.

[*3*] In his iacebat multitudo magna languentium, cæcorum, claudorum,
aridorum, expectantium aquæ motum.

[*5*] Erat autem quidam homo ibi triginta et octo annos habens in infirmitate
sua. [*Some MSS. omit* habens.]

[*6*] Hunc cum vidisset Iesus iacentem, et cognovisset quia iam multum tempus haberet, dicit ei: Vis sanus fieri?

[*7*] Respondit ei languidus: Domine, hominem non habeo, ut cum turbata
fuerit aqua, mittat me in piscinam: dum venio enim ego, alius ante me descendit.

[*8*] Dicit ei Iesus: Surge, tolle grabatum tuum, et ambula.

[*9*] Et statim sanus factus est homo ille: et sustulit grabatum suum, et am-
bulabat. Erat autem sabbatum in die illo.

[*10*] Dicebant ergo Iudæi illi, qui sanatus fuerat: Sabbatum est, non licet tibi
tollere grabatum tuum.

[*11*] Respondit eis: Qui me sanum fecit, ille mihi dixit: Tolle grabatum tuum,
et ambula.

[*12*] Interrogaverunt ergo eum: Quis est ille homo, qui dixit tibi, Tolle
grabatum tuum, et ambula?

[*13*] Is autem, qui sanus fuerat effectus, nesciebat quis esset. Iesus enim
declinavit a turba constituta in loco.

[*14*] Postea invenit eum Iesus in templo, et dixit illi: Ecce sanus factus es:
iam noli peccare, ne deterius tibi aliquid contingat.

[*15*] Abiit ille homo, et nunciavit Iudæis quia Iesus esset, qui fecit eum
sanum.

þa cwæð he) to þam earman, Wylt þu beon hal?
*(Se lama him andwyrde, La leof,   *f. 239
ic næbbe nænne mannan þe) mage me
int(o þam wæterscipe don æfter þære styrunge,   35
and) þonne ic earming (þyder cume,
þonne cymð sum oðer ma)n ǽr into þam wætere.
Þa cwæþ (se Hælend him to, Aris) hal of ðam bedde,
and ber þin legerbed (gangende heonon.)
Se man þa sona mihtiglice wearð gehæl(ed,   40
and bær his leger)bed on his bæce, and eode.
Hit wæs þa Sæternes-(dæg þa þis ge)worden wæs;
þone dæg wurþodon þa Iudeiscan (mid freolse,)
æfter Moyses ǽ, and hí to þam men cwædon
þe ðær (gehæled) wæs, Hit is halig resten-dæg;   45
ne most ðu styrigan (þine bed)dinge.
Se man him andwyrde anrædlice and cw(æð,
Se ðe) mé gehælde, hé het me niman
min bed and gán; and hi (ongun)non hine axian,
Hwæt is se man þe het þe niman (þin bed) and gán?   50
and se þe þær gehæled wæs nyste hwæt se Hæl(end wæs,
and se) Hælend þa eode of þære meniu.
Syþðan eft se (Hælend ge)seah þone mann
binnan þam temple, and him (bebead þas) word:
Efne nu þu eart gehæled, heald (þe nu heonon forð,)   55
þæt þu ne syngie, þy læs þe þe sum þing
(wyrse gelimpe; and se) man þa eode,
and sæde þam Iudeiscum (þæt 'se' Hælend hine gehælde.)
    We habbað nú gesæd sceortlice þis god(spel
anfealdum and)gite, and we eac willað eow secgan   60
þæt gast(lice andgyt, æfter) Agustinus trahtnunge,
sceortlice (swaþeah, þæt ge ne beon) gehefegode.

---

32 wilt *F.*   38 Aris] *no cap. F.*   39 gangende] *alt. to* and gang *F*; *H has*
traces of an initial g.   42 Hyt *F.*   43 wurðedon *F.*   44 menn
(*over line*) *F.*   45 Hit] *no cap. in MSS.*; hyt *F.*   ys *F.*   ræste(n)-dæg
(n *erased*) *F.*   46 styrian *F.*   47 andwyrde (*over line*) *F.*   49 *second*
and] *om. F.*   52 þa eode] eode þa *F.*   mænigo *F.*   53 mann] mann(an)
H, last two letters erased; man *F.*   60 andgyte *F.*   wyllað *F.*   61 *before*
agustinus, *at end of a line,* sanctus *in a different though contemporary hand F.*

---

62 [*Though the sentiment is frequent in Ælfric, cf. Alcuin's Commentaria (from*
Bede's hom.):] Sed utriusque nobis sunt breviter exponenda mysteria, ne prolixæ
lectionis prolixa quoque explanatio cuiquam forte gravior existat.

Se wæterscipe wæs b(eworht mid fif porticum,)
and hæfde getacnunge, swa swa se tr(ahtnere segð,
Iudeisces) folces, þe wæs befangen þa   65
mid (fif ǽlicum bocum, þe Moy)ses him sette
be Godes sylfes* (dihte, þæt hi singian ne sceoldon.   * Last word
                                                          visible,
On þam porticum lagon alefode and adlige,   f. 239.
blinde and healte, and on handum forscrunce[n]e.

Swa wæron þa Iudei wanhale on mode,   70
and on heora geleafan alefode) *forþearle,   * First word
                                                         visible,
for þ(am ðe Moysæs ǽ ne mihte hi geriht)wisian,   f. 239ᵛ.
oþþæt Crist sylf cóm (cuðlice to mannum,
and us gerih)tlæhte mid geleafan and gife,
and eac (þa Iudeiscan þe on hi)ne gelyfdon.   75
þá beoþ blinde on mode þe ne (magon geseon)
þæs geleafan leoht, þeah hí locion brade;
and (þa beoð heal)te on heortan þe þæs Hælendes beboda
unriht(lice farend)e ne gefyllað mid weorcum;
and þá beoþ deafe þé (Drihtnes) hæsum   80
nellað gehyrsumian, þeah þé hí þa gehyron.
(Se hæfð) forscruncene hand þé næfð mildheortnysse (weorc,
and) biþ únwæstmbære, and æfre fordrugod.

67 hi singian] *altered to* hy syngian *F.*   69 forscruncenne *F.*   74 gyfe *F.*
77 locian *F.*   78 bebodu *F.*   83 byð *F.*   fordruwod *F.*

63–67 [*Augustine, In Ioan. Ev., Tract. xvii*] Piscina illa et aqua illa populum
mihi videtur significasse Iudæorum. . . . Aqua ergo illa, id est populus ille,
quinque libris Moysi, tanquam quinque porticibus claudebatur. [*Bede's restatement, in Alcuin, supplies Ælfric's final clause*:] Probatica piscina, quæ quinque
porticibus cingebatur, populus est Iudæorum, legis undique custodia, ne peccare debeat, munitus.

68–75 [*Alcuin (Bede)*] Tales in quinque porticibus iacebant, sed non nisi in
piscina[m] angelo veniente sanabantur, quia *per legem cognitio peccati, gratia
autem remissionis non nisi per Iesum Christum facta est* (*Rom. iii. 20 sqq.*). . . .
Gratia autem Evangelii . . . per fidem ac mysterium Dominicæ passionis sanat
omnes languores iniquitatum nostrarum, a quibus in lege Moysi non potuimus
iustificari.

76–83 [*Alcuin (Bede)*] *Cæci* erant, qui necdum perfectum fidei lumen habebant: *claudi* erant, qui bona, quæ noverant, operandi gressibus implere nequi-
bant: *aridi*, qui quamlibet oculum scientiæ habentes, pinguedine tamen spei et
dilectiones egebant. [*Ælfric's inclusion of the deaf was probably suggested by the
preceding sentence in Bede and Alcuin*] . . . catervas quæ, legis verba audientes,
suis se hanc viribus implere non posse dolebant. [*Ælfric's independent treatment
of the* aridi *springs from his interpretation of the passage from Luke immediately
below. Neither Augustine nor Alcuin alludes to it.*]

Be swilcum (cwæð se Hæ)lend on his halgan godspelle,
þá þá sum lama (læg þær þæ)r hé lærde þæt folc: 85
Astrece þine hand; and he hál wearð (sona,
and astr)ehte his swyþran, þe forsearod wæs oþ þæt.
Swilce (he wære gemán)od mid þam mihtigan wundre,
astrece þine (hand, þe ær wæs unc)ystig,
to ælmysdædum earmum þear(fum.   90
Swilce wanhal)e lagon wiðinnan þam porticon,
ac (se ælmihtiga Hælend þ)e of heofenum astah
mancyn to (alysanne mihte hi g)ehælan
on sawle and on lichaman, þurh (his soðan gyfe.
Hys) nama is Hælend, for þan þe he gehælþ (his folc,   95
swa swa se eng)el cwæþ be him, ær þan þe hé acenned (wære:
He gehælþ hys fol)c fram heora synnum.
Micele (mare wundor is þæt he w)olde beon mann

84 his] *om. F.*   87 hys *F.*   88 Swilce] *Both MSS. capitalize.*
92 heofonum *F.*   96 ðam *F.*

84–90 [*Luc. vi. 6–10*] Factum est autem et in alio sabbato, ut intraret in synagogam, et doceret. Et erat ibi homo, et manus eius dextra erat arida. ... Et circumspectis omnibus dixit homini: Extende manum tuam. Et extendit: et restituta est manus eius.

[*Cf. Bede, In Luc. vi. 10*] Sananda manus arida iubetur extendi, quia infructuosæ debilitas animæ nullo melius ordine quam eleemosynarum largitate curatur.

91 [*Alcuin (Bede)*] Tales in quinque porticibus iacebant.

91–94 [*Augustine*] Ingressus est locum ubi iacebat magna multitudo languentium . . . ; et cum esset medicus et animarum et corporum, et qui venisset sanare omnes animas crediturorum, de illis languentibus unum elegit quem sanaret. [*Ælfric develops the concession, deferring the main clause.*]

95–97 [*Not in immediate sources. The allusion is to Matth. i. 21, part of which line 97 translates:*] Et vocabis nomen eius Iesum: ipse enim salvum faciet populum suum a peccatis eorum.

98–114 [*Augustine, with different order and emphasis*] Magis gaudere quam mirari debemus, quia Dominus noster et salvator Iesus Christus homo factus est, quam quod divina inter homines Deus fecit. Plus est enim ad salutem nostram quod factus est propter homines, quam quod fecit inter homines: et plus est quod vitia sanavit animarum, quam quod sanavit languores corporum morituriorum. . . . Corporum enim salus quæ vera exspectatur a Domino erit in fine in resurrectione mortuorum: tunc quod vivet, non morietur; tunc quod sanabitur, non ægrotabit; tunc quod satiabitur, non esuriet aut sitiet; tunc quod renovabitur, non veterascet. Nunc vero in illis factis Domini et salvatoris nostri Iesu Christi, et cæcorum aperti oculi, morte clausi sunt; et paralyticorum membra constricta, morte dissoluta sunt; et quidquid sanatum est temporaliter in membris mortalibus, in fine defecit: anima vero quae credidit, ad vitam æternam transitum fecit. [*Ælfric's distinction between visible and invisible miracles was probably suggested by the passage directly below.*]

on þisum life, (and alysan us þurh hine,
þ)onne þa wundra wæron þe he worh(te betwux mannum; 100
and selran) us wæron þa ungesewenlican *(wundra, *f. 240
þurh þa he adwæs'c'te þa dyrnan leahtras
urra sawla, þonne þa gesewenlican wundra,
þurh þa ðe wæron gehæ)lede þa þe eft swulton.

(Witodlice seo sawul þe fram) synnum bið gehæled, 105
and on gel(eafan þurhwunað, færð of) þisum life to Gode;
and se brosnigenda l(ichama, þeah þe) he beo gehæled,
bið mid deaþe fornumen (and to duste) awend.

Hé bið swáþeah gehæled to ansundre (hæle 'eft')
on Domes-dæg, þonne hé of deaþe arist, 110
and syþ(ðan ne swylt,) ne seoc ne gewyrð,
ne him hingrian ne mæg, n(e him þurst) ne deraþ,
ne he ne forealdað, ac bið ece syþþan,
(on sawle) and on lichaman, orsorh deaþes.

On þam wætersci(pe wæron) twá wundorlice mihta, 115
an þurh þone engel, oþer (þurh þo)ne Hælend.
Æfter þæs engles styrunge eode (in se ðe) mihte,
and wæs sona gehæled fram his seocnysse,
(and se þe) syþþan cóm swanc on idel,
for þan þe se eng(el getacno)de ures Hælendes tocyme, 120
se þe on his (tocyme cydde) his mihte,
and mid wundrum astyrode (þæt Iudeisce folc,
swa) þæt hi andodon ongean his lare,
oþþæt h(i syrwdon hu hi hyne) beswicon.

An wæs gehæled æfter þ(æs engles tocyme, 125
and æn)ne gehælde se Hæle'n'd on his tocy(me,

---

99 þysum F. 100 wundra] om. F. 104 þurh þa ðe] sic F, probably
correct; see note. 105, 108, 109 byð F. 110 dæg'e' F. 120 þe] om. F.

115–16 [Alcuin (Bede)] Duo pariter miracula humanæ sanitatis leguntur,
unum invisibiliter per angelicam administrationem, alterum per dominicam
præsentiam visibiliter exhibitum.

117–24 [Augustine] Post aquam turbatam mittebat se unus qui poterat, et
sanabatur solus: post illum quisquis se mitteret, frustra faceret. Quid sibi ergo
hoc vult, nisi quia venit unus Christus ad populum Iudæorum; et faciendo
magna, docendo utilia, turbavit peccatores, turbavit aquam præsentia sua, et
excitavit ad passionem suam?

125–9 [Augustine] Ibi sanabatur unus, significans unitatem; postea quisquis
veniret, non sanabatur: quia quisquis præter unitatem fuerit, sanari non poterit.
[Augustine proceeds to the second miracle, but Ælfric's phrasing is better explained

for ðære annysse) ures geleafan;
and swá hwá swá bið bu(ton þære annysse)
Cristes gelaþunge, ne becymþ ðam n(án hǽl.

þurh þæs wæ)teres styrunge wæs eac getacno(d   130
þæs Hælendes þrowung,) þurh þá hæl becom
eallum m(ancynne þe on anum) geleafan
Criste gehyrsum(iað mid haligre drohtnun)ge.

Ænne hé gehælde þa* (of eallum þam untrumum,   * Last word
se ðe mid anum worde eaðelice mihte   visible,
                                                          f. 240.
hi ealle gehælan; ac he wolde swiþor   136
þurh þæt an wundor awreccan h[e]ora mod,
and heora sawla onlihtan þurh þæt) *syllice tacn.   * First word
                                                      visible,
(Eahta and þrittig wintra wunode se) bedryda   f. 240ᵛ.
on þam legerbedde, (anbidigende his hæle,   140
oð)þæt Crist sylf cóm, þe sceortlice b(eleac
ealle halige b)ec on twam bebodum:
þæt is, þæt ðu lufige and mi(d geleafan wurði)ge
þone ælmihtigan Drihten mid ealre þin(re heortan,)
and syþþan þinne nextan swá swa þe sylfne.   145
Lege (þas twa beb)oda to þam twam læs feowertigum
þæs langsu(man legere)s þæs laman beddrydan,

128 byð F.   137 heeora F.   138 tacen F.   145 necstan F.
147 bedrydan F.

---

by the restatement in Alcuin (Bede):] In [secundo miraculo] etiam ipso unus commendatur sanatus, . . . ut [Salvator] doceret, præter unitatem catholicæ fidei
nullum cuilibet locum patere salutis.

130–3 [Alcuin (Bede)] Motus ergo aquae passionem Domini . . . insinuat.
Et . . . per eandem passionem redempti sunt credentes. [Cf. also the quotation
from Augustine at lines 117–24.]

134–8 [Augustine] Tot iacebant, et unus curatus est, cum posset uno verbo
omnes erigere. Quid ergo intelligendum est, nisi quia potestas illa et bonitas illa
magis agebat quid animæ in factis eius pro salute sempiterna intelligerent, quam
quid pro temporali salute corpora mererentur?

139–50 [Augustine] Numerum triginta octo annorum in illo languido volo
exponere. . . . Charitas implet Legem. Ad plenitudinem Legis in omnibus
operibus pertinent quadragenarius numerus: in charitate autem duo præcepta
nobis commendantur . . .: Diliges Dominum Deum tuum ex toto corde tuo, et ex
tota anima tua, et ex tota mente tua; et, Diliges proximum tuum tanquam teipsum.
In his duobus præceptis tota Lex pendet et Prophetæ (Matth. xxii. 37 ff.). . . . Si
ergo quadragenarius numerus habet perfectionem Legis et Lex non impletur
nisi in gemino præcepto charitatis, quid miraris quia languebat qui ad quadraginta, duo minus habebat? [Alcuin (Bede)] A qua nimirum perfectione duo
minus habet, qui a Dei et proximi dilectione, quam legis pariter et Evangelii
scriptura commendat, vacuus incedit.

þonne bið þær fullice (feowertig-g)etel.
Fram þære fulfremednysse færð se man (æmptig,
se ðe) næfð þá soþan lufe his Scippendes and manna.   150
Soþ(lice þis gete)l wæs gesett gefyrn,
þa þa Moyses fæste feowertig (daga,
and Gode)s ǽ sette be Godes sylfes dihte;
and Helias se witiga (eall swa lange) fæste,
on þam wæs seo witegung witodlice getacnod;   155
(ac hi ne mihton) þurh hí sylfe swylc fæsten þurhteon,
ac (him sealde þa mihte) se þe mæg ealle þing.
Eft þa ure Hæ(lend on hys andweardnys)se fæste
feowertig daga, þurh his (agenne fultum;
þurh þ)one wæron getacnode þa towerdan (godspell   160
þe he sylf gefad)ode þurh his feower godspelleras,
(mannum to lare and to) geleafan trymminge.
Ðis wæs se (ordfruma ures Lenc)tenes,
and þus gegrundweallod þurh (God sylfne ær,
and us is t)o healdenne forþi þæt halige fæsten   165
(þyssere tide, swa us tæcð u)re scrift.
    Nu is oþer fæsten (us eac to healdenne,
swa sw)a se apostol Paulus on his (pistole awrat,
þæt we us forha)bbon fram arleasnysse
and fram *(yfelum lustum þysre worulde,   *f. 241
and syferlice lybban symble) gemetlice,   171
(rihtlice and arfæstlice, anbidigend[e] edleanes

148 -getæl F.   149 mann F.   150 hys F.   153 gesette F.
154 elias F.   witega F.   155 witudlice F.   156 swilc F.   157 After
þing, a later hand adds don F.   160 toweardan F.   162 tryminge F.
165 forðy F.   172 anbidigendum F.

151–66 [Augustine] Quadragenarius numerus sacratus nobis in quadam perfectione commendatur . . .: testantur sæpissime divinæ Scripturæ. . . . Nam et
Moyses quadraginta diebus ieiunavit (Exod. xxxiv. 28), et Elias totidem (III
Reg. xix. 8), et ipse Dominus noster et salvator Iesus Christus hunc ieiunii
numerum implevit (Matth. iv. 2). Per Moysen significatur Lex, per Eliam
significatur Prophetæ, per Dominum significatur Evangelium. . . . Sive ergo in
Lege, sive in Prophetis, sive in Evangelio, quadragenarius numerus nobis in
ieiunio commendatur.

167–76 [Augustine] Ieiunium autem magnum et generale est, abstinere ab
iniquitatibus et illicitis voluptatibus sæculi quod est perfectum ieiunium: ut
abnegantes impietatem et sæculares cupiditates, temperanter, et iuste, et pie vivamus
in hoc sæculo. Huic ieiunio quam mercedem addit Apostolus? Sequitur, et dicit:
Exspectantes illam beatam spem, et manifestationem gloriæ beati Dei, et salvatoris
nostri Iesu Christi (Tit. ii. 12, 13).

þæ)s eadigan hihtes ur(es Hælendes tocymes,
on þam we under)foð þæt ece lif mid him,
gif we nu gehyr(sumiað his hæsum) mid weorcum,   175
and þá þé hine forseoð he (besencð on helle-)grund.

þis fæsten ǽr Eastran wé fæstað m(id geswince,)
and wé freolslice syþþan fiftig daga lybbað,
oþ þ(a halgan) Pentecosten þe se Halga Gast on cóm
on fyr(es gelicnysse,) and þone geleafan getrymede,   180
ǽrest þam apostol(um, and eft) þurh hí mancynne,
swilce wé on þisum life swinc(on, and on) ðam towerdan
   blission,
underfangenre mede (on þam) ecan freolse.

þreo þing bebead se Hælend þam (bedry)dan:
þæt is, aris, and ber þin legerbed, and gang.   185
Hé geh(ælde) his untrumnysse mid þam þe he het hine arisan,
(and swa)þeah seo dæd getacnode sum þing,
swilce he þam s(eocan) sæde þisum andgite:
Asceac þe of hraþe ([þ]a sleacnysse)
fulra leahtra, þé þu gefyrn on lage,   190
(and gearca þe sylf)ne to þære sawle mægnum;
and swaþ(eah næs genoh þam) seocan bedrydan
þæt hé hál up aris(e, ac het hyne þa gyt)
beran his legerbedd, and eac gán þa(non.
Ber þin leger)bed, þæt is, beo geþyldig,   195

---

175 gyf *F.*   177 Þys *F.*   eastron *F.*   182 þysum *F.*   toweardan *F.*
185 ys *F.*   bær *altered to* ber *F.*   186 hyne *F.*   188 þysum andgyte *F.*
189 of hraþe] raðe of *F.*   þa sleacnysse] asleacnysse *F; H retains the upper
part of a letter that was probably* þ.   194 bæran *altered to* beran *F.*   hys
F.   legerbed *F.*   195 Bær *altered to* Ber *F.*

177–83 [*After identifying Paul's promised reward with the number ten, by
which forty becomes fifty, Augustine adds:*] Unde cum labore celebramus Quadra-
gesimam ante Pascha; cum lætitia vero, tanquam accepta mercede, Quinqua-
gesimam post Pascha. [*Augustine goes on, by a train of thought that Ælfric omits,
to mention the reward of the Holy Spirit at Pentecost.*]

184–91 [*Augustine*] Tria dixit, *Surge, tolle grabatum tuum, et ambula.* Sed
Surge, non operis imperium fuit, sed operatio sanitatis. [*Alcuin (Bede), partially
disagreeing:*] Surge enim dicitur, vitiorum torporem, in quibus diu languebas,
excute, et ad exercitum virtutum, quibus perpetuo salveris, erigere.

192–201 [*Augustine*] Sano autem duo imperavit, *Tolle grabatum tuum, et
ambula.* [*Alcuin (Bede)*] *Tolle grabatum tuum:* porta diligens proximum tuum,
patienter eius infirma tolerando. [*Augustine*] Quid dictum est ab Apostolo?
Invicem onera vestra portate, et sic adimplebitis legem Christi (*Galat.* vi. 2).
[*Alcuin (Bede) quotes the usual form of this text*, Alter alterius onera portate, *etc.*]

and forber þine (nextan, swa swa) þu betst mæge, [. . .?]
teonfullan dæda oþ([þe . . .] word,)
Swá swá se apostol Paulus cwæð o(n sumum pistole:
Al)ter alterius onera portate, et (sic adimplebitis legem) Christi:
Berað, ic bidde, eowre byrþ(ena eow betwynan,   200
and) ge swa gefyllað soþlice Cris*(tes ǽ;   * Last word
þis belycð ægðer ge lufe ge hatunge.   visible,
                                 f. 241.
Ure ælc sceal mid lufe oðrum fylstan,
and eac ure yfelnysse us betwynan forberan,
þæt) *Godes (ǽ on us swa beo gefylled.   * First word
Soðlice Crist)es æ is seo soþe (lufu,   visible,
and seo ne byð gefylled buto)n we swá dón   f. 241ᵛ.
þæt we ure byrþena (b[e]ron us betwyn)an.
Crist het hine gán, þæt is on godra (weorca
stap)um forðstæppan, and né standan idel.   210
He bær (þa his bed) bliþelice gangende,
and þá Iudeiscan ceorodon (for ðam) Sæternes-dæge,
þone hí miclum wurþodon æfter (Moyses) ǽ,
for þan þe se ælmihtiga God ealle þing gesceop,
(gesewenlic)e and ungesewenlice, ealle on six dagum,   215
and on þone (seofoða)n geswác his weorces,
and þone dæg gehalgode, and het (on his) ǽ syþþan
þone dæg freolsian, for þære digelan ge(tacn)unge
Cristes þrowunge, swa swa hit cuþ wearð syþþan.

---

196 forbær *altered to* forber *F.*   bæst *F.*   197 teonfullan word *only, no sign of omission F. See note on 196–7.*   198 Swá] *no cap. F.*   paulus] *om. F, perhaps rightly: cf. Augustine's Latin.*   199 honera *F.*   202 þis] *cap. F.*   204 forbæran *altered to* forberan *F.*   208 bæron *F. Cf. the variants at lines 194 sqq.*   213 micclum *F.*   wurþedon *F.*   214 ðam *F.*   216 hys *F.*   218 diglan *F.*   219 hyt *F.*

202–5 [*Not explicitly in either of Ælfric's sources.*]
206–10 [*Augustine*] Lex ergo Christi charitas est, nec charitas impletur nisi invicem onera nostra portemus. [*Alcuin (Bede)*] Ambula autem; . . . quotidianis bonorum operum passibus de virtute in virtutem progredere, nec . . . intentionem recti incessus avertens.
211–19 [*Alcuin (Bede)*] Persequebantur autem eum quasi legis auctoritatem simul et divinæ operationis exempla secuti; quia et Dominus sex diebus mundi perfecta creatione, *septimo requievit ab omnibus operibus suis* (*Gen. ii. 2*), et populum sex diebus operari, septimo vacare præceperit (*Exod. xxxv. 2*). [*Later, speaking of the creation, Bede and Alcuin have the phrase,*] cuncta visibilia et invisibilia. [*Augustine*] In eo quod *Deus in die septimo requievit*, ipsum Dominum et salvatorem nostrum Iesum Christum . . . magno sacramento significavit.

(God ge)sceop his gesceafta on syx dagum ealle,   220
and geswac (on þone) seofoþan, swa þæt he syþþan ne gesceop
nane oþre (gesceafta, ac) þa sylfan geedniwað
on mannum and on ny(tenum mihtiglic)e oþ þis.

He gesceop þa twegen men, and (ealle tida gesette,)
ac he ne gesceop na syþþan seldcuþe (gesceafta,   225
of þam ealdan) dihte þe he æt fruman gesette;
ac (he gescipð ælce dæge ed)niwe sawla,
and on lichaman geliffæst, (swa swa we leorniað) on bocum,
and þa sawla ne beoð na(hwær gesceapene
æ)r þan þe God hi asent to þam gesceape(nan lichama[n]   230
on he)ora moddra innoþum, and hi swa men (wurþað.

Nu ge ma)gon tocnawan þæt ure sawla ne cumað
(of fæder ne of meder,) ac se heofonlica Fæder
gescipð (þone lichaman and hine gel)iffæst mid sawle;
and he ealle *(g)esceafta (geedniwað symble,   *f. 242
ge on fixum ge on fugelum ge on fe)ðerfetum n(ytenum,   236
for ðam ðe þa ærran for ylde at)eoriaþ;
and hé ge(wissað þas woruld mid welwillendum dih)te,
þeah ðe ure yfelnys him oft (abelge,
and we þonne swin)gla for urum synnum þrowiaþ.   240

Nu sm(eagað menn for)oft hwær hit eal becume
þe fram Adame w(æs oð ðis) gesceapen,
ac hí nyton þæt se Ælmihtiga micel w(ile habban)
into his heofonlican rice, swá swa him gerisa(n mæg,)
þæt hé micclum werode mihtiglice rixige;   245
and ea(c ealles) to fela forfaraþ þurh synna.

Se ylca resten-(dæg,) swa swa we ræddan lyttle ǽr,

220 six *F.*   224 menn *F.*   225 selcuðe *F.*   230 þam *F.*
lichamam *F.*   231 modra *F.*   241 eall *F.*   243 ælmihtiga]
ælmihtiga scippend *F.*   micel wile] wile micel *F.*   245 rixie *F.*
247 ræsten- *F.*   ræddon *F.*   lyte *F.*

220–31 [*Alcuin (Bede)*] Conditor in die septima non ab opere mundanæ
gubernationis et annuæ, immo quotidianæ rerum creatarum substitutionis, sed
a nova creaturarum institutione cessavit. [*Alcuin*] Non incognita animarum
genera, sed eiusdem substantiæ animas, quæ in primo homine condita est,
reformat.

232–46 [*Not in Ælfric's immediate sources.*]

247–50 [*Augustine*] At ubi impleta sunt omnia opera eius, sexta sabbati *in-clinato capite reddidit spiritum* (*Ioan. xix. 30*), et in sepulchro sabbato requievit
ab omnibus operibus suis.

getacnode þone (dæg þe) ure Drihten [forðfaren
on byrgenne læg] for u(re aly)sednysse,
and geswac þæra wundra þe he worhte on his (life,)   250
and on þam Sunnan-dæge arás of deaþe gesund,
and is n(u) se Sunnan-dæg syþþan gehalgod
þurh ures Driht(nes) ærist, þe on þam dæge arás,
and wé hine wurþiað (Gode to) wyrðmynte,
and syþþan geswac þæs Sæte(rnes-dæges fre)ols.   255

On þam ealdan resten-dæge, þe we (ær embe spræcon,)
ne worhton þa Iudei nan þeowtlic (weorc,
and se an) getacnode eal ure lif,
þe is gastlic (ræsten-dæg, on þam) wé Gode sceolon
symle þeowian, and sy(nna forbugan,)   260
þe synd þeowtlice weorc, and on þeowte (gebringað
heora) wyrcendras a to worulde.

þa Iu(deiscan freolsodon) þone foresædan resten-dæg,
and oft (bemændon þa ða) men wæron
gehælede on þam dæge fram (urum Hælende.)   265
þa axode he hi on sumne sæl* (be sumum wæter-   * Last word
seocum men   visible,
    f. 242.
hwæðer he on þam freolsdæge þe hi swa f)*reoli(ce   * First word
wurðedon   visible,
    f. 242ᵛ.
moste beon gehæled fram þam miccl)an br(oce.
Hi suwodon þa ealle, and se Hæland sona)

248–9 forðfaren on byrgenne læg] *sic F*; læg forðfaren on byrigene *H (irregular
allit.*)   250 geswac] geswa *F*.   252 ys *F*.   253 þe] þe he *F*.   254 wur-
mynte *F*.   256 ræsten- *F*.   257 iudeiscan *F*.   þeowlic *F. In H the
t is partly rubbed out.*   258 eall *F*.   259 ys *F*.   260 symble *F*.
261 synt *F*.   þeow'e'tlice, þeow'e'te *H*.   263 ræsten- *F*.

251–5 [*Not in Ælfric's immediate sources.*]
256–62 [*Alcuin (Bede)*] Sabbato quippe carnali, quod iuxta litteram custodie-
batur, populus ab omni opere servili die septima vacare præceptus est; spiritale
autem Sabbatum est in luce gratiæ spiritalis, quæ septiformis accipitur; quia
non una, sed omni die, nos ab inquietudine vitiorum manere feriatos oportet.
Si enim iuxta vocem dominicam, *omnis, qui facit peccatum, servus est peccati*
(*Ioan. viii. 34*), patet liquido, quia peccata recte opera servilia intelliguntur.
263–75 [*Luc. xiv. 2–6, to which Augustine alludes in order to draw a distinction
which Ælfric disregards*] Et ecce homo quidam hydropicus erat ante illum. Et
respondens Iesus dixit ad Legisperitos, et Pharisæos, dicens: Si licet sabbato
curare? At illi tacuerunt. Ipse vero apprehensum sanavit eum, ac dimisit. Et
respondens ad illos dixit: Cuius vestrum asinus, aut bos in puteum cadet, et non
continuo extrahet illum die sabbati? Et non poterant ad hæc respondere illi.

þone wæter(seocan gehælde on heora gesih)þum,   270
and axode hi syþþan, swylc(e mid bigspelle,
Hwæt l)a, nelle ge, gif hwylc-eowres assa fylþ,
(oððe oxa, o)n pyt, ardlice hine up ateon
on þam halgan (ræsten-dæ)ge? And hi þa ne mihton
nan þing him geand(wyrdan,) for þan þe hi wæron oferswyþde.

Se gehæleda (mann ge)mette þone Hælend   276
syþþan on þam temple, and hé (him sæ)de þas word:
Nu þu eart gehæled, geheald þe wið (synna,)
þæt þe sum þing ne gelimpe on þinum life wyrse.

(Mid) þam he geswutelode þæt he for synnum wæs gebro(cod,)
ac swáþeah ne beoð ealle untrume   281
for synnum (ges)wencte, þeah þe hi sume beon.

Sume beoþ geuntru(mode) þæt hi þe eadmodran beon,
sume for fandunge, (sume for Go)des wundrum,
for þan þe Godes domas swi(ðe digle sint,   285
and æ)fre rihtwise on eallum his dædum.

Se ge(hæleda man þa, sy)þþan he þone Hælend gespræc,
cydde (þam Iudeiscum þæt) Crist hine gehælde,
and hine mærsode, (his mihte herigen)de.

þam sy wuldor on ecnysse mid (his ælmihtigan Fæ)der   290
and þam Halgan Gaste on anre God(cundnysse, AME)N.

---

271 swilce *F.*   272 gyf *F.*   hwilc- *F.*   273 pytt *F.*   275 ðam *F.*
oferswiððe *F.*   278 gehealt *F.*   285 ðam *F.*   286 ellum *F.*
287–91 *Wanley prints this concluding passage from H.*   287 syððan þe
Wanley (incorrectly).   288 cydde *altered to* kydde *F.*   289 gemærsode
F.   heriende *F.*   290 si *F.*

276–86 [*Alcuin (Bede)*] Inveniens in templo quem sanaverat, Dominus ait illi:
Ecce sanus factus es, iam noli peccare, ne deterius tibi aliquid contingat. Quibus
verbis aperte monstratur, quia propter peccata languebat. . . . Quod non ita
sentiendum est, quasi omnis qui infirmatur, ob peccata infirmetur. [*Alcuin*]
Sæpe infirmatur homo, ne extollatur in donis Dei . . .: sæpe ut probetur, tribu-
latur . . .: quibusdam vero infirmitas pro gloria Dei datur. . . . Novit Dominus,
pro quo quemlibet iubeat infirmari, vel dimittat sæpe occulto hominibus iudicio,
sed numquam iniusto.
287–91 [*Ælfric's independent conclusion.*]

NOTES

5. *Godes dyrling.* Ælfric had described John the Apostle as 'Cristes dyrling' in the homily on his assumption, *CH* I. 58. In Assmann's homily XIII, not by Ælfric, he is introduced as 'synderlice Cristes dyrling'. The English word has lost some of its original brightness; the special affection it points to rests on John's introduction of himself as the disciple whom Jesus loved (*quem diligebat Iesus, Ioan.* xiii. 23; xxi. 20).

6. *Cristes moddrian sunu.* On this bit of legend, habitual with Ælfric, see the note on I. 5.

10–16. In this passage Ælfric has added the following details not found in the gospel: (1) that the pool was near the temple, (2) that the porches were built by Solomon, (3) that they were made of 'fæstum weorcstanum', and (4) that the sacrificial victims were washed in the pool. The quotation from Alcuin given as a source sufficiently accounts for the fourth addition and, by implication, for the first. The ultimate authority is Eusebius's *Onomasticon,* translated by Jerome under the title, *De Situ et Nominibus Locorum Hebraicorum* (Migne, *PL* XXIII. 884 sq.; Greek and Latin texts in *Eusebius Werke,* ed. E. Klostermann, III[1]. 58 sq.). The second and third additions are perhaps natural inferences by Ælfric, in view especially of the allusions to Solomon's porch in the temple at *John* x. 23 and *Acts* iii. 11 and v. 12. Bede gives some slight support in his commentary on *Nehemiah* iii. 1, where, speaking of the building of the sheep-gate, he notes that where the Vulgate ('nostri codices') has 'portam gregis', the Old Latin ('vetus translatio') has 'portam et piscinam probaticam', and identifies the latter with the 'probatica piscina' of our present text. (Migne, *PL* XCI. 887.) Ælfric might have assumed that the porches of the pool, like much else that was restored under Nehemiah, had originally been the work of Solomon. Even if independent, Ælfric's inference was not without precedent. According to Wordsworth and White, p. 495, six Gospel codices of centuries VII–IX, two of them Irish, the others of north-western Europe, have the *capitulum* for *John* v. 1–15, 'In porticu salamonis', etc. Ælfric's third addition, the 'fæstum weorcstanum', recalls the numerous references in *I Kings* to the great hewn stones used by Solomon, e.g. vi. 36, where the Vulgate has, 'Et ædificavit atrium interius tribus ordinibus lapidum politorum.'

Ælfric's paraphrase of verse 2 is so free that one cannot tell whether he was familiar with the frequent variant in the Vulgate text, *super probatica* instead of *probatica.* The passage from Alcuin cited for lines 14–16 seems to imply the standard reading.

10. *wæs gehæfd.* Cf. *CH* I. 86/21, *þær wæron gehæfde hate baþe*; *CH* II. 506/26, *Ðær wæs ða gehæfd gehende ðære byrig swilce halig stow*; and *LS* III. 324 sqq., *Hwæt þa Basilius to þære byrig ferde, Nicea gehaten, on þære wæs gehæfd þæt foresæde mynster.* It is clear from the alliteration of these passages that the past participle *gehæfd* must receive some weight, though its meaning has been weakened to a point where it resists definition.

Thorpe contents himself with 'there were' and 'there was'; Skeat finds
a good stylistic equivalent in 'was situated'. Bosworth–Toller, under
gehabban, quoting the first passage above, gives 'kept' for the past participle, presumably in the sense 'kept in use'; and the Supplement, quoting
the last passage, under xi-a, proposes 'carried on' as an institution, though
perhaps 'maintained' or 'kept in use' would be nearer. These latter meanings have been adopted tentatively for the glossary, but with the conviction that they are too precise. We can still say, in the active voice, 'In that
city they had a pool' or 'a shrine' or 'hot baths' or 'a monastery'. A trans-
lator would surely follow Thorpe's 'there was' or Skeat's 'was situated'.

11. *Bethsaida*. This is the reading of the modern Vulgate and the
majority of early manuscripts of it. The 'Bethesda' of the Authorized
Version occurs in many Greek and a few Old Latin manuscripts. See
Nouum Testamentum . . . Latine, ed. Wordsworth and White. The Lindisfarne MS. has 'bethsaida' with 'bethesda' in the margin; the Rushworth,
'bethsaida'; the manuscripts of the West Saxon Gospels, 'bethsaida' or
'betzaida'.

18–23. Verse 4 in the Vulgate has an unusual number of variants,
possibly a sign that it is an interpolation. The two variants quoted may
seem a little closer to Ælfric's version than the standard reading. These
variants are reported by Wordsworth and White from E, an early manuscript of Tours.

23. *fram swa hwilcere untrumnysse swa he wære gehæfd*. This clause copies
the ellipsis of the Latin, *a quacumque detinebatur infirmitate*, since *fram*
can be used to translate *a* in both senses. Wyclif used a similar construction, 'of what euere siknesse he was holdun', which is echoed in the
Rheims translation of 1582. An easier construction appears in the West
Saxon Gospels, 'fram swa hwylcere untrumnysse swa he on wæs'. Still
easier is Tyndale's, followed by the Authorized Version: 'of whatsoever
disease he had'.

33. *La leof*. Although *la leof* is the most frequent form of respectful
address in Ælfric, it does not usually fill a half-line. One might expect *la
leof hlaford*, as in vi. 10. But a rough estimate of the space in H suggests
that it agreed with F. If there is an error it goes back to a common
ancestor.

55–57a. Cf. Ælfric's earlier translation of this verse, *CH* I. 350: 'Efne
nu ðu eart gehæled, ne synga ðu heonon-forð, þylæs ðe ðe sum ðing
wyrse gelimpe'; and also the more firmly alliterated recasting of it below,
lines 278–9.

98 sqq. With the contrast in this passage between visible and invisible
miracles compare the contrast in Ælfric's early homily for the middle of
Lent, *CH* I. 184, between the usual and the unusual miracles, to the
advantage of the former. Compare also homily iv. 64 sqq., 'Dæghwamlice
he wyrcþ ðas ylcan wundra gyt', etc.

104. *þurh þa ðe*, 'through which'. The occurrence of the relative *þa ðe*, as a parallel to plain *þa* in line 102 and in contrast to the complex *þa þe*, 'those that', in the second half of 104, looks at first like a scribal error; but Ælfric uses both forms of the relative freely, and the chances are that he himself chose *þa þe* here for its rhythm. In 102, *þurh þa* is followed by weakly stressed syllables and another such syllable would hardly be an advantage. In 104, *þurh þa þe* is followed by the partially stressed first syllable of *wǣron*. The addition of *þe* provides an alternation of stress and makes the whole sequence easier.

156–7. Ælfric had made the same reservation about the forty-day fasts of Moses and Elias in his homily for the first Sunday in Lent, *CH* I. 178.

164. *gegrundweallod*. The only other occurrence of this word, according to the dictionaries, is in the Stowe Psalter, edited by J. Spelman, *Psalterium Davidis Latino-Saxonicum Vetus*, 1640, *Psal*. xxiii. 2, where *gegrundweallode* translates *fundavit*. Ælfric uses *grundweall* in his *Grammar* (p. 31/3; p. 220/1; and p. 289/13) and four times in succession in a homily (*CH* II. 588/18 sqq.). He also uses *gegrundstapelod* in the life of Saint Agatha (*LS* VIII. 21).

196–7. These two lines are puzzling. I take 'þine nextan' as accusative plural, rendering the accusative singular of the Latin, 'porta . . . proximum tuum', and I think the likeliest way to fill out the lacuna of H in the next line is by reading 'teonfullan dæda oþþe tallican word'. The word *tāllic* occurs several times in Ælfric and the verb *tǣlan* alliterates with *tēonful* in *LS* XXI. 359. But the accusatives 'dæda' and 'word' cannot without awkwardness be taken as parallel to 'þine nextan', and the use of the weak declension in the ending of 'teonfullan' suggests that the definite article or a possessive (*heora*?) should have preceded. I suspect that between lines 196 and 197 a whole line had dropped out from the text in a common ancestor of the two manuscripts.

212–75.   Ælfric had developed most of the ideas in this passage on the Jewish Saturday and the Christian Sunday, particularly in the part extending to line 255, in his comment on the third commandment, *CH* II. 206, 208. There is a further treatment of the distinction in lines 220–31, between the original creation and the constant renewal of all creatures, in Ælfric's *Hexameron*, 358–75, where the language is similar. That God shapes the child's body in the mother's womb and gives it a soul is explained at greater length in *De Initio Creaturæ*, *CH* I. 20/12–18, and again in *De Fide Catholica*, *CH* I. 292/25–30. Because of the emphasis on the Jewish prohibition of *þeowtlic weorc* in lines 256–75, I think it is to this passage rather than to *CH* II. 206 that Ælfric refers in Belfour VII, p. 70/7. Belfour's homily has been assigned by Clemoes (*Chronology*, 215) to Wednesday after the fourth Sunday in Lent because of its pericope, *John* ix. 1 sqq. Thus it belongs to the same season as the two just mentioned.

247. *swa swa we rǣddan lyttle ǣr*. At lines 218–19.

272. Ælfric's *hwylc-eowres*, 'of any one of you', a possessive genitive of the interrogative or indefinite *hwylc eower*, 'which of you, anyone of you', is unrecognized in the dictionaries and grammars, so far as I am aware, although the Lindisfarne gloss to *Luke* xiv. 5 seems to offer this construction as an alternative: 'huelc *vel* huæs iueres', that is, either *huelc-iueres* or *huæs iueres*. In the West Saxon gospels, as in the second alternative of Lindisfarne, both words are inflected, 'hwylces eowres'. Ælfric has *swa hwylc eower swa*, 'whichsoever of you', at XIII. 215. See Glossary under *swa*.

286. *and*. One might expect *ac*, corresponding to Alcuin's *sed*.

III[1]

FERIA VI IN SECUNDA EBDOMADA QUADRAGESIMÆ

Matth. xxi. 33–46

THIS is one of the shortest of Ælfric's homilies and appears to be based on only one, or at most two authorities apart from the Bible. The main source, certainly, is the fortieth homily in the interpolated homiliary of Haymo printed by Migne: *Feria Sexta Post Reminiscere, PL* cxviii. 244–7. There is evidence that this interpolated homiliary was already in being as early as the tenth century, and it appears that Ælfric had a copy of it.[2] The fortieth homily is one of thirteen pieces excerpted from an unprinted Carolingian commentary on *Matthew*, whose unidentified author I shall call pseudo-Haymo. At many points this homily is much the same as its principal source, the commentary by Jerome; but Ælfric has used nothing of Jerome's that is not also in pseudo-Haymo, and he has used several elaborations in pseudo-Haymo that are not in Jerome. He has not used anything peculiar to Bede, who likewise drew on Jerome for his commentaries on the parallel texts in *Mark* and *Luke*.

Another homily for the same day on the same text is to be found in the collection of Paulus Diaconus as printed by Migne, *PL* xcv. 1252–5. It is probably the work of Haymo's distinguished pupil, Hericus of Auxerre.[3] Although it also draws upon Jerome, it seldom comes as close as the pseudo-Haymo to Ælfric's ideas and expressions. The conclusion is an exception and I have quoted it below at line 176, but with some hesitation, for I am not sure that any of Hericus's homilies had been incorporated in Ælfric's copy of Paul's homiliary.

---

[1] On the group of homilies for Fridays in Lent, see above, pp. 226–8.

[2] See above, p. 157, notes 1 and 2, and pp. 160–1.

[3] On Ælfric's use of Paul's homiliary, see above, pp. 156–9; and on the attribution to Hericus, p. 159, n. 2.

FERIA VI IN SECUNDA EBDOMADA
QUADRAGESIMÆ

Homo erat pater familias qui plantauit, et re*li*qua.

Ure Drihten sæde oft swiðe digle bigspell;
þa on sumne sæl sæde he þis bigspel
his leorningcnihtum and þam geleaf[leas]um Iudeiscum:
Sum hiredes ealdor wæs, þe het settan wineard,
and hine behégode, and het delfan þærinne   5
ane winwringan, and worhte anne stypel,
and betæhte þone wineard his tilium syððan,
and ferde on ælþeodignysse to fyrlenum lande.
Eft þa ða þæs wineardes wæstmas genealæhton,
þa sende he his þeowan to ðam foresædum tilium,   10
þæt hi underfengon þæs wineardes wæstmas.

Text based on F (CCCC 162), pp. 252–8. Collated with H (Cotton Vitellius
C. v), ff. 242^v–5^v. As in the preceding homily, H had originally the better text,
but its superiority is so slight as not to offset the awkwardness of its many
lacunae. Although only the large lacunae at top and bottom of the pages are
regularly indicated among the various readings, at doubtful points it is noted
that H agrees, or disagrees, or has no reading.

F's use of capitals at beginnings of sentences and speeches has been regularized, especially as some of its capital forms, notably those of *h* and the runic *þ*
and *p*, can be distinguished from minuscule forms only by their being very
slightly larger.

Excluded variants: (1) H has *i* where F has *y* in *byð, gyf, hyne, hys, hyt, ys,
þys.* (2) H has *for þan þe* where F has *for þam þe.*

Sup.: FR. VI EMDOMADA II. (Ðis spel gebyrað on) þone frige-dæg on
þære oþre (lencten-wucan). EVVANGELIVM. (Homo erat pater) familias qui
plantauit uinea*m.* Et re*li*qua. H (*the bracketed portions from Wanley's* Catalogus,
p. 211).

1 Ure . . . oft] *no longer in H but confirmed by Wanley.*   bigspel *H.*
2–3 sumne] *end of f. 242^v in H; top of f. 243 illegible except for* (s)æde h(e) . . .
(geleaflea)sum.   3 geleafsumum *F.*   5 behegode *both MSS.*   6 anne]
ænne *H.*

SOURCES. 1–11 [*Matth. xxi. 33*] Aliam parabolam audite: Homo erat paterfamilias
qui plantavit vineam, et sepem circumdedit ei, et fodit in ea torcular, et ædificavit turrim, et locavit eam agricolis, et peregre profectus est.
[*34*] Cum autem tempus fructuum appropinquasset, misit servos suos ad
agricolas, ut acciperent fructus eius. [*Rushworth MS.*, tempus adpropinquasset
fructum viniae.]

þa gelæhton þa tilian heora hlafordes þeowan,
and sumne beswungon, sumne eac ofslogon,
sumne oftorfedon soðlice mid stanum.

Eft se hlaford syððan sende oðre þeowan,   15
micele ma him to, and þa manfullan tilian
dydon *sona embe hi swa swa embe þa oðre.   *p. 253
He sende þa æt nextan his sunu to, and cwæð,
Hi 'wyllað' forwandian witodlice minne sunu.

þa tilian þa gesawon þone sunu, and cwædon,   20
þes ys se yrfenuma; uton hine ofslean,
and his yrfweardnyss ure byð syððan.
Hi gelæhton þone sunu þa and gelæddon of þam winearde
and hine ofslogon. Hwæt secgce ge,
hu deð þæs wineardes hlaford embe þa wælhreowan tilian,   25
þonne he cymð him to? þa cwædon þa Iudeiscan,
þa yfelan tilian he yfele fordeð,
and betæcð his wineard oðrum tilium syððan,
þe him wæstmas agyfað on gewissum timan.

Se [Hælend] him sæde þa be þam hyrnstane þus: 30
Ne rædde ge on bocum be þam hyrnstane,
þone þa weallwyrhtan aworpen hæfdon,
þæt se is geworht on ðæs wealles hyrnan?
þys ys þurh 'God' gedon, and hyt ys wundorlic

---

14 oftorfodon H.   15 after Eft] ða over line H (perhaps syððan was
omitted; no reading at margin).   19 willað H.   21 ofsclean H.   22 yrfewerd-
nys H.   24 secgce] sic F; no reading H.   29 agifað H.   timan] no reading H.
30 hælend] sic H; om. F.   30, 31 hyrnstane] repeated in both MSS.
34 god over line F; on the line H.

12–17 [35] Et agricolæ, apprehensis servis eius, alium ceciderunt, alium
occiderunt, alium vero lapidaverunt.
[36] Iterum misit alios servos plures prioribus, et fecerunt illis similiter.
18–22 [37] Novissime autem misit ad eos filium suum, dicens: Verebuntur
filium meum.
[38] Agricolæ autem videntes filium, dixerunt intra se: Hic est heres, venite,
occidamus eum, et habebimus hereditatem eius. [Rushworth MS., et nostra erit
hereditas.]
23–29 [39] Et apprehensum eum eiecerunt extra vineam, et occiderunt.
[40] Cum ergo venerit dominus vineæ, quid faciet agricolis illis?
[41] Aiunt illi: Malos male perdet: et vineam suam locabit aliis agricolis, qui
reddant ei fructum temporibus suis.
30–35 [42] Dicit illis Iesus: Nunquam legistis in Scripturis: Lapidem, quem
reprobaverunt ædificantes, hic factus est in caput anguli? A Domino factum
est istud, et est mirabile in oculis nostris:

on eowrum gesihþum, and ic secge eow forþi 35
þæt Godes rice byð eow ætbroden,
and byð þære þeode geseald þe him syllað wæstmas,
and se ðe on þone stan fylþ, he byð tobrocen,
and se ðe se stan offylþ, se byð tocwysed.

Hwæt þa bisceopealdras, þa þa hi þis bigspel gehyrdon, 40
and þa sunde‵r′halgan sona oncneowon
þæt he hit sæde be him, and sohton him betwynan
on heora sundor-rununge hu hi hyne beræddon,
ac hi ondredon þa mænigu þe him mid wæs þa,
for ðam ðe þæt folc hæfde *hine for witegan.   *p. 254

We habbað anfealdlice gesæd eow nu þis godspell, 46
and we willað geopnian eow þæt andgyt nu,
for ðam þe ge ne cunnon ealle tocnawan þa digelnysse,
buton mán eow secge þæra snotera lareowa
trahtnunge be þam, swa swa hit on bocum stent. 50

Se hiredes ealdor witudlice þe hæfde þone wineard
is se heofonlica God, þe hæfde gelogod
þa Iudeiscan þeode on þam selestan earde
þysre worulde middan, and sette him á,
þæt hi hine [ænne] æfre wurþian sceoldon 55

---

35 eowrum] *H uncertain; see note.*   36 biþ *last word visible f. 243 H.*
39 -fylþ *first word visible f. 243ᵛ H.*   41 sunder-] *corrected from* sundel- *F.*
43 sundor-rununge *both MSS.*   44 mæniu *H.*   46 godspel *H.*
47 geopnian] *only* -nian *visible H.*   andgit *H.*   51 witodlice *H.*   54 þisre
H.   him *altered to* hym *F.*   55 ænne] *sic H; om. F.*

35–39 [43] ideo dico vobis, quia auferetur a vobis regnum Dei, et dabitur
genti facienti fructus eius.

[44] Et qui ceciderit super lapidem istum, confringetur: super quem vero
ceciderit, conteret eum.

40–45 [45] Et cum audissent principes sacerdotum, et Pharisæi parabolas
eius, cognoverunt quod de ipsis diceret.

[46] Et quærentes eum tenere, timuerunt turbas: quoniam sicut prophetam
eum habebant.

51–80 [ps.-Haymo] Omnipotens etenim Deus Pater, conditor et gubernator
familiarum suarum est. Vinea illius, domus Israelitica est. Hoc enim nomine
solet appellari eadem gens in sacro eloquio, sicut Isaias dicit (v. 1–7): Cantabo
dilecto meo canticum patruelis mei vineæ suæ. Vinea facta est mihi in loco uberi, etc.
usquequo dixit: Vinea Domini sabaoth, domus Israel est. Omnipotens ergo Deus
vineam plantavit, quia eiectis de terra promissionis habitatoribus suis Chana-
næis, in eamdem gentem Israeliticam collocavit. [Ælfric treats the whole passage
freely in lines 51–63, then quotes with some exactness several verses from the passage
in Isaiah to which pseudo-Haymo refers, as indicated below.]

mid halgum biggen`c'gum, swa swa þa fif bec tæhton
þe Moyses him awrat, se mæra heretoga,
þe fram Egipt[a] lande hi lædde to ðam earde,
and hi ana þa hæfdon andgyt embe God,
and ealle oðre þeoda þeowdon deofolgyldum.   60

þa het God hi oft þurh his halgan witegan
wineardes naman, for þam ðe hi wyrcan sceoldon
góde wæstmas [Gode], swa swa gód wineard.

Be þam wineard[e] cwæð se witega Isaias:
Ic abad þæt min wineard bære me wæstmas,   65
and he þa forðbrohte abroðene berian;
nu æteow[e] ic eow hwæt ic þam winearde do:
Ic tobrece his hege, and him fram abrede,
and hyne man toberð and tobryt hys wæstmas;
ic towurpe his weal and he byð fortreden;   70
ic hine aweste, and he ne byð gescreadod
oððe bedolfen, ac him deriað bremelas
þe him on weaxað, and wilde þornas,
and ic eac beode þam uplicum wolcnum
*þæt [hi] nænne renscur him on ne rinon.   *p. 255

Godes wineard soðlice is Israhela hiwræden,   76
and ic abad heora þæt hi worhton dom,
and efne hi worhton unrihtwisnysse.

Rihtwisnysse ic abad, and hi worhton hream:
þis sæde se witega be þam ungesæligum Iudeum.   80
    þone wineard he behegode, þæt is Israhela folc,

---

56 biggengum *H.*   58 egiptan *F; no reading H.*   60 þeowodon *H.*
63 Gode] *not in F; H has . . . de; see note.*   64 winearde] wineard *F;* win . . . *H.*
67 æteowde *F; only . . . e H.*   69 and tobryt] *f. 244 H. (nothing else legible
until line 71* ic hine).   75 hi] *sic H; om. F.*

64–80 [*Is. v. 4*] . . . exspectavi ut [vinea mea] faceret uvas, et fecit labruscas.
    [5] Et nunc ostendam vobis quid ego faciam vineæ meæ: auferam sepem eius,
et erit in direptionem; diruam maceriam eius, et erit in conculcationem.
    [6] Et ponam eam desertam; non putabitur et non fodietur; et ascendent
vepres et spinæ; et nubibus mandabo ne pluant super eam imbrem.
    [7] Vinea enim Domini exercituum domus Israel est; . . . et exspectavi ut
faceret iudicium, et ecce iniquitas; et iustitiam, et ecce clamor.
    81–92 [*ps.-Haymo*] 'Et sepem circumdedit ei,' id est muros urbium et custodiam
angelorum. 'Et ædificavit turrim.' Turrim, id est templum illud augustissimum,
quod Dominus in medio Ierusalem ædificavit, primum per Salomonem. . . . 'Et
fodit in eo torcular.' Torcular significat altare. Quoniam sicut in torculari uvæ
exprimuntur, ita et in altari sanguis hostiarum et victimarum effundebatur. 'Et

mid mærlicum burgum, and mid engla [hyrdrædena.]
Se stypel þe he getimbrode, þæt wæs þæt stænene tempel
þe se snotera Salomon gesette on Hierusalem
mid wundorlicum cræfte, to wurðmynte Gode,   85
and seo winwringe getacnode þæt weofud þær-[wið]innan,
on þam man offrode Gode on ða ealdan wisan
mænigfealde lac mid geleafan symle.

God betæhte þone wineard þam wisum bocerum
and þam Sunderhalgum þe heoldon his æ,   90
þæt hi him wæstmas agéafon godra weorca,
and he ferde syððan on fyr[lenne] wræcsið.

Manega þær geþugon of ðam mancynne Gode,
þeah þe hi sume ungesælige wæron,
and Crist forsawon, and eac besyrwdon.   95

He cidde eac him, and on sumne sæl cwæð,
Wa eow bocerum and eow Sunderhalgum,
ge hiweras þe heofonan rice
ætforan mannum belucað, and ge sylfe ín ne farað,
ne þam ne geðafiað þe in faran woldon.   100

Ge teoðiað eowre wyrta, and witudlice forlætað
þa maran beboda þe eow bebyt seo æ,
rihtne dom and geleafan, and mildheortnysse weorc.

þas þing gedafenode soðlice *to donne,   *p. 256
and eac þa oðre na to forlætene.   105

Lytle ær we sædon þæt se hlaford ferde

---

82 hyrdrædena] *sic H*; hiwredæne (*sic*) *F* (*the error probably due to association
with line 76*).   83 getimbrode] timbrode *H*.   templ *H*.   85 wyrðmynte
H.   86 weofod *H*.   þær-wiðinnan *H*; þær byð innan *F*.   87 on þa ealdan
wisan *both MSS*.   88 menigfealde *H*.   91 goddra *H*.   92 fyrlenne]
sic H; fyrnlene *F*.   97 Wa] *no cap. in MSS*.   98 ge hiweras] *so both
MSS. originally; altered in H to* eow hiwerum.   101 witodlice *H*.   104 geda-
fenode] ged . . ., *bottom f. 244 H*.   105 forlætene] *sic F*.   106 se
hlaford] .e hla . . ., *top f. 244ᵛ H*.

---

locavit eam agricolis,' id est commendavit eam scribis et Pharisæis, ut fructum
bonorum operum ex lege reportarent. 'Et peregre profectus est.'
93–105 [*Not in ps.-Haymo.*]
97–105 [*Matth. xxiii. 13*] Væ autem vobis scribæ et Pharisæi hypocritæ, quia
clauditis regnum cælorum ante homines! Vos enim non intratis, nec introeuntes
sinitis intrare. . . . [*23*] . . . Qui decimatis mentham, et anethum et cyminum,
et reliquistis quæ graviora sunt legis, iudicium, et misericordiam, et fidem! Hæc
oportuit facere, et illa non omittere.
106–14 [*ps.-Haymo*] 'Et peregre profectus est.' Non mutatione locorum, quia

on fyrlene wræcsið syððan he þone wineard betæhte.

Ne færð God swaðeah feorr ahwyder aweg,
se ðe on ælcere stowe hys andweardnysse cyð;
ac he let þone wineard on heora gewealde,   110
and let hi habban cyre agenes willan,
and hí na ne nydde on 'n'aðre healfe,
for ðam ðe ælc man hæfð agenne cyre
hwæt he lufige on his lifes timan.

Se hiredes ealdor sende, swa swa we sædon ær,   115
his men to ðam winearde, wolde hys wæstmas habban,
for ðam ðe se heofonlica God him sende gelome to
heahfæderas and witegan, wolde hi gerihtlæcan,
ac þa Iudei ofslogon sume of þam witegum,
and sume beswungon, swa swa us segð þis godspell,   120
and sume hi stændon mid stiðre reðnysse.
He sende eft ma þeowan to ðam manfullan tilian,
and hi swa him þenedon swa swa þam oðrum.

He sende þa æt nextan hys agenne sunu tó,
for ðam ðe se ælmihtiga God swa mildheort wæs us   125
þæt he his agenne Sunu asende of heofonum
mancyn to alysenne, and þa manfullan Iudei
swa dyrstige wæron þæt hi dorston hine acwellan,
and Crist swa alysde þa ðe gelyfað on hyne,
and he ne wiðerode na ongean, ac wæs gehyrsum hys Fæder, 130
for ðære micclan lufe þe he to mancynne hæfð,
þæt he sylfwilles sealde hys lif for us.

---

107 fyrlene] *sic F; no reading H.*   109 (and) werdnysse *H.*   112 naþre *H.*
118 to *written and crossed out before* witegan *F.*   120 godspel *H.*   122 manfullum (tiliu)m *H.*   123 þenodon *H.*   126 heofe(num) *H.*

Deus ubique est, et nusquam abest; . . . sed abiisse dicitur, quia cultoribus vineæ
operandi arbitrium suæ voluntatis reliquit.

115–23 [*ps.- Haymo*] Misit servos suos ad agricolas, Aaron videlicet et Moysen.
'Et agricolæ, apprehensis servis eius, alium ceciderunt.'Ceciderunt etenim Moysen
er Aaron, licet non verberibus, sed tamen moribus et verbis. Nam etiam eos
lapidare voluerunt. . . . Ceciderunt etenim David. . . . Alios etiam prophetas
quosdam occiderunt, quosdam vero lapidaverunt. 'Iterum misit alios servos
plures prioribus.' Servi qui secundo mittuntur, chorum prophetarum significant.
'Et fecerunt illis similiter', id est, quosdam lapidaverunt, sicut Naboth; quosdam ceciderunt, sicut Isaiam, secantes eum serra lignea: quosdam verberaverunt,
sicut Jeremiam.

124–32 [*Not in ps.-Haymo. Cf. Ioan. iii. 16; Eph. ii. 4; Phil. ii. 8.*]

He cwæð to ðam Iudeiscum, Hwæt deð þæs hire*des   *p. 257
   ealdor
be þæs wineardes tilium? and hi ne wendon þa gyt
þæt hi hyt sylfe wæron, and sædon him to andsware,   135
' þa yfelan tilian he yfele fordeð,
and betæcð his wineard oðrum tilium syððan,
þe him wæstmas agyfað on gewissum timan.'
Rih[t]lice hi demdon heora agenne dom.
Soðlice gyf hi wiston þæt hi hyt sylfe wæron,   140
noldon hi andwyrdan swa amberlice be þam.

Witodlice se hyrnstan þe se Hælend foresæde,
þe hylt þa twegen weallas, ys se Hælend sylf,
þe gefegde togædere of twam folcum hy[s] cyrcan,
manega of Iudeiscum and ma of hæðenum folce,   145
to anre gelaþunge on soðum geleafan.

Manega ætspurnað mid mislicum synnum
æt þam hyrnstane, ac 'hi' habbað forgyfennysse,
þa ðe mid dædbote heora Drihten gladiað.
Oþer is þæt mán [sic] fealle uppon þone stán,   150

---

133 Hwæt] *no cap. F, no reading H.*   134 git *H.*   136 þa] *no cap. in MSS.*
138 agifað *H.*   timan] *no reading H.*   139 Rihlice *F.*; (Ri)htlice *H.*
140 Soðlice] *f. 245; three lines of H destroyed; no reading until* sylf, *line 143.*
142 hyrnstan *altered to* hyrnestan *F.*   144 hys] hyr *F.; no reading H.*
147 ætspornaþ *H.*   148 hi] *over line F; on the line H.*   forgifen(nysse) *H.*
150 man *H.*   uppan *H (but* uppon *lines 152, 153; no reading line 151).*

133–41 [*ps.-Haymo*] Interrogat Dominus scribas et Pharisæos, quid facturus
sit paterfamilias adveniens illis agricolis, non ut ignorat quid facturus sit, sed
ut ipse ex sua responsione eos convincat. Sua enim sententia convicti sunt.
142–6 [*Ibid.*] 'Lapidem tunc reprobaverunt,' id est Christum. . . . Sed
lapis 'factus est in caput anguli.' Angulus duos parietes nectit, et Christus factus
et in caput anguli, qui duos populos ex diverso venientes coniunxit in semetipso,
faciens pacem his qui prope erant, et his qui longe.
147–54 [*Ibid.*] Aliud est super lapidem cadere, et aliud sub lapide. Super
lapidem cadit, id est super Christum, qui peccando illum offendit, spem tamen
veniæ per poenitentiam habendo. Quicunque enim Christum negaverit, super
illum cadit, hoc est animadversio divina super eum irruit, et penitus conteret
eum, ut non remaneat ex eo testa, unde aqua hauriri possit. Potest et aliter
intelligi. In præsenti peccatores super lapidem cadunt, qui confringuntur per
poenitentiam. Lapis autem super eos in die iudicii cadet, quia Dominus Iesus
cum omnibus virtutibus superius ad iudicium veniet. [*In 147–9 Ælfric supplies
a transition by anticipating much of ps.-Haymo's second sentence. Perhaps the word*
offendit *reminds him of I Peter ii. 8, where the* lapis angularis *is identified with the*
lapis offensionis *of Isaiah viii. 14. Although Ælfric's distinction in 152–4 emphasizes the first of ps.-Haymo's interpretations, the reference to eternal punishments
seems to reflect the second.*]

and oðer is þæt se stan uppon hyne fealle.

Se fylþ uppon þone stan, se ðe syngað on Crist,
and se ðe Criste wiðsæcð, se stan fylþ uppon hyne,
and hine ealne tocwyst on þam ecum witum.

He cwæð þa æt nextan, swa swa we cwædon ær,   155
'þæt Godes rice byð eow ætbroden,
and byð þære þeode geseald þe him syllað wæstmas.'

Him is soðlice ætbroden seo boclice lár,
and eall seo deopnyss þe be Drihtne sprycð,
and is geopenad eallum Cristenum   160
þe hine wurðiað mid weorcum and geleafan.

'Hwæt þa bisceopealdras, þa ða hi *þis bigspel gehyrdon,
and þa Sundorhalgan sona oncneowon   [*p. 258
þæt he hit sæde be him, and sohton him betwynan
on heora sundor-rununge hu hi hyne beræddon,   165
ac hi ondredon þa mænigu þe him mid wæs þa,
for ðam ðe þæt folc hæfde hine for witegan.'

þeah þe hi heardheorte wæron and hetole on mode,
and noldo[n] gelyfan on þone lifigendan Crist,
þeah hi oncneowon þæt he cwæð be him   170
þa larlican bigspel, and gebulgon hi sona,
and woldon hine besyrwan, gyf hi wiston hu
for þære mæniu þe him mid ferdon,
and his lare gehyrdon, and his wundra gesawon,
and hyne wurðedon swa swa mærne witegan.   175
Ure geleafa is mara þon[n]e þære mænigu wære,

159 eal *H.* deopnys *H.*   160 geopenod *H.*   162 biscop(ealdras) *H.*   163
sunder(halgan) *H.*   166 mæniu *H.*   169 noldoon *F;* noldon *H.*   170 oncneo-
wan *H.*   173 meniu *H.*   þ[e], *bottom f. 245 H.*   176 þone *F; no reading H.*

158–61 [*Ibid.*] 'Auferetur a vobis regnum Dei', id est scientia Scripturarum,
et remanebit vobis sola ariditas litteræ. 'Et dabitur genti,' id est gentili populo,
facienti fructus eius, videlicet opera illius.

168–75 [*Ibid.*] Licet duri corde essent scribæ et Pharisæi, et licet in
Christum credere noluissent, aperte tamen intelligebant parabolas eius ad se
pertinere. Et ideo quærebant eum tenere, sed timuerunt turbas, quia sicut
prophetam eum habebant.

176–87 [*Not in ps.-Haymo, who may nevertheless have suggested Ælfric's conclusion
by calling attention to the fickleness of the common people. A conclusion like Ælfric's
occurs at the end of the homily on this text in the collection of Paulus Diaconus as
printed by Migne, PL XCV. 1255:*] Veneremur eum, non sicut simplices turbæ
ut prophetam, sed ut Deum et Dominum prophetarum, salvatorem et redemp-
torem nostrum, qui vivit et regnat, *etc.* [*See above, p. 247.*]

for ðam ðe we gelyfað on ðæs lifigendan Godes Sunu,
þæt he wæs æfre God mid his þam ecan Fæder,
and þam Halgan Gaste, on heofona rice wunigende,
and wæs man geworden þa ða he sylf wolde   180
for ure alysednysse, þæs we him æfre þanciað.

Uton smeagan nu georne þæt we sume wæstmas
godra weorca Gode agyfan,
and mid urum geleafan hine æfre wurþian,
þæt we mid þam Hælende habban þæt ece lif,   185
swa swa he behet þam ðe hyne lufiað;
þam si wuldor and lof on ecere worulde, amen.

178 his þam] *first words visible in H, f. 245ᵛ.*   179 (he) ofonan *H.*
183 agifon *H.*   184 wurþion *H.*   185 habbon *H.*   187 sy *H.*
on ecere worulde] *sic both MSS.*

NOTES

3. *geleaf[leas]um.* The *geleafsumum* of F can hardly be right, for Jesus
was addressing the scribes and Pharisees in the temple. H shows clearly
the final -*sum* of what was probably *geleafleasum.*

5. *behegode.* BT lists *behegian* 'to behedge, hedge around, *circumsepire*',
without saying where it occurs. Actually it seems to be unique in this
passage, which Toller cited out of Wanley's Catalogue after the publication of BTS. See *MLR* XVII (1922), 166. Cf. *ymbhegian* in BT (citing
Ælfric's *Grammar*) and *hegian, gehegian* in BTS.

29. *on gewissum timan.* Here and at line 138 below the phrase is probably
plural, agreeing with the Latin *temporibus suis.* Cf. *CH* I. 18/26, *on
asettum tyman,* and II. 94/3, *on alyfedum timan,* both most naturally
construed as plural. In fact it seems to be the practice in the best of the
Ælfric manuscripts to use -*um* in the dative plural for all strong nouns,
but to prefer -*an* for weak nouns. Examples are not very common, but
I have noticed the following in the *Catholic Homilies*: *adligendum lichaman* (I. 86/22), *mid urum lichaman* (II. 52/12), *twam wucan* (II. 30/30),
buton . . . Noe anum, and his seofan hiwon (II. 58/34). In contrast is the
phrase, *mid þinum hiwum* (I. 20/34), and one instance of -*on* with a foreign
noun, *apostolon* (II. 48/11).

30. *hyrnstane.* Cf. note on line 142 below.

35. *eowrum.* One expects *urum* for the Latin *nostris*, especially since this
is a direct quotation from *Psal.* cxvii. Indeed the authority for *eowrum*
is slight, for the second manuscript, H, has lost all but faint traces of the
first letter, and Ælfric does not repeat the verse, as he does most of the
others, later in the homily. Yet the *and* at the beginning of the next clause
accords with *eowrum* (since it suggests that what precedes is not the second
part of the quotation but the first part of Jesus's application of it to the

scribes and Pharisees), and the traces of the first letter in H look more like *e* than *u*. Perhaps Ælfric himself or an early scribe misconstrued or deliberately altered the gospel.

43. The word *sundor-runung*, 'private consultation', 'secret counsel', is not in the dictionaries, but Ælfric's use of *runung* and of *sundor-spræc* is recorded in BT. Note especially his phrase, *on synderlicum runungum*, of the secret conversations of the guards at Christ's sepulchre, in Assmann VI. 161 (p. 79). Cf. also *Andreas* 1161, *gesæton sundor to rune*, and *Wanderer* 111, *sundor æt rune.*—Here there seems to be a play on *sunderhalgan*, line 41.

53–54. *on . . . middan*. In BTS, under *on-middan*, are two examples, both from Ælfric, of phrases where the governed noun comes between *on* and *middan*, though neither is as extreme as this.

63. MS. H probably had *gode wæstmas gode*, 'good fruits for God', which fits the space better than *gode wæstmas to gode*. Either of these readings seems preferable to the flat *gode wæstmas*, which fails to show the metaphorical sense in which *wæstmas* is to be taken. A more extended play on 'good' and 'God' will be found in the opening lines of homily VIII.

67. The sense requires *æteowe* (Latin *ostendam*).

71. *gescreadod*. Cf. Ælfric's comments on the vineyard in his homily for Septuagesima Sunday, *CH* II. 74/12 sqq., where *screadian* alone and with various prefixes is used for the idea of pruning. The meaning survived until the eighteenth century. See *OED*, *shred*, v.

82. The form *hyrdrædena* of H is probably to be taken as a careless spelling of the dative or instrumental singular, *hyrdrædene*, although it is conceivable that the scribe understood it as an accusative plural. The accusative after *mid* when agency is involved is comparatively rare, and the preceding phrase clearly establishes the prevailing dative-instrumental.

92. Note Ælfric's rather heavily charged expressions for the Latin *peregre profectus est* (*ferde on ælþeodignysse to fyrlenum lande* at line 8 above, and here *ferde on fyrlenne wræcsið*). He uses the same expression, *fyrlen wræcsið*, to describe the journey to England which was contemplated by Gregory the Great but feared by the Roman people, *CH* II. 122/14.

141. *amberlice*. MS. F is our sole authority for this word, of which there is no record in the dictionaries. The word is probably to be associated with the adjective *ambyre*, which has survived uniquely in the phrase *ambyrne wind* (acc. sing.). Since the phrase occurs in a familiar passage, the report of Ohthere in Alfred's *Orosius* (ed. Sweet, p. 19/13), it has attracted wide attention, and there have been conflicting opinions about its meaning. An early interpretation as 'favourable wind', adopted by Sweet in his *Reader*, was challenged in the corrections appended to BTS, p. 756, where modern Icelandic *andbyrr*, 'contrary wind', was cited in

support of the opposite meaning, 'unfavourable wind'. But the first interpretation has been vindicated by E. Ekwall in an article, 'Old English *ambyrne wind*', in *Mélanges de Philologie offerts à M. Johan Melander* (Uppsala, 1943), pp. 275–84, reprinted in Ekwall's *Selected Papers* (Lund, 1963), pp. 129–37; and accordingly the meaning 'favourable' for the adjective is held to be confirmed in the revision of Sweet's *Reader* by C. T. Onions (14th ed., 1959, p. 200). Ekwall shows that the context demands that the wind be favourable (though not necessarily in a high degree), that the modern Icelandic *andbyrr* is not a satisfactory analogue, and that although there is not enough evidence to make the etymology certain, there are several plausible ways of accounting for an adjective *ambyre* with the sense 'favourable' when applied to wind. Ekwall prefers to derive the word from the prefix *and* and the noun *byre*, for which he cites the meanings 'opportunity' and also 'time, period'. He maintains that in some Old English words *and-* signifies, not 'against', but 'having a useful purpose' (better perhaps 'fitting' or 'appropriate', for opposition or confrontation includes the idea of matching as well as that of antagonism). On the basis of this etymology Ekwall would take the adjective as a *bahuvrihi* formation meaning 'with (affording) good opportunity', or more generally 'useful, helpful, serviceable'. One might suggest 'suitable, appropriate, opportune' as a more satisfactory range of meaning, for it not only accords with the demands of *ambyrne wind* and with Ekwall's proposed etymology, but yields a satisfactory explanation of *amberlice* in the present context. If we take *amberlice* as a combination of *ambyre* (either the adjective or a corresponding noun) and *lice*, with reduction of *-byre* to *-ber* through loss of secondary stress before the suffix, its range of meanings ought to include 'aptly, appropriately, opportunely'. Here the meaning 'appropriately' comes very near to what one would expect Ælfric to say. The scribes and Pharisees, caught off guard, have pronounced a just sentence against themselves. If they had known that they themselves were meant, they would not have answered so appropriately about the matter.

142–6. Cf. *CH* I. 106/11 sqq.: 'Soðlice se sealm-sceop awrát be Criste, þæt he is se hyrn-stan þe gefegð þa twegen weallas togædere, forðan ðe he geþeodde his gecorenan of Iudeiscum folce and þa geleaffullan of hæðenum, swilce twegen wagas to anre gelaðunge.' The word *hyrnstan* (lines 30, 31, 142, 148) has been cited in the dictionaries only three times: from the preceding passage, from a gloss published by Napier (BTS), and from Orm (*OED*, hern, hirn, sb.).

IV

DOMINICA III IN QUADRAGESIMA

Luc. xi. 14–28; *Matth.* xii. 22 sq.

To this homily belongs the distinction of two modern editions, the first of which antedates Thorpe's edition of the *Catholic Homilies*. Both are indirect products of the researches of N. F. S. Grundtvig, who brought to Copenhagen, as the fruit of several journeys to England, a number of transcripts of Old English materials, among them a transcript of the present homily as it stands in MS. N (Cotton Faustina A. ix). Grundtvig's transcript was the basis of both editions, the first by L. C. Müller in his *Collectanea Anglo-Saxonica*, Copenhagen, 1835, pp. 19–27, the second by George Stephens in his *Tvende Old Engelske Digte*, Copenhagen, 1853, pp. 81–99, where the text is arranged in metrical half-lines and accompanied by a correspondingly metrical and alliterative translation. Since these editions are neither entirely satisfactory for students of Ælfric nor readily available, it has seemed advisable to include the homily here. Müller's and Stephens's readings, having no independent value for the establishment of the text, are not included in the apparatus, but a detailed comparison of their texts with N is given at the head of the notes.

A brief extract from Ælfric's translation of the gospel, lines 41–55, has also been printed as it appears in MS. G by Rubie D.-N. Warner, *Early English Homilies*, p. 58.

The principal source of the exegesis is Bede's commentary, *In Lucæ Evangelium Expositio*. The relevant section of this commentary (*Luc.* xi. 14–28) was treated as a separate homily in the collection of Paulus Diaconus (both as originally constituted and as in Migne), and also in the collection attributed to Smaragdus, *PL* CII. 135 sqq.

Characteristically, however, Ælfric did not limit himself to a single source. Bede himself has drawn upon much of Jerome's commentary on the corresponding passage, *Matth.* xii. 22–30, 43–

45; and Ælfric, who sometimes takes account of the variant readings of this other passage, makes independent use of Jerome at certain points where Bede has a different comment. He also uses Haymo, whose homily for the third Sunday in Lent (no. XLII) is a rewriting of Bede's commentary, spelling out many of its condensed interpretations and adding several elaborations. With most of the added matter Ælfric has little to do, but he picks up a number of small suggestions.

Ælfric's allusion at line 75 to an earlier work may refer to *De Falsis Diis* (our XXI), or to *LS* XVIII, as explained in the note. Now apparently this is one of the earliest of Ælfric's additional homilies, since it appears in MS. E and, though with rubric and Latin text only, in F, both of which have early texts of the *Catholic Homilies* and very little of Ælfric's later work. Clemoes has argued (*Chronology*, 221, 224) that both *De Falsis Diis* and the presumably somewhat later homily IV may have been composed before the entire set of *Lives* was ready for publication. Although a subordinate argument, based on the enumeration of the eight deadly sins, has been questioned in the note on 249–51, the main contention is by no means improbable. Without pressing for an exact chronology one may suppose that the homily was roughly contemporary with the *Lives* and not far removed from our II, III, V, and VI.

Eight full copies of the homily have survived in addition to the little excerpt in G, and there is a trace of another copy. In MS. F (CCCC 162), p. 258, between the homilies here numbered III and V, stand the rubric and Latin text. (See above, p. 23.) Perhaps the exemplar had lost a gathering at this point and the scribe of F reproduced what remained without any attempt to fill the gap.

MS. Q (CCCC 188), an early copy of an augmented version of Ælfric's First Series, provides an excellent basis for the text, although in this particular homily it is rivalled in correctness by M (ULC Ii. 4. 6). I count as probable errors in Q only the following: 44 *cwæþ* for *cweþ*, where indeed a correction to *cweþ* was probably intended though imperfectly executed; 183 *burh* for *inburh*, of which there is something to be said in a moment; 239 *deofles* for *deofle*, and 266 *wearða* for *wearð ða*. There are a few mildly erratic spellings: 1, 62 *þæræ* for *þære*; 60 *earmann* for *earman*; 61 *bendas* for *bendes*; 207 *tostencge* for *tostence*; and 116 *seccaþ* for *secgaþ*. This last I have altered to *secgaþ*, the spelling of the majority of the manuscripts, to avoid confusion, but *seccaþ* appears as a rare alternative spelling in several of the manuscripts—for example, in N's text of the present homily at line 23. The punctuation of Q, which is followed in the designation of sentences but not in smaller matters, is very sound, but the accent-marks, which are duly reported, are as spasmodic as usual and of uncertain significance. Occasionally they seem downright freakish, as, for instance, 17 *geséah*, 22 *stapolfǽst*, 38 *on þam ðé*. For further instances, see the note on XI. 53.

The errors of Q are, it is clear, so slight and so easily corrected that it might have served as exemplar for any of the other manuscripts, but since not one of its little idiosyncrasies has been reproduced, there is no reason to assume such a relationship. The only error it shares with other manuscripts, *burh* for *inburh* at line 183, may go back to a careless slip in Ælfric's original or in a fair copy that was responsible for all the later progeny. At line 34 all the manuscripts except H have *inburh* (or *innburh*) correctly, and H, with *burh*, has an unattached marginal *in* that was probably intended as a correction; but at line 183 H alone has *inburh* as a primary reading: in T it appears as a correction, with *in* above the line. The chances are that H's *inburh* is also a correction made at some stage in the transmission of the text, not an inheritance from Ælfric's original; for if C, which has *burh*, is indeed related to H more closely than to other manuscripts, these two probably shared an ancestor that had *burh*. Correction would be relatively easy, because the passage at line 183 is a repetition of the passage at line 34. Indeed the scribe of H, if he made the imperfect correction in the earlier passage, might well have remembered the difficulty when he came to the second passage and made the correction himself.

Much less is disclosed about the relationship of the eight principal manuscripts than might be hoped. In the light of what has been said in the Introduction, we might suppose that these manuscripts would represent some four successive issues of the homily: E an early one; MNO a second; Q, with T, a third; H (the work of the interpolator) a fourth. The twelfth-century C, though it draws on early sources for the original series of *Catholic Homilies*, draws on late ones for some of the additional homilies and might thus have a late text here. The conjectural pattern just outlined may in fact be correct, but there is positive confirmation in the various readings for two pairs only: a very close relation between

N and O, and a somewhat less close relation between H and C. One reason for the lack of evidence is the extraordinary correctness of two manuscripts, not only Q but M also. If M and NO had a common ancestor short of Ælfric's original (as is almost certain), or Q and T (as is probable), there were simply no inherited errors or deviations to reveal the fact. Clearly, however, if Ælfric issued the homily on successive occasions, he did not introduce any discoverable revisions. The variants of E on the one hand and H on the other do not support such a notion.

N and O share a number of errors that do not appear elsewhere. Besides the small omissions at 88, 130, 136, 207, 237, 246, 257, 261 may be noted the altogether ridiculous substitution of *deofle* for *folce* at 132 and of *unwerie* for *unwæterige* at 217. At many other points these two manuscripts depart in little ways from the rest, so that their close relationship is obvious. Each, however, has enough unique errors to preclude the notion that one is copied from the other.

C and H share a relatively small number of minor errors. There are small omissions at 90 (*eac*), 141 (*god*), 143 (*sædon*), 172 (*a*), 177 (*þæt is on englisc*), 240 (*to*), 273 (*þa*), 294 (*þæt halige*), some of which are certainly errors, besides a few other correspondences. It is not an impressive list, but sufficient, I think, to establish a relationship. C, which is much later than H, cannot be a copy, for H has errors of its own. The relationship of these two manuscripts may seem surprising, in that C has connexions with the south-east, and H (though doubtfully) with the south-west. But it is to be noted that, in homily xi, C shows a comparable association with U. Now U (probably written at Canterbury) and H are geographically separated, but the interpolated homilies of H and the homilies of U are derived from a comparably late textual tradition. In this respect C's alliance with U in xi and its alliance with H here are in accord.

E, as might be expected, stands almost entirely apart, and I do not take as evidence of textual affinity its few points of agreement with the deviations of C and H. At 141, like them, it omits *god*, but the omission springs, I think, from a grammatical misunderstanding that must have afflicted two scribes independently. At 116 and 118 it agrees with C and H in writing *adræfde* for the *adræfe* of the other manuscripts. But lines 116–18 repeat a portion of the gospel-text from 23–25, and there the most reliable manuscripts have *adræfde* at 23 and *adræfe* at 25. There is obviously room for scribal confusion here and it is impossible to be sure that any manuscript has Ælfric's reading throughout. E has *adræfde* at 25 in agreement with H (somewhat obscure), N, and O, where C has *adræfa*; and at 138, where the present tense is plainly called for by the Latin quotation in the previous line, E has *adræfde* in company with H but not C, and N and O have the preterite of another verb. Under the circumstances these instances of agreement on the part of E cannot be accepted as indicative of its line of inheritance.

Of the eight principal manuscripts, H alone has pointed the text by half-lines and has done so with almost perfect consistency. Such pointing is to be found in K (Thorpe's manuscript of the *Catholic Homilies*) in the passages of rhythmic prose that occur here and there in the Second Series; in W (Skeat's manuscript of the *Lives of Saints*); in the interpolated homilies of H (as here); in U; and occasionally elsewhere.

Three of the manuscripts, C, E, and T, contain among them some ten Middle English glosses. Those in C are of the late twelfth or early thirteenth century. Those in E and T are of the early thirteenth, in the well-known 'tremulous' hand of a Worcester scribe, who was likewise responsible for a large number of Latin glosses in these two manuscripts.[1] The Middle English glosses are as follows:

42 woriend: walconde *C*.   60, 61 fram: of *E* (*twice*).   74 for-þearle: vel suðe *E* (= OE swiðe).   90 sellic: vncuð *T*.   97 syrwig-endan : vuele *(sic) E*.   163 wealcen: þencen *C*.   190 forgægednysse: gulte (*?erased*) *E*.   260 mægðe: cunne *C*.   282 untwilice: iwislice *C*.

There is a much earlier gloss in the margin of T, f. 58ᵛ, opposite line 77 of our text, in a hand resembling the main scribe's. The OE word *prut* is probably an interpretation of the name *Baal*.[2]

The Latin glosses in T and corresponding glosses in E are printed below the text. The rest of E's glosses, omitted by mistake when this edition went to press, are listed separately on p. 285 below. All these glosses are, I believe, in the tremulous hand.[3]

---

[1] On the Worcester glosses and corrections, see above, pp. 185–8.

[2] Jerome defines *Baalim* as *habentes, sive ascendentes, vel superiores* (*De Nominibus Hebraicis, PL* XXIII. 812).

[3] Certain Latin marginalia in T are in a different hand of about the same period. This hand wrote the less relevant list of sins cited first for lines 249–51, besides some topic phrases and sentences suggested by the Old English which have not been reported.

DOMINICA III IN QUADRAGESIMA

Erat Iesus *eiciens demoniu*m. *Et reliqua.*

On þǽræ mǽran tíde þe se míldheorta Hǽlend
wunode mid mannum on soðre menniscnysse,
wundra wyrcende, þa wearð him gebroht tó
sum witseoc man, wundorlice gedreht;
him wæs soðlice benǽmed his gesihð and spræc, 5
and hé swa dumb and ablend deoflice wedde.

Text based on Q (CCCC 188), pp. 123–31. Collated with C (CCCC 303), pp. 30–34; E (CCCC 198), ff. 316–21; H (Cotton Vitellius C. v), ff. 73–75^v; M (ULC Ii. 4. 6), ff. 75^v–83; N (Cotton Faustina A. ix), ff. 63–69; O (CCCC 302), pp. 129–37; T (Hatton 114), ff. 57–63^v; and G (Cotton Vespasian D. xiv), f. 67^v, this last a mere excerpt corresponding to lines 41–55 below. For Müller's and Stephens's editions, based on N, and Warner's edition of the excerpt in G see the introductory comment.

Excluded variants: (1) Most instances of the following minor variations in spelling: double and single consonants, final as in *man(n)*, *eal(l)*, *-nys(s)*, medial as in *mic(c)lum*; *y* and *e* in *-nyss*, *-ness*; *o* and *e* medially in *heofonum*, *heofenum*; *wunodon*, *wunedon*, and the like; *i* and *y* for EWS *i* or *ie*, long or short; *ig* and *i* medially in such words as *worigende*, *woriende*; and the interchange of *þam*, *þan*, *þon*, especially in *for þam þe*. (2) A number of typically late spellings in C, chiefly levelled endings.

Sup.: QUADRAGESSIMA *MT. Title as in* Q *but added later* E. EWANGELIUM SECUNDUM IN DOM*INICA* [3 quadrag.], *the words in brackets added by a modern hand,* C. demonium] demonia C; demonium, et illud erat mutu*m* EN.

1 þæræ] þære *EHMNOT*; þæra C. mærran E; mære C. 2 wunodo C. menniscnesse N. 3 gebroht to] gebrohto N; to gebroht CH. 4 wundorlic T. 5 gesyhð *OT*; geseohþ C. spræc] is spæc (*on erasure*) M; his spræce O. 6 he] *om.* E. ablænd N; blænd O. deofollice E; deofolice O. awedde C.

Latin Glosses in T and E. (*Ten ME glosses are listed above, p. 263; additional Latin glosses in* E, *below, p. 285.*) 4 witseoc: demonium (*sic*) T; demoniacus E. 5 benæmed: auferre T.

Sources. 3–11 [*Matth. xii. 22 sq.*] Tunc oblatus est ei dæmonium habens, cæcus, et mutus, et curavit eum ita ut loqueretur, et videret. [*Some MSS. add* et audiret; *cf. line 10.*] Et stupebant omnes turbæ. [*Ælfric uses this fuller account to supplement the first verse of his basic text,* Luc. xi. 14:] Et erat eiiciens dæmonium, et illud erat mutum. Et cum eiecisset dæmonium, locutus est mutus, et admiratæ sunt turbæ.

Hwæt þá se mildheorta Críst þurh his godcundan mihte
þone mann gehælde, and ðone hetelan deofol
him fram adræfde þe hine drehte oð ðæt,
and he þa, gewittig, wel spræc and gehyrde,   10
and eall séo meniu micclum þæs wundrode.
þa sǽdon þa Iudeiscan þæt ure Drihten scéolde
þá wundra wyrcan on þæs deofles mihte
þe men hataþ Béélzebúb, ac hí lugon forðearle.
Sume hí woldon éác þæt hé sum syllic tacen   15
of heofonum æteowde, ac he cwæþ him tó,
þa ða he geséah heora syrwiendan geþohtas:
Ælc cynerice þe bið on him sylfum todæled
bið soðlice toworpen, and ne wunaþ ná on sibbe,
and híwræden fealð ofer hiwrædene.   20
Gif se sceocca soðlice is on him sylfum todæled,
hú mæg þonne standan his ríce staþolfǽst?
Ge secgaþ þæt ic adræfde deofla of mannum
þurh ðæs deofles mihte þe menn hataþ Beelzebúb,
and gif ic on his naman adrǽfe deofla of mannum,   25

---

7 godcundlican *O*; godcunde *C*.   8 gehælde] gehælan *H*.   hetolan
EHMNOT; hetole *C*.   10 gewitti *M*.   geherde *C*.   11 mæniu
CNO.   wundrodon *E*; wundroden (n *added later*) *T*.   12 iudeiscean *MO*.
13 wyrcean *MHO*; wircan *C*.   14 mæn *C*.   hateð *CT*.   Zebub *capital-
ized in Q only*.   forðearle] forðealle *C*.   15 sellic *T*.   tacn *EHMNO*.
16 ateowode *C*.   heom *CE*.   17 hyra *T*.   syrwienda *C*.   geþohtes *C*.
18 kynerice *C*.   19 wunaþ] wunenæd *C*.   20 hiwrædden, hiwræddene *T*.
21 scucca *T*; sceocce *C*.   soðlice] *om. C*.   22 staloð- *M*.   23 seccað *N*;
secgeað *O*.   adræde *O*.   24 hateð *CT*.   25 adræfde *EH*(?)*NO*.

Latin glosses: 14 forþearle: valde *ET*.   17 syrwiendan: *insidias, mala*
(*marg.* malas) *T*; insidiantes, [m]alas *E*.   18 todæled: diuisu*m ET*.   20
hiwræden, -e: domu*s*, domu*m ET*.

12–26 [*Luc. xi. 15*] Quidam autem ex eis dixerunt: In Beelzebub principe
dæmoniorum eiicit dæmonia.
    [*16*] Et alii tentantes, signum de cælo quærebant ab eo.
    [*17*] Ipse autem ut vidit cogitationes eorum, dixit eis: Omne regnum in se-
ipsum divisum desolabitur, et domus supra domum cadet.
    [*18*] Si autem et Satanas in seipsum divisus est, quomodo stabit regnum
eius?
    [*18*] Quia dicitis in Beelzebub me eiicere dæmonia.
    [*19*] Si autem ego in Beelzebub eiicio dæmonia: filii vestri in quo eiiciunt?
[*Ælfric here omits the rest of the verse*, Ideo ipsi iudices vestri erunt. *See line 124
below.*]

on hwæs naman adræfaþ eowre suna þonne?—
þis *sæde se Hælend be his apostolum,   *p. 124
þe wæron 'heora' suna and heora siblingas,
and hi deofla adræfdon on heora Drihtnes naman,
and fela wundra worhton on ðæs folces gesihðe.—   30
Ða cwæþ sé Hælend to þam heardheortum folce:
Witodlice gif ic aflyge on Godes fingre deofla,
Godes ríce becymð soðlice on eow.
Ðonne sé stranga healt his inburh fæste,
þonne beoð on sibbe þa ðing þe he sylf hæfð.   35
Ac gif sum strengra cymð and hine oferswið,
ealle his wæpna he gewinð þonne
on þam ðé he truwode, and todælð his hereréaf.
Se þe nys mid me, he bið ongéan mé,
and se þe mid me ne gaderaþ, hé towyrpð soðlice.   40

26 hwæs] wæs H.   eowra T.   suna] synna E.   27 'bi' (later) E.   28 sibblin-
gas H.   29 hi] heo E.   drihtenes HO.   30 feala NO; feola E.
worton N.   31 cwæþ om. H.   heardheortan EHT.   32 aflige
CEHMNOT.   34 inburh] burh H (corrected in margin?); innburh MO.
feaste C.   35 beoð] bið C.   þincg E.   36 Ac] And N.   gyf HT;
geof C.   sum om. C.   oferswyþ E.   37 wepna M.   38 truwode]
ontruwode E.   his] om. C.   hereræf C.   39 first me] me cwæð crist E.
beoð C.   ongeanes E.   40 towurpð T.

Latin glosses: 26 adræfað: eiciunt T.   32 aflige: eicio ET.   34 stranga:
fortis T.   healt: custodit T.   inburh: atrium ET.   38 truwode: confidebat
ET.   herereaf: spolia ET.

27–30 [Bede, In Luc. xi. 19 (restating Jerome)] Dixit hoc utique de discipulis
suis, illius populi filiis. . . . Illi expulsionem dæmonum Deo assignant.
32–55 [Luc. xi. 20] Porro si in digito Dei eiicio dæmonia: profecto pervenit
in vos regnum Dei.
[21] Cum fortis armatus custodit atrium suum, in pace sunt ea, quæ possidet.
[22] Si autem fortior eo superveniens vicerit eum, universa arma eius auferet,
in quibus confidebat, et spolia eius distribuet.
[23] Qui non est mecum, contra me est: et qui non colligit mecum, dispergit.
[24] Cum immundus spiritus exierit de homine, ambulat per loca inaquosa,
quærens requiem: et non inveniens dicit: Revertar in domum meam unde
exivi.
[25] Et cum venerit, invenit eam scopis mundatam, et ornatam.
[26] Tunc vadit, et assumit septem alios spiritus secum, nequiores se, et
ingressi habitant ibi. Et fiunt novissima hominis illius peiora prioribus.
[27] Factum est autem, cum hæc diceret: extollens vocem quædam mulier
de turba dixit illi: Beatus venter, qui te portavit, et ubera, quæ suxisti.
[28] At ille dixit: Quinimmo beati, qui audiunt verbum Dei, et custodiunt
illud.

þonne sé unclæna gast gǽþ ut of ðam men,
þonne færð hé worigende on únwæterigum stowum
secende him reste, ac hé soðlice ne fint.
þonne cw[e]þ se fula gást þæt he far῾an´ wylle
into his huse, of þam ðe hé ut ferde,   45
and cymþ ðonne tó, and áfint hit gedæft.
He genimð him þonne tó seofan oðre gástas
wyrsan þonne he sylf sy, and hi wuniaþ mid þam men,
and bið þæs mannes wise wyrse þonne hit ær wære.
Mid þam ðe he þis clypode, þa cwæþ him sum wíf to   50
of þære menigo mid micelre stemne:
Eadig is se innoð þe ðe to mannum gebær,
and gesælige syndon þá bréost þe þu gesuce.
Hire andwyrde se Hǽlend: Gyt synd eadigran
þa ðe Godes wórd gehyrað and hit gehealdaþ.   55
    We gegaderiað þæt andgyt to þisum godspelle
be þam twam godspellerum, Lucam and Matheum,
and we wyllað sceortlice secgan eow þæt andgit.
Ure Drihten gehælde þá þurh his heofonlican mihte
þone earmann wodan fram his wodnysse,   60

---

41 *Beginning of excerpt in G, Warner p. 58. Prefixed is the phrase,* Se helend
cwæð *on his godspelle. Variants in spelling are not ordinarily recorded.*   gæþ
ut] gewitt *T.*   42 fearð *C.*   unwætergum *O*; wæterigum *E.*   stowe *C.*
43 seccende *O.*   ne] hi ne *CH*; nane ne *OT.*   fint] fint na on þam soþfæstum
mannum nane wununge *E.*   44 cwæþ (*alt. to* cweþ?) *Q*; cweð *CET*; cweðð
G; cwyþ *HMNO.*   46 cymþ *altered from* cwyþ *Q.*   afintt *H*; fint *EOT.*
after hit] him *over line T.*   47 seofon *EHMNO.*   48 he] he hi *O.*   self *C.*
after hi] inn farað and *T.*   49 bið] bið þænne *H.*   hit] heo *EGH.*   wære]
wæs *E*; wæron *G.*   50 þis] þuss *G.*   cleopode *E.*   51 of] on *H.*   meniu
EHMO; mæniu *N*; maniu *C.*   mid] mid mid *O.*   stæmne *CG.*   52 is]
his *H.*   þe] se *E.*   manne *G.*   53 gesælig synd *E.*   breosta *G.*   gesuce]
suce *CEHO*; suca *G.*   54 andwyrde] andswarede *G.*   Gyt synd eadigran]
and cwæð.   Eadige synd *E*; Eadige synden *G*; Gyt syndon eadigre *C.*
55 hit] hio *H. Excerpt in G ends with this line. (Next sentence in Warner is set apart
in MS. and is a modification of a sentence in CH I. 304. 5 sqq.)*   56 gegadriað *O.*
godspellum *O.*   57 be] of *H.*   Lucum *N.*   58 secgean *MO.*   60 earman
EHMNOT; earm̄ *C.*   *after* wodan] man *over line C.*

Latin glosses: 41 gewitt: exierit *T.*   46 gedæft: tranquillum *ET.*

59–71 [*Bede, In Luc. (Jerome, In Matth.*)] Tria ergo signa simul in uno
homine perpetrata sunt. Cæcus videt, mutus loquitur, possessus dæmone libe-
ratur. Quod et tunc quidem carnaliter factum est, sed et quotidie completur in
conversione credentium, ut, expulso primum dæmone, fidei lumen aspiciant,
deinde ad laudes Dei tacentia prius ora laxentur.

and fram his dumbnysse þæs deoflican bendas,
and fram þæræ blin`d´nysse þe hine ablende se deofol,
*'and eall seo meniu micclum þæs wundrode.'   *p. 125
Dæghwamlice he wyrcþ ðas ylcan wundra gyt,
æfter gastlicum andgite, on Godes gelaþunge,   65
on soðre gecyrrednysse synfulra manna.

þonne se ungeleaffulla þe læg on his synnum
gebihþ to his Drihtne mid soþre dædbote,
and ðone deofol forlæt þe hine forlædde on ǽr,
þonne bið hé geclænsod fram þam unclænan gáste,   70
and hæfð þæs geleafan leoht, and heráð his Drihten.

' þa sædon þá Iudeiscan þæt ure Drihten sceolde
þa wundra wyrcan on þæs deofles naman
þe men hatað Beelzebúb, ac hí lugon 'for'ðearle.'
Hwilon ær we sǽdon be þisum sceandlican deofle.   75
Ða hæþenan leoda gelyfdon on hine
and heton hine Beel, sume Báál,
and se ylca hæfde yfelne tonaman,
þæt is Zebub, for ðære sceandlican offrunge.
Ðá hæþenan him offrodon swa swa healicum gode   80
sceap and hryðeru, and ofslogon þá;

61–62 þæs . . . blindnysse] *om. C.*   61 deofolican *E.*   bendes *EHMT.*
62 þære *EHMNOT.*   ablænde *N.*   63 mænigu *N;* mæniu *CO.*   wundrodon
T; wrund`r´ode *C.*   64 wundra] wundro *T; om. N.*   65 gastlican *T.*
66 on] and on *T.*   mana *E.*   67 *after* ungeleaffulla] man *over line C.*
þæ *O.*   læg *with* ligeð *over line T.*   67–68 his synnum gebihþ to] *om., in*
margin sunne went t[o] *C.*   68 gebigþ *alt. to* gebihþ *Q;* gebyhð *EHMNO;*
gebygð *alt. to* gebuhð *T.*   drihtene *HO;* drihtenne *N (for* drihtene?).
69 forlet *H.*   on ær] ær *C.*   70 unclænum *CH.*   gaste *om. H.*   71
and he hæfð *O.*   þæs] his *T.*   72 sædan *EN.*   iudeiscean *EMO.*
73 wyrcean *EMO;* wircan *C.*   74 hateð *T.*   75 Hwilum *T.*
scandlican *T;* sceandlicum *E.*   76 hæþenan] he þan *E.*   leode *E.*
77 and *inserted before* sume *T.*   79 ðere *C.*   sceanlican *N;* scandlican *T.*
80 Ða] þe þa *O.*   hæðenum *C.*   81 scep *CN.*   hruðeru *H.*

Latin Glosses: 66 gecyrrednysse: *conuersione ET.*   69 forlædde:
seduxit *T.*   76 leoda: gentes *ET.*   79 offrunge: *immolatio T.*

76–89 [*Bede*] Non hæc aliqui de turba, sed Pharisæi calumniabantur et
Scribæ. . . . Illi . . . hæc . . . sinistra interpretatione pervertere laborabant, quasi
non haec divinitatis, sed immundi spiritus opera fuissent, id est Beelzebub, qui
deus erat Accaron. Nam Beel quidem, ipse est Baal. Zebub autem, musca vocatur.
. . . Beelzebub ergo Baal muscarum, id est, *vir muscarum,* sive *habens muscas*
interpretatur, ob sordes videlicet immolatitii cruoris, ex cuius spurcissimo ritu
vel nomine principem dæmoniorum cognominabant.

þa gewunedon þær fleogan to þære fulan offrunge,
and his bígengas þa hine heton Beelzebub,
þæt is fleogena Bél, oððe se ðe fleogan hæfð,
for þan ðe zebub is gesǽd fleoge.   85
Nu sǽdon ða Iudeiscan, urum Drihtne to teonan,
þæt hé sceolde adrǽfan déofla of mannum
on ðises godes naman, þe is gramlic deofol,
and nætfð náne mihte menn to gehǽlenne.
'Sume hi woldon éac þæt hé sum syllic tacen   90
of heofonum æteowde,' ac hi his fandodon swá.
þa Iudeiscan gesawon swutele tacna
on þam wódan men þe ðær wæs gehǽled,
and swaþeah woldon wundra geséon
ufon of heofonum, mid ungeleaffulnysse   95
fandiende Cristes, 'ac hé cwæþ him to,
þa ða he geseah heora syrwigendan geþohtas:
Ælc cyneríce þe bið on him sylfum to*dæled   *p. 126
bið sóðlice toworpen, and ne wunað ná on sibbe,
and hiwrǽden fealð ofer hiwrǽdene.'   100
Gif se woruldlica cyning winð wið his léoda,

82–85 *om. C.*   82 gewunodon *MNOT.*   83 biggengas *EHNO.*
þa hine] hine þa *N.*   84 fleogana *T.*   beel *E.*   85 þan ðe] ðon *T;* þam
ðe *EMO.*   fleoga *EN.*   86 seaden *C.*   iudeiscean *EM.*   drihtene *HO.*
87 adrefan *H.*   deofla of mannum] of mannum deofla *T.*   88 godes *om.*
NO.   89 menn] *om. C.*   gehælende *H;* gehælanne *T.*   90 eac]
om. CH.   sellic *T.*   tacn *EHMNO.*   91 ætewde *C.*   92 þa]
swa þa *O.*   iudeiscean *EMO.*   swytele *H;* swytela *T.*   tacne *E.*   93 þar *O.*
95 ufan *HT;* ufor *C.*   96 fandigende *E.*   he] *om. H.*   heom *CEO.*
97 hyra *T;* hyre *E.*   syrwiendan *HMNT;* syrwienda *C.*   100 and] ac *NO.*
hiwrædden, hiwræddene *T.*   fealð *EM.*   101 woruldlica] woruld *E.*
wið] *om. CM* (ongen *over line C*).   leode *CEHMNOT.*

Latin glosses: 82 offrunge: *immolatio T.*   83 bigengas: *colentes T;* cul-
tores *E.*   85 is gesæd: *dicitur T.*   86 teonan: *scandalum, contumelia*
ET (schandalu*m E*).   87 adræfan: *eicere ET.*   91 his: illu*m T;* eu*m E.*
100 hiwræden: *domus ET.*   101 winð: *pugnat T;* pu*n*gnat *E.*

80–85 [*Haymo, Hom. XLII, restates Bede more clearly*] Propter effusionem
autem sanguinis, qui ibi frequenter effundebatur, multæ muscæ in eodem loco
congregabantur. Unde congruum nomen ei impositum est Beelzebub, id est
princeps muscarum, sive *vir habens muscas. Zebub* enim musca dicitur.
92–96 [*Haymo*] Superflue, qui ea quæ oculis vident, credere nolunt, de in-
visibilibus signa quærunt. Qui enim cæcum videntem, mutum loquentem a Deo
curatum credere nolebant, ad callida argumenta se converterunt, quærentes
signum de cælo. [*Bede (Jerome) more remote in expression.*]

and þa leoda wiðeriað wið heora cynehlaford,
þonne cymð heora sacu him to aworpennysse,
and þæt cynerice bið raðe swa toworpen,
and gif þæs hiredes hlaford hatað his cnihtas   105
and him onwinnende bið, hi wurþaþ sóna totwæmede.
Ða cwæþ se Hælend him to be þam hetelan deofle þus:
'Gif se sceocca soðlice is on him sylfum todæled,
hu mæg þonne standan his ríce staðolfæst?'
Nele nán deofol adræfan oðerne,   110
ac hí ealle syrwiað mid heora searucræftum
mid anrædum mode hu hi men beswicon
to hellicum suslum, þær ðær hi sylfe wuniað,
and heora ríce is on þam reþum witum
æfter Domes-dæge a bútan ende.   115
'Ge sec[g]aþ þæt ic adræfe deofla of mannum
þurh ðæs deofles mihte þe menn hatað Béélzebub,
and gif ic on his naman adræfe deofla of mannum,
on hwæs naman adræfað eowre suna þonne?—
þis sæde se Hælend be his apostolum,   120

102 leode CT.   103 heom CEH.   104 hraðe CEMN.   swa] om. E.
105 hlaford] heafod E.   106 heom E.   wyrðað H; weorþað T; bið C.
107 heom CEO.   hetolan MNO; hatelan E.   109 standan his rice staðolfæst]
his rice standen staðelfæst C.   110 Nel O.   111 mid heora searucræftum]
om. H.   heora] his C.   searo- MN; seara- E; sære- C.   112 hi] om. O.
beswicon] beswican magon H; beswicon magon O.   113 susle CO.
þær þar O.   wuniað] onwuniaþ E.   115 buton CN.   116 seccaþ
Q; secgeað MO; secgað CEHNT.   adræfde CEH.   118 adræfde CEH.
119 adræfð C.   eowra E.   suna] sunum C; synna E.

Latin glosses: 102 wiðeriað: aduersantur ET.   103 sacu: contentio T;
prelium E.   aworpennesse: destructione ET.   106 totwæmede: diuisi
ET.   108 todæled: diuisus ET.   111 syrwiað: insidiatur T; insidian-
tur E.   112 mid anrædum mode: unanimi, constanter T.   anrædum:
constanti E.   116 adræfe: eicio T.   119 adræfað: eiciunt T.

101–6 [Ælfric separates cynerice from hiwræden or hired as suggested by Matth.
xii. 25:] Omne regnum divisum contra se, desolabitur; et omnis civitas, vel
domus divisa contra se, non stabit. [Jerome] Non potest regnum et civitas contra
se divisa perstare. . . . [Haymo] Si . . . regnum in seipsum divisum fuerit, ut aliud
rex, aliud principes, aliud duces, aliud milites sentiant, desolationem patitur.
Similiter domus si divisa fuerit, ut aliud vir, aliud uxor, . . . aliud servi, et aliud
domini sapiant, utique et ipsa ruinas patietur.
110–15 [Not in Bede, Jerome, or Haymo.]
120–3 [Bede, as above, 27–30. Haymo much closer:] Filios eorum discipulos
suos dicit, qui sine dubio ex eorum progenie nati erant, quibus iam potestatem

ðe wæron heora suna and heora siblingas,
and hi deofla adræfdon on heora Drihtnes naman,
and fela wundra wrohton on þæs folces gesihðe.—
Ideo ipsi iudices uestri erunt:
Forþam ða ylcan beoð eft eowre déman.'   125
þa halgan apostolas þe þam Hælende folgodon
on soðre láre sceolon eft beon
ealles manncynnes déman on þam micclan dæge,
ge þæra Iudeiscra ge oðra leoda,
þeah ðe hí comon of þam yfelan cynne   130
þe Criste wiðsóc and eac swilce ofsloh.
    'Ða cwæþ se Hǽlend to þam heardheortum folce:
Witodlice gif ic aflige on Godes fingre deofla,
Godes ríce *becymð soðlice on eow.'   *p. 127
Godes finger soðlice getacnode þone Halgan Gást,   135
swa swa Matheus awrát, þisum wordum cweþende:
Si in spiritu Dei eicio demones:
Gif ic on Godes Gaste deofla adræfe.

121 þæ O.   sunas C.   122 drihtenes HO.   123 feala ENO.
worhtan C; worhton EHMNOT.   gesyhðe EOT; geseohþe C.   125 þam]
ðan COT.   beoð] bið C.   eft] om. E.   eowere MN.   126 halgan] om. H.
hælend O.   127 eft beon] beon eft C.   128 ealle N.   129 þara E; þære CO.
second ge] ge eac T.   130 yfelan] om. NO.   131 crist CE.   wiðsocon
O.   ofslogon OT.   132 hærd- C.   -heortum] *sic* T; *alt. from* -heortam Q;
no reading H; -heortan CEMNO; *cf.* 31.   folce] deofle NO.   133 fingra E.
134 becymð soðlice] soðlice becymð C.   136 cweþende] om. NO.   137 dei]
dei aguntur T.   138 deoflu T.   adreafa C; adræfde EH; afligde N;
afligede O.

    Latin glosses: 126 folgodon: secuti *sunt* T.   133 witodlice: porro ET.
aflige: eicio ET.

effugandi dæmones dederat, atque calcandi super omnem potestatem inimici,
dicens: *In nomine meo infirmos curate, leprosos mundate, cæcos illuminate, dæmones
eiicite (Matth. x. 8, inexactly).*
    124 sq. [*Ælfric here quotes and translates that part of Luc. xi. 19 which he has
omitted earlier (above, line 26).*
    126–31 [*Haymo, following Jerome on Matth. xii. 27*] Id est, . . . discipuli mei,
qui curationes dæmonum Deo et non Beelzebub assignant, *iudices vestri erunt,*
tunc scilicet, quando venerit Filius hominis, et *sederit in sede maiestatis suæ sede-
bunt et ipsi super sedes duodecim, iudicantes duodecim tribus Israel (Matth. xix. 28,
inexactly).*
    135–8 [*Haymo*] Digitus Dei, Spiritus sanctus intelligitur, quod Matthæus
evangelista manifestius declarat, cum dixit: *Si autem ego in Spiritu [Dei] eiicio
dæmones (Matth. xii. 28).*

þes finger oferswiðe soðlice þá drymen
on Egipta lande ætforan Faraó,   140
þa ða hí wunnon wið Moysen and God,
woldon wyrcan gnættas, ac God him forwyrnde;
and hi ða oferswiðe sædon openlice:
Digitus Dei est hoc: Ðis is Godes finger.

Mid þisum fingre wæron éac swilce awritene   145
Moyses tabulan on þam munte Syná;
on ðam tabolum wæron tyn word awritene,
þæt is seo ealde ǽ, eallum mannum to steore,
ge þam ealdan folce ge us þe nu syndon.

Godes hánd soðlice is ure Hælend Críst,   150
þurh ðone he gescéop ealle gesceafta,
and Godes finger is witodlice se Halga Gást,
þurh ðone adræfde ure Drihten ðá deofla,
and þurh ðone syndon geliffæste ealle lybbende gesceaftu,
and ðurh ðone se halga Fæder his halgum todælð   155

---

139 drymen] þrymen *N*; ðry menn *O*.   140 egypta *CEHMO*.   pharao
CMT; pharaho *E*; farrao *O*.   141 moyses *O*.   and] and wið *NT*;
and wid *O*.   god *om. CEH*.   142 hig *before* woldon *E*.   wyrcean *HO*;
wyrcen *C*.   heom *CE*.   143 and] *om. NO*.   oferswyðe *N*; oferswiððe *O*; oferswiþdon *E*.   sædon] *om. CH*.   openlice] openlice, and hi þa
oferswiðde clypodon *H*.   144 Digitus dei est hoc] *om. E*.   Ðis] þæt *O*.
is] his *M*.   145 swilce] *om. E*.   awritene] *om. NO*.   146 sina *N*; synai *H*;
synay *C*.   147 ðam] twam *E*.   tabulum *EM*; tabulam *H*; tabulan *CN*;
tabulon *O*.   ten *T*; tien *C*.   148 ælde *C*.   ellum *C*.   stiore *C*.   149 *after*
syndon] Fela manna nyton hwæt æ is; nu secge we hwæt seo æ is, þæt is, seo
ealde godes lagu, and eac seo niwe. *T*.   151 gescop *CN*.   153 deoflu
ET; deoflæ *C*.   154 sind *N*; synd *O*.   geliffæst *N*; geliffeste *C*.   gesceafta
EHMO; gesceafte *C*.   155 ðone] ðone þe *M*.   halegum *C*.

Latin glosses: 139 oferswiðde: uicit *T*.   drymenn: *incantatores T*; magos *E*.
141 wunnon wið: *certauerunt contra T*; certabant *E*.   143 oferswiðde: victi
T; superati *E*.   153 adræfde: eiecit *T*.   154 þone: illum *T*.

139–49 [*Bede, In Luc.* (*Jerome*)] Iste est digitus quem confitentur et magi,
qui contra Moysen et Aaron signa faciebant, dicentes, *Digitus Dei est iste* (*Exod.
viii. 19*). Quo et tabulæ lapideæ scriptæ sunt in monte Sina. [*The corresponding
passage in Haymo is closer to Ælfric at one point*:] De hoc etiam digito magi
in Ægypto superati dixerunt: etc.
150–2 [*Bede* (*Jerome*)] Igitur manus et brachium Dei Filius est, et digitus
eius Spiritus Sanctus. . . .
150–7 [*Freely composed except as above, but Haymo quotes Psal. xxxii. 6*:]
Verbo Domini cæli firmati sunt, et spiritu oris eius, omnis virtus eorum. [*He
continues with I Cor. xii, as in next, enumerating the gifts, which include prophecy.*]

menigfealde gyfa and micele mihta,
and þurh þone witegodon ealle witegan be Criste.
Nis us nán lim swa gewylde to gehwilcum weorce
swa us syndon ure fingras, and forði is gehaten
se Halga Gást Godes finger   160
for þam menigfealdum gifum þe God gifð his halgum
þurh ðone Halgan Gást, be þam þe him gewyrð.
Ne sceal nán mann wenan, ne on his mode wealcan,
þæt ure Hælend sy on his heofonlican mihte
læsse þonne his Fæder for ðan ðe hé is gehaten   165
Godes hand on bocum; ac he is God Ælmihtig,
and sé Halga Gast is on ðam heofonlican þrymme
æfre ælmihtig God on anre Godcundnysse
mid þam hal*gan Fæder and þam Hælende Criste,   *p. 128
hi ðry an ælmihtig God æfre rixiende,   170
and heora ríce ne bið næfre todæled
ne næfre toworpen, ac wunað a on ecnysse.
'Profecto peruenit in uos regnum Dei:
Witodlice Godes ríce becymð on eow.'
Crist sylf is Godes ríce, swa swa he cwæþ on oðre stowe: 175

156 menifealde *M*; mænigfealde *NO*; mænigfealda *ET*; manigfealde *C*.
gyfa *from* gifa *Q*.   158 gewulde *H*.   gehwilcum] ælcum *EM*.   159 forþy
N.   161 meni- *M*; mænig- *ENT*; mæni- *O*; manig- *C*.   halgan *N*.
162 gewurð *C*; gewyrh *E*.   164 si *H*.   heofen- *M*.   165 his] on his *C*.
þam *EM*.   is] his *O*.   167 on] of *C*.   heofonlican *M*; heofonlicim *E*.
168 ælmihti *M*.   169 and þam hælende criste] *om. E*.   170 ðreo *C*; ðry is
O.   ælmihti *M*.   171 ne bið næfre] næfre ne byþ *E*.   todælð *C*.   172
næfre] *om. CT*.   a] *om. CH*.   173 Perfecto *O*.   174 becymð *C*.

158–62 [*Bede (Aug. quæst. in ev. s. Luc.)*] Digitus Dei vocatur Spiritus Sanctus,
propter partitionem donorum quae in eo dantur unicuique propria, sive hominum sive angelorum. In nullis enim membris nostris magis apparet partitio,
quam in digitis. [*Haymo, restating same point*] Sicut in nullis aliis membris
tantam partitionem habemus, quantam in digitis, sic et Spiritus sancti dona
diversa sunt, . . . teste Apostolo, qui ait: *Alii quidem per Spiritum datur sermo
sapientiæ*, etc. . . . *Hæc autem omnia operatur unus atque idem Spiritus, dividens
singulis prout vult.* (*I Cor. xii. 8–11*.)

163–72 [*Bede (Jerome)*] Patris et Filii et Spiritus Sancti una substantia est.
Non te scandalizet membrorum inæqualitas, cum ædificet unitas corporis.

175–82 [*Jerome, In Matth. xii. 28*] Vel seipsum significat, de quo in alio loco
scriptum est: *Regnum Dei intra vos est* (*Luc. xvii. 21*). . . . Est et tertium regnum
Scripturæ sanctæ, quod aufertur a Iudæis, et tradetur genti facienti fructus eius
(*Matth. xxi. 43*). [*Not in Bede. Haymo gives first half, not second.*]

Regnum Dei intra uos est:
þæt is on Englisc, Godes ríce is betweox eow.
Godes rice is eac Godes gelaþung,
þæt is eall Cristen folc þe on Crist gelyfð,
and hé hí gebringð eac to ðam heofonlican ríce,   180
ge of Iudeiscum cynne þe on Críst gelyfdon,
ge of oðrum leodscipum þe his geleafan healdað.
' þonne se stranga healt his [in]burh fæste,
þonne beoð on sibbe þa ðing þe he sylf hæfð.
Ac gif sum strengra cymð and hine oferswið,   185
ealle his wæpna he gewinð þonne
on ðam ðe he truwode, and todælð his hereréaf.'
Deofol is se stranga þe ure Drihten embe spræc,
ðe hæfde eall manncynn on his andwealde þá
ðurh Adames forgægednysse, ac Godes Sunu com,   190
strengra þonne he, and hine gewylde,
and his wepna him ætbræd and tobræc his searocræftas,
and his hereréaf todælde þe he mid his deaðe alysde

177 þæt is on englisc] *om. CH.*   betwux *MNO*; betwyx *HT*; betwix *C.*
178 eall *after* eac *H.*   gelaðunge *T.*   179 on criste *C.*   gelifð *N.*
180 hig *T.*   gebringð eac] bringð eac *H*; eac gebringð *E.*   heofen- *M.*
181 iudeiscum] þam iudeiscan *N*; þam iudeiscean *O*; iudeiscean *E*; iudeiscan *C.*
182 his] is *O.*   183 hilt *N.*   inburh] *sic HT* (in *over line T*); burh *CENOQ*
buruh *M.*   feaste *C.*   184 bið *C.*   þa] ealle þa *NO.*   þingc *E.*   heafð *C.*
185 strængre *C.*   oferswyð *N.*   187 truwade *O*; getruwode *E*: truwede *C.*
hereræf *C.*   188 ymbe *ENOT.*   189 his] is *O.*   anwealde *CEHMNOT.*
þa] *om. O.*   191 strængra *C.*   192 wæpna *CEMNOT*; *no reading H.*
ætbryt *E.*   seara- *HNO*; sære- *C.*   193 herehræf *C.*   todealde *C.*

Latin glosses: 183 burh *E*, `in´burh *T*: atrium *ET.*   187 ðam: quibus *ET.*
truwode: confidebat *ET.*   189 þe: qui *T.*   190 forgægednesse: preuari-
catione *T*; transgressione *E.*   193 hereréaf: spolia *ET.*

188–96 [*Bede*] Fortem, diabolum: atrium vero illius, mundum qui in maligno
positus est appellat, in quo usque ad Salvatoris adventum male pacato potiebatur
imperio, quia in cordibus infidelium sine ulla contradictione quiescebat. . . .
Si autem fortior illo superveniens vicerit eum, etc. De seipso quippe loquitur, quod
. . . fortiori potentia victor homines a dæmonio liberaret. Arma in quibus male
fortis ille confidebat, astutiæ dolique sunt nequitiæ spiritalis. Spolia vero eius,
ipsi homines sunt ab eo decepti. Quæ victor Christus distribuit, quod est insigne
triumphantis, quia *captivam ducens captivitatem, dedit dona hominibus.* [*Ephes. iv.*
8. Ælfric develops only the motif of the Harrowing of Hell from the last sentence.
Haymo is closer only near the beginning:] Fortem armatum, diabolum dicit, cuius
atrium erat mundus, per quem prævaricationem primi hominis sibi subiugaverat.

þa ða hé Adam and Efan and heora ofspring genám,
swiðe micelne dǽl, of þam manfullum deofle,   195
and gelædde hí of helle up to heofonan ríce.
   '*Qui non est mecum aduersum me est*:
Se ðe nys mid me, he bið ongean me,
and se þe mid me ne gaderaþ, he towyrpð soðlice.'
Ures Drihtnes dæda and þæs deofles ne magon   200
nateshwón geþwærian ne béon gelice,
for þan ðe se Hælend wyle us gehealdan æfre,
and se deofol wile us fordón gif he mæg.
*Crist tihð to mihtum symle and deofol to mandǽdum, *p. 129
ac wé sceolon gehyrsumian urum Hælende symle,   205
þe is ure hyrde, na þam hetelan wulfe,
þe þæs anes cepð, hu hé us tostencge
mid mislicum leahtrum fram ðam míldan Hælende.
Eac þá manfullan menn þe mistihtaþ oðre
to deofollicum weorcum wiðeriað ongean Críst,   210

194 þa ða] þa *NO*.   he] þe *N*.   euan *CEHMO*.   ofspryncg *C*.   195 swyðe
ENOT.   micel *E*.   manfullan *NOT*; manfulne *C*.   196 up] in *NO*;
upp *H*.   heofonan] hēfan *C*.   198 *after* ongean me] cwæð crist *E*.
199 gegaderað *NO*.   towurpð *T*; towyrp *MN*.   200 drihtenes *NOT*.
magan *M*.   201 gehwærian *M*; geþwæran *O*; geþwærlæcan *E*; *om. C*.
ne] ne ne *NO*; *om. C*.   202 þam *EM*.   gehealden *T*; gehælden *C*.
204 tyhð *H*; tyht *MT*; tiht *C*; tihð us *E*; tiht us *NO*.   mihtum] rihtwisnesse
NO.   symble *EHM*.   deofol] se deofol *EM*.   204–5 and . . . symle]
om. H.   205 sceolan *T*; sculon *C*.   gehersumigen *C*.   hælendum *C*.
symble *EM*.   206 na] and na *T*.   hetolan *EM*.   207 anes] *om. NO*.
kepð *T*; cypþ *CE*.   hwu *C*.   tostence *EHMOT*; tostentte *N*; tostince *C*.
208 mistlicum *ENO*; mystlicum *C*.   ðan *M*.   mildan] *om. E*.   209
oðrum *C*.   210 deoflicum *HNO*; deoflum *C*.   weorce *NO*.   wiðeriað]
þe wiðeriað *EO*.

Latin glosses: 195 manfullum: *iniquo ET*.   199 towyrpð: dispergit *ET*.
201 geþwærian: concordare *ET*.   203 fordon: damnare *T*.   204 mandæ-
dum: malo opere *T*.   207 tostence: dispergat *T*; disperdat *E*.   208 mislicum: variis *T*.   209 manfullan: *iniqui T*.   menn: homines *T*.

200–11 [*Bede (Jerome)*] Non putet quisquam de hæreticis dictum et schis-
maticis, quanquam et ita ex superfluo possit intelligi [*as by Ælfric at* 209–11],
sed ex consequentibus textuque sermonis, ad diabolum refertur, et quod non
possint opera Salvatoris, Beelzebub operibus comparari. Ille cupit animas
hominum tenere captivas, Dominus liberare. . . . Ille trahit ad vitia, hic ad virtutem revocat. Quomodo ergo possunt habere concordiam inter se, quorum opera
divisa sunt?
205–8 [*Haymo*] Et ideo quia cum illo non colligit, dispergit, sicut de eo alibi
sub figura lupi dicitur: *Et lupus rapit, et dispergit oves (Ioan. x. 12)*.

and mid him ne gaderiað, ac swiðor towurpaþ.

'Ðonne sé unclæna gást gæþ ut of þam men,
þonne færð hé worigende on unwæterigum stowum,
secende him reste, ac hé soðlice ne fint'
on þam clǽnheortum him gecweme wununge.   215
He forlæt þá clǽnan mód þe Críste þeowiað,
þa ðe þurh syfernysse syndon unwǽterige,
and him reste secð on þam receleasum,
þe on oferflowednysse and fulnysse lybbað,
swa swa ure Drihten be þam deofle gecwæþ: 220
Sub umbra, inquit, dormit in secreto calami, et locis humentibus.
Ðæt is on urum gereorde, he gerest hine on sceadewe,
and on þæs reodes digolnysse, and on fuhtum stowum.
Ðæs deofles rest bið on deorcum sceadewum
for ðan ðe hé slæpþ on ðam sweartum ingehýdum   225
þe ðæs geleafan leoht on heora lífe nabbað;
and ða ðe þurh híwunge beoð swa hole swa réod,

---

211 swyðor *EHT*; swiðar *C*.   toweorpað *ENOT*; towyrpað *H*; towurpð *C*.
214 ne] nane ne *O*.   215 clænheortum] clænheortam *C*; clænan heortu*m T*;
clænum heortum *E*; clænum men *O*.   216 forlet *HM*.   clænan mod]
clænmodan *NO*; clænan *E*.   þewiad *C*.   217 unwæterige] unwerie
NO; unwæterigende *E*.   218 receleasum] receleasum mannum *NO*.
219 -flowen- *NO*; -flowend- *H*.   220 swa swa] swa *NO*.   gecwæþ]
cwæð *CHNOT*.   221 inquit] *om. H*; inquid *ENO*.   222 gereste
CNO.   223 *first* and] *om. NO*.   hreodes *HMNOT*.   digel- *CN*; dihel-
O.   224 bið] is *NO*.   sceaduwum *M*; stowum *C*.   225 for ðam *EH*;
for ðon *CT*.   sweartan *HNO*; swearton *C*.   226 hyre *E*.   nabað *N*.
227 ðe] *om. EM*; ða *T*; ðæ *O*.   beoð] bið *C*.   hreod *CHMNOT*.

Latin glosses: 213 -wæterigum: humen*tibus ET*.   223 fuhtum: hum*entibus
ET*.   225 sweartu*m* ingehydu*m*: superbis *T*.   ingehydu*m*: i*n*tenti*one T*';
i*n*tenti*one* conciencie *E*.   226 þe: *qui T*.   227 hiwunge: simulati*one*
ET (*preceded by* ficticia *E*).   hole: *co*ncaui *ET*.

216–19 [*Bede*] De [malo catholico] tempore baptismatis spiritus immundus
qui in eo prius habitaverat . . . eiiciatur, locaque inaquosa peragret, id est, corda
fidelium, quæ a mollitie fluxæ cogitationis expurgata sint, callidus insidiator
exploret. . . . Sed bene dicitur: *Quærens requiem et non inveniens*. Quia castas
mentes effugiens, in solo diabolus corde pravorum gratam sibi potest invenire
quietem. [*Haymo supplies a phrase or two*:] Tunc ambulat per loca arida, et
inaquosa, id est, corda aliorum Christianorum tentando, qui aridi sunt per
abstinentiam: et inaquosi, a fluxu libidinis alieni. . . .Castas et puras mentes
effugiens, tenebrosas et libidinosas quærit.

220–30 [*Bede*] Unde de illo Dominus: *Sub umbra* (inquit) *dormit in secreto
calami, et locis humentibus* (*Iob. xl. 16*). In umbra, videlicet, tenebrosas conscien-
tias: in calamo, qui foris nitidus, intus est vacuus, simulatrices: in locis humentibus, lascivas mollesque mentes insinuans.

wiðutan scinende and wiðinnan æmtige,
and þa ðe fuhtiende beoð on fulre gálnysse,
on swilcum hé macað symle his wununge.   230
Sé deofol bið adræfed þurh ures Drihtnes mihte
of þam hǽþenan men þonne hine man fullað;
þonne secð he gehwær him sylfum wununge,
ac hé ne fint on þam clænum him gecweme wununge.

'Ðonne cweþ sé fúla gást þæt hé faran wylle   235
into his húse of þam þe hé ut férde,'
into þam Cristenan men gif *hé his Cristendom ne healt   *p. 130
mid godum bigengum, swa swa he Gode behét:
þæt hé deofl[e] wiðsóce and his weorcum and getotum.
'He cymþ þonne to and afint hit' aswapen,   240
and eac swilce æmtig and eall him 'gedæft'.

Sé man bið geclænsod fram his unclænum synnum
þurh þæt halige fulluht on þæs Hælendes naman;
ac gif he æmtig bið æfter his fulluhte fram eallum   godum
    weorcum,
and ðurh hiwunge gefrætewod þam fúlan deofle,   245
'þonne genimð he him to seofan oðre gastas
wyrsan þonne hé sylf sy, and hi wuniað mid þam men,

---

229 ðe] *om. O.*   230 symble *CEH.*   231 adrefed *H*; adræfð *C.*
drihtenes *O.*   232 heþenan *T*; *om. C.*   man] me *O.*   fulleð *T.*   233
secgð *NO*; geseceð *C.*   gehwar *O.*   234 clænan *EN*; clænan men *O*;
clæne *C.*   235 cwyð *HMNO.*   237 ne] *om. N.*   238 biggengum
HOT; biggængum *C.*   god *O.*   239 deofle] *sic CEHMNOT*; deofles *Q.*
getogum *NO*; his getotum *C*; geþohtum *H.*   240 to] *om. CH.*   hit] *om. O.*
241 swilce] *om. E.*   æmti *M*; eamtig *C.*   geðæft *C.*   245 gefreetewoð *C.*
246 to] *om. NO.*   seofon *EMNOT.*   247 silf *N.*   si *H.*

Latin glosses: 229 fuhtigende: humidi *ET.*   231 adræfed: eicietur *T*;
eiectus *E.*   232 fulleð: baptizat *T.*   233 gehwær: ubique *T.*   238 bigengum: cultu *ET.*   239 getotum: pompis *ET.*   241 gedæft: tranquillum
ET.   245 hiwunge: simulatione, (sp)ecie (?)*T*; simulatio *E.*   (bið)
gefrætewod: ornatur *T.*

231–4 [*Ælfric makes further use of the passage quoted above for lines 216–19.*]
237–9 [*Bede*] Timendus est iste versiculus, non exponendus. Ne culpa quam
in nobis extinctam credebamus, per incuriam nos vacantes opprimat. [*Ælfric
avoids Bede's comment and a more pedestrian one in Haymo but all agree about the
meaning. See note on 239.*]
240–1 [*Ælfric's recapitulation of Luc. xi. 25 is expanded to include the parallel
verse, Matth. xii. 44, where the word* vacantem (æmtig) *is added. Bede makes the
comparison.*]
242–5 [*Bede*] Mundatam videlicet a vitiis pristinis per baptismum, vacantem
a bonis actibus per negligentiam, ornatam simulatis virtutibus per hypocrisin.

and bið ðæs mannes wise wyrse þonne hit ǽr wære.'
Ða séofon gastas syndon þa seofan heafodleahtras,
gyfernyss and forlír, gytsung and yrre,   250
asolcennyss and unrotnyss, idelgylp, and eahteoðe is modignyss.
Gif ðas heafodleahtras habbað stede on þam menn,
þonne næfþ Godes gást nane wununge on him,
ac hé bið eall deofles gif he geendaþ on ðam,
and him wære sélre þæt hé soðlice ne cuðe   255
þære soðfæstnysse weg, þonne hé sceolde abúgan
fram þære soðfæstnysse to ðam sweartan deofle eft.
    Se Hælend cwæþ to þam héardheortum Iudéiscum:
Sic erit et generationi huic pessime:
þus gewyrð witodlice þissere wyrstan mægðe.   260
Ða þa þæt Iudeisce folc underfeng Godes ǽ,
þa férde sé fula gást fram þam folce aweg;

---

248 wyse *N.*   hit] hio *H.*   ær] æt *O.*   wære] wæs *E.*   249 seofan]
seofon *CEMNO.*   hæfod- *C.*   250 gyfernysse *C.*   forligr *CM*; forliger
EHOT; forligger *N.*   gitsung *CO*; and gitsung *N*; gitsunga *E.*   251 and
asolcennys *CN* (-nes *N*).   unrotnyss] *om. C*; unrotnesse *NO.*   and idelgylp
CHNOT (ydel- *C*; -gilp *N*).   eahtoðe *EMN.*   modignysse *C*; -nesse *O.*
253 nafð *C.*   wunuge *M*; wunungge *O.*   255 þæt] þæt he gefullod nære,
þonne he wære, and þæt *T.*   256–7 weg . . . soðfæstnysse] *over line T.*
257 þære] *om. NO.*   soðfest- *C.*   258 -heortan *CENOT.*   iudeiscan *N.*
260 gewurþ *CE.*   þysse *C.*   261 godes] *om. NO.*

Latin glosses: 249–51 *T has two lists in margin*: (1) Gula, auaricia, cup*iditas*,
for*nicatio*, accidia, etc.; (2) Gula, lux*uria*, auaric*ia*, ira, accidia, *in*vidia, *in*anis
gloria, superbia. *The second list* (*in the tremulous hand*) *corresponds to the order
in the text and to glosses in E, though* invidia *has replaced* tristitia.   260
gewyrð: erit *ET.*   wyrstan: pessime *T.*   mægðe: generat*ioni ET.*

249–51 [*Bede*] Per septem malos spiritus, universa vitia designat. [*Haymo*]
Alios septem nequiores secum assumit, id est septem vitia principalia, quæ sunt
superbia, gula, fornicatio, avaritia, ira, tristitia, vana gloria. [*See note.*]
255–7 [*Bede, modifying II Petr. ii. 21*] Melius quippe erat ei viam veritatis
non cognoscere, quam post agnitionem retrorsum converti.
258–68 [*Bede* (*Jerome*)] Quo autem generaliter hæc parabola tendat, ipse
secundum Matthæum Salvator exposuit, ubi ea terminata mox subdidit dicens,
Sic erit et generationi huic pessimæ (*Matth. xii.* 45). . . . Immundus quippe spiritus
exivit a Iudæis, quando acceperunt legem, et . . . ambulavit per gentium solitu-
dines. Quæ cum postea Domino credidissent, ille . . . dixit, *Revertar ad domum
meam pristinam unde exivi. . . . Et veniens, invenit vacantem, scopis mundatam.*
Vacabat enim templum Iudæorum, et Christum hospitem non habebat. . . .
Quia igitur Dei et angelorum præsidia non habebant, et ornati erant superfluis
observationibus Pharisæorum, revertitur ad eos diabolus, et septenario sibi
numero dæmonum addito habitat pristinam domum, et fiunt posteriora illius
populi peiora prioribus.

ac hé cyrde eft to him mid þam seofon heafodleahtrum
þa ða hí Críste wiðsócon and to cwale gedydon,
and Godes æ swa awurpon þe witegode embe Críst,   265
and heora wise wearð [ð]á wyrse þonne æror,
for þan ðe hí wiðsocon þam soðfæstan Hælende,
mancynnes Alysend, and mislice hine tældon.

'Mid þan ðe hé þis clypode, þa cwæþ him sum wíf to
of þære menio mid micelre stemne: 270
Eadig is se *innoð þe ðe to mannum gebær,   *p. 131
and gesælige syndon þa bréost þe ðu gesuce.'

þurh ðises wifes stemne wurdon þa gescynde
þa arleasan Iudéiscan, Drihtnes wiðersacan,
and heora geleafleast þurh hire geleafan.   275

Eac þæra gedwolmanna þe dwelodon embe Críst,
and sædon þæt hé nære on soðre menniscnysse,
ealle heo oferswiðde mid soðum geleafan,

---

263 heom CEO.   seofan C; seofanfealdum NO.   heafod-] heafdum O.
264 wiðsocan CO.   cweale O.   265 towurpon NO.   ymbe CENO.
criste T.   266 wearð ða] sic EHMNOT; wærð ða C; wearðá Q.   æror]
heo æror wære H; hit æror wæs T; ærror E.   267 soðfæston E.   268 alysende H.   mistlice CENOT.   269 þam CEMNOT.   þa] þam C.
him sum wif to] sum wif him to C.   270 meniu EM; mæniu CNO.
stæmne CM.   271 is] om., wes over line C.   272 brist C.   gesuce] suce
CENO.   273 stæmne CM.   þa] om. CH.   gescende T; gesceonde C.
274 arleasan] om. E.   iudeiscean M.   drihtenes HNO.   275 heora]
heor N; heare C.   geleafleaste NO; geleaflæst C.   276 þara T.   dwelodon
CEHNT.   ymbe CEOT.   crist] om. N.   278 heo] he N; he hi O.
oferswyðde NO.   soðrum M.

Latin glosses: 268 tældon: reprehenderunt T.   273 gescende: scandali-
zati T.

273–81 [Bede] Magnæ devotionis et fidei hæc mulier ostenditur, quæ Scribis
et Pharisæis Dominum tentantibus simul et blasphemantibus, tanta eius
incarnationem præ omnibus sinceritate cognoscit, tanta fiducia confitetur, ut et
præsentium procerum calumniam, et futurorum confundat hæreticorum per-
fidiam. Nam . . . hæretici . . . negando Mariam semper virginem sancti Spiritus
operante virtute, nascituro ex humanis membris Deo carnis suæ
materiam ministrasse, verum consubstantialemque matri filium hominis fateri
non debere dixerunt. Sed si caro Verbi Dei secundum carnem nascentis a
carne virginis matris pronuntiatur extranea, sine causa venter qui eam por-
tasset, ubera quæ lactassent, beatificantur. . . . [Haymo simplifies the comment on
the heretics:] Futurum eorum errorem destruit, qui dicturi erant Dominum non
veram carnem ex Maria virgine assumpsisse. Si enim ventre portatus, uberi-
busque est lactatus, patet profecto quod consubstantialem carnem matris
suscepit.

for ðan ðe sé innoð wæs eadig soðlice
þe Godes Sunu abær, and ða breost þe hé séac on his cíldháde 280
wæron gesǽlige, swa swa héo sǽde.

Ðis wíf getacnode úntwylice mid wórdum
and mid anrædum geleafan ealle Godes Gelaþunge,
þæt is 'eal' Cristen folc þe on Críst nu gelyfð,
and ægþer ge mid mode ge mid muþe hine he%rað,   285
on soðum geleafan þone soðfæstan Hǽlend.

'Hire andwyrde sé Hǽlend: Gyt syndon eadigran
þa ðe Godes wórd gehyrað and hit gehealdaþ.'

Eadig is Maria þæt arwyrðe mæden,
þæt heo Godes Sunu abǽr bliðe to mannum;   290
ac heo is swaþeah git swyþor eadig,
for ðan ðe heo Godes word lufað and healt.

Eac syndon eadige þá ealle þe gehyrað
þæt halige Godes wórd and hit healdað mid lufe.

Uton herian urne Drihten, and þæt halige Godes wórd   295
eac swilce lufian and mid geleafan gehéaldan.

Ðæs us geunne se ælmihtiga Wealdend,
se ðe á rixað on ecnysse; amen.

---

279 þam *EM*. ædig *C*.   280 gebær *O*.   282 untweolice *T*; untweonlice
N; unntweolicelice *O*; untwilice *C*.   283 anrædan *T*.   283–6 ealle ...
geleafan] *om. C*.   284 on crist nu] nu on crist *NO*.   gelyfað *H*.   285 and
erased N; *om. EO*.   heriað *EHOT*.   286 hælend *om. O*.   289 arwurðe
CEMNO.   290 heo] hi *C*.   suna *H*.   gebær *O*.   bliðe] swa bliðe *NO*.
292 þam *EM*; ðon *C*.   293 gehyrað] gehyrod *C*; gelyfað and gehyrað *NO*.
294 þæt halige] *om. CH*.   halie *M*.   295 drihtne *C*.   halie *M*.   godes
word] *om.*, word *over line T*.   297 us] *om. C*.   ealmihtiga *C*.   298 a
rixað] leofað and rixað a *T*.   on ecnysse] a on ecnysse *E*.

Latin glosses: 283 anrædum: *constanti ET*.   287 eadigran: beaci*us T*.

282–6 [*Bede*] Et nos igitur ... extollamus vocem cum Ecclesia catholica, cuius
hæc mulier typum gessit. ... [*Haymo*] Spiritualiter autem mulier ista sancta
significat Ecclesiam, quae inter turbas Iudæorum, paganorum et hæreticorum
credula voce Dominum Christum confitetur.

289–94 [*Bede*] Pulchre Salvator attestationi mulieris annuit, non eam tantum-
modo quæ Verbum Dei corporaliter generare meruerat, sed et omnes qui idem
Verbum spiritaliter auditu fidei concipere, et boni operis custodia vel in suo vel
in proximorum corde parere, et quasi alere studuerint, asseverans esse beatos.
Quia et eadem Dei genetrix, et inde quidem beata, quia Verbi incarnandi ministra
est facta temporalis, sed inde multo beatior quia eiusdem semper amandi custos
manebat æterna. [*Haymo simplifies helpfully but leaves out the substance of 291–2.*]
Ac si dixisset: Iuxta tuam sententiam principaliter beatus ille venter est qui me
portavit: sed et omnes beati, qui audiunt verbum Dei et custodiunt illud.

NOTES

1–298, *the texts of Müller and Stephens*. Since Grundtvig's transcript of MS. N was the sole authority for the texts of this homily printed by Müller and Stephens, they have reproduced most of the idiosyncrasies of N, including its numerous omissions of single words, as at lines 64, 88, 130, 136, 143, 145, 207, 246, 257, 261, 276, and the odd readings, *unwerie* for *unwæterige* at 217, *getogum* for *getotum* at 239. But in the following respects they differ from N:

1. Both Müller and Stephens have properly emended the readings of N at the following points:

3 gebrohto] gebroht to	199 towyrp] towyrpð
61 bendas] bendes	275 heor] heora
132 deofle] folce	

2. Stephens has properly added the following emendations where Müller adhered to the manuscript:

139 þrymen] drymen	237 healt] ne healt
201 ne ne] ne	278 he] heo

3. The spelling has been silently normalized in some nineteen instances, as *worhton* for *worton* (30), *Lucam* for *Lucum* (57), *drihtne* for the improperly abbreviated *drihtenne* (68), *tostencce* for *tostentte* (207), *secð* for *secgð* (233), and others of even less consequence. Very likely Grundtvig made some of these little changes in his transcript. In one instance the normalizing is in error: at lines 70 and 242 both editors have *geclænsed* for N's grammatically correct *geclænsod*.

4. Both texts have the following errors or omissions, often no doubt because of a fault in the transcript:

Sup.: *Latin text om.*	197 adversum] adversus
18 þe] þæt	207 cepð] cerð
27 þis] þes	221 inquid (*for* inquit)] *om.*
94 geseon] *om.*	221 *Latin* et (*ampersand*)] æt
103 him] *om.*	251 eahtoðe] eahtode
115 æfter] æft	278 oferswiðde] oferswiððe

5. The following errors are peculiar to Müller's text:

16 sq. to, þa þa] to þam, þa
154 ðone] þon (*Stephens* þon[e], *showing an error in the transcript*)
219 -flowen-] -flower- (*Stephens emends to* -flowed-)
263 eft] oft
289 arwurðe] arwurde

6. Stephens's text has one independent error, *in* for *on* at 280.

7. Both editors punctuate incorrectly on several occasions, and twice they treat independent words as compounds:

34 inburh fæste] inburh-fæste (*and* burh-fæste 183)
298 a rixað] arixað (*where N itself ran the words together,* árixað)

10. *gehyrde*. Ælfric's inclusion of the sense of hearing is natural enough with reference to a man said to be mute and therefore assumed to be deaf, and he may not have needed the *audiret* that is added to some of the texts of the verse in Matthew; but his omission of the sense of sight appears a little careless in view of his earlier mention of the man's blindness and his return to that theme, under Bede's guidance, at line 62. Probably at this point he was turning back from Matthew to Luke, who does not mention that the man was blind.

12, 72, 87. On this use of *sceolde* to emphasize the unreliability of a reported assertion, see the glossary under *sceolan*, b.

23. *adræfde*. All manuscripts agree on the past tense here, though the Latin favours the present. At line 116, where this verse is repeated, the present is used in Q and four other manuscripts. At lines 25 and 118 the present also prevails. One manuscript, E, has the past tense at all three places, 25, 116, and 118, whereas N and O, closely related to one another, have it only at 25, and the other pair, C and H, have it only at 116 and 118. Ælfric himself may have been responsible for the past tense in 23; its irregular occurrence in the other three places is probably to be attributed to the independent action of three scribes, of whom one was responsible for the readings of E, another for those inherited by N and O, a third for those inherited by C and H. Still another odd pattern appears at line 138, where Ælfric uses the present, *adræfe*, to translate a parallel verse from *Matthew*. Here E, true to form, has the past tense. H, apparently independently, has it also, whereas C has the present. N and O also have the past tense, but evidently their ancestor had substituted the alternate verb, *afligde*, which Ælfric himself had used in the present tense at line 133.

31. *heardheortum*. In the early manuscripts of Ælfric the strong ending *-um* is often preferred to the weak *-an* in the dative singular masculine or neuter of adjectives preceded by the definite article. Very likely Ælfric himself was responsible. Cf. line 132 below.

34. *inburh*. BT and BTS cite this word only as a gloss for *atrium* (the word that it here translates) or *vestibulum*, and define it as 'hall, vestibule'. As a compound the word suggests the entrance to a stronghold, which fits the present context readily enough. In the glosses to Lindisfarne and Rushworth, and in the West Saxon Gospels, the word for *atrium* at this point is *cafertun*, which Ælfric himself uses on occasion (*CH* I. 422/26; II. 248/27). Stephens, in his edition, p. 83, following Müller, treats *inburh-fæste* as a compound and translates it freely as 'high-towering castle', but undoubtedly *fæste* is either an adverb or the accusative singular feminine of the adjective *fæst*. Possibly this passage is responsible for the curious entry in BT; 'inburh-fæst; *adj. Stationed in a hall*; atriensis; scil. atrii janitor, seneschallus, lictor, Lye.' Lye may have found the combination in one of the manuscripts of this homily and misunderstood it.

46. *gedæft*. Ælfric uses both *dæftan* and *gedæftan*, 'to put in order, prepare', in other homilies (*CH* I. 212/34; 362/8; II. 316/7; *LS* IV. 369).

49. *hit ær wære.* Although *wise* is feminine, the *hit* seems idiomatic. Conceivably, however, the minority reading *heo, hio* here and at line 248 (where H alone has *hio*) is Ælfric's and not just a scribal emendation.

61. *bendas.* The genitive in *-as* is certainly not favoured by Ælfric, but it has been allowed to stand as a sporadic variant of the period, familiar enough to students of the poetical manuscripts.

71. *heraŏ.* This is the regular form of the third singular present indicative of *herian* in the Ælfric manuscripts. For the general tendency of the present tense of weak verbs in *-ian* in the first class to be assimilated to the second class in late West Saxon, see S–B, 410, 5; Cpb, 752.

75. *Hwilon ær.* Ælfric had mentioned Beelzebub very briefly as *Bel* when speaking of Daniel in his homily on St. Clement (*CH* I. 570/24), but the reference here is probably to *De Falsis Diis*, our XXI. 354–431, where he tells at length the story of Daniel's exposure of the fraud practised by the priests of Bel; or possibly to *LS* XVIII. 85 sqq., describing Elijah's discomfiture of other priests of the same god, there called Baal.

81. *sceap and hryŏeru.* A mere formula for animals customarily sacrificed. In homily XXI. 356, Bel is said to receive forty sheep a day. In the homily on St. Clement mentioned in the preceding note the lions of Daniel xiv. 31 (which normally received, according to the Vulgate and homily XXI. 462, two sheep and two corpses a day) are said to have received 'twa hryŏeru and twa scep'.

137. *Si in spiritu dei aguntur,* MS. T. The irrelevant *aguntur* that appears in this one manuscript may be due to a scribe's absent-minded recollection of *Rom.* viii. 14: *Quicumque enim Spiritu Dei aguntur, ii sunt filii Dei.*

139–44. Cf. homily I. 258 sqq. and the note on I. 267–74.

149. The definition of *æ* as *seo ealde Godes lagu and eac seo niwe,* which is quoted in the apparatus as part of the interpolated explanation in T, states the meaning to be inferred from Ælfric's habitual use of the word, and shows that already in the eleventh century, in the neighbourhood of Worcester at any rate, it was somewhat unfamiliar.

239. *deofle.* It is barely possible that the genitive *deofles* of Q is authentic, for the genitive is sometimes used with *wiŏsacan,* and there is at least one instance of it in Ælfric: *CH* I. 144/23: *hi wiŏsacaþ Cristes tocymes,* a reading supported by the three manuscripts closest to Ælfric, K, A, and Q (Thorpe's Gg. 3. 28, Royal 7 C. xii, and CCCC 188), though at least one other, E (CCCC 198), has the dative. But the meaning here is different, and the dative seems to be supported not only by all the other manuscripts and by dative *weorcum* and *getotum,* but by Thorpe's manuscript in a precisely parallel passage, *CH* II. 52:

Se mæsse-preost axaŏ þæt cild, and cweŏ, 'Wiŏsæcst ŏu deofle?' Đonne andwyrt se godfæder þæs cildes wordum, and cweŏ, 'Ic wiðsace deofle.' Þonne axað he eft, 'Wiðsæcst ðu eallum his weorcum?' He cweð, 'Ic wiðsace.' He axað þriddan siðe, 'Wiðsæcst ðu eallum his getotum?' He cwyð, 'Ic wiðsace.' Þonne hæfð he wiðsacen, on ðisum ðrym wordum, deofle and eallum leahtrum.

BT has one example, indeed, in which dative, accusative, and genitive are used successively in the same sentence: *Se fæder wiðsoc his bearne, and ðæt bearn wiðsoc ðone fæder, and æt nextan ælc freond wiðsoc oðres* (*LS* XXIII. 110 sq.). But Skeat's manuscript, Cotton Julius E. vii (our W), here the only authority, is neither so early nor so carefully written as Thorpe's of the *Catholic Homilies*, and the account of the seven sleepers, in which this sentence occurs, is not the work of Ælfric.

249–51. Ælfric's list of the eight deadly sins is conspicuously at variance with Haymo's in order and in number, and stands in a relation to other lists in Ælfric that has been considered significant. Hence it is well to look carefully at the facts. Bede had referred to only seven sins, representing the seven other spirits accompanying the devil, without saying which they were. Haymo, revising and expanding Bede, listed seven, not eight. He put *superbia* first, following throughout the order in the pseudo-Alcuin *De Octo Vitiis Principalibus* (*PL* CI. 632–7, attached as a second part to Alcuin's *Liber de Virtutibus et Vitiis*), but omitting *accidia* before *tristitia*. Ælfric, on the other hand, apparently reasoning that the devil himself could represent the eighth sin, included *accidia* (*asolcennyss*) and saved *superbia* (*modignyss*) for the last. His order corresponds almost exactly with that of Cassian, *Collatio* v, *De Octo Principalibus Vitiis* (*PL* XLIX. 609 sqq.), the only difference being that *accidia* and *tristitia* have changed places as in pseudo-Alcuin. The exact order of Cassian is given in Ælfric's lists at *CH* II. 218 and *LS* XVI. 267 sqq., whereas in *De Doctrina Apostolica* (our XIX. 127–9) and in the second Old English letter for Wulfstan (Fehr, *Brief* III. 147 sqq.) we find pride in first place and the exact order of pseudo-Alcuin throughout. Thus the present passage stands between the other pairs, resembling *CH* and *LS* in the position assigned to *superbia*, but XIX and the letter for Wulfstan in putting *accidia* before *tristitia*. Since the shifting of *superbia* from last place to first is much more striking than the transposition of the other two sins, it is natural to feel that this passage belongs with *CH* and *LS*. Hence Dr. Clemoes has deduced (*Chronology*, 225 sq.) that the present homily is earlier than *De Doctrina*, which agrees with the definitely late letter for Wulfstan. Yet I question whether this deduction should be allowed to outweigh the evidence of the style; for the part of *De Doctrina* in which the list occurs is non-rhythmical and would normally be classed with the bulk of the *Catholic Homilies* as early composition. We must bear in mind, not only that Ælfric might have changed the order of the list in *De Doctrina* when he added the rhythmical conclusion, but that the order in the present passage might have been dictated primarily by Ælfric's desire to assign the sin of pride to the devil himself. This would have required him to assign the other sins to the seven companion spirits and it would have been natural to name them first. Moreover Max Förster has

made it clear (*Anglia*, XVI. 46–48) that Ælfric was acquainted with both
Cassian and pseudo-Alcuin, hence with both orders, from the beginning.
(On the history of these orders, see Morton Bloomfield, *The Seven Deadly
Sins*, 69–72, and on Ælfric's use of them, 112 sq.). Already in both *CH* and
LS, though he names pride last, he has characterized it as the beginning
and end of all evil. This is very different from Cassian, who had interpreted the same passage in *Luke* in the opposite way, identifying the chief
devil with the first sin in his list, *gastrimargia* or *gula* (Ælfric's *gyfernyss*),
which he associates with the flesh-pots of Egypt and regards as the fleshly
foundation of all other, even spiritual, corruption. (*Collatio* V, cap. XXV,
PL XLIX. 640 sq.) Hence it is questionable whether Ælfric changed from
one order to the other as a matter of principle or even of habit at some
particular moment in his career. The substitution of *invidia* for *tristitia*
in the glosses of T and E is in accord with the gradual triumph of the
former, which according to Bloomfield (p. 72) was first introduced by
Gregory the Great.

Additional Latin glosses in E: 9 adræfde: eiecit, expulit.   15 syllic tacn:
mirabile singnum.   19 byþ toworpen: desolabi*tur*, destr*uetur*.   21, 108
sceocca: satanas.   21 todæled: diuisus.   23, 116 Ge: vos.   23, 25 adræfde:
eicio.   26, 119 synna (*for* suna): filii.   28, 121 suna: filii.   32 Witodlice:
porro.   37, 186 gewinþ: auferet.   38 on þam: *in* q*ui*bus.   todælþ:
dist*ri*buet.   40 towyrpþ: disp*er*git.   46 gedæft: scopis mundata*m*.
48, 247 wyrsan: neq*ui*ores.   hi: illi.   53 Eadig *or* gesælig: beata.   56
andgit, 65 andgyte: intellectu*m*.   59, 82, 83 þa: *tunc.*   61 þæs: ill*ius.*
63 þæs: h*oc.*   65 æfter: sec*undum.*   68 gebyhþ: *conuertit.*   73 þa: illa.
74 forþearle: valde.   75 Hwilon ær: paulo ante.   77 heton: vocaba*nt.*
95 ufon: desup*er.*   97 syrwigendan: *in*sidiantes.   98 todæled: diuisu*m.*
99, 104, 172 byþ toworpen: destr*uetur.*   100 hiwrædene: domu*m.*   101
leode: Gente*m.*   102 wiðeriað: *pre*liantur.   103 aworpennysse: desolat*i*one.
105 hiredes heafod: p*ate*rfamilias.   106 onwinnende: *pre*liando, iminendo.
110 adræfan: expell*ere.*   111 searacræftum: machinis.   114 reþum: seua.
119, 186 þonne: *tunc.*   129 (*twice*), 149, 181 ge: eciam.   131 wiðsoc:
negau*er*v*n*t.   eac swilce: similiter.   133 deofla: demonia.   141 wunnon:
*pre*liaba*nt.*   142 wyrcan: facere.   143 hi: illos.   148 steore: discip[l]ina,
doct*ri*na.   155, 187 todælþ: diuidit.   162 be þam þe him gewyrh: p*ro* vt
uolu*n*t (*sic*).   163 wealcan: uol*u*ere.   187 on: *in.*   herereaf: spolia.
192 ætbryt: *contriuit,* aufert.   201 geþwærlæcan: *con*uenire.   207 cypþ:
insidi*atur.*   210 wiþeriað: adu*er*santur.   211 toweorpaþ: disp*er*gu*n*t.   217
unwæterigende: n*on* humidi.   219 fulnysse: fetido.   227 þa: illi.   229
fulre: fetido.   230 symble: se*m*per.   250 gifernyss: Gula.   forliger:
luxuria.   gitsunga: auaricia.   yrre: ira.   251 asolcennyss: accidia.
unrotnyss: *tri*sticia, *in*vidia.   idelgylp: *in*anis glo*ri*a.   modignyss: sup*er*bia.
256 abugan: declinare.   283 anrædum: diligenti.   289 arwyrðe: honorabili*s.*
296 eac swilce: similit*er.*   297 þæs: h*oc.*

FERIA VI IN TERTIA EBDOMADA QUADRAGESIMÆ

Ioan. iv. 5–42

MUCH of the interest of this homily depends on the literal presentation of the gospel story, which is unusually long and full of dramatic touches. For the interpretation Ælfric selects carefully, passing over altogether the section dealing with the Samaritan woman's husbands and so concentrating attention on a few relatively simple and familiar themes.

The principal source of the interpretation is Augustine's commentary on the text, *In Ioannis Evangelium Tractatus* xv. 6 sqq. A homily in Smaragdus's collection (*PL* CII. 141–5) is simply an abridgement of this portion of Augustine's commentary and leaves out some passages that Ælfric seems to have used. Two other expositions of the gospel may have been consulted: Alcuin's *Commentaria* and *Homilia* xcv in the interpolated collection of Paulus Diaconus (*PL* xcv. 1272 sqq.). The latter, a free adaptation of Augustine, probably by Hericus of Auxerre,² seems especially relevant at only two points in Ælfric's homily (118–22, 141–7), and at these points Alcuin's commentary could have provided all that was needed to supplement Augustine. Hence Alcuin is quoted rather than Hericus, especially as the homily is not one of those in the oldest manuscripts of the collection and may not have been available to Ælfric. The relevant portion of Alcuin's commentary, on the other hand, appears as a homily for the third Friday in Lent in the interpolated version of Haymo's homiliary (Hom. XLVII, *PL* CXVIII. 273 sqq.). On Ælfric's use of this collection, see above, pp. 157–61.

For the text we are dependent, as in II and III, on the well-preserved F (CCCC 162), which has two or three gross omissions,

---

¹ On the group of homilies for Fridays in Lent, see above, pp. 226–8.
² See above, p. 159, n. 2.

and the fire-damaged H (Vitellius C. v), originally the more accurate copy, though not without a few slips. Indeed there are signs
that both H and F are descended from a faulty ancestor: both
apparently had *ræscendes* at line 29 until H was emended to
ræsendes; both have a questionable *and* in line 40; and the spacing
makes it probable that H (which cannot now be read at this point)
shared with F the omission of a seemingly necessary *byrig* in line
88. These slight indications are somewhat strengthened by the
corruption that seems to underlie both manuscripts in homily II
at lines 196–7.

*Uenit Iesus in ciuitatem Samarie qu[æ]
dicitur Sichar, et *reliqua*   *p. 257+

Se godspellere Iohannes sæde on þysum godspelle
þæt Crist ure Hælend, þa þa he her on life wæs,
come on sumne sæl to Samarian byrig,
to ðæs heahfæderes wurþige þe wæs gehaten Iacob;
þone wurþig he forgeaf Iosepe his suna,   5
and þær wæs se wæterpytt þe ðær worhte Iacob.
Se Hælend þa sæt þær, of ðam siðfæte werig,
wið ðone wæterpytt, and hit wæs þa middæg,
and his discipuli eodon into ðære byrig,
þæt hi him mete bohton, and he abad þær þa hwile.   10
þa com þær betwux þam of Samarian byrig

Text based on F (CCCC 162), pp. 258, 257+, 258+, 259–62. (Two successive
leaves are numbered 257 on the recto.) Collated with H (Cotton Vitellius C. v),
ff. 245ᵛ–9ᵛ. Because of the many gaps in H, an effort has been made, as in
Homily III, to state not only its ascertainable variants but, at other points where
the text of F might be questioned, whether it agrees or has no reading. F's use
of capitals has been regularized. See above, p. 248.

Excluded variants: (1) H has *i* where F has *y* in *byð, gyf, hys, hyt, þys, þyses,
þysne, þysre, þysum, ys*; (2) H has both *hyre* and *hire, buton* and *butan*; (3) H has
for þan þe where F has *for þam þe*.

Sup.: FR. VI. IN EBD. III. (Ðis spe)l sceal on frige-dæg on þære þriddan
lencten-wucan. EVG. (V)en(it) IHs in ciuitatem samariæ quæ dicitur sichar.
H (*with bracketed letters from Wanley, Catalogus, p. 211; Wanley omits* þriddan).
TERTA *F.*   QUADRAGESIMÆ] XL *F.*   quæ] qui *F.*

1–2 Se . . . hælend] *quoted by Wanley; all but* Se *and* crist *still legible; Wanley
misprints* Hælende.   4 worþige *H.*   5 worþig *H.*   forgef *H.*
6 -pyt *H.*   8 -pytt] *no reading H.*

SOURCES. 1–8 [*Ioan. iv. 5*] Venit ergo in civitatem Samariæ, quæ dicitur Sichar;
iuxta prædium, quod dedit Iacob Ioseph filio suo.

[*6*] Erat autem ibi fons Iacob. Iesus ergo fatigatus ex itinere, sedebat sic
supra fontem. Hora erat quasi sexta.

9, 10 [*8*] (Discipuli enim eius abierant in civitatem ut cibos emerent.)

11–20 [*7*] Venit mulier de Samaria haurire aquam. Dicit ei Iesus: Da mihi
bibere.

[*9*] Dicit ergo ei mulier illa Samaritana: Quomodo tu Iudæus cum sis, bibere
a me poscis, quæ sum mulier Samaritana? non enim coutuntur Iudæi Samari-
tanis.

an wif to ðam wæterscipe, wolde wæter feccan,
and se Hælend hyre cwæð to, Syle me drincan.
þæt wif him cwæð to andsware, Hwi wilt þu me þæs biddan,
þonne þu eart Iudeisc, and ic Samaritanisc wif?   15
Nellað þa Iudeiscan mid nanum Samaritaniscum
etan oððe drincan. Hyre andwyrde se Hælend,
Gyf þu cuþest Godes gyfe, and wistest hwa þe cwæð to,
Syle me drincan, wen ys þæt þu bæde hine
and he wolde þe syllan of þam liflican wætere.   20
þæt wif him cwæð þa to, þes wæterpyt ys deop,
and þu hlædfæt næfst; hwanon hæfst þu liflic wæter?
Eart þu la furðor þonne ure fæder Iacob,
þe us þysne pyt forgeaf?—and he sylf þærof dranc,
and hys *bearn and nytenu. Hyre andwyrde se Hælend,   *p. 258+
Ælcum þæra þyrst eft þe of þysum wætere drincð,   26
and þam ne þyrst on ecnysse þe of þam wætere drincð
þe ic him sylle, ac hit soðlice wyrð
wylspring on him ræ[s]endes wæteres
to ðam ecan life. [H]im andwyrde þæt wif,   30
Hlaford, syle me of þysum liflican wætere,
þæt me heonon forð ne þyrste, ne ic her ne þurfe hladan.
þa cwæð se Hælend hyre to, Gang clypa þinne wer,

16 mid] *bottom f. 245ᵛ, H.*   17 -de se Hælend] *first words visible f. 246, H.*
22 hlædfæt *both MSS.*   29 ræscendes *both MSS.; altered to* ræsendes *H.*
30 Him] *sic H*; and him *F.*

[10] Respondit Iesus, et dixit ei: Si scires donum Dei, et quis est, qui dicit tibi: Da mihi bibere: tu forsitan petisses ab eo, et dedisset tibi aquam vivam.

21–32 [11] Dicit ei mulier: Domine, neque in quo haurias habes, et puteus altus est: unde ergo habes aquam vivam?

[12] Numquid tu maior es patre nostro Iacob, qui dedit nobis puteum, et ipse ex eo bibit, et filii eius, et pecora eius?

[13] Respondit Iesus, et dixit ei: Omnis, qui bibit ex aqua hac, sitiet iterum: qui autem biberit ex aqua, quam ego dabo ei, non sitiet in æternum:

[14] sed aqua, quam ego dabo ei, fiet in eo fons aquæ salientis in vitam æternam.

[15] Dicit ad eum mulier: Domine, da mihi hanc aquam, ut non sitiam: neque veniam huc haurire.

33–43 [16] Dicit ei Iesus: Vade, voca virum tuum, et veni huc.

[17] Respondit mulier, et dixit: Non habeo virum. Dicit ei Iesus: Bene dixisti, quia non habeo virum:

[18] quinque enim viros habuisti, et nunc, quem habes, non est tuus vir: hoc vere dixisti.

[19] Dicit ei mulier: Domine, video quia Propheta es tu.

[20] Patres nostri in monte hoc adoraverunt, et vos dicitis, quia Ierosolymis est locus, ubi adorare oportet.

and cum hider þonne. Heo cwæð him to andsware,
Næbbe ic nanne wer. þa cwæð se Hælend,   35
Wel þu cwæde, [wif,] næbbe ic nanne wer;
fif weras þu hæfdest, and þone þe [þu] nu hæfst,
nis [sé] þin wer; þæt þu sædest soðlice.

þæt wif him [cwæð þa to,] Hlaford, ic geseo
þæt þu witega eart; and ure fæderas woldon   40
on þysum munte hi gebiddan, and ge secgað
þæt on Hierusalem si seo stow
þær þær gedafenað to gebiddenne.

þa cwæð se Hælend hyre to, Wif, gelif [þu] me
þæt se tima cymð þonne ge eow ne gebiddað   45
[ne] on þysum munte ne on Hierusalem
to ðam heofonlican Fæder:
for ðam [þe] ge gebiddað þæt ge nyton; we us gebiddað [þæt we
    witon,]
for ðam þe se hæl is of Iudeiscum folce;
ac se tima cymð, and nu is soðlice,   50
þonne þa soðan biddendras gebiddað [hi] to ðam Fæder
on gaste and on soðfæstnysse, and God Fæder secð
swilce biddendras þe him to gebiddað.

God soðlice is gast, and þam ðe him to gebiddað
gedafenað to ge*biddanne on gaste and on soðfæstnysse. *p. 259
þæt wif him cwæð þa to, Ic wat þæt us cymð   56

---

36 wif] sic H; om. F.   37 second þu] sic H; om. F.   38 sé] sic H; om. F.
39 cwæþ þa to] sic H; 'to' cwæð F.   40 and both MSS.   42 sy H.
44 þu supplied by conjecture; no reading H; cf. line 162.   46 first ne] sic H;
om. F.   48 þe] sic H; om. F.   þæt we witon] sic H; om. F.   49 se both
MSS. (H later has seo hæl).   51 biddendras both MSS.   hi] sic H; om. F.
52 first on] last word visible f. 246, H.   55 soðfæstnysse] first word visible
f. 246ᵛ.

44–55 [21] Dicit ei Iesus: mulier crede mihi, quia venit hora, quando neque
in monte hoc, neque in Ierosolymis adorabitis Patrem.

[22] Vos adoratis quod nescitis: nos adoramus quod scimus, quia salus ex
Iudæis est.

[23] Sed venit hora, et nunc est, quando veri adoratores adorabunt Patrem in
spiritu et veritate. Nam et Pater tales quærit, qui adorent eum.

[24] Spiritus est Deus: et eos, qui adorant eum, in spiritu et veritate oportet
adorare.

56–65 [25] Dicit ei mulier: Scio quia Messias venit (qui dicitur Christus);
cum ergo venerit ille, nobis annunciabit omnia.

[26] Dicit ei Iesus: Ego sum, qui loquor tecum.

se ðe is gehaten Mæssias, þæt is Hælend Crist,
and þonne he cymð he cyð us ealle þing.
Hyre andwyrde se Hælend, Ic hit eom þe þe to sprece.

Mid þam þa comon Cristes leorningcnihtas,   60
and hi wundrodon þæt he to wifmenn spræc;
heora nan [swaþeah nolde] befrinan
hwæt heo þær wolde, oððe hwæt he hire to spræce.

þæt wif þa forlet hyre wæterfæt þær,
and eode into ðære byrig, and to ðam burhwarum cwæð,   65
Cumað and geseoð soðlice þone man
þe me ealle 'þa' þing sæde þe ic æfre gefremode;
cweþe ge, la leof, hwæðer he sylf Crist sy.
And seo burhwaru þa eode ut ardlice to him.

þa bædon his leorningcnihtas hine betwux þam, cweþende,   70
Ett, leof lareow. And he him andwyrde þus:
Ic hæbbe mete to etenne þone þe ge nyton.

Hys discipuli þa sædon digellice him betwynan,
Hwæðer ænig man him brohte mete hider?

Se Hælend him cwæð þa to, Min mete is soðlice   75
þæt ic þæs willan wyrce þe me hider asende
þæt ic hys weorc gefylle. La hu ne secge [ge]

57 messi(as) *H.*   61 (wi)mmen *H.*   sprec *H.*   62 swaþeah nolde]
sic *H*; nolde swaðeah *F* (*spoils alliteration*).   65 -warum *both MSS.*
67 *before first* þe *H has a gap of two letters, probably* se.   þa þing *H.*   68 ge
la] *no reading H; hardly room for more than* ge.   70 leornincnihtas *H.*
75 cwæð þa] þa cwæþ *H.*   77 ge] *sic H; om. F.*

[*27*] Et continuo venerunt discipuli eius: et mirabantur quia cum muliere
loquebatur. Nemo tamen dixit: Quid quæris, aut quid loqueris cum ea?
[*28*] Reliquit ergo hydriam suam mulier, et abiit in civitatem, et dicit illis
hominibus:
66–77 [*29*] Venite, et videte hominem, qui dixit mihi omnia quæcumque
feci: numquid ipse est Christus?
[*30*] Exierunt ergo de civitate, et veniebant ad eum.
[*31*] Interea rogabant eum discipuli, dicentes: Rabbi, manduca.
[*32*] Ille autem dicit eis: Ego cibum habeo manducare, quem vos nescitis.
[*33*] Dicebant ergo discipuli ad invicem: Numquid aliquis attulit ei manducare?
[*34*] Dicit eis Iesus: Meus cibus est ut faciam voluntatem eius, qui misit me,
ut perficiam opus eius.
77–87 [*35*] Nonne vos dicitis, quod adhuc quattuor menses sunt, et messis
venit? Ecce dico vobis: Levate oculos vestros, et videte regiones, quia albæ sunt
iam ad messem.
[*36*] Et qui metit, mercedem accipit, et congregat fructum in vitam æternam:
ut, et qui seminat, simul gaudeat, et qui metit.

þæt feower monðas synt gyt ær þam þe gerip cume?
Efne ic se`c´ge eow, sceawiað þas eardas,
for ðam þe hi synd gearwe to [ge]ripe nu,   80
and se þe ripð þæt gerip, se underfehþ mede,
and he gaderað wæstm into ðam ecan life,
þæt hi samo`d´ blission, se ðe sæwþ and se ðe ripð.
On þam is soð word gecwæden, þæt *oðer is se ðe sæwð   *p. 260
and oðer se ðe ripð. Ic sende eow to rippanne   85
þæt þæt ge ne beswuncon; oðre hit beswuncon,
and ge ferdon in to heora geswincum.
Of þære burhware þa Samarian [byrig]
manega menn gelyfdon on þone lifigendan Hælend
for ðæs wifes gecyðnysse þe heo cydde be him,   90
þæt he hyre sæde swa hwæt swa heo gefremode.
þa þa seo burhwaru him com to, þa bædon hi hine georne
þæt he þær wunode, and he wunode þær twegen dagas,
and micele ma gelyfdon for hys mæran lare,
and to ðam wife cwædon, þæt we for þinre spræce ne gelyfað; 95
we sylf[e] gehyrdon and soðlice witon
þæt þes is soðlice Hælend middaneardes.
    Langsum trahtnung belimpð to ðysum godspelle,
and ge ne magon undergytan ealle þa deopnysse
buton man hit eow secge sceortum andgyte,   100

78 synt . . . þe] *no reading* H.   79 secge H.   80 hy synd H.   geripe]
sic H; ripe F.   83 samon *corrected to* samod F.; samod H.   84 gecweden H.
85 ripenne H.   86 *first* beswuncon] *bottom f. 246ᵛ, H.*   88 (bu)ruhware,
first word visible f. 247, H.   byrig *supplied by conjecture*; *no reading* H, *but
there would hardly have been room for* byrig *unless* menn *in the next line was omitted.
See note.*   89 lyfigendan H.   95 þæt *both MSS.*   96 sylfe H; e
erased F.   soðlice *both MSS.*   97 hælend soþlice H.   99 under-
gitan H.   100 andgite H.

[37] In hoc enim est verbum verum: quia alius est qui seminat, et alius est
qui metit.
[38] Ego misi vos metere quod vos non laborastis: alii laboraverunt, et vos in
labores eorum introistis.
88–97 [39] Ex civitate autem illa multi crediderunt in eum Samaritanorum,
propter verbum mulieris testimonium perhibentis: Quia dixit mihi omnia
quæcumque feci.
[40] Cum venissent ergo ad illum Samaritani, rogaverunt eum ut ibi maneret.
Et mansit ibi duos dies.
[41] Et multo plures crediderunt in eum propter sermonem eius.
[42] Et mulieri dicebant: Quia iam non propter tuam loquelam credimus:
ipsi enim audivimus, et scimus quia hic est vere Salvator mundi.

þe læs þe seo deopnys eow drecce to swiðe.

Se Hælend wæs werig, þeah þe hit wundorlic si.

His heofonlica Fæder þurh hine gesceop
ealle gesceafta buton geswince;
ne swanc se Fæder ne se Sunu naðor   105
on þam micclan weorce, ac Crist wæs werig swaþeah
on þære menniscnysse, æfter mannes gecynde,
and his untrumnys [(is ure trum)nys:
his trumnys] us gesceop, and his untrumnyss us alysde.

On þære sixtan tide he sæt werig æt þam pytte,   110
and on ðære syxtan ylde þysre worulde
he com to middanearde mancynn to alysenne.

þær com of Samarian byrig, *swa swa we sædon eow ær, *p. 261
þæt wif to þam Hælende, and heo hæfde getacnunge,
for ðam þe heo ælþeodig wæs fram Iudeiscum cynne,   115
ealre þære Gelaþunge þe on Criste nu gelyfð,
of eallum leodscipum þe to geleafan bugon.

Se Hælend bæd drincan, swa swa ge gehyrdon ær,

---

101 þe læste *H.*   deopnyss *H.*   102 sy *H.*   108–9 *bracketed passage*
om. F; . . . nys. his trumnys *H; see note.*   110 syxtan *H.*   112 [man]cyn *H.*
116 on criste] on crist *H?* (*The letters not clear.*)   118 gehyrdon] geh . . .,
last letters visible f. 247, H.

102–9 [*Augustine, In Ioan. Ev.*] Invenimus . . . fortem et infirmum Iesum:
fortem, quia *in principio erat Verbum, et Verbum erat apud Deum, et Deus erat
Verbum: hoc erat in principio apud Deum.* Vis videre quam iste Filius Dei fortis
sit? *Omnia per ipsum facta sunt, et sine ipso factum est nihil*; et sine labore facta
sunt. Quid ergo illo fortius, per quem sine labore facta sunt omnia? Infirmum
vis nosse? *Verbum caro factum est, et habitavit in nobis.* (*Ioan. i. 1–2, 3, 14.*)
Fortitudo Christi te creavit, infirmitas Christi te recreavit. . . . Condidit nos
fortitudine sua, quæsivit nos infirmitate sua. . . . Ideo *fatigatus ab itinere* quid est
aliud, quam fatigatus in carne? . . . Illius infirmitas nostra est fortitudo.

110–12 [*Augustine*] Quare ergo hora sexta? Quia ætate sæculi sexta. . . .
Fatigatus venit, quia infirmam carnem portavit. Hora sexta, quia ætate sæculi
sexta. Ad puteum, quia ad profunditatem huius habitationis nostræ. . . .

113–17 [*Augustine*] Samaritani ad Iudæorum gentem non pertinebant:
alienigenæ fuerunt. . . . Pertinet ad imaginem rei, quod ab alienigenis venit ista
mulier, quæ typum gerebat Ecclesiæ: ventura enim erat Ecclesia de Gentibus,
alienigena a genere Iudæorum.

118–22 [*Augustine*] Ille autem qui bibere quærebat, fidem ipsius mulieris
sitiebat. [*Alcuin, Commentaria*] Sed scilicet, sitiebat Deus mulieris illius fidem,
quoniam Samaritana erat, et solet Samaria idololatriæ imaginem sustinere; ipsi
enim separati a populo Iudæorum, simulacris mutorum animalium, id est, vaccis
aureis animarum suarum decus addixerant. Venerat autem Iesus Dominus noster,
ut gentium multitudinem, quæ simulacris servierat, ad munimentum fidei
Christianæ et incorruptæ religionis adduceret.

æt þam Samaritaniscan wife, for ðan ðe he gewilnode
hire geleafan, þæt heo gelyfde on hine,   120
and þæt gedwyld forlete þæs deoflican bigengas
þæra hæþenra goda þæt hi oð ðæt wurðedon.
þa wundrode þæt wif þæt he wolde drincan
of hyre fæte, for ðam ðe þa Iudeiscan
noldon næfre brucan nanes þinges mid þam hæþenum,   125
ne of heora fatum furðon næfre drincan,
and hi rihtlice swa dydon, for þam soðan biggenge
þæs ælmihtigan Godes þe hi on gelyfdon,
þæt hi ne wurdon befylede þurh þa fulan hæþenan.
Crist cwæð to þam wife, 'gyf þu cuþest Godes gyfe:'   130
Godes gyfu is se Halga Gast;
soðlice þone Gast forgyfð God hys gecorenum,
swa þæt he him on wunað and gewissað hi symble
to Godes willan and to godum weorcum,
and þæt ys þæt wæter [þe] he þam wife behet,   135
and he cwæð be þam wætere þe wæs on þam pytte,
'Ælcum þæra þyrst eft þe of þysum wætere drincð,
and þam ne þyrst on ecnysse þe of þam wætere drincð
þe ic him sylle, ac hit soðlice wyr[ð]
wylspring on him ræ[s]endes wæteres   140
to ðam ecan life;' and þæt is soðlice
swa swa ure Hælend cwæð ær his þrowunge:

---

121 bigengas] *sic F.*   122 oð ðæt] *first words visible f. 247ᵛ, H.*   wur-
þod(on) *H.*   127 bigenge *H.*   130 gife *H.*   131 gifu *H.*
132 forgifð *H.*   133 symle *H.*   135 þe] *sic H; þe altered to þæt F.*
139 wyrð] *sic H; wyrcð F (cf. 28).*   140 ræscendes *F; no reading H (cf. 29).*

123–9 [*Augustine*] Videtis alienigenas: omino vasculis eorum Iudæi non
utebantur. Et quia ferebat secum mulier vasculum unde aquam hauriret, eo
mirata est, quia Iudæus petebat ab ea bibere, quod non solebant facere Iudæi.
[*Ælfric's addition at 127–9 may owe something to Alcuin above.*]

130–5 [*Augustine*] Si scires, inquit, *donum Dei.* Donum Dei est Spiritus sanctus. [*Neither Augustine nor Alcuin, who has the same interpretation, seems responsible for Ælfric's elaboration, 132 sqq.*]

141b–7 [*The citation of a parallel passage may have been prompted by Alcuin:*]
Hanc enim recte intelligimus aquam vivam . . . sicut idem Ioannes testatur alio
loco dicens: *Quoniam stabat Iesus, et clamabat: Si quis sitit, veniat et bibat. Qui
credit in me, sicut dicit scriptura, flumina de ventre eius fluent aquæ vivæ. . . .*
Cuius aquæ vivæ interpretationem ita subiicit: *Hoc autem dicebat,* inquit, *de
Spiritu, quem accepturi erant hi, qui in eum credituri erant.* (*Ioan. vii. 37–39.*)
[*Alcuin's text of verse 37, like some copies of the gospel, omits* ad me *after* veniat,
just as Ælfric omits me.]

*Ælcum þe þyrst[e], cume to and drince.

Se ðe gelyfð on me, swa [swa] gewritu se'c'gað,
of his innoðe flowað liflices wæteres flod;   145
þis sæde se Hælend be þam Halgan Gaste,
þe þa underfengon þe on hine gelyfdon.

He is se liflica wylspring, and þa[m] ðe he on wunað
ne þyrst on ecnysse, ac þæt ece lif
him bið forgyfen on heofonan rice.   150

þæt wif nyste þa gyt hwilc wæter he mænde, and cwæð,
'Hlafurd, syle me' drincan 'of þysum liflican wætere,
þæt me heonon forð ne þyrste, ne ic her ne þurfe hladan.'

Heo wolde þa iu beon buton geswince,
ac heo ne gehyrde þa gyt hwæt se Hælend cwæð   155
on sumre oðre stowe to his apostolum:
Cumað to me, ealle þe geswincað
and gehefegode synd, and ic eow gereordige.

   Ge ne magon understandan þa micclan deopnysse
ealles þyses godspelles, swa swa we ær sædon,   160
and we forþi gescyrtað be sumum dæle þysne traht.

He cwæð to ðam wife, 'Wif, gelyf þu me
þæt se tima cymð þonne ge eow ne gebiddað
ne on þysum munte ne on Hierusalem
to ðam heofonlican Fæder: 165
for ðam ðe ge gebiddað þæt ge nyton; we us gebiddað þæt we
    witon,
for ðam [þe] se hæl is of Iudeiscum folce.
Ac se tima cymð, and nu is soðlice,

---

143 Ælcum] *cap. both MSS.* (*see note*).   þyrste] *sic H*; þyrst *F* (*see note*). *Two
letters, probably* me, *erased after* to *F*; *no reading H but hardly space for* me.
144 swa swa gewritu] *sic H*; swa swa writu (?) *altered to* swa gewritu *F*.   148 þam]
sic H; þa *F*.   150 forgi(fen) *H*.   151 hwylc *H*.   152 Hlafurd] *no
reading H*.   drincan *both MSS*.   153 her] *bottom f. 247ᵛ*, *H*.   156
stowe] . . . we, *first letters visible f. 248*, *H*.   160 ær] eow ær *H* (*perhaps
correct*).   166 gebyddað *H*.   167 þe] *sic H*; *om. F*; *cf. line 49*.
se hæl] *no reading H*.

151–8 [*Augustine*] Et illa nondum intelligebat, et non intelligens, quid
respondebat? [*Her reply quoted.*] Ad laborem indigentia cogebat, et laborem
infirmitas recusabat. Utinam audiret, *Venite ad me, omnes qui laboratis et onerati
estis, et ego vos reficiam* (*Matth. xi. 28*). Hoc enim ei dicebat Iesus, ut iam non
laboraret: sed illa nondum intelligebat.

161 [*Ælfric skips verses 16–20 of the gospel (lines 33–43 above), and the corresponding sections (18–23) of Augustine's exposition.*]

þonne þa soðan biddendras gebiddað hi to ðam Fæder
on gaste and on soðfæstnysse, and God Fæder secð   170
swilce biddendras þe him to gebiddað.
God soðlice is gast, and þam ðe him to gebiddað
*gedafenað to gebiddenne on gaste and on soðfæstnysse.'   *p. 263
Nu ne þurfe we astigan to sticolum muntum
mid earfoðnysse, us to gebiddanne,   175
swilce God si gehendor on þam hean munte
þonne on þære dene, for hyre deopnysse.

Se heaga munt getacnað þa heagan modignysse,
and seo dene eadmodnysse, þe ure Drihten lufað,
and we sceolon us gebiddan mid soðre eadmodnysse,   180
gyf we willað þæt us gehyre se heofonlica God,
se ðe on heannysse wunað, and behylt þa eadmodan,
and byð symble gehende þam ðe mid soðfæstnysse
him to clypiað on heora gedrefednysse.

Ne we ne þurfon secan ofer sæ ne ofer land,   185
mid widgilre wórunge, þone welwillendan God,
þone þe þæt arfæste mod mid him æfre hæfð,
and he bið æfre anweard eallum weldóndum
on ælcum lande þær hys geleafa byð.

Witodlice þa Iudeiscan þe þa wurþedon God   190
gebædon hi to Gode binnan þam temple,
and Crist cwæð to þam wife, 'we us gebiddað þæt we witon,
for þam [þe] se hæl is of Iudeiscum folce.'
Se hæl ys soðlice ure Hælend Crist,

---

173 Gedafenað *F*; gedafnaþ *H*. gebiddenne *both MSS.*   175 gebiddenne *H*.   176 sy *H*.   (hea)gan *H*.   183 symble *both MSS.*   186 wel-]
last word visible f. 248, H.   188 anweard] *sic F.*   weldón(den)dum *F(?)*
192 wife] *first word visible f. 248ᵛ, H.*   193 þe] *om. F; no reading H; but*
cf. lines 49, 167.   (se)o hæl *H (cf. line 49).*   194 Seo hæl *H.*

174–90 [*Augustine*] O si invenirem, dicebas, montem aliquem altum et soli-
tarium! credo enim quia in alto est Deus, magis me exaudit ex alto. Quia in
monte es, propinquum te Deo putas, et cito te exaudire, quasi de proximo cla-
mantem? *In excelsis habitat*, sed *humilia respicit* (Psal. cxii. 5, 6). *Prope est*
Dominus. Quibus? forte altis? *His qui obtriverunt cor* (Psal. xxxiii. *19 in Augus-*
tine's own version.). Mira res est: et in altis habitat, et humilibus propinquat. . . .
Superbos longe videt, eo illis minus propinquat, quo sibi videntur altiores. . . .
Convallis humilitatem habet. Ergo intus age totum. Et si forte quæris aliquem
locum altum, aliquem locum sanctum, intus exhibe te templum Deo. [*Ælfric's*
comment on the needlessness of travel in 185–6 is not explicit in Augustine.]
194–7 [*Not in Augustine or Alcuin, who here follows Augustine.*]

se ðe of Iudeiscum cynne com of Marian,   195
þe wæs þæs cynecynnes, and þone Kyning gebær
heofonan and eorðan to ure alysednysse.
þyss wiston þa witegan þe hit witeg'od'on toweard,
and of þam cynne comon Cristes apostoli,
and manega oðre, þe æfter his æriste   200
heora æhte beceapodon, and eall þæt wurð lédon
æt ðæra *apostola fotum, and folgodon Criste   *p. 264
buton gytsunge, and heora bigleofa
wæs gemæne him eallum mid þam apostolum.

    þæt wif cwæð to Criste, Ic wat þæt Mæssias cymð,   205
se ðe ys Crist gecweden; and he cwæð to hire,
'Ic hit eom þe to ðe sprece;' and þa comon his leorningcnihtas.
Messias on Ebreisc, Christus on Grecisc,
unctus on Leden, ys on Englisc gesmyrod;
þæt ys ure Hælend, þe mid þam Halgan Gaste   210
wæs on þære menniscnysse mihtiglice gesmyrod
mid seofonfealdre gyfe, swa swa us sæde se witega
Isaías on [his] witegunge, þa þa he wrat be Criste.

    þæt wif forlet þa sona hyre wæterfæt þær standan,
and efste to ðære byrig and bodade ymbe Crist.   215
Mid þam þe heo gehyrde of þæs Hælendes muþe,
Ic hit eom, se ðe to ðe sprece,

---

    196 cyning H.   198 þis H.   towerd H.   201 æhta H.   203 (gi)tsunge
H?   205 messias H.   207, 217 spræce alt. to sprece F.   208 (ch)ristus H?
212 gyfe] no reading H.   213 his] sic H; om. F.   215 embe H.

    198–204] [Augustine, Alcuin] Nos adoramus quod scimus. Ex persona Iudæ-
orum dictum est, sed non omnium Iudæorum, non reproborum Iudæorum: sed
de qualibus fuerunt Apostoli, quales fuerunt Prophetæ, quales fuerunt illi
omnes sancti, qui omnia sua vendiderunt, et pretia rerum suarum ad pedes
Apostolorum posuerunt (Act. iv. 34 sq.). [Ælfric glances in 204 at Act. iv. 32,
sed erant illis omnia communia; the entire passage, 194–204, has a slightly different
point from Augustine's.]
    208–9 [Augustine, Alcuin] Messias autem unctus est; unctus græce Christus
est; hebraice Messias est.
    210–13 [This elaboration is not in Ælfric's immediate sources. The allusion in
213 is to Is. xi. 1–3. See note.]
    214–15 [Ælfric has skipped verse 27 and now sums up 28–29 freely.]
    216–22 [Augustine, Alcuin] Audito, Ego sum qui loquor tecum, et recepto in cor
Christo Domino, quid faceret, nisi iam hydriam dimitteret, et evangelizare
curreret? Proiecit cupiditatem, et properavit annuntiare veritatem. [Earlier, § 16,
Augustine has interpreted the water as voluptas sæculi and the water-pot as
cupiditas.]

þa efste heo swiðe ham to ðære byrig,
and began to bodienne þam burhwarum embe Crist.
Heo forlet hyre wæterfæt, þe hæfde getacnunge   220
woruldlicre gewilnunge, and wearð þa bydel,
and cydde soðfæstnysse þam ceastergewarum,
and 'manega' þa 'gelyfdon on þone lifigendan Hælend
þurh þæs wifes gecyðnysse þe heo cydde be him.'
        'þa bædon his leorningcnihtas hine betwux þam, þus
        cweþende: 225
Ett, leof lareow; and he him andwyrde þus:
Ic hæbbe mete to etanne þone þe ge nyton.'
Her ge magon gehyran þæt ure Hælend æt,
þonne his leorning*cnihtas hine laðedon to mete,   *p. 265
þeah þe sum mæssepreost, þe we meldian nellað,   230
ætsoce mid gedwylde þæt ure Drihten ne æte
næfre on þysum life, ac he leah forþearle.
He ne cuðe na þa Cristes boc þe us cyð ymbe þæt,
þæt ure Hælend æte swa swa oðre men doð,
ge ær his þrowunge ge æfter his æriste.   235
He æt soðlice and dranc, for ðam ðe he soð man wæs;
he æt buton gyfernysse and dranc buton druncennysse,
and eall his lif wæs gelogod buton synnum,
and nan leahter næfd'e' nænne stede on him.
        He cwæð, 'Min mete is þæt ic þæs willan wyrce   240
        þe me hider asende þæt ic his weorc gefylle.'
Hys gastlica mete ys mancynnes alysednyss,

---

219 bodienne] *no reading* H.   burhwarum *both MSS.*   embe *both MSS.*
222 ceaster-] *bottom f. 248ᵛ,* H.   224 þæs] *first word visible f. 249,* H.
225 þus cweþende] *no reading* H. (*cf. line 70*).   227 etenne H.   229 mæte
alt. to mete F.   233 embe H.   237 gifernysse H.   238 eal H.
239 næfde H. nan(ne) H.   242 alysednys H; alysednyss(e) F (e *erased*).

---

223 f. [*Ælfric moves ahead to verse 39 before returning to 31–38.*]
228–39 [*Not in Ælfric's immediate sources. Lines 233–4 probably refer especially
to such passages as Matth. xi. 19, Luc. xxiv. 43. The theme of the passage, and lines
238–9 recall such a text as Hebr. iv. 15*: Non enim habemus pontificem qui non
possit compati infirmitatibus nostris; tentatum autem per omnia pro similitudine, absque peccato.]
242–6 [*Augustine, Alcuin] Meus,* inquit, *cibus est ut faciam voluntatem eius qui
misit me.* Ergo et potus ipse erat in illa muliere, ut faceret voluntatem eius, qui
miserat eum. Ideo dicebat, *Sitio, da mihi bibere;* scilicet ut fidem in ea operaretur,
et fidem eius biberet, et eam in corpus suum traiiceret: corpus enim eius
Ecclesia.

and him þyrste on þam wife hyre geleafan,
and he symble gewilnað urre sawla hælu,
and his Fæder willan he worhte þa, 245
þa he þa burhware gebigde to geleafan.

He cwæð, 'Ic secge eow, sceawiað þas eardas,
for ðam ðe hi synd gearwe to geripe nu,
and se ðe ripð þæt gerip, se underfecð mede,
and he gaderað wæstm into þam ecan life, 250
þæt hi samod blission, se ðe sæwð and se ðe ripð.
On þam is soð word gecweden, þæt oþer is se ðe sæwð,
and oðer se ðe ripð; ic sende eow to ripanne
þæt þæt ge ne beswuncon; oðr[e] hyt beswuncon,
and ge ferdon in to heora geswincum.' 255
þa heahfæderas and þa witegan þe embe þone Hælend cyddon,
þ[a] wæron þa sæderas þe seowon Godes lare,
and þæt gelyfede folc þe þa gelyfde on God
wæs þæt gerip soðlice þæt Crist *embe sæde, *p. 266
and þa apostoli wæron witodlice þa rifteras 260
þe þæt gerip gaderodon into Godes berne
heofonan rices, þær hi gehealdene beoð,
þæt hi samod blission, þa sæderas and þa rifteras,
on þære ecan blisse for heora geswince.
Soðlice ure Hælend þurh hine sylfne eft 265

244 symle H.   ure H.   245–6 þa, þa] þa. ða (sic) followed in H by two
letters erased, probably þa, which may well have been authentic; þa þa without
punctuation F.   249 underfecð] no reading H.   253 ripanne] no reading H.
254 beswu'n'con (twice) H.   oþre] sic H; oð(e)r F (e erased, but not restored
to proper position).   256 heahfæd(eras), last word visible f. 249, H.
257 first þa] þe F.   260 wæron] first word visible f. 249ᵛ, H.

256–64 [*Augustine, Alcuin*] Qui laboraverunt? Ipse Abraham, Isaac, et
Iacob. Legite labores eorum: in omnibus laboribus eorum prophetia Christi;
et ideo seminatores. Moyses et cæteri Patriarchæ et omnes Prophetæ, quanta
pertulerunt in illo frigore quando seminabant? Ergo iam in Iudæa messis parata
erat. . . . Illa vero messis iam matura erat, quo prius missi sunt discipuli, ubi
Prophetæ laboraverunt. Sed tamen, fratres, videte quid dictum sit: *Simul
gaudeat et qui seminat et qui metit.* Dispares temporis labores habuerunt: sed
gaudio pariter perfruentur, mercedem simul accepturi sunt vitam æternam.
265–78 [*Augustine, Alcuin, a passage which occurs within the preceding paragraph*] Quid inde factum est? De ipsa messe eiecta sunt pauca grana, et semina-
verunt orbem terrarum, et surgit alia messis quæ in fine sæculi metenda est.
De ista messe dicitur, *Qui seminant in lacrymis, in gaudio metent (Psal. cxxv. 5).*
Ad istam ergo messem non Apostoli, sed Angeli mittentur: *Messores*, inquit,
Angeli sunt (Matth. xiii. 39). Ista ergo messis crescit inter zizania, et exspectat

and þurh his apostolas and heora æftergengan
seow þa godspellican lare and geleafan on his folce,
and þæt sæd nu wyxt [oþ] þysre worulde geendunge,
gemenced wið coccel, þæt synd þa manfullan
þe betwux þam gelyfedum lybbað her on worulde.   270
Englas beoð þa rifteras on ende þysre worulde,
swa swa Crist sylf sæde on sumon his godspella,
and hi gaderiað onsundron þa synfullan menn,
and þa ðe unrihtwisnysse worhton on heora life,
and wurpað hi gebundenne into þam byrnendan fyre,   275
þær bið wop and wanung on ealra worulda woruld.
þonne scinað þa rihtwisan, swa swa sunne deð nu,
on heora Fæder rice; þis sæde se Hælend.

Seo burhwaru gelyfde, swa swa we sædon ær,
ærest þurh þæt wif; and eft, þa þa hi comon   280
to Criste sylfum þær þær he sæt,
þa bædon hi þæt he wunode þær sume hwile,
and he him getiþode, and twegen dagas þær wunode,
lærende þæt folc, oððæt hi gelyfdon fullice,
and to ðam wife cwædon þe him cydde ær be him,   285
We ne gelyfað nu þurh þine 'ge'cyðnysse;
'we sylf[e] gehyrdon and to soðan witon
þæt þes ys Hælend soþlice mid*daneardes.'   *p. 267
On þone we eac gelyfað, se ðe alysde us.
Si him wuldor and lof á to worulde, amen.   290

---

267 seow`on' H (wrongly).   268 wext H.   oþ] sic H; on F (oþ is needed
to give point to line 271).   269 gemenged H.   272 sumon both MSS.
godspell(:)e H (a letter erased, probably a).   273 men H.   275 gebundene H.
276 woruld(e) F; woruld H.   279 buruhwaru H.   286 gecyþnysse H.
287 sylfe] sic H; sylf(e) F.   290 Sy H.   worulde] bottom f. 249ᵛ, H.
The amen would have been at top of f. 250.

---

purgari in fine. [Ælfric modifies the idea at the beginning and expands the passage
cited from Matthew, as indicated below.]
269 f. [Matth. xiii. 38] Zizania autem filii sunt nequam.
271–8 [Matth. xiii. 39] Messores autem angeli sunt.
[40] Sicut ergo colliguntur zizania, et igni comburuntur, sic erit in consum-
matione sæculi:
[41] mittet Filius hominis angelos suos, et colligent de regno eius omnia
scandala, et eos qui faciunt iniquitatem.
[42] Et mittent eos in caminum ignis. Ibi erit fletus et stridor dentium.
[43] Tunc iusti fulgebunt sicut sol in regno Patris eorum.
279–90 [A mere summary of the gospel with conventional ending.]

NOTES

9, 73. *discipuli.* Ælfric frequently uses this Latinism instead of the corresponding English word, *leorningcnihtas.* He uses the Latin *-i* for the nominative plural, the Old English *-um* for the dative plural (homily xx. 282, and *CH* II. 266/33; 320/13). For a similar mixture of forms in the plural of *apostol,* where, however, the nominative has both *-i* and *-as,* see the glossary and lines 199, 202, 204, 260, and 266 of the present homily.

13. *Syle me drincan.* There seems no way to tell whether *drincan* is here the infinitive or an inflected case (presumably accusative) of the weak noun, *drinca,* m. (occasionally *drince,* f.). The same ambiguity recurs at lines 19, 118 (*bæd drincan,* where *drincan* might be infinitive, or accusative or genitive of *drinca*), and 152. The West Saxon Gospels have the same ambiguous *drincan* in this passage, and BT, under *sellan,* III. a, cites two similar passages from the *Riddles* (12/5 and 72/8 in Krapp–Dobbie) where *drincan* is regarded as the infinitive. The dictionaries offer no parallels with *etan,* but a parallel occurs in xxv(*c*). 8, *ge sealdon me etan,* and there is a somewhat similar construction with *þicgan* in *Leechdoms* (II. 184/10): *Ealle ða mettas ge drincan* (acc. pl.) *ða ðe habban hát mægen and scearp sele þicgean* (a sort of complementary infinitive). This construction occurs several times in the *Leechdoms*: see BT, *þicgan,* II. One would certainly suppose that the Latin *bibere* in Ælfric's sources would have prompted him to use the infinitive (as does the Authorized Version, 'Give me to drink'), and one might argue that when the substance to be drunk (water, milk, wine) is not directly named, the infinitive is more expressive than the vague noun. An example apparently in favour of the noun appears in BT under *gifan,* in a passage from the *Psalms* (*Paris Psalter,* 79/5), where *us drincan gifest* translates *potum dabis nobis.* I am not sure, however, that the passage as a whole does not favour interpreting *drincan* as infinitive and indeed it is so regarded by the *OED* under *give,* II. 6. b.

29, 140. *ræsendes.* That both manuscripts apparently had *ræscendes* until H was corrected may indicate a tendency to confuse *ræsan* and *ræscan,* but almost certainly *ræsendes* is right. The West Saxon Gospels at this point have *forþræsendes* for the Latin *salientis,* and Ælfric's Grammar (ed. Zupitza, p. 191) has '*prosilio* ic forþ aræse'.

40. *and.* This word seems intrusive, but both manuscripts have it and the passage is not repeated later.

45–55. The use of reflexive pronouns with *gebiddan* in these lines is not altogether consistent, but the repetition of the passage in lines 163–73 appears to confirm the readings here chosen. In the second passage F has all but one of the words that are here supplied from H, and H itself confirms most of the readings that are here rendered doubtful by its lacunæ. One might expect *ge eow gebiddað* in line 48, and of course both manuscripts may be descended from a faulty ancestor.

65. *burhwarum.* Here and at 219 (paralleled by 222 *ceastergewarum*) the word is dative plural, pointing to a nominative plural *burhware*, 'citizens', but at lines 69, 88, 92, and 279 we have the collective singular, *seo burhwaru.* At 246, *þa burhware* might be either accusative singular feminine or accusative plural.

88. *Samarian [byrig].* It seems essential to logic as well as rhythm and alliteration to supply *byrig.* Unfortunately Ælfric did not repeat this line later, but compare lines 3, 11, and 113. If H did not contain the word, as the spacing suggests, the two manuscripts had a common faulty ancestor.

96, 97. The first *soðlice* is rendered doubtful by the *to soðan* in the repetition at line 287. Line 288 tends, moreover, to confirm the order of H in 97, *hælend soðlice.* But one can hardly be sure that Ælfric himself did not vary.

108. *is ure trumnys.* What is missing in H can be supplied with some confidence, for Ælfric is translating Augustine's *illius infirmitas nostra est fortitudo.*

143. *Ælcum þe þyrste.* In this elliptical construction, the dative *ælcum* acquires the status of a relative pronoun by the addition of *þe* and is governed by *þyrste*, leaving the subject of *cume* and *drince* unexpressed. Compare lines 26, 27 in this homily, and also homily VI. 10: *þone þe þu lufast ys nu geuntrumod*, where a scribe has emended to *se þe.* In another homily Ælfric had translated *Si quis sitit* by the somewhat easier idiom, *Swa hwam swa ðyrste* (*CH* II. 274/3), where, incidentally, the subjunctive *ðyrste* helps to confirm the reading of H against the indicative *þyrst* of F.

152. *drincan.* This word is not present in the corresponding passage, line 31 above. It seems impossible to tell whether it is Ælfric's addition or a scribe's.

186. *mid widgilre worunge.* Is Ælfric making a particular attack on pilgrimages? There is nothing in his source about travel apart from climbing mountains.

210–13. Ælfric's statement that the Saviour was anointed with the sevenfold gifts of the Holy Spirit and his reference to Isaiah are not in his immediate sources. Cf. his own composition, *De Septiformi Spiritu*, Napier's *Wulfstan*, VIII, p. 56 sq.:

> Isaias se witega awrat on his witegunge
> be ðam halgan gaste and be his seofonfealdum gifum. . . .
> þas seofonfealdan gifa soðlice wunodon
> on urum hælende Criste eall be fullum þingum
> æfter þære menniscnysse swiðe mihtiglice.

See the references on this subject in Bethurum's *Wulfstan*, pp. 304 sq.

230. *sum mæssepreost.* Presumably a local heretic. Compare Ælfric's comment on the priest who preached polygamy, *O. E. Hept.*, p. 76 ('Preface to Genesis', 12 sqq.).

FERIA VI IN QUARTA EBDOMADA QUADRAGESIMÆ

Ioan. xi. 1–45

ÆLFRIC'S homily on the raising of Lazarus has survived in three versions, two of which are here presented in full. The first version, lines 1–208, 292–373, is represented by three manuscripts, F (CCCC 162), C (CCCC 303), and H (Cotton Vitellius C. v). F and C give the first version only, as did the original scribe of the appended section of H in which the homily stands. But the scribe who interpolated H from beginning to end has here introduced an extra passage, lines 209–91, thus establishing the second version. In his usual fashion, he put the interpolation on an extra leaf, erasing and copying just enough of the original text to join new and old neatly together into a continuous whole. Unfortunately H has not only lost many readings because of the Cottonian fire, but had earlier (before Wanley's time) lost the last eighteen lines altogether. Probably at least one gathering had disappeared from the end of the codex, for the old table of contents indicates that two more homilies followed this one.

Although F provides a more satisfactory basis for the text than the twelfth-century C or the partially burnt H, its version of this homily has been marred by someone (evidently of the twelfth century) who undertook to revise it. Sometimes the reviser merely underscored words he wished to delete; sometimes he erased them. His own substitutions are written above the lines and in the margins. Fortunately the erasures are often so incomplete that most of the letters can still be read.

Evidence for the relationship of the three copies of the first version is very slight though it suggests that F and C are more closely related to one another than to H. At two points F and C agree in manifest error: at line 10 they have *lufodest* for *lufast* in

---

[1] On the group of homilies for Fridays in Lent, see above, pp. 226–8.

opposition to the gospel and to the situation (for Lazarus is not
yet dead); and at line 363 they have a disordered syntax stemming
from the failure of some scribe to recognize the limits of a quotation. Now at line 10 H supplies the true reading, *lufast*; but it has
no reading at all for line 363, which fell within the missing conclusion. Hence there is only one point, line 10, where F and C can
be shown to be united in error against H. There may be some
confirmation of the nearness of F and C at line 32, where F changes
discipuli to *leorningcnihtas*, the reading of C. Alliteration strongly
favours *discipuli* as Ælfric's choice, but the change to the native
English equivalent may have been made by two editors independently. Unfortunately H has no reading here. I have adopted the
order of words supported by H and C against F at lines 337 and
343, not only because of the conjectured relationship of the manuscripts but because in both instances the order seemed superior,
though ever so slightly.[1]

It is B (Bodley 343) alone that contains the third version of the
homily, which has been printed as no. XIV in Belfour's *Twelfth
Century Homilies*, pp. 136–40. This is a self-contained excerpt from
the second version (that is, it draws on both the original version
and the interpolation), developing the theme of redemption without regard to a particular gospel text. It begins with the three dead
raised by Christ and their significance for the redemption of the
sinful soul. This passage corresponds roughly to lines 170–208,
but with considerable rearrangement and rewriting. Next comes
all but the last paragraph of the interpolation (lines 209–83),
dealing with the unforgivable sin against the Holy Spirit, presented
without substantial alteration. After the interpolation comes a final
paragraph consisting of lines 318–27, which form an appropriate
conclusion.

The first section of B, as just described, has undergone so much
change that collation has seemed inadvisable. The other two sections, in spite of the late spellings and other small alterations,
follow the text as established by the older versions line by line and
are therefore collated. For the interpolation B has been of considerable value as a guide to the missing words and letters in H.
Belfour's text has been freshly compared with the manuscript and

---

[1] It is not surprising that C and F should be related, since both manuscripts
are connected with the south-east. Moreover, the section of C that contains this
homily runs closely parallel in content to F. C cannot, however, be a copy of F.

one or two trifling errors corrected, but it must still be consulted
for a complete view of the third version, including all B's peculiarities of spelling and its careful differentiation of the two kinds of *g*.

The last eight lines of the interpolation (284–91) are omitted
from B's version but turn up in an unexpected quarter as the first
eight lines of a self-contained little composition on good and bad
intentions called *De Cogitatione*. This piece appears in P (Hatton
115) and in S (Hatton 116), and was printed from S by Napier in
Anglia X (1888), 155. It contains altogether twenty-nine lines of
rhythmic prose in Ælfric's characteristic style, and there can be
little doubt that he wrote it, as Clemoes has already recognized
(*Chronology*, 219). If I am right in my conjecture about the short
pieces contained in MSS. P, R, and S (as stated above, p. 57, in
the description of P), Ælfric may have composed *De Cogitatione*
independently and kept it in reserve for some future use. If so it
was ready to hand when he was interpolating the Lazarus homily
and he inserted as much of the passage as he thought appropriate.
His use of a passage already composed would help to explain the
very slight relation at this point to Augustine's sermon.

Within the eight lines that appear in the interpolation in H the
only consequential variant is *hetela* for *swicola* in the first line.
Clearly *swicola* yields better alliteration, but I have allowed *hetela*
to stand on the chance—a rather remote one, perhaps—that Ælfric
made the substitution himself. For the reader's convenience
I have reprinted the rest of *De Cogitatione* in the note on line 284
of the present homily.

The Latin sources bear out the indications in the manuscripts of
a sharp distinction between the first version of the homily and the
interpolation. For the first version Ælfric probably began with
the interpolated Haymo, in which the homily for the fourth Friday
in Lent is simply Alcuin's commentary on *John* xi. 1–45. But in
homilies II and V we have seen Ælfric going behind Alcuin, or the
excerpts from him in Haymo, to Augustine's tractates on *John*;
and if he took the same route here he found that Alcuin at this
point had merely abridged Augustine. No matter what the route,
it is certain that Ælfric made vigorous use of Augustine's Tractate
XLIX. 1–25. Before taking up the gospel narrative verse by verse,
Augustine comments generally on the great reputation of the
miracle of the raising of Lazarus and on the moral significance
of the thee dead raised by Christ. This section of the tractate,

which has strongly affected Ælfric's homily, is altogether missing in Alcuin's abridgement. Since Alcuin on his side has nothing that is not also in Augustine, his demonstrable contribution is reduced to zero and Augustine alone figures as the chief source of the first version.

Nowhere in the forty-ninth tractate does Augustine mention the sin against the Holy Spirit. But in *Sermo* LXXI (*PL* XXXVIII. 445–67) he comments at length on this matter as it is set forth in *Matthew* xii. 31 sq. This sermon is the ultimate if not the immediate source of Ælfric's interpolation.

There is an obvious connexion between the interpolation and the original homily. The three dead raised by Christ have been regarded, under Augustine's guidance, as typifying three stages of death experienced by the soul as it proceeds in sin from secret willingness to open performance, and finally to habitual sin. The raising of Lazarus shows that even habitual sinners can be redeemed if only they repent. It is this condition, present in Augustine's exposition and of course axiomatic in all discussions of the forgiveness of sins, that leads to a consideration of *Matthew* xii. 31 sq., where Jesus says that all sins may be forgiven except the sin of blasphemy against the Holy Spirit. Augustine, in *Sermo* LXXI, explains this unforgivable sin as the sinner's stubborn refusal to repent.

In composing his interpolation, however, Ælfric was not making the connexion for the first time. There is a curious parallel with his early homily for the seventeenth Sunday after Pentecost (*CH* I. 490–500). That homily deals with another of the three dead raised by Christ, the young man of Naim,[1] *Luke* vii. 11–16. Here, as Max Förster has pointed out (*Anglia* XVI. 25), Ælfric starts out with the interpretation of the gospel in Bede's commentary on *Luke*, but presently he introduces the subject of the three dead. For this he turns, not to Augustine, but to Bede's condensed and rewritten version of Augustine in his commentary on the third person raised, the daughter of Jairus, as described in *Luke* viii. 41–56 and *Mark* v. 22–43. Bede's long paragraph on the subject occurs first in the commentary on *Luke* and again, with only slight revisions, in that on *Mark* (ed. Hurst, *In Lucam* III. 1052–1101; *In Marcum* II. 461–509).[2] Ælfric does not stop here, however.

---

[1] A.V. *Nain*, but Ælfric follows the Vulgate spelling.
[2] Bede's commentaries on *Luke* vii. 11–16 and viii. 41–56 were included in Paul the Deacon's homiliary, II. 76 and II. 96 respectively. See above, p. 156.

Having considered the forgiveness of sins as expounded by Bede, he turns to the one unforgivable sin as expounded by Augustine in *Sermo* LXXI, thus anticipating the interpolation in the later homily. Indeed it is hard to tell whether, in composing the interpolation, he did not merely rewrite, in rhythmic prose, his own earlier exposition; but the reference to heretics in the interpolation, though it is only obliquely related to Augustine's sermon, makes me believe that he turned once more to the Latin source. Both of Ælfric's versions of Augustine are greatly abridged, and it is possible that he was using some intermediate Latin abridgement rather than the original *Sermo*, though I have not encountered any such document. (Bede does not mention the unforgivable sin in the passages to which Ælfric is directly indebted in the early homily, and his interpretation of it elsewhere in his writings is markedly different from Augustine's. See, for example, his commentary on *Luke* xii. 10 and, later, on *Mark* iii. 28 sq.)

Ælfric's dependence on Augustine's tractate for the first version of his homily on Lazarus is clear not only from the many small correspondences but from the arrangement, for although the proportions are very different the order is roughly the same. Augustine devotes three introductory sections to general topics (miracles, the three dead raised by Christ, the death and redemption of the soul) before proceeding to a verse-by-verse exegesis of the gospel. He deals with verses 1–45 in twenty-two sections. Ælfric, after giving a translation of these verses, begins his exposition with the general topics of Augustine's first three sections. Though he abridges somewhat, he allows these topics to fill 134 lines (lines 111–208, 292–327 as printed), about three-quarters of the remaining space. Then he turns, with Augustine, to the verse-by-verse exegesis; but he reduces this to a mere thirty-six lines, followed by a seven-line conclusion. His explicit comments are limited to some nine of the forty-five verses (3–9, 25, 26).

There are other passages in Augustine that might have contributed something to Ælfric's first version, and likewise a few works of later writers, though in no case have I found evidence persuasive enough to warrant their being cited as sources. Thus Augustine treats the theme of the three dead and the redemption of sinners very elaborately in *Sermo* XCVIII (Migne, *PL* XXXVIII. 591 sqq.), which starts with the raising of the young man of Naim, *Luc.* vii. 11–15. He treats the same theme very briefly in the first

book of his commentary on the Sermon on the Mount (Migne, *PL*
XXXIV. 1247). These passages have many points of correspondence
with the passage in the tractate, but as a whole they are much less
close to Ælfric. Among later writers Bede was clearly influential,
since his commentaries had been Ælfric's primary source for the
earlier sermon, already mentioned, on the young man of Naim;
but here it is plain that Ælfric has Augustine, not Bede, before him.

At first sight a very likely source is another treatment of the
raising of Lazarus: Homily CII, for the Fourth Friday in Lent, in
the Migne version of Paul the Deacon's homiliary, *PL* XCV. 1299–
1307. This homily, which is probably by Hericus of Auxerre, is
heavily indebted to Augustine, but it presents the materials of his
tractate in another order and with many small variations, some of
which come from other passages in Augustine. After a brief introduction on miracles, similar to that of the tractate, this homily
takes up the gospel verse by verse, leaving to the end the theme of
the three dead.

In spite of many general correspondences, I have found only
one point in Hericus's homily where it comes closer to Ælfric
than Augustine's tractate. In lines 346–8, where Ælfric is commenting on verse 9 of his text, he elaborates Augustine's interpretation,
that Christ is the day, by a reminiscence of *Ioan.* viii. 12, *Ego sum
lux mundi,* &c. Hericus has a somewhat similar elaboration of
Augustine, with direct quotation of the same text (Migne, *PL*
XCV. 1301). Yet Ælfric does not include any of the particulars of
Hericus's passage beyond the gospel quotation. It is possible,
therefore, that he introduced the allusion independently.[1]

It is difficult to decide whether Ælfric himself should be credited
with the third version of the homily. As printed by Belfour from
B, it has clearly acquired features that belong to a later period:
levelled endings and other small changes of form or spelling which
reflect the twelfth century. These little changes are easily discounted, and in most of the Belfour homily we can discern Ælfric's
work shining through line for line and usually word for word. The
problem is largely confined to the first nineteen lines in Belfour's
text, which are considerably rewritten, and secondarily to a few
lines that follow these, where the reviser is modifying the opening
of Ælfric's interpolation, chiefly by omitting phrases.

---

[1] On Ælfric's use of the collection of Paulus, see above, pp. 156–61; and on
the attribution to Hericus, p. 159, n. 2.

The first nineteen lines in Belfour constitute an abridgement and partial rewriting of lines 170–208, with here and there a reminiscence of 160–9. Certain features of this passage accord well enough with the idea that the reviser was Ælfric himself. Almost all the words can be found in the earlier versions, even *unforwondodlic* (Belfour, line 11), which is mistakenly printed at the beginning of a sentence rather than at the end of the preceding one. (Cf. 166, *Se ðe . . . unforwandodlice singað.*) The use of *betacnian* for *getacnian* is no doubt a later substitution, and perhaps the compound *sunnepoht*, but on the whole the few expressions not found in the earlier versions seem well within Ælfric's range. Moreover, some of the revised passages make very good alliterative lines in Ælfric's manner.

On the other hand, the metrical structure is at fault at several points. In Belfour's line 4, the phrase *pare sunfule sawle* is quoted directly from line 173, but the reviser now jumps to 176 and leaves the half-line incomplete. Later, at Belfour's lines 9 and 10, one otherwise acceptable metrical line made from two (172, 173) is unbalanced by an extra phrase, *on hyre life*, which does not occur anywhere in our text. These and a few other instances look like the work of someone who was willing to disregard, on occasion, the niceties of Ælfric's style. At the beginning of the revised interpolation (Belfour 19–23), as revealed by the table of variants in this edition, there has been considerable abridgement, and this has resulted in a similar weakening of the metrical structure. If one looks only at Belfour's text one sees that the sense is satisfactory and the sentence-rhythms not displeasing, but comparison with the earlier text reveals that here and there the alliterative pattern is weakened or the line-balance mildly disturbed.

One way to explain the conflicting evidence is to suppose that a revision made originally by Ælfric has been partially distorted by alterations, chiefly abridgements, made by a later editor. On the whole, however, it seems a little more probable that this essentially rather mechanical piece of excerption and revision was the work of an early successor, one who was familiar enough with Ælfric's work to approximate its vocabulary and style at the few points where he chose to rewrite it, but was content for the most part to copy what lay before him, and was not much troubled if his little abridgements (almost entirely confined to the first twenty-three lines in Belfour's text) weakened the metrical form of the original.

Even if Ælfric was not responsible for the third version, his continued interest in the theme of the three dead and the forgiveness of sins is clear. Having introduced the theme at first in his homily on the young man of Naim, he treated it again in the first version of his Lazarus homily. Afterwards, following the path already marked out in the earlier homily, he added the interpolation to produce the second version here printed. Whoever put together the brief, self-contained discourse represented in B was focusing attention on the part of the Lazarus homily that Ælfric himself had thought about most carefully. It is essentially Ælfric's own synthesis of two arresting passages in Augustine.[1]

---

[1] There is a separate edition of Augustine's *Sermo* LXXI by P. Verbraken in the *Revue Bénédictine*, LXXV (1965), 54–108. The passages of the *Sermo* quoted below, from the Maurist text in *PL* XXXVIII, sections 6 and 18–21, are included in lines 134–40, 365–89, 409–10, 438–47, and 461–2 of Verbraken's text. The few differences between these texts are not significant for Ælfric.

FERIA VI IN *QUARTA* EBDOMADA
QUADRAGESIMÆ

Erat quidam languens Lazarus, et *reliqua*

On þam halgan godspelle þe ge gehyrdon nu rædan
us segð be Lazare, þe seoc læg
þa he wæs on Bethania-wic wuniende (þa),
(and) wæs Marðan broðor and Marian (soðlice),
*and þæt wæs seo Maria þe mid micelre arwurðnysse

Except for the interpolation in lines 209–91, the text is based on F (CCCC
162), pp. 274–84. It is collated with H (Cotton Vitellius C. v), ff. 250–3, 254^{r-v},
which breaks off at line 357, having lost the conclusion; and with C(CCCC 303),
pp. 38–43. The interpolation is based on H, ff. 253–4, which alone of these three
manuscripts contains it. Likewise collated, however, for the greater part of the
interpolation and for lines 318–27 of the original homily is the otherwise divergent homily in B (Bodley 343), ff. 166^v–7^v, Belfour xiv. Collated for the end of
the interpolation, 284–91, are the first eight lines of the short *De Cogitatione*
in P (Hatton 115), f. 59, and S (Hatton 116), p. 380.

Round brackets enclose erasures in F (most of them apparently made by
a reviser in the twelfth century) and the usual gaps in H. In the interpolation
the gaps of H have been filled by comparison with B, but B's late readings are
often normalized in the text, its actual readings relegated to the table of variants.
In the original homily the combined authority of F and C has encouraged an
even more selective notice of H's gaps than in homilies iii and v. F's use of
capitals has been regularized. See above, p. 248.

Excluded variants: (1) Both H and C prefer *i* to *y* in such words as *biþ*, *his*,
hit, *is*, *þis*. (2) Where F has *for ðam ðe*, H has *for þan þe*, C either *for þan þe* or
for þon þe. (3) C's late spellings have been treated selectively; B's are given only
when its readings have been used as the basis for the text.

Sup.: (FR.VI. EBD QUARTA.) þis spel (gebyrað on þone feorþan frige-
dæg on Lencten. EVG.) Erat q*uidam* (longuens [*sic*] Lazarus. et reliqua.) *H, the
bracketed portions from Wanley,* Catalogus, *p. 211.* Ewangeli*um* de lazaro. in
quadragesima. Secundum iohannem. *C* (*Latin text as in* F).

1 gehyrdon] herdon *C.* nu] *om. H* (*according to Wanley, whose record of
lines 1–2 shows no other variants*). 2 sægð *C.* 3 first þa] *erased H.*
(wuni)gende þa *H*; wunigenda þa *C*; *second* þa *erased F.* 4 and wæs *CH.*
In F *the corrector substitutes* þes lazarus *for* and. marthan *CH.* soðlice]
sic C; no reading (*though the space is right*) *H; in* F *there may have been a shorter
word: the space of the erasure should not have contained more than five letters.*

SOURCES. 2–7 [*Ioan. xi. 1*] Erat autem quidam languens Lazarus a Bethania, de
castello Mariæ, et Marthæ sororis eius.

[2] (Maria autem erat, quæ unxit Dominum unguento, et extersit pedes eius
capillis suis: cuius frater Lazarus infirmabatur.)

mid deorwurðre sealfe urne Drihten smyrode,
and mid hyre fexe wipode hys fet.

þa ða (he) seoc læg, þa sændon his geswustra
to þam Hælende sona, secgende (mid sarnysse),
La leof hlaford, (þon)e þe þu luf[a]st   10
ys nu geuntrumod. He him andwyrde and cwæð:
Nis þeos untrumnyss na to deaðe,
ac for Godes wuldre, þæt Godes Sunu sy
gewuldrod þurh hine. Se Hælend lufode
soðlice Marthan, and Marian hire swuster,   15
and Lazarum heora broþur, and þa þa he geaxode be him
þæt he geuntrumod wæs, þa wunode he
twegen dagas on þære ylcan stowe,
and æfter þam cwæð to his leorningcnihtum,
Uton faran nu eft to Iudea lande.   20
þa cwædon his leorningcnihtas, (La leof lareow,)
nu for feawum dagum sohton þa Iudeiscan
þe to stænenne, and þu eft nu wylt
þyder ongean faran? And he him andwyrde,
La hu næfð se dæg twelf tid'a' on him?   25
And se ðe gæð on dæg, se ne ætsp[y]rnð na,
for þam ðe he gesicð þises middaneardes leoht.

---

7 feaxe C; *no reading* H.   his fet wipode H.   8 he *altered to* lazar*us* F.
sendon H; seandon C.   9 mid sarnysse CH.   10 La leof hlaford *not
erased, but* Drihten *over line* F.   þone CH; *altered to* se F.   lufast] *sic* H;
lufodest FC.   11 He *underscored,* Se hælend *over line* F.   12 untrumnys
H; untrumnesse (!) C.   14–15 lufode soðlice FH; soðlice lufode C.
16 broþor CH.   20 iudean C.   21 cwæðo his leorningcnihtu*m* (!) C.
La leof lareow C; H *retains final* -eow; *altered to* Drihten hlaford F.   23 (þe
to stæ)nenge (!) H.   24 ongean faran FH; faran *ongean* C.   and he
underscored, Se hælend *over line* F.   26 ætspyrnð] *sic* CH; ætspryrnð F.
27 gesihð C; *no reading* H.

8–18 [*3*] Miserunt ergo sorores eius ad eum dicentes: Domine, ecce quem
amas infirmatur.

[*4*] Audiens autem Iesus dixit eis: Infirmitas hæc non est ad mortem, sed pro
gloria Dei, ut glorificetur Filius Dei per eam.

[*5*] Diligebat autem Iesus Martham, et sororem eius Mariam, et Lazarum.

[*6*] Ut ergo audivit quia infirmabatur, tunc quidem mansit in eodem loco
duobus diebus.

19–27 [*7*] Deinde post hæc dixit discipulis suis: Eamus in Iudæam iterum.

[*8*] Dicunt ei discipuli: Rabbi, nunc quærebant te Iudæi lapidare, et iterum
vadis illuc?

[*9*] Respondit Iesus: Nonne duodecim sunt horæ diei? Si quis ambulaverit
in die, non offendit, quia lucem huius mundi videt:

⁊ þæꞃ ꞃeo mariᵹa þe miᵹ miceꞁꝛe aꞃꝛuꞃᵹ
ᵹeꞃꝛuꞃᵹꞃe ꞃeuꞇe uꞃne ᵹꞃihꞇ ⁊ miꞃꞃoᵹe
feꞃꞇe ꞃiꞃoᵹe hyꞃ ꝛeꞇ; þaᵹa *lazar* ꞃeoꞇ ꞇeᵹ. þa
ᵹeꞃꝛuꞃꞇꞃa ꞇoþam hæꞇenᵹe ꞃona ꞃeꞇᵹenᵹ
ꞃyꞃᵹ; Ꞁa Ꞁeoꝼ hꞀaꝼoꞃᵹ *ᵹꞃihꞇ* ꞃe þe þu Ꞁuꝼoᵹeꞃ
unꞇꞃumoᵹ; hꞇ him anᵹꞃyꞃᵹe ⁊ᵹeꞃꝛ; Nꞇ
nyꞃꞃ naꞇoᵹeaᵹe. aꞇꝼoꞃᵹoᵹeꞃ ꝛuꞇoꞃe þᵹoᵹe
ᵹeꝛuꞀoꞃoᵹ þuꞃh hine; Se hæꞀenᵹ Ꞁuꝼoᵹe ꝛ
ꞇhan ⁊mariᵹan hiꞃe ꞃuꞃꞇæꞃ ⁊Ꞁazaꞃum
þuꞃ ⁊ þaþahe ᵹeaꝼoᵹe behim þ he ᵹeunꞇ
þa ꞃunᵹoᵹe he ꞇꝛeᵹen ᵹaᵹaꞃ onþæꝛe yꞀca
þam ꞇꝛæᵹ ꞇohiꞃ Ꞁeoꞃninᵹꞇnihꞇum; ᴠꞇ
eꝛꞇ ꞇoiuᵹea Ꞁanᵹe; þaꞇꝛæᵹon hiꞃ Ꞁeoꞃnin
ᵹꞃihꞇ hꞀaꝼoꞃᵹ. nu ꝛoꞃ ꝛꞇꞃapum ᵹaᵹum ꞃohꞇa
þe ꞇoꞃꞇæꞃnenne; ⁊ þueꝛꞇ nu wyꞀꞇ þyᵹeꞃ onᵹ

Corpus Christi College, Cambridge, MS. 162, p. 275. Homily VI, 5 sqq. in the handsome main hand, with alterations by a later scribe.

Se ðe gæð on niht, se soþlice ætspyrnð,
for þam þe leoht nis on him. And he eft þa cwæð,
Lazarus ure freond liþ nu and slæpð,   30
ac ic wille faran þyder, þæt ic hine awecce.
þa cwædon hys discipuli, Drihten, gyf he slæpð,
he byð gehealden. (And) se Hælend sæde
be Lazares deaðe, þe læg þa forðfaren;
*hi wendon soþlice þæt he be slæpe sæde.   *p. 276
'He cwæð þa openlice (oðre word him to:)'   36
Lazarus is forðfaren, and ic for eow blissige,
þæt ge gelyfon, for ðam þe ic næs þær;
ac uton faran to him. And Thomas cwæð þa,
(þæs tonama wæs Didimus,) to hys geferum,   40
Uton we eac faran, þæt we swelton mid him.
Se Hælend þa ferde, and (hi) forð mid him,
and comon on þone feorðan dæg þæ(s) þe he bebyrged wæs
'to Bethanian (wic), þær he bebyrged wæs,'
þanon wæron to Ierusalem fiftene furlang.   45
Manega þa com'on' of þam Iudeiscum
to Marþan and Marian, and mid him wæron,
þæt hi hi gefrefrodon for heora broður deaðe.

31 *after* wille] nu *over line F.*   awrecce *H.*   32 discipuli *not erased,
but* leorningcnihtas *over line F;* leorningcnihta*s C; no reading H.*   sleapð *C.*
33 *after* sæde] þis *over line F.*   34 leag *C.*   35 sleapa *C.*   36 *Whole line
inserted in upper margin by original scribe F.*   oþre word him to *CH; erased F.*
38 þæt] þæt þæt *C.*   39 *after* uton] nu *over line F.*   40 þæs tonama
wæs didimus *CH; erased F.*   41 *after* swelton] forð *inserted at end of line F.*
42 feorde *C.*   hi *erased,* his leorningcnihtas *over line F.*   43 þæs *altered
to* þær *F.*   bebyrged] gebered *C;* bebyrged *H (original hand on erasure?).*
44 bethanian wic *H;* bethania wic *C;* wic *erased F.*   45 wæron *underscored,*
syndon *over line F.*   hierusalem *CH.*   fiftyne *H.*   46 *after* manega] mænn
inserted at end of line F.   *after* iudeiscum] folce *inserted over line F.*   47 him
altered to hiom *F;* heom *C.*   48 broþor *C; no reading H.*

28–29 [*10*] si autem ambulaverit in nocte, offendit, quia lux non est in eo.
[*11*] Hæc ait, et post hæc dixit eis: Lazarus amicus noster dormit: sed vado
ut a somno excitem eum.
[*12*] Dixerunt ergo discipuli eius: Domine, si dormit, salvus erit.
[*13*] Dixerat autem Iesus de morte eius: illi autem putaverunt quia de dormi-
tione somni diceret.
[*14*] Tunc ergo Iesus dixit eis manifeste: Lazarus mortuus est:
[*15*] et gaudeo propter vos, ut credatis, quoniam non eram ibi. Sed eamus
ad eum.
39–48 [*16*] Dixit ergo Thomas, qui dicitur Didymus, ad condiscipulos:
Eamus et nos, ut moriamur cum eo.

Martha þa gehyrde þæt se Hælend wæs cumen,
and eode him togeanes, and Maria sæt æt ham.　　50
þa cwæð Martha sona swa heo geseah þone Hælend,
Hlafurd, gyf þu her wære, nære min broþur dead;
ac ic swaðeah wat þæt God þe getiþað
swa hwæs swa þu hine bitst. And se Hælend cwæð,
þin broþur arist. And Martha him cwæð to,　　　55
Ic wat þæt he arist on þam æriste,
on þam endenextan dæge. Hyre andwyrde se Hælend,
Ic eom ærist and lif; se ðe gelyfð on me,
þeah þe he dead si, he leofað swaþeah;
and ælc þæra þe leofað and on me gelyfð,　　　　60
ne swylt he on ecnysse; gelyfst þu þis, Martha?
Heo andwyrde and cwæð, Witudlice, hlafurd,
ic gelyfe þæt þu eart Crist, Godes Sunu,
þe on þysne middaneard to mannum come.
He'o' eode þa sona, syððan heo þys cwæð,　　　　65
and clypode hyre swuster, mid (swigan) cwe*þende,　　*p. 277
Se (lareow) ys her, and he þe clypað.
Heo aras þa sona and eode to him,

---

49 geheorde *C*.　　　52 Hlaford *H*; Drihten *over line before* Hlafurd *F*.
broþor *H*; broðer *C*.　　55 broðor *C*; *no reading H*.　　　57 ændenixtan *C*.
58 gelefhð (!) *C*.　　59 si] *no reading H*.　　*after* si] on þison lyfe *over line F*.
60 gelyfð] geleofð *C*.　　　61 þis *underscored*, ðyses *over line F*; þis *H*; þises *C*.
62 Witodlice *H*.　　hlaford *CH*; hlafurd *crossed out F*.　　　63 *before* godes]
þæs lyfigenden *over line F*.　　64 *before* þe] þu *over line F*.　　66 *after* swuster]
marian *over line F*.　　swigan *CH*; *erased*, stilnesse *over line F*.　　cwæþende *alt.*
to cweþende *F*.　　67 lareow *CH*; *erased*, hælend *over line F*.

[*17*] Venit itaque Iesus: et invenit eum quatuor dies iam in monumento
habentem.
[*18*] (Erat autem Bethania iuxta Ierosolymam quasi stadiis quindecim.)
[*19*] Multi autem ex Iudæis venerant ad Martham, et Mariam, ut consola-
renter eas de fratre suo.
49–59 [*20*] Martha ergo ut audivit quia Iesus venit, occurrit illi: Maria autem
domi sedebat.
[*21*] Dixit ergo Martha ad Iesum: Domine, si fuisses hic, frater meus non
fuisset mortuus:
[*22*] Sed et nunc scio quia quæcumque poposceris a Deo, dabit tibi Deus.
[*23*] Dicit illi Iesus: Resurget frater tuus.
[*24*] Dicit ei Martha: Scio quia resurget in resurrectione in novissimo
die.
[*25*] Dixit ei Iesus: Ego sum resurrectio, et vita: qui credit in me, etiam si
mortuus fuerit, vivet:

and se Hælend þa gyt wæs on þære ylcan stowe
þær Martha him spræc to, oððæt Maria com.   70
þa eodon þa Iudei æfter Marian,
for þan ðe hi gesawon þæt heo swa raðe aras,
(and) cwædon þæt heo wolde wepan æt þære byrgenne.
Maria þa sona swa heo þone Hælend geseah,
þa feoll heo to hys fotum, and him þus cwæð to: 75
Hlaford, gyf þu hær wære, nære min broður dead.
þa ða se Hælend geseah hi sarlice wepan,
and þa Iudeiscan wepende þe hire mid comon,
þa (grymette) he on gaste, and hyne sylfne gedrefde,
and cwæð, Hwær lede ge hine? (And) hi cwædon him to,   80
Hlafurd, cum and geseoh. And þa weop se Hælend.
þa sædon þa Iudeiscan, Gesixst þu, hu he hine lufode.

---

69 git *H.*   wæs *om. H* (*probably inserted after* stowe, *where there is no reading*).
72 gesagon *H.*   hraþe *H*; hraða *C.*   73 and *erased F; om. C; no reading H.*
hi woldon (*wrongly*) *C; no reading H.*   *after* wolde] þa *over line F.*   byrigene
H; byrigenne *C.* (*So in line 85.*)   75 feol *CH.*   76 Hlafurd *C.*   her *CH.*
broþor *CH.*   79 grymette (?) *erased,* geomerode *over line F*; grymmette *H*;
grimette *C.*   he *om. C.*   gedræfde *C.*   81 Hlaford *CH.*   82 gesixst
þu] gehu (!) *C.*

60–70 [*26*] et omnis, qui vivit, et credit in me, non morietur in æternum.
Credis hoc?
    [*27*] Ait illi: Utique Domine, ego credidi, quia tu es Christus filius Dei vivi,
qui in hunc mundum venisti.
    [*28*] Et cum hæc dixisset, abiit, et vocavit Mariam sororem suam silentio,
dicens: Magister adest, et vocat te.
    [*29*] Illa ut audivit, surgit cito, et venit ad eum:
    [*30*] nondum enim venerat Iesus in castellum: sed erat adhuc in illo loco, ubi
occurrerat ei Martha.
71–79 [*31*] Iudæi ergo, qui erant cum ea in domo, et consolabantur eam, cum
vidissent Mariam quia cito surrexit, et exiit, secuti sunt eam dicentes: Quia vadit
ad monumentum, ut ploret ibi.
    [*32*] Maria ergo, cum venisset ubi erat Iesus, videns eum, cecidit ad pedes
eius, et dicit ei: Domine, si fuisses hic, non esset mortuus frater meus.
    [*33*] Iesus ergo, ut vidit eam plorantem, et Iudæos, qui venerant cum ea,
plorantes, infremuit spiritu, et turbavit seipsum,
80–88 [*34*] et dixit: Ubi posuistis eum? Dicunt ei: Domine, veni, et vide.
    [*35*] Et lacrymatus est Iesus.
    [*36*] Dixerunt ergo Iudæi: Ecce quomodo amabat eum.
    [*37*] Quidam autem ex ipsis dixerunt: Non poterat hic, qui aperuit oculos
cæci nati, facere ut hic non moreretur?
    [*38*] Iesus ergo rursum fremens in semetipso, venit ad monumentum. Erat
autem spelunca: et lapis superpositus erat ei.
    [*39*] Ait Iesus: Tollite lapidem. Dicit ei Martha soror eius, qui mortuus
fuerat: Domine, iam foetet, quatriduanus est enim.

Sume of him sædon, La hu ne mihte (se) don,
(se) ðe þone blindan gehælde, þæt þes eac ne swulte?
Se Hælend eft grymetende com to ðære byrgenne,   85
and cwæð to þam ymbstandendum, Doð him of þone stán.
Martha cwæð to Criste, Hlaford (leof), he stincð,
for ðam ðe feower dagas synt syððan he bebyrged wæs.
Se Hælend hyre cwæð to, La hu ne sæd[e] ic þe
þæt gyf þu gelyfst, þu gesihst Godes wuldor?   90
Hi ahofon þæt hlid þa of þære þryh raðe,
and se Hælend cwæð, upahafenum eagum,
Fæder, ic þancige þe, for ðam ðe þu me gehyrdest;
ic soðlice wat þæt þu me symle gehyrst,
*ac for ðam folce ic sæde þe her onbutan stent,   *p. 278
þæt hi gelyfon þæt þu me asendest.   96
þa þa he þis cwæð, þa clypode he hlude,
Lazare, ueni foras: Lazarus, cum hider ut.
And he forð stop sona, se ðe forðfaren wæs,
bewunden swaþeah, swa swa hit gewunelic wæs,   100
handum and fotum, and his heafud wæs befangen
mid swatclaðe, swa swa he geled wæs.
þa cwæð se Hælend to ðam ymbstandendum,
Tolysað hys bendas, and lætað hine gán.
And he þa leofode lange syððan,   105

---

83 se *erased*, þes *over line F.*   85 grymetende *underscored*, geomerigende *over
line F.*   87 *before* cwæð] þa *over line F*; cwæþ þa *H*; cwæð *C.*   Hlaford *crossed
out,* leof *erased,* Drihten *over line F.*   88 synt] syndan *C*; *no reading H.*
89 sæd *F*; sæde *C*; *no reading H.*   90 gelifest *C.*   geseohst *C.*   wuldor]
wundor *C.*   91 þæt hlid þa *om. C.*   þruh *C.*   hraþe *CH.*   92 *after*
cwæð] þa *over line F.*   93 geherdest *C.*   94 wat] *sic FC*; *no reading H.*
95 ðam *underscored,* þisen *over line F.*   96 gelyfon *altered from* gelyfdon *F*;
gelyfon *CH.*   98 cum hider ut *not erased, but* ga forð *over line F.*   101 (hea)fod
H; hæfod *C.*   102 gelegd *C*; *no reading H.*   104 bændes *C.*

89–98 [*40*] Dicit ei Iesus: Nonne dixi tibi quoniam si credideris, videbis
gloriam Dei?
   [*41*] Tulerunt ergo lapidem: Iesus autem elevatis sursum oculis, dixit: Pater
gratias ago tibi quoniam audisti me.
   [*42*] Ego autem sciebam quia semper me audis, sed propter populum, qui
circumstat, dixi: ut credant quia tu me misisti.
   [*43*] Hæc cum dixisset, voce magna clamavit: Lazare veni foras.
99–104 [*44*] Et statim prodiit qui fuerat mortuus, ligatus pedes et manus
institis, et facies illius sudario erat ligata. Dixit eis Iesus: Solvite eum, et sinite
abire.
105 sq. [*Ælfric's addition.*]

halre þonne he ær wæs, þurh þæs Hælendes mihte.
Manega þa eornostlice of þam Iudeiscum
þe comon to Marian and Marthan hire swuster
and gesawon hu se Hælend heora broþur arærde
gelyfdon on hyne for þam (liflican) tacne.   110
  Betwux eallum þam wundrum þe ure Hælend worhte
ys þyss miccle wundor mærlicost geþuht,
þæt he þone stincendan Lazarum to life arærde;
ac gyf we behealdað hwa hyne arærde,
þonne mage we blissian swiðor þonne wundrian.   115
Se arærde þone man se ðe man geworhte;
he ys se ancenneda Sunu þæs ælmihtigan Fæder,
þurh þone synd gesceapene ealle gesceafta;
and la, hwilc wu[n]dor is þéah þe to life arise
an mann þurh hyne, þonne ælce dæge beoð   120
manega acennede þurh *hys mihte on worulde?   *p. 279
Micel‘e’ mare miht ys menn to [ge]scippenne
þonne to arærenne þone þe ǽr wæs.
He gemedemode swaþeah þæt he menn gesceope,
and eac þæt he arærde hi eft of deaðe.   125
He gesceop ealle menn, and sume arærde,
se ðe eaðe mihte ‘ealle gif he wolde
deade arǽran þurh his (drihtenlican) mihte;’

---

106 halra *CH*. he] *om. C.*   107 *after* iudeiscum] folce *over line F.*
109 broþor *CH*.   110 *after* gelyfdon] ða *over line F.*   liflican *erased*,
mærlican *in margin F.*   113 lyfe *H*.   114 behældæð *C*.   117 a‘n’cen-
ne(da) *H*; acennede *C*.   119 wundor *CH*; wuldor *F*.   þe] *om. C.*
120 man *CH*.   dæg *H*.   beoð] bið *C*.   121 *after* manega] men *over line F.*
122 menn] man *C*; *no reading H*; a *above* e *F*.   gescippenne] *sic H*;
gesceppenne *C*; scippenne *F*.   123 arænne (!) *C*.   126 men *H*.   arearde *C*.
128 arearon *C*.

107–10 [*45*] Multi ergo ex Iudæis, qui venerant ad Mariam, et Martham, et
viderant quæ fecit Iesus, crediderunt in eum.
111–18 [*Augustine, In Ioan. Ev.*] Inter omnia miracula quæ fecit Dominus
noster Iesus Christus, Lazari resurrectio præcipue prædicatur. Sed si attendamus quis fecerit, delectari debemus potius quam mirari. Ille suscitavit
hominem, qui fecit hominem: ipse enim est Unicus Patris, per quem, sicut
nostis, facta sunt omnia.
119–28 [*Augustine*] Si ergo per illum facta sunt omnia, quid mirum est si
resurrexit unus per illum, cum tot quotidie nascantur per illum? Plus est homines
creare quam resuscitare. Dignatus est tamen et creare et resuscitare; creare
omnes, resuscitare quosdam. . . . Audisti enim quia Dominus Iesus mortuum
suscitavit: sufficit tibi ut scias quia si vellet, omnes mortuos suscitaret.

ac he heold witodlice þæt weorc him sylfum
oð ða geendunge þysre worulde,   130
swa he sylf sæde on sumon godspelle,
þæt se tima cymð þonne ealle þa deadan
þe on byrgenum beoð gehyrað swutellice
Godes Sunu stefne, and gað of heora byrgenum—
to lifes æriste, þa ðe gód worhton;   135
to genyðerunge æriste, þa ðe yfel worhton.

Is swaþeah oðer ærist on urum sawlum
þe ure Hælend deð dæghwamlice on mannum,
þonne seo sawul arist of ðære synna deaðe,
for ðam se ðe syngað, hys sawul ne leofað,   140
buton heo þurh andetnysse eft acucige,
and þurh dædbote hyre Drihten gladige.

Ælc man ondræd him deaðes tocyme,
and feawa him ondrædað þære sawle deað.

For ðæs lichaman life, þe langsum beon ne mæg,   145
swincað menn swiðe, on sæ and on lande,
þæt hi deaðe ætbærston, and beoð swaþeah deade
on sumne timan, (þeah þe h`i´ sume hwile ætfleon;)
and hi nellað swincan þæt hi ne singian,

---

132 deadan] dæde *C.*   133 beoð] bið *C.*   geheorad (!) *C.*   134 suna *H.*
stemne *H.*   *after* and] hio *over line F.*   byrgenum] beogenum (!) *C.*   136 *before*
to] and *over line F.*   139 ðære synna] ðære synne *C; no reading H.*
141 acwucie *C.*   142 hyre] hirne (!) *C.*   143 ondræt *CH.*   *before*
deaðes] þæs lichames *over line F.*   144 him] hi`o´m *F;* heom *C (no*
reading H, but regularly him).   þæra *H.*   146 swincð man (?) *C;* swincaþ
men *H.*   147 dæðe *C.*   (ne) ætbærston *F* (ne *rightly erased);* ætberstan
H; ætberston *C.*   148 hi] *altered from* he *F (still visible despite erasure).*
149 swincan] geswican *C;* swincan *H.*   singian] sengian *C; no reading H.*

129–36 [*Augustine*] Et hoc quidem sibi ad finem sæculi reservavit. Nam . . .
veniet hora, sicut ipse ait, *quando omnes qui sunt in monumentis audient vocem* eius:
et procedent . . . qui bene fecerunt, ad resurrectionem vitæ; qui male egerunt, ad
resurrectionem iudicii (*Ioan. v. 28, 29*). [*Ælfric seems to follow the Vulgate directly,*
which has vocem Filii Dei, bona fecerunt, mala egerunt.]

137–42 [*Ælfric's independent transition, partially suggested by Augustine*:] Si
attendamus mirabiliora opera Christi, omnis qui credit, resurgit: si attendamus
omnes, et intelligamus detestabiliores mortes, omnis qui peccat moritur.

143–51 [*Augustine*] Sed mortem carnis omnis homo timet, mortem animæ
pauci. Pro morte carnis quæ sine dubio quandoque ventura est, curant omnes ne
veniat: inde est quod laborant. Laborat ne moriatur homo moriturus, et non
laborat ne peccet homo in æternum victurus. Et cum laborat ne moriatur, sine
causa laborat; id enim agit ut multum mors differatur, non ut evadatur: si
autem peccare nolit, non laborabit, et vivet in æternum.

þæt heora sawla lybban on þam ecan life   150
buton geswince, and byð se *lichama   *p. 280
æfter Domes-dæge to ðam ylcan gebroht,
on sawle geliffæst syððan áá to worulde.

Ondræde swa þu ondræde, se deað þe cymð to;
ys forþi wislicor þæt þu warnige georne   155
þæt þu yfele ne swelte, on synnum geendod,
and syððan ecelice on sawle and on lichaman
æfre cwylmige on endeleasum witum,
and sweltan ne mage swaðeah næfre.

We willað secgan eow nu be þære sawle deaðe,   160
þæt [he] ys þreora cynna, þeah þe hit eow cuð ne si.

Se þe yfel geþengð and yfel dón wile,
him ys se deað wiðinnan digollice on his sawle;
and se þe yfel wile and þæt yfel gefremað,
he byð þonne openlice yfele déad.   165

Se ðe gewunolice and unforwandodlice singað,
and hys yfel gewidmærsað þurh yfelne hlisan,
se ys bebyrged on [bismer]fullum leahtrum,
and he fule þonne stincð on his fracodum dædum.

Nu segð us seo Cristes boc þæt Crist ure Hælend   170
þry men arærde of deaðe to life,

150 lybbon *H*; libban *C*.   151-3 and . . . worulde *crossed out F.*
153 aa *om. H*; a *C*.   155 warnige þe *C*; *no reading H.*   156 swylte *C.*
158 endelæsu*m C.*   160 *before* We] Leofan men (?) *over line F.*   eow nu
secgan *C.*   161 he *CH*; *om. F.*   ðrira *C.*   sy *CH.*   162 geþencð *CH.*
163 digellice *H.*   164 yfele (*twice*) *C.*   166 gewunelice *CH.*   syngaþ *CH.*
167 yfelne] yfele *C.*   168 bis(merful)lum *H*; bismærfullu*m C*; his
mánfullum (!) *F.*   169 deadu*m C.*   170 seo] si *C.*

151-9 [*Ælfric's independent elaboration of the preceding.*]

160-208 [*Ælfric rearranges materials from a consecutive passage in Augustine dealing with the three dead raised by Christ as types of the death and resurrection of the soul.*]

160-9 [*An anticipatory summary based on materials introduced later and separately by Augustine:*] Peccatum, mors est animæ. Sed aliquando in cogitatione peccatur. Delectavit quod malum est; consensisti, peccasti; consensio illa occidit te: sed intus est mors, quia cogitatum malum nondum processit in factum. . . . Si autem non solum malæ delectationi consensisti, sed etiam ipsum malum fecisti, quasi mortuum extra portam extulisti: iam foris es, et mortuus elatus es. . . . Qui autem peccare consuevit, sepultus est, et bene de illo dicitur, *fetet*: incipit enim habere pessimam famam, tanquam odorem teterrimum.

170-3 [*Augustine*] Tres tamen mortuos a Domino resuscitatos in Evangelio legimus. . . . Bene intelligimus tres illos mortuos quos in corporibus suscitavit, aliquid significare et figurare de resurrectionibus animarum quæ fiunt per fidem.

and þa þry getacnodon þone þryfealdan deað
þære synfullan sawle, þe syngað on þreo wisan:
on yfe'lre' geþafunge oððe yfelum geþohte,
on yfelre fremminge, and on yfelum gewunan.   175
Ure Drihten arærde anes ealdormannes dohtor,
seo ðe læg dead digellice on his huse,
and næs þa gyt geferod forð openlice,
and heo soðlice getacnode *þære sawle deað   *p. 281
þe byð wiðinnan hyre þurh þæt yfele geþanc,   180
and ne bið geopenod þurh yfele fremmincge.
He arærde anne cniht þa þa he com to anre byrig
Naim gehaten, and he wæs geferod
on þæs folces gesihþe, and him folgode seo modor,
dreorig wepende; ac ur'e' Drihten sona   185
hi swæslice gefrefrode, and hyre sunu arærde,
and betæhte þære meder, swa swa he mildheort wæs.
þes deada getacnode þære sawle deað
þe syngað openlice, swilce heo ferige on folces gesihþe
hyre deadan on bære, and byð þonne cuð   190
hyre synfulla deað þurh þa openan synna.
Gyf þu syngodest, þu hit soðlice behreowsa,
and Crist arærð þe, þæt þu cucu byst on G[o]de,

---

173 þe] þe þe C.   þri wisum C.   174 before on] þæt is over line F.
175 gefremunga C.   181 geopenod 'þa gyt' H.   fremminge CH.   184 seo]
sy C.   185 dryrig C.   186 gerærde C.   187 moder C.   swa
swa . . . wæs underscored, hys (sic) over wæs F.   191 synna FH; synan (!) C.
192 singodes (!) C.   behreowsa FH; bet and bet and bhreowsa (sic) C.
193 gode C; göde F; góde H. See note.

174, 175 [Augustine does not supply this summary, though he provides its elements.]
176–81 [Augustine] Resuscitavit filiam archisynagogi adhuc in domo iacentem. . . . Intus est mors; quia cogitatum malum nondum processit in factum.
Talem animam resuscitare se significans Dominus, resuscitavit illam puellam
quæ nondum erat foras elata, sed in domo mortua iacebat, quasi peccatum
latebat.
182–91 [Augustine] Resuscitavit iuvenem filium viduæ extra portas civitatis
elatum. . . . Si autem non solum malæ delectationi consensisti, sed etiam ipsum
malum fecisti, quasi mortuum extra portam extulisti: iam foris es, et mortuus
elatus es. Tamen et ipsum Dominus resuscitavit, et reddidit viduæ matri suæ.
192–5 [Augustine] Si peccasti, poeniteat te: et resuscitat te Dominus, et reddet
Ecclesiæ matri tuæ.
193b [Cf. Rom. vi. 11] Ita et vos, existimate vos mortuos quidem esse
peccato, viventes autem Deo, in Christo Iesu Domino nostro.

and betæcð þe þinre meder, þæt ys, [his] gelaþung'e',
on þære þu wære gefullod, and on þære þu scealt geþeon.   195
Se þridda deada (wæs) þe ure Drihten arærde
Lazarus (se Iudeisca), se læg bebyrged
fule þa stincende, swa swa we her beforan sædon;
and he hæfde getacnunge þæs synfullan mannes,
þe hæfð him on gewunan hys yfelan dæda,   200
and stincð þurh unhlisan and yfelne gewunan.

Swylcra ys to fela þe on synnum licgað,
forlorene on þeawum and ofhrorene mid leahtrum,
and nellað gehyran þa halgan lare,
and þincð him æþryt þæt he embe þæt þence,   205
hu he arise of þam reocendan meoxe;
is him leofre to licganne on his lichaman lustum
þonne he ænig þing swince and hys softnys'e' forleose.

Witodlice ure leofa Hæ(lend mæg, swa swa ælmihtig God,)
ða sawla aræran þe ðuss ðryfealdlice syng(iað,   210
swa swa he þas þry) deadan þurh his drihtenlican mihte
to life arærde, [him sylfum to lofe.]

---

194 moder C.   his CH; þære over line F.   gelaþunge H; gelaþung C.
196 þreodde C.   arearde C.   197 'wæs' lazarus F.   198 her altered from ær
F; her C; no reading H.   199 syn'n'(fullan) H.   204 geheran C.   205
aþrit C.   þeance C.   206 whu (!) C.   hreocendan C.   207 leofre] leofra
to lifra (!) C.   licgenne H; last word on f. 252ᵛ, the final ne added by the scribe
who revised the volume. He wrote the whole of the following leaf, beginning on his
lichaman lu. . . .   208 softnysse C; no reading H.   forlyse C.   209–91]
The text of these lines is from the fire-damaged H, f. 253, line 2, to f. 254, the first
word. Gaps, indicated by round brackets, are supplied conjecturally by comparison
with B, f. 167ʳ⁻ᵛ, which corresponds roughly for all but the last eight lines. Actual
readings of B, when not accepted, are recorded among the variants. See the introductory comment and headnote.   209 Witodlice ure leofa] Ac ure B.   almihtig
B.   210 þe . . . syngiað] om. B.   211 swa swa] swa B.   deadan] deaden
dyde B.   212 to life arærde] om. B.   to lofe (him sylfum) H (?); him sylfe
to lofe B.

196–201 [Augustine] Resuscitavit Lazarum sepultum quatriduanum. . . .
Tertius mortuus est Lazarus. . . . Qui autem peccare consuevit, sepultus est, et
bene de illo dicitur, fetet: incipit enim habere pessimam famam, tanquam
odorem teterrimum.

202–8 [Augustine] Tales sunt omnes assueti sceleribus, perditi moribus. Dicis
ei, Noli facere. Quando te audit quem terra sic premit, et tabe corrumpitur, et
mole consuetudinis prægravatur? [Ælfric develops this very freely.]

209–16 [Ælfric's independent transition. Lines 213–16 give the orthodox
elaboration of the Omne peccatum . . . remittetur hominibus at the start of the
passage quoted below. Augustine's sermon attributes this doctrine to the church and
defends it without stating it at length.]

Is nu swyðe to witenne þæt nis næfre nan synn
to ðam swiðe (micel þæt man) ne mæg gebetan
her on ðisum life, gif he ða dædbote deð   215
(be þæs gyl)tes mæðe, on Gode truwien[d]e.
Ure Hælend swaðeah sæde (on his) godspelle
þæt se mann ðe tallic word cwyð ongean ðone Halga(n Gast,)
and hine hæfð to hospe, næfð he his næfre forgyfenysse,
ne (on) ðissere worulde, ne on ðære toweardan.   220
Oft gedwolmenn sp(ræ)con dyselice be Criste,
ac hi hit eft gebetton, and gebugon to hi(m) mid soðum geleafan,
and he heom sealde forgyfenysse, swa swa he sylf sæde:
Ðeah ðe hwa secge be me tal oððe hosp,
hit byð him forgyfen, gif he hit behreo'w'sað;   225
ac se ðe be ðam Halgan Gaste hosp gecwyð oððe tal,
ðonne byð his synn æfre endeleas.

Se ælmihtiga Fæder, þe ealle ðing gesceop,
hæfð ænne Sunu of him anum acenned
unasecgendlice, þone soðfæstan Hælend;   230
and se Halga Gast nis na gehaten Sunu,

---

213 Is . . . synn] Nis swaðeah nan synne *B.*   214 to . . . man] swa swiðe
mycel *þæt* mon *B.*   215 her . . . life] *om. B.*   dædbote] bote *B.*   216 bi
þes gyltes *B.*   on gode truwienne *H*; and on gode trywige *B.*   217 swaðeah
sæde] sæde swaðæh *B.*   218 þæt . . . cwyð] þe ðe tallice word sæð *B.*   halig
gast *B.*   219 his næfre] næfre þærof *B.*   221 Ofte dwolmen specon *B.*   222
betton and bugon *B.*   mid soðe bileafæ *B.*   223 sylf sæde] sæde him sylf *B.*
225 byð him] him bið *B.*   226 se ðe be] þe þe *B.* (*Belfour emends to* þe
be; *better* þe þe be).   gecwyð] cw̄ (*for* cwyð *or* cweð) *B* (*Belfour* cwæð).
227 ðonne . . . æfre] his synne bið soðlice *B.*   231 and] ac *B.*

217–20, 224–7 [*Matth. xii. 31*] Ideo dico vobis: Omne peccatum et blasphemia remittetur hominibus, Spiritus autem blasphemia non remittetur.
[*32*] Et quicumque dixerit verbum contra Filium hominis, remittetur ei; qui
autem dixerit contra Spiritum sanctum, non remittetur ei neque in hoc sæculo,
neque in futuro.

221–3 [*Probably suggested by several passages in Augustine, Sermo LXXI, e.g.*:]
Nam quicumque verbo Dei crediderunt, ut Catholici fierent, utique aut ex
Paganis, aut ex Iudæis, aut ex hæreticis in gratiam Christi pacemque venerunt:
quibus si non est dimissum quod dixerunt verbum contra Spiritum sanctum,
inaniter promittitur et prædicatur hominibus, ut convertantur ad Deum, et sive
in Baptismo sive in Ecclesia pacem remissionemque accipiant peccatorum.
[*But Ælfric does not say that his heretics had spoken against the Holy Spirit.*]

228–41 [*Aug. Sermo*] Nostis, charissimi, in illa invisibili et incorruptibili
Trinitate, quam fides nostra et catholica Ecclesia tenet et prædicat, Deum
Patrem non Spiritus sancti Patrem esse, sed Filii; et Deum Filium non Spiritus
sancti Filium esse, sed Patris; Deum autem Spiritum sanctum non solius Patris,
aut solius esse Filii Spiritum, sed Patris et Filii.

for ðan þe se an Fæder is æfre unbegunnen,
and his ancenneda Sunu of him sylfum æfre,
and se Halga Gast is heora begra Willa and Lufu,
æfre hiom betwynan, of hiom bam gelice.   235
Nu nis se Fæder heora begra fæder,
for ðan þe heora oðer is suna, and se oðer nis na suna.
Eft se ylc(a) Sunu nis na heora begra suna,
þæs Fæder and þæs Gastes, on ðære godcundnesse.
Ac se Halga Gast ana is heom bam ge(mæ)nelice,   240
ðam ælmihtigan Fæder and his ancennedan Suna,
and ðurh ðone Gast beoð ealle synna forgyfene.
Se wisa Fæder witodlice gesceop and geworhte
ðurh his halgan Wisdom, þe his Sunu is,
ealle gesceafta; and he hi soðlice geliffæste   245
þurh ðone Ha(l)gan Gast, ðe is heora begra Lufu.
Heora weorc beoð æfre untodæledlice,
and hi habbað ealle ane godcundnysse,
and ealle an (ge*cynd and ænne mægenþrymm.   *f. 253ᵛ.
Ac) ðæra synna forgyfe(nyss stent on þam Halgan) Gaste,   250
and he deð forgyfenysse ðam dæd(betendum mannum,
and) heora mod onliht mid his liðan forgyfennysse,

---

234 willa and] om. B.   235 hiom betwynan] bitweonæn heom B.
236 nis] nis na B.   237 heora] ðe B.   238 ylcæ B.   239 gastes]
halig gastest B.   240 ana is] is ane B.   imænelic B.   242 ðone gast]
halgæ gast B.   244 þe his sunu is] þæt is his sune B.   245 he hi] heom B.
geliffæste] lif bifeste B (Belfour life).   246 lufu] lufe and willæ B.   247 bið
æfre untodæledlic B.   248 habbað ealle] alle habbæð B.   249 first and
over line B. gecund and ane mægnþrymme B.   250 forgyfenesse stont
on þam halige gaste B.   251 ðam] om. B   dæþbetendum monnum B.

---

242 [See below, on lines 250 ff.]
247–9 [Aug. Sermo] Et hanc Trinitatem, quamvis servata singularum pro-
prietate et substantia personarum; tamen propter ipsam individuam et insepara-
bilem æternitatis, veritatis, bonitatis essentiam vel naturam, non esse tres deos,
sed unum Deum.
250–68 [Aug. Sermo] Ac . . . insinuatur nobis in Patre auctoritas, in Filio
nativitas, in Spiritu sancto Patris Filiique communitas, in tribus æqualitas. . . .
Est ergo Pater Filio veritati origo verax, et Filius de veraci Patre orta veritas, et
Spiritus sanctus a Patre bono et Filio bono effusa bonitas: omnium est autem
non impar divinitas, nec separabilis unitas. [Ælfric substitutes much from his own
habitual statements about the Trinity.]
250–5 [Aug. Sermo] Primum itaque credendum beneficium est benignitatis
Dei in Spiritu sancto remissio peccatorum. [And section 19i s headed, Peccatorum
remissio datur per Spiritum sanctum.]

(and hi syððan) gefrefrað, for ðan ðe he is Frofergast.

Swa swa seo acen(nednyss to) Criste anum belimpð,
swa belimpð seo forgyfenyss to ðam (lifigendan) Gaste,   255
se ðe is ælmihtig God æfre unbegunnen,
of ðam Fæder (and of þam Su)na, heora begra Lufu.

Be ðam ge magon witan þæt he is eallweal(dend God,
þonne) he swa mihtig is þæt he mæg forgyfan
ealra manna synna (þe hiom soð)lice behreowsiað   260
heora misdæda, on eallum middanearde.

Se (Hælen)d ana, ðe is gehaten Crist,
underfeng þa menniscnysse and for us (mannum) ðrowode;
nu hæbbe we ða alysednysse ðurh ðone leofan Drihten,
and ure synna forgyfenysse þurh ðæne Halgan Gast;   265
and ðeah eall seo Ðrynnyss on soðre annysse
ægðer ðyssera dæda us deð untwylice,
for ðan þe hi ealle wyrceað æfre an weorc.

Se mann cwyð hosp and tal ongean ðone Halgan Gast
se ðe næfre ne geswicð synna to wyrcenne,   270
and wunað on his yfele oð ende his lifes,
and forsyhð þa forgyfenesse ðæs soðfæstan Gastes,
and him sylfum swa belycð þone liflican weg
to ðære miltsunge ðæs miltsiendan Gastes
mid his heardheortnysse his hetelan modes.   275
Behreowsiendan mannum gemiltsað se Halga Gast,
ac ðam he ne miltsað næfre þe his gyfe forseoð.

253 and heom syððan frefræð B.   254 acennednesse belimpæþ to criste
ane B.   255 lifigendæ B.   258 ge] we B.   259 þenne B.   260 heom B.
261 heora . . . middanearde] and heoræ misdedæ her on weorldæ B.
263 monnum B.   266 ðrynnyss] þrymme is B.   267 ægðer . . . deð] and
heo us þæs dæda doþ B.   268 wyrceað] wurcð B.   æfre] om. B.   269 cwyð]
sæð B.   togean B.   271 and . . . lifes] and on heom wunæd oð his lifes ende B.
273 and . . . belycð] and binimæð him selfum swa B.   274 to ðære] buton
B.   miltsiendan] mihtige B.   276 Ðe halgæ gast mildsæð bereowsiende
monnum B.   277 ðam he ne miltsað] heom ne mildsæþ he B.

269–77 [Aug. Sermo] Contra hoc donum gratuitum, contra istam Dei
gratiam loquitur cor impoenitens. Ipsa ergo impoenitentia est Spiritus blasphemia, quæ non remittetur neque in hoc sæculo, neque in futuro. Contra
Spiritum enim sanctum, quo baptizantur quorum peccata omnia dimittuntur, et
quem accepit Ecclesia, ut cui dimiserit peccata, dimittantur ei (Ioan. xx. 23),
verbum valde malum et nimis impium, sive cogitatione, sive etiam lingua sua
dicit; quem patientia Dei cum ad poenitentiam adducat, ipse secundum duritiam
cordis sui et cor impoenitens thesaurizat sibi iram in die iræ et revelationis iusti
iudicii Dei, qui reddet unicuique secundum opera eius (Rom. ii. 4–6).

Nu sceolon we biddan mid gebigedum mode
þone ælmihtigan Fæder, þe us ðurh his Wisdom gesceop,
(and) us eft alysde ðurh ðone ylcan Sunu,   280
þæt he ure synna fram us adyle(gie)
þurh ðone Halgan Gast, and us gehealde wið deofol,
þæt we him gegán þe us (ær) geworhte.

Se hetela deofol, ðe syrwð embe manncyn(n),
asent yfele geðohtas and þwyrlice ongean God   285
on ðæs mannes heortan, þæt he mæge hine gebringan
on orwennysse, þæt he ortruwian sceole
be Godes mildheortnysse for þam manfullum geðohtum;
ac wite nu gehwa þæt ða yfelan geþohtas
ne magon us derian gyf hig us ne ge(lici)að,   290
and gyf we hig onscuniað, and to urum Drihtene *clypiað.   *f. 254

Ne sceal nan man swaðeah, þeah he synfull si,
geortruwian hyne sylfne for hys synna micelnysse,
ne se goda man ne sceal for hys godnysse
'gedyrstlæcan to swiðe, ne dyslice' hyne ahebban,   295
ne þone synfullan forseon, for þam hit (swa) getimað foroft
þæt se synfulla mann his mandæde behreowsað,
and hyne Drihten arærð, swa swa he dyde Lazarum,

279 fæder] god B.   280 eft] om. B.   281 fram us adylegie] all
adiglæde B.   283 him gegan] to him gan B.   geworhte] wrohte B. Here B
skips to 318. For 284–91 H is supported by the first eight lines of 'De Cogitatione'
in P and S. See note.   284 hetela] swicola PS.   ymbe S.   mancynn PS.
286 mage PS.   287 orwenesse S.   288 -nesse S.   manfullan P.
290 gif PS.   hi PS.   geliciað] liciað PS.   291 gif PS.   hi PS.
onscuniað] ascuniað S.   drihtne PS.   292 From here on the text is once
more based on F. Ne . . . si] And ne sceal nan (man, þeah þe he si) synfull H
(?). With synfull, the interpolating scribe stops. What follows in H is in the hand
of the original scribe.   295 swyþe H.   296 for þan H; for þon C.
swa oft getimaþ H; swa getimað foroft C.   297 mandæda H; mandeade C.
298 arerð C.

Latin glosses in P and S: 284 syrwð: circuit, insidiatur PS   285 a(-sent):
semper P.   þwyrlice: praua P, peruersas S.   287 orwennysse: desperatione PS.   ortruwian: diffidere PS, desperare S.   288 manfullan, -um:
iniquos P, iniqui S.   289 gehwa: unusquisque S.

284–91 [Aug. Sermo] De nullo enim desperandum est, quamdiu patientia Dei
ad poenitentiam adducit. [Ælfric is largely independent.]
292–300 [Augustine, In Ioan. Ev.] Novimus, vidimus, quotidie videmus
homines, pessima consuetudine permutata vivere melius, quam vivunt qui
reprehendebant. . . . Videmus multos, novimus multos: nemo desperet, nemo de
se præsumat. Et desperare malum est, et de se præsumere.

and he leofað þonne bet on his lifes rihtinge
þonne þa lybbon þe his líf ær tældon.   300
Be swilcum we rædað on sumum godspelle,
þæt an synful wif wæs swiðe fordón mann,
and heo ofaxode þa þæt ure Hælend 'wæs'
mid anum Sunderhalgum, se hatte Símon.

þa com þæt wif þyder, and to Criste genealæhte,   305
licgende æt his fotum, gelomlice wepende,
and mid hyre tearum hys fet aþwoh,
and mid hyre fexe hi fo(rh)tlice wipode,
and mid deorwurðre sealfe hí syððan smyrode,
swa swa hyt gewunelic wæs on Iudeiscre þeode.   310
þa cwæð se Hælend be hyre þæt hyre wæron forgyfene
manega synna, for ðam þe heo micclum lufode.
Se mann þe ortruwað, and endeleaslice syngað,
and on his heardheortnysse his líf geendað,
se byð gewislice dead þam wyrstan deaðe,   315
for ðam þe he færð of þysum frecenfullan life
to ðam ecan deaðe for hys endeleasum synnum.
Be þrym deadum we rædað þe ure Drihten arærde,

299 leofð C.   301 swylcum CH.   302 man CH.   304 sunderhalgan H.   symon CH.   305 (þ)yþer H.   genealeahte C.   307 tærum C.
308 forhtlice CH; *entire word underscored,* rh *erased, alt. to* 'fet' *lice* F.
309 deorwyrðre H.   312 heo] heo hine C.   312 *sq.* lufode . . . ortru-]
The interpolator of H *erased the original scribe's work at this point, writing the
given words in his own smaller hand on the erasure and above the line, so as to add,
before* Se mann, *the words* And forþi swa swa we ær sædon.   315 gewi's'slice
H (*the correction by the interpolator.*)   318 Here B resumes. þrim H.

301–12 [*Augustine at point where omission is indicated in preceding quotation*:]
Detestabaris hominem: ecce ipsa soror Lazari (si tamen ipsa est quæ pedes
Domini unxit unguento, et tersit capillis suis quos laverat lacrymis) melius susci-
tata est quam frater eius: de magna malæ consuetudinis mole est liberata. Erat
enim famosa peccatrix: et de illa dictum est, *Dimittuntur ei peccata multa,
quoniam dilexit multum* (*Luc. vii. 47*). [*Ælfric refrains from mentioning the possibility that this woman is the sister of Lazarus, and refers independently to the
beginning of the story in Luke, as indicated below.*]
302–9 [*Luc. vii, 37*] Et ecce mulier, quæ erat in civitate peccatrix, ut cognovit
quod [Iesus] accubuisset in domo Pharisæi, attulit alabastrum unguenti;
[*38*] et stans retro secus pedes eius, lacrymis coepit rigare pedes eius, et
capillis capitis sui tergebat, et osculabatur pedes eius et unguento ungebat. [*The
name Simon is in verse 40.*]
313–17 [*Ælfric's independent elaboration.*]
318–21 [*Augustine, near the beginning of his tractate*:] Nam cum multa fecisset
Dominus Iesus, non omnia scripta sunt; sicut idem ipse sanctus Ioannes

ac hys wundra næron awritene ealle,
ac þa áne man wrat þe mihton genihtsumian   320
mannum *to hæle, and to heora geleafan,   *p. 283
and þa ðe hæfdon healice getacnunge,
þe wurdon geopenode eft þurh þone Hælend.
Hys apostoli arærdon and heora æftergengan
manega menn of deaðe, ac se ylca Drihten   325
dyde (þæt) þurh hi, swa swa he dyde ǽr
þurh hyne sylfne on hys andweardnysse.

þa geswustra cyddon Criste be Lazare
þæt he licgende wæs, and he wunode swaðeah
on þære ylcan stowe, anbidigende swa lange   330
oððæt he forðfaren wæs, and ferde syððan to him.
He nolde hine gehælan, ac wolde hine aræran,
and þurh þæt miccle wundor his mihta geswutelian.

His leorningcnihtas woldon gelettan þone Hælend,
þæt he ne ferde to ðære frecednysse   335
þær þa Iudeiscan woldon hyne berædan,
and he forþi [ær þanon] siþode.

þa halgan apostoli woldon þam Hælende
þone ræd tæcan þæt he ne þorfte sweltan,
se þe sylfwilles com þæt he sweltan wolde,   340
þæt hi sylfe ne swulton, ne we eac soðlice,
þam yfelan deaðe þe he us of alysde.

Se Hælend cwæð þa [him to], Se dæg hæfð twelf tida,
and se ðe færð on dæg, hys fot ne ætspyrnð,
for þam ðe he [þæt] leoht gesihþ þyses middaneardes.   345

---

320 ana *H.*   322 'he'afdon *C.*   323 þe wurdon] þa wæren *B.*   eft
om. B.   324 arærden *B, transposed to follow* æftergengan.   326 dyde
þæt *CH;* dude þæt *B.*   þurh heom *B.*   327 þurh him sylfum *B.   B concludes with* andweardnesse.   333 wurdor (!) *C.*   337 ær þanon] *sic H;*
ær þonen *C;* þanon ær *F.*   343 him to] *sic H;* heom to *C;* to him *F.*
344 fearð *C.*   fot] fod (!) *C.*   345 þæt] *sic CH; om. F.*   liht *C.*
geseohð *C.*   þeoses *C.*

---

evangelista testatur multa Dominum Christum et dixisse et fecisse quæ scripta
non sunt (*Ioan. xx. 30*): electa sunt autem quæ scriberentur, quæ saluti credentium sufficere videbantur.

324–7 [*Not in Augustine. The injunction to raise the dead is given to the disciples
at Matth. x. 8, and at Marc. xvi. 17 sq. believers are promised power to work
miracles in the name of Jesus.*]

332–3 [*Augustine*] Ille distulit sanare, ut posset resuscitare.

338–42 [*Augustine*] Voluerunt enim consilium dare Domino ne moreretur,
qui venerat mori, ne ipsi morerentur.

He is se soða dæg, and þæt soðe leoht
ealles middaneardes, and se man þe him filigð,
ne gæð he na on þeostrum, ac hæfð lifes leoht.
His twelf apostoli synt þa twelf tida
þe ðam dæge folgiað Drihtne Hælende,   350
þeah þe se swicola Iudas, þe hyne syððan *belæwde,   *p. 284
of þam· wurðmynte afeolle; ac þær feng oðer tó,
Mathias se eadmoda, and wearð eft gefylled
þæt twelffealde getel on þam twelf apostolum.

Se Hælend cwæð to Marthan, Lazares swuster,   355
'Ic eom ærist and lif; se ðe gelyfð on me,
þeah þe he dead si, he leofað swaþeah,
and ælc þæra þe leofað and on me gelyfð,
ne swylt he on ecnysse.' And he sæde on oðre stowe,
Ego sum Deus Abraham et Deus Isáác et Deus Iacob: 360
Ic eom Abrahames God and Isááces and Iacobes.
Nis ná God deadra manna, ac is libbendra;
ealle menn him lybbað. [Se] þe on hine gelyf[ð],
þeah þe he dead si, he sceal libban swaþeah,
and se ðe ne gelyfð on hyne, þeah þe he lifes si,   365
he ys dead swaþeah þam yfelan deaðe.

---

347 fyligð *H.*   348 heefð (!) *C.*   liht *C.*   349 synd *CH.*
350 filgiað *C.*   351 beleawde *C.*   352 wyrð- *H.*   353 afylled *C.*   354
getæl *C.*   355 swyrter (!) *H.*   356 gelyfð] lyfð *C.*   357 sy *CH.*   leofað]
lyfað *C*; leofaþ *H, bottom f. 254ᵛ. The rest of H is lost.*   358 gelyfð] geleofað
C.   359 swylt he] swelt he na *C.*   362 Næs *C.*   363 Se] *not in FC. See
note.*   gelyfð] gelyfað *FC.*   365 sy *C.*

346–54 [*Augustine*] Quo ergo pertinet, *Nonne duodecim horæ sunt diei*? Quia
ut diem se esse ostenderet, duodecim discipulos elegit. Si ego sum, inquit, dies,
et vos horæ, numquid horæ diei consilium dant? Horæ diem sequuntur, non dies
horas. Si ergo illi horæ, quid ibi Iudas? Et ipse inter duodecim horas? Si hora
erat, lucebat; si lucebat, quomodo diem ad mortem tradebat? Sed Dominus in
hoc verbo non ipsum Iudam, sed successorem ipsius prævidebat. Iuda enim
cadente successit Matthias, et duodenarius numerus mansit (*Act. i. 26*).
346–8 [*Ioan. viii. 12*] Ego sum lux mundi; qui sequitur me non ambulat
in tenebris, sed habebit lumen vitæ.
359–66 [*Augustine*] *Qui credit in me, etiamsi mortuus fuerit*, sicut Lazarus
mortuus est, *vivet*; quia non est Deus mortuorum, sed vivorum. De olim mortuis
patribus, hoc est de Abraham, et Isaac, et Iacob, tale responsum Iudæis dedit:
*Ego sum Deus Abraham, et Deus Isaac, et Deus Iacob, non est Deus mortuorum, sed
vivorum: omnes enim illi vivunt (Matth. xxii. 32; Luc. xx. 37, 38*). Crede ergo;
et si mortuus fueris, vives: si autem non credis, et cum vivis, mortuus es.
363 b–4 [*Cf. 58 b, 59 supra.*]

We ne durran gelencgan na leng þysne traht,
ne eow geswencan na swiðor mid þam,
þe læs þe eower sum ceorige on mode;
ac uton biddan ealle ur`n´e Drihten Crist   370
þæt [he] ure sawla fram synnum arære,
and us þæt ece lif on ende forgyfe;
þam si wuldor and lof á to worulde, amen.

367 gelencgan] længan *C*   læng *C*.   368 gesw**can**can *C*.   371 he]
sic C; *om. F*.   synne *C*.   373 sy *C*.   wurulde *C*.

367–73 [*Ælfric's independent conclusion*.]

NOTES

10. *þone þe þu lufast*. The relative *þone þe*, governed by *lufast*, parallels
the Latin, *quem amas*, and leaves the subject of *ys* to be inferred. That this
usage was not accepted by everyone is suggested by the revision of *þone*
to *se* in F. For parallels see the note on v. 143, p. 302 above.

22. *sohton þa Iudeiscan þe to stænenne* ('quærebant te Iudæi lapidare',
Ioan. xi. 8). This idiom is recorded once in BTS, *secan*, I. 3, from the
gloss of the same verse in the Lindisfarne Gospels, and is recognized as
Old English by the *OED*, *seek*, 11. There is no doubt, from the *OED*'s
quotations, that *seek* eventually governs the infinitive phrase, and the
accusative noun or pronoun (which is usually but not always present) is
regarded as object of the infinitive. But it seems possible that in the earliest
examples, all of which have an accusative between *seek* and the infinitive,
or even before *seek*, the accusative is felt to be the object of *seek* and only
secondarily, by ellipsis, the object of the infinitive. Thus the *OED*'s first
quotation, from the West Saxon Gospels, *John* vii. 30, *Hig hine sohton to
nimanne*, may mean 'they sought him in order to take (him)', and Ælfric's
clause, here under discussion, may mean 'the Jews were seeking thee in
order to stone (thee)'. It is hard to tell, however, even if the expression
originated as is here suggested, how early it had acquired its modern
meaning. The fact that Ælfric inserts *þa Iudeiscan* after *sohton* may be
significant, since he thus makes *þe to stænenne* seem like a semi-independent phrase. For this reason I have entered the idiom in the glossary with
a definition similar to that in the *OED*.

185. *dreorig wepende*. Ælfric uses another inflexion of this expression,
dreorig wepan, in *CH* II. 142/13. The adjective, where one might expect
an adverb, keeps in view the subject as well as the verb and increases the
descriptive force of the phrase. Perhaps there is a touch of poetic elevation
as well. Cf. *Beowulf* 27, *felahror feran*.

189. *on folces gesihþe*. If this phrase were certainly authentic I should
prefer to rearrange the lines, putting *þe syngað openlice* by itself or treating

it as a third member of the preceding line. But *on folces gesihþe* is not needed here for the sense; it looks like a careless repetition from 184. If so it is another instance of the descent of F and H (and now C also) from a faulty ancestor. Cf. note on homily II. 196–7, and the introductory comment on homily v (above, pp. 245 and 287).

193. *on Gode.* Two manuscripts, F and H, put accents over the *o*, which may indicate that the scribes took the word for the common noun 'good', though there are many instances in these manuscripts of *gód* where the sense is clearly 'God'. Here the notion of being alive in God is supported by such passages as *Rom.* vi. 11 (quoted as a source) and *Act.* xvii. 28: *In ipso enim vivimus, et movemus, et sumus.*

209, *ænig þing.* For this adverbial use of the phrase cf. the negative in Assmann IX. 47, p. 103, *Ne wanda þu nan ðing,* and *LS* XXIII. 71, *nan þingc ne wandode* (*De Septem Dormientium,* not by Ælfric).

249. *ænne mægenþrymm.* If this was the original reading, B's *ane mægnþrymme* is simply a levelled form of it. Possibly, however, the original reading was *ane mægenþrymnysse.* Ælfric uses both words in similar contexts. For *mægenþrymm* cf. *Letter to Wulfgeat,* Assmann I. 25 (p. 2); and *Interrogationes,* 524; these lines are repeated by the compiler of our homily XIa at lines 19 and 212 respectively. For *mægenþrymnyss,* cf. *Hexameron,* 63, and *Old and New Testament,* 31.

284. The remainder of *De Cogitatione* is here reproduced and arranged in metrical lines. The whole was previously printed by Napier in *Anglia* X (1888), 155, from S (Hatton 116), pp. 380–1. S is again the basis, with variants from P (Hatton 115), f. 59.

> And se man þe gód deþ mid gódum ingehyde
> þæt he oþrum men fremige on féo oðð́e on læne,   10
> and seo lǽn becume to sumon laþe þam men,
> he bið swaþeah orsorh þe hit him ǽr alænde,
> and he hæfð his mede his modes góódnesse,
> þeah þe hit þurh ungelimp þam oðrum derode.
> Eft se þe yfel deþ mid yfelum geþance,   15
> þeah þe seo yfele d[ǽd] oþrum men fremige,
> se yfela hæfð swaþeah þurh his yfelan willan
> þa écan geniþerunge for his arleasnesse,
> swa swa þa Iudeiscan þe urne Drihten acwealdon,
> us to alysednesse and him to forwyrde,   20
> for heora syrwunge embe þone soþan Hælend.
> Eall swa þa ehteras æfter Cristes þrowunge,
> þe þa martiras ofslogan on mistlicum witum,
> fremodon þam halgum, and hi gebrohton to heofenum,

11 sumum P.   menn P.   12 byð P.   13 godnysse P.   14, 15 om.
P.   16 dǽd] *sic* P; deþ S.   18 genyðerunge P.   -nysse P.   20 -nysse P.
heom P.   22 Eal P   23 martyras P.   ofslogon P. mislicum P.
24 heofonan P.

and hi sylfe fordydon on þere deopan helle.   25
Swa éac ure ælc æt þam ælmihtigan Gode
underfehð þa mede be his modes fadunge,
swa yfel, swa gód, swa hweþer swa he lufode,
for þam þe Crist agylt ælcum be his dædæ.

25 þære P.   28 hwæðer P.   29 þan P.   agylt] *marked for separation
as a gylt in P, perhaps correctly.*   dæde P.

290. The same sentiment occurs in one of Ælfric's early homilies: 'Ne
magon ða yfelan geðohtas us derian, gif hi us ne liciað.' (*CH* I. 156/28–29.)
Similarly Fehr, *Brief* II. 96.

301–12. Ælfric does not follow Augustine in suggesting the possibility
that the woman at Simon's house (*Luke* vii. 37 sqq.) was the same as
Lazarus's sister Mary, of whom the very gospel that Ælfric has translated
says, she was the Mary who anointed our Lord with ointment and wiped
his feet with her hair (*John* xi. 2 and Ælfric, above, lines 5–7). But this
verse in *John* is often held to be sufficiently explained by the later passage
in the same gospel (xii. 3) where Mary performs these acts for Jesus at
supper in Bethany. There is then no need to identify Mary with the woman
at the house of Simon. The actions of the two women are similar but the
meanings assigned to these actions and the characters of the two women
may be considered very different. If Ælfric consulted the homily in the
collection of Paulus Diaconus he rejected it at this point, for it goes
beyond Augustine in flatly identifying the two (*PL* xcv. 1299–1300).
Gregory, *Hom. in Evang.* xxxiii, and Bede in his commentary on *Luke*
vii. 36 sqq., both make the same identification, and Bede argues for it.

Ælfric relates the whole story completely and in almost literal translation (*Luke* vii. 36–50) in the homily for the dedication of a church printed
by Brotanek as his no. 1. The story is there introduced (instead of a less
pertinent comparison in Ælfric's source) to point a contrast in hospitality
between the sinful Zacchæus and the selfrighteous Simon. The contrast
is reinforced by the parallel between Zacchæus and the woman. Since
Brotanek 1 is non-rhythmical except for a few short passages, it was
probably written a little earlier than homily VI and represents Ælfric's
first treatment of the story. Because of the difference in style the resemblances in diction are all the more striking. Note especially the following
excerpts from Brotanek, pp. 9–10, in which I have italicized certain additions to the gospel that reappear, with differences, here:

Verse 38: heo aþwoh his fet mid hyre tearum, and mid hyre fexe
           adrigde . . . and mid þære deorwyrþan sealfe gesmyrede, *swa
           swa heora gewuna wæs.*
Verse 44: þis wif aþwoh mine fet *forhtlice* mid hire tearum, and mid hire
           fexe drigde.

In one respect Ælfric's abridged version here is inaccurate. The gospel,
in verse 38, pictures the woman standing at Jesus's feet behind him (*stans
retro secus pedes eius*), evidently behind the couch on which he was reclin-

ing at Simon's table; and in his original translation (Brotanek, p. 9) Ælfric says that she 'stod æt þæs Hælendes fotum'. Here, however, where he is writing more freely, he pictures her 'licgende æt his fotum', not so much, I suppose, for the sake of the alliteration, as because he imagines Jesus as standing or sitting. She would then have to lie down, not merely as a penitent, but in order to touch his feet.

Ælfric returned to the story once more in his rather late homily on the Nativity of the Virgin, Assmann III. 434–43. The treatment is even freer than here, but the following lines show the same image, and the last two are almost identical with 309–10 here:

> Sum synful wif iu, swa swa þæt godspel us segð,
> gesohte Cristes fet and mid swiðlicum wope
> his fet aþwoh and mid hyre fexe wipode
> and gelome hi cyste, licgende æt his fotum,
> and mid deorwyrðre sealfe hi syððan smyrode,
> swa swa hit þeawlic wæs on ðære þeode.

363. *Se þe on hine gelyfð.* This appears to be the obvious remedy for the nonsense of C and E, which have simply *þe on hine gelyfað* as if the antecedent of *þe* were *ealle menn.* But the quotation from *Luke* ends with *lybbað.* What follows corresponds to Augustine's *Crede ergo,* &c., as given under *Sources.*

VII

DOMINICA QUARTA POST PASCHA

Ioan. xvi. 5–14

I

FIVE homilies, here numbered VII–X and XII, for consecutive Sundays from the fourth after Easter to the first after Pentecost, appear to have been issued by Ælfric towards the middle of his career, somewhat after the completion of the *Lives of Saints* and before the augmented version of the First Series marked by MS. Q; probably, therefore, a short while before he became abbot. The chief witness for this is MS. M, in which all five appear; for M, as explained in the Introduction, is descended from a temporal set that must have been sanctioned if not designed by Ælfric, since it appears to have contained everything that he had written for the Sundays between Septuagesima and the first after Pentecost up to the date of issue of the master copy. If we leave out of account the unreliable Rogationtide homilies of M, we find that the five homilies here considered, together with homily IV, are the only ones in the volume that do not belong to the *Catholic Homilies* or the *Lives of Saints*. Homily IV had probably been issued by Ælfric a few years earlier, since it appears in E and is announced by rubric in F. The other five, apart from the little excerpt from VIII in the otherwise textually early but unreliably eclectic J, appear only in manuscripts containing other elements that are textually later than M. Four of the five, VII–X, are in the closely related N, which, by stopping at Pentecost, leaves us to wonder whether or not its exemplar contained XII. All five appear again in U, but this time VII has an interpolation and a sixth homily, for the third Sunday after Easter (Assmann VI), makes its unique appearance just before. Evidently we are dealing with a later, augmented issue. Three of the five appear in other manuscripts: VIII in B (which mixes very early and very late texts), and as a brief excerpt in J; IX in T (Junius 121); and XII again in B.

The textual relations of the manuscripts in these homilies are what we might expect from the general picture. In IX there is strong evidence that M and N are more closely related to each other than to U. They agree in omitting a metrically important phrase, *on his fundunge*, at line 4; in adding metrically excessive words at line 51; in omitting *gast* at line 85 (a repetition of line 6), and in transposing *and he* to the syntactically absurd *he and* at line 121. We are dealing here, it seems, with scribal errors, not with alternative readings of an earlier version. In VII, VIII, and X there are few revealing errors, but such evidence as there is brings M and N together in contrast to U. At VII. 38, M and N have *onlocigendum*, perhaps an earlier reading for U's *onhawigendum*, and at 179 they share a minor error, the omission of *him*; in VIII. 204 they are probably wrong (though possibly following an earlier version) in reading the usual *sædon* instead of *ræddon*; and in X. 70 they add a grammatically inappropriate *is* after *ac*. (I do not include *læsse* for the grammatically proper *læssa* at X. 153 because comparatives in the predicate often show levelling of masculine -*a* to -*e* in the best Ælfric manuscripts.) In XII, which is not in N, M stands alone in contrast to U and B, as explained in detail on p. 476 below.

B figures also as a witness for VIII—the fourth, where the fifth, J, has too brief a passage to reveal its affiliations. Here too U and B are closely related in contrast to M (here seconded by N). They agree in omitting *lage and his halgan* at line 17 and a large part of the Latin text at lines 27–28, probably because the scribe of a common ancestor allowed his eye to skip from *lage* to *lare* at 17 and from one *uobis* to another at 27–28. Eye-skip is an unsure guide, since it is a mistake likely to be made by more than one scribe; but the double correspondence here points to a common inheritance, and this is strongly supported by the evidence of XII.

In IX there is also a fourth manuscript, T, which stands apart, like U, from the shared errors of M and N, but may not be closely related to U. The evidence is meagre and hard to interpret. At line 129 U and T share what is probably an error, the omission of *sylf*, but it is the sort of error that might seem at first sight like a reasonable alternative or even an improvement, so that it might easily have been made independently by two scribes. Certainly the variation at line 72, where M and U have *hwilon*, N and T *hwilon ær*, must have been caused by the similar action of two independent scribes, because the pairing here cuts across the otherwise firm association of M and N. Probably M and U, which are usually more accurate than N and T, preserve Ælfric's reading, and N and T have independently added *ær* because it so frequently follows *hwilon*. (B has the same alteration at VIII. 103.) At line 134 the pairing is what we expect. M and N have *inweardlicre*, U and T *incundre*. But which of these equally Ælfrician words was Ælfric's choice? Or did he first write *inweardlicre* and later change it to *incundre*? This seems possible, but it is perhaps more likely that he wrote the slightly less familiar *incundre* and a scribe substituted *inweardlicre*. According to either theory *incundre* is a correct reading and its presence in U and T proves only that they are descended from Ælfric's original, though according to the first theory this original was a revised version.

It is obvious that U, by virtue of the interpolation, contains a revised version of VII, but whether the revision extended, here or in the other homilies, to small alterations must remain in doubt. Against such putative instances of revision as I have mentioned at VII. 38 and IX. 134 must be set the fact that a few rather inconspicuous errors in these homilies are common to all the manuscripts. Apparently they were in Ælfric's own fair copy (not necessarily a copy in his own hand) and were allowed to remain there uncorrected when he added the passage to VII. In VII. 13 all three manuscripts omit what appears to be a needed *swa*, though all three have it in the repetition at line 45. In VIII. 96 all four manuscripts fail to translate *fiat* in a text where it is followed by a purposely differentiated *fiet*, and although the translation as a whole can be understood, the failure coincides with a metrically incomplete line. In IX all four manuscripts have an incomplete line (perhaps improperly added) at 91, and at 102 a *his* where one expects a parallel *þæs*. It is possible that Ælfric made some small alterations without attending to these minor lapses, but one can hardly be certain.

II

The five homilies as they appear in M mark one stage in Ælfric's progress toward a complete Temporale. In the First Series of *Catholic Homilies* the sermons for the first two Sundays after Easter are very short and there are none for the other Sundays until Pentecost. The real burden in this part of the church year is carried by the three Rogation days and Ascension Thursday, each of which has a homily. Ælfric's Second Series adds three more homilies (the second subdivided) for the Rogation days, but nothing for any of the first six Sundays after Easter, or for Pentecost. The Sunday after Pentecost was altogether unprovided for. Thus the five homilies help to fill a conspicuous gap. Only one of them, that for Pentecost, has an earlier rival; and here the seeming duplication is understandable. The first homily for Pentecost had dealt with the basic story in the early chapters of the *Acts of the Apostles*, and had expounded the mysteries of the Holy Spirit. The second deals with the gospel-text (*John* xiv. 23–31) for the day.

Eventually, as testified by U, Ælfric enlarged this part of the Temporale still further. He closed the gap after Easter by supplying a homily for the third Sunday (Assmann VI), composed still another homily, the big *Sermo in Octavis Pentecosten* (our XI) to mark, as it were, the combined significance of Pentecost and its octave (already coming to be regarded as Trinity Sunday), and made substantial additions to the short homilies for the first, second, and fourth Sundays. The main steps in this growth are marked by M, Q, and U, which alone has Assmann VI and the addition to our VII.

There are references in all but one of the added homilies (Assmann VI, our VIII, IX, X, and XII) to Ælfric's previous writings. These help to confirm his authorship but their value for the chronology of his works is not very great. Assmann VI refers at line 181 to previous writings concerning the calamities that befell the Jews after they had put Christ to death—chiefly the destruction of Jerusalem by the Romans under Titus. Ælfric had dealt with this theme first in the homily for the eleventh Sunday after Pentecost, *CH* I. 402, 404, and a second time (according to the most probable chronology) in his homily for Friday in the fifth week of Lent (Assmann V. 66–95). A briefer treatment of the theme occurs in Assmann IV, *In Natale Unius Confessoris*, 239–48; but this must be dated within the period when the younger Æthelwold, for whom it was written, was bishop of Winchester (1006–12). It is a question whether it is earlier or later than Assmann VI, about which we know only that it should have been composed later than the five homilies in M.

In VIII. 103–5 there is a reference to a story about Gregory the Thaumaturgist that is told in *De Falsis Diis*, XXI. 575 sqq. In IX. 72 there is a reference to the passion of Peter and Paul, *CH* I.

364 sqq., and at 144 to the passage on the Holy Spirit and his
sevenfold gifts in Ælfric's first homily for Pentecost, *CH* I. 318–
26, esp. 326. (That this cannot well be a reference to *De Septiformi
Spiritu* is explained in the note on IX. 144.) In X. 105–6 there is a
reference to another part of the same Pentecost homily, *CH* I.
310 sqq., esp. 314. Thus all these references are to comparatively
early work and tell us nothing we should not otherwise have
guessed.

In XII. 224 there is reference to two earlier homilies, and this is
a little more valuable, because though one of the two belongs to
the Second Series (*CH* II. XIII), the other is our XX, *De Populo
Israhel*, which is thus given, though vaguely, a chronological
position.

Another vague chronological inference is made in the note on
IX. 52, where it is suggested that Wulfstan added a few words
in one copy of the homily and perhaps remembered it when he
was composing his *Polity*. But Jost's date for the *Polity* (1008–10)
is at least six or eight years later than the probable date of IX, so
that nothing very definite is indicated.

III

As already mentioned, homily VII, like VI, exists in two versions,
of which the second is distinguished by an interpolation in Ælfric's
style. The interpolation, lines 94–161, is found in U alone, pp.
92–95, and there it is misplaced, being introduced after line 28,
two lines before the conclusion of the gospel for the day, a wholly
inappropriate spot. In U the same scribe writes the entire homily,
including the interpolation, consecutively, so that one must look
for the source of the error in an ancestor of U. Now the content of
the interpolation makes it plain that it should follow line 93, where
it has been printed below, and it seems probable that the error was
purely mechanical. The passage, containing 68 metrical lines (81
manuscript lines in U), has been misplaced by 65 metrical lines
(80 manuscript lines in U). If this passage had been written on a
single leaf, as could easily have happened if it had been destined
for insertion in one of the larger codices, it might have been inserted by mistake one opening too early, causing a heedless scribe
to make such a copy as we have in U.

The chief source of the original homily is Alcuin's *Commentaria*

in Ioannis Evangelium, PL c. 950–4. Ælfric may have consulted it
directly, or indirectly in the homily excerpted from it to deal with
the gospel of the day. This homily is found in the collection of
Smaragdus, *PL* cii. 296–9, and also in that of Rabanus Maurus, *PL* cx.
209–13. Alcuin draws mainly on Augustine's commentary on *John*
and on a homily of Bede's, numbered ii. 11 in Hurst's edition (ii. 6
in Migne's). Bede's homily was in the original collection of Paulus
Diaconus, no. ii. 22, for the fourth Sunday after Easter, and in the
Migne edition, no cxxxix, for the same day. Hence Ælfric could
hardly have failed to read it; but I have found no evidence that he
made use of anything in it that Alcuin did not include. For direct
use of Augustine, on the other hand, whose treatment of the text is
spread over tractates xciv–c, there is positive testimony in lines
177–80, where Ælfric gives the substance of a passage in Tractate
xcv. 4 that Alcuin lacks.[1] Finally, there is Haymo, whose very similar Homily lxxxvii is a modification of Bede's with a good many
additions, some of which correspond partially to Alcuin's. In view
of Ælfric's habit of consulting Haymo it would be strange if he
had overlooked this homily, and I think there is enough verbal
similarity at 32–38 to warrant a quotation. There is general correspondence at many other points, but nowhere else does Ælfric
seem to have preferred Haymo's way of saying things to Alcuin's
or Bede's, and at several points his exposition is totally different
from Haymo's.

It is not so easy to assign a precise source to the interpolation,
which consists of two parts. For the first part, lines 94–126, which
comments on the folly of the unbelieving Jews by means of a verse
from *Psalm* lxiii, the ultimate source seems to be Augustine's
Enarratio on that psalm, *PL* xxxvi. 767 sq. (There is a vague
parallel also in the *Enarratio in Psalmum lvi*, *PL* xxxvi. 669.) For
the second, lines 127–61, there may be a hint in the same commentary but no more than a hint. Ælfric points out how much
confirmation of their faith was given to the disciples by Christ
during the forty days between his resurrection and his ascension.
Much is made of his presence among them in the flesh and the
completeness of his bodily form, which sets the example for
the resurrection of the body on the Last Day. The function of the

---

[1] The same passage may be found in the commentary on *John* falsely attributed to Bede, but in this section that commentary is a mere copy, slightly
abridged, of Augustine.

passage as a pendant to the discussion of the sin of disbelief seems to be to show how much Christ did to dispel disbelief, first in his disciples, and then, through them, in us. That, certainly, is the function of the passage by Augustine quoted as a source at line 127. But Ælfric appears to be drawing upon his general knowledge of the Scripture and of scriptural exegesis as he develops the passage—at any rate I have not come upon a source for most of the details of his exposition.[1] In the course of it he makes vivid and particular the Saviour's presence in the flesh during the forty days. Even in the earlier half of the interpolation he has inserted many details not in Augustine, and in his reference to the chief priests and elders who tried to suppress the news of the resurrection he draws, independently of Augustine, on his own knowledge of the Scripture, in particular on *Matthew* xxvii and xxviii.

In fact his account of the watchmen at the tomb is very close to what he says about them in the homily for the Sunday preceding this, Assmann VI, with the second part of which the interpolation as a whole has an interesting relation. Assmann's homily consists of two parts. The first part, lines 1–148, is a straightforward exposition of *John* xvi. 16–22, based on Bede's homily on that text (ed. Hurst, II. 13), with a sentence or two from Alcuin's Commentary at the end. This part is comparable, then, to homily VII as originally composed. The second part, 149–87, introduces an apocryphal story about Joseph of Arimathea with some preliminary ridicule of the slayers of Christ in their effort to suppress the news of the resurrection. This part, like the interpolation in VII, brings out certain aspects of the resurrection and supplies details of the events that followed it during the forty days before the Lord's ascension. Thus both passages, though each has its own individuality, direct attention to the historical period now under seasonal review.

It is likely enough that the whole of Assmann VI and the interpolation in our homily VII, since they survive uniquely in U, were composed rather late in Ælfric's career. Their resemblance suggests that they were composed at about the same time.

---

[1] I should not be surprised to find a source elsewhere in Augustine, who makes much of the resurrection of the body in *Sermo* CCXLII and neighbouring sermons, and in *Ep.* 205 *ad Consentium* (*CSEL* LVII. 323–39). Cf. also Bede, Hom. II. 9, and his commentary on *Luc.* xxiv. 39, 40. The latter concludes with the same quotation as Ælfric's (*Luc.* xxi. 18).

DOMINICA *QUARTA POST* [PASCHA]

Uado ad eum qui me misit

Manega godspel syndon gesette to mæssan
of ðære langsuman spræce þe ure leofa Hælend spræc
on þære nihte þe he belǽwed wæs,
swa swa Iohannes awrát, þe hit wiste eall.
Án þæra godspella is þe we nú embe sprecað,   5
*and eow secgan wyllað þæs Hælendes agene wórd,   *f. 202ᵛ
swa swa he sylf sæde.
He cwæð to his folgerum on þære foresædan nihte,
Ic fare nú to þam þe me asende hider,
and eower nán ne befrínð hwider ic fare nú,   10
ac eower heorte únrotsað for ðan þe ic eow þis sæde.
Ic secge eow soðfæstnysse, þæt eow sylfum fremað

Text of original homily, lines 1–93, 162–226, based on M (ULC Ii. 4. 6),
ff. 202–7ᵛ. Collated with N (Cotton Faustina A. ix), ff. 162ᵛ–5ᵛ, and U (Trinity B.
15. 34), pp. 90–92, 95–103. Interpolation, lines 94–161, occurs uniquely in U,
pp. 92–95, where it is misplaced to follow line 28.

Excluded variants: (1) U and N usually have *hy* for *hi* in the plural. In U *hi*
was sometimes written originally and altered to *hy*. (2) U and N have *him* in the
dative plural, where M has *heom*. In U this is usually altered to *hym*. (3) U
usually has *sæcg-*, *sæg-* for *secg-*, *seg-* in the verb *secgan*, and *sænd-* for *send-* in
the verb *sendan*. (4) The manuscripts often have single for historically double
consonants at the end of *mann*, *godspell*, *eall*, &c.

U normally points the text by half-lines. A few instances of erratic pointing
are noted among the variants. M's use of capitals has been regularized.

Sup.: PASCHA] *sic N*; PASCA *U*; OCT*AVAS* PASCHAE *M*.   *after*
misit] ET RELIQVA *N*.

5 godspella`re´ *N* (re *in later hand*).   spræcað *altered to* sprecað *U*.   6
sæcgan *U* (*so frequently; not noted hereafter*).   willað *N*.   8 folgerum]
leorningcnihtum *N*.   9 asænde *U* (*so frequently; not noted hereafter*).
10 acseþ *in later hand over* befrynð *N*.   hwyder *N*.

SOURCES. 8–10 [*Ioan. xvi.* 5] . . . Nunc vado ad eum, qui misit me; et nemo ex
vobis interrogat me, Quo vadis?

11–21 [*6*] Sed quia hæc locutus sum vobis, tristitia implevit cor vestrum.

[*7*] Sed ego veritatem dico vobis: expedit vobis ut ego vadam: si enim non
abiero, Paraclitus non veniet ad vos: si autem abiero, mittam eum ad vos.

[*8*] Et cum venerit ille, arguet mundum de peccato, et de iustitia, et de iudicio.

[*9*] De peccato quidem: quia non crediderunt in me:

[*10*] De iustitia vero: quia ad Patrem vado: et iam non videbitis me:

þæt ic [swa] fare. And he heom sǽde eft,
Gif ic eow fram ne fare, ne cymð eow se Froforgast.
Gif ic soðlice fare, ic asénde hine to eow.   15
Mid þam þe he cymð, he þreað þysne middaneard,
ægþer ge be synne ge be rihtwisnysse,
and be soþum dóme, sona swa he cymð.
Be synne he þreað, for ðan þe hí ne gelyfað on mé;
be rihtwisnysse he þreað, for ðan *þe ic nú fare   *f. 203
up to minum Fæder, and ge me ne geseoð.   21
Be dóme he þreað, for ðan þe nú is gedémed
þam yfelan ealdre þises middaneardes.
Gít ic hæbbe soðlice eow to secgenne fela þing,
ac ge ne magon hit [u]nderstándan, ne on móde aræfnian.   25
þonne se soðfæstnysse Gást cymð, he tæcð eow ealle soðfæst-
      nysse.
Ne sprecð hé na of him sylfum, ac sprecð swa hwæt swa he
      gehyrð;
and þa þing þe gewurðaþ, witodlice he cyð eow.
Me soðlice he mærsað, for ðan þe he of minum
þa þing underfehþ þe he eow bodaþ.   30
      We secgað nú swutellicor þas gesetnysse:
þæt se Hælend sæde þæt he siðian wolde

13 swa *not in MSS.: supplied from line 45.*   him *N;* him *altered to* hym *U.*
14 frofer- *U.*   16 *over* þreað] teþ *for* þreateþ *N;* ceastað *U (later*
hands).   19 þrea'te'ð *N;* ceastað *over* þreað *U.*   hy *N;* hi *altered to* hy,
heo *over line U.*   20 -nesse *N.*   þrea'te'ð *N;* ceasteð *over* þreað *U.*
20 sq. *U points after* up; *but after* fare *when sentence is repeated at* 94.   22 ceastað
over þreað *U.*   23 yfelum *N.*   maistre *over* ealdre *U.*   24 Gyt *N;*
Get *U.*   þinga *U.*   25 understandan] *sic NU;* na understandan *M.*
aræfnian] geþolien *on erasure N;* geþencan *over line U (later hands).*   26 þonne
se]'Ac' þonne seo (!) *U.*   soðfæst- *N.*   28 cyð eow] cyð, *followed by erasure*
of not more than two letters and full stop, U. *Here U introduces passage printed after*
line 93 below.   29 hereþ *over* mærsað *N.*   31 swutelicor *N. No MS.*
punctuates after gesetnysse.   32 *First* þæt *originally* þe *U.*   faran *over*
siðian *N.*

22–28 [*11*] De iudicio autem: quia princeps huius mundi iam iudicatus est.
[*12*] Adhuc multa habeo vobis dicere: sed non potestis portare modo.
[*13*] Cum autem venerit ille Spiritus veritatis, docebit vos omnem veritatem.
Non enim loquetur a semetipso: sed quæcumque audiet loquetur, et quæ ventura
sunt annunciabit vobis.
29–30 [*14*] Ille me clarificabit: quia de meo accipiet, et annunciabit vobis.
32–38 [*Alcuin, Commentaria (Aug. XCIV. 3)*] Significat sic se iturum ad eum,
qui misit illum, ut nullus interrogaret, quod palam fieri visu corporis cernerent.
. . . Nubes enim suscepit eum, quando ascendit ab eis; et euntem in cælum non

to his heofonlican Fæder þe hine asende;
and his geférum næs to befrínenne nan néod,
þonne *hi gesawon swutellice ealle   *f. 203ᵛ
hu he upp astáh eaþelice to heofonum,   36
and þæt wolcn underfeng wurðlice hine,
heom on[haw]igendum, úngedwimorlice.
'Eower heorte unrotsað for ðan þe ic eow þis sǽde.'
Him wæs lað to forlætenne þone leofan Hælend,   40
and hi uneaðe mihton his neawiste aberan,
for ðan þe hi næron þa gít gefréfrode
þurh þone Halgan Gást, swa swa hi syððan wæron.
'Ic secge eow soðfæstnysse, þæt eow sylfum fremað
þæt ic swa fare; and he heom sǽde eft,   45
Gif ic eow fram ne fare, ne cymð eow se Fróforgást.'
Eow fremað micclum þæt ic mín mennisce híw
eowrum gesihþum afyrsige, þæt ge syððan magon
þurh geleafan habban máran lufe to mé,
and gewilnian on móde þære upplican *wununge,   *f. 204
þyder þe ic siðige me sylf nú ærest.   51
'Gif ic eow fram ne fare, ne cymð eow se Froforgást.'
Swiðe eaþe he mihte, mid him þa wuniende,

---

34 acsiene *over* befrinnenne (*sic*) N.   35 hy N; hi *altered to* hy U (*so both*
MSS. frequently; not noted hereafter).   seghen *over* gesawon N.   swutelice N.
37 weolcn U.   38 him N; hym U.   onhawigendum] *sic* U; onlocigendum MN; *see note.*   40 [H]eom *over* Him N; Him *altered to* Hym U.
(*These changes not noted hereafter.*)   41 neaweste U.   42 gyt NU.
46 frofer- U. (*So hereafter.*)   47 swyþe *over* micclum (*perhaps for* swyþe
micclum) N.   mennisc N.   51 fare *over* siðige N.   53 Swyðe N.   mid
him þa wunigende *emended to* þa he mid hym wunigende wæs U.

---

verbis quæsierunt, sed oculis viderunt. [*Haymo, Hom. LXXXVII, PL CXVIII.*
517] Visa autem ascensionis gloria, non necesse habuerunt interrogare quo
pergeret, quia, sicut Lucas narrat in Actus apostolorum, *videntibus* cunctis
elevatus est, et nubes suscepit eum ab oculis eorum (*Act. i. 9, except* illis *for* cunctis).
40–43 [*Alcuin* (*Aug. XCIV. 4*)] Videbat utique, quid illa sua verba in eorum
cordibus agerent: spiritalem quippe nondum habentes interius consolationem,
quam per Spiritum sanctum fuerant habituri, id quod exterius in Christo vide-
bant, amittere metuebant.
47–51 [*Alcuin* (*Bede*)] Expedit, ut forma servi, vestris subtrahatur aspecti-
bus, quatenus amor divinitatis aptius [*Bede* artius] vestris infigatur mentibus.
Expedit, ut notam vobis formam cælo inferam, quatenus per hoc maiore desi-
derio illuc suspiretis.
53–57 [*Alcuin* (*Bede*)] Non quia non poterat ipse in terra positus dare Spiritum discipulis, hæc loquitur; cum aperte legatur, quia post resurrectionem
apparens eis, *insufflavit et dixit eis: Accipite Spiritum sanctum* (*Ioan. xx. 22*).

him on eorðan forgifan þone ylcan Froforgást,
swa swa he dyde syððan, þa þa he of deaþe arás: 55
he bléow on heom eallum, þus heom secgende:
Underfoð nú on eow þone Halgan Fróforgast;
and þam mannum þe ge syllað synna forgifennysse,
þam beoð sona forgifene heora synna gewiss;
þam þe ge nellað forgifan, þam ne beoð forgifene.   60
Swilcne anweald he forgeaf eallum his apostolum;
ac hi ne mihton habban swa micele gewilnunge
to þam heofonlican lífe, ǽr ðan þe se Hælend,
heom onlocigendum, [upp] to heofonum astáh;
and he heom asende syððan of heofonum   65
*þone Halgan Gast, swa swa he heom behét.   *f. 204 v
Se Halga Gast wunode on þam halgum witegum
þe witegodon embe Crist on þære ealdan ǽ,
and éac he wæs soðlice on Cristes apostolum;
ac he ne cóm ná swa swutellice swa swa he syððan dyde,   70
on scínendre beorhtnesse, swilce býrnende fýr,
to þam Godes bydelum þe bodedon mancynne.
    'Mid þam þe he cymð, he þreað þisne middaneard
ægðer ge be synne ge be rihtwisnysse,
and be soðum dóme, sona swa he cymð.'   75
Be eallum þisum þingum þreade se Hælend,

---

54 forgyfan *N*; for- *underscored for deletion U.*   ylcan *underscored U.*
58 forgifennesse *N*; forgifenysse *U.*   59 forgifenne *U.*   60 nyllað *U.*
61 Swylce (*sic*) *U.*   62 miccle *U.*   64 upp] *sic U*; up *N*; *om. M.*
65 *U has point after* syððan, *not* asende; *another point after* heofonum.
70 swutelice *N.   U has point after* na *instead of* swutellice.   71 beorhtnysse
NU.   swylce *NU.*   73 þreað *corrected to* þreateð *by later hand N.*
þysne *U.*   76 þrea'te'de *N.* (*So line 83.*)

58–60 [*Ioan. xx. 23*] Quorum remiseritis peccata, remittuntur eis; et
quorum retinueritis, retenta sunt.

62–72 [*Alcuin (Bede)*] Sed quia ipso in terra posito, et corporaliter conver-
sante cum eis, non valebant ad illum erigere mentem, ad sitienda munera
gratiæ cælestis. Ascendente autem illo ad cælos, et illi pariter omne desiderium
suum illo transferebant. . . . [*Alcuin (not Bede)*] Non quod antea Spiritus sanctus
non esset in cordibus discipulorum, vel etiam in antiquorum sanctorum: sed
manifesta plenitudine ante sic non fuit datus, quomodo post ascensionem die
decima in centum viginti nomina transmissus legitur.

76–84 [*Alcuin (not Bede), from Aug. XCV. 1*] Nunquidnam Christus, dum esset
in mundo, non arguit mundum de his omnibus, quæ sequuntur? Sed Christus
solam Iudæorum gentem arguit; Spiritus vero sanctus in discipulis eius toto
orbe diffusis, non unam gentem intelligitur arguisse, sed mundum.

mid mannum wunigende, þa ðe his wórd gehyrdon;
ac he ne þreade swaðeah þurh hine sylfne þa gít
buton þæt Iudeisce cynn, þe he tó cumen wæs,
and mid þam þe he wunode and fela tácna geworhte.   80
Se Halga Gást *soðlice, syððan he asend wæs   *f. 205
his halgum apostolum and on heom wunode,
þreade endemes ealne middaneard
be þam ðrim þingum þe se Hælend sǽde.
'Be synne he þreað, for ðan þe hí ne gelýfað on mé.'   85
Seo ungeleaf[f]ulnyss is þæra synna ordfruma,
þæt man ne gelyfe on þone lifigendan Hælend;
and se geleafa is ordfruma ealra goddra mihta,
for ðan þe se geleafa ús gelǽt to heofonum.
Micel synn him wæs þe gesáwon his wundra,   90
þæt hi noldon gelyfan on þone leofan Hælend,
þe ða déadan arǽrde þurh his drihtenlican mihte,
and fela oðra wundra geworhte heom ætforan.

Be þam sang se witega and se sealmwyrhta iú,
ǽr þan þe se Hælend her on worulde mann wǽre,   95
and cwæð be ðam Iudeiscum and be heora dyrstinysse þus:
Sagitte paruulorum facte sunt plage eorum.
Se witega cwæð be him
þæt heora weorc wǽron, and þa wunda gelice,
þe hy on ðam Hælende hetelice afæstnodon,   100
þæra cildra sceotungum þe sceotiað mid reodum
on heore (*sic*) geonglicum plegan on heora plegstowe.
Hwæt is swa idellic, oððe swa untrumlic,

78 gyt *U.*   79 butan *U.*   80 þam] *om. N.*   81 asænd *N.*
85 Be synne] Be sume, Be *erased N.*   þreað *altered over line to* þreatede *N.* (*So line 94.*)   þam *U.*   gelyfað *altered to* gelyfdan *N.*   on me] *om. U; altered to* on þæne hælend *N.*   86 ungeleaffulnys *N*; ungeleaffullnes *U.*   87 lyfigendan *U.*   88 godra *N.*   90 syn *N.*   94–161 *Only in U, pp. 92–95.*
98 heom *in later hand over* him.   99 wunda *wrongly altered to* wundra.

86–89 [*Alcuin (Bede)*] Peccatum incredulitatis quasi speciale posuit, quia sicut fides origo virtutum, ita solidamentum est vitiorum in incredulitate persistere. . . .
90–93 [*Ælfric's own elaboration.*]
97, 113 [*Ps. lxiii. 8, 9. The Latin in the text corresponds to the Vulgate.*]
101–2 [*Augustine, Enarratio in Psal. lxiii*] Nonne *sagittæ infantium factæ sunt plagæ eorum?* Nostis quemadmodum sibi faciunt de cannitiis sagittas infantes.
103–12 [*This rhetorical piece, not in the Enarratio just cited, may have been prompted by some unidentified source. Cf. Augustine's Enarratio in Psalmum lvi,*

swa swa þæt man fordeme þone soþan Deman,
and þone gebinde þe unbint eall mancynn,   105
and þone wylle ofslean þe ure synna forgyfð,
and þa deadan arærde þurh his drihtenlican mihte?—
and we ealle beoð arærde eft þurh hine on Domes-dæg.

Swylce wæron soðlice þæra Iudeiscra syrwunga
ongean *þone Hælend þæt hy hine acwealdon,   *p. 93
for þan þe he oferswiðde þone sylfan deað swa   111
mid his halgum æriste, us to alysednysse.

Et infirm[ate] sunt contra eos lingue eorum:
And heora tungan wæron geuntrumode swyðe
ongean hy sylfe: þus sæde se witega.   115

Swyþe untrume wæron heora tungan gewiss,
þa ða hy sylfe sædon be ðam soðan Hælende,
Gif he Godes Sunu is, gange he of þære rode.

And þa weardmenn syððan þe besæton his byrgene
cyddon þæt Crist aras cucu of þære byrgene.   120

Læ(s)san þinges hy bædon on heora geleafleaste,
þæt Crist þa gán sceolde cucu of ðære rode;
ac he soðlice aras syððan of ðæm deaðe,
to maran wundrunge, gewunnenum sige
of ðæm ealdan deofle, (and) alysde us   125
fram þam ecan deaðe and þæs deofles anwealde.

---

108 *Medial point after* eft.   113 infirmitate(s), *the* s *erased.*   120 *Points*
after cyddon *and* cucu.   121 *First* s *of* læssan *erased.*   122 *Point after* cucu
instead of sceolde.   124 *Entire line underscored for deletion.*   125 and
in later hand before of, *other* and *erased.*   126 of *in later hand before* þæs.

Migne, PL XXXVI. 669:] Vidit Dominum in Spiritu iste propheta humilia-
tum, . . . ligno suspensum: . . . et post illam iam omnem humiliationem, et
illorum furorem, resurrexisse eum, et illa omnia quæ fecerant Iudæi sævientes
facta esse inania; et elatus gaudio, tanquam videret fieri, *Exaltare,* inquit, *super*
cælos, Deus (*lvi.* 6). Homo in cruce, et super cælos Deus. Remaneant in terra
sævientes, tu in cælo esto iudicans. Ubi sunt qui furebant? ubi sunt *dentes*
eorum arma et sagittæ (*lvi.* 5)? Nonne *sagittæ infantium factæ sunt plagæ eorum*?
Alio enim loco psalmus hoc dicit, volens eos ostendere inaniter sævisse, et
inaniter in furias præcipitatos esse.

116–26 [*Aug., En. in Psal. lxiii*] Ecce resurrexit Dominus qui occisus erat.
Transibant ante crucem, vel stabant, et intuebantur illum. . . . Tunc caput
agitabant dicentes: *Si Filius Dei est, descendat de cruce* (*Matth. xxvii.* 40). . . .
Quid tibi videtur qui de cruce non descendit, et de sepulcro surrexit? . . .
Posuerunt custodes milites ad sepulcrum. Concussa terra Dominus resurrexit:
miracula facta sunt talia circa sepulcrum, ut et ipsi milites qui custodes adve-
nerant, testes fierent, si vellent vera nuntiare.

Eow is nu eac to witenne, and we wyllað eow sæcgan,
þæt ure leofa *Hælend her on life wunode   *p. 94
æfter his agenum deaðe, syððan he of deaðe aras,
mid his halgum apostolum, and he hy wissode   130
mid mænigfealdre lare hu hy læran sceoldon
eall manncyn to geleafan, þæt hy rihtlice gelyfdon,
and to fulluhte gebugon fram heora fyrnlicum synnum,
þæt hy þæt éce lif mid him habban mihton,
swa swa he eallum behet þam þe hine lufiað.   135

He æt þa sylf and dranc openlice mid him,
þæt he swa geswutolode þæt he soðlice leofode
æfter his agenum deaðe, þe he oferswiðde mid mihte,
and he feowertig daga wæs wunigende mid him,
þæt hy hine handledon and mid handum grapedon   140
on his handum and fotum, hu he gefæstnod wæs,
and eac on his sídan hy sceawodon his dolhswaða,
and hy mihton geseon þæt he soðlice aras
on ansundum lichaman, oferswiðdum deaðe.

Ealle his lima he hæfde, *and hæfð butan twyn;   *p. 95
on his fotum he stod, and þa næron butan sceancan;   146
his sidan hy grapodon, and he soðlice hæfde
ge innoð ge breost, butan þam þe ne magon
ænige sidan beon to geswuteligenne.

Innoð he hæfde éac, þa ða he æt and dranc;   150
and tungan he hæfde, þa ða he to him spræc;
and he næs butan toðum, þe mid þære tungan swegdon;
and þrotan he hæfde, þa ða hy gehyrdon his stæmne;
and his handa hæfdon, þe hy gegrapedon,

134, 136, 139, 151 him *altered to* hym.   136 him *in later hand before*
sylf.   138 his *in later hand before* mihte.   145 mid gewisse *in later hand*
over butan twyn.

127–61 [*No close source identified beyond the gospels, but cf. Aug., loc. cit.*:]
Lætabitur iustus in Domino (*Ps. lxiii. 11*). Iam non est tristis iustus. Tristes enim
erant discipuli crucifixo Domino. . . . Resurrexit; etiam apparens tristes invenit.
Tenuit oculos duorum in via ambulantium, ne ab eis agnosceretur, et invenit eos
gementes et suspirantes. . . . Ecce iam resurrexit, ecce iam loquitur: nondum
agnoscitur, ut lætius agnoscatur. Postea aperuit oculos eorum in fractione panis:
agnoscunt eum (*Luc. xxiv. 16–46*), lætantur, exclamant. . . . Nuntiatur cuidam
duriori, Visus est Dominus, resurrexit Dominus: adhuc ille tristis est, non
credit. *Nisi misero*, inquit, *manum meum, et tetigero cicatrices clavorum, non
credam*. Præbetur et corpus tangendum, mittit manum, contrectat, exclamat,
Dominus meus et Deus meus (*Ioan. xx. 25–28*).

earmas and exla, on ansundum lichaman.   155
Ne mihte nan wana beon þam welwillendan Hælende
ænig his limena æfter his æriste,
þonne he us eallum behet þæt æfter urum deaðe,
þonne we on Domes-dæg of deaðe arisað,
þæt us ne bið forloren forðon þæt læste hær   160
on urum lichaman, be ðam þe we on life hæfdon ǽr.
    'Be rihtwisnesse he þréað, for ðan þe ic nú fare
up to minum Fæder, and ge me ne geseoð.'
Ðæt is seo riht*wisnys, þæt man rihtlice gelyfe   *f. 205ᵛ
on þone soðan Hælend, þone gesáwon his folgeras,   165
and on hine gelyfdon, and mid lufe wurðodon.
We ne gesáwon hine, ac we swaðeah gelyfað
mid rihtum geleafan, ús to rihtwisnysse,
on þone soðan Scyppend, þe ús gescéop to mannum,
and ús eft alysde fram deofles anwealde.   170
    'Be dóme he þréað, for ðan þe nu is gedémed
þam yfelan ealdre þyses middaneardes.'
þone hetolan deofol he hét middaneardes ealdor,
for ðan þe he hæfð ofer þa únrihtwisan
micelne ealdordóm, þe þisne middaneard lufiað   175
swiðor þonne þone Scyppend þe gescéop þysne middaneard.
Næfð se deofol swaðeah on his anwealde nateshwon

155 exla *altered from* axla.   162 *The text is once more based on M.* rihtwisnysse *NU.* [þrea]tede *over* þreað *N.*   165 gesehon *over* gesawon *N.*
167 seghon *over* -sawon *N.*   168 rihtwisnesse *N.*   172 þisses *U.*   173 mid-
danerdes *U.*   174 ðam *NU.*   176 þisne *N.* (*So line 178.*)   177 *U has*
point after anwealde *instead of* swaþeah, *and another after* nateshwon.

160–1. [*Luc. xxi. 18*] Et capillus de capite vestro non peribit.
164–70 [*Alcuin (Bede)*] Iustitia discipulorum Christi erat, quod Dominum,
quem verum hominem cernebant, verum quoque Dei Filium esse crediderunt:
et quem sibi corporaliter ablatum noverant, certo semper amore colebant. Iustitia
ceterorum fidelium, id est, eorum, qui Dominum in carne non viderunt, hæc est:
quod eum, quem corporali intuitu nunquam viderunt, Deum et hominem verum
corde credunt et diligunt. [*Ælfric, in simplifying, altogether neglects to add* (*as do
Bede and Alcuin*) *that the unfaithful world is to be reproved by comparison with
the righteousness of the faithful.*]
173–86 [*Alcuin (slightly amplifying Bede)*] Principem mundi diabolum dicit,
quia primatum in cordibus infidelium tenuit, quos hic mundi nomine voluit
intelligi: qui ordine perverso, mundum potius, quam mundi Creatorem diligunt;
qui iudicatus est a Domino, qui ait: *Videbam Satanam sicut fulgur cadentem de
cælo.* Iudicatus est ab eo, cum et ipse dæmonia eiiceret, et discipulis daret
potestatem calcandi supra omnem virtutem inimici (*Luc. x. 18, 19*).
177–80 [*Augustine, In Ioan. XCV. 4*] Non enim cæli et terræ, et omnium quæ

ealne *þysne middaneard; ac se ælmihtiga God   *f. 206
áh ealne embhwyrft, and þa ðe [him] on wuniað,
and þa þe árwurðiað hine mid weorcum á.   180
Ðam deofle wæs gedémed þurh ures Drihtnes ðrowunge,
swa þæt he him of anam Ádames ofspring,
and forgeaf his apostolum þone anweald ofer hine,
þæt hi mihton adræfan deoflu of ðam wódum,
and eall þæs deofles miht hi mihton fortredan,   185
and se yfela ne mihte heom ahwar derian.
'Gýt ic hæbbe soðlice eow to secgenne fela þing,
ac ge ne magon hit understándan, ne on móde aræfnian.'
Fela þing he sæde syððan his apostolum,
æfter his æriste, þe hi ær ne mihton   190
eaðe understándan, ær ðan þe hi gesáwon
þone Hælend mid heom hálne æfter deaþe,
etende and drincende, *heom onlocigendum,   *f. 206ᵛ
and his lare heom secgende mid swutelum spræcum.
'Ðonne se soðfæstnesse Gást cymð, he tæcð eow ealle soðfæst-
    nysse.'   195
Ða halgan apostolas þurh þone Halgan Gást

---

179 him] sic U; om. MN; N has þar over line.   184 deofla N.   ðam
om. N.   186 ahwær U.   187 Git N.   þinga U. U has points after
sæcgenne and þinga; none after soðlice.   188 þolian over aræfnian N.
189 þinga U.   191 þon U.   195 soðfæstnysse NU.

---

in eis sunt, est diabolus princeps, qua significatione intelligitur mundus, ubi
dictum est, *Et mundus per eum factus est*: sed mundi est diabolus princeps, de
quo mundo ibi continuo subiungit atque ait, *Et mundus eum non cognovit* (*Ioan.
i. 10*), hoc est homines infideles, quibus toto orbe terrarum mundus est plenus:
inter quos gemit fidelis mundus, quem de mundo elegit, per quem factus est
mundus.

183–6 [*Ælfric here supplements Alcuin as already quoted by details from the
text to which Alcuin(following Bede) alludes, Luke x. 17–19*:] Reversi sunt autem
septuaginta duo cum gaudio, dicentes: Domine, etiam dæmonia subiiciuntur
nobis in nomine tuo. Et ait illis: Videbam Satanam sicut fulgur de cælo cadentem.
Ecce dedi vobis potestatem calcandi supra serpentes, et scorpiones, et super
omnem virtutem inimici; et nihil vobis nocebit.

189–94 [*Not in Ælfric's immediate sources.*]

196–206 [*Alcuin* (*Bede, with some minor variations*)] Certum est autem, quod
veniente desuper Spiritu, Apostoli maiorem multo scientiam veritatis, quam car-
nales eatenus potuere, consecuti sunt. . . . Non tamen putandum est, in hac vita
quempiam omnem veritatem posse comprehendere. Unde et ipse beatus Paulus
Apostolus . . . ait: *Ex parte*, inquit, *cognoscimus, et ex parte prophetamus; cum
autem venerit quod perfectum est, evacuabitur quod ex parte est.* (*I Cor. xiii. 9*).
Intelligendum est ergo, quod ait de Spiritu, *docebit vos omnem veritatem*, quasi

wurdon swa gelǽrede þæt hi witodlice sprǽcon
mid eallum geréordum úncuðra þeoda,
and hí lǽran mihton mancynn on worulde
of ðam ealdum bócum þe hí ǽr ne cuðon   200
under Moyses lage, mid micclum andgite
gástlicra getácnunga, swa swa him God onwreah.

Ac nán mann ne mæg on middanearde swaðeah
becuman on his lífe to ealre soðfæstnesse,
ær ðan þe he sylf becume to þam soðfæstan Gode,   205
swa swa se þeoda lareow Paulus ús sæde.

    'Ne sprecð he na of him sylfum, ac sprecð swa hwæt swa he
        gehyrð.'

Se Halga Gást ne sprycð *ná, swa swa se Hælend cwæð, *f. 207
buton of ðam þe he is on ánre godcundnysse.

He is seo micele Lufu and se mihtiga Willa   210
þæs Fæder and þæs Suna, of heom bám gelíce,
and ealle þa witegan witegodon þurh hine,
and þa halgan apostolas þurh hine sprǽcon,
micclum onbryrde and gebylde þurh hine.

    'And þa þing þe gewurðað witodlice he cyð eow.'   215
þis is swa we ǽr sǽdon, þæt seo witegung is of him,
and þa þing þe becómon he cydde him foran tó,
and heora mód onlihte mid his micclan gife.

    'Me soðlice hé mærsað, for ðan þe he of minum
    þa þing underfehð þe he eow bodaþ.'   220

---

198 uncuðre N.   204 on] to U.   soðfæstnysse NU.   208 sprecð NU.
209 butan U.   210 mycele N.   214 miclum U.   gebylde 'wæren' N.
217 þe wæren to cumene in margin for becomon N.   219 mærsað] hereð
N (later hand on erasure).   he] om. N.   219–20 for ðan þe . . . bodaþ] om. U.

---

diceret: Diffundet in vestris cordibus caritatem, quæ vos omnem veritatem faciet
amare: cuius magisterio intus edocti, proficiatis de virtute in virtutem, dignique
efficiamini pervenire ad vitam, in qua vobis æterna claritas summæ veritatis et
veræ sublimitatis, id est, contemplatio vestri Conditoris appareat. [*The last sentence reduced to almost nothing in line 205.*]

    208–11 [*Alcuin (modified from Bede)*] Non enim loquitur Spiritus a semetipso,
fortassis, quia non est a semetipso, sed a Patre. Nam Filius natus est a Patre, et
Spiritus sanctus procedit a Patre: non enim loquitur a semetipso, id est, sine
Patris et Filii communione. Non enim divisus est Spiritus sanctus a Patre et
Filio, sed unum opus est Patris et Filii et Spiritus sancti.

    212–14 [*Ælfric's elaboration, though prompted by what follows.*]

    215–18 [*Alcuin (modified from Bede)*] Constat enim nonnullos Sanctorum in
Spiritu sancto futura prædixisse. [*Ælfric develops this concession, not the main
interpretation.*]

Se Halga Gást mǽrsode Cristes menniscnysse,
for ðan þe his gifu is on Godes halgum wunigende,
and Godes lufu is agoten on urum heortum
*þurh þone ylcan Gast, þe is Godes Lufu,   *f. 207ᵛ
of ðam Fæder and of ðam Suna, him symle gemǽne,   225
on ánre mægenþrymnysse, á to worulde. AMEN.

221 hereþ *over* mǽrsode *N.*   223 *U has point after* agoten, *none after*
lufu *or* heortum.   224 ilcan *U.*   225 æfre *over* symle *N*; symble *U.*
226 weorulde *U.*

221–6 [*Alcuin (modified from Bede)*] Spiritus clarificavit Christum, cum
impleti gratia spiritali doctores sancti tot et tanta miracula in nomine Christi
fecerunt.... Clarificat, dum caritatem in cordibus nostris diffundit. [*Ælfric's close,
though it imitates Alcuin in celebrating the Trinity, is independent in expression.*]

NOTES

24, 187, 189. *fela þing.* This reading, supported by the related pair of
manuscripts, M and N, has exactly the same manuscript authority as the
fela þinga of U. The same opposition recurs in homily VIII. 23, where U
is supported (without gain in authórity) by the related B; and again in
x. 185—at x. 24 there is no reading for U. Ælfric generally uses the parti-
tive genitive with *fela*, but not always. In BTS, under *fela*, are a number
of examples from the *Catholic Homilies* and the *Lives of Saints* where *fela*
is treated as an adjective modifying either a singular or a plural noun.
There is even one example of *fela þing*, from *LS* XXXI. 1009, where a
following pronoun, *hit*, shows that the phrase is singular, 'many a thing'.
Here it translates *multa* and may as easily be taken as a plural, 'many
things'. I think *fela þing* is more likely to have been Ælfric's choice than
fela þinga because it avoids the jingle of a rhymed ending and fits easily
into a familiar group: *ænig þing, nan þing, sum* (pl. *sume*) *þing*, and *ealle
þing.* (See Glossary, *þing.*)

38. *heom on*[*haw*]*igendum, ungedwimorlice.* Ælfric here enhances the
formality of his dative absolute (rendering the *videntibus illis* of *Act.* i. 9)
by repeating its rhythm almost exactly in *ungedwimorlice.* The phrase
heom onlocigendum occurs at lines 64 and 193 below in more purely
expository passages. Here it is a question whether to read *onlocigendum*
with M and N or *onhawigendum* with U. Since M and N probably had
a common ancestor not shared by U, the weight of manuscript evidence is
the same for each reading. There is something to be said for *onhawigendum*
as formed from the less common of the two verbs and at the same time
a verb that Ælfric himself uses on several occasions (see BT, *hawian*).
Even *onhawian* appears in the form *onhawoden* in *LS* II. 261. Possibly,
however, Ælfric was responsible for both readings: MS. U, which

inherited the interpolation, may also have inherited a minor revision. This possibility has seemed to strengthen the case for *onhawigendum* enough to warrant its adoption in the text, though *onlocigendum* should be kept in mind as a respectable alternative, well attested as Ælfrician by the agreement of all three manuscripts at lines 64 and 193, and by its occurrence in the *Catholic Homilies* and *Lives of Saints*. (See Glossary.) The rhythmic repetition in this line is probably of more account than the alliteration, which is primarily, I think, on the prefixes, *on-* and *un-*. Supplementary alliteration is provided by *-loc-* and *-lice* in one reading, and in the first half only by *him* (the spelling of U) and *-haw-* in the other.

The word *ungedwimorlice* was cited from this passage in U by Napier in *COEL* ('Contributions to Old English Lexicography'). He defined it as 'clearly, without any delusion'. Ælfric elsewhere has *gedwimor*, 'an illusion, delusion, apparition, phantom', and *gedwimorlice*. See BT, our XXIX. 14 and 119, and the glossary.

41. *aberan.* Napier (*COEL*) defined this tentatively as 'to do without'. The word does not occur elsewhere with this meaning but the context will hardly allow any other. Alcuin's Latin confirms the basic sense of the passage, and his *amittere*, though different in meaning, may have suggested *aberan* by its form.

59, 116. *gewiss.* The neuter form of the adjective is used in these two places (and in VIII, XII, XV, and XVI, as indicated in the glossary) with unmistakable adverbial force. The dictionaries of Old English do not record this use, but there is an example of it at *CH* I. 376/17. The *OED*, under *iwis*, has quotations for the adverb dating from 1160.

103. *idellic.* Napier (*COEL*) cited this passage as evidence for the word.

145. *butan twyn.* The dative *twȳn* for *twēon*, which appears here in the unique copy, U, and at X. 114, where the three manuscripts, M, N, and U, concur, implies nominative *twȳ* as mutated variant of *twēo*. Professor Campbell, in his *Old English Grammar*, § 619. 2, footnote, treats *twȳ* with caution as a form that 'does not occur before 1200 (Bodleian MS. of OE Boethius)', but if the dative *twȳn* is accepted as evidence, the date must be moved back more than two centuries. The phrase *butan twyn* appears in *CH* I. 190/18, and *twȳn* is the reading, not only of Thorpe's MS., but also of MS. Royal 7 C. xii, which can be dated very close to 990 (Clemoes, *Chronology*, 243, n. 2). A nominative *twy* is also cited by BT from the gloss to Defensor's *Liber Scintillarum*, ed. Rhodes, p. 48/10. The gloss is usually dated about the middle of the eleventh century.

154. *his handa hæfdon . . . earmas and eaxla.* A surprising variation but clearly deliberate: there is a similar train of thought in 146b.

157. *limena.* This form, unless merely scribal, may have been preferred for its extra syllable. Another instance of the weak form of the genitive plural is cited in BT from *Solomon and Saturn*, I. 102a, where the extra syllable is metrically necessary.

185. *eall þæs deofles miht.* Although the accusative is demanded by the construction, the form *eall . . . miht* is nominative. Ælfric normally has accusative singular *mihte,* though *miht* was once regular because of the i-stem; and *ealle* is certainly to be expected. Perhaps Ælfric preferred the rhythmic effect of the uninflected form and thought it was acceptable because of the word-order. Either *miht* or *mihte* gives a play on the following *mihton . . . mihte.* There is an erasure after *miht* in MS. N, but I think the scribe had merely written *mihton* by mistake.

VIII[1]

DOMINICA QUINTA POST PASCHA

Ioan. xvi. 23–30

THIS homily has already appeared in print in the late-twelfth-century version of MS. B edited by Belfour, *Twelfth Century Homilies*, pp. 12–22. The first nineteen lines had been printed earlier, from J, where they appear as an isolated paragraph, by James W. Bright in *Modern Language Notes*, V (1890), col. 91. Bright quoted the paragraph as an illustration of the tendency to interpret the word 'gospel' without regard for its etymology, though he recognized that the true etymology was here included along with the false.

Ælfric has ranged about very freely in seeking materials for this homily. For the basic exposition of the gospel he depends chiefly on Bede, Homily II. 12 in Hurst's edition, but he supplements it now and then from Haymo's Homily LXXXIX on the same text.[2] His numerous elaborations are drawn from several other sources. In the prefatory lines, where he is commenting on the meaning of 'godspell', he seems to allude to the Epistle for the day, which is taken from the first chapter of James and includes the injunction to be doers of the word and not hearers only. A little later, Ælfric makes a substantial addition to the exegesis of the gospel. The passage on prayer has unusual importance for this fifth Sunday after Easter, which is immediately followed by the three Rogation Days. At line 73 Ælfric begins to expatiate on the efficacy of prayer beyond the scope of the homilies by Bede and Haymo. The Epistle

---

[1] On matters relating generally to homilies VII–X and XII, see VII, introduction, pp. 333–7 above.

[2] Alcuin's exposition of this text, which is excerpted from his *Commentaria* as a homily in the collection of Smaragdus, Migne, *PL* CII. 301–3, does not correspond very closely and is relevant only at points where Bede or Haymo could have supplied what is needed. A brief recollection of Gregory the Great, *Hom. in Evang.* XXVII, is noticed at lines 59 and 69 and discussed in the note on 59–72. This is one of three illuminating observations on the sources which I owe to the kindness of Dr. J. E. Cross, who has studied the homily in Belfour's edition and allows me to take advantage of his findings.

for Monday, from the fifth chapter of James (of which Ælfric himself makes explicit mention in his second homily for Rogation Monday, *CH* II. 330/13), has already suggested a somewhat kindlier notion of prayers for a friend than is brought to mind by Bede or Haymo, and now furnishes very clearly the example of Elias. Ælfric goes beyond the Epistle for certain details, but follows its pattern and its emphasis. Now he prepares the ground for three post-Biblical *exempla* by quoting *Mark* xi. 23 concerning the moving of mountains. Bede's commentary on that verse apparently gave him the lead by telling how Gregory the Thaumaturgist moved a mountain, not into the sea, but just far enough on land to give him room for a church.[1] Ælfric already knew the account of this and two other miracles of Gregory's as told by Rufinus in his version of Eusebius's *Ecclesiastical History*. He had used one of the others in *De Falsis Diis* (our xxi), and now turns back to Rufinus for details of the miracle introduced by Bede and for the miracle of the disappearing lake. These two miracles are followed by a third from an entirely different source. It tells how the prayers of a humble monk thwarted the plans of Julian the Apostate by barring the way to his demonic messenger. Ælfric had told of Julian's death in his first homily on the Assumption of the Virgin (*CH* I. xxx, pp. 448 sqq.) and again in the life of St. Basil (*LS* III. 205–91). He mentions him on several occasions elsewhere (as *LS* VII. 394 sqq.; xxv. 833; xxxi. 19, 95). Perhaps we owe his introduction here in part to a link with the name Gregory. In the life of St. Basil (*LS* III. 16 sqq.) Ælfric mentions that Julian and a certain Gregory, who afterwards became bishop and performed many miracles, had been fellow students with Basil in Athens. The Gregory concerned was Gregory Nazianzen, but Ælfric's description makes one think of the earlier Gregory the Thaumaturgist. Whether or not Ælfric confused the two, the association of names may have helped to bring about his reference to Julian here. The actual miracle he found in a collection on which he frequently drew, the *Vitæ Patrum*.

After these conspicuous *exempla* Ælfric returns to the exegesis of Bede and Haymo, but a little later he enlarges independently on a familiar theme. At line 183 he follows Haymo's suggestion by quoting a relevant verse from another part of the same Gospel:

---

[1] Ælfric's use of Bede's commentary here was brought to my attention by Dr. Cross.

John x. 30. Then he leaves Haymo behind as he comments on its importance as testimony concerning the Trinity. His exposition, with its insistence on the grammatical implications of the text, stems from Augustine, though his immediate source, as I explain in the note on the passage, is hard to determine.

Finally, at lines 228–35, Ælfric adds a comparison between God and the sun which he had already developed in *De Fide Catholica* (*CH* I. xx. 286/29 sqq.). On the ultimate source, which Dr. Cross has traced to Augustine, see the note on this passage.

A number of small decisions are required to establish the text of this homily. As I have indicated in the introduction to VII (above, pp. 333–5), the manuscripts are so related as to form two pairs, MN and BU, with J an independent fifth for the first nineteen lines. U and B agree in a clear error at line 17 (against M, N, and J) and again at 26–27. At line 70 two distantly related manuscripts, N and B, one from each pair, agree in reading *ponne*, which seems better than the *swa ponne* of M and the void of U. At line 201 N, U, and B are obviously correct in opposition to M, whose scribe jumped from one *for us* to another and omitted half a line. Elsewhere the decisions are delicate. At line 2 the *gemæne* of M is supported by N and J and seems entitled to stand against the equally plausible *mæne* of U and B. At line 23 the odds are nearly even between the *fela ping* of MN and the *fela pinga* of BU, but I incline toward the former as at VII. 24 (see the note on that line).

At lines 91, 227, and 233 the syncopated forms of the present third singular in M and N are definitely to be preferred to the unsyncopated forms of U and B. Johannes Hedberg has shown, in *The Syncope of the Old English Present Endings: A Dialect Criterion* (*Lund Studies in English*, XII, 1945), that unsyncopated forms of the second and third singular in the present indicative are rare in Ælfric manuscripts and tend to appear mostly in manuscripts written after the author's lifetime and in non-West-Saxon territory. U in fact stands alone with unsyncopated *sægest* at 46 and 238, *forgifeð* at 58, *sprecest* at 205; and (in a later alteration of *bitst*) has *bidest* to match B's *bidæst* at 69. B in turn has *becymeð* at 96, *iheræð* at 155, *spæcest* at 237. (For other such forms in U, see X. 39; XII. 156; XIII. 75, 78, 86, 91, 102, 107, 205; XV. 176; XVI. 223, 269.)

On the other hand, the readings of U and B have been preferred at line 41, where the pronoun *ge* supplies alliteration and is confirmed by line 214, and also at line 204, where *ræddon*, as the note explains, seems more likely to be Ælfric's choice than the customary *sædon* of M and N. Here, indeed, it is conceivable that U and B have inherited a revised reading.

DOMINICA QUINTA POST [PASCHA]

Sume menn nyton gewiss, for heora nytennysse,
hwí godspell is gecweden, oþþe hwæt godspell gemǽne.
Godspell is witodlice Godes sylfes lár,
and ða word þe he spræc on þissere worulde,
mancynne to láre and to rihtum geleafan;   5
and þæt is swyðe gód spell, þurh Godes tócyme
ús to gehyrenne þæt we habban móton
þa heofonlican wununge mid him sylfum ǽfre,
swa swa he þam eallum behét þe hine lufiað,
on rihtwisnysse and on rihtum geleafan   10
and on soð*fæstnysse hine sécende.   *f. 208
Nu sceole we gehýran þæt halige godspell
mid onbryrdnysse, ús to beterunge,
and eac we sceolon witan hwæt ða wórd mǽnon,
þæt we magon hi awendan to weorcum þe eað: 15

Text based on M (ULC Ii. 4. 6), ff. 207ᵛ–15ᵛ. Collated with N (Cotton
Faustina A. ix), ff. 165ᵛ–9ᵛ, U (Trinity B. 15. 34), pp. 103–18, B (Bodley 343),
ff. 6ᵛ–8 (printed by Belfour, *Twelfth Century Homilies*, pp. 12–22), and J (Cotton
Cleopatra B. xiii), f. 57ᵛ (the first nineteen lines only; printed by J. W. Bright,
Modern Language Notes, V [1890], col. 91).

Excluded variants: (1) N and U usually have *hy*, B *heo*, for *hi* in the plural.
In U *hi* was sometimes written originally and altered to *hy*. (2) N and U have
him in the dative plural, where M and B have *heom*. In U this *him* is usually
altered to *hym*. (3) U and B usually have *sæcg-*, *sæg-* for *secg-*, *seg-* in the verb
secgan. (4) The manuscripts often have single for historically double consonants
at the end of *mann*, *godspell*, *eall*, &c. (5) Since B has been printed, its numerous
variations in spelling are not recorded unless they correspond to those in other
manuscripts. Disregarded also are its frequent omissions of the prefix *ge-*
(usually *i-* when present) and its regular *sægen* for *sawon* or *sewen*.

U normally points the text by half-lines. A few instances of erratic pointing
are noted among the variants. M's use of capitals has been regularized.

Sup.: PASCHA] PASCA *U*; OCTAB*AS* PASCHAE *M*; OCTAV*AS*
(PASCHÆ *om.*) *N*. No title *J*; *simply* EWANGELIUM *B*.
   1 niton *J*.   nytenysse *JU*.   2 gemæne] mæne *BU*.   4 worlde *U*.
6 and] *om. U*.   swiðe *BJNU*.   7 gehurenne *N*.   10–11 and on
rihtum . . . soðfæstnysse] *om. J*.   11 hine secende] *om. B*.   beoð *after*
secende *J*.   14 mænan *JU*; mænen *B*.   15 awændan *U* (*so line 19*).
þe eað] *om. B*.

SOURCES. 7–11 [*A restatement of many texts. Cf. especially Ioan. iii. 16; xiv. 2,
15, 21.*]

for ðan þe se bið wís þe mid weorcum geswutelað
þa halgan Godes lage and his halgan láre,
and se bið unrihtwis þe heorcnað þæra wórda,
and nele hí awéndan to weorcum, him to þearfe.

On þære Frigenihte þe ætforan Eastron bið   20
hæfde ure Hælend, ær ðan þe he þrówode,
swiðe langsume spræce wið his leorningcnihtas,
and heom fela þing sæde on his fúndunge þa;
and Iohannes se godspellere hit gesette on Cristes béc,
þe his láre gehýrde; and he cwæð him þa þus tó: 25

EUUANGELIUM

*Amen, amen, dico uobis, si quid petieritis Patrem   *f. 208ᵛ
in nomine meo, dabit uobis. Et reliqua.

Soð, soð ic eow secge, gif ge sylfe hwæs biddaþ
æt minum halgan Fæder eow on minum naman,   30
he hit forgyfð eow untwylice hraðe.

Ne bæde ge nán þing gít on minum naman;
biddaþ and ge underfoð, þæt eower bliss beo full.

Ic spræc to eow on bigspellum, ac nú bið se tíma
þæt ic on bigspellum eow to ne sprece,   35
ac ic cyðe eow swutellice be þam soðan Fæder.

On þam dæge ge biddað on minum naman geornlice,
and ic ne sæde eow gít þæt ic sylf wylle biddan
þone ylcan Fæder, for eow þingiende.

---

16 *first* þe *altered to* þæt *U.*   17 laga *N.*   lage and his halgan] *om. BU.*
19 hi] heom *B.*   *second* to] *om. J.*   þearfe *is the last word in J.*   23 þing] *om.*
N.; þinga *U;* þingæ *B.*   25 þa ðus to] to ðus þa *B.*   26 EUUANGELIUM]
om. BU; after Latin text N.   27–28 si quid . . . uobis] *om. BU.*   27 quid]
quis *N.*   30 eow] *om. B.*   31 forgifð *NU;* gifð *B.*   untweolice hraðe
added in margin of U by contemporary scribe.   32 gyt *BNU.*   35 spræce
altered to sprece *U.*   36 swutelice *NU (so usually).*   38 gyt *BNU.*
Later hand in U inserts mi *before* sylf.   wille *N.*   39 ilcan *U.*

16–19 [*Cf. Iac. i. 22:*] Estote autem factores verbi, et non auditores tantum,
fallentes vosmetipsos.

27–31 [*Ioan. xvi. 23, as given.*]

32–39 [*24*] Usque modo non petistis quidquam in nomine meo: Petite, et
accipietis, ut gaudium vestrum sit plenum.

[*25*] Hæc in proverbiis locutus sum vobis. Venit hora cum iam non in proverbiis loquar vobis, sed palam de Patre annunciabo vobis.

[*26*] In illo die in nomine meo petetis: et non dico vobis quia ego rogabo
Patrem de vobis:

Se sylfa Fæder lufað eow, for ðan þe ge lufedon me,   40
and [ge] gelyfdon þæt ic fram Gode férde.

Ic férde fram þam Fæder and com to *middanearde;   *f. 209
ic forlǽte eft middaneard and ic fare to þam Fæder.

þa sǽdon his folgeras mid swiðlicre blisse,
Efne þu sprecst nú swutellice, leof,   45
and þu nateshwon ne segst nan bigspell nú ús.

Nu we witon soðlice þæt þu wást ealle þing,
and þe nis nán néod þæt þe hwá áhsige;
on ðam we gelyfað, þæt þu fram Gode cóme.

We habbað nú gesǽd sceortlice on Englisc   50
þis halige godspell, swa swa ge gehyrdon nú,
þa nacedan wórd ána; ac we nú wyllað
mid fægerum andgite hi gefrætewian eow,
þæt hi lícweorðe beon to láre eow eallum,
gif ge þæt gastlice andgit mid gódum willan underfoð.   55

    'Soð, soð ic eow secge, gif ge sylfe hwæs biddaþ
æt minum halgan Fæder eow on minum naman,
he hit forgifð eow untwýlice hraðe.'

*Se Hælend wæs geháten fram his cildháde Iesus,   *f. 209ᵛ
fram þam halgan engle, ǽr ðan þe he acenned wurde,   60
and se bitt on his naman se ðe him hǽlu bitt,
for ðan þe Iesus is Hælend gecweden.

Bide þe nú hǽlu on þæs Hælendes naman,
modes and lichaman, oþþe for leofne fréond,

---

41 ge] *sic BU*; *om. MN. Cf. 214.*   46 sægest *U*; sægst *B.*   nu us nan
bigspel *B.*   48 axige *BU.*   49 *U, unlike the other MSS., has point after*
on ðam, *not before.*   52 nacodan *U.*   willað *N.*   53 hi] heom *B.*
58 forgifeð *U*; gifð *B.*   60 wurde] wære *B.*   61 *first* bitt] bið hal *B.*

40–49 [*27*] Ipse enim Pater amat vos, quia vos me amastis, et credidistis,
quia ego a Deo exivi.

[*28*] Exivi a Patre, et veni in mundum: iterum relinquo mundum, et vado
ad Patrem.

[*29*] Dicunt ei discipuli eius: Ecce nunc palam loqueris, et proverbium
nullum dicis.

[*30*] Nunc scimus quia scis omnia, et non opus est tibi ut quis te interroget:
in hoc credimus quia a Deo existi.

59–62 [*Gregory, Hom. in Evang. XXVII. 6*] Quia nomen Filii Iesus est, Iesus
autem salvator, vel etiam salutaris dicitur, ille ergo in nomine Salvatoris petit,
qui illud petit quod ad veram salutem pertinet. [*Similarly Haymo, Hom.*
LXXXIX] Nomen vero eius Iesus est, id est salvator sive salutaris. Ille ergo in
nomine Iesu petit, qui animæ suæ salutem quærit. [*Bede, Hom. II. 12, states the*
same idea more obliquely.]

64 [*For the reference to physical health and prayers for the sick cf. Iac. v. 14–*

and se Fæder þe tiðað untwýlice þæs,   65
gif ðu andsæte ne bist and þine gebedu him.
Gif ðu þonne yfel bist, þu most yfeles geswícan,
and to þam godan Fæder mid gódnysse gebúgan.
And gif ðu yfeles bitst ænigum oðrum menn,
þu ne bitst na [þ]onne swa swa se Hælend bebéad,   70
ac mid yfelum móde þu yfeles gewilnast,
þæt nis nán hǽlu on þæs Hǽlendes naman.
Micele þing abǽdon þa mǽran *apostolas   *f. 210
æt þam halgan Fæder æfter þæs Hǽlendes upstige,
þa ða hí arǽrdon þa deadan on heora Drihtnes naman,   75
swa swa he sylf ǽr dyde;
and hi menigfealde wundra geworhton on his naman,
and hi þa hǽþenan leoda to his geleafan gebigdon.
Hwilon éac se witega þe wæs Helias gehátᵉn
bæd þone ælmihtigan God for manna yfelnyssum   80
þæt he rénscúras forwyrnde to feorðan healfan geare;
and he eft syððan abǽd þæt God asende rénscuras
and eorðlice wǽstmas, for ðan þe hí awendon þa
heora mód to Gode mid máran geleafan.

---

66 and] ne *U.*   and . . . him] *om. B.*   68 góodnysse *U.*   69 yfele
U.   bitst *altered by later hand to* bidest *U*; bidæst *B.*   70 bitst] bist *BU*;
bist *altered to* bitst *N.*   þonne] *sic N*; þenne *B*; swa þonne *M*; *om. U.*   bead *B.*
73 abædon] abidon *B.*   mæron *N.*   74 æfter] æt *B.*   þæs] þam *B.*
77 mænig- *N.*   79 elias *NU.*   gehaten heliæs *B.*   80 þone] þenne *B.*
81 to] *om. B.*   82 abæd] bed *B.*   asænde *U.*   83 awændon *U*;
wændon *B.*

16:] Infirmatur quis in vobis? inducat presbyteros ecclesiæ, et orent super eum,
. . . et oratio fidei salvabit infirmum, et alleviabit eum Dominus; et si in peccatis
sit, remittentur ei. Confitemini ergo alterutrum peccata vestra, et orate pro
invicem ut salvemini; multum enim valet deprecatio iusti assidua.
66–68 [*Bede, Hom. II. 12*] Quotiescumque ergo petentes non exaudimur,
ideo fit, quia vel contra auxilium nostræ salutis petimus, . . . vel . . . ipsi male
vivendo auditum a nobis iusti iudicis avertimus.
69–72 [*Gregory, Hom. in Evang. XXVII. 7*] Quod est gravius, alius postulat
mortem inimici, eumque quem gladio non potest persequi, persequitur oratione. . . . Quisquis itaque ¦sic orat, in ipsis suis precibus contra conditorem
pugnat. [*Not in Bede or Haymo. See further the note on this whole passage, 59–72.*]
75 [*Cf. Act. ix. 40 sq.; xx. 10–12.*]
79–84 [*The story of Elijah is in III Reg.* (*I Kings*) *xvii sq., but Ælfric's summary
of it is guided by Iac. v. 17 sq.:*] Elias homo erat similis nobis passibilis; et oratione oravit ut non plueret super terram, et non pluit annos tres et menses sex.
Et rursum oravit, et cælum dedit pluviam, et terra dedit fructum suum. [*See
note.*]

Be þam micclum bénum þe menn magon abiddan,   85
þa ðe Gode liciað, cwæð se leofa Hælend
on sumum oðrum godspelle to his halgum apostolum:
*Amen, dico uobis, quia si quis dixerit huic monti,   *f. 210ᵛ
Tollere et mittere in máre, et non hesitauerit in corde suo,
sed crediderit, quia quodcumque dixerit fiat fiet ei: 90
Soð ic eow secge, gif hwa segð on eornost,
and cwyð to anum munte on minum naman þus,
far ðu on Godes naman feor út on sǽ,
and gif him na ne tweonað þæt he þæs tiða beo,
ac gelyfð on heortan, swa hwæt swa he gecwyð,   95
[. . .] hit becymð and gewyrð.
Micel bið seo bén þæt se múnt aweg fare
of his agenum stede þurh ænigne mannan;
ac we magon eow secgan þæt hit soðlice gewearð
þurh ænne haligne wer, swa swa we hér secgað: 100
    Sum halig bisceop wæs gehaten Gregorius,
swiðe micel lareow on micclum geþingðum,
be þam ic sæde hwilon, on sumum oþrum spelle,
*hu he þone hæþenan god, þe nane godcundnysse næfde,   *f. 211
adrǽfde mid his tocyme of his anlicnysse aweg.   105
Se ylca Gregorius wolde Gode arǽran

85 biddon B.   86 cweð N.   90 fiat] om. B (fiæt for fiet).   91 sægeð
BU.   92 cwæð B.   94 twynað N.   95 ac] 7 ac B. All MSS. omit
punctuation after heortan.   gecwyð] cwæð B.   96 No indication of loss in
MSS.; see note.   bicymeð B.   98 mannan] man N.   100 swa swa]
swa BU.   102 mucel N.   103 hwilon ær B.   105 -nyse N.

88–96 [Marc. xi. 23. The Vulgate has quicumque for si quis.]

99 sqq. [Bede, In Marcum, commenting on preceding verse and defending Christians against the charge of having too little faith to accomplish this miracle, cites an
approximation to it:] Legimus factum precibus beati patris Gregorii Neocæsariæ
Ponti antistitis, viri meritis et virtutibus eximii, ut mons in terra tantum loco
cederet quantum incolæ civitatis opus habebant. Cum enim volens ædificare
ecclesiam in loco apto videret eum angustiorem esse quam res exigebat, eo quod
ex una parte rupe maris, ex alia monte proximo coartaretur, etc. [Except for
in loco apto, which may have suggested 109, this version is not quite as close to
Ælfric as the one below. See note on 97–131.]

106–18 [Rufinus, addition to Eusebius, Eccl. Hist. VII, after 28, 2; ed. Momm-
sen p. 954, on Gregory the Thaumaturgist] In quodam loco ruris angusti cum
res posceret ecclesiam construi, rupes quædam vicini montis ex parte orientis
obiecta, ex alia vero præterfluens fluvius, spatium quantum ecclesiæ sufficeret
denegabat. Et cum alius omnino non esset locus, . . . ille fide plenus pernoctasse
in oratione dicitur. . . . [Reference to the Lord's promise about moving mountains,
partly from Matth. xvii. 19, partly from Marc. xi. 23.] Cumque hæc plena fide ac

halig mynsterlíf gehénde ánre éá;
ac þær wæs to gehénde swiðe heah clif onemn,
and wæs se stede myrige to þam mynsterlífe,
gif he rúmra wære to þam Godes weorce.   110
Ða mearcode se bisceop on þam múnte þone dǽl
þe he habban wolde to þæs weorces rýmette,
and bæd þa þone Ælmihtigan, þe mæg þæt he wile,
þæt he ahófe þone múnt be his mearcunge,
þæt he mihte macian his mynster on þam rýmette;   115
and God þa sóna ascéaf þone múnt
butan geswínce, swa swa he gewilnode;
and se halga wer worhte him ðær mynster.
    Ða wæron twegen gebroðra, welige on lífe,
and hæfdon ænne fixnoð *on anum brádum mere,   *f. 211ᵛ
heom bám gemǽne, to micelre tilunge;   121
ac þær wurdon oft æt þam wæterscipe
mænigfealde ceastu and manslihtas,
and micele gefeoht for ðan fixnoðe.
    Hwæt ða se bisceop wearð geúnblissod   125
for ðam blódes gyte, and abæd þá æt Gode
þæt he worhte þæne wæterscipe to wynsumum eorðlande;

107 gehænde U.   ea] sæ B.   108 to over line U.   to gehende swiðe]
bi halfes an swiðe B.   110 weorcum N.   113 mæg] mæg don B.   wyle
BNU.   115 rymete U.   119 gebroðra] breðræn B.   120 fiscnoð N
(fisc- regularly in N).   121 mycelre N.   122 oft] eft U.   123 menig- U.
124 þam BNU.   125 geunblissod] unbliðe B.   127 þone BNU.
yrþlande BNU.

devotione deposceret, ad lucem coeuntibus populis inventa est rupes importuna
secessisse tantum, quantum spatii ad condendam quærebatur ecclesiam.

119–31 [Ibid., pp. 953–4] Stagnum quoddam erat in Ponti regionibus situm,
piscibus copiosum, ex quorum captura prædivites redditus dominis præsta-
bantur. Ista possessio duabus fratribus sorte hereditatis obvenerat. Sed pecuniæ
cupiditas . . . fraternam necessitudinem violavit. Coibatur a fratribus tempore
captionis non tam ad capiendos pisces quam ad homines decipiendos, cædes
ac bella movebantur, humanus sanguis pro piscibus fundebatur. Sed Dei
providentia adfuit aliquando auxilium adventusque Gregorii, videt proelia et
mortes virorum furentesque germanos. . . . In conspectu omnium virgam, quam
tenebat in manu, ad primas litoris undas defigit et ipse positis genibus palmas
tendit ad cælum atque his verbis excelso supplicat Deo: . . . 'Præcipe . . . ut
nunquam in hoc loco vel piscis appareat vel aqua resideat, sed sit campus aratri
patiens ac frugum ferax et custos in æternum fraternæ concordiæ perseveret.'
Simul ut ille orandi finem fecit, statim se unda subducens et cursu velociore
refugiens a conspectu superno iussa discedere abyssis suis redditur et arentem
campum germanis iam concordibus dereliquit. Sed et in hodiernum frugum
ferax esse dicitur solum, quod ante fuerat navium ferax.

and þæt wæter sona gewende of ðam fixnoþe,
and wæs se mere awend to wídgillum felda,
swa þæt man erode ealne þone fixnoð,   130
and þær corn weox æfre wynsumlice syððan.

Iulianus se wiðersaca, þe wæs ærest Cristen,
and to preoste besceoren for ðæs caseres ege,
awearp his geleafan and gelyfde on deofolgyld
syððan he his sylfes geweold; and he wearð casere,   135
and lufode þa drýcræft and þæs deofles þeowdóm;
*and he þa manega martyras acwealde,   *f. 212
and wann wið þone Hælend, oþþæt he forférde.

He asende ænne deofol to sumum lánde hwilon,
on sumum ǽrende, þæt he árdlice ferde;   140
and se deofol þa be his sánde férde,
and cóm eft him tó embe tyn daga fyrst.

þa cwæð se casere him tó, Hwí come þu swa late?
Se deofol him andwyrde, Ic wearð yfele gelett
þurh ænne haligne munuc, se hatte Publius;   145
ic ne mihte na faran forð on þin ærende,
for ðan þe se munuc, mid his micclum gebedum,
forwyrnde me þæs weges, and ic wende nú ongéan
butan ælcum ærende, ungewiss eft to þe.

128 gewænde U.   129 widgyllum NU; brade B.   131 weox corn B.
134 he awearp B.   deofolgild N.   135 sylfes] syfes N.   137 martiras
NU.   138 wan NU; fæht B.   139 asænde U.   hwilon to sume londe B.
140 sumum] sum B.   ardlice] heardlice B.   141 Entire line in margin of
U in contemporary hand.   142 to him B (so line 143).   144 andswyrde B.
gelet N.   146 forð faran N.   147 gebedum] bene B.   148 wænde U.
149 unwis B.

132–8 [No specific source for this epitome has been found. Some of the details are
in Ælfric's earliest account of Julian, CH I. 448/23 sqq.]

139–52 [Vitæ Patrum VI. ii. 12] Temporibus Iuliani apostatæ, cum descen-
deret in Perside, missus est dæmon ab eodem Iuliano, ut velocius vadens in Occi-
dentem, afferret ei responsum aliquod inde. Cum autem pervenisset ille dæmon in
quemdam locum, ubi quidam monachus habitabat, stetit ibidem per dies decem
immobilis, eo quod non poterat ultra progredi. . . . Et regressus est sine effectu
ad eum qui miserat illum. Dixit autem ei Iulianus: 'Quare tardasti?' Respondit
ei dæmon et dixit, 'Et moram feci, et sine actione reversus sum; sustinui enim
decem dies Publium monachum, si forte cessasset ab oratione ut transirem, et
non cessavit, et prohibitus sum transire, et redii nihil agens.' Tunc impiissimus
Iulianus indignatus dixit: Cum regressus fuero, faciam in eum vindictam. Et
intra paucos dies interemptus est a providentia Dei. Et continuo unus ex præ-
fectis qui cum eo erant, vadens vendidit omnia quæ habebat, et dedit pauperibus,
et veniens ad senem illum, factus est monachus magnus, et sic quievit in Domino.

And se casere wearð on þam wege ofslagen,   150
and sum his þegna, þe þis þa gehyrde,
gewende to þam munuce, and wearð munuc him sylf.
Swilce þing *maciað þa mæran gebedu   *f. 212ᵛ
þurh þone soðan God, þe symle wile well,
and gehyrð þa gebedu on his halgena neode,   155
and his þearfena clypunga uncuðlice ne forsihþ.
  þæt godspell us segð þæt se Hælend sæde,
'Ne bæde ge nan þing gytt on minum naman.'
Forðí hí ne bædon on þæs Hælendes naman,
for ðan þe hi hæfdon hine sylfne mid heom,   160
his láre brúcende, and ne bædon na swiðe
þa ungesewenlican þing, þonne hi hine gesáwon.
  'Biddaþ, and ge underfoð, þæt eower bliss beo full.'
Ðære ecan blisse he hét hi þa biddan,
for ðan þe nanum menn ne bið full bliss on his lífe,   165
þæt him ne eglige æfre sum þing hér.
  'Ic spræc to eow on bigspellum, ac nu bið se tíma
þæt ic on bigspellum eow tó ne sprece,
ac ic cyþe eow swutellice *be þam soðan Fæder.'   *f. 213
On bócum is gewunelic bigspell to secgenne,   170
þæt is oþer ðing on wórdum, and oþer on getácnungum,
and se Hælend heom spræc to swiðe gelóme
on manegum bigspellum, heora móde to trymminge;

151 þegena *NU*; þegenæ *B*.   152 gewænde *U*.   153 swylce *BNU*.
macigað *U*.   154 symble *U*; simle *N*.   wyle *BNU*.   155 iheræð *B*.
156 clypunge *N*.   forsyhð *N*.   158 gyt *BNU*.   159 -þy *BU*.
160 for þon þe *U*.   161 *before* his] 7 *inserted U*.   164 hi] heom *B*.
165 full blis *U, altered later to* fullice seo mucel blis.   166 eglige] *glossed*
irez *U* (*see note*).   168 to eow *B*.   172 heom spræc to] to heom spæc *B*.

159–62 [*Bede*] Non petierunt eatenus in nomine Salvatoris, quia dum ipsum
Salvatorem visibili præsentia complecterentur, minus ad invisibilia salutis dona
mentis intuitum erexerant.
  164–6 [*Bede*] Plenum ergo gaudium beatitudinem perpetuæ pacis appellat.
Nam ut taceamus de gaudio reproborum, . . . habent sancti etiam in præsenti
gaudium de spe cælestium bonorum. . . . Sed non est plenum gaudium, quod
fletu variante miscetur. [*Haymo has the same interpretation in different words.
Perhaps the following is closer than Bede*:] Plenum ergo et perfectum gaudium
esse non potest, ubi fragilitas mutabilitatis ita variatur, ut vix unius horæ spatio
gaudium nobiscum permanere possit.
  170 f. [*Haymo*] Proverbia quædam similitudines dicuntur, quæ ad obscu-
riores quasque sententias intelligendas necessariæ ab auctoribus adhibentur, ut
saltem per visibilia invisibilia cognoscere queant.

ac he sǽde heom nú þæt he swutellice wolde
be þam halgan Fæder heom bodian and cyþan,   175
for ðan þe he sylf deþ þæt his halgan geseoð
his Fæder on his wuldre, þonne hí wuniað mid him,
swa swa ða englas geseoð hine soðlice nú.

'On þam dæge ge biddaþ on minum naman geornlice.'
On ðam lífe is án dæg, þe næfre ne geéndaþ,   180
and on dæge hi biddað, þa þe þonne biddað,
ná on sweartum þeostrum þissera costnunga;
ac þæs Hælendes wórd heom beoð þonne cuðe,
þe þus sǽde to heom on sumum his godspella:
Ego et Pater unum sumus: 185
Ic and min *Fæder syndon witodlice án.   *f. 213ᵛ
þæt is, soðlice, án God, on ánre godcundnysse,
and him bám is gemǽne ǽfre an soð Lufu,
þæt is se Halga Gást, þe gæð of him bám.
He cwæð, wyt syndon, for ðan þe se Sunu   190
is ǽfre swa wunigende, and ne awent ná of ðam,

---

175 halgum *BU*.   177 wuldre] wundre *U*.   178 nu soðlice *B*.
181 hi] *om. B*.   182 þyssera *U*.   184 godspella] *originally* godspelle *M*;
godspellæ *B*.   186 syndon] beoð *B*.   190–3 *om. B*.   190 wit *U*.
191 wuniende *N*.   awænt *U*.

174–8 [*Not in Bede or Haymo, who follow Augustine's warning against so
simple an interpretation, though Bede takes it up and seems to defend it against
Augustine with respect to the next verse.*]

180–2 [*Bede*] Possumus horam quam pollicetur in futura vita intelligere. . . .
In die etenim petunt, quia non inter tenebras pressurarum, ut nostra in præsenti,
sed in luce sempiternæ pacis, et gloriæ, beatorum spirituum pro nobis intercessio
funditur.

183–6 [*Haymo, though he differs in his interpretation of* illo die:] *Illo die in
nomine meo petetis.* Quod est dicere: Illo die cum Spiritus sanctus adveniens
cognoscere vos fecerit quia *ego et Pater unum sumus* (*Ioan. x. 30*), in nomine
meo petetis quia æqualem Patri me esse cognoscetis, et omnia me dare posse
cum Patre credetis.

190–9 [*Augustine, In Ioan. Ev. Tract. XX. 3*] Quia Pater et Filius non sunt
duo dii, sed . . . Deus unus, Pater et Filius, charitate complexi, unusque charitatis
Spiritus eorum est, ut fiat Trinitas Pater et Filius et Spiritus sanctus. [*Tract.
XXXVI. 9*] Una substantia est, una divinitas, una coæternitas, perfecta æqualitas,
dissimilitudo nulla. . . . Cum dicit: *Ego et Pater unum sumus*, utrumque audi, et
unum, et *sumus*, et a Charybdi et a Scylla liberaberis. In duobus istis verbis quod
dixit, *unum*, liberat te ab Ario; quod dixit, *sumus*, liberat te a Sabellio. Si *unum*,
non ergo diversum; si *sumus*, ergo et Pater et Filius. [*Tract. XXXVII. 6*]
[Sabelliani] dicunt ipsum esse Patrem qui est Filius; nomina diversa, unam vero
esse personam. Cum vult, Pater est, inquiunt; cum vult, Filius; tamen unus est.
[*Cf. also Bede, Hom. I. 8, as quoted above for Hom. I. 151–60; and see note.*]

ne heora nán ne bi‎ð abróden to oþrum,
þæt he elles beo of ‎ðam þe he ǽr wæs.

He cwæ‎ð, wyt syndon án, for ‎ðære ánnysse,
þæt seo án godcundnyss, and seo án mægenþrymnys,   195
and þæt án gecynd þe him is gemǽne
nele geþafian þæt hi þry godas syndon,
ac án ælmihtig God ǽfre on ‎ðrym hádum;
and þis oncnawa‎ð þa halgan þonne hí hine geseo‎ð.
Næs na se halga Fæder to menn geboren for ús,   200
[ne he ne þrowode for us,] ac þrówode se Sunu,
se ‎ðe þa menniscnysse ána underfeng;
and hér ge magon gehyran þæt hi *syndon þrý,   *f. 214
and án God swa‎ðeah, swa swa we ǽr [r]æd[d]on.

‎Ðæt godspell sprec‎ð for‎ð on þus þæs Hælendes wórd: 205
'And ic ne sǽde eow gyt þæt ic sylf wylle biddan
þone ylcan Fæder, for eow þingiende.'
On þære menniscnysse þe he mid is befangen,
he bit for his halgum his heofenlican Fæder;
and on his godcundnysse, on þære þe he G[o]d is,   210
he getiþa‎ð ealle þing æfre mid þam Fæder;
and we habba‎ð on þam Suna swi‎ðe gódne þingere.

'Se sylfa Fæder lufa‎ð eow, for ‎ðan þe ge lufedon me,
and ge gelyfdon þæt ic fram Gode férde.'

---

194 wit *BU.*   syndon] beo‎ð *B.*   195 -þrimnys *N.*   197 syndon]
beon *B.*   198 þrim *NU*; ‎ðreo *B.*   199 icnawæ‎ð *B.*   201 ne . . . us]
sic *BNU*; *om. M.*   203 syndon] beo‎ð *B.*   204 ræddon] *sic BU*;
sædon *MN.*   205 spreceþ *U.*   207 ilcan *U.*   209 heofonlican *NU.*
210 god] *sic BNU*; gód *M.*   214 ge] *om. B.*

200–2 [*Augustine, In Ioan. Ev. Tract. XXXVI. 8*] Sabelliani . . . vocantur et
Patripassiani, qui dicunt ipsum Patrem passum fuisse. [*Tract. XXXVII. 7*]
Gratias Domino quia et ipse Arianus recessit ab errore Sabelliano, et non est
Patripassianus; non dicit ipsum Patrem indutum carne venisse ad homines,
ipsum esse passum, ipsum resurrexisse, et quodammodo ad se ascendisse.

208–12 [*Haymo*] Rogat ergo Patrem per humanitatem, quia omnia postulata
dat cum eo per Divinitatem. (*Cf. also Bede, Hom. II. 12*) Quia Dominus noster
Iesus Christus et Deus et homo est, modo summa deitatis, modo humanitatis
humilia loquendo designat. Quod enim dicit non rogaturum se Patrem de
discipulis, propter consubstantialem Patri divinitatis suæ potentiam dicit, in
qua non Patrem ipse rogare, sed rogata cum Patre consuevit donare. Quod vero
Petro ait, *Ego autem rogavi pro te, ut non deficiat fides tua* (*Luc. xxii. 32*), et de
illo Ioannes, *Advocatum*, inquit, *habemus apud Deum Patrem Iesum Christum
iustum* (*I Ioan. ii. 1*), propter dispensationem dictum est assumptæ humanitatis,
cuius cum triumphum Patris ostendit oculis, pro nostra infirmitate propitius
intervenit. [*See note.*]

Hér ge magon gehyran þæt se ðe næfð þone Sunu,   215
þæt he næfð þone Fæder þe hine asende;
and se Fæder lufað þa þe gelyfað on Crist,
and se bið gesælig þe swylce lufe underfehþ.
'Ic ferde fram þam Fæder, and com *to middanearde;*f. 214ᵛ
ic forlǽte eft middaneard, and ic fare to þam Fæder.'   220
He cóm to middanearde, and wæs mann gesewenlic,
se ðe ungesewenlic mid þam soðan Fæder wæs;
and he forlét middaneard, mid þam þe he up astáh
on þære menniscnysse to þam úngesewenlican;
ac he wunað swaðeah, oþ þissere worulde énde,   225
mid his halgum mannum on þære godcundnysse,
swa swa he sylf behét, se ðe ne wǽgð næfre.

Gif ðu þises wundrast, hu he wunian mage
mid mannum on eorðan, and éac swilce on heofenum,
scéawa be þære sunnan, þe is Godes gesceaft,   230
hu heo mage aséndan hyre scinendan leoman
fram hire upplican ryne ofer ealne middaneard.

Se sunbeam bescinð þe swutellice eallne;
and ne mæg se Eallwealdend, gif ðu hine lufast,
*his leoman þe aséndan, and éac þe lufian?   *f. 215

' þa sǽdon his folgeras mid swiðlicre blisse,   236
Efne þu sprecst nú swutellice, leof,
and þu nateshwón ne segst nán bigspell nú ús.'
Hwæt mage we eow secgan swutellicor be þysum

216 asænde U; sende B.   218 se] om. B.   swilce N.   220 fare] fare
eft B.   222 se ðe ungesewenlic in margin of U in contemporary hand.   soðan]
om. B.   224 menniscnusse N.   225 þyssere U.   227 wægeð BU.
228 mæge U.   229 swylce U.   heofonum NU.   231 asændan U;
sendon B.   232 hyre N.   233 bescineð U; biscinæð B.   235 senden B.
237 spæcest B.   238 sægest U; sægst B.   us nu B.   239 magon U.
þissum U.

215–18 [Not in Bede or Haymo.]
221–4 [Bede] Exivit a Patre et venit in mundum, quia visibilis mundo
apparuit in humanitate, qui erat invisibilis apud Patrem in divinitate. . . .
Reliquit mundum, et rediit ad Patrem, quia humanitatem quam induit, per
ascensionem ad invisibilia perduxit.
225–7 [Haymo] Non dereliquit electos, cum ad Patrem rediit, sicut ipse alibi
ait: Ecce ego vobiscum sum omnibus diebus usque ad consummationem sæculi (Matth.
xxviii. 20). . . . Rediens ad Patrem per humanitatem, mansit cum electis per
divinitatem.
228–35 [Not in Ælfric's immediate sources. Cf. CH I. 286/29 sqq., and see
the note on this passage.]
239–41 [Not in Bede or Haymo.]

þonne ða apostolas hit gesæd habbað,   240
swa swa ge gehyrdon nú on þissere segene?
'Nu we witon soðlice þæt þu wast ealle þing,
and þe nis nán néod þæt þe hwá áxige.'
Ful soð hi sædon be þam soðan Hælende,
þæt he ealle þing wát, swa swa eallwealdend God;   245
and þæt is seo swutelung his soðan godcundnysse,
þæt he mæg asmeagan ealra manna heortan,
and ure geþohtas þurhseon ealle;
and we ne ðurfon áxian hu he sylf dón wylle.

þa apostoli sædon þa, swa swa we sceoldon dón,   250
'On þam we gelýfað, þæt þu fram Gode cóme.'
And we *sceolon gelyfan on þone lyfigendan Hælend,   *f. 215ᵛ
þæt se Fæder ús lufie þe hine asende,
and ure heortan onlihte mid þæs Halgan Gastes gife,
þam is æfre an wuldor and án wurðmynt, AMEN.   255

241 sægene *U*; sæcgene *B*.   243 axie *U*; axiæ *B*.   244 soðam *N*.
246 -nesse *N*.   249 wille *N*.   250 sceolon *BN*.   252 lifigendan
N; lifigenddn (!) *U*; lifigende *B*.   253 lufige *BNU*.   asænde *U*; sende *B*.
255 wyrðmynt *N*.

244–9 [*Bede*] Apertum namque divinitatis indicium est, cogitationum nosse
secreta, Salomone affirmante, qui Deo supplicans ait: *Tu enim solus nosti corda
omnium filiorum hominum* (*III Reg. viii. 39*). [*Haymo*] Proprium namque est Deo
cogitationes hominum intueri, Scriptura testante. . . .
250–5 [*Not in Bede or Haymo.*]

NOTES

20. *on þære Frigenihte*, 'on the night between Thursday and Friday'.
This passage was cited for the idiom by Napier in *COEL* ('Contributions to Old English Lexicography'). See BTS for other examples.

23. *fela þing.* Cf. note on VII. 24.

59–72. Dr. J. E. Cross has very kindly brought to my attention Ælfric's
use of Gregory, *Hom. in Evangelia* XXVII, both here and (as first pointed
out by Max Förster) in his earlier homily, *In Natale Unius Apostoli* (*CH*
II. XL), where there is also a passage on praying in the name of the
Saviour (Thorpe, p. 528). Curiously, the earlier passage is already based
on a combination of Gregory and Bede, though the selection is different
from that in the later passage. It is Bede's homily II. 12 (or Haymo's
parallel homily LXXXIX) that has furnished Ælfric, in the earlier passage,
with the reference to *Prov.* xxviii. 9, and to the reward that the virtuous
may expect even when their prayers for sinners are not answered. That

Ælfric was thinking partly of Gregory in composing the later passage is indicated by the fact that Gregory, not Bede or Haymo, refers to prayers directed against enemies. The fountainhead of all these interpretations is Augustine, *In Ioan. Ev. Tract.* LXXIII, but there is nothing to show that Ælfric had consulted that passage.

79–84. With this passage compare Ælfric's allusion to the Epistle of James and to the story of Elias in his homily for Rogation Monday, *CH* II. 330/12–20. The passage from the Epistle quoted as a source for line 64 comes just before that on Elias.

96. This deficient line would be properly balanced by a translation of *fiat* to match the translation of *fiet*: perhaps 'becume hit and gewurðe'. The omission may have resulted from a scribe's misunderstanding of the parallelism or from mere eye-skip. For a list of places where all extant manuscripts of this group of homilies seem to agree in error see VII, introduction, p. 335 above.

97–131. The introduction of Gregory the Thaumaturgist and the basis of Ælfric's stories about him need a word of explanation. Apparently a major portion of the big passage on the efficacy of prayer was suggested to Ælfric, as Dr. Cross has conjectured, by Bede's reference to Gregory's feat in his commentary on *Mark* xi. 23. That Ælfric had in mind some of the details in Bede's version of the miracle is suggested, as pointed out under *Sources*, by partial correspondence with the phrase *in apto loco*; and in most respects Bede gives the same account as Ælfric. But one of his details is erratic: he describes the building-site as bounded, on the side opposite the mountain, by the sea (*rupe maris*), whereas Ælfric follows the usual account in representing the boundary as a river. There are two main Latin versions of these stories about Gregory: one in Rufinus, as indicated under *Sources*, the other in the life of Gregory attributed to Gregory of Nyssa and printed in the *Bibliotheca Casinensis*, III (1877), Florilegium Casinense, pp. 168–79. For the two stories that Ælfric tells here either version might have been consulted, and both support Ælfric against Bede. But there is a third story that Ælfric had already told at the end of *De Falsis Diis* (XXI. 575–648). He refers to it here at line 103. Now this story is clearly derived from Rufinus, because Rufinus, and not the life, provides Ælfric with the setting in the Alps. Hence it is reasonable to suppose that Ælfric turned to Rufinus once more when Bede had reminded him of Gregory. Rufinus, unlike the life, gives just the three stories that Ælfric uses, one in *De Falsis Diis*, the other two here. One feature of Ælfric's story of moving the mountain seems to be original: somewhat anachronistically he converts the *ecclesia* of the Latin authorities into a *munuclif*.

120. *fixnoð*. The various meanings of the word in this homily and in XIV were cited for their meanings by Napier in *COEL*. See Glossary, *fiscnoþ*.

125. *geunblissod*. This unique example of *ge-unblissian* 'to make unhappy' was cited by Napier in *COEL*.

127. The mutated *yrþ-* of B, N, and U is presumably Ælfric's form, but *eorþ-* is on record as a possible variant. See BTS, *irþland*.

166. The faintly written or partially erased gloss above the line after *eglige* in MS. U, if it is *irez*, must be the present third singular of *ire* 'to anger, irritate', though the *OED* cites only one example (*c.* 1420) of this verb. The *z* is surprising, but occurs frequently beside *th* in the verbal endings of the *South English Legendary* in MS. Laud 108 (ed. Horstmann, EETS, O.S. 87), which is variously dated *c.* 1280–1300 and considered south-western (*MED*, p. 12; Serjeantson, *RES* III. 322, suggests northern Wiltshire). Luick, *Historische Grammatik*, §763, Anm. 3, follows Horstmann in attributing the *z* to French scribal practice. Other glosses in U (mostly earlier, I think) look south-western. See above, pp. 79–80.

187–204. Ælfric's interpretation of the verse, *Ego et Pater unum sumus*, is fundamentally that of Augustine, as may be seen from the various excerpts given under *Sources*; but Ælfric may actually have had other passages, indeed other authors, in mind. Bede's Homily II. 24 includes a long comment on the verse (ed. Hurst, lines 148 sqq.; Migne, *PL* XCIV. 246 sq.) based entirely on Augustine. It might have prompted a good deal of Ælfric's passage, though certain details in Bede's Homily I. 8 (in a passage already quoted for I. 151–60) better explain Ælfric's remarks at the expense of the Sabellians in lines 190–3. Alcuin's comment on the verse (*PL* C. 893–4) is Augustinian, but leaves out some features of Ælfric's interpretation.

192. *abroden*, 'changed'. A meaning not hitherto recorded for *abregdan*, though known for *bregdan*. See Glossary.

197. *syndon*. The subjunctive meaning is confirmed by the substitution of *beon* in B. See note on I. 162.

204. *ræddon*. This reading of U and B seems preferable to the *sædon* of M and N because it is both more precise and less usual: a scribe's alteration of *ræddon* to *sædon* is more probable than the reverse. There is support for *ræddon* in II. 247, where both manuscripts, F and H, have the word. Its meaning, an unusual one, seems to be exactly the same in both passages. On both occasions Ælfric is referring to an interpretation he has presented shortly before. In homily II he has said that the day on which God rested after the six days of creation prefigures the day when Christ rested in the tomb. Here he has explained the mystery of the Trinity. I take it, then, that *swa swa we ær ræddon* in these passages means 'as we (I) explained before'. This meaning is recorded in BT with particular reference to explaining a riddle, but the limitation does not seem essential.

205. *sprecð forð on þus,* that is, 'goes on speaking thus'. See Glossary, *forþ*, and BTS, *forþ*, 2b and 3a.

206–12. Ælfric's translation of *et non dico vobis quia ego rogabo Patrem de vobis* gives a different meaning from that which Bede and Haymo assume. They take the statement as a denial (though perhaps a qualified denial) that Jesus will pray to the Father for the disciples, and Bede therefore attempts to reconcile this denial with other statements (*Luc.* xxii. 32 and I *Ioan.* ii. 1) that represent Jesus as an intercessor with the Father. As man, he intercedes; as God, he bestows. Ælfric accepts this doctrine, but so translates the gospel as to make it agree with the other texts. His translation seems to mean, 'And I have not yet told you [but you are now to learn] that I myself will pray', &c. Thus the burden of the passage is taken to be that Jesus will act as an intercessor, and the qualification, that in so far as he is God he grants all things with the Father, becomes a gratuitous addition rather than a direct implication of the text.

228–35. This passage on the sun, for which there is no hint in Bede or Haymo, is so much like the passage in *De Fide Catholica* (*CH* I. 286/29 sqq.) that no other immediate source need be sought. But Dr. Cross has traced the earlier passage to Augustine, *Sermo* cxx, in an article entitled 'Ælfric and the Mediæval Homiliary—Objection and Contribution', Kungliga Humanistiska Vetenskapssamfundet i Lund, *Scripta Minora*, 1961–2, no. 4, Lund, 1963, pp. 26 sqq.

IX[1]

DOMINICA POST ASCENSIONEM DOMINI

Ioan. xv. 26–xvi. 4

THE chief interest of this homily lies in the tangential passage at the head of the exposition, lines 20–82. It seems to be aimed at those in high station, including the king, and falls into two parts. The first part, lines 20–63, takes as its point of departure the openness of the Saviour's disclosures and warnings to his disciples in the gospel of the day, showing by another text that it was his habit to speak openly, both to his companions and to men in general. This habit is now treated as an example to counsellors. They are to speak openly, not in secret whispers, and the king is to call upon them and to heed their advice. And now the king in turn comes under examination. The king of a Christian people is Christ's vicar, whose duty it is to protect his people against an attacking army and to pray for victory to the Saviour, as did all kings who pleased God. Every king is holy if he protects God's people, and governs them with love and justice, and is ready to give his life if need be, as did Christ, for his people's protection.

Thus the discourse still turns upon Christ's example, but it has moved some distance from the point of departure. The second part of the passage, lines 64–82, seems to change the subject very abruptly. It cites the verses in *Matthew* where Jesus elicits from Peter the belief of the disciples, that he is no mere prophet but the Son of God. The text might have been quoted pertinently as an example of the testimony of the disciples, since the gospel of the day says they are to give such testimony later. But Ælfric thinks once more of the example set by Christ, this time an example to men that they should have concern for their reputations and beware of setting bad examples. Evidently we have another admonition to men in high station.

[1] On matters relating generally to homilies VII–X and XII, see VII, introduction, pp. 333–7 above.

As a sign of Ælfric's concern for the political and military troubles of his day this passage associates itself with at least five others: with the contrast he draws between the days of Edgar and those of Ethelred in two passages in the *Lives of Saints* (XIII. 147–77; XXI. 444–63); with the comments on the kings of Hebrew and Roman history, followed by the pointed praise of Alfred, Athelstan, and Edgar, at the close of the homily drawn from *Judges* (*O.E. Hept.* 414–17); with the advice to kings in our XXII; and with the comment on the extracts from *Maccabees* (*LS* XXV) in *On the Old and New Testament*: 'rædon gif ge wyllað eow sylfum to ræde!' (*O.E. Hept.* 51/837–8). Related also are the two passages dealing with the three pillars of the throne, *oratores, bellatores, laboratores* (*LS* XXV. 812 sqq. and *Old and New Testament*, 1207 sqq.). In the first passage the emphasis is on the *oratores*, who are to be protected from military service that they may fight against the invisible enemy; but in the second passage it is the *bellatores* whose service to the realm is emphasized, and for whose right to bear arms in a Christian society St. Paul's authority is cited. The dates of composition of these passages range from perhaps the mid-nineties (*LS* XIII) to some years after 1005, when Ælfric was an abbot (*Old and New Testament*). The manuscript evidence (VII, introduction, p. 333) points to a time soon after 1000 for this homily, roughly the same period, we may suppose, as the homily on *Judges*, or only a little later.

A fundamental theme in the passages just mentioned, as in Wulfstan's *Sermo ad Anglos* and in several of the laws for which he was responsible, is that all authority is from God, as is all power over men and all victory in battle. A king and his people cannot hope to prosper unless they win God's favour by right action and by prayer. The theme is Biblical and Augustinian, but in certain specific elaborations of it with respect to the king, Ælfric seems to be indebted to two more recent Latin treatises.

One of these treatises is the *De Duodecim Abusivis Sæculi*, wrongly attributed to Cyprian in many of the early manuscripts. It was almost certainly composed in Ireland in the seventh century, as demonstrated by S. Hellmann, 'Pseudo-Cyprianus de XII abusivis saeculi' (*Texte und Untersuchungen zur Geschichte der altchristlichen Literatur*, Reihe 3, Bd. 4, Heft 1, Leipzig, 1909, pp. 1–62). The text may be found in Hellmann, pp. 32–60, and in Migne, *PL* iv. 947–60, where it is entitled *De Duodecim Abusionibus Sæculi*.

Among Ælfric's surviving works is a translation of this treatise, slightly abridged, into rhythmic prose. It is properly an independent composition and has been printed as such from the twelfth-century MS. G. by Warner, *Early English Homilies*, pp. 11–16; but MSS. R and S contain a text more nearly Ælfrician in spelling as the second part of an unauthorized compilation, *De Octo Vitiis et de Duodecim Abusivis*, the whole of which is printed from R by Morris, *Old English Homilies*, pp. 296–304. Neither Morris's nor Warner's text of the *De Duodecim Abusivis* is adequate. A separate, annotated edition, based on all the manuscripts, of which I have given a list above, p. 63, is surely to be desired.

Ælfric's translation probably belongs to the years when he was at work on the *Lives of Saints*, but his acquaintance with the Latin original is already apparent in the rhythmical homily for Rogation Monday in the Second Series (*CH* II. xxi). This has a passage on kings and bishops (Thorpe 318 sq.) that draws freely on *De Duodecim Abusivis*, as was properly recognized by Jost (*Polity*, p. 37) though he made the unjustified inference that the translation was earlier than the sermon. In the *Lives of Saints* there is a second echo of the treatise, this time in a passage (xiii. 116–27) listing the twelve abuses with one alliterative line for each in language that seems to depend for most of its terms on the translation.

In the present homily, which should be dated several years later, Ælfric selects only a few points from the *De Duodecim Abusivis*. All these are to be found in the treatment of the ninth abuse, which is defined as *rex iniquus* and contains prescriptions for the just king as well as a list of calamities brought on by unjust kings. The most directly relevant passages of the original are quoted under *Sources* and a line or two of the translation in the note on lines 50–51. Here it may be said in general that three of Ælfric's points, that the king should act according to the advice of his counsellors, that he is to defend his people against an attacking army, and that he is to govern with love and justice, are supported by the *rex iniquus* passage.

Two other points that Ælfric makes were probably suggested to him by a different work, the ninth-century *Liber de Rectoribus Christianis* by Sedulius Scottus (ed. S. Hellmann, *Quellen und Untersuchungen zur lateinischen Philologie des Mittelalters*, I, München, 1906, pp. 21–91; and Migne, *PL* CIII. 291 sqq.). This work is often classed with roughly similar treatises by three other ninth-century Carolingian authors, Smaragdus, Jonas of Orléans,

and Hincmar of Rheims, but Ælfric seems to owe little to any of
them except Sedulius. In general Sedulius agrees with the *rex
iniquus* passage of pseudo-Cyprian, of which he makes use; but his
much longer treatise has other matter besides. It is probably from
him that Ælfric derived his statement that the king is Christ's vicar,
'Cristes sylfes speligend', and also his emphasis on prayer as a pre-
requisite for victory. What Sedulius says about the king as God's
vicar is quoted under *Sources*, and his remarks on prayer are discussed in the note on lines 52–54. Sedulius also adds greatly to the
weight of what the *rex iniquus* passage has to say about good
counsel. In chapter vi of his treatise (Hellmann's edition, pp. 37–
40) he deals at length with the question of counsel, making three
points: the king should trust above all in God's counsel as set
forth in the scriptures; he should trust in many counsellors rather
than in his own judgement (as Ælfric suggests at lines 34–35,
before he has mentioned the king); and he should trust in good
counsellors only, those who are good servants of God. The correspondences here have not seemed close enough to warrant quotation, but it is evident that Ælfric would readily have subscribed
to what Sedulius says and may very well have been encouraged by
it. Ælfric's own remarks throughout this passage seem to be
directed to the needs of his time as he sees them. Hence it is not
surprising that they should stand at some remove from Latin
authorities.

In Ælfric's exaltation of the king as Christ's vicar there is
obviously no immediate concern with the relative authority of
king and pope, though the expression itself implies that the king,
within his own sphere, is not subordinate to anyone on earth, and
Sedulius, in the passage quoted as Ælfric's probable source, is
explicit about the king's authority over the church. Both Sedulius
and Ælfric are chiefly concerned to impress the king with his
responsibility for the spiritual as well as the material needs of his
people, and neither of them seems to feel any contradiction in the
famous story of Ambrose and Theodosius (which Sedulius tells in
chapter xii and Ælfric in our xxvi), though another might have
used it to show that bishops are superior to kings. The more
serious controversy between Church and State was to emerge a
little after Ælfric's time, but the earliest recorded reference to the
king as God's vicar (*God's*, as by implication in Sedulius, not
Christ's, as in Ælfric) involves an assertion of the king's superiority

to the bishop, though it is achieved by a very questionable distinction between two of the persons of the Trinity. A certain Cathvulfus, thought to be an Anglo-Saxon, wrote as follows to Charles the Great: 'Memor esto ergo semper, rex mi, Dei regis tui cum timore et amore, quod tu es in vice illius super omnia membra eius custodire et regere, et rationem reddere in die iudicii, etiam per te. Et episcopus est in secundo loco, in vice Christi tantum est.'[1]

Ælfric's use of *Cristes* instead of *Godes* certainly has nothing to do with the sort of distinction made by Cathwulf. It may have been prompted in the first place by the convenient alliteration with *cyning* in line 48, and was clearly useful as a support for Ælfric's definition of the holy king (lines 55–60) as one who will give his own life, if need be, for the protection of his people, as the Saviour gave himself for us.

The phrase *Cristes speligend* has not received attention as Ælfric's even though, as I point out in the note on line 48, it was quoted from our manuscript M by Abraham Whelock in his edition of Bede; for Whelock was not in a position to identify the author. Hence the designation of the king as *Cristes gespeliga* in the *Institutes of Polity* (ed. Jost, I. Polity a, 2, p. 40) and in a contemporary law (VIII Æthelred 2, 1, Liebermann, *Gesetze der Angelsachsen*, I. 263), both of which have been attributed to Wulfstan, has been traced back to Cathwulf (Liebermann, II. 549, under *König*, 6, d) or to Sedulius (Jost, loc. cit.) without consideration of Ælfric as an intermediary. Yet Wulfstan's general tendency to borrow from Ælfric, and the use of *Cristes* where Cathwulf demands *Godes* and Sedulius implies it, suggest that Wulfstan is echoing Ælfric here also. This may seem all the more likely when we notice that the revised versions of *Polity* printed by Jost in adjacent columns (pp. 40, 41) have substituted for *Cristes gespeliga* the phrases *folces frofer, and rihtwis hyrde ofer cristene heorde*, and that Ælfric, immediately after calling the king *Cristes speligend,*

---

[1] *Monumenta Germaniae Historica*, Epistolae, IV. 503. The idea that the king is God's vicar was traced back by A. J. Carlyle to the pseudo-Augustinian *Quæstiones Veteris et Novi Testamenti* (now attributed to 'Ambrosiaster'), especially *Quæst*. xci. 8 (ed. A. Souter, *CSEL* L. 157; also in *PL* xxxv. 2284). On the whole subject see Sir R. W. and A. J. Carlyle, *A History of Mediæval Political Theory in the West*, I (by A. J. Carlyle, 1903), chaps. xiii–xv, xvii, xviii; and Walter Dürig, 'Der theologische Ausgangspunkt vom Herrscher als Vicarius Dei', *Historisches Jahrbuch*, LXXVII (1958), 174–87. Ælfric's acquaintance with one of Ambrosiaster's *Quæstiones* is shown in our XXIX.

had called him *hyrde* (line 50). Possibly Wulfstan had second thoughts about the propriety of *Cristes gespeliga* and made the substitution with Ælfric still vaguely in mind. For later appearances in English documents of the idea of the king as vicar of the deity, see Liebermann, *Gesetze*, II. 549, under *König*, 6, g.

At line 83 Ælfric begins to comment on the gospel of the day verse by verse. His first remarks, on the Trinity, are untraced, but after line 110 he follows two parallel sources with hardly an interruption. The first of these is Bede's Homily II. 16 in Hurst's edition, the second Haymo's Homily XCVIII, on the same text. Since they are much alike it is hard to tell which Ælfric is using, but except for a few lines he seems to have depended chiefly on Bede.

As I have already said in the introduction to VII (p. 334), the four manuscripts here involved include one pair, M and N, that has several common errors. In this homily such errors occur very plainly at lines 4, 51 (an unwarranted addition), 85, 121. There are probably other errors or unauthorized changes in M and N at 45, 50, and 134. At 57 and 129 I have allowed their reading to stand, but it may be wrong.

The points just mentioned, 57 and 129, are the only ones where the other two manuscripts, U and T, share readings that can plausibly be regarded as errors, and their testimony is too uncertain to establish U and T as a subordinate pair. In most respects T seems to be a law unto itself. It changes the order of words some twenty-six times, including the order in a Latin quotation at line 37, and once, before line 52, includes an extra line. As I have explained in the note, this line appears to be an interpolation and some of its features suggest the possibility that it was added by Wulfstan; but elsewhere the changes are not like those that Wulfstan made in *De Falsis Diis*, *De Septiformi Spiritu*, and other compositions of Ælfric's.

At two points, 23 and 72, the two less reliable manuscripts, N and T, otherwise not closely related, agree in readings that are probably not authentic but are plausible enough to be regarded as independent emendations or half-conscious substitutions.

The glosses in T are all, I think, in the 'tremulous' hand of the thirteenth-century Worcester scribe. (See above, pp. 185–8.) Variations in ink, size, and firmness, even in interpretation, suggest intermittent glossing over a period of years.

DOMINICA POST ASCENSIONE[M] DOMINI

Cum autem uenerit Paraclitus. Et reliqua.

Se Hælend hér on life, mid his halgum apostolum
and mid mannum wunigende, manega wundra wyrcende,
on þære ylcan nihte þæs ðe he on merien þrówode,
sæde his folgerum [on his fundunge] þus:
þonne se Froforgást cymð þe ic eow asénde 5
fram minum Fæder, se ðe [is] soðfæstnysse Gást,
and se soðlice for[ð]stæpð of ðam soþan Fæder,
he cyð gecyðnysse swiðe cuðlice be mé,

Text based on M (ULC Ii. 4. 6), ff. 257ᵛ–64. Collated with N (Cotton Faustina
A. ix), ff. 182ᵛ–6, U (Trinity B. 15. 34), pp. 198–211, and T (Junius 121), ff.
130ᵛ–6ᵛ.

Excluded variants: (1) N and U usually have *hy* for *hi* in the plural. In U *hi*
was sometimes written originally and altered to *hy*. (2) N and U have *him* in the
dative plural, where M and T have *heom*. In U *him* is usually altered to *hym*.
(3) T usually has *for þam þe* instead of *for þan þe*. (4) T has *hyra* for *heora*.
(5) U has *sæcg-, sæg-* for *secg-, seg-* in the verb *secgan*. (6) The manuscripts often
have single for historically double consonants at the end of *mann*, *godspell*,
eall, &c.

U normally points the text by half-lines. A few instances of erratic pointing
are noted among the variants. M's use of capitals has been regularized.

Sup.: ASCENSIONEM] *sic NTU*; ASCENSIONE *M. Before* et reliqua]
quem ego mittam uobis a patre *TU*; *the same plus* spiritum ueritatis *N*.

2 wuniende *NT*.   manega] and manega *T*.   windra *alt. to* wundra *U*.
3 þæs *om. T*.   mergen *TU*.   4 on his fundunge] *sic TU*; *om. MN*.
5 frofer- *U*.   asænde *U*.   6 fæder] *om. N*.   is] *sic NTU*; *om. M*.
7 se] he *T*.   forð-] *sic NTU*; for- *M*.   -stepð *U*.   8 swyðe *NT*.

Glosses in T, Latin: 4 fundunge: recessu.   5 froforgast: paraclitus.
6 soðfæstnysse: ueritatis.   7 forðstæpð: procedit.   8 cyð: perhibebit.
gecyðnysse: testimonium.

SOURCES. 5–19 [*Ioan. xv. 26*] Cum autem venerit Paraclitus, quem ego mittam
vobis a Patre, spiritum veritatis, qui a Patre procedit, ille testimonium perhibebit
de me:
    [*27*] Et vos testimonium perhibebitis, quia ab initio mecum estis.
    [*xvi. 1*] Hæc locutus sum vobis, ut non scandalizemini.
    [*2*] Absque synagogis facient vos: sed venit hora, ut omnis, qui interficit vos,
arbitretur obsequium se præstare Deo.
    [*3*] Et hæc facient vobis, quia non noverunt Patrem, neque me.
    [*4*] Sed hæc locutus sum vobis: ut cum venerit hora eorum reminiscamini,
quia ego dixi vobis.

þæt is, þæt he bið gewitnyss eallra minra weorca.
And ge éac cyþað gecyðnysse be mé,   10
for ðan þe ge fram anginne mid me wunedon.
Ic spræc þas ðing to eow þæt ge ne beon geæswicode.
Hi geútlagiað eow of heora gesam*nungum,   *f. 258
ac se tíma becymð þæt þa þe eow ofsleað
þæt hi wénað þæt hi gearcion Gode þénunge swá;   15
and þas ðing hi doð on heora gedwýlde,
for ðan þe hí ne cunnon minne Fæder ne mé.
Ac ðas þing ic spræc to eow þæt ge béon gemýndige,
þonne heora tíma cymð, þæt ic hit eow sǽde.
Se Hǽlend spræc openlice ǽfre to his geférum,   20
and oft to folces mannum on his micclan láre,
wolde þæt menn wiston wið hwæt hí hí warnian sceoldon,
and hwæt menn dón sceolon on heora Drihtnes willan,
þa þe his wórd wyllað mid weorcum gefyllan.
Ge magon gehyran hu he sylf cwæð be ðam: 25
Ego palam locutus sum mundo. Et reliqua.
Ic spræc openlice to þisum middanearde;
ic tǽhte on gesamnunge symle, and on ðam temple,
þær ðær *þa Iudeiscan ealle ætsomne cómon,   *f. 258ᵛ
and ic on digelnysse nán þing ne spræc.   30

---

9 ealra *NT*.   11 wunodon *T*.   14 becymð] cymð *T*.   15 *first*
þæt] *om. T*.   gearcigan *U*; gearkion *T*.   18 sprece (*alt. from* spræc) *T*.
gemyndig *U*; gemyndie *T*.   19 tyma *T*.   eow hit *N*.   sæde] 'ær' sæde *T*.
20 æfre openlice *T*.   21 mycelan *T*.   22 wearnian *U*.   23 sceoldon *T*;
sceo'l'don *N*.   24 willað *U*.   27 þyssum *U*.   28 symle on gesamnunge *T*.   symble *U*. *U has point after* symble, *not before*.   29 *Entire
line*] þær ealle þa iudeiscan tosomne comon *T*.   30 digel- *altered to* dygel-
U; digol- *T*.   gespræc *U*.

Glosses in T, Latin: 10 ge: vos.   cyþað: p*er*hibebitis.   11 ge: vos.
fram anginne: ab i*n*itio.   wunedon: estis.   12 þæt: vt.   ne: n*on*.   beon
geæswicode: scandalizemini.   13 Hi: illi.   geutlagiað eow: absq*ue* faci-
ent vos.   gesamnungum: sinagogis.   14 þæt þa þe: vt omn*is* q*ui*.
ofsleað: interficit.   15 wenað: arbitr*etur*.   gearkion: p*r*estare.   gode: deo.
þenunge: obseq*uium*.   16 hi: illi.   gedwylde:errore.   17 ne cunnon:
non nouer*unt*.   18 ge: vos.   beon gemyndie: reminiscamini.   22 wið:
contra.   24 þa ðe: q*ui*.

20–82 [*No source for this passage as a whole has been found*.]
26–30 [*Ioan. xviii. 20*] Ego palam locutus sum mundo; ego semper docui in
synagoga, et in templo, quo omnes Iudæi conveniunt; et in occulto locutus sum
nihil.

Hé sealde éac bysne soðlice mid þam,
þæt witan sceolon cyðan heora wórd openlice,
and þa ðe manegum rǽdaþ, ná mid rúnungum,
for ðan þe manega magon máran rǽd fíndan
þonne ǽnlypige magon mid ágenum gewille.   35
Be þam ylcan ús manað Godes wisdóm on bócum:
Omnia cum consilio fac, et post factum non pænitebis:
Gefada ealle þing fægere mid geþeahte,
and æfter þære dǽde þe ne ofðingþ nán þing.
Ne se wita ne sceal his wísdom behydan,   40
gif he rǽd cunne, swa swa hit cwyð be þam:
Sapientia abscondita et thesaurus occultus,
quæ utilitas in utroque?
Se behydda wisdóm and se bedigloda goldhórd,
hwilc fremu *is ænigu[m] on aðrum þæra?   *f. 259
And þæs behófað se cyning þæt he clypige to his witum,   46
and be heora rǽde, na be rúnunge fare,
for ðan þe se cyning is Cristes sylfes speligend

---

31 soðlice bysne *T. U has point after* soðlice, *none elsewhere in line.*
32 sceoldon *corrected to* sceolon *U.*   33 *Entire line*] na mid runungum þa
ðe manegum rǽdað *T.*   35 ænlipige *NU;* ænlypie *T.*   36 þus *after*
bocum *T.*   37 fac cum consilio *T.* penitebis *TU.*   40 Ne sceal
na se wita *T.* se *over line U.*   43 que *U.*   44 bediglode] *N has unerased*
o *under* l.   45 hwylc *TU.* freme *U.* ænigum *TU;* ænigum menn *MN.*
46 And] *om. T.* cing *U.* clipige *N;* clypie *T.*   47 fare] *earlier, after*
and *T.* rununga *NU;* runungum *T.*   48 spiligend *U;* speliend *T.*

Glosses in T, *Latin:* 32 witan: sapientes.   33 þa ðe: qui.   rædað:
consiliantur.   35 ænlypie: singuli.   38 Gefada: fac.   40 wita:
sapiens.   41 ræd: consilium.   44 bedigloda: occultus.   45 fremu:
vtilitas.   46 Ðæs: hoc.   48 speligend: vice gerens, vicarius.

37–39 [*Eccli. xxxii. 24. Vulgate differs slightly:* Fili, sine consilio nihil facias,
et post factum non pænitebis.]
42–45 [*Eccli. xx. 32. Vulgate differs slightly:* Sapientia absconsa, et thesaurus
invisus, quæ utilitas in utrisque?]
46–47 [*Cf. pseudo-Cyprian, De XII Abusivis Sæculi, Nonus abusionis gradus,
ed. Hellmann, pp. 51–52:*] Iustitia vero regis est ... senes et sapientes et sobrios
consiliarios habere, magorum et hariolorum et pythonissarum superstitionibus
non intendere.
48–50a [*Sedulius Scottus, De Rectoribus Christianis, cap. XIX, ed. Hellmann,
p. 86:*] Oportet enim Deo amabilem regnatorem, quem divina ordinatio tam-
quam vicarium suum in regimine ecclesiæ suæ esse voluit et potestatem ei super
utrumque ordinem prælatorum et subditorum tribuit, ut singulis personis ea
quæ iusta sunt decernat.

ofer ðam Cristenan folce þe Crist sylf alýsde,
him to hyrde gehalgod, þæt he hi healdan sceol[e],   50
mid þæs folces fultume, wi[ð] onfeohtend[n]e here,
and him sige biddan æt þam soðan Hælende,
þe him þone anweald under him sylfum forgeaf,
swa swa ealle cyningas dydon þe gecwémdon Gode.

Ælc cyning bið hálig þe gehylt Godes folc,   55
and mid lufe gewissað, ná mid wælhreownysse,
ac æfre æfter rihte, ná mid anwilnysse,
and wyle éac syllan, gif hit swa micel néod bið,
his agen líf æt nextan for his leode ware,
*swa swa se Hælend sealde hine sylfne for ús,   *f. 259�v
þeah þe he mihte eall mancynn ahreddan   61
butan his agenum deaðe, and of ðam deofle [ge]niman
his ágen handgeweorc, gif he swa dón wolde.

Se Hælend befrán hwilon his halgan apostolas
hu woruldmenn sǽdon hwæt he him sylf wǽre.   65
Hi andwyrdon him þus: Sume secgað þæt þu sy
Iohannes se fulluhtere, sume Helias,

---

49 cristenum *NTU*.   50 and is *before* him *T*.   sceole *TU*; sceolde *MN*.
hi healdan sceole] *after* fultume (51) *T*.   51 wið] *sic TU*; wið yfele menn
and *MN* (men *N*).   onfeohtendne] *sic NU*; feohtendne *T*; onfeohtende *M*.
52 *before* and] and ælc unriht on his leode alecgan *T*.   54 *þa before* cyningas *T*.   gode gecwemdon *T*.   55 hali *T*.   gehealt *TU*.   56 gewisað *N*.
57 ac] *om. TU* (*perhaps written, then erased in U*).   58 wule *N*.   eac wile *T*.
mycel *NT*.   62 buton *T*.   ðam] *om. T*.   geniman] *sic. NTU*; niman *M*.
63 *after* agen *an erasure in U*.   64 hwilon befran *T*.   65 wuruld- *U*.
66 sy] seo *U* (*no punct. following; point after* iohannes, 67).   67 elias *T*.

Glosses in *T*, *Latin*: 51 feohtendne: dimicante.   52 (*added line*) leode:
regione.   sige: victoriam.   56 gewissað: regit.   57 anwilnysse: obsti-
natio*ne*.   58 syllan: dare.   59 leode: re*n*gno, regione.   60 sealde:
dedit.   62 buton: sine.   geniman: assum*ere*.   64 befrán: inqu*isiu*it.
67, 68 sume: alii.

50b–51 [*Pseudo-Cyprian, ibid.*] . . . patriam fortiter et iuste contra adversarios
defendere.
52–54 [*Ibid.*] . . . per omnia in Deo confidere. [*But see commentary for influence
of Sedulius, op. cit., cap. XV.*]
64–71 [*Matth. xvi. 13*] Venit autem Iesus in partes Cæsareæ Philippi, et inter-
rogabat discipulos suos, dicens: Quem dicunt homines esse Filium hominis?
[*14*] At illi dixerunt: Alii Ioannem Baptistam, alii autem Eliam, alii vero
Ieremiam, aut unum ex prophetis.
[*15*] Dicit illis Iesus: Vos autem quem me esse dicitis?
[*16*] Respondens Simon Petrus dixit: Tu es Christus, Filius Dei vivi.

sume Hieremias, oþþe sum witega.

Ða cwæð se Hælend heom tó, Hwæt secge ge hwæt ic sí?

Petrus him andwyrde mid ánrædan móde,   70

þu eart se soða Crist, þæs lifigendan Godes Sunu.

þas wórd we sǽdon hwilon on sumon oþrum spelle
mid swutelum andgite; ac we secgað nu hér
þæt se Hælend sealde swá bysne ús mannum
þæt we sceolon witan hwilc wórd *we sylfe habbað,   *f. 260
oþþe hwilcne hlísan on ures lifes þeawum,   76
and gerihtlæcan ús æfre to beteran,
þæt we yfele bysne oðrum mannum [n]e syllon
on ǽnigre wohnysse oþþe anwilnysse;
for ðan þe seo yfele bysen byð openlice forwýrd.   80
Eft sæde se Hælend, Ic sealde eow bysne,
þæt swa swa ic eow dyde, þæt ge dón sylfe swá.

Nu sǽde se Hælend, swa swa ús segð þis godspell,
'Ðonne se Frófergast cymð þe ic eow asénde
fram minum Fæder, se ðe is soðfæstnysse [Gast,]   85
and se soðlice forðstæpð of ðam soþan Fæder,
he cyð gecyþnysse swyðe cuðlice be me,
þæt is, þæt he byð gewitnys ealra minra weorca.'
Mannum næs ná swa cuð on swa micelre swutelunge
be þære halgan þrynnysse, ær þæs Hælendes tócyme   90
*on his menniscnysse,   *f. 260ᵛ

---

68 oðer *added and erased after* sum U.   69 heom to] to hym U.   *second*
hwæt] *þæt* U.   sy *NTU*.   70 anrædum *TU*.   72 ær *after* hwilon *NT*.
sumum *NU*.   73 andgyte *TU*.   75 sceoldon *altered to* sceolon U.
hwylc *TU*.   76 hwylcne *NTU*.   78 ne] *sic NTU*; æfre ne M.   syllan
U.   80 bið *NTU*. U *has point after* bið, *not before*.   81 bisne N.   82 þæt . . .
dyde *om. N*.   sylfe] eall *T*.   83 Nu . . . hælend] Se hælend sæde *T*.
84 frofor- *NT*.   asænde U.   85 gast] *sic TU*; *om. MN*.   86 forstæpð
T; forðstepð *U*.   87 swiðe *TU*.   88 bið *NTU*.   eallra U.

Glosses in T, Latin: 68 oððe: aut.   70 anrædum: *constanti*, (*and faintly*
in margin) sapienti corde, finita mente.   73 andgyte: intellectu.   76 hlisan:
famam.   79 anwilnysse: obstinatione.   80 bysen: norma.   forwyrd:
interitus *vel* damnatio.   82 ge: vos.   84 froforgast: paraclitus.
84 asende: mitto.   86 forstæpð: procedit.   87 cyð: perhibebit.   gecyðnysse: testimonium.

---

81 f. [*Ioan. xiii. 15*] Exemplum enim dedi vobis, ut quemadmodum ego feci
vobis, ita et vos faciatis.
89–109 [*Not in Bede or Haymo, though both talk of the Trinity.*]

ac he mannum geopenode oftrǽdlice mid wordum
be his heofonlican [F]æder and be þam Halgan Gáste,
and he sylf spræc to mannum, þæt secgende swutelice,
swa swa ge gehyrdon her on þisum godspelle.   95
On oþre stowe he sǽde, swa swa Matheus awrát,
to his halgum apostolum, þus heom bebeodende:
Euntes ergo docete omnes gentes, baptizantes eos
in nomine Patris, et Filii, et Spiritus sancti; et reliqua:
Farað eornostlice to fyrlenum lándum;   100
lǽrað ealle [þ]eoda, and mid geleafan fulliað
on þæs Fæder naman, and his Suna witodlice,
and þæs Halgan Gastes; þus cwæð se Godes Sunu.
Her is micel swutelung þæs soðan geleafan,
hu se Hælend sylf hit sǽde,   105
and bead þæt ealle þeoda sceoldon *swa beon gefullode   *f. 261
on þa halgan þrynnysse and soðe ánnysse;
and þes án geleafa is eallum to healdenne,
þam mannum þe habbað ænigne myne to Gode.

He cwæð þæt he sylf wolde aséndan þone Gást,   110
þære soðfæstnysse Gást, þe of ðam Fæder forðstæpð,
for ðan þe se Frofergást forðstæpð of heom bám,
heora begra Lúfu, gelíc him on mihte.

---

93 fæder] *sic NTU*; fædfæder *M.*   94 swutollice *T.*   95 ðyssum *U.*
U has point after her, *not before.*   99 et reliqua] *om. N.*   101 þeoda] *sic*
NTU; leoda *M.*   102 witodlice] *om. T.*   104 mycel *T.*   105 sylf]
syf *N.*   hit] *om. T.*   106 beon swa *T.*   gefullade *U.*   108 is] his *N.*
to healdenne eallu*m T.*   109 mine *N.*   110 asændan *U.*   þone gast]
om. T.   111, 112 -stepð *U.*   112 frofor- *T.*   forð-] for- *N.*
113 gelic him on mihte] heom bam gelic on mihte *T.*

Glosses in T, Latin: 92 rædlice: mox, certe.   94 þæt secgende: hoc
dicendo.   95 ge: vos.   97 bebeodende: predicante, precipiente.
100 eornostlice: *ergo.*   101 þeoda: Gentes.   108 þes: iste.   109 myne:
memoria*m.*   110 asendan: *mittere.*   111 forðstæpð: procedit.
112 froforgast: paracli*tus.*
ME: 92 rædlice: iwislice. (*Written faintly in margin; cf. Latin* certe.)

98–103 [*Matth. xxviii. 19, as given.*]
110–13 [*Bede, Hom. II. 16*] Notandum autem inprimis, quod Dominus
spiritum veritatis, et a se mittendum esse testatur, et eundem mox a Patre pro-
cedere subiungit. . . . Cum enim eiusdem Spiritus gratia datur hominibus,
mittitur profecto Spiritus a Patre, mittitur et a Filio: procedit a Patre, procedit
et a Filio: quia et eius missio ipsa processio est, qua ex Patre procedit et Filio.
[*Haymo, Hom. XCVIII, has a similar passage.*]

þone asende se Sunu, and sǽde þæt he sceolde
gecyðnysse cyþan be Criste swutelice.   115
Hi begen hine sendon, and he sylfwilles cóm,
for ðam þe se ylca Gást, þurh his godcundnysse,
swa swa ælmihtig Wealdend swiðe wíde todælþ
his gástlican gifa ofer Godes folce
on eallum middanearde swiðe mihtiglice;   120
[and hé] his seofonfealdan gifa besǽwð on ús mannum,
be þam þe him *gewyrð, and we ús sylfe gearciað   *f. 261ᵛ
mid estfullum móde, þæt hé mid ús wunige.
Micel lét se Hǽlend þæs Halgan Gastes gecyðnysse,
þæt is, his gewitnysse, for ðon þe he wurðode begen   125
þone heofenlican Fæder and þone Halgan Gást
oft on his menniscnysse on þisum middanearde,
swa swa us swiðost segð Iohannes gesetnys
on þære feorðan Cristes béc, þe Iohannes sylf awrát.
Se Halga Gast cydde gecyðnysse [be] Criste   130
ǽrist þam apostolum on þære upflóra,
þa þa he on fýres gelicnysse befeng hi ealle

---

114 asǽnde *U*.   115 swutollice be criste *T*.   116 sǽndon *U*; sende *T*.
117 þan *U*.   ilca *U*.   118 ælmihti *T*.   120 mihtilice *T*; mihtlice *N*.
121 and he] *sic TU*; he and *MN*.   gifu *U*.   besǽwð] becwæð *U*.   123 wunie
T.   124 Mycel *T*.   125 ðan *NU*; ðam *T*.   126 heofon- *NTU*.
127 ðissum *NU*.   129 feorðe *N*.   cristes *om. N*.   sylf *om. TU (rightly?)*
130 be] *sic NTU*; mid *M*.   131 ǽrest *NTU*.   upflore *U*.   132 hi
ealle befeng *T*.

Glosses in *T, Latin*: 114 þone: illu*m*.   115 gecyðnysse: testimoniu*m*.
121 seofonfealdan gifa: septiforma dona.   besǽwð: seminat.   122 be ðam
þe hi*m* gewyrð: pro ut uult.   123 estfullum mode: deuoto a*n*imo.
124 gecyðnysse: testimoniu*m*.   125 wurðode: honorau*i*t.   128 gesetnys:
testimoniu*m*.   130 cydde: p*er*hibuit.

116–23 [*Bede*] Venit et sua sponte, quia sicut coæqualis est Patri et Filio, ita
eandem habet voluntatem cum Patre et Filio communem. *Spiritus* enim *ubi vult
spirat* (*Ioan. iii.* 8), et sicut apostolus, enumeratis donis cælestibus, ait: *Hæc
omnia operatur unus atque idem Spiritus, dividens singulis prout vult* (*I Cor. xii 11*).
124–9 [*Not in Bede.*]
130–8 [*Bede*] Adveniens autem Spiritus testimonium perhibuit de Domino,
quia discipulorum cordibus aspirans, omnia quæ de illo erant scienda mortalibus,
clara luce illis revelavit. . . . *Ille* ergo, inquit, *testimonium perhibebit de me, et vos
testimonium perhibebitis*: quia quæ spiritu intus docente perceperunt, hæc abiecto
timore pristino foris loquendo et aliis ministrabant. Ipse namque Spiritus corda
eorum et scientia veritatis illustravit, et ad docenda quæ nossent culmine virtutis
erexit.

[and hy ealle onælde, swa swa man isen deð,
butan ælcere dare,] mid [incundre] lufe.

Hi wurdon þa gewissode wundorlice mid his gife   135
be Cristes menniscnysse, and hí cénlice bodedon
cyningum and ealdormannum embe þæs Hælendes fǽr;
and on ealre soðfæstnysse he hi symle getrymde.

His gifa syndon *micele on seofonfealde wísan: *f. 262
on wisdome and on andgite and on wíslicum geþeahte,   140
on modes ánrædnysse mid micelre strengðe,
on soðum ingehyde and on árfæstnysse,
on Godes ege éac mid underþeodnysse;
be þysum we sǽdon swutelicor iú ǽr.

Mid gódum inngehyde he gladaþ ure mód,   145
and þurh hine we oncnawað hwæt ús to dónne is,
and he ús gestrangað to þære fremminge,
þæt we for earfoðnysse ure anginn ne forlǽton;
and se ðe Cristes Gast næfð, nis he ná Cristes mann.

'And ge éac cyþað gecyðnysse be me,   150
for ðan þe ge fram anginne mid me wunedon.'
Ðurh þone Halgan Gast hi wurdon gebylde,

133 *sq.* and . . . dare] *sic NU and substantially T; om.* M.   133 hi *T.*
deð isen *T.*   134 incundre] *sic TU;* inweardlicre *M.;* inwerdlicre *N.*
135 gyfe *T.*   137 ymbe *U.*   138 and *om. N.*   symble *U.*   140 on
om. T.   andgyte *TU.*   141 mycelre *T.*   143 and *before* on *U.*
144 ðisum *NU;* þissum *T.*   iu ær swutollicor *T.*   145 ingehyde *NTU.*
gegladað *U.*   151 wunodon *T.*

Glosses in T, *Latin:* 134 butan: sine.   dare: lesione   incundre: *intimo.*
136 cenlice: audac*ter,* acri*ter.*   137 fær: actu*m.*   138 getrymde:
edifica*uit,* roborau*it.*   140 andgyte: *intellectu.*   geþeahte: *consilio.*
141 modes anrædnysse: *constancia,* (*marg.*) unanim(itas), m*entis const*(ancia)?
strengðe: fortitudo.   142 ingehyde: sciencia.   arfæstnysse: pietate.
143 ege: timore.   underþeodnysse: (*faintly in marg.*) subiecti*one.*   144 iu
ær: sup*erius.*   145 ingehyde: sciencia.   148 angin: *inicium.*
151 anginne: initio.   152 gebylde: audaces (*consentientes erased*).

139–43 [*Is. xi. 2*] Et requiescet super eum spiritus Domini: spiritus sapientiæ,
et intellectus, spiritus consilii et fortitudinis, spiritus scientiæ et pietatis; et
replebit eum spiritus timoris Domini.

145–8 [*Bede*] Unde recte apud Esaiam, spiritus idem fortitudinis et scientiæ
nuncupatur. Est etenim spiritus scientiæ, quia per ipsum quæ recte agere, vel
etiam cogitare debeamus, agnoscimus: est et fortitudinis, quia etiam per ipsum,
quæ bene novimus ut operemur, accipimus, ne adversitate aliqua a bonis, quæ
cepimus, repellamur.

152–62 [*Bede*] Cum data Spiritus gratia etiam hoc fiduciam discipulorum

and éac heora ánrædnyss eall wæs gestrangod
þurh þæt þæt hi wunedon mid þam wuldres Drihtne,
on ealre his fare, fram frymðe *his láre,   *f. 262ᵛ
and mihton buton twéon bodian mancynne   156
þæt þæt hi gehyrdon and hi sylfe gesáwon.
Be þam cwæð Petrus on his bodunge iú:
Of deaþe he arás on þam þriddan dæge,
and ús he wæs geswutelod; ná eallum folce,   160
ac we ðe æton mid him, and éac swilce drúncon,
æfter ðam þe he arás of ðam deaþe gesúnd.
Crist wolde habban him sylfum to gewitan
þa halgan witegan þe witegodon be him
on þære ealdan gecyðnysse, ær ðan þe he cóme to mannum,   165
and eft syððan his apostolas, swa swa we sædon nú hér;
and þa halgan martyras syndon his gewitan,
þe heora líf sealdon, for his geleafan ofslagene;
and ælc þæra þe soð tæcð on soðfæstre láre
is Cristes [ge]wita wið ða unrihtan gedwolan   170
þe gedwýld lufedon oþþe gýt lufiað.
      'Ic spræc þas þing *to eow þæt ge ne beon geæswicode. *f. 263
Hí geútlagiað eow of heora gesamnungum.'

153 wæs] wearð U.   154 wunodon T.   156 butan TU.   mancynne
bodian T.   157 second hi] heom T.   159 he over line T.   161 ac] om.
U.   swylce NU.   ac . . . druncon] ac us þe mid him æton and druncon T.
162 aras . . . gesund] of deaðe aras gesund T.   166 æror before nu N.
her] ær U.   167 martiras T.   syndan U.   168 ofslagene U.   169 ælc]
æl N.   ðara U.   on] on his U.   170 gewita] sic NTU; wita M.   ge-
dweolan U.   173 geutlagiað] N has unerased a under i.

    Glosses in T, Latin: 153 anrædnys: constancia.   158 iu: superius.
162 gesund: incolumis.   163 gewitan: testes.   168 ofslagene: interfecti.
170 wið: contra.   172 þæt: vt.   ne: non.   beon geæswicode: scandalizemini.   173 gesamnungum: sinagogis.

iuvit, quod ab initio erant cum Domino, ideoque quæ apud illum viderunt et
audierunt, absque ulla ambiguitate prædicare valebant. . . . Hinc [Petrus] gentibus Christum evangelizans, confidenter aiebat (Act. x. 40 f.): Hunc Deus
suscitavit tertia die, et dedit eum manifestum fieri, non omni populo, sed testibus
præordinatis a Deo: nobis, qui manducavimus et bibimus cum illo, postquam surrexit
a mortuis.
    163–71 [Not in Bede. Perhaps suggested by the next sentences in Peter's sermon,
Act. x. 42 f., which are quoted by Haymo, Hom. XCVIII: Et præcepit nobis
prædicare populo, et testificari quia ipse est qui constitutus est a Deo iudex
vivorum et mortuorum. Huic omnes prophetæ testimonium perhibent, remissionem peccatorum accipere per nomen eius omnes qui credunt in eum.

Se bið geǽswicod þe on orwennysse
þurh yfele gebysnunga hihtleas befylþ,   175
and byð þonne beswicen on synlicum gylte,
gif he únwǽr byð wið ða yfelan bysne.
Nú warnode se Hǽlend wið þæt his apostolas,
and cwæð þæt þa ehteras of heora gemótum
hí woldon geútlagian, and mid ealle adrǽfan,   180
swa swa þa Iudeiscan dydon eft syððan—
beswungon þa apostolas, and him swiðe forbudon
þæt hi nán ðing ne bodedon be þam Hǽlende nahwar;
ac hí noldon geswícan swaðeah þære bodunge,
cwædon þæt hit gedafenað Drihtne to gehyrsumienne   185
swiðor þonne mannum; and hi swá éac dydon.
   'Ac se tíma becymð þæt þa ðe eow ofsleað,
[þæt] hi wénað þæt hi gearcian *Gode þenunge swá.'   *f. 263 ᵛ
þa Iudeiscan wéndon þe wunnon wið ðone Hǽlend

175 *transposed* hihtleas befealð þurh yfele gebysnunga *T.*   176, 177 bið
NTU.   177 bið unwǽr *T.*   178 apostolum *T. U has points after* þæt
and apostolas, *then a full stop after* cwæð!   181–2 *U has points after* dydon,
beswungon *and* apostolas.   182 swyðe *T.*   183 nahwar be ðam
hǽlende *T.*   nahwǽr *U.*   184 swaðeah *transposed to precede* noldon *T.*
geswicon *U.*   þæra *N.   U has point after* swaðeah, *not before.*   185 gehyr-
sumigenne *NU. U has point after* drihtne, *not before.*   186 swyðor *T.*
eac swa *T.*   188 *first* þæt] *sic NU;* and *M;* *om. or erased* T.   gearcion *T.*
swa gode þenunge *T.   U has point after* wenað, *not* gearcian.

   Glosses in T, Latin: 174 on orwennysse: *in desperatione.*   175 hihtleas:
sine spe.   befealð: *cadit.*   178 wið: *contra.*   179 gemotum: *sinagoga.*
180 adræfan: *eicere.*   185 gedafenað: *oportet, dec*et.   drihtne: *do*mino.
to gehyrsumienne: *obedire.*   187 ofsleað: *inter*ficiu*nt.*   188 wenað:
*arbit*re*tur (sic).*   gearcion: *p*restare.   gode: *deo.*   þenunge: *obsequiu*m.
189 wendon: *arbit*r*abant.*   wunnon: *certaue*ru*nt,* dimicabant.   wið: *contra.*

174–86 [*Haymo, in part*] Scandalizari autem est aliquem in persecutione a fide
deficere vel a prædicatione cessare. . . . Ut autem fortiores eos redderet, non
solum persecutiones eis prædixit, sed etiam eiusdem genus persecutionis ostendit.
. . . Quod autem a Synagoga frequenter eiecti sunt, liber Actuum Apostolorum
pleniter declarat, in quo legitur: *Quia statuentes eos in concilio, denuntiaverunt
eis, ne cuiquam homini loquerentur, neque docerent in nomine Iesu; quando illi ibant
gaudentes a conspectu concilii, quoniam digni habiti sunt pro nomine Iesu contumeliam
pati* (*Act. v. 40 f.*).
189–98 [*Bede, in part*] Arbitrabantur autem obsequium se Deo præstare Iudæi
in eo, quod ministros novi testamenti odiis insequabantur et mortibus. . . .
Cuius memor admonitionis beatus martyr Stephanus flexis genibus pro his, qui
se interficiebant pia voce supplicabat, dicens (*Act. vii. 60*): *Domine, ne statuas
illis hoc peccatum.* Arbitrabantur ergo legis æmulatores obsequium se præstare
Deo, dum præconibus gratiæ neces inferrent.

þæt hí Moyses lage mihton swa gefyllan,   190
mid þam þe hí acwealdon Cristes bydelas,
þe þæt godspell bodedon under [Godes] gife,
on þære niwan gecyðnysse, þe ða Iudeiscan ne cuðon.

þa oftórfodon hi Stephanum mid stanum oð deað,
and þone rihtwisan Iacob mid heora reðnysse,   195
and þone oþerne Iacob hi éac beheafdedon,
and besetton éhtnysse on þa oðre apostolas,
and mid niðfullum hatungum heora láre onscunodon.

'And þas ðing hi doð on heora gedwylde,
for ðan þe hi ne cunnon minne Fæder ne me.'   200
Ða Iudeiscan noldon urne Drihten oncnáwan
mid soðum geleafan, þæt he Godes Sunu is,
ac mid anwilnysse his wórdum *wiðcwædon,   *f. 264
and nabbað nú naðor ne þone Fæder ne hine,
swa [swa] he sylf sæde on sumum oðrum godspelle: 205
Se ðe me hatað, he hatað minne Fæder.

'Ac þas ðing ic spræc to eow þæt ge beon gemýndige,
þonne heora tíma cymð, þæt ic hit eow sæde.'
Se Hælend hi warnode wið þa tóweardan gefeoht,
for ðan þe gehwá mæg micele eað acúman   210
þa earfoðnyssa þe him ǽror beoð cuðe,
þonne þa fǽrlican þe him fǽringa becumað.

---

191 þe] þy U.   192 godes] sic NTU; cristes M.   gyfe T.   194 oftorfedon N.   oð deað] om. T.   195 r(a)eðnysse U (a erased).   196 beheafdodon TU; behæfdedon N.   198 niðfullum] fullum N.   199 ðing
over line U.   205 swa swa] sic TU; swa MN.   211 æror] ær U.

Glosses in T, Latin: 193 gecyðnysse: testamentum.   196 oþerne: alterum.
199 gedwylde: errore.   200 ne cunnon: non noverunt.   203 anwilnysse:
obstinatione.   207 beon gemyndige: reminiscamini.   208 þonne: cum.
209 wið: contra.   gefeoht: agonia.   210 gehwa: quisque.   acuman:
vincere, probare.   212 þonne: quam.   færlican: subita.

194–8 [A recasting of CH I. 402/16–19; see note.]
201–6 [Bede] Quicumque Filii credulitati obstinata mente resistunt, nec
Patrem nosse probantur. Unde etiam idem Ioannes veritatem divinæ unitatis
insinuans, ait (I Ioan. ii. 23): Omnis qui negat Filium, nec Patrem habet.
206 [Ioan. xv. 23] Qui me odit, et Patrem meum odit.
209–12 [Bede, on xvi. 1 above] Curavit namque pius magister futura discipulis
pravorum bella prædicere, quo minus hæc eos venientia possent offendere, quia
solent nimirum levius ferri adversa, quæ possunt ante prænosci. Nam quæ im-
parato ac non prævidenti animo mala ingeruntur, gravius hunc sæpe ab integri-
tatis suæ statu deiiciunt.

And micel frofor him wæs on þam gefeohte eft,
þæt se sylfa hi warnode þe him symle mihte
on þam gewinne gehelpan, þæt hi hæfdon sige,   215
and æfter þam sige heom gesælþe forgifan,
and þone écan wurðmynt on wuldre mid him,
se ðe á rixað on écnysse. AMEN.

213 mycel *T.*   frofer *U.*   214 symble *U.*   217 wyrðmynt *NT.*

Glosses in T, Latin: 215 gewinne: agone.   sige: victoria*m.*

213–17 [*Bede*] Magno pondere pensandum est, quod ait, *Ego dixi vobis*, ego
qui . . . in tribulatione vos semper adiuturus, qui æterna vobis præmia post
tribulationem daturus sum. Magnum quippe certantibus levamen, magnam
consolationis gratiam præstat, quando ille certamina eadem futura prædixisse
reminiscitur, qui et milites suos ne vinci possint adiuvare, et ne incassum vincant
immortalem post proelia solet rependere palmam.

NOTES

3. *on þære ylcan nihte þæs ðe he on merien þrowode*, 'on the very night
after which, on the morrow, he suffered.' It looks as if Ælfric had here
combined the ordinary use of *þæs ðe* as a temporal conjunction, 'after',
with the idiom *þæs on merien*, 'the next morning'. (Cf. BT, *se*, V, 2, and
Glossary, *se*, *mergen*.) The same expression occurs at Assmann VI. 6.

4. *on his fundunge.* The omission of this alliterating phrase in M and
N is a fair illustration of the ease with which some of Ælfric's lines can
be shortened without apparent loss of meaning. Yet the phrase states an
important reason for the long speech of which the gospel for the day is
a part. It occurs also at VIII. 23, in a similar introduction.

8. *cuðlice.* The word was cited from this passage by Napier in his
'Contributions to Old English Lexicography'. He took it as accusative
singular feminine of the adjective in the sense 'certain, evident', which
gives a firmer meaning than the formally identical adverb.

31–47. I have suggested above, p. 375, that Ælfric's plea for outspoken
advice from counsellors may owe something to Sedulius Scottus, *De
Rectoribus Christianis*, cap. vi. Sedulius emphasizes, among other things,
the advantages of seeking counsel from many persons, somewhat as
Ælfric does in lines 34–35. But Ælfric's contrast between open counsel and
whisperings (presumably the secret suggestions of imprudent or self-
seeking individuals) suggests both the plight of the ill-counselled Ethelred
and Ælfric's hope that the actual members of the *Witan* might gain in

power and wisdom. As early as the homily on the prayer of Moses (*LS* XIII. 128 sqq.) Ælfric had this problem in mind:

> þissere worulde hæl is þæt heo witan hæbbe,
> and swa ma witena beoð on bradnysse middaneardes,
> swa hit bet færð æfter ðæs folces þearfa.
> Ne bið se na wita þe unwislice leofað,
> ac bið open sott þeah þe him swa ne ðince.

And as the passage proceeds Ælfric directs his admonition to both the secular lords and the leaders among the clergy. Not long after the date of the present homily Wulfstan, as a member of the *Witan*, was to exert the kind of influence Ælfric had in mind, though without noticeable advantage to Ethelred.

48–53. These lines on the king as Christ's vicar were quoted by Abraham Whelock in his edition of Bede, *Historiæ Gentis Anglorum Libri V*, Cambridge, 1643, p. 151/29 sqq., from MS. M, whence they were cited by BT under *speligend*. Whelock wanted to show by his quotation that the Anglo-Saxon Church had preferred to regard the king as directly subject to God rather than to the pope, whereas the letter of Pope Honorius to Edwin, quoted by Bede at II. 17, had subtly implied the contrary. For a discussion of the phrase *Cristes speligend*, its antecedents and its relation to Wulfstan's phrase, *Cristes gespeliga*, see the introduction to this homily, pp. 375–7.

50b–51. *þæt he hi healdan sceole . . . wið onfeohtendne here.* Ælfric's translation of the injunction in pseudo-Cyprian quoted under *Sources* partially anticipates the choice of words here: '[he sceal] fæstlice winnan wið onsigendne here, and healdan his eðel' (*Old English Homilies*, ed. Morris, I. 303).

52. The extra words preceding this line in MS. T, *and ælc unriht on his leode alecgan*, constitute an acceptable Ælfrician line with the very rare but not unexampled alliterative pattern *aa : bb* (Introduction, p. 124), and supply a theme that is dominant in the *rex iniquus* passage of pseudo-Cyprian, on which Ælfric has just drawn. It was probably composed by someone who recalled Ælfric's own translation of the *rex iniquus* passage, near the beginning of which we read, '[se cyning] sceal wissigan mid wisdome his folce, and unriht alecgan' (*Old English Homilies*, 302). The phrase *unriht alecgan* occurs also, with different inflection, in *LS* XVI. 67. Yet I question whether Ælfric himself was responsible for the line, not simply because of the unusual alliterative pattern, but also because it breaks the logical continuity between lines 51 and 52, and even more because it is absent from both the M–N and the U texts, which appear in general to be derived from two different states of Ælfric's originals, a middle and a late state respectively. That T should have preserved an original reading or received an authentic addition not represented in either M–N or U seems unlikely.

I am tempted to attribute the line to Wulfstan, especially since T is a

Worcester manuscript that includes copies of some of Wulfstan's own compositions. The alliterative pattern accords better with his freely grouped two-stress phrases than with Ælfric's pairs, and in his writings, though alliteration is less constant than in Ælfric's, the internal alliteration of a single phrase is very common and that of consecutive phrases less of a rarity than in Ælfric. (See McIntosh, *Wulfstan's Prose*, 8–11, with quotation from the *Sermo ad Anglos*; also *Polity* I. 12 and Bethurum IX. 146.) The sentiment would have seemed at least as important to Wulfstan as to Ælfric, and the expressions are equally within his range. The combination *ælc unriht* occurs at least three times in Wulfstan's acknowledged works (Bethurum, xa. 11 and XIII. 103, followed by *ascunian*; xc. 139, followed by *gebetan*). The combination *unriht alecgan* occurs also in certain laws for the wording of which Wulfstan was at least partly responsible (Liebermann, V Æthelred 33, 1; Cnut 1020, 3; II Cnut 7, 1 and 11, 1). For the relevant passage in V Æthelred there is a further link. Karl Jost, in his *Wulfstanstudien* (p. 43, n.), has pointed out that this passage shows the influence of the *rex iniquus* passage, particularly of a sentence or two that Ælfric did not include in his translation. Hence there is all the more reason to suppose that Wulfstan, out of his familiarity with both Ælfric and the *rex iniquus* and his interest in the problem, might have made the addition that has come down to us in the text of MS. T. Whether he actually did so must remain uncertain.

52–54. *and him sige biddan . . . swa swa ealle cyningas dydon þe gecwemdon Gode.* Ælfric could have found support for these words not only in some of his own writings but also in Sedulius Scottus, *De Rectoribus Christianis*, cap. xv (ed. S. Hellmann, pp. 66–72), which begins as follows:

> Unde, si quando bellici rumores crebrescant, non tam in armis corporalibus et fortitudine confidendum, quam assiduis ad Dominum orationibus est insistendum Deique sunt imploranda suffragia, cuius in manibus consistit salus, pax atque victoria.

Sedulius cites as examples Moses's victory over Amalek (described by Ælfric, *LS* XIII), Hezekiah's over Sennacherib (*LS* XVIII), Jehoshaphat's over the children of Moab and Ammon, the various victories of the Maccabees (*LS* XXV), then jumps over the centuries to the Christian emperors, Constantine (whose victory over Maxentius Ælfric describes, *CH* II. 304) and Theodosius the Great (whose victory by the aid of a tempest Ælfric mentions in the epilogue to *Judges*, *O.E. Hept.* 415). The list concludes with victories gained by St. James and St. Germanus, which Ælfric seems not to have touched upon anywhere. In the epilogue to *Judges* Ælfric refers to English kings who were victorious by God's aid, but though he might have mentioned the miraculous victory of Oswald (*LS* XXVI), he focuses attention on Ethelred's line, on the hard-won victories of Alfred and Athelstan and on the victorious peace of Edgar. See further the introduction to XXII below.

59. *his agen lif . . . for his leode ware.* Ælfric attributes such a sacrifice to St. Oswald: *he ofslagen wearð for his folces ware*, *LS* XXVI. 147; and

also to St. Edmund, who refuses to flee from his enemies even though he will not defend himself with weapons: *ic wolde swiðor sweltan gif ic þorfte for minum agenum earde, LS* XXXII. 79 sq.

72. *on sumon oþrum spelle.* In the homily on the passion of Peter and Paul, *CH* I. 364 sqq.

144. *be þyssum we sædon . . . iu ær.* Almost certainly Ælfric is referring to his first homily for Pentecost, *CH* I. XXII, in which there is a long passage (Thorpe 318 sqq.) dealing with the significance of the Holy Spirit, mentioning his general gifts (322) and concluding with an enumeration of the sevenfold gifts (326). The *iu ær* especially points to this early homily rather than to the specialized little treatise, *De Septiformi Spiritu*, which, to judge by its association with Wulfstan and its occurrence in manuscripts, should have been composed even later than the present homily, certainly not a long time before it. There is a similar reference to the sevenfold gifts in XI. 69, this time with the clause, *swa swa we sædon eow on sumum spelle ær*; and here the reference to a *spell* seems to indicate the early homily rather than *De Septiformi Spiritu*. The one clear reference to the latter is in *On the Old and New Testament*, 48–50, where it is called a *gewrit* and there is particular mention of Isaiah, who is named in it and not in the early homily. Actually the Pentecost homily has a fuller presentation of the gifts of the Holy Spirit than *De Septiformi Spiritu*, because although it gives Isaiah's list without comment, it has had a great deal to say in advance about the general gifts of the Spirit enumerated by St. Paul. (In Clemoes, *Chronology*, 232, it is argued that the references in IX and XI are to N's composite homily for the third Sunday after Easter, for the dubious character of which see the introduction to XIX.)

194–8. Ælfric's first treatment of this theme occurs in his homily for the eleventh Sunday after Pentecost, *CH* I. 402/16–19:

hi oftorfodon mid stanum ðone forman Godes cyðere Stephanum, and Iacobum, Iohannes broðer, beheafdodon. Eac ðone rihtwisan Iacobum hi ascufon of ðam temple, and acwealdon, and ehtnysse on ða oðre apostolas setton.

This passage is part of an account of the destruction of Jerusalem that supplements, from Rufinus, Ælfric's digest of Gregory's *Hom. in Evang.* XXXIX, as Max Förster has pointed out(*Anglia* XVI. 9 and 54). Evidently the passage quoted stuck in Ælfric's head, for there is a final reminiscence of it in *On the Old and New Testament*, 1233 sq.:

and hi acwealdon Cristes apostolas,
þone gingran Iacob and þone rihtwisan Iacob,
and Stephanum oftorfedon mid heardum stanum.

Ælfric deals separately with the passions of these three martyrs in *CH* I. III (Stephen); *CH* II. XVIII (James the Just); and II. XXXI (James, son of Zebedee). (On Jerome's identification of James the Just, to which Ælfric adheres, and Ælfric's nevertheless unorthodox view that Jesus and James the son of Zebedee were cousins, see note on I. 5b.)

XI[1]

DOMINICA PENTECOSTEN

Ioan. xiv. 23–31

APART from two little *exempla* introduced at line 159, this homily is a straightforward exposition of its pericope. Ælfric's chief guide seems to have been Haymo's *Homilia* C. But Haymo himself made use of at least two earlier authorities. One of these was Gregory the Great, whose *Homilia* XXX of the series *in Evangelia*, intended for Pentecost, begins with an exposition of the appointed gospel but stops after the first part of verse 27, *Pacem relinquo vobis, pacem meam do vobis.* The other authority was Augustine in his commentary on *John*, *Tractatus* LXXVI–LXXIX. Even in the first part of the homily Haymo modifies what he takes from Gregory by suggestions from Augustine; and in the second part, where Gregory's comment is not available, he draws rather heavily on Augustine. Yet he reworks ideas from both these authorities and adds a good deal that is more or less independent of them.

Now it appears that Ælfric, though strongly influenced by Haymo, went behind him to these older authorities on several occasions. In the first part of his homily he sometimes prefers Gregory to Haymo or takes suggestions from both almost concurrently. In the second part, though he less frequently sets Haymo aside, he seems to draw a few notions from Augustine. There is, to be sure, a homily for Pentecost attributed to Smaragdus (Migne, *PL* CII. 328–31) in which several of the relevant passages from Augustine appear, but not quite all of them; and the same can be said of the commentary by Alcuin. I am inclined to believe, therefore, that Ælfric turned to Augustine directly.[2]

[1] On matters relating generally to homilies VII–X and XII, see VII, introduction, pp. 333–7 above.

[2] Or, what is virtually the same, to the alternative version of Alcuin's commentary on *John* falsely attributed to Bede (Migne, *PL* XCII). This part of the pseudo-Bede is a mere copy of Augustine's tractates with a few trifling omissions. I am uncertain whether Ælfric ever made use of this commentary, since the latter part of it (from *Ioan.* xiii on), where alone it differs from Alcuin's, cannot be

Ælfric had already made use of Gregory's Homily xxx in at least two other homilies. In his first homily on Pentecost (*CH* I. xxii) he had used passages on the Holy Spirit; and in his second homily for Rogation Monday (*CH* II. xxi), as I have mentioned in the note on line 31, he had used the exposition of two verses of the gospel (*Ioan*. xiv. 23, 24).[1] Now, where these same verses occur, he echoes the Rogation homily, but there is enough fresh borrowing from Gregory to indicate either a vivid recollection or a rereading of the original. See further the notes on 49–56 and 59–64.

For the story of Arius, Ælfric need not have gone beyond his own previous accounts. The basic one, in *CH* I. 290, probably owes something to Haymo's *Historiæ Sacræ Epitome*, Migne, *PL* cxviii. 863, though Ælfric rarely depends on this work elsewhere and was certainly familiar with Haymo's chief sources, Rufinus and the *Historia Tripartita*.[2] There is brief mention of Arius in *LS* xvi. 206 sq., and again a somewhat fuller account in the first Latin letter to Wulfstan and its English translation (Fehr, *Brief* 2, sec. 51–55; *Brief* II. 54–58), which may be a little later than this homily. The three main accounts—in *CH*, this homily, and the letters—have the same taunt, which runs thus in *CH*: ' þa geswutulode God þæt he wæs swa geæmtogod on his innoðe swa swa he wæs ær on his geleafan.' Dr. J. E. Cross has recently come upon the probable source of this taunt in Bede's comment on the death of Judas, *Acts* i. 18, where he points to the similar death of Arius and finds in the manner a just retribution for both: 'sicut sensu inanes vixerant sic quoque ventre vacui perirent.'[3] When, some-

distinguished, at the points where I have been able to test it, from Augustine himself. Max Förster credits Ælfric with using it in three homilies (*Anglia* XVI. §§ 58, 61, 65), but only at one of these, *CH* II. xl, 47 sqq. (Förster § 61) is the part of the commentary that differs from Alcuin's in view. Here, contrary to Förster's statement, there is no significant difference between pseudo-Bede and Augustine's tractates 83–85. For further details see above pp. 161–2.

[1] Förster noted the borrowing from Gregory in I. xxii (*Anglia* XVI, § 55), but overlooked that in II. xxi.

[2] On the probable debt to Haymo's *Epitome* for some features of the story of the death of Arius see J. E. Cross, 'Ælfric and the Mediæval Homiliary', Kungliga Humanistiska Vetenskapssamfundet i Lund, *Scripta Minora*, 1961–2, no. 4, p. 32 sq.; and on Ælfric's general debt to Haymo, C. L. Smetana, *Traditio* XVII. 457–69; but surely it is not true, as Father Smetana suggests, p. 469, that 'Aelfric knew Rufinus and the "wyrd-writeras" only through Haymo', a generalization questioned by Cross also, loc. cit. At several points in this edition where I have cited Rufinus or the *Historia Tripartita* as sources, Haymo's *Epitome* is either blank or inadequate.

[3] *Bedae Venerabilis Expositio Actuum Apostolorum et Retractatio*, ed. M. L.

what later, Ælfric adverts to the death of Arius in the homily for a confessor, Assmann IV. 195–202, he drops the taunt, but in other details echoes the earlier accounts.

Immediately after the account of Arius in Assmann IV Ælfric has added, as in the present homily, an account of Olympius. The two versions are very much alike, that in Assmann a little longer and easier but not more detailed except in the statement, probably a mere inference, that Olympius was a bishop. The brief account quoted from Isidore's *Chronicon* gives all the details Ælfric needed. A slightly more elaborate account in the chronicle of Victor Tununensis for the year 498 (Migne, *PL* LXVIII. 949) has nothing pertinent to add and diverges crucially, if the printed text is right, by reading *invisibiliter* instead of *visibiliter*.

W. Laistner (Mediæval Academy of America, Cambridge, Mass., 1939), p. 12. Dr. Cross has generously allowed me to mention this interesting find, which he has communicated to me privately.

DOMINICA PENTECOSTEN

Si quis diligit me, et reliqua

Iohannes se godspellere, þe ðis godspell awrát,
sǽde þæt se Hǽlend hér on þisum lífe
on sumne sǽl sprǽce to his apostolum ðus:
Se ðe me soðlice lufað, he hylt mine sprǽce,
and mín Fæder hine lufað, and wyt becumað to him,   5
and mid him wuniað witodlice begen.
Se þe me ne lufað, ne hylt he mine sprǽce.
And seo sprǽc þe ge *gehyrdon, nis heo na min sprǽc, *f. 276ᵛ
ac þæs ylcan Fæder þe me asende.
Ic sprǽc ðas þing to eow mid eow nú wunigende.   10
Se halga Froforgást þe min Fæder asent
on minum naman eow, he eow tæcð ealle þing,
and eow ealle þing geswutelað, swa hwæt swa ic eow secge.

Text based on M (ULC Ii. 4. 6), ff. 276–82ᵛ. Collated with N (Cotton Faustina A. ix), ff. 192ᵛ–6ᵛ, and U (Trinity B. 15. 34), pp. 232–44.

Excluded variants: (1) N and U often have *hy* for *hi* in the plural. In U *hi* was sometimes written originally and altered to *hy*. (2) N and U have *him* instead of *heom* in the dative plural. In U this has usually been altered to *hym*. (3) U has *sæcg-, sæg-* for *secg-, seg-* in the verb *secgan*. (4) The manuscripts often have single for historically double consonants at the end of *mann, godspell, eall*, etc.

U normally points the text by half-lines. A few instances of erratic pointing are noted among the variants. M lacks sentence capitals only at 121 and 205.

Sup.: DOMINICA PENTECOSTEN] EODEM DIE DE EVANG*ELIO N. Before* et reliqua] mandata mea seruabit *N.*
4 Se ðe] þe þe *N.*   5 wit *U.*   9 asænde *U.*   10 *second* eow] eow (eow) *U.*   11 frofer- *U.* asænt *U.*   12 *second* eow] om. *U.*

SOURCES. 4–10 [*Ioan. xiv. 23*] Si quis diligit me, sermonem meum servabit, et Pater meus diliget eum, et ad eum veniemus, et mansionem apud eum faciemus.
[*24*] Qui non diligit me, sermones meos non servat. Et sermonem, quem audistis, non est meus: sed eius, qui misit me, Patris.
[*25*] Hæc locutus sum vobis apud vos manens.
11–21 [*26*] Paraclitus autem Spiritus sanctus, quem mittet Pater in nomine meo, ille vos docebit omnia, et suggeret vobis omnia, quæcumque dixero vobis.
[*27*] Pacem relinquo vobis, pacem meam do vobis: non quomodo mundus dat, ego do vobis. Non turbetur cor vestrum, neque formidet.
[*28*] Audistis quia ego dixi vobis: Vado, et venio ad vos. Si diligeretis me, gauderetis utique, quia vado ad Patrem: quia Pater maior me est.

Ic forlǽte eow sibbe, and mine sibbe eow sylle.

Ne forgife ic eow swa swa þes middaneard gifð.   15

Ne beo eower heorte gedréfed, ne ne forhtige nateshwón.

Ge gehyrdon þæt ic sǽde soðlice nu eow,

þæt ic sylf nu fare, and ic cume to eow.

Gif ge me lufedon, ge witodlice blissodon,

for ðam þe ic fare to minum Fæder nu,   20

for ðan þe se Fæder is máre þonne ic sý.

And nu ic hit eow secge ær ðan þe hit gewurðe,

þæt ge þonne his gelyfon þonne hit gedón bið.

Ne sprece ic ná *fela þing heonon forð to eow.   *f. 277

Ðises middaneardes ealdor to me sylfum becóm,   25

and he nán þing næfð eallunga on me;

ac oncnáwe þes middaneard þæt ic minne Fæder lufige,

and swa swa he bebod me gesette, swa ic dó untwýlice.

Se Hælend us sǽde on þisum halgan godspelle

þæt 'se ðe me lufað, he hylt mine sprǽce.'   30

þære lufe fándung is þæs weorces fremming,

þæt is þæt God wile þa weorc habban æt ús,

þæt we mid gódum weorcum hine wurðian á,

na mid nacodum wórdum butan þære fremminge,

for ðan þe seo lufu sceall beon geswutelod mid dǽdum.   35

'And min Fæder hine lufað, and wit becumað to him,

and mid him wuniað witodlice begen.'

Gesælig bið se mann þe swilce cuman underféhð,

---

14 forlæta *U*.   15 swa.swa (swa) *corrected by regular scribe to* swa.swa
þes *U*. (*U has point before first* swa *at 127*.)   gifð] forgifð *N* (*cf. 127*).
19 blissedon *N*.   20 for ðan þe *U*.   21 is.mare *U*.   23 his] is *N*.
24 *entire line om. U*.   25 þisses *U*.   middaneardes] middan *N*.   ealder *N*.
28 untwylice *underscored N*.   29 ðyssum *U*.   31 lufu *N*.   is. þæs *U*.
32 wyle *U*.   34 nacedum *U*.   35 sceal *NU*.   geswutelad *U*.
36 wyt *N*.   38 swylce *U*.

22–28 [*29*] Et nunc dixi vobis prius quam fiat: ut cum factum fuerit, credatis.
[*30*] Iam non multa loquar vobiscum. Venit enim princeps mundi huius, et
in me non habet quidquam.
[*31*] Sed ut cognoscat mundus quia diligo Patrem, et sicut mandatum dedit
mihi Pater, sic facio.
31 [*Gregory, Hom. XXX in Ev.*] Probatio ergo dilectionis exhibitio est operis.
[*Haymo, Hom. C, echoes with adjectives*: veræ dilectionis, boni operis.]
38–40 [*Haymo*] Sed læto corde accipiendum est quod infertur: *Et mansionem
apud eum faciemus.* Ad quorumdam vero corda Deus venit, sed mansionem non
facit; quia eos per compunctionis gratiam visitat, sed cum hora compunctionis
transierit, et ad iniquitatem redeunt, Deum a corde suo repellunt. . . . Conside-

gif he mid unþeawum hí aweg *ne adrifð,   *f. 277ᵛ
ne mid sweartum synnum, swilce cuman him fram.   40
Ne hi ne cumað ná butan heora begra Lufu,
þæt is se Halga Gást, þe hi asendon begen
on þysum ylcan dæge ofer ða apostolas,
þæt Godes lufu wære wuniende mid heom,
for ðon þe hi on eorðan embe God þa sméadon,   45
and his willan gefremedon mid þæs weorces fremminge
on manegum wísum, on wundrum and tácnum,
þurh ðone ylcan Gást æfre gestrangode.
God syl[f] afándað ælces mannes heortan,
hwæðer se mann wylle his wununge habban,   50
oþþe leahtras lufian, þe Gode mislíciað;
and nán mann ne bið fram Gode forlæten,
buton he sylf forlǽte his lufe him ǽr fram,
and bið þonne his gylt þæt hine God swa forlǽt,
for ðan þe he ne rohte on his receleaste   55
Godes wununge on him, ne éac his *néosunge.   *f. 278

Se Hælend ús sæde on þysum soðum godspelle,
'Se ðe me ne lufað, ne hylt hé mine sprǽce.'
Ne bið seo lufu idel, gif heo God lufað,
ac wyrcð mihtilice micele þing æfre,   60
and gif heo wyrcan nele, nis heo þonne lufu.
Godes lufu sceal beon geswutelod on ús

39 adrifeð U.   40 swylce U.   him altered to hym (though sing.) U.
41 lufe U.   42 asændon U.   43 ðissum U.   ilcan U.   44 wunigende U.   45 for ðan þe NU.   god(e) N.   48 ilcan U.   49 sylf]
sic NU; sylfð M.   50 wille N.   51 mislicað U.   53 butan U.
54 forlætt U.   57 ðisum NU.   60 mihtiglice NU.   61 wyrcean U.

randum ergo summopere est quanto studio mansionem suæ mentis præparare
debet, qui tantum ac talem hospitem suscipere desiderat. [Derived from Gregory,
but in details closer to Ælfric.]
    41-43 [Haymo] Nisi Deus trinitas esset, nequaquam pluraliter diceret, Et ad
eum veniemus. Ubicumque enim venit Pater, venit Filius, venit Spiritus sanctus.
. . . Quia sicut ait Apostolus: Charitas Dei diffusa est in cordibus nostris per Spiritum sanctum, qui datus est nobis (Rom. v. 5).
    49-56 [Cf. the passage already cited for 38-40.]
    59-64 [Gregory] Nunquam est Dei amor otiosus. Operatur etenim magna, si
[verus amor] est; si vero operari renuit, amor non est. De dilectione conditoris,
lingua, mens, et vita requiratur. [The first two sentences are echoed, with some
elaboration, in Haymo. The third, which precedes the first two in Gregory, is not
in Haymo.]

on muðe and on móde and on þæs mannes lífe,
þæt he Godes spræce mid gódnysse gefylle.

'And seo spræc þe ge gehyrdon, nis heo na min spræc, 65
ac þæs ylcan Fæder þe me asende.'

Se Hælend, þe ðis spræc, is geháten Wórd,
of ðam Fæder acenned, and he syl[f] cwæð forðí
þæt seo spræc nære þe he þa spræc to him
his sylfes agen spræc, [ac] his Fæder spræc, 70
þonne he is þæs Fæder Wórd þe wið hi þa swá spræc;
and heom bám synd gemǽne, butan ælcere twéonunge,
ægðer ge wórd *ge weorc, and witodlice ealle þing.   *f. 278ᵛ

'Ic spræc þas ðing to eow mid eow nú wunigende.'

He wæs ða mid heom wunigende lichamlice, 75
and he heom fram férde swiðe fús to heofonum,
to his écan myrhðe, þe he ǽfre hæfde,
and he [w]unode swaðeah [witodlice mid him]
þurh his godcundnysse, and hí gewissode á.

'Se halga Frofergást, þe min Fæder asent 80
on minum naman eow, he eow tæcð ealle þing,
and eow ealle þing geswutelað, swa hwæt swa ic eow secge.'

Se Halga Gást is gehaten Paraclitus

---

66 ilcan *U.*   asænde *U.*   68 sylf] *sic NU*; sylfð *M.*   forðig *U.*
70 ac] *sic U*; ac is *MN.*   71 is] (h)is *N.*   75 *U has point after* wunigende,
not before.   76 swiðe fus *underscored U.*   78 wunode] *sic NU*; gewu-
node *M.*   witodlice mid him] *sic NU* (him *changed to* hym *U*); mid heom
witodlice *M.*   79 hi] hy *N*; he'o' *U.*   a] *om. U.*   80 asænt *U.*

67–71 [*Gregory*] Scitis, fratres charissimi, quia ipse qui loquitur, unigenitus
Filius, Verbum Patris est, et ideo sermo quem loquitur Filius non est Filii, sed
Patris, quia ipse Filius Verbum est Patris. [*Haymo has same idea but is influenced by Augustine's more complicated exposition, In Ioan. Ev. Tract. LXXVI.*]
72 sq. [*Not explicit in Ælfric's sources.*]

75–79 [*Haymo*] Nunquid non erat mansurus cum discipulis, quibus alibi
promisit, dicens: *Ecce ego vobiscum sum omnibus diebus usque ad consummationem
sæculi* (*Matth. xxviii. 20*)? Erat utique, sed [cum] ait: *Hæc locutus sum vobis,
apud vos manens,* de præsentia corporali dicit, per quam post modicum ab eis
recessurus erat. . . . Qui ergo in articulo passionis hæc loquebatur, mansurus cum
eis semper per divinitatem, recessurus loquitur per humanitatem. [*Restated from
Gregory, seemingly a little closer to Ælfric.*]

83–86 [*Haymo*] Patet profecto . . . quare eumdem Spiritum Paracletum nomi-
net: παράκλητος Græca locutione, Latine *consolator* sive *advocatus* dicitur. Bene
consolator dicitur, quia mentes fidelium, ne inter adversa huius sæculi deficiant,
spe cælestium consolatur præmiorum. [*Gregory has same definition; his comment
on* consolator *seems at least equally pertinent:*] Consolator autem idem Spiritus
vocatur, quia de peccati perpetratione moerentibus, dum spem veniæ præparat,
ab afflictione tristitiæ mentem levat.

on Grɛciscre spræce, and on Leden Consolator,
þæt is Fréfrigend on Englisc, for ðan þe he gefréfrað   85
þæra manna heortan þe heora synna behreowsiað,
and he sylf gedeþ ealra synna forgifennysse
on eallum middanearde, þurh his micclan gife,
*and hé gegladað ælcne þe on Gode truwað,   *f. 279
and ealle þa englas þe eardiað on heofenum   90
he éndemes gegladað to Godes lufe ǽfre,
for ðan þe he sylf is soðlice Godes lufu,
þæs Fæder and þæs Suna, him symle gemǽne,
of him bám ǽfre, anes gecýndes.

He wearð asend þá, swa swa se Hælend sǽde,   95
fram ðam halgan Fæder, and fram his Suna éac,
on fýres gelicnysse swiðe hlúde swégende
ufan of heofenan ofer ða apostolas
on þysum ylcan dæge on ánre upflóra;
on ðam húse wæron hundtwelftig manna ðá,   100
þæs Hælendes folgeras, þe him folgodon on lífe;
on þam wæs þæt anginn ealles Cristendomes,
and hí eallne middaneard, þurh ða micclan gife
þæs Halgan Gástes, to Gode gebigdon.

We habbað gesǽd swutellicor be þisum   105
on þam *oðrum spelle þe hér tó gebyrað,   *f. 279ᵛ
on þam man mæg gehyran be þam Halgan Gáste,
se ðe hit rǽdan wyle, oþþe rǽdan gehyrð.

Buton se Halga Gást nú eowre heortan onlihte
mid his gástlican gife, ne gáð ure wórd aht   110

---

85 frefriend *NU.*   89 *U has point before* ælcne, *not after.*   90 heofonum *NU.*   91 lufu *N.*   92 lufe *N.*   93 sunu *N.*   symble *U.*
95 asænd *U.*   98 heofonan *N;* heofonum *U.*   99 upflore *altered to*
upflora *U.*   100 *U has point after* manna *instead of* ða.   101 folgedon
NU.   103 ealne *NU.*   gifu *U.*   105 swutelicor *NU.* (swutelic-
regularly both MSS.)   þysum *N;* ðyssum *U.*   106 gebyreð *U.*   108 wile
N.   109 halga] haga *N.*   onlyhte *N.*   110 gæð *U.*   (n)aht *U* (?).

87–94 [*Largely independent of Gregory and Haymo.*]
95–108 [*Independent of Gregory and Haymo. For 97–99 cf. Act. ii. 1–4; and
for 100, Act. i. 15.*]
109–15 [*Haymo, restating Gregory*] Et recte Spiritus sanctus omnia docere
dicitur, quia in vacuum laborat sermo doctoris exterius, nisi interius sit Spiritus
sanctus, qui illustret cor auditoris. [*Gregory*] Ecce unam loquentis vocem omnes
pariter auditis, nec tamen pariter sensum auditæ vocis percipitis.

innto eowre heortan, eow to onbryrdnysse,
ne to nánre beterunge butan his gife.

Ealle ge gehýraÞ þas ane rǽdinge,
and swaðeah butan twýn ne beoÞ ealle eowre mód
gelíce onlihte þurh Þas láre éndemes,   115
for Þan þe se Halga Gást þurh his godcundnysse
his gife eow forgifÞ be þam þe he wyle;
he is ælmihtig God, and he ealle þing gehylt
mid þam Fæder and þam Suna, on anre godcundnysse.

Se Hælend þa sǽde his apostolum þus: 120
'Ic forlǽte eow sibbe, and mine sibbe eow sylle.'
Sibbe he forgeaf symle his apostolum,
and sibbe he lufaÞ on geleaf*fullum mannum,   * f. 280
mid soÞfæstnysse, á butan swicdome.

He forlét hi on sibbe, and heom syÞÞan forgeaf   125
his þa écan sibbe on his rice mid him.

'Ne forgife ic eow swa swa Þes middaneard forgifÞ.'
Þes middaneard forgifÞ þa gewítendlican þing,
and he forgifÞ þa écan þam þe hine lufiaÞ.

'Ne beo eower heorte gedréfed, ne ne forhtig[e] nateshwón.
Se Hælend hi gefréfrode mid his fægerum wordum,   131
nolde þæt hi wurdon wiðinnan gedréfede

---

111 into NU.   115 Þas] his N.   U has point after lare instead of
endemes (N has point after endemes).   117 gifu U.   wile N.   121 first
sibbe] on sibbe N.   sille N.   122 Sybbe N.   simble U.   124 U has
points before and after á   125 forlæt U.   127 U has point before swa swa
(cf. 15).   forgifÞ] gifÞ NU (cf. 15).   130 forhtige] sic NU; forhtige ge M
(cf. 16).

---

117 [Cf. I Cor. xii. 11:] Hæc autem omnia operatur unus atque idem Spiritus,
dividens singulis prout vult.

122-6 [Gregory] Hic relinquo, illic do. Sequentibus relinquo, pervenientibus
do. [Haymo] Ac si diceret: Do præsentibus, relinquo futuris. Sive inchoantibus
relinquo, perseverantibus do. Et quia perfectior erit pax in futuro quam in
præsenti, bene cum additamento dixit: Pacem meam do vobis. [Ælfric seems to
base his own simpler and clearer explanation on these suggestions. Gregory's exposition of the gospel does not proceed beyond this point.]

128 sq. [Not in Haymo, nor in Augustine.]

131-8 [Perhaps vaguely suggested by Haymo:] Sed hunc eorum dolorem
benigne pius magister consolatur, cum dicit: Non turbetur cor vestrum neque
formidet pro eo quod dixi: vado et venio ad vos. Si enim contristatur quis quia
ego vado, lætificari debet quia venio, iuxta illud quod alibi dicit: Non turbetur
cor vestrum: Creditis in Deum, et in me credite. . . . Quia si abiero et præparavero
vobis locum, iterum veniam et accipiam vos ad meipsum, ut ubi sum ego, et vos sitis
(Ioan. xiv. 1, 3).

for his fúndunge þá and his fær to heofenum,
and he heom þus sæde, swa swa ðis godspell ús segð:
'Ge gehyrdon þæt ic sæde soðlice nú eow   135
þæt ic sylf nú fare, and ic cume to eow.'
For ðan þe he ða férde, and he gefette hi eft
to þære écan blisse, swa swa he heom behét.

'Gif ge me lufedon, ge witodlice blissodon,
for ðan *þe ic fare to minum Fæder nú,   *f. 280ᵛ
for ðan þe se Fæder is máre þonne ic sý.'   141
Hí lufodon hine ealle, and swaðeah forhtodon,
for ðan þe he swa fús wæs fram heom þá to heofonum,
ac hi mihton blissian on móde þæs ðe swiðor,
þæt he to wuldre férde of ðisum gewinnum,   145
and þæt hi sylfe moston syððan him fylian.
On þære menniscnysse is se Fæder máre,
and be þære he spræc swá ǽr his ðrówunge,
ǽr ðan þe he sylf wæs gewuldrod mid his ǽriste,
and swa is gecweden be Cristes menniscnysse.   150
Be þam ðe he soð God is, he wæs symle acenned
of ðam ælmihtigan Fæder, eal swa mihtig swa he,
for ðam þe se Ælmihtiga ne mæg beon na læsse;
be þam þe he mann wæs, he wæs of Marian acenned;

133 heofonum *NU.*   135 *U has point after* gehyrdon, *none after* sæde.
137 eft] *om. U.*   140 nu to minum fæder *N. U has point after* fæder *instead
of* nu.   142 lufedon *NU.*   143 *U has point after* þa *instead of* wæs.
144 blission *N. U has point after* mode *instead of* blissian.   149 *U has point
after* gewuldrod *instead of* wæs.   150 menisc- *N.*   151 symble *U.*
153 for ðan þe *U.*   læssa *U (see note).*

142–6 [*Haymo*: *cf. the passage just quoted and the following*:] Inde turbari et
formidari poterant, quod quem totis visceribus diligebant a se recessurum
audiebant. . . . Non negat se a discipulis diligi, sed eorum fragilitati conde-
scendens, illorum mentes humanas ad amorem divinum præparat.

147–50 [*Haymo*] Altera est natura divinitatis, et altera humanitatis. . . . In
natura humanitatis, qua minoratus est paulo minus ab angelis, minor esse creditur Patre, per quam loquitur: *Quia vado ad Patrem, quia Pater maior me est.*

151–8 [*Haymo*] In natura quoque divinitatis non a Deo factus, sed ex Deo
creditur natus, Deus de Deo, lumen de lumine, coæternus et consubstantialis
Patri. [*Augustine, In Ioan. Ev. Tract. LXXVIII*] Agnoscamus geminam sub-
stantiam Christi: divinam scilicet qua æqualis est Patri, humanam qua maior
est Pater. . . . Quis est ergo per quem factus est mundus? Christus Iesus, sed in
forma Dei. Quis est sub Pontio Pilato crucifixus? Christus Iesus, sed in forma
servi. Item de singulis [anima et carne] quibus homo constat. Quis non est de-
relictus in inferno? Christus Iesus, sed in anima sola. Quis resurrecturus triduo
iacuit in sepulcro? Christus Iesus, sed in carne sola.

be þam þe he lichama wæs, he læg bebyrged;   155
on þam ðe he déad wæs, *he arás of deaþe,   *f. 281
þæt is on ðam menn, þe mihte béon déad,
for ðan þe his godcundlice miht ne mihte beon déad.

Arrius hatte iú sum healic gedwola,
se wolde lytlian þone leofan Hælend,   160
þæt he únmihtigre wære on his mægenþrymme
þonne se halga Fæder wæs on his godcundnysse;
ac þam gedwolan becóm, for his micclum gedwýlde,
swyðe bysmorlic deað, swa swa béc us secgað,
swa þæt him aéode út eall his innoð togædere   165
þa ða he to gange éode, and he swa earmlice swéalt,
swa æmtig on innoðe swa swa his geleafa wæs,
[for ðan] þe he wolde wanian on his gewitleaste
þæs Hælendes mihte, þe ne mæg beon gewanod.

Olimpius wæs geháten sum oðer gedwola,   170
se sæt him on bæðe, and hé ungesæliglice
spræc mid gedwylde, for ðan þe he gedwola *wæs,   *f. 281ᵛ
hæfde him to hospe þa halgan Ðrynnysse,
ac him cóm fýr to færlice ehsynes,
and forbærnde his líc eall on þam baþe to colum,   175
þæt he mihte witan hwæne he tælde.

We sceolon gelyfan on þone lyfigendan Hælend,
þæt he ælmihtig God is æfre mid þam Fæder,
and mid þam Halgan Gáste, on ánre godcundnysse;
seo godcundnys ne mæg næfre beon gelytlod.   180

---

155 bebyriged *N.*   159 gedweola *U* (*similarly* eo *for* o *163, 170, 172*).
162 wæs] *om.,* wære *after* godcundnyse [*sic*] *N.*   163 gedwilde *N.*
164 swiðe *NU.*   bismorlic *NU.*   166 sweolt *N.*   167 emtig (*altered
from* æmtig?) *U.*   168 for ðan þe] *sic NU;* þe *M.*   wunian *altered to*
wanian *U.*   171 ungesælilice *U.*   174 fyr to] to fyr *U.*   eahsynes *N.*
176 hwæne] hæne *N.*   177 gelufan *N.*   lifigendan *N.*   180 godcundnys]
godnys *U.*   glytlod *N;* gelytlad *U.*

159–69 [*Haymo, on preceding verse*] *Quia Pater maior me est.* Quam sententiam
male Arius interpretatur, qui ausus est dicere Filium Dei in divinitate minorem
esse Patre, . . . infelix. . . . [*For Ælfric's other treatments of the death of Arius and
for his jibe in 167, see the introductory comment; for his tone, cf. Augustine, loc. cit.,
on the same verse:*] Hoc attendat Arianus, et attentione sit sanus: ne contentione
sit vanus, aut, quod est peius, insanus.

170–6 [*Isidore, Chronicon, 113*] [*5714*] Anastasius regnat annis xxvii. . . .
Per idem tempus apud Carthaginem Olymp[i]us quidam Arianus, in balneis
sanctam Trinitatem blasphemans, tribus igneis iaculis, angelo immittente,
visibiliter est combustus.

Ðis godspell segð gít forð þæt se Hælend sæde ða,
'And nu ic hit eow secge ær ðan þe hit gewurðe,
þæt ge þonne his gelýfon þonne hit gedón byð.'
þis is swutellice gesæd, and he sæde forð gít,
'Ne sprece ic na fela þing heonon forð to eow,'   185
for ðan þe he þæs on merien for mancynne ðrówode,
and ne spræc na leng on þam lífe wið hí.
'Ðises middaneardes ealdor to me sylfum becóm,
and he nán ðing *næfð eallunga on mé.'   *f. 282
þæt wæs se sylfa deofol, þe on ðam synfullum rixað,   190
and is yfel ealdor árleasra manna,
se cóm to þam Hælende, cunnode gif he mihte
ænige synne oþþe sumne gylt
on Criste afíndan, ac he ne fúnde nán þing,
swa swa se Hælend her him sylf sæde   195
nú on þisum godspelle þe ge gehyrdon nú.
Se deofol þa forléas þæt he gelæht hæfde
to his anwealde æror of Adames cynne,
eall þæt on God gelyfde, and hi alysde Crist,
se ðe butan synnum únscyldig þrówode,   200
and he sigefæst swa siðode heonon
mid þam hereréafe þe he on helle gefette,
ealle his gecorenan of Adames cynne.
Se hælend cwæð þa gýt on þises godspelles énde,
'Ac oncnáwe þes middaneard þæt ic minne Fæder lufige,   205

181 git altered to get U.   U has point after hælend instead of ða.
182 hit eow secge] eow secge hit N.   183 gelyfan U.   bið NU.
185 þinga U.   heonan U.   186 mergen N; merigen U.   188 þisses U.
190 sylfa] yfela U.   ricxað U.   195 U has point after nu (196), not sæde.
196 ðissum U.   199 hi] hy N; he U.   200 unsyldig N.   201 heonan U.
202–3 gefette, ealle om. U.   204 git U.   ðisses U.

186 sq. [Haymo] Iam non multa loquar vobiscum, de corporali locutione dicit.
Nam in articulo passionis discipulis hæc loquens, pauca corporaliter erat eis
locuturus.
190–203 [Aug. LXXIX] Venit enim princeps mundi huius: quis, nisi diabolus?
Et in me non habet quidquam: nullum scilicet omnino peccatum. Sic enim ostendit
non creaturarum, sed peccatorum [later called hominum impiorum], principem
diabolum, quos nunc nomine mundi huius appellat. [Haymo] Iste ergo princeps
mundi ad Dominum venit, quando eum quasi hominem mori conspiciens, eius
animam sicut cæteras, quas per originale peccatum tenebat, se rapere posse
æstimavit. Sed in eo non reperit quidquam. . . . Inde ergo potestatem, quam in
cæteris retinebat, amisit, quo gladium suæ percussionis contra eum in quo nihil
invenit exacuit. [Augustine names Adam but is otherwise less close to Ælfric. The
specific allusion to the harrowing of hell in 201–3 is not in Augustine or Haymo.]

and swa swa hé bebod me gesette, *swa ic dó úntwylice.'   *f. 282ᵛ
On þam we magon tocnáwan þæt Crist lufode his Fæder,
on þam þe he wæs gehyrsum his Fæder oþ deað,
and be his bebode he ús swa alysde,
sylfwilles swaðeah; þam sy á wuldor   210
mid þam Halgan Gáste on ecnysse, AMEN.

206 he] *om. N.*   bebod me gesette] bebead. and me gesette *U.*   210 si *N.*

207–10 [*Haymo*] Spontanee passionem sustinuit, ut et Patris obedientiam impleret, et nos a mortis interitu liberaret. Quod ergo ait: *Sed ut cognoscat mundus
quia diligo Patrem*, tale est ac si diceret: . . . in hoc me ostendo Patrem diligere,
qui cum possim mortem vitare, pro eius amore mortem subire non differo,
quoniam non veni voluntatem meam facere.

NOTES

4–7. Cf. the translation of part of the same text (*Ioan.* xiv. 23 and half
of 24) in Ælfric's homily for Monday in Rogation Week, *CH* II. 314/24–
26, and 316/14–15, which I arrange in metrical lines:

> Se ðe me lufað, he hylt min bebod,
> and min Fæder hine lufað for ðære hyrsumnysse;
> and wit cumað him to, and him mid wuniað. . . .
> Se ðe me ne lufað, ne hylt he mine word.

31. *Þære lufe fandung is þæs weorces fremming.* Exactly the same words
occur in the homily cited above, *CH* II. 314/28 sq. That they are there,
as here, a direct translation from Gregory's thirtieth homily on the gospel
is clear from some of the succeeding lines, especially p. 316/7–11:

> Menn dæftað heora hus, and wel gedreoglæcað,
> gif hi sumne freond onfon willað to him,
> þæt nan unðæslicnys him ne ðurfe derian;
> and we sceolon us clænsian fram unclænum dædum,
> þæt se mihtiga God on urum mode wunige.

Cf. Gregory (Migne, *PL* LXXVI. 1220 sq.):

> Certe si domum vestram quisquam dives ac præpotens amicus intraret,
> omni festinantia domus tota mundaretur, ne quid fortasse esset quod
> oculos amici intrantis offenderet. Tergat ergo sordes pravi operis, qui
> Deo præparat domum mentis.

Max Förster, in *Anglia* XVI. 58, listed this homily as one for which he
had found, and expected to find, no source. Very likely he was right with
respect to the homily as a whole, which looks like a collation put together
independently of any one source. But it certainly has sources: among them
Gregory, as has just been shown, and a little further on (at p. 318/32 sqq.)
De Duodecim Abusivis, as I have said in the introductory comment on
homily IX, p. 374 above.

49-56. This passage, though more elaborate, is similar in sentiment to a passage in the homily cited above, *CH* II. 316/11–13:

> se [*sc.* God] ðe ænne gehwilcne þurh his Gast geneosað,
> and ða fulan forlæt for heora fracodnysse,
> leohtes bedælede, for ðan ðe hi ne lufiað hine.

59–64. In this passage Ælfric follows Gregory more extensively than he had done in the earlier homily cited above, where only a little of his comment (*CH* II, 316/15 sq.) corresponds:

> Godes lufu geswutelað hi sylfe mid weorcum,
> and gif heo ydel bið, nis heo ðonne lufu.

The first of these lines is partially echoed by line 35 in our homily.

106. *on þam oðrum spelle.* That is, in the homily for Pentecost at *CH* I. 310 sqq. The coming of the Holy Spirit to the apostles is described on p. 314.

153. *læsse.* MS. U has here the correct masculine form *læssa*, but the *læsse* of M and N has been allowed to stand in view of the similar instances at lines 21, 141, 147, and 161, where all manuscripts have final -*e*. A similar tendency is already apparent in Thorpe's MS. of *CH*, our K. See, for example, *CH* I. 282/34–284/6, where in seven printed lines there are four comparatives in -*e* and one in -*a* as predicate modifiers of the deity, besides one in -*e* as modifier of the neuter *hwæt*. Evidently there was a strong tendency in late West Saxon to level the comparative to -*e* in all genders of the nominative singular, at least when it stood alone as a predicate adjective. I can make no pronouncement on Ælfric's own practice, for although the *Grammar* (Zupitza, p. 46) seems to maintain the old distinction, the examples are not predicate adjectives.

SERMO AD POPULUM, IN
OCTAVIS PENTECOSTEN DICENDUS

ONE of the reasons for the distinctive title of this homily is doubtless that it does not expound a pericope for the day, as do the other
homilies of the Temporale here edited, numbers I–X and XII–XVII.
Instead it presents two subjects on which a lay congregation in
particular might not be adequately informed. At the beginning it
surveys the principal events commemorated by the church
between Christmas and Pentecost, carrying the story from Christ's
nativity to his crucifixion, resurrection, ascension, and, finally, his
sending of the Holy Spirit to the apostles. But this half-lyrical
summary, which ends (as it should for the Sunday after Pentecost)
with a brief celebration of the Trinity, fills less than a fifth of the
total space. All the rest of the homily is devoted to what is in store
for men after death, both now and at the end of the world. Ælfric
thus spells out the consequences for man of the Christian story he
has outlined at the beginning. In doing so he also develops the
theme of Christ's Second Coming at the Judgement with which the
story is at last to be concluded.

For this major section of the homily I have been able to present
a Latin source much closer than usual. The credit for discovering
it belongs to Miss Enid M. Raynes, who very generously communicated to me in advance the substance of her illuminating
article, 'MS. Boulogne-sur-Mer 63 and Ælfric', *Medium Ævum*
XXVI (1957), 65–73. In this article she points out, among other
features that establish a close connexion between the Boulogne
MS. and Ælfric, that the first item in the volume, ff. 1–10, is the
direct source of nearly everything in the present homily from line
94 to the end.

Miss Raynes distinguishes between the first part of the Boulogne
MS., ff. 1–34, and the second, ff. 35–86. Both parts are entirely
in Latin. The second part, containing four pieces attributed to
St. Augustine, exhibits a style of writing that should belong to the
late tenth or early eleventh century. The style of the first part looks

a little later, though still to be dated, presumably, in the first half of the eleventh century. Both parts contain features of English as opposed to continental script, but they need not always have formed a single volume, and it is the first part only of which the content shows signs of being associated with Ælfric and Archbishop Wulfstan. The manuscript was described and some of these signs were pointed out by Bernhard Fehr in his introduction to *Die Hirtenbriefe Ælfrics*, pp. x–xiv. Others have now been added by Miss Raynes, who suggests that the first part of the manuscript is a copy of one 'which Ælfric kept for his personal use and in which he entered Latin sermons for translation and other items of interest'. This suggestion is supported by several of the items in the miscellany, of which the first three are the most important. The second, ff. 10–13, is a uniquely preserved copy of a Latin letter from Ælfric to Wulfstan, printed by Fehr as *Brief* 2a, pp. 222–7. The third, ff. 13–18, is a Latin version of Ælfric's nativity sermon in the *Lives of Saints*, no. 1. Both Miss Raynes and Mr. Neil Ker (*Catalogue*, no. 162, 4) have suggested that this Latin sermon, which corresponds to its Old English counterpart very exactly at many points, was composed by Ælfric himself. I am inclined to agree with them, but for reasons set forth in the Introduction (p. 4) think it best to reserve judgement. But it is the first item, hardly less significant in its way, with which we are here concerned.

This first item, ff. 1–10, is headed, *Hunc sermonem ex multis excerpsimus de libro qui dicitur Pronosticon. In Christi nomine*. Miss Raynes has described it accurately as 'an unpublished series of excerpts, mainly taken from *Prognosticon Futuri Sæculi* by Julian, Archbishop of Toledo (680-90), with some passages from other sources'. The three books of Julian's work, on death, the life of the soul between the death of the body and the resurrection, and the life of soul and body that begins with the resurrection and the day of judgement, are designed to answer most of the questions that can be asked about these matters. The work is a thoughtful compilation from several earlier authorities, of whom Augustine is the most conspicuous. There are many passages from Julianus Pomerius, several from Gregory the Great, and in the first book a number, conspicuously eloquent, from Cyprian. Migne's edition of the *Prognosticon*, *PL* xcvi. 461–524, gives very helpful notices of Julian's sources.

The author of the excerpts in the Boulogne MS. has followed the principal themes of Julian in nearly their original order, but there are occasional dislocations of sentences that cause trouble for anyone who tries to identify them in the original. Apparently the excerptor would sometimes pass over something only to be reminded of it sharply a little later and bring it in at a new place. Sometimes he deliberately rearranged a passage, or substituted his own words, usually by way of abridgement, for the original, but on the whole he copied what lay before him. On rare occasions he seems to have added something pertinent from another source. I think it could be shown that several of these small additions are of a sort that Ælfric himself would have been likely to make. He was almost certainly the excerptor, and in attending to the differences between Julian's original, the Latin excerpts, and the Old English homily we can observe an intelligible progression.[1] What one notices in the excerpts is chiefly the construction of an orderly digest. In the English homily the process of adaption is carried much further. Even though this is one of Ælfric's longest sermons, it omits large passages of the excerpts, keeping for the most part to the things that come closest to the concerns of a relatively simple congregation. But at the same time there is expansion at precisely the points where such a congregation might be profitably instructed or inspired. Most notably Ælfric has turned directly to the Bible to repeat in all its detail the address of the Lord to the righteous and the sinful from *Matthew* xxv.

In quoting sources I have tried to indicate the relation of the excerpts in the Boulogne MS. to Julian's *Prognosticon* as it appears in *PL* xcvi by referring to both whenever they correspond; but in these instances the basis of the text of the quotation is the Boulogne MS.[2] I have ordinarily followed the spelling of the manuscript, but I have printed the consonantal *u* as *v*, and although I have preserved the spelling *e* for earlier *æ* I have altered *ae*, which sometimes appears, to the digraph *æ*. The punctuation is modernized, though seldom radically altered.

No source has been indicated for the introductory section on the

---

[1] Not that the excerpts were made expressly for the homily. They had already served, apparently, as incidental sources for homilies in the First and Second Series. See Milton M. Gatch's article, *JEGP*, LXV (1966), 482–90, and my notes on lines 153–9 and 305–38.

[2] I wish to thank the librarian of the Bibliothèque publique at Boulogne-sur-Mer for permitting me to make use of photostats of the excerpts.

liturgy, lines 1–93. I have not come upon any direct source and am inclined to suppose that Ælfric was here writing freely on the basis of themes long familiar to him.

Homily XI is unusually well represented in the surviving manuscripts, with six complete copies (in Q, R, T, U, V, and C), one fragment (f^b), and one long excerpt (M). No doubt the broad human interest of the piece is partly responsible, but we must also reckon with the fact that, unlike most of Ælfric's later additions to the Temporale, it was included in the enlarged edition of the First Series represented by Q as well as in the late Temporale represented by U. It was not, on the other hand, in the earlier Temporale represented by M, for the excerpt in M occurs in the erratic Rogationtide section and its textual affinity, as explained below, is probably with the RT pair. Since the copy in the variously derived C is textually allied with U and V, and the homilies in f^b, though it has no revealing readings for XI, are generally of a late type textually, we may assume that this homily was composed at some time after the issue of M's ancestral set (perhaps 1002 or 1003), and probably not long before Ælfric's release of the set marked by Q. It may very well have been issued for the first time in that set.[1] The liturgical review at the beginning is entirely appropriate to the revised First Series, for the holy occasions noted are Christmas, Epiphany, Candlemas, Lent, Passiontide, Easter, Ascension, Pentecost, and the octave of Pentecost. All these occasions except the last are treated in homilies that were in the First Series as originally constituted, and the last is now marked by this added homily.

The relationship of the various manuscripts is not entirely clear, but five of them form two subordinate groups that can readily be distinguished. As I have explained in the Introduction, there are reasons for supposing that R served as the exemplar for several of the Ælfric homilies in T. The three closely associated volumes of T (Junius 121, Hatton 113 and 114) were written at Worcester in the second half of the eleventh century. The somewhat earlier R, though it was probably written elsewhere, was at Worcester

---

[1] Separate publication (as suggested by Clemoes, *Chronology*, 230) is not impossible, but it is not indicated by the evidence of the manuscripts, nor by the title *Sermo*, which occurs in K's titles for the *Catholic Homilies* four times (I. 1, 11; II. 111, xv), each time applied to a general discourse not dependent on a pericope. Ælfric may of course have had more than one reason for calling a piece *Sermo*.

soon after the middle of the century. Our homily XI, as it stands in Hatton 113, not only has a great many small deviations that it shares with R in opposition to the other manuscripts,[1] but at certain points it has strong indications of being a direct copy of R. Thus at lines 72, 74, 240, and 518, where the original reading of R agrees with all the manuscripts except T, it has received contemporary additions above the line, and these same additions are incorporated in the text of T. One might hesitate to accept this as proof of direct copying, since it would seem at first sight that R might have been 'corrected' by comparison with T or the exemplar of T. But I cannot find any good reason to introduce this added complication, and the correction of R by comparison with T itself is certainly out of the question. For on several occasions T has unsatisfactory readings corresponding to R and then corrects them (125, 168, 265, 475, 518, 560). If R had been corrected from T one would expect to find these corrections. Moreover, there is nothing in the text of T to indicate an exemplar other than R. The scribe of T corrects a few obvious blunders in spelling and often prefers his own system of spelling, but in every other respect he has produced what looks like a direct copy. For corroborative details from other homilies see the Introduction, p. 76.

The other group consists of three manuscripts, the nearly contemporary U and V and the much later C. The three share omissions at 69–70 and 436, minor substitutions at 361 and 436, variant forms at 17, 235, 333, 370, 465, and 505. A small omission at 324 is shared by C and U where V has omitted the entire passage. U and V share substitutions apart from C at 408 and 527. The evidence for the pairing of these two is much slighter than for R and T, but their near relation is supported by small agreements in spelling and corroborated in other homilies, as I have explained in the description of V (Introduction, p. 82). The somewhat more distant connexion of the variously derived C makes no difficulty.[2] There is reason to associate U and C with the south-east, and I

---

[1] e.g. substitutions at 43, 169, 274, 325, 363, 407, 427; omissions at 69, 98, 120, 176, 188, 318, 564; added words or parts of words at 6, 31, 66, 94 (twice), 241, 284, 537; transpositions at 176, 180, 413, 431, 494–5 (clauses transposed), 515. There are a few more trivial correspondences, such as omission or addition of *ge-* and change of numbers or inflexion: 102, 213, 297, 396.

[2] At line 24 C and U share an error not in V (*ænlicum* for *ælicum*), but in U the error, a very obvious one, is corrected by erasure and we must suppose that V (unless it was actually copied from U, which is doubtful) made the correction independently.

have argued in the Introduction that the earlier part of V, with which we are here concerned, was produced in the same region.

That U and the early quires of V were in close proximity shortly after they were written is suggested by a curious correspondence at 196. In U a corrector has added in the margin, to follow the verb *geandettan*, the words *his scriftan*. In V another corrector has added, above the line, *his scrifte*. Perhaps this correspondence is mere coincidence, but the script of the corrector of U is surprisingly similar in style to that of the main scribe of V. They are not, I believe, the same, but they look like products of the same scriptorium at the same period.

One would expect Q to represent one issue of the homily and U another; but U's deviations from Q do not look like the author's revisions and it is probable that Ælfric made no changes in his basic text, whatever small deviations may have occurred inadvertently in the copies that left his hands. The omission, at 69–70, of the reference to an earlier treatment of the gifts of the Holy Spirit (that is, in the first homily for Pentecost, *CH* I. xxii, as I have explained on p. 392 above) is certainly not Ælfric's, and probably not even deliberate, for it is untidily made: 71 should have been omitted also. Very likely a scribe's eye skipped from *mannum* at 68 to *mannum* at 70.

Q, written earlier than the rest and more nearly correct, stands somewhat apart. Once, at 79, it has the right reading where all the rest have introduced a plausible but on second thoughts clearly erroneous *and*.[1] It has a few errors of its own (at 120, 313, 449, 466, 554) but is not united in error with any other manuscript except, probably, in the title (where Q and V must have made the same omission independently) and in one other place where the correspondence is puzzling. At 193 a demonstrative *þa* which is not strictly necessary but is rhetorically useful and is supported by parallel instances at 186 and 188 is present in M as well as CUV but omitted in Q and RT. It would not be surprising if such a trifling omission had already been made in the fair copy of the revised First Series from which both Q and R, though by different lines, are presumably descended; but in that case it is hard to see why M has the correct reading; for M, at a few points, shows a

---

[1] Apparently more than one scribe was misled. Actually Q is supported by the original reading of M (to which *and* is added) and by H in the corresponding part of xia (195).

connexion with RT that is closer than Q's. This peculiarity of M is yet to be set forth. Meanwhile I conclude that Q and R have omitted *þa* independently, or, more probably, that M, which has signs of being an intelligently written though not always faithful text, has restored *þa* by the analogy of the parallels I have mentioned. At one point, finally, line 210, Q shares with all the other manuscripts a deficiency that must go back to Ælfric himself or a basic copy.

The association of M with RT is difficult to gauge. At 159 Q and CUV have the unusual reading *hæftnyssum*, M and RT the ordinary and acceptable *ehtnyssum*. I have explained in the note on the line my reasons for believing that Ælfric's choice here was *hæftnyssum*. If I am right, then M and RT have an unauthorized reading in common, and since it does not seem probable that they have arrived at this substitution independently, we may suppose that they had a common, already divergent ancestor. I know of no reason why this should not be so, for although the main part of M is textually remote from R, M's extract from XI belongs to the unreliable Rogationtide section and is embedded in a homily that is partly non-Ælfrician. Perhaps the compilation was not made till after Ælfric's death, when any one of the lines of descent from his original might have supplied an exemplar. But at other points in XI M's relations are not clearly indicated. M and RT show the expected agreement in some inconsequential variants at 319 and 409; but at 151, 370, and 420 R had at first the same reading as Q and changed it to a reading in which M and T concur. Since M is too early a manuscript to have inherited a change made first in R, we must suppose that these particular changes were made independently by someone responsible for the excerpt in M and by the corrector of R. This is likely enough if we consider the nature of the variants. The addition of *he* at 151, though ill-advised, is plausible, and was introduced also (again independently, it seems) by the corrector of C. (In C and M, but not in R, and differently in T, the consequences of the first change are recognized and induce a second.) Again, substitution of the indicative for the subjunctive at 370 and elimination of a usefully correlative but not indispensable *oððe* at 420 are 'improvements' that might occur to anyone. The variants exhibited by M at 139, 141, 144, 161, 172, 174, 220, 232, 246, 259 (indicative for subjunctive), 261, 328–31, 335, 349, 361, 375, 377, 384, 391, 392, 395, 404, 407, 409, 426, 429,

443, 454 show a strong tendency toward editorial revision such as
we might expect of a compiler, and it is likely enough that such
a man would occasionally hit on the same change as someone else.[1]
Hence I do not regard these instances where M seems closer to T
than to R as indicative of the lines of descent, any more than the
one instance previously discussed where (at 193) M agrees in a
correct reading with CUV and thus seems to put Q with RT in
a group that excludes M. Very tentatively I suggest the following
diagram, where 'A. Text 1' and 'A. Text 2' represent successive,
though probably not intentionally altered, issues of an authorized
text of the homily.

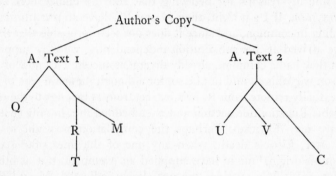

The fragment, f^b, cannot be placed.

The two Worcester manuscripts, R and T, have corrections and
glosses in later hands.[2] The many Latin and the few vernacular
glosses are printed separately in the apparatus. Most of them are
in the well-known 'tremulous' hand of a glossator at Worcester
in the early thirteenth century. I have called attention to a few
that are in a similar but firmer hand, perhaps the same man's at
an earlier period, and to a few others in markedly different hands.

The few vernacular glosses of U and C (late Old or early Middle
English) are included with the others. Those in U are in hands
of a rather early style (1100–1150?), and are meant as substitutions, for Ælfric's words are marked for deletion. The four
glosses in C are in a twelfth century hand (c. 1150?), somewhat
like that of the main text.

---

[1] A reviser of U has made comparable changes at 220, 328–31 (less thoroughly),
349, 384, 392, 395.
[2] On the systematic revisions of spelling in the Worcester MSS. (not here
reported) and the Worcester glosses, see the Introduction, pp. 185–7.

SERMO AD POPULUM IN

OCTAUIS PENTECOSTEN [DICENDUS]

Wé wyllað eow secgan sume swutelunge nú
be þam halgum tídum ðe we héaldað and weorðiað
on geléaffullum cyrcum mid Godes lofsangum,
þæt ge sum andgit þæron tocnawan magon,
hú eall ðæs geares ymbegang Gode Ælmihtigum ðeowað.   5
Ærest wé worðiað ón Middewintres Dæge
ures Hælendes acennednysse,

Text based on Q (CCCC 188), pp. 215–33. Collated with R (CCCC 178), pp.
54–73; T (Hatton 113), ff. 102ᵛ–15ᵛ; U (Trinity B. 15. 34), pp. 249–81; V
(CCCC 421), pp. 99–150; C (CCCC 303), pp. 203–11; M (ULC Ii. 4. 6), ff.
217ᵛ–27ᵛ (an excerpt, lines 139–454); and fᵇ (Jesus 15), f. iʳ⁻ᵛ (a fragment, lines
526–74).

Another manuscript, H (Cotton Vitellius C. v), includes the first part of the
homily in a compilation printed separately below as XIa.

Excluded variants: (1) Interchange of short i and y in andgit, bið, gif, him (sg.),
his, hit, libban, micel, sind, siððan, -spring, swilce, þissere, þisum, will-. (2) Interchange of long i and y in swið-. (3) Substitution of hy or heo for hi in the nom.
acc. plural. U and V usually have hy, occasionally heo. (It has seemed best to
report the distinctive dative plural heom of C, M, and T, and the corresponding
instances of hym in R, U, and V.) (4) Substitution of æ for e in the present
stem of secgan; frequent in U and V. (5) Single for double final consonants
in cynn, full, mann, etc. (6) Interchange of þam, þan, þon in for þam þe: C prefers
þon, the others þam or þan. (7) Interchange of -ness(e) (especially common in C
and U, frequent in V) and -nyss(e) (preferred by the rest). (8) Interchange of e
and o in the second syllable of heofon-, hetol-. (9) The following alternations in
the preterite and past-participial endings of weak verbs of the second class:
-ade/-ode; -edon/-odon; -ad/-od. R, U, and V favour -ade, -ad. (10) Interchange of
-an/-on, and in late manuscripts (V and esp. C) -en in the preterite plural of all
verbs. R, T, and V prefer -an to -on. (11) Several late or merely careless spellings
in C. The range of its spellings is better represented elsewhere in this edition
(VI, XIX, XXI).

Sup.: DICENDUS] sic RTU; om. QV. (See note.) Title replaced by SERMO
QUANDO VOLUERIS DE TEMPORIBUS C.

1 sæcgan UV (not noted hereafter); seggan C.   2 wurðiað RT.   4 ge
over line R.   5 geares] 'middan' geares T.   ymbgan'g' R; ymbgang T.
6 weorðiað UV; wurþiað CRT.   on] om R.   dæge] mæssedæge RT.
7 acennenysse R.

Glosses: Latin in R and T; Middle English in R, T, U, and C.
Latin: 4 ge: vos T (cf. infra 409).   andgit: intellectum RT.   5 þeowað:
ministrat R.   7 acennednysse: natiuitatem RT.

hú hé to mannum cóm on soðre menniscnysse
mid flæsce befángen for ure alysednysse
of þam halgan mædene Maria geháten,   10
seo ðe ana is ægþer ge mæden ge modor.

On þam twelftan dæge þære tíde ymbeganges
we wurðiað mid lofsangum hu ða geleaffullan cyningas
of eastdæle comon ðe Criste lác brohton,
and hu he wearð gefullod fram þam fulluhtere Iohanne   15
on ðære éá Iordane on ðam ylcan dæge,
þeah ðe he unsynnig wære, ac hé wolde sylf swa
gehalgian ure fulluht mid his halgan lichaman,
and ealle wæterstréamas mid his ingange.

On þam feowerteogoðan dæge fram his acennednysse,   20
ðe wé cweðað on Englisc Cándelmæssedæg,
bær þæt hálige mæden (his modor) Maria
ðone heofonlican Æþeling to þam halgan temple
mid þam ælicum lácum, swa swa sé ælmih*tiga God   *p. 216
ǽr Moysen bebéad, þam mæran heretogan,   25
and sé ealda Symeon him sealde ðær bletsunge,
and be him witegode, and eac seo wudewe Anna.

On Lengtenes anginne we éác swylce wurðiað
mid urum lofsangum hu sé léofa Hælend
on þam westene fæste feowertig daga tosomne,   30
and hu hine ðær costnode sé hetela deofol,
ac hé wearð oferswiðed þurh þone soðan Hælend.

Eft wé weorðiað on ufeweardan Lengtene
on halgum rædingum þæs Hǽlendes ðrowunge,

10 þam over line Q.   11 moder UV, modeer C.   13 weorðiað CUV.
14 coman RTV.   brohtan V.   15 gefullad V.   16 ilcan RV.
17 ðe] om. CUV.   18 gehalg'i'an Q.   lichamon R.   20 -teogeþan V.
acennednednysse R.   21 candelmæssandæg V.   22 his modor] sic
RT; erased Q; his moder CU; om. V.   23 heofolican R.   haligan RT.
24 ænlicum U (erased); ænlican C.   27 wyde'we' R; wydewe TV; wudewa C.
28 lenctenes IV; leangeenes (!) C.   swylce] erased U.   29 lofsange V.
31 hu (he) hine R.   se hetela] se awyrda and se hetola R; se awyrgeda and
se hetola T.   32 hælend] scyppend V.   33 wurðiað CRT.   ufewer-
dan R; ufeweardene C.   lenctene RTV.

Glosses, Latin: 14 lác: munera R.   15 fram: a R.   20 acennednysse:
natiuitatis T.   23 æþeling: illustrem RT.   24 ælicum: legalibus RT.
lacum: muneribus T.   25 bebead: precepit R.   heretogan: dux R.
30 westene: deserto RT (desertis T?).   tosomne: continue RT.   31 hetola:
exosus RT.   32 oferswiðed: victus R.   34 rædingum: lectione R.

hu hé wæs gefæstnod for urum synnum on róde   35
on Langgan Frigedæge mid feower næglum,
and gewundod mid spere syððan he gewit[e]n wæs,
and hú hé wæs bebyrged on þam ylcan dæge,
and ús swa alysde mid his agenum deaðe.

Hé arás eft of deaðe on þam Easterdæge,   40
mid þam ylcan lichaman ðe hé ǽr on ðrowode
to ecum ðingum awend, mid undeadlicnysse,
and wé wurðiað þá tíd wurðlice mid sangum
seofon niht on án, swilce hit án dæg sy,
for ðære micelan mærðe mancynnes alysednysse.   45

On ðam feowerteogoðan dæge þæs ðe hé of deaðe arás,
hé astáh to heofonum to his halgan Fæder,
mid þam ylcan lichaman ðe hé of deaðe arærde,
ætforan his apostolum, þe him folgodon on lífe;
and we éac wurðiað wurðlice þone dæg   50
on Ðunresdæg on ðære Gangwucan,
for ðam ðe he geopenode ús infær to heofonum
mid his agenum upstige, gif we hit géearnian willað.

Eft ðæs ymbe týn niht on urum ðeowdome
we mærsiað þone dæg mid mærlicum *wurðmynte   *p. 217
þe wé hátað Pentecosten, on ðam com sé Halga Gást   56
of heofonum swegende ofer ða halgan apostolas,
on fyres gelicnysse, and afylde þæt hus
ðær þær hí inne sæton, and séalde heora ælcum
swa micele mihte, þæt hi mihton sprecan   60
mid eallum gereordum ðe on eorðan syndon,
and hí éac gebylde to ðære godspellic[an] bodunge,

36 langan *RT*; langum *CUV*.   37 gewiten] *sic RTUV*; gewitan *QC*.
38 ilcan *CRTV*.   40 -dæg *R*.   41 ilcan *CRTV*.   þrowade *RTV*;
þrowde *C*.   43 weorþiað *RT*.   wurðlice] wuldorlice *R*; wuldor'ful'lice *T*.
45 miccllan (!) *R*; micclan *T*.   46 -tegoðon *R*; -teogeðan *V*.   deaðæ *U*.
47 algan *U*.   48 ilcan *RTV*; ylcam *C*.   50–51 *om. C*.   54 ten *U*;
tin *C*.   55 wyrð- *T*; wurh- *C*.   59 ðær þær] þær *V*.   alcum *R*; ælca *C*.
60 mihton] mehton *U*; mihten *R*; mihto *C*.   sprecon *CRT*.   62 -lican]
sic RTUV; -licen *C*; -licum (!) *Q*.

Glosses, Latin: 37 gewiten: mortuus *R*.   42 awend: *conuer*sus *R*.
44 on án: iugit*er RT*.   52 infær: *in*gressu*m T*.   54 ðeowdome: officio
RT.   55 mærsiað: celebram*us RT*.   mærlicum: *in*genti *R*.   57 swegende:
sonando *R*.   61 gereordum: lingua *R*; l*in*guis *T*.   62 gebylde: audaces
fecit *RT*.   bodunge: *p*redicatione *T*.
ME: 37 gewiten: dead *T*.   61 syndon: beoð *R*.

swa þæt hí unforhte ferdon geond ðas woruld,
and ða hæþenan gebigdon to þæs Hælendes geléafan,
and fela wundra worhton, and gefullodon mancynn.　　65
Seofon dagas we wurðiað mid urum sange on cyrcan
ðone halgan tocyme þæs Halgan Gástes,
for ðære seofonféaldan gife þe hé gifð mannum,
swa swa wé sædon éow on sumum spelle ǽr,
hú he todælð his gifa on geleaffullum mannum　　70
be þam ðe he sylf wile, for ðan ðe hé soð God is.
On ðyssere wucan wé wurðodon ðas tíd,
and nu todæg wé heriað þá hálgan þrynnysse
mid úrum ðeowdome, and on ðyssere wucan
oð Sunnanæfen wé singað be þam,　　75
and wé belucað swa mid urum lofsangum
þone halgan geléafan þe wé habbað to Gode,
for ðan ðe wé gelyfað on þone lyfiendan God,
on ðá halgan þrynnysse, þé heofonas gewylt
and ealle gesceafta, án ælmihtig Scyppend,　　80
swa swa gewrita cyðað on Cristenum bócum,
and ðá halgan fæderas, fram frymðe middaneardes.
Æfre wæs sé Fæder witodlice mid þam Suna,
and éac sé Halga Gást, on eallum his færelde,
for ðan ðe hi ðrý sind án þrymwealdend God　　85
on anre Godcundnysse *æfre rixiende,　　　　*p. 218
on anum gecynde, ealle gelíce mihtige;
ac sé sunu ána soðlice underfeng
ða menniscnysse of us, þe hé us mid alysde.
Eall ðæs géares ymbegang herað God Ælmihtigne,　　90

63 heo *C*.　　65 worhtan *CRT*.　　gefulloden *V*; fullodon *C*.　　66 sange]
sangu*m* *C*; lofsongum *R*; lofsangum *T*.　　69–70 *om.* *CUV*.　　69 eow]
om. RT.　　72 ðisre *U*; þisse`re´ *R*; þissere *T*; þisse *C*.　　*after* tid] þe nu
wæs. be þam halgan gaste *R* (*over line*), *T*.　　74 *after* and] swa forþ *R* (*over
line*), *T*.　　þissere *RT*.　　75 oð] *on C*.　　76 lofsange *V*.　　78 gelefað *V*;
geleueið *C* (*C often has* ei *for* a).　　lifiendan *RT*; lifigendan *UV*; lifigende *C*.
79 *before* on] and *R* (*over line*), *CTUV*.　　ða] *om. C*.　　gewealt *CUV*.
81 gewritu *RTUV*; gewrity *C*.　　82 middangeardes *U*.　　86 ricsiende *T*
(c *corrected to* x *over line*).　　89 of us] *om. T*.　　90 geares] `middan´geares
T.　　ælmihtine *T*; ealmigtinne *C*.

Glosses, Latin: 63 unforhte: *imperterriti RT*.　　geond: per *R*.　　64 gebigdon: *conuerterunt RT*.　　68 gife: *gratia T*.　　70 todælð: diuidit *R*.
71 be þam þe: prout *R*.　　73 þrynnesse: *trinitatem R*.　　74 þeowdóme:
officio *R*.　　83 witodlice: certe *RT*.　　84 færelde: Gressu *R*.　　86 ricsiende: rengnates [*sic*] *T*.

and wé mid urum ðeowdome geðwærlæcað þam tídum,
ac wé nellað nu secgan na swiðor embe ðæt,
ac wé wyllað embe us sylfe secgan hwæthwega.

Sé frumsceapena mann, swa swa wé sædon eow oft,
Adám ure fæder, wæs ðurh God swá gesceapen   95
þæt hé béon mihte butan synnum æfre,
and éac butan deaðe, gif he his Drihtne gehyrde;
and gif hé syngode, hé sceolde béon deadlic;
and hé wúrde gesælig gif he ná ne syngode,
þa ða hé soðlice mihte synna forbugan,   100
and hé wurde earming, ða ða hé eaðelice mihte
synna forbugan, gif hé syngode.
Ðá cóm sé ealda deofol mid andan afylled,

---

92 ymbe *CRTUV*.   93 ymbe *RTUV*.   secgan] nu secgan nu *C*.   hwæ-
thwæga (*altered to* -hwega) *V*; hwætwega *C*.   94 *before* Se] *Leofan men*
RT.   sædon] ær sædon *RT*.   98 syngode] 'ne' syngode *R*; gesyngode
UV.   *second* he] *om. RT*.   99 na] *om. C*.   100 soðlice mihte] mihte
soðlice mihte (*second* mihte *crossed out*) *C*.   101–2 *crossed out in U; over line*
in 12th c. hand and al his ofsprung.   eaðelice mihte] *tr. C*.   102 syngode]
gesyngode *RT*.   103 se ealda] sealde *C*.

Glosses, Latin: 91 þeowdome: officio *RT*.   geþwærlæcað: *concordamus RT*.
93 hwæthwega: par*um R*; par*umper T, written more firmly (by tremulous hand?)*
with aliquid *over* hwæt, *and* hyye(?) *in another hand over* hwega.   97 gehyrde:
obediu*it R*; pareret *T*.   100 forbugan: declinare *RT*.   101 earming:
miser *R*.   102 forbugan: declinare *R*.
ME: 99 wurde: were *RT*. (*Similarly R at 101, 299, 461, 532; T at 101, 335,*
461.)

SOURCES. *On the Boulogne Excerpts (BE), a manuscript source discovered by Miss*
Enid Raynes, see above, pp. 407–9.
94–102 [*B(oulogne) E(xcerpts) f. 1, Julian's Prog(nosticon) I. iii*] Γrimus igitur
homo ea naturæ qualitate creatus est ut inmortalitatis ac mortis admodum
capax, nec sic inmortalis fuerit ut etiam si peccaret mori non posset, nec ita
mortalis ut si noluisset peccare morti succumberet. Arbitrii quoque libertati
donatus est, ut iure aut beatus esset qui noluisset peccare cum posset, aut miser
[qui] cum potuisset vitare peccatum, non aliqua necessitate sed propria voluntate
peccasset. [*For Ælfric's reference to obedience in 97, Miss Raynes cites Prognosticon*
I. ii, not included in excerpts:] Sed ita conditus est homo, ut perfunctus obedien-
tiæ munere, sine interventu mortis, angelica eum immortalitas sequeretur,
æternitasque beata; inobedientem autem, mors plecteret iustissima.
103–10 [*BE f. 1. not Prog*] Tunc diabolus invidia plenus suasione decoepit
[*sic*] hominem, ut contra vetitum manducaret, fieretque mortalis, sicut scriptum
est: *Invidia autem diaboli mors introivit in orbem terrarum (Sap. ii. 24). Deus*
mortem non fecit, nec letatur, inquit, *in perditione vivorum (Sap. i. 13)*. [*The next*
two sentences in BE, from Prog I. i and ii, quote Rom. v. 12 and insist on the in-
heritance of original sin; cf. line 106.]

and beswác ðone mann, þæt hé syngode wið God,
and his bebod tobræc þe he him bebéad to healdenne, 105
and hé wearð ðá déadlic, and eall his ofspring syððan.
Ne gescéop God þone déað, ne hé soðlice ne blissað
on manna forwyrde, swa swa gewritu secgað.
Inuidia autem diaboli mors intrauit in orbem terrarum:
Ac ðurh þæs deofles ándan sé deað com on ðas woruld. 110
On ðréo wisan he cymð, swa swa hit fullcuð is:
Mors acerba, mors inmátura, mors naturalis.
Ðæt is on Englisc, sé bitera deað,
sé ungeripoda deað, and se gecyndelica.
Sé bitera deað is gecweden þe bið on cildum, 115
and se ungeripoda deað, on geongum mannum,
and se gecyndelica, þe becymð þam *éaldum. *p. 219
Ælc man him ondræt þæs lichaman deað,
and feawa him ondrædað þære sawle deað.
þam lichaman men tiliað, þe la[n]ge lybban ne mæg, 120
and ne tiliað þære sawle þe ne swelt on ecnysse.
Ne becymð na yfel deað þam ðe ær wel lyfode,
ac se hæfð yfelne déað ðe þam déaðe folgode,

---

104 gód *V*. 107 gescop *V*. 109 mors intrauit] intrauit 'mors' *C*.
110 weoruld *RU*. 111 he] heo *V*. 112 immatura *C*. 114 ungeri-
poda] unripæ *C*. gecyndelica] -lic *C*; *followed by* deað *CV*. 116 se]
om. C. geongum] 'gun'gum *R*. 117 gecyndelice deað *C*. þam ealdum]
on ealdum mannum *C*. 118 him *altered to* hym *U*. 119 him *altered
to* hym *U*; hym *V*. 120 lange] *sic CUV*; la ge *Q* (*see note*); *om. RT*.
121 saule *U*. swylt *RU*. 122 leofode *CUV*. 123 folgade *V*.

Glosses, Latin: 104 wið: *contra R*. 105 bebead: *imperauit R*. 108 forwyrde: *interitu RT*. 113 bitera: *acerba* (*tremulous hand?*) *T*. 114 ungeripoda: *immatura* (*tremulous hand?*) *T*. gecyndelica: *naturalis* (*tremulous
hand?*) *T*. 118 þæs: *illius R*. 120 tiliað: *curant R*.
ME: 105 bebod: *heste R*.

111–17 [*BE f. 1, Prog I. v*] Tria sunt genera mortis: id est, acerba, inmatura,
naturalis. Acerba infantium, inmatura iuuenum, matura, id est naturalis, senum.
118–21 [*BE f. 1, Prog I. xi*] Mortem carnis omnis homo timet, et mortem
anime pauci. Pro morte carnis quæ sine dubio quandoque ventura est curant
omnes ne veniat: inde est quod laborant. Laborat ne moriatur homo moriturus,
et non laborat ne peccet homo in eternum victurus. [*From Augustine: cf. above,
Hom. vi. 143 sqq.*]
122–8 [*BE f. 1^{r–v}, Prog I. xii*] Mala mors putanda non est quam bona vita
precesserit, nec enim facit malam mortem nisi qui sequitur mortem. Non itaque
multum curandum est eis qui necessario morituri sunt, quid accidat ut moriantur,
sed moriendo quo ire cogantur.

and on yfelum dædum deofle gecwemde.

Ne ðearft ðu ná hogian hu ðu sceole sweltan,   125
ac hoga ðu swiðor hu ðin sawol sceole
æfter þam forðsiðe faran be gewyrhtum,
oððe to reste, oððe to reþum wítum.

Twegen deaðas synd, swa swa us secgað béc:
an is ðæs lichaman deað, þe eallum mannum becymð,   130
oðer is ðære sawle déað, þe ðurh synna becymð,
na eallum mannum, ac þam mánfullum anum,
and heora sawul lósað fram þam écán lífe,
and ne swelt ðeah næfre on ðære hellican susle,
ac bið æfre geedniwed to þam ecum witum.   135

þysum déaðe ætwindað, swa swa ure Drihten cwæþ,
ða ðe his wórd héaldað, (and) hí habbað þæt ece líf
mid þam sóðan Hælende, þe hí gehyrsumedon on lífe.

Ælc man ðe Godes freond is sceolde swyðe æfstan æfre
mid godum weorcum, þæt he Gode gecwemde,   140
and to þam éarde becume ðe us behaten is,
þæt is heofonan ríce, swa swa Críst us behét.

Hwa dórste æfre gewilnían þæs wynsuman éardes,

---

125 na] nu RT (corrected to na T).   scyle V (and 126).   126 sawul RT;
sawel V; sawle C.   127 gewyrhton U; gewyrhtan C.   129 swa swa] swa V.
133 sawl R; sauwl U; sawel V; sawle C.   134 swylt RTV.   135 geedni-
wod TUV; -að R; -æð C.   þan R.   ecan altered to ecvm Q; ecan
RT.   137 and] sic RT; erased Q; om. CUV.   138 gehyrsumodon RT,
gehersomoden C.   139 Here begins the extract in M.   swyðe] georne M.
efstan CMRTU; efestan V.   140 goodum R.   141 becumen T;
become M.   142 heofena V; heofonum C.   143 durste V.

Glosses, Latin: 128 reþum: crudel' RT.   witum: pen(:) R (how inflected?).
132 mánfullum: iniquis RT.   133 losað: perit R.   134 susle: supplicio RT.   135 (bið) geedniwa[d]: renouatum (?) R; renouatur T (both
probably the tremulous hand, though unusually firm and clear in T).   136 ætwindað: euadent RT.   139 efstan: festinare RT.   143 wynsuman:
amenum R; iocunda T.

129–38 [BE f. 1ᵛ, restated from Prog I. xii] Due namque sunt mortes: una
corporis et altera anime. Sed mortem corporis nemo evadit, anime vero mortem
omnes electi evadunt, sicut Dominus ait: Si quis sermonem meum servaverit,
mortem non videbit in eternum (Ioan. viii. 51).

139–52 [Not in BE; but cf. BE f. 2, Prog I. xiv:] Porro cum mundus oderit
Christianum, quid amas eum qui te odit, et non magis sequeris Christum qui te
et redemit et diligit? Patriam nostram paradisum computemus. . . . Quid non
properamus et currimus ut patriam nostram videre . . . possimus?

and swa miceles wurðmyntes, gif se welwillend[a] Hælend
us ne behete þone heofonlican eard,   145
and forði cóm to middanearde þæt hé mancynn alysde,
ægðer ge weras ge wíf, and ðá unwittigan cíld,
*and ða gehádodan menn þe healdað heora clænnysse,   *p. 220
and wið déofles costnunge dæghwamlice campiað;
nu ne mæg Godes behát beon ús alogen,   150
ðe us hæfð beháten heofonan ríces myrhðe,
for his arfæstnysse, na for úre godnysse.

   Micel héap andbidað þǽr ura holdra freonda
ures tocymes to him, hóhfull git embe ús,
órsorh be him sylfum, woldon ús geséon   155
on ðære ylcan blisse ðé hí on wuniað.
Hwá nele nú efstan to ðære ecan blisse
fram þyssere earfoðnysse ðe wé on wuniað,
fram déofles hæftnyssum to þam arfæstan Drihtne?

144 micelan M.   wyrðmyntes TV; wurðscipes M.   welwillenda] sic
MRTUV; welwillende QC.   145 heofonlicne C.   146 forðig M; forði
'he' R.   middam- M.   mancynn alysde altered to wolde mancynn alysen R.
147 unwitegan U; unwitigan C; ungewittigan M.   149 costnunga MRT;
costnungæ U.   150 nu ne mæg] ne mæg nu C.   151 ðe] þe 'he' CR;
þe he M; þæt he T.   heofonan] heofona U; heofena V; þæt is heofonan CM
(þæt is over line C).   152 na] and na CV.   na for ure godnesse added in
margin U.   goodnysse R.   153 heap] heap 'manne' C.   anbidað CUV.
ðar M.   ure RTUV; hure C.   holdra] ældra C.   154 hym RUV;
heom CMT.   hohfull] and hohfulle M.   gyt MRT; get CUV.   ymbe
MUV.   155 orsorh] and orsorge M.   hym RUV; heom CMT.
156-7 ylcan . . . ðære] om. C.   156 ilcan V.   158 on wuniað]
anwuniað, followed by 157 sqq. C.   we] we 'nu' T.   159 hæftnyssum]
ehtnyssum MRT.   drihtene M.

   Glosses, Latin: 147 unwittigan: insensatos RT.   149 campiað: militant
RT.   150 behát: promissum R.   (beon) alogen: fallere R.   152 arfæstnysse: pietate R.   153 héap: caterua RT.   andbidað: expectat R.
154 hohfull: tristes T.   155 orsorh: securi RT.   157 efstan: properare RT.   159 ehtnyssum: persecutione RT.   arfæstan: pio R.
   ME: 150 alogen: fals T.   152 arfestnysse: mildheornesse C.   154 hohfull: careful R.

153-6 [BE f. 2ʳ⁻ᵛ, Prog I. xiv] Magnus illic nos carorum numerus expectat,
parentum fratrum filiorum frequens [BE sequens] nos et copiosa turba desiderat,
iam de sua incolomitate secura, adhuc de nostra salute sollicita. Ad horum con-
spectum et complexum venire, quanta et illis et nobis in commune letitia est.
157-9 [BE f. 2, Prog I. xiv] Obsessa mens hominis, et undique diaboli infes-
tatione vallata, . . . vix resistit. . . . Tot persecutions animus cotidie patitur, tot
periculis pectus urguetur, et delectat hic inter diaboli gladios diu stare, cum
magis concupiscendum et optandum sit ad Christum subveniente velocius morte
properare? Quis non ad letitiam venire festinet?

Is swáðeah micel néod þæt ða ðe manegum fremiað,   160
þæt héora líf béo þæs ðe leng mid ús,
and mid heora fultume ús gefyrðriun to Gode.

Se syrwienda deofol swicað æfre embe ús,
and on þæs mannes forðsíðe fela cnottan him bryt;
ac sé mann behófað micclum gebeda   165
gehádodra manna, þe him foreðingian
on his forðsíðe, þæt hé þam féonde ætberste;
for ðam ðe we rædað on bócum þæt sé reða féond come
swilce egeslic dráca tó ánum licgendum cnihte,
wólde his sáwle habban for his synnum to helle,   170
ac ðǽr comon munecas tó on ðæs mannes forðsíðe,
and geornlice bædon for þam geongan cnihte,
oððæt hí swa afligdon þone feondlican dracan,
and sé cniht gewyrpte, and wunode on lífe,
oððæt hé his synna gebette, and eft syððan gewát,   175
ac he ne geséah ðone dracan ðá, for ðan ðe hé oferswíðed wæs.

Man scéal éac syllan þam seocan men husel,

161 þæs] *om. M.*   lengc *V*; læng *C.*   162 gefyrðrian *CRTUV*; gefyr-
ðrion *M.*   gŏde *V.*   163 Se *altered over line to* þe *R* (*12th c.*).   syrwianda *R*; syrwigenda *MV.*   ymbe *CMRTV.*   164 and on] æt *C.*   forðsiðe]
om. C.   brytt *M*; bret *CV.*   165 se mann] þam men *C.*   miclum *UV*;
micclan *C.*   166 -þingion *MV.*   167 feondum *M.*   168 ðe] *om. R;*
over line T.   169 egeslic] reðe *RT*; 'an' egeslic *C.*   170 saule *U.*
171 coman *V.*   *after* to] and preostas *added in later hand U.*   172 bædan
R; gebædon *T.*   þam ... cnihte] ðone ... cniht *M.*   173 afligde'n' *T*;
afly'g'don *C.*   174 *after* gewyrpte] and wearð to munuce gehalgod *M.*
176 ða] *om. RT.*   oferswiðed wæs] wæs oferswiðed *R*; wæs 'ær' oferswiðed
T.   177 sceall *T.*   husl *U.*

Glosses, Latin: 160 manegum: *multis T.*   fremiað: *proficiunt R.*
162 gefyrðrian: *promoueantur* [*sic*] *R; promoueant T.*   163 syrwianda: *insi-
dians RT.*   swicað: *decipit, fraudatur RT.*   164, 167 forðsiðe: *exitu R.*
166 foreþingian: *intercedant R.*   167 ætberste: *euadet RT.*   168 reða:
atrox R; crudelis T.   169 reðe: *crudelis T.*   173 oð þæt: *donec T.*
afligdon: *fugauerunt* [*sic*] *RT.*   174 gewyrpte: *conualuit RT.*   175 gewát:
obiit RT.   176 oferswiðed: *victus R.*
ME: 163 syrwienda: swycola *U.*   164 bryt: breideð *R.*

160–2 [*BE f. 2, not Prog*] Nulli enim fidelium optandum est in ista vita diu
permanere, nisi forte vita eius multis prosit ad salutem.
163–76 [*BE f. 2ᵛ, Prog I. xvii*] Nititur namque diabolus extrema vite hominis
suis laqueis innectere, sed necesse habet Christianus in ipso exitu sibi adesse
frequens fratrum oratio; quia quosdam legimus in hora transitus sui ab adsis-
tente et insidiante diabolo fraternis precibus et psalmodie frequentia liberatos.
[*Ælfric's exemplum is not in BE.*]

*þá hwíle ðe he hit þicgan mæg, ær ðam ðe hé sáwlige,   *p. 221
for ðan ðe ús secgað béc þæt he hit sceole ðicgan,
ac hé his ne mæg onbyrian gif hé bið gewiten ǽr.   180
Tó goddra manna forðsiðe God asent his englas,
þæt hí heora sawla onfón on heora forðsiðe,
and gelǽdon to reste, swa swa wé leorniað on bócum,
and Críst him tæcð wununge be heora gewyrhtum.
Ða ðe góde beoð, and Gode ǽr gecwemdon,   185
on eallum godum weorcum, ða wuniað mid Gode,
and ða ðe ne beoð ful góde, ne afeormode mid ealle
fram eallum heora synnum, þa sceolon to wítum faran,
and on þám wítum þrowian, oððæt hí wurðon clæne,
and þurh ðingrædene ðanon alysde.   190

178 ðan *CU.*   saulige *U.*   179 sceolde *U*; scolde *V.*   180 his] hi (!)
C. gewiten ær] *tr. RT.*   181 godra *CTUV*; goodra *R.*   183 gelæ-
dan *RUV.*   184 hym *RUV.*   tæcð] betæceð *C.*   185 goode *R*; gode
'men' *T.*   Gode] gðde *V.*   gecwemdan *R.*   186 goodum *R.*   Gode]
gðde *V.*   187 ful gode] full goode *R*; full gode *C.*   *second* ne *erased U.*
afeormade *V*; afyrmode *C.*   188 eallum] *om. RT.*   scylon *V*; sceolan *RT.*
189 wurðon] weorðon *U*; weorðan *CV*; wurdon *M.*   190 alysede *M.*

Glosses, Latin: 178, 179 þicgan: sumere *RT.*   178 sawlige: moria*tur R.*
180 onbyrian: Gustare *RT.*   181 forðsiðe: obitu *R.*   182 onfón: re-
cipia*nt R.*   187 afeormode: purgati *RT.*   188 witum: purgariu*m*
[*sic*] *R.*   189 þrowian: pati *R.*   190 þingrædene: *intercessiones RT.*
ME: 180 gewiten: dead *RT.*   188 witum: pine *T.* (*Similarly T at 465,*
R at 189, 209, 215, 227, 238, 331, 452.)

181–3 [*BE f.* 2ᵛ, *Prog I. x*] Cum in evvangelio mentio divitis et Lazari pauperis
ageretur, sic scriptum est: *Contigit mori inopem illum* (*et*) *ferri* [*MS. blotted*;
Prog, et deferri] *ab angelis in sinum Abrahe* ((*Luc. xvi. 22, Old Latin*). Qua
sententia verissime confirmatur quod in separatione sanctarum animarum et
egressu a corpore, angelorum semper habeantur excubiæ. Et quod ab eisdem
angelis animæ eorum excipiantur perducendæ ad Deum quem coluerunt. [*Last
sentence restates the conclusion of Prog. I. x*].

185–94 [*Cf. Prog II. x, not included in BE*] Spiritus illi qui nec tam perfectæ
sanctitatis hinc exeunt, ut ire in paradisum statim post depositionem suorum
corporum possint, nec . . . ita in suis criminibus perseverant, ut cum diabolo et
angelis eius damnari mereantur, Ecclesia hic pro eis efficaciter supplicante,
poenis medicinabilibus expiati, corpora sua cum beata immortalitate recipient.
. . . [*Cf. BE f.* 3ᵛ, *Prog II. ix*] Tempus quod inter hominis mortem et ultimam
resurrectionem interpositum est anime abditis receptaculis continentur, sicut
unaquæque digna est vel requie vel erumna, pro eo quod sortita est in carne cum
viveret. [*Also BE f.* 4ᵛ, *Prog II. xiii*] Sicut enim credimus animas sanctorum esse
in cælo . . . sic oportet ut et iniquorum animas in inferno per omnia esse cre-
damus. [*Prog II. xiii adds,*] Nam sicut electos beatitudo glorificat, ita credi
necesse est, quod a die exitus sui ignis reprobos exurat.

Ða fordónan synfullan þé deofle gehyrsumodon
on eallum synnum, and forsáwon heora Drihten,
and swá geendodon, [þa] sceolon to helle
swa raðe swá hi gewitað, and ðær wunian æfre.

Gif sé man wólde huru, þonne hé séoc bið,   195
to Gode gecyrran, and his synna geandettan
mid sóðre bereowsunge, sé sóðfæsta Dema
him wolde mildsian, þæt he moste huru
on Dómes-dæge þam deofle ætwíndan.

Nis na eallum mannum se gemænelica deað   200
gelíce earfoðe, ac foroft bécymð
þam synfullan men sumera synna forgyfennys,
þurh ðone earfoðan déað þe hine swá swíðe drehte,
and ðurh ðone ógan þæs egeslican deaðes.

Sume éac blissiað on heora forðsiðe foróft,   205
þonne hí witodlice geseoð þæt hi sceolon to reste,
and glad[a]ð þonne seo sawul, and swa gewít of lífe.

Sumera *manna sáwla siðiað to reste   *p. 222
æfter heora fórðsiðe, and sume farað to wítum,
be þam ðe hi geworhton ǽr,   210

193 þa] sic CMUV; om. QRT.   sceolan RT; scylon V.   to helle] to helle
faran V.   194 hraðe CMRTV.   þar RT.   196 geandettan] geandettan 'his scriftan' U; . . . 'his scrifte' V.   197 behreowsunge MRTUV;
bereowsynga C.   198 miltsian CRU; 'ge'miltsian T.   199 -dæg M.
202 synfullum V.   forgyfennys] -gyf- from -gif- Q; -gifennys M; -gifennyss
R; -gyfennyss'e' T; -gifnes U; -gifenes V; -gyfnesse C.   203 hyne RT;
hina C.   205 Sume 'vel halige men' T.   206 sceolan RT; scylon V.
207 gladað] sic CMRTUV; gladiað Q.   sawl CR; sawule T; sawel V.
208 saw(u)la T.   210 geworhtan C; worhtan RT.   ær] ær 'her on lif[e]' U.

Glosses, Latin: 191 fordónan: damnati RT.   192 forsawon: contempserunt R; spreuerunt [sic] T.   194 hraþe: mox R.   gewítað: transeunt R;
obiunt T.   195 séoc: infirmus T.   196 geandettan: confiteri RT.
198 miltsian: misereri R.   199 ætwindan: euadere RT.   201 foroft:
persepe R.   202 sumera: aliquarum R.   204 ógan: tremore [sic] R;
timorem T.   egeslican: terribilis R.   206 witodlice: certe RT.   207 gewit:
transit R; obit T.   208 siðiað: transeunt R.
ME: 208 siðiað: Goþ T.

200–4 [BE f. 2ᵛ–3, Prog I. vii] Contigit etiam plerumque ut per asperam
mortem carnis liberetur anima a peccatis. . . . Ita esse credendum est quod
plerumque de culpis minimis ipse solus pavor egredientes iustorum animas
purget.
205–7 [BE f. 3, Prog I. vii] Quidam vero in ipso suo fine hilarescunt, æter-
norum contemplatione bonorum.
208–13 [For the general doctrine see the passages already cited for lines 185–94.]

and béoð eft alysede þurh ælmesdǽda,
and swiðost þurh ða mæssan, gif him man fore déð,
and sume beoð fordemede mid þam déoflum to helle,
and se ðe ǽne cymð to helle, ne cymð hé nǽfre ðanon,
and se ðe ǽne cymð to reste, ne cymð hé nǽfre to wítum. 215
    Seo sawul hæfð soðlice, swa swa ús secgað béc,
þæs lichaman gelicnysse on eallum hyre limum,
and heo gefret softnysse oððe sarnysse,
swa hwæðer swa héo on bið, be þam ðe heo geearnode ǽr.
Sume leahtras béoð on ðisum lífe gebette, 220
and sume æfter déaðe, swa swa ure Drihten sǽde;
ac ða micclan synna ne magon þær béon gebette,
ne þam fordónan ne fremað þæt þæt him man fore deð,
for ðan ðe hé his ne geearnode ǽr on his lífe.
Ðá leohtan gyltas and ða lytlan synna 225
beoð þonne afeormode þurh ðæt witniendlice fýr,

211 alysde V.   þur R.   213 deoflum] deofle RT.   214 om. C.
216 sawl CV.   soðlice] om. C.   217 lichoman RT.   hire CRUV;
heora altered to hyre T.   219 hweðer V.   bið] lið C.   220 leahtras]
leahtres C; synna M.   222 miclan UV; miccle C.   225 lutlan
altered to lytlan U; litla C.   226 witnigend- MUV.

Glosses, Latin: 211–12 þurh ælmesdæda, and . . . þurh ða mæssan: per ele-
mosinas et per factas missas T (not the trembling hand).   212 swiðost:
maxime R.   218 gefret: sentit RT.   220 leahtras: crimina R; vica
[sic] T.   223 fordónan: damnatis RT.   fremað: proficit R.   224 his:
hoc R.   226 afeormode: purgati R.   witniendlice: puniendo R; cru-
ciendo T.
ME: 220 leahtras: synna U.

211, 212 [Perhaps suggested by BE f. 3, Prog I. xxi] Cum enim Deo sacrificia
pro spiritibus defunctorum offeruntur, pro valde bonis gratiarum actiones sunt;
pro non valde malis propitiationes sunt. . . . Quibus tamen prosunt aut ad hoc
prosunt ut sit plena remissio, aut certe ut tolerabilior fiat ipsa dampnatio.
214, 215 [BE f. 3ᵛ, restated from Prog II. xiv] Anima denique quæ semel in
infernum proiecta fuerit, ibidem erit perpetuo permansura. Et exaltata ad
gloriam semel, numquam perveniet ad supplicium.
216–19 [BE f. 3ᵛ, Prog II. xv, xvi] Anima namque, a corpore separata, sensi-
bus suis non erit privata. Anima autem similitudinem corporis habet, et in eadem
corporali similitudine requiem sentit perfertque tormenta.
220–6 [BE f. 3ᵛ–4, Prog II. xix restated] Constat namque quasdam culpas in
hoc seculo, quasdam vero in futuro posse relaxari, quia Dominus ait in evvangelio, Si quis in Spiritum sanctum blasphemiam dixerit, neque in hoc seculo remittetur ei neque in futuro (Matth. xii. 32). Leviores quidem culpe ut stipula ligna pur-
gatorio igne consumentur; graviora vero crimina eterno supplicio dampnentur.
223 [BE f. 3, Prog I. xxi, by implication] Cum enim Deo sacrificia pro spiritibus defunctorum offeruntur, . . . pro valde malis etiam si nulla sint adiumenta
mortuorum, qualescumque tamen sunt consolationes viventium.

and nis nanes cynnes wíte on þyssere worulde swá téart
swa swa þæt foresæde fyr þé afeormað þa gymeleasan.
Sume beoð þær lange, sume lytle hwile,
be þam ðe him fore beoð his frynd hér on lífe,   230
and be þam ðe he geearnode ǽr on his lífe,
and ælc mæg tocnawan oðerne on þam lífe,
and ða ðe to reste becumað oncnawað soðlice
ge þa ðe hí ǽr cuðon ge þa ðe hí na ne cuðon,
for ðan ðe hí on weldædum wæron ær gelice.   235
And þa halgan sáwla þé on heofonum wuniað
gebiddað for ús ðé on *eorðan wuniað,   *p. 223
and éac for ðam sawlum ðe syndon on witum,
and hí habbað gemynd heora hóldra fréonda,
and wé magon éac þingian ðam ðe on wítum beoð,   240
and swiðust þurh mæssan, swa swa ús secgað béc,

---

227 þissere *CMRT*.   228 geomel'e´asan *V*; gimeleason *C*.   230 hym
RU; heom *M*.   freond *CTV*.   232 ælc] ælc mann *M*.   234 *first*
cuðon] cuðan *V*; cnywan *C*.   *second* cuðon] cuðan *RV*.   na] *om. C*.
235 ðan] þam *RT*; ði *CU*; ðy *V*.   238 ðan *M*.   240 ðam] þan *C*;
'for´ þam *R* (*early correction*); for ðam *T*.   241 swiðost *MUV*; swiðest *C*.
mæssan] ða mæssan *RT*.

Glosses, Latin: 234 *first* ge: eciam *R*.   235 weldædum: bonis actibus *R*.
239 gemynd: recordationem *R*.

227, 228 [*BE f. 4, Prog II. xix*] Et ipse ignis purgatorius multo gravior erit
quam quicquid homo potest pati in hac vita.
229–31 [*Cf. Prog II. xxii, not in BE*] Puto quod . . . omnes qui per graves
purgatorias poenas salvi esse creduntur, non uno eodemque spatio temporis
cruciatus spirituum sustinebunt. . . . Sed tanto illis minus vel maius ignis purga-
torii extendetur supplicium, quanto hic minus vel amplius bona temporalia
dilexerunt.
232–5 [*BE f. 4, Prog II. xxiv*] Non est ergo dubitandum quod se defunctorum
spiritus in illa regione pariter recognoscant. Possunt enim et boni bonos et mali
malos cognoscere. Fit autem in electis quiddam mirabilius, quia non solum eos
cognoscunt quos in hoc mundo noverant, sed velut visos ac cognitos recogno-
scunt bonos quos numquam viderunt, quos in operibus semper noverunt.
236–42 [*BE f. 4, Prog II. xxv*] Orant pro inimicis suis anime beatorum eo
tempore, ut ait sanctus Gregorius, quo possunt ad fructuosam penitentiam eorum
corda convertere, atque ipsa conversione salvare. Et quomodo pro illis tunc
orabitur qui iam nullatenus possunt ad iustitie opera ab iniquitate commutari?
Eadem itaque causa est cur non oretur tunc pro hominibus eterno igne dampn-
natis, quæ nunc etiam causa est ut non oretur pro diabolo angelisque eius eterno
supplicio deputatis. [*BE f. 4, Prog II. xxvi*] Est igitur anime post mortem et
sensus integer et memoria plena, et recordans quos amavit in seculo commen-
dare eos potest precibus Christo.

ac þam ðe on helle beoð ne gehelpð nán foreþingung.

þa halgan sáwla syndon soðlice on blisse,
on anfealdum gyrlum þære écan blisse,
for ðan ðe hí lybbað nú butan heora lichaman,　　　　　245
ac hí onfoð heora lichaman, þeah ðe hé formolsnod wære,
eft on ðam micclan dæge, þurh heora Drihtnes mihte,
and hi beoð þonne gefretewode mid fægerum lichaman,
and þæt bið þæt oðer réaf ðære ecan myrhðe,
and hí beoð þonne éce, and æfre undéadlice,　　　　　250
ge on sáwle ge on licháman, gesǽlilice mid Gode,
and heora lichama bið ðonne swiðe leoht and wynsum,
ðeah ðe hé him hefig wǽre hér on lífe ǽror.

Dæghwamlice hí willniað þæt Domes-dæg cume hraðe,
þæt hí magon blissian on twyfealdre blisse,　　　　　255
on sáwle and on lichaman, ac hí sceolon swaðéah
be Godes willan abídan heora gebro[ð]ra getel,
and ðæra haligra manna ðe of middanearde cumað to him,
oððæt þær swa fela béon swá God foresceawode on ǽr,

---

242 gehylpð *CM*; hylpð *R*; helpð *T*.　　244 *om. C.*　　gyrlan *M.*
245 hyra *U.*　lichoman *RT.*　　246 lichoman *RT.*　he] heo *V.*　ær *before*
formolsnod *M.*　　247 miclan *UV.*　drihtenes *M.*　　248 gefrætewode
MRTU; gefretewade *V*; gefrætewede *C.*　　251 lichoman *RT.*　gesælig-
MRTUV; gesæglig- *C.*　göde *V.*　253 he] *om. C.*　　254 wilniað
MRTUV; wilniad *C.*　255 twi- *CMT.*　256 on . . . lichaman] and
sawle and lichaman *C.*　lichoman *T.*　scealan *R*; scylon *V*; scelon *C.*
257 gebroðra] *sic MRTU*; gebrora *Q*; broðra *V*; brodra *C.*　getæl *CRTV.*
258 þar(a) *V* (a *erased*).　hym *UV*; heom *M.*　　259 feala *R.*　beoð *M.*
on *erased U.*

Glosses, Latin: 242 þam: illis *R.*　　244 (on) anfealdum gyrlum: (*in*) simplici
veste *RT.*　245 butan: sine *R*; þreter *T.*　　246 formolsnod: corrup-
tum *T.*　248 gefrætewode: ornati *RT.*　　249 reaf: vestis *RT.*
252 wynsum: iocundum *R*; iocundus *T.*　254 hraðe: cito *R.*　259 oðþæt:
donec *RT.*

ME: 244 gyrlum: murhþe *U* (*a substitution*).　　246 formolsnod: forroted
R.　254 hráðe: sone *T.*

243–53 [*BE f. 4^v, condensed from Prog II. xxxv and xi*] Anime denique
beatorum exute corporibus sola iocunditate spiritus perfruuntur, quæ prima
stola (*Apoc. vi. 11*) quietis atque felicitatis est. Secunda vero stola erit cum
receptis corporibus de anime et carnis inmortalitate letabuntur, tam ineffabili
facilitate ut sit eis corpus gloria, quod ante sarcina fuit.

254–60 [*BE f. 4^v, Prog II. xxxvii, condensed*] Et cotidie desiderant sancti
resurrectionem corporum suorum et dupplicationem beatitudinis sue, sed tamen
expectant donec impleatur numerus fratrum et conservorum suorum (*Apoc.
vi. 11*).

ða ða hé ærest gescéop ealle þas woruld.   260
Nú hí sceawiað soðlice heora Scyppendes beorhtnysse,
and nis forðí nán gesceaft þe hi geseon ne magon,
ge on héofonum ge on eorðan, ge ða ðe on helle béoð,
ac híra bliss ne bið ná swaðeah gewanod,
þurh ðæt þæt hí geseoð þá synfullan on wítum,   265
ac hí ðanciað þæs ðe swiðor heora Scyppende æfre,
þæt hé hi swa ahredde fram þam réðum witum.

þá *halgan sáwla geséoð swutollice ealle ðing,   *p. 224
ac ða arleasan sáwla ðe on suslum wuniað
ne magon gewitan hwæt géwyrð mid us;   270
hi habbað swaðéah hóge be heora freondum on lífe,
þeah ðe hit naht ne fremige, ne heora freondum ne him.

Nis nánum men nú cuð, ne cucum né deadum,
ne nanum gesceafte, swa swa sé Hælend sǽde,
Hwenne sé miccla dóm eallum mannum becume,   275

260 ða ða] ða ðe *U*; þa þa þe *C*.   gescop *T*.   261 soðlice] *om. M*.
262 forþy *R*.   ge'se'on *Q*.   263 *first two* ge's*] ne *M*.   heofenan *M*.
264 heora *CMRTUV*.   swaðeah na *M*.   265 ðæt þæt] ðæt *R*; ðæt 'þe'
T.   267 he] *om. C*.   reþan *altered to* reþum *R*.   268 swytellice *U*;
swutelice *MV*.   269 sawle *CT*.   s'u's'l'um *Q*.   270 gewitan] witan *M*;
gewiton *C*.   gewurð *CMV*.   mid] be *V*.   272 fremie *T*.   hym *RUV*;
heom *MT*.   273, 299, 300, 302 *over* cuc-] *id est* cwi *T* (*11th c*).   274 sæde]
cwæð *RT*.   275 Hwænne *CMRTU*; Hwonne *V* (*QUV have capital*).
micla *UV*; micele *C*.

Glosses, Latin: 261 sceawiað: vide*n*t *R*; aspiciu*n*t *RT*.   267 ahredde:
libe*r*aui*t T*.   reðum: seuo *T*.   269 arleasan: i*m*pii *RT*.   suslu*m*: supplicio *RT*.   270 gewitan: scire *R*.   gewyrð: fiet *R*.   272 fremige:
proficiat *R*.   273 cúð: notu*m R*.
ME: 271 hoge: care *R*.

261–7 [*BE f. 4ᵛ, Prog II. xxxi, xxxii partly restated*] Cum igitur sancti reg-
nantes in celo Creatoris sui claritatem semper videant, nichil in creatura agitur
quod videre non possint. Et quod reproborum tormenta conspiciunt non potest
minuere letitiam ipsorum, sed tanto maiores Ereptori suo gratias referunt quanto
vident in aliis quod ipsi perpeti potuissent si ab illo relicti fuissent.

268–70 [*BE f. 4ᵛ, Prog II. xxxi, heading*] Non enim impiorum sed sanctorum
tantum anime norunt quid possit a viventibus agi in seculo.

271, 272 [*BE f. 4, Prog II. xxvii restated*] Est quoque cura defunctis de suis
caris vivis, sicut de divite legitur qui rogabat Abraham mittere Lazarum ut
moneret fratres suos, ne et ipsi devenirent in locum tormentorum (*Luc. xvi.
27, 28*).

273–5 [*BE f. 4ᵛ–5, Prog III. i, summarized*] Iudicii enim tempus vel diem
nullus hominum neque angelorum novit. [*Prog quotes Marc. xiii, 32*] De die
autem illo vel hora nemo scit, neque angeli in cælo, neque Filius, nisi Pater solus.
[*Cf. Matth. xxiv. 36.*]

for ðan ðe God sylf gescéop gesceafta swa swa hé wolde,
be nánes oðres dihte, ne éac sé dæg ne cymð
þyssere worulde geendunge be æniges mannes ræde,
ac þurh his anes forescéawunge þe ealle ðing gescéop.
Ure Hælend sæde him sylf be þam dæge   280
þæt woruldmen bytliað and begað heora tilunge,
and wæpmen wífiað, and wífmen ceorliað,
oðþæt sé miccla dæg eallum mannum becymð,
and se Hælend sylf cymð mid his scinendum englum,
and séo sunne forsweorcð, and soðlice sé móna,   285
for ðam ormætan leohte þæs mihtigan Drihtnes.
Understandað nú, men, hu micel miht is on Criste,
þonne seo sunne and sé móna ne magon syllan nán leoht,
for þam godcundan leohte ðe gæþ of þam Hælende.
Engla werod berað þá beorhtan róde him ætforan,   290
and his slagan geseoð hwæne hí ofslogon ær,

276 sylfa *T*; self *C*.   gescop *T*.   278 weorulde *R*.   281 worold- *U*;
weoruld- *R*.   teolunge *CUV*; bigleofan and heora tilunge *M*.   283 micla
V; mycele *C*.   284 sylf] him sylf *RT*.   285 forswyrcð *MUV*;
forsweocð *R*; foreswicð *C*.   286 ormætum *CRTUV*.   mihtigan] ælmihtigan *CM*.   drihtenes *M*.   289 ðan *U*.   -cunddan *R*; -cunde *C*.

Glosses, Latin: 277 dihte: dispositi*one R*.   279 foresceawunge: *pro-*
visione RT.   281 bytliað: funda*nt R*.   begað: excercent(*sic*) *RT*; colunt *T*.
285 forsweo[r]cð: obscuratur *RT*.   286 ormætu*m*: *immenso RT*.   mihtigan: potentis *R*.   290 werod: chorus *R*; corus *T*.   291 slagan: *perem-*
tores R; *interemtores T*.   hwæne: que*m RT*.
ME: 277 dihte: rede *R*.

280-3 [*Luc. xvii. 26-30*] Et sicut factum est in diebus Noe, ita erit et in
diebus Filii hominis. . . . Uxores ducebant, et dabantur ad nuptias. . . . Similiter
. . . . in diebus Lot. . . . Plantabant, et ædificabant. . . . Secundum hæc erit qua
die Filius hominis revelabitur.
283, 284 [*Joel ii. 31; Act. ii. 20*] . . . dies Domini magnus. . . . [*Apoc. vi. 17*]
. . . dies magnus iræ. . . . [*Matth. xxv. 31*] Cum autem venerit Filius hominis in
maiestate sua, et omnes angeli cum eo. . . .
285-9 [*BE f. 5*ʳ⁻ᵛ, *Prog III. v*] De hoc adventu dixit Iohannes Crisostomus:
Tunc, inquit, quando venturus erit Christus, *sol obscurabitur, et luna non dabit*
lumen suum (*Matth. xxiv. 29*). Tanta enim erit eminentia splendoris in Christo
ut etiam clarissima celi luminaria pre fulgore divini luminis abscondantur.
290-5 [*BE f. 5*ᵛ, *Prog III. v*] Exercitus denique angelorum et archangelorum
precedent eum, illud triumphale vexillum miro fulgore coruscans preferentes.
Tunc plangent omnes tribus terre (*Matth. xxiv. 30*) videntes ipsam crucem,
cognoscentesque peccatum suum. Quid autem miraris si crucem adferens veniat
ubi et ipsa vulnera ostendet tunc, quoniam *videbunt*, inquit, *in quem compunxe-*
runt (*Ioan. xix. 37*, Old Latin).

and hé æteowð þá wúnda gewislice him;
þonne wepað þá synfullan and swíðe héofiað,
þa ðe on heora lífe ðone Hælend forsawon,
and oncnawað heora synna mid sorhfullum móde.   295
Ðonne ofergæþ án fyr ealle ðas woruld,
and sé engel blæwð þa seofoðan býman,
þæt is seo æftemyste, and ealle men arísað
*þe æfre wúrdon on lífe mid lichaman cuce,   *p. 225
and eal swa hraðe beoð þá cúce ðe cumað þonne of helle 300
swa swa ðá lybbendan beoð þé on lífe beoð gemette.
Ða cucan béoð ofslagene sóna mid þam fyre,
ac hi beoð þærrihte eft acucode
on ecum lichaman, swa swa ða oðre,
and hí ealle ðonne beoð on anre ylde syððan,   305
on þære ylde þé Críst wæs ða ða hé ðrowode,
wæron hí on ylde déade, wæron hí on cildháde.

292 ætywð *V*; æteoweð *M*; æteawð *C*.   gewislice *M*; gewilice (!) *C*.
hym *RUV*; heom *M*.   293 and] *erased U*.   296 an] *erased U*.   297 encgel
T.   byme *RT*.   298 -meste *MTUV*.   300 *after* of helle] *id est* of
ðam oþran life *T* (*marg.*).   301 þe on life beoð] *om. M*.   beoð] beoð þonne *V*.

Glosses, Latin: 292 æteowð: ostendet *RT*.   gewislice: certe *RT*.   293 heofiað: lugent *RT*.   294 forsáwon: *contempserunt R*; spreuerunt *T*.
295 sorhfullum mode: dolenti *animo R*.   298 æftemyste: vltima *RT*.
300 hraðe: promti [*sic*] *R*.   305 þonne: tunc *R*.   306 þrowode: passus
est R.   307 ylde: etate *R*.
ME: 293 heofiað: forhtyað (*meant as substitution but erased*) *U*.

---

296 [*Perhaps this common belief, derived in part from II Petr. iii. 10, 12, was
suggested by BE f. 5ᵛ, not in Prog*] *Ignis in conspectu eius exardescet* (*Psal. xlix. 3*).
. . . Non erit iste tuus ut focus tuus, sed sicut precedens iudicium in diebus Noe
per diluvium factum est sic erit subsequens iudicium per ignem in adventu
Christi (*cf. Matth. xxiv. 37*). [*The psalm itself is quoted in Prog III. iv.*]
297–301 [*BE f. 6, Prog III. xv*] Novissime autem id est septime claro tube
strepitu personante, mortui suscitantur, corpora quæ prius habuerunt corrupti-
bilia incorrupta recipientes. Et tanta fiet celeritate resurrectio mortuorum, ut
vivi quos in corporibus suis consummationis tempus invenerit mortuos de
inferis resurgentes prevenire non valeant.
302–4 [*BE f. 7, added to excerpt from Prog III. x*] Ipsi vero qui viventes rep-
periuntur in die iudicii, sicut docet pater Agustinus, in ipso raptu nubium
(*I Thess. iv. 17*) momentaneam mortem gustabunt, et sic in terram ibunt quia
corpus exanime terra est, et iterum statim in ipsis nubibus spiritum vite accipient.
305–7 [*BE f. 6, Prog III. xx, restated*] Resurgent ergo omnes homines . . . *in
mensura . . . etatis plenitudinis Christi* (*Ephes. iv. 13*), hoc est in illa etate et in illo
robore ad quam Christus pervenit in mundo.

Ælc man hæfð swaðeah his agene lenge,
on ðære mycelnysse þe hé man wæs ǽr,
oððe hé beon sceolde, gif hé fulweoxe,　　　　　　　　　310
se ðe on cíldháde oððe samweaxen géwat.
Swa swa God gescéop on sawle and on lichaman
ge [w]æpmen ge wífmen, and geworhte hí to men,
and hé ægðerne hád eft syððan alysde,
swa hé éac on Dómes-dæg of déaðe hí arærð,　　　　　315
ge weras ge wíf, and hí wuniað æfre swa,
butan ælcere galnysse, ge góde ge yfele,
and nán wer syððan ne gewifað næfre,
né wíf ne céorlað, ne hí cild ne gestrynað.
Né ðá halgan ne beoð þe tó heofonum sceolon　　　　320
on ænigre awyrdnysse, oððe wanhále,
oððe ánégede, þeah ðe hé ǽr wære
lama on his lífe, ac his lima beoð
him ealle ánsunde, on scinendre beorhtnysse,

308–31 *om. V.*　　　308 lencge *M*; længe *C.*　　　310 scolde *T.*　-weoxe]
-wæxoe (!) wæra *C.*　　　311 -weahsen *R*; -weaxan *C.*　　　312 gesceop] 'hy'
gesceop *T.*　　　313 wæp-] *sic CMRTU*; gæp- *Q.*　　　314 he] *om. M.*
317 ælcre *R.*　　goode *R.*　　　318 ge- *erased T.*　　næfre] *om. RT.*
319 geceorlað *MRT* (ge- *erased T*).　　　321 oððe wanhale] oððe 'halte oððe'
wanhale *U.*　　322 aneagede *CMU.*　　ðe] *om. C.*　　324 him] *om. CU.*

Glosses, Latin: 311 gewat: obiit *RT.*　　　314 had: sexu*m RT.*　　　317 ge:
ecia*m R.*　　galnysse: libidine *T.*　　　319 gestrynað: gen*erant RT.*
321 awyrdnysse: labe *R*; lesione *RT.*　　wanhale: debiles *R.*　　324 ansunde:
integri, *incolumes R.*
ME: 311 samweaxen: halfwaxen *RT.*　　318 wer: mon *U.*　　324 ansunde:
gesunde *U*; ihole *T.*

308–11 [*BE f. 6, Prog III. xx, restated*] Resurgent ergo omnes homines tam
magni corpore et in illa statura in qua erant viventes, vel futuri erant si vixissent.
312–19 [*BE f. 6ᵛ, Prog III. xxiv*] Dominus dixit in evvangelio, *In resurrectione
enim nec femine nubent, nec viri uxores accipient.* (*Matth. xxii. 30*). Ex quibus
sacratissimis verbis apertissime patet quod ibi non sexus sed concubitus desit,
nec carnis sit natura mutanda, sed eius concupiscentia finienda. Sicut enim
omnipotens Deus utrumque sexum condidit, instituit, ac redemit, sic etiam
utrumque in resurrectione restituet.
320–4 [*BE f. 6, Prog III. xxii*] Resurgent itaque omnium sanctorum corpora
omni felicitate et gloria inmortalitatis conspicua, sine ulla corruptione, sine
difficultate, vel onere aut deformitate. [*BE f. 7, Prog III. xxviii, modified*] Sic et
cetera [monstra] quæ amplius vel minus aliquid habuerunt, vel [qui] debiles vel
ceci fuerunt, cum integro numero membrorum corporis sine deformitate
resurgent.

and grapiendlice on ðam gastlican lichaman.   325
Ðá wiðercorenan soðlice, ðe wuniað æfre on suslum,
hwæt sceal him ænig wlite on þam sweartan fyre,
þonne hé æfre heofað, and egeslice gristbitað,
and wolde gif he mihte wurðan to nahte,
oððe béon déad, ac he ne bið swaðeah,   330
ne he of þam wítum ne mæg wurðan æfre alysed?

Ælc man scéal arísan þonne *þe æfre on lífe wæs;   *p. 226
wære he on wætere adruncen, oððe hine wílde deor æton,
oððe hine fýr forbærnde færlice to dúste,
and ðæt dúst wurde toworpen mid blædum,   335
swað[ea]h sé ælmihtiga God mæg hine eft aræran,
se ðe ealle þas woruld geworhte of nahte,
and se ðe þises ne gelyfð, ne bið his geleafa naht.
Man bewint þone déadan gewunelice mid réafe,
ac ðæt réaf ne arist na ðe hraðor mid þam men,   340

325 grapigend- *M.*   lichaman] limum *altered to* liman *R;* liman *T.*
327 hym *RU;* heom *CM.*   þam] *om. C.*   328 hi . . . heofað *M.*   heofað
and] hafað *C.*   -bit'i'að *U;* -bitiað *M.*   329 wolde'n' *U;* woldon *M.*   he]
hi *M.*   mihte'n' *U;* mihton *M.*   wurðan] gewurðon *M.*   330 deade *M.*
he] hi *M.*   beoð *M;* bið *altered to* beoð *U;* bioð *C.*   331 he] hi *M;*
he'o' *U.*   magon *M;* mæg'en' *U.*   wurdon *M;* wurðon *C.*   alysede *M;*
alysd *C.*   332 life] lif *R.*   333 adruncen] druncen *R.*   deor *in margin U.*
æton] 'fr'æte *U;* æte *CV.*   335 wurde] wære *M.*   toworpen] 'wide'
toworpen *U.*   mid blædum] *erased U.*   336 -ðeah] *sic CMRTUV;*
-ðæ'a'h *Q.*   340 arisð *V.*   hraðor] hraðor 'eft' *T;* raðor *M.*

Glosses, Latin: 325 grapiendlice: palpabiles *R.*   326 wiþercorenan: reprobi *R.*   suslum: supplicio *RT.*   327 wlite: decor *RT.*   328 þonne:
ex quo *R.*   heofað: luget *R;* flet *T.*   egeslice: terribiliter *T.*   335 blædum: flatu *RT.*   338 þyses: hoc *R.*   339 bewint: inuoluit *R.*   reafe:
veste *RT.*

ME: 328 heofað: saryge beoþ *U.*   331 wurðan: beon *R. (Cf. 99 supra.)*

---

325 [*BE f.* 6, *added to passage from Prog III.* xx, *perhaps suggested by III.*
xviii] Corpus nostrum inmortalitatis gloria sublimatum subtile erit per effectum
spiritalis potentiæ, sed palpabile per veritatem nature.

326–31 [*BE f.* 6ᵛ, *Prog III.* xxiii, *abridged*] De reprobis vero quid dicendum
est, nisi quod ubi erit dentium stridor æternus et incessabilis fletus, inaniter
quæritur corporum decus.

332–8 [*BE f.* 7, *Prog III.* xxix, *restated*] Etsi a bestiis devorentur, sive igne
concremantur et in auras aspergantur, potens est tamen eos in puncto temporis
reformare, qui de nichilo mundum creavit.

339–42 [*Elaborated from BE f.* 7, *Prog III.* xxvi, *condensed*] Et si indumenta
fuerint, spiritalium corporum spiritalia erunt.

for ðan ðe hé ne behófað þæs huxlican réafes,
ac þære gastlican gyrlan ðe him God forescéawað.

God asent þonne his englas, and hi gegaderiað him to
ealle his gecorenan of eallum middanéarde,
and standað ða gódan men on Godes swiðran hánd,   345
and ðá wiðercorenan on his wynstran hánd.

þonne sitt se Hǽlend on his heofonlican ðrymsetle,
mihtig and wuldorful, and mílde þam gódum,
egeslic and andrysne þam earmum synfullum,
and ealle men geséoð swutollice þone Hǽlend   350
on ðære menniscnysse, ac ne moton swaðeah
ða earman synfullan geséon his godcundnysse;
ða godan ána geseoð þá godcundnysse.

His twelf apostolas, þe him folgodon on lífe,
sittað þonne éac on twelf domsettlum,   355

341 ðe] om. V.   he ne] he him ne C.   342 gastlican gyrlan] transposed
then corrected R.   344 middangearde M.   345 goodan R.   347 sit
CTV.   -settle RT.   348 goodum R.   349 andrysne] andredendlic
U (later hand on erasure); angrislic M; andrisne C.   350 swutelice CMUV.
351 menisc- U.   motan V.   353 om. C.   'ah' þa godan U. goodan R.
355 -setlum CMUV.

Glosses, Latin: 341 ne behofað: non indiget R.   huxlican: vili R; vilis T.
reafes: veste T.   342 gyrlan: indumento R; indumentum T.   foresceawað:
preuidet R.   343 þonne: tunc R.   345 goodan: boni R.   swiðran:
dextra R.   346 wiðercorenan: reprobi R.   wynstran: sinistra R.
347 þrymsettle: trono RT.   348 wuldorfull: gloriosus RT.   349 egeslic:
terribilis R.   andrysne: horribilis RT.   355 twelf dómsettlum: sedibus
duodecim T.
ME: 341 huxlican: forrotendan U.   342 gyrlan: scrydes U.

343, 344 [Matth. xxiv. 31] Et mittet angelos suos cum tuba et voce magna, et
congregabunt electos eius a quatuor ventis, a summis cælorum usque ad
terminos eorum.
345, 346 [BE f. 8, Prog III. xxxvi, a modification of Matth. xxv. 32 sq.]
Separatis igitur per angelica ministeria bonis a malis, et electis quidem a dextris,
reprobis vero a sinistris adstantibus. . . .
347, 348 [Matth. xxv. 31] Cum autem venerit Filius hominis in maiestate
sua, . . . tunc se debit super sedem maiestatis suæ.
348, 349 [BE f. 6ᵛ, Prog III. vii] Redemptor humani generis cum apparuerit,
et mitis iustis et terribilis erit iniustis.
350-53 [BE f. 6ᵛ, Prog III. viii, abridged] Humanitatem namque eius et iusti
et iniusti visuri sunt; divinitatem vero eius non videbunt nisi soli iusti.
354-59 [BE f. 7ᵛ, Prog III. xi-xiii condensed] Sedes igitur habebunt apostoli
in quibus Christo iudicante sessuri sunt, iuxta quod ipsa Veritas ait: . . . sedebitis
et vos super sedes duodecim . . . (Matth. xix. 28). Et non solum duodecim apostoli,
sed . . . omnes sancti qui perfecte mundum reliquerunt cum Domino residentes
ceteros iudicabunt.

and ealle ða hálgan weras ðe ðas woruld forleton,
and woruldlice æhta mid ealle forsawon,
sittað on dómsetlum soðlice mid him,
and hí mid þam Hælende mancynne þonne demað.
Ðær beoð feower gefylcu on þam micelan flocce: 360
þæt forme gefylc bið þe we hér foresædon,
þe sittað mid þam Hælende on heora héahsettlum;
him ne bið na gedemed, ac hí *démað mid Críste   *p. 227
eallum oðrum mannum mihtelice on wuldre.
Ðæt oðer werod bið þæra woruldmanna   365
ðe on gódum weorcum Gode ǽr gecwemdon,
and mid ælmysdǽdum geearnodon æt Gode
þá heofonlican wununge and þæt éce wuldor;
hí ne demað nánum men, ac him bið gedémed,
swa þæt hí habbon heofonan ríces wuldor.   370
Ðæt þridde werod bið witodlice þonne
þæra Cristenra manna ðe cuðon heora geléafan,
ac hí gremedon God mid gramlicum dǽdum,
and fullice lyfedon on fulum synnum æfre:

356 weoruld *R*.   357 woroldlice *U*; woruldlic *C*.   358 -settlum *RT*.
360 gefilcu *CU*; gefylcea *M*.   mycelan *RV*; micclan *M*; micclein (!) *C*.
flocce] folce *M*.   361 gefilc *CU*; gefylce *M*.   þe] þæt þe *M*.   her] ær
CUV.   362 heahsetlum *CMU*; domsetlum *V*.   363 hym *U*; heom *V*.
criste] þam hælende *RT*.   365 þara *UV*.   366 goodum *R*.   367 ælmes-
CMTUV; ælmæs- *R*.   369 hym *UV*; heom *MT*; hiem (!) *C*.   370 hab-
bon] habban *altered to* habbað *R*; habbað *MT*; habban *CV*.   heofona *CUV*.
372 þara *UV*.   373 gremodon *RT*; gegremedon *UV*.   374 ful(l)ice
U (l *erased*); fulice *MV*.   leofodon *M*; leofedon *C*.   on] *om. C*.

Glosses, Latin: 357 forsawon: spreuer*unt R*; contemps*er*u*nt T*.   360 gefylcu:
pop*uli RT*.   365 werod: ordo *RT*.   369 hi: illi *R*.   371 werod:
ordo *RT*.   witodlice: c*er*te *RT*.
ME: 360 gefilcu: werod *U*.   361 gefilc: werod *U*.

360 [*Prog III. xxxiii, not explicit in BE*] Duæ enim differentiæ vel ordines
hominum erunt in iudicio collectorum, hoc est electorum et reproborum, qui
tamen in quatuor dividuntur.
361–4 [*BE f. 7ᵛ, Prog III. xxxiii*] Igitur perfectorum sanctorum primus ordo
erit, qui cum Domino iudicat, et non iudicatur, sed regnat.
365–70 [*BE f. 7ᵛ, Prog III. xxxiii*] Alius quoque est ordo electorum quibus
dicitur, *Esurivi, et dedistis mihi manducare* (*Matth. xxv. 35*). Hi iudicantur et
regnant.
371–83 [*BE f. 7ᵛ, Prog III. xxxiii, modified*] Item reproborum ordines duo
sunt, unus eorum, qui Dei cognitionem habuerunt sed fidem dignis operibus non
exercuerunt, isti iudicabuntur et peribunt, quibus dicetur a Domino, *Esurivi et
non dedistis mihi manducare. Ite, maledicti, in ignem æternum* (*Matth. xxv. 41, 42*).

moröslagan and mándǽdan, and unmǽöfulle gitseras, 375
wigleras and wiccan, and unlybwyrhtan,
þéofas and réaferas, and öa réöan drýmen,
þá forsworenan men, and öa swicelan wedlogan,
öa fúlan forlíras, and öá fracodan myltestran
öe acwellaö heora cíld ær þan öe hit cuö béo mannum; 380
hi ne dydon nán gód Gode to wurömynte,
ne náne ælmessan, ac geendodon on synnum;
him biö þonne gedémed mid þam déofle to helle.
þæt féoröe gefylc biö öæra fulra hæöenra
þe náne cyööe ne hæfdon to þam heofonlican G[o]de, 385
ne Crístes geleafan ne cuöon on heora lífe;
hí adrugon heora líf on déofles biggengum,
and hi butan Godes ǽ æfre syngodon,
and eft butan Godes ǽ on écnysse forwuröaö,
mid þam léasan Cristenum æfre cwylmigende. 390
Ne mæg þonne nán man nahwar béon behydd,

375 þæt syndon *before* moröslagan M.   gytseras MRT; gytseres C.
376 unlybb- RT.   377 reaferas] öeodscaþan. ryperas. and reaferas M.
378 swicolan MRTV; swicolon C.   wedd- M; wet- C.   379 and þa
fulen C.   forligras MRT; (for)lig'e'ras U; forligeras V; forlygras C.
380 *first* öe] þa þe C.   öam MRT.   381 hi ... wurömynte] hi ne do 'ö
gode' nan god to wurhmente C.   dydan RTV; dyden U.   good R.   wyrö-
mynte TV.   383 hym RUV; heom M.   384 gefylc] gefylce M.   þara
V; þære C.   hæöenra 'monna' U; hæöenra manna M.   385 ne hæfdon]
næfdon MRTV; nafdon C.   þan CRT.   Gode] gode CMRTUV; góde Q.
386 cuþan RT; cyöan C.   387 bigencgum V; beggungum C.   388 syn-
goden V; syngedum (!) C.   390 leasum MRT.   cristenan CUV.
cwylmiende CRTV.   391 Ne] Witodlice ne M.   nahwar] on domes dæg
nahwar M; nahwær UV₋; nawær C.   behyd V.

Glosses, Latin: 375 moröslagan: homicidii R.   mandædan: op*erarii iniqui-*
tatis R.   376 unlybbwyrhtan: venefici RT.   377 reþan: atroces T.
drymen: *incantatores* RT.   379 forligras: libidinosi R.   fracodan myltestran: fragiles mere*trices* RT.   380 cuö: notu*m* R.   384 hæöenra:
iudeor*um* (!) R.   385 cyööe: noticia*m* R.   387 biggengum: cultu RT;
ex*cercitatione* T.   389 forwuröaö: *intereunt* RT.   390 leasum: falsis R.
cwylmiende: *cruciando* R; *cruciantes* T.   391 behydd: occultu*m* R.

ME: 375 unmæöfulle: grædi R.   379 fracodan myltestran: fulan horan
and byccan U.   384 gefylc: werod U; folc R.   387 adrugon: ledden RT.
biggengum: larum U; hersumnesse C.   388, 389 æ: lagu U.

384-90 [*BE f. 7ᵛ-8, Prog III. xxxiii, restated*] Alter quoque ordo reproborum
est paganorum videlicet, qui Dei cognitionem non habuerunt, qui sine lege
peccaverunt et sine lege peribunt.
391-404 [*BE f. 8, Prog III. xxxvi*] Tunc libri aperti erunt, id est conscientie
singulorum manifestabuntur. Iohannes enim apostolus dicit, *Vidi mortuos*

ac ealle beoð þær þé æfre cuce wæron,
and þær béoð æteowde ure eallra geðohtas,
and ealle ure dǽda eallum þam werodum;
þæt ðe ǽr wæs gebet ne bið þær na ætéowed,   395
ac ða ungebettan *synna beoð þær geswutelode;   *p. 288
hi beoð þonne ofsceamode, and sorhfulle on móde,
þæt hí ær noldon andettan heora synna,
and dǽdbote gedón be heora lareowes dihte.

þær béoð ealle gelice, ge sé hlaford ge se ðeowa,   400
se rica and sé héana, on þam rihtan dóme,
and ðǽr nan man ne mæg ne ne mót
habban nane gewitnysse þe hine betelle,
for ðan ðe his dǽda beoð undígle ðonne eallum.

Ðonne cweð sé Hǽlend of his halgan ðrymsettle   405
to ðam gódum Cristenum ðe Godes willan gefremedon,

---

392 ealle] ealle 'men' U; ealle hi M.   393 ealra MRTUV; alre C.
394 weredum UV; werode M.   395 þæt] 'and' þæt U; and þæt M.
wæs] byð M.   396 unbettan RT.   geswutelade R; geswytelode U.
397 ofsceomode M; ofsceamedo C.   398 noldan RV; nolden altered to
noldan T.   heora scriftan in margin to follow synna U.   400 (h)laford T.
404 undigele M.   eallum] eallum mannum M.   405 cwyð MRUV;
abbreviated cw̅ C.   halgum CMU.   -setle CMRUV.   406 goodum R.
willan] om., weorc over line C.

Glosses, Latin: 392 þær: ibi R.   cuce: víui T.   393 æteowde: ostensi
R; aperti T (not the tremulous hand?).   394 werodum: populo R.
395 Ðæt: hoc R.   æteowed: ostensum RT.   398 andettan: confiteri T.
399 dædbote gedon: penitere, penitenciam agere R.   gedon: agere T.
403 betelle: excusat, defendat R.   404 undigle: in aperto R.   405 þrym-
setle: trono RT.   406 gefremedon: fecerunt RT.

ME: 394 werodum: folke T.   398 andettan: scrifen R.   399 dihte:
wissinge R.   401 heana: pouere R.   403 betelle: werie T.   404 undigle: opene T.

---

magnos et pusillos, et aperti sunt libri. Et alius liber apertus est qui est vite uniuscuiusque. Et iudicati sunt mortui ex his scripturis librorum secundum facta sua.
(Apoc. xx. 12). . . . In isto autem libro de quo dicit, alius liber apertus est qui est
vitæ uniuscuiusque, quædam vis est intellegenda divina qua fiet ut cuique opera
sua vel bona vel mala cuncta in memoriam revocentur, et mentis intuitu ita
celeritate cernantur, ut accuset vel excuset scientia conscientiam, atque simul et
omnes et singuli iudicentur [Ælfric's development is in large part independent.
The distinctions in 395–9 are not in BE, nor in Prog.]
405–29 [Matth. xxv. 34–40; BE f. 8 quotes 34–36; Prog III. xxxvi]
405–11 [34] Tunc dicet Rex [BE, Prog Christus] his qui a dextris eius erunt:
Venite benedicti Patris mei, possidete paratum vobis regnum a constitutione
mundi.

ðe stándað on his swiðran héalfe, þus secgende him to:
Uenite, benedicti Patris mei, Et cetera:
Cumað, ge gebletsodan mínes heofonlican Fæder,
and habbað þæt ríce ðe eow gegearcod wæs　　　　　410
fram þam forman anginne þissere worulde.
Me hingrode soðlice, and gé mé gereordodon.
Eft ða ða me þyrste, ge sealdon me drincan.
Éác ic wæs cuma, and ge me underfengon.
Ic wæs éác swilce nacod, and ge me scry[d]don.　　　　　415
Ic wæs eac swilce untrum, and ge me geneosodon.
On cwearterne ic wæs, and ge cómon to me.
þonne andswariað hi ðam arfæstan Deman þus:
Eala ðú Drihten léóf, hwænne gesáwe wé ðe
oððe hungrienne and wé ðe feddon,　　　　　420
oððe eft þurstine and wé ðe scencton?
Oððe hwænne wǽre ðu cuma and wé ðe [underfengon,

407 healfe] *om. M.*　　secgende] cweðende *RT.*　　hym *UV;* heo*m M.*
408 cetera] *reliqua UV.*　　409 gebletsode *MRT;* gebletsoden *C.*　　mines...
fæder] to mines fæder rice *M.*　　heofenlican *V;* heofonlica *U;* heofonlices *C.*
411 worolde *U;* weoralde *R.*　　413 seoldon *M.*　　sealdon me] *transposed RT.*
415 eac *over line,* swilce *erased U.*　　scryddon] *sic CMRTU;* scryddan *V;*
scry(:)don *Q.*　　416 swilce] *erased U.*　　and ge me geneosodon] *erased U.*
417 ic wæs and] *erased U.*　　and] *om. C.*　　419 Eala] *cap. in CRTV only.*
hwonne *RV;* hwanne *C.*　　420 oððe] *erased R; om. MT.*　　hungrigne *R;*
hungrine *MT;* hungriende *C. See note.*　　421 Oððe *QRT.*　　þurstigne
CMRUV.　　scencton] sealdon drincan *M.*　　422–3 underfengon ... ðe] *sic*
UV; the same exc. unscrydd *CMRT; om. Q.*

Glosses, Latin: 407 swiþran: dext*ra R.*　　409–50 ge: vos (*T 12 times, R 15*
times).　　410 gegearcod: paratu*m R.*　　412 gereordodon: refecistis *RT.*
414 cuma: hospes *RT.*　　416 untrum: in*firmus R.*　　geneosodan: visitastis
R; visitasti *T.*　　417 cwearterne: carc*ere RT.*　　418 arfæstan: pio *R;*
piis *T.*　　419 Eala ðú: o tu *R.*　　420 hungrigne: esurient*em R.*
422 cuma: hospes *RT.*

ME: 411 anginne: frymþe *U.*　　412 gereordodon: feddon *U.*　　416 untrum: seoc *T.*　　418 arfæstan: rihtwise *C.*

412–17 [35] Esurivi enim, et dedistis mihi manducare: sitivi, et dedistis mihi
bibere [*this clause not in BE, Prog*]: hospes eram, et collegistis me:
　　[36] Nudus, et cooperuistis [co- *om. BE*] me: infirmus, et visitastis me: in
carcere eram, et venistis ad me.
　　418–25 [37] Tunc respondebunt ei iusti, dicentes: Domine, quando te vidimus esurientem, et pavimus te: sitientem, et dedimus tibi potum?
　　[38] Quando autem te vidimus hospitem, et collegimus te: aut nudum, et
cooperuimus te?
　　[39] Aut quando te vidimus infirmum, aut in carcere, et venimus ad te?

oððe hwænne wære þu unscryd and we ðe] scryddon?
Hwænne wære þú untrum and wé ðe genéosodon,
oððe on cwearterne and wé comon to ðe?   425
Ðonne andwyrt se Cyning þam arfæstan and cweð:
Sóð ic eow secge, þæt ge me sylfum dydon
þas foresǽdan ðing, swá oft swa ge hí dydon
anum of *ðisum lyttlum minra gebroðra.   *p. 229
þæt is soðlice swá to understandenne: 430
swa oft swa ge ælmessan dydon anum lytlan ðearfan
of Cristenum mannum, þæt ge dydon Criste,
for ðan ðe Crist sylf is Cristenra manna héafod,
and eft ða Cristenan syndon Cristes lima.

Ðonne cweð sé Dema éft to ðam dréorigan héape   435
ðe stent on his wynstran hánd, Gewitað heonan
fram me, ge awyrigedan, into þam ecan fyre
ðe is ðam deofle gegearcod, and eallum his englum.
Mé hingrode soðlice, and ge me ne gereordodon;

---

424 Oððe hwænne *CM*.   and we ðe geneosodon] *erased U*.   425 Oððe *Q*.
comon to ðe] ðe comon to *M*.   426 andwyrt] andwyrd *C*; andweardað *U*;
andswarað *M*.   cyning] hælend *M*.   arfæstum *MRT*.   cwyð *MRT*; *abbreviated* cw̄ *C*.   427 Soð] Soðlice *RT*.   429 lytlum *RUV*; lytlum 'þearfum' *T*; litlum *C*; lytlingum *M*.   430 soðlice] *om. V*.   431 ælmessan
dydon] dydan ælmessan *RT*.   lytlum *RT*; litlum *C*.   433 s'y'lf *Q*.
435 cwyð *MRUV*.   dreorian *MU*; dryrian *C*.   436 stænt *CU*.   his] ða
CUV.   Gewitað] *no cap. MSS*.   heonan] *om. CUV*; heonon *M*.   437 aweri-
gedan 'gastas' *U*; awergedan *C*; awyrgedan *MRT*.   438 ealum *R*.

Glosses, Latin: 424 untrum: infirmus *RT*.   geneosodon: visitauimus *RT*.
425 cwearterne: carcere *RT*.   426 andwyrt: respondet *R*.   arfæstum:
piis *RT*.   435 heape: caterue *RT*.   436 wynstran: sinistra *R*.   gewítað: discedite *R*.   heonan: hinc *R*.   439 gereordodon: refecistis *R*.
ME: 426 arfæstan: rihtwisen *C*.   435 dreorigan: sori *R*.   439 ne
gereordodon: etan ne sealdon *U*.

426–9 [*40*] Et respondens Rex, dicet illis: Amen dico vobis, quamdiu fecistis
uni ex his fratribus meis minimis, mihi fecistis.
430–4 [*Not in BE or Prog. For 433–4 cf. Col. i. 18*: Et ipse est caput corporis
ecclesiæ; *and I Cor. xii. 27*: Vos autem estis corpus Christi, et membra de
membro.]
435–54 [*Matth. xxv. 41–46*]
[*41*] Tunc dicet et his qui a sinistris erunt: Discedite a me maledicti in ignem
æternum, qui paratus est diabolo et angelis eius.
[*42*] Esurivi enim et non dedistis mihi manducare: sitivi, et non dedistis mihi
potum:
[*43*] Hospes eram, et non collegistis me: nudus, et non cooperuistis me:
infirmus, et in carcere, et non visitastis me.

eft ic wæs ðurstig, and ge me ne scencton. 440
Eac ic wæs cuma, and ge me ne underfengon;
ic wæs eac swilce unscryd; nolde ge me scrydan.
Ic wæs untrum and on cwearterne; ne come gé to me.
þonne andwyrdað þá synfullan þam soðan Deman ðus:
Eala ðu soða Drihten, hwænne gesawe we ðe 445
hungrinne oððe þurstigne, cuman oððe nácodne,
untrumne oððe on cwearterne, and we ne ðénodon ðé?
Ðonne andwyrt sé Dema þam earmum forscyldegodum:
Soð ic eow secge, me sylfum ge his forwyr[n]don
swa oft swa ge his forwyrndon ánum of þisum lytlum. 450
    Ðonne gewítað þá earmingas and ðá arléasan synfullan
into þam ecan wíte mid þam áwyrgedan déofle,
and ðá rihtwisan farað forð mid þam Hælende
to þam ecan lífe, mid his engla werodum.
On ðisum wordum wé magon gewíslice tocnawan 455
ðæt ða synfullan beoð besencte ærest on helle,
mid þam awyrgedum deoflum, ðær ðær hí wunian sceolon,

442 unscrydd *MRT.* noldan *UV.* scrydon *CRT.* 443 Ic wæs] Ic
wæs eac *M.* cweartern *R.* comon *MU*; coman *V.* ge] ge 'na' *T.*
444 þonne] *cap. CMRTV*; *no cap. QU.* 445 hwonne *V.* 446 hungrinne]
hungrigne *R*; hungrine *CMT. See note on 420.* þurstine *T.* 447 untrumne oððe] *transposed M.* 448 earman *MV.* forscyldgodu*m RT*;
forscildegodon *M.* 449 sylfon *CUV.* forwyrndon] *sic MRTUV*;
forwyrdon *Q*; forwyr'n'don *C.* 450 litlum *CRT*; *plus* 'ðearfum' *T*,
'þearfan' *U.* 452 ecum witum *CV.* 454 to] into *M.* weredu*m MR*;
weoredum *T. Here ends the extract in M.* 457 sceolan *CRT*; scylan *V.*

Glosses, Latin: 441 cuma: hospes *R.* 443 untrum: *infirmus R.* cweartern: carc*ere R.* 444 andwyrdað: respond*ent R.* 445 Eala þu: o tu *R.*
446 cuman: hospit*em T.* 447 untrumne: infirm*um R.* cwearterne:
carc*ere R.* þenodan: ministr*auimus RT.* 448 andwyrt: respond*et R.*
earmu*m*: miseris *R.* forscyldgodu*m*: reis, da*m*natis *R*; criminosis, scel*e*ratis *T.*
449 his: hoc *R.* 450 hys: hoc *R.* 451 gewitað: discedu*nt RT.*
arleasan: imp*ii RT.* 453 rihtwisan: iusti *T.* 454 weredu*m*: choro *RT.*

444–50 [*44*] Tunc respondebunt ei et ipsi, dicentes: Domine, quando te
vidimus esurientem, aut sitientem, aut hospitem, aut nudum, aut infirmum, aut
in carcere, et non ministravimus tibi?
[*45*] Tunc respondebit illis, dicens: Amen dico vobis: Quamdiu non fecistis
uni de minoribus his, nec mihi fecistis.
451–4 [*46*] Et ibunt hi in supplicium æternum: iusti autem in vitam æternam.
[*Quoted BE f. 8^v, Prog III. xxxvi, with* impii *for* hi.]
455–8 [*BE f. 9, Prog III. xliv, abridged*] Precurrit ergo impiorum dampnatio,
et post sequitur electorum remuneratio, dicente Christo, *Ibunt impii,* etc.

and ðá halgan syððan síðiað to heofonum.

Be ðære ylcan endebyrdnysse *awrát éac Iohannes ðus: *p. 230
Heora ælcum wæs gedemed be his agenum weorcum;   460
þonne sé déað and seo héll wurdon asende
into þam bradan mere ðæs brastligendan fyres.
Sé deað and séo hell is se déofol sylf,
for ðan ðe he is ealdor ðæs ecan déaðes,
and hé is sé ordfruma eallra dæra wítena.   465
[þa cwæð eft Iohannes be ðam arleasum mannum:]
Ælc ðæra manna wæs aworpen into ðam widgillan mere
ðæs brádan fýres, ðe on ðære líflican béc
æror næs awríten on þam ecan gemynde,
swa swa ðæra halgena naman ðe mid þam Hǽlende wuniað 470
syndon awritene on ðære wuldorfullan béc,
þæt is séo forestihtung fram frymðe mid Gode.
On ánum fýre hí byrnað on þam byrnendan mere,

458 syþiað *T.*   459 ilcan *RTV.*   462 inn- *RT.*   brastliendan
RT; brastlienden *C.*   464 and for þon þe *C.*   465 ealra *CRTUV.*
witena] wita *CUV* (*a letter or two erased after the word in U*).   466 *in*
CRTUV, om. *Q; supplied from U.*   eft *over line U.*   arleasan *V*; arleasun (!) *C.*
467 þara *RV*; þære *C.*   inn- *RT.*   w(id)gillum *U*; widgillum *V*; widgellan *C.*
mǽre *V.*   469 æror *altered to* ær on *R*; ærror *C.*   awritem *U*; awriton *C.*
470 þara *V*; þære *C.*   472 forestihting *RT*; forstihtung *C.*   473 byrnen-
du*m UV*; byrnende *C.*

Glosses, Latin: 458 syþiað: vadu*nt T.*   459 Be þære . . . endebyrdnysse:
De hac ordine *R.*   endebyrdnysse: ordine *T.*   464 ealdor: p*r*inceps *RT.*
465 ordfruma: auctor *R*; origo *T.*   witena: pena*rum R.*   466 arleasum:
impiis *RT.*   467 widgillan: spatioso *R* (-a ?)*T.*   469 æror (ær on): p*r*ius
R.   gemynde: memoria *R.*   471 wuldorfullan: glorioso *R.*   472 forestihting: p*r*edestinati*o RT.*

ME: 458 siðiað: fareð *R.*

459–65 [*BE f. 8ᵛ, Prog III. xxxviii, restated*] Sequitur Iohannes in Apocalipsi
dicens: *Et iudicati sunt singuli secundum opera sua; et mors et infernus missi sunt
in stagnum ignis* (*Apoc. xx. 13, 14*). Mors et infernus diabolus intelligitur, quia
ipse est auctor mortis omniumque poenarum.
466–72 [*BE f. 8ᵛ, Prog III. xxxix, modified*] Sanctus Iohannes scripsit in
Apocalipsi ut qui non fuerint inventi in libro vitæ scripti mittantur in stagnum
ignis. [*Ælfric follows the Vulgate,* Et qui non inventus est in libro vitæ scriptus,
missus est in stagnum ignis, *Apoc. xx. 15.*] Et Agustinus dicit quod liber ille
predestinationem significat eorum quibus æterna vita dabitur, quia Deus
oblivionem non patitur, ut libri recitatione indigeat.
473–7 [*BE f. 8ᵛ, elaborated from Prog III. xli and xl*] Unus quippe ignis erit
utrisque, et demonibus et impiis hominibus. . . . Ergo sempiterno igne ardebunt
et mori omnino non poterunt, quia eterna erunt corpora omnium bonorum scilicet
et malorum post communem resurrectionem.

ðá earman menniscan menn, and ðá modigan déoflu;
þæt fyr bið ðonne écé, and hi écelice byrnað,   475
ac héora lichaman ne magon næfre forbyrnan,
for ðan ðe hí beoð éce æfter þam æriste.

Nu smeagað sume men hu ðá ungesæligan déoflu
magon ðær gefrédan ðæs fýres bryne on him,
þonne hi syndon gastas, and nabbað nanne lichaman.   480
Wé secgað nu to sóþan þæt ðæs mannes sáwul
is belocen on his lichaman ða hwíle ðe hé lybbende bið,
and héo of þam lichaman né mæg be hyre agenum dihte,
ac ðæron forberð, swa betere swá wyrse,
blisse and sárnysse, and þonne héo úte bið,   485
ne gefret sé lichama nane sarnysse.

Eall swa eaðelice mæg sé ælmihtiga God
belúcan ðá déofla on þam deorcan fyre,
þæt hí ðæron cwylmion, and ofcuman ne magon;
and sé ðe þá halgan englas on heofonum gegladað,   490
sé mæg éac gedreccan [þa] *déoflu on þam fyre,   *p. 231
ðeah ðe hí gastas syndon, forscyldegode ealle.

Ðæra manna wíte bið swa gemetegod þurh God

---

475 hi ecelice] hetelice (!) C.   forbyrnað RT (for *erased* T).   479 gefredon CRT.   hym UV; hine (!) C.   480 nænne RTUV; nenne C.
481 ðas R.   sawel V; sawle C.   483 hire CRTUV.   484 forbyrð RT.
488 deofla] *altered from* deoflu Q; deoflu UV.   þam] *om.* C.   489 cwylmian
RTV.   491 þa] *sic* CRTUV; *om.* Q.   492 syndan V.   forscyldgode
RT; forscildegode C.   493 Ðara V.   gemetgod RT; gemetogod C.

Glosses. Latin: 479 gefredon: sentire T.   480 þonne hi syndon: *cum* sint
RT.   484 forbyrð: *patitur* RT.   485 sarnysse: dolorem T.
486 gefret: sentit T.   489 cwylmian: *cruciantur* RT.   492 forscyldgode: *criminosi* RT; malingni T (*another hand*).   493 wíte: pena R.   bið
gemetgod: *temperetur* RT.
ME: 478 smeagað: þencheþ R; þencþ T.   479 gefredan: þolian U.
483 dihte: wille R.   486 ne gefret: næf[ð] U.

478–92 [*BE f. 8ᵛ–9, Prog III. xli restated*] Sanctus itaque Augustinus de poena
demoniorum sic ait: Cur enim non dicamus, quamvis miris tamen veris modis,
etiam demones incorporeos posse poena corporalis ignis affligi, si animas [animæ]
hominum nunc possint includi corporalibus membris in quibus patiuntur dolores.
[*BE cont., not Prog*] Et nos dicimus quod omnipotens Deus, qui sanctos angelos
in cælesti regno remunerat et letificat, potest etiam dampnatos angelos eterni
ignis cruciatibus affligere.
493–503 [*BE f. 9, Prog III. xlii, shortened and rearranged*] Tanto igitur
quisque hominum ibi tolerabiliorem habebit dampnationem, quanto hic minorem habuit iniquitatem, quia ipse ignis, pro diversitate meritorum, aliis erit

þæt se ðe hwónlicor syngode, þæt hé hwonlicor ðrowað,
and se ðe swiðor syngode, þæt hé swiðor ðrowige,   495
and be his ágenum geearnungum ælc man ðær ðrówað.

Ðæt líðoste wíte and þæt leohtoste
bið ðam únwittigum cíldum ðe wǽron ungefullode,
þe náne oðre synne ðurh hí sylfe ne geworhton,
buton þære ánre ðé Adám þurhtéah,   500
and ðurh ðá ane wæs eall mancynn fordón,
buton þam ðe gelyfdon on ðone lyfiendan Hǽlend,
and wurdon gefullode fram ðære fyrnlican synne.

Né magon þá fordemdan, ne furðon ðá deoflu,
þa blisse géséon þe bið mid ðam halgum,   505
syððan hí gebrohte béoð on þam brádan fýre,
ac hi ðær béclysede cwylmiað on éccnysse.

Iohannes sé Godspellere, on his gastlican gesihðe,
cwæþ þæt he gesáwe syððan æfter ðisum,
eall-níwe heofonan and eall-níwe eorðan,   510
for ðan ðe þes middanéard bið mid þam brádan fýre
ðe on Cristes tocyme cymð swa færlice
eall geedníwod, and éac seo sunne

494–5 se ... ðrowað, se ... ðrowige] *transposed RT.*   495 swiðer *V (first only),* *C (twice).*   496 ge-] *om. CUV.*   497 liðeste *V.*   leohteste *CV.*
500 butan *RTU.*   502 butan *RTUV.*   lifigendan *RTUV;* lifiende *C.*
503 gefullude *U.*   from *R.*   504 furðan *altered over line to* forðan *RT;*
forðæn *C.*   deofla *U;* deoflen *C.*   505 bið] beoð *CUV.*   506 fure *altered to* fyre *U.*   507 þar *R.*   á *over line before* on *V.*   ec- *CRTUV.*
508 gastlicum *UV;* gaslice (!) *C.*   509 þissum *UV.*   511 þam bradan] bradum *C.*

Glosses, Latin: 494 hwonlicor: minus *RT (firmer hands).*   498 unwittigum: *insensatis RT.*   500 þurhteah: *perpetrauit RT.*   503 fyrnlican: originali *RT* (-gen- *T).*   504 ne furðan: *nec etiam R; nec eciam T.*
507 cwylmiað: *cruciantur RT.*   510 niwe: *nouum (twice) T.*   511 þes: *iste RT.*   513 (bið) geedniwad: *renouatur RT.*

---

levior, aliis gravior. Mitissima omnium poena erit eorum qui, preter peccatum quod originale traxerunt, nullum insuper addiderunt.

504–7 [*BE f. 9, Prog II. xxxii and III. li*] Credendum vero est quod ante retributionem extremi iudicii iniusti in poenis quosdam iustos in requie conspiciunt, ut eos videntes in gaudio, non solum de suo supplicio sed etiam de illorum bono crucientur. Post iudicium autem nesciunt quid agatur in gaudio beatorum.

508–18 [*BE f. 9, Prog III. xliv, xlvi, xlviii, restated*] Et ilico [Iohannes] adiecit: *Et vidi celum novum et terram novam (Apoc. xxi. 1).* . . . . Et hoc quod dicit, *celum novum et terram novam,* non alia creanda sunt, sed hec ipsa renovantur per ignem. Et in celo novo et terra nova omnino non erunt nisi electi.

and se móna soðlice be seofanfealdum beoð
beorhtran þonne hi nú syndon, be þan ðe us secgað béc;　　515
and on ðære niwan heofonan, and on ðære niwan eorðan
né beoð nane oðre buton Godes gecorenan,
þe his halgum gegearcode fela eardungstówa.

Æfter ðysum dome ure Drihten færð
to his heofonlican Fæder, mid þam halgum mannum　　　　520
ðe hé on middanearde of þære móldan arærde,
and betæchð hí his Fæder, swa hit stent *on bócum:　　　*p. 232
Cum tradiderit regnum Patri suo:
þæt is on urum gereorde, þonne he betæhcð ríce his Fæder;
for ðan ðe hí beoð Godes ríce, and hi rixiað mid Gode.　　525
Crist him gelæst þonne, swa swa hé him on lífe behét,
ða ða hé clypode of eorðan to his ælmihtigan Fæder:
Fæder mín, ic wylle þæt ðá wunion mid me
ðe ðu me forgeafe of ðisum middanéarde,
ðær ðær ic sylf eom, þæt hi geséon magon　　　　　　530
míne beorhtnysse, ðe ðu me forgeafe,
for ðan ðe ðu lufudest me, ær ðam ðe middanéard gewurde.
Sé Hǽlend soðlice is his halgena heafod,

514 seofon- *RUV*; vii *T*.　　-fealdan *U*; -fealdon *C*.　　515 ðam *RTUV*.
ðe] *om. R; over line T*.　　secgað bec] *transposed RT*.　　517 butan *CRTUV*.
518 þe] 'for *þam*' *þe R*; for ðam þe 'he' *T*; þe he *C*.　　halgum *altered to*
halgan *R*; halgan *CT*.　　'is' gegearcod(e) *R*.　　521 hé *over line Q*.
522 betæcð *RTUV*; betæht *C*.　　swa hit] swa swa hyt *RT*.　　524 betæcð
CRTUV.　　524–5 his fæder . . . rice] *in margin U*.　　525 godes] on
godes *C*.　　ricsiað *RT*.　　göde *V*.　　526 hym *R (first), U (twice)*;
heom *(twice) V*.　　swa swa] *Here begins the fragment in f^b*.　　527 cleopode
V.　　of] ofer *UV*.　　fæder] gode *C*.　　528 wille *CRUf^b*. wunian *CRTV*.
530 seolf *altered to* sylf *f^b*; silf *C*.　　531 breoht- *f^b*.　　532 lufodest
RTUVf^b; lufedast *C*.　　*second* ðe] þæ *R*.　　533 halgana *f^b*; halgene *C*.

Glosses, Latin: 527 *first* þa: *tunc R*.　　532 ær þam þæ: *ante R*.

513b–15 [*Ultimately from Is. xxx. 26*] Et erit lux lunæ sicut lux solis, et lux
solis erit septempliciter sicut lux septem dierum, in die qua alligaverit Dominus
vulnus populi sui, et percussuram plagæ eius sanaverit. [*See note.*]
519–25 [*BE f. 9^{r-v}, Prog III. xlv*] Iam vero post iudicium pergit hinc Christus
rex noster, et ducet secum ad celum corpus cui caput est (*Col. i. 18*), et offert
regnum Deo et Patri (*I Cor. xv. 24*).
526–32 [*BE f. 9^v, Prog III. lii, modified*] Sicut ipse in mundo promisit suis
sequacibus dicens ad Patrem: [Pater, quos dedisti mihi,] volo ut ubi ego sum
et ipsi sint mecum, ut videant claritatem meam, [quam dedisti mihi, quia
dilexisti me ante constitutionem mundi.] (*Ioan. xvii. 24, the bracketed portion
not in BE.*)
533–41 [*BE f. 9^v, Prog III. lii, lv, recast*] Si enim capitis membra sumus et

and hí mid him rixiað, his englum gelíce,
and hi God geséoð, swa swutellice swa swa englas,   535
swa swa Iohannes cwæþ to ðam Cristenum mannum:
Wé hine soðlice geseoð swutellice swa swa hé is.
And eft sé apostol Paulus on his pistole cwæð:
Nu we menn geseoð swilce þurh sceawere,
and on rǽdelse, ac we eft geseoð   540
fram ansyne to ansyne on þam ecan lífe.
Eft cwæþ sé Hælend on his halgan godspelle,
þær ðær ic sylf beo, ðær bið mín ðen,
and se ðe me ðénað, hine gé(ar)wurðað mín Fæder.
Manega becumað of middanearde to heofonum   545
Godes halgena, for ðan ðe hé habban wile
micel werod mid him, swa swa hit wel geríst,
and hí beoð geendebyrde ælc be his geearnungum,

534 ricsiað *RT*.   535 swutollice *RT*; swutelice *C*.   537 swutellice]
swa swutollice *RT*; swutelice *Cf*^{b}.   538 æft *f*^{b}.   cwæð on his pistole *C*.
539 urne drihten *over line after* geseoð *T*.   540 on] *om*. *C*   redelse *f*^{b}.
æft *f*^{b}.   hine *over line after* geseoð *C*.   541 anseone *U* (*twice*).   to
ansyne] *om*. *C*.   542 Eft . . . hælend] Se hel*end* cwæð *C*.   hel*end f*^{b}.
544 gearwurðað] *sic CRTUVf*^{b} (-ar- *erased Q*).   545 Manæga *f*^{b}.
546 halgana *f*^{b}.   547 gerisð *V*.   548 geendebirde *f*^{b}.

Glosses, Latin: 540 on rædelse: enin*g*mate *R*; *in* enin*g*mate *T*.   541 fram
ansyne to ansyne: facie ad facie*m RT*.   544 þenað: ministrat *R*.   geár-
wurðað: honorificabit *R*; honorificat *T*.   545 Manega:m*ul*ti *R*.
547 werod: t*ur*bam *T*.   gerist: dec*et*, oport*et*, congru*it RT*.   548 geendebyrde: ordinati *RT*.
ME: 547 werod: folc *R*.

unus in se et in nobis est Christus (*I Cor. xii. 12 sqq*.), utique ubi ipse ascendit et
nos ascensuri sumus. Similes ergo tunc angelis erimus, quia sicut illi nunc vident,
ita et nos Deum post resurrectionem videbimus. Sicut Paulus ait: *Videmus nunc
per speculum in enigmate; tunc autem facie ad faciem* (*I Cor. xiii. 12*). Et Iohannes
apostolus dixit, *quoniam videbimus eum sicuti est* (*I Ioan. iii. 2*).
542–4 [*Ioan. xii. 26, not in BE nor in Prog*] Ubi sum ego, illic et minister meus
erit. Si quis mihi ministraverit, honorificabit eum Pater meus.
545–7 [*Not explicit in BE or Prog. Cf. supra, Homily II. 241 sqq.*]
548–57 [*BE f. 9*^{v}, *partly Prog III. lviii*] Gradus honorum atque gloriarum qui
in illa vita futuri sunt, ut ait sanctus Agustinus, quis est idoneus cogitare?
Quanto magis dicere? [*BE alone*] Hinc Paulus apostolus ait: *Stella autem ab
stella differt in claritate; sic et resurrectio mortuorum* (*I Cor. xv. 41 sq*.). [*BE, Prog*]
Et nullus inferior invidebit superiori, . . . nec aliquis ordo vult esse quod non
accepit, sicut nec in corpore nostro vult digitus esse oculus, . . . sed unumquod-
que membrum totius corporis, pacata compagine, hoc quod accepit possidet (*cf.
I Cor. xii*). [*BE alone*] Sic habitabitur tunc illa superna civitas Hierusalem summa
concordia et caritate quæ numquam cadit, in qua valde magnus civis habebitur
qui minimus estimabitur.

and éác gewuldrode on þam micelan wurðscipe,
be ðam ðe hí on life lufodon heora Scyppend;   550
and ðar ne bið nán ánda on heora ænigum,
ac hí ealle beoð on anre geðwærnysse,
and on sóðre sibbe symle wunigende.
Ðær bið swiðe micel and swiðe mære *on [w]uldre   *p. 233
sē þe læst bið geðuht on þam lífe wunigende,   555
and he ne gewilnað nanes wuldres furðor
ofer þæt ðe he hæfð þurh ðæs Hælendes gife.
Ælc man mæg ðær geséon oðres mannes geðoht,
ne him næfre né hingrað, ne hefigmod ne bið,
ne him ðurst ne derað, ne hine ne drehð nan ðing,   560
ac hí ealle beoð on anre blisse mid Criste,
hine lufigende buton toforlætennysse,
and hine herigende butan werignysse,
and Crist sylf ðonne bið him eallum ælc ðing,
and him naht wana ne bið, þonne hi hine habbað.   565
Hé is heora ríce, and líf, and wurðmynt,

549 micclan *RTf*ᵇ; miclan *C*.   wurðscype *T*.   551 þær *CRTUVf*ᵇ.
552 anræ *R*.   553 on] *om. f*ᵇ.   sybbe *f*ᵇ.   symble *RTUV*.   wuniende
CR.   554 mere *f*ᵇ.   wuldre] *sic CRTUVf*ᵇ; woruld'r'e *Q*.   555 wuniende
CR.   556 wuldræs *f*ᵇ.   557 hefð *f*ᵇ.   ðes *Cf*ᵇ (*over line C*).   gyfe *f*ᵇ.
558 Elc *f*ᵇ.   559 nefre *f*ᵇ; neafre *C*.   ne he hefigmod *T*.   560 dærað *R*.
last ne] *om. R*; *over line T*.   drecð *UV*; dreceð *R*; drecað *T*.   561 anre]
om. C.   562 lufiende *R*; luuiende *C*.   butan *RTUV*.   -lætenysse *RT*;
-lætennesse *UV*.   563 buton *Cf*ᵇ.   weryg- *f*ᵇ.   564 ðonne] *om. RT*.
hym *U*; heom *V*.   ælc] æl *f*ᵇ (*perhaps* c *cut off by binder*).   565 hym *UV*.
566 wyrðmynt *V*.

Glosses, Latin: 549 gewuldrode: glorificati *RT*.   550 be þam þe: quemadmodum *T*.   552 geþwærnysse: *con*cordia *RT*.   553 sibbe: pace *RT*.
554 on wuldre: glorie *T*.   556 wuldres: gloriam *R*.   furðor: vl*terius R*.
557 gife: gracia *R*.   559 hefigmod: *grauis T*.   562 toforlætenysse:
i*ntermissione RT*.   563 werignysse: fatigati*one RT*.
ME: 554 wuldre: glorie *T* (*or Latin genitive, as conjectured above?*)

558–65 [*BE f. 9ᵛ, first sentence from Prog III. lx; the OE reverses the order*]
Finis igitur desideriorum nostrorum Christus tunc erit, qui sine fine videbitur,
sine fastidio amabitur, sine fatigatione laudabitur. . . . [*BE alone*] Patebunt etiam
cogitationes nostrae invicem nobis, et non egemus sustentari cibis aut poculis,
quia non erit ibi esuries aut sitis (*cf. Apoc. vii, 16*) ubi erit *Deus omnia in omnibus*
(*I Cor. xv. 28; quoted in Prog III. lxi*).
566–74 [*BE f. 9ᵛ–10, a small part as indicated from Prog III. lxi, lxii*] [*BE
alone*] Ipse denique regnum, ipse possessio erit electorum suorum, . . . in quo . . .
est [*BE, Prog*] vita et salus et copia et gloria et honor et pax et omnia bona.
[*BE, Prog paraphrased*] Ibi erit nobis dies eterna, [*BE alone*] ibi dupplicia, id

heora hǽl and wuldor, sibb and genihtsumnys,
and ðær soðlice bið an éce dæg, ðe næfre ne geendað,
and hí be twyfealdan beoð þonne gewuldrode
on sáwle and on lichaman, and hí scínað æfre   570
swa beorhte swa sunne on heora Fæder ríce.
Se ðe leofað and rixað mid his leofan Suna
and ðam Halgan Gáste, on ánre godcundnysse,
án ælmihtig God, á butan ende, AMEN.

567 hel f^b.   wuldo f^b.   sib CUV; sybb f^b.   568 ðer f^b.   nefre f^b.
569 twyfealdum RT; twefealdan C.   gewuldrodode T.   570 scynað Cf^b.
572 ricsað RT; rixat C.   573–4 on anre . . . ende] on ealre worulde worulda
buto ælcum ende C.   574 ælmihti f^b.

Glosses, Latin: 567 hǽl: salus RT.   wuldor: gloria R.   sibb: pax R.
genihtsumnyss: habundancia R; sufficiencia T.   569 be twyfealdum:
duppliciter T.   gewuldrade: glorificati R.

---

est binas stolas possidemus, et letitia sempiterna erit nobis et fulgebimus sicut
sol in regno Patris nostri (*cf. Matth. xiii. 43*), qui vivit et regnat sine fine. Amen.

NOTES

Title. The DICENDUS of RTU looks authentic because it removes all
danger of ambiguity by its grammatical nicety. Since one can gather the
essential meaning of the title without it, a scribe might easily decide to
leave it out, whereas only a remarkably fussy scribe would be likely to
add it if it were missing. I conclude that RT and U have inherited the
correct reading, by separate lines of descent, from the author's original,
and that Q and V (which likewise have separate lines) have independently
omitted it.

19. *wæterstreamas*. This seemingly inevitable compound is rare. It was
cited from the present passage in U by Napier in *COEL* ('Contributions to
Old English Lexicography') and thence found its way into BTS. Another
occurrence, in the *Paris Psalter, Psalm* lxxvii. 44, is recorded in BT.

53. *géearnian*. The accentuation of the prefix ge- recurs at lines 270,
311, 505, and 544 in Q and constitutes a seemingly freakish extreme.
Perhaps it is simply a careless extension of the scribe's tendency to accent
the vowels of such monosyllables as *ne, se*. Here and frequently elsewhere
he leaves a space after *ge* as if it were a separate word. Perhaps he absent-
mindedly confused it with the pronoun. Cf. what is said of Q's accents
in the introduction to IV, p. 261.

69. *swa swa we sædon eow on sumum spelle ær*. Presumably in the first
homily for Pentecost, *CH* I. XXII. The sevenfold gifts are enumerated at

p. 326 in Thorpe's edition, but lines 70 and 71 suggest rather an earlier passage, 322/24–31. Cf. note on IX. 144.

69, 70. On the omission of these lines in C, U, and V see the discussion above, p. 412, where it is argued that the omission is due to eye-skip on the part of the scribe of a common ancestor rather than to editorial revision by the author or by anyone else.

94. *swa swa we sædon eow oft.* For example, in *De Initio Creaturæ, CH* I. 12 sqq.; *Epiphania Domini, CH* I. 112; *Nativitas Domini, CH* II. 6; and doubtless in several other places. Especially close in phrasing to 95–103 is a passage in Ælfric's *Hexameron*, 413–19. The present passage is a little closer to the Latin from which both appear to be derived, probably because in the *Hexameron*, which was pretty surely composed earlier, Ælfric was influenced by other sources as well.

112. *Mors acerba, mors inmatura, mors naturalis.* This triad was borrowed by Julian from Isidore's *Etymologiæ,* Lib. XI, cap. ii, 32 (*PL* LXXXII. 418). Ælfric has rightly apprehended that the underlying figure is that of fruit, which is bitter to the taste when it first appears on the tree and still unpalatable when it has attained to its full size but has not mellowed.

120. *la ge,* Q. This nonsensical reading (for *lange*) may have arisen in an earlier copy in which the scribe wrote *la* instead of *lan* at the end of a line and *ge* at the beginning of the next. If the mistake was in the common ancestor of Q and R, it explains the absence of *lange* in R and T. The scribe of Q copied *la ge* mechanically, but someone in the line of R was a little more attentive and chose to amputate.

153–9. Compare the following passage from Ælfric's homily, *In Natale Unius Apostoli, CH* II. 526/30–33:

> Micel heap holdra freonda ure andbidað þær, orsorh be him sylfum, carful gyt for ure hælðe. Uton forði efstan to urum eðele, þæt we magon ure frynd geseon, and ure siblingas gegretan.

This is clearly an earlier treatment of the same Latin passage, though the selection of detail is different. The second sentence, for example, depends in part on a Latin sentence immediately preceding the description of the multitude of friends that awaits us: 'Quid non properamus et currimus ut patriam nostram videre et parentes salutare possimus?' (The passage containing this sentence is quoted as an illustration for lines 139–52, which are not taken directly from the Boulogne Excerpts and may, in their reference to the man who is God's friend, have been suggested by the talk of God's friends in the earlier homily.) Although the ultimate source of the Latin passage is Cyprian's *De Mortalitate,* cap. xxvi (*Opera Omnia,* ed. G. Hartel, *CSEL* III, Pars I [1868], 313), Ælfric probably needed to go no further than his own excerpts from the *Prognosticon,* which he seems to have made long before he composed the earlier homily. (See above, p. 409, note 1.) There is nothing like the passage in Ælfric's principal source for that homily, which Max Förster correctly identified (*Anglia* XVI. 12) as Gregory's *Homilia XXVII in Evang.* (*PL* LXXVI. 1204 sqq.).

159. *hæftnyssum.* This unusual word, instanced twice in the singular (see Glossary) but not elsewhere recorded as Ælfric's, would presumably mean 'bonds' or 'snares' in the plural. I have allowed it to stand as genuine, though with some hesitation, for the following reasons: (1) it is the *durior lectio.* (2) Although the *persecutiones* of the Latin source seems at first to point clearly to *ehtnyssum*, which is a very common word in Ælfric's writings, there are images of a siege a little earlier that could have prompted the choice of *hæftnyssum.* (3) The initial vowel of *ehtnyssum* is not needed because alliteration is already supplied by *deofles—Drihtne.* (4) If *hæftnyssum* is an unauthorized substitution it points to an otherwise unsupported association of MS. Q with the group CUV in opposition to M, R, and T. But if *ehtnyssum* is the substitution we leave Q independent of CUV and find instead that M is in association with the closely connected RT. This seems the more likely association, since it does not conflict with other evidence, whereas what is generally known of Q indicates that it should not be closer to CUV than to R. See the introductory comment, p. 413 above.

162. *to Gode.* I have followed the evidence of the manuscripts in interpreting this expression as *to Gode* rather than *to gōde.* The manuscripts all tend to distinguish *gōd* by spelling it *gód* or *good* or *góód.* Here six of them have simply *gode*, which is a negative indication that they understood the word as *Gode.* In the seventh, V, someone has made use of the rare cup-shaped accent over the vowel, *gŏde*, a positive vote for *Gode*, as strongly attested by the same manuscript at lines 185–7 below, where the three inflected instances of *gōd* are all correctly supplied with acute accents, *góde, gódum, góde,* and the two instances of *Gode* are correctly supplied with the breve, *gŏde.* Additional instances of *gŏd(e)* occur at lines 104, 251, and 525, all incontestably *God(e)*; at line 467 there is an equally incontestable instance of *mĕre.* Thus this sign appears to be unambiguous, unlike the acute accent, which not infrequently appears over short vowels, either through scribal carelessness or through confusion of functions. V itself, for instance, has *gód* at line 107 where *God* is manifestly correct, and *góde* for *Gode* is an occasional feature of nearly every manuscript. The context at line 162 also favours *to Gode*, especially in view of the contrast between God and the devil in 159. The Latin *ad salutem* might seem at first sight to point the other way, but neither phrase translates it literally and its ultimate meaning is better served by *to Gode.*

193. *þa sceolon.* This reading is favoured by the parallel constructions at 186 and 188. It occurs in four manuscripts, the group CUV and M; whereas Q and RT have *sceolon* alone. This division of manuscripts, as I have explained above, pp. 412–13, is not easily accounted for, because there is some evidence that M is more closely related to RT than either of these to Q. If so we must suppose that Q and RT have omitted *þa* independently, or that the omission occurred in an ancestor of Q, RT,

and M, but M reintroduced *þa* on the strength of the parallels at 186 and 188. This seems probable in view of the general character of M.

210. *be þam ðe hi geworhton ær*. This line is clearly deficient, but the words supplied by V over the line, *her on life*, are lacking in alliteration. One would expect rather, *be þam ðe hi geworhton on þissere worulde ær*. Ælfric may have neglected to complete the line, or an omission may have occurred in a very early and influential copy.

296. The *one* fire that shall overrun the whole world is not explicitly introduced at this stage in the *Prognosticon* and is merely inferential in the Bible. Ælfric seems to be thinking of a sequence similar to that in the alphabetic hymn on the Last Judgement quoted by Bede, *De Arte Metrica*:

> Flamma ignis anteibit iusti vultum Iudicis,
> Cælos, terras, et profundi fluctus ponti devorans.

Essentially this is simply a combination of inferences from *Psal*. xlix. 3, and *Apoc*. xxi. 1. The fire is dwelt upon at length in the OE *Christ* III (*The Last Judgment*), 956 sqq. Cf. Ælfric himself, *CH* I. 616: 'Heofonlic fyr ofergæð ealne middangeard mid anum bryne, and ða deadan arisað of heora byrgenum mid ðam fyre.'

305–38. The topics in these lines had already been treated in a different order in Ælfric's homily for the first Sunday after Easter, *CH* I. 236/5–238/4. There Ælfric argues first that the creator of the universe will have no difficulty in restoring the bodies of the dead. The argument (which is quoted in full above, p. 110) is based on Gregory, *Hom*. xxvi *in Evang.*, and differs greatly in detail from its counterpart here (332–8). The remainder of the earlier passage, however, owes nothing to Gregory's homily. It takes up in succession the ideal condition of the resurrected body (as here, 305–11, 320–5), the indifference of the whole question of bodily condition for the wicked (as here, 326–31), and the absence of marriage, even sexual desire, in heaven (as here, 312–19, though without mentioning the persistence of male and female forms). Ælfric's elaborations indicate (as Dr. Gatch shows in the article cited above, p. 409, note 1) that he had already made his excerpts from the *Prognosticon*.

310 sq. *fulweoxe* and *samweaxen*. It is a question whether to treat *fulweoxe* as one word or two, but in the context is seems to me slightly better to treat it as one, with reduced stress on *ful*. With the past participle *weaxen* we are on firmer ground, and there is no doubt that *samweaxen* is a compound. It occurs here only, so far as the dictionaries tell us, having found its way into them by way of Napier's citation of this passage from U in his *COEL*.

333. *wære he on wætere adruncen*. This detail, not included in the *Prognosticon*, is included in similar words in a Blickling Homily on the Day of Judgement (ed. Morris, p. 95/15, 'Þeah þe hie ær . . . on wætere adruncan'). It occurs also, differently expressed, in a similar list in Ælfric's homily on the martyrs, *CH* II. 544/1:

Ne bið þæs mannes lichama næfre swa swiðe fornumen on fyre, oððe on sæ, oððe ðurh deora geslit, þæt he ne sceole eft arisan ansund þurh ðæs Scyppendes mihte, ðe ealle ðing of nahte gesceop.

It is evident that Ælfric was familiar with the idea independently of the sources he was using at the moment. In the earlier homily he has added the sentence just quoted to a paragraph based on Gregory's *Homilia XXXV in Evang.* (cf. Max Förster, *Anglia* XVI. 4). In composing the present homily his first step (if he made the Boulogne Excerpts) was to rewrite a passage in the *Prognosticon* taken directly from Augustine, making it a little more traditional and simpler in expression. The ideas of this revision can be found in both Augustine and Gregory, but probably not the exact words. Then, in writing the Old English homily, Ælfric slightly enlarged the Latin of the Excerpts in accordance with a familiar list of alternatives. Recently J. E. Cross has traced the development of this theme from *Apoc.* xx. 13 (*Et dedit mare mortuos qui in eo erant*) through several of the early Christian writers, Greek and Latin, to Old English homilists, and, as he believes, to the author of *The Wanderer*. See his article, 'On the Wanderer Lines 80–84', *Vetenskaps-Societetens i Lund Årsbok*, 1958–9, pp. 75–110.

339–42. Ælfric had already made this point in very similar language in the Easter homily of the First Series, *CH* I. 224/5–8:

þeah man deadne mannan mid reafe bewinde, ne arist þæt reaf na ðe hraðor eft mid þam men, ac he bið mid þam heofenlicum reafe gescryd æfter his æriste.

343–458. The part of this narrative that follows *Matth.* xxv. 32 sqq. is anticipated in Ælfric's sermon for the first Sunday in Lent, *CH* II. 106–8.

375–80. With this list of offenders compare the list of offences in xvi. 73–83, and see the note on that passage. The word *unmæðfull* 'immoderate, greedy', 375, was cited by Napier from this passage in T in *COEL*. It is the only occurrence on record.

420. *hungrienne*. I have allowed this form to stand because it is supported by Q and UV, and if it is taken as the present participle, *hungriendne*, with loss of *d* before the ending, it is supported by C's *hungriende*, for C has many levelled endings. The Latin *esurientem* suggests that this participial form might have been chosen by Ælfric. But there is a good deal of evidence on the other side. (1) The verb normally has mutated *hyn-* or *hin-*. (2) At 446 all the manuscripts agree in giving the adjective *hungrigne* (*hungrinne*, *hungrine*), as do M and RT here. (3) In Ælfric's earlier homily, *CH* II. 108, Thorpe's manuscript has *hungrine* and *hungrinne*. It is possible, of course, that Ælfric introduced a variation at 420, but it is also possible that the scribe who made a fair copy of his original deviated here from the usual spelling of the adjective, perhaps with the participle vaguely in mind, and that this odd spelling was interpreted as the participle by the scribe of C.

465. *witena*. This weak genitive plural of *wīte* 'punishment' appears, among other places, in *CH* II. 310/27.

513*b*-15. Ælfric's addition concerning the brightness of the sun and moon has a parallel in his earlier treatment of the new heaven and earth in his homily for the second Sunday in Advent, *CH* I. 618: 'þonne bið seo sunne be seofonfealdum beorhtre þonne heo nu sy, and se mona hæfð þære sunnan leoht.' This too is an addition to Ælfric's immediate Latin source, which Max Förster correctly identified (*Anglia* XVI. 9) as Bede's commentary on *Luke* xxi. 33. Ælfric's earlier addition is a little closer to the passage from *Isaiah* quoted under *Sources*, but he was probably familiar with many partial repetitions of the prophecy.

539. The word *sceawere* 'mirror', translating *speculum*, is rare in Old English. BT cites it only from a gloss (Wright–Wülker, *Old English Vocabularies*, I. 152/38, *speculea*: *sceawere*), and BTS only from this passage, which was quoted from MS. U by Napier in *COEL*, and from the translation of Alcuin's *De Virtutibus et Vitiis* in MS. Cotton Vespasian D. xiv (our G). BTS brackets this citation because MS. G is of the twelfth century, but the translation may go back to a late Old English original. The relevant passage occurs in Assmann's edition, *Anglia* XI (1889), 374/78, and in Warner, *Early English Homilies*, p. 94/4. Three Middle English examples are recorded in the *OED*, *shower*, sb.[2], 2.

559. *hefigmod*. This word, though formed like such traditional poetical words as *deormod*, *wraðmod*, *sarigmod*, and *werigmod*, has been recorded in the sense 'heavy-hearted, sad' only as it appears in this passage. Napier cited it from U in *COEL*.

XI*a*

DE SANCTA TRINITATE ET DE
FESTIS DIEBUS PER ANNUM

WHOEVER compiled this homily has joined together, at some points interwoven, three passages that can be found separately in Ælfric's extant writings and three shorter passages (probably segments of a single passage) that appear nowhere else but are equally characteristic of Ælfric. Among the three recognizable passages is the greater part of the opening section of homily XI, the review of festivals and other holy occasions from Christmas to the octave of Pentecost. Here it dominates the middle part of the homily and is responsible for part of the title, *De Festis Diebus per Annum*. One could argue that this passage, though rivalled in length and surpassed in scope by another, was in fact the basic one, to which the others had been added for the fuller development of its themes. Hence I have printed the whole piece here as a pendant to XI. To print the whole, not simply the unique passages, has seemed advisable even though I think Ælfric did not put it together, for it is well to have the evidence on view. Besides, the compilation has a good deal of interest in its own right.

The homily stands first, by obvious design, in MS. H, to which it has been added by the interpolator who so greatly enlarged what had previously been a straightforward copy of Ælfric's First Series and a few appended homilies. Thus it directly precedes *De Initio Creaturæ* (here assigned to be read *ante natale domini*) and two Christmas homilies, the one that belongs to the First Series and our I. It makes a good introduction to these three homilies in particular and to the carefully ordered annual series that follows; for, by adding other matter to the liturgical survey of the *Sermo in Octavis Pentecosten* at both ends and in the middle, it embraces all the essentials of the creed, gives full weight to the doctrine of the Trinity, and at the same time brings out the role of the Second Person in relation to man from the creation to the last judgement, dwelling especially on the life of Christ on earth as man's redeemer. The *Sermo's* references to the octave of Pentecost as the

time of the discourse are removed, so that we look forward to the
unfolding of the year from the Christmas season, and stop with
the octave of Pentecost because the celebration of the Trinity is a
natural climax and conclusion.

The recognizable members of this compilation are: (1) lines 6–80
of the *Sermo*, which appear, slightly altered and interspersed with
other matter, in the middle section, lines 75–196; (2) the introductory portion of Ælfric's *Letter to Wulfgeat*, Assmann 1. 8–84, of
which lines 8–61a appear consecutively at the beginning, 61b–64
are replaced by twenty unfamiliar lines, to be described later, and
65–84 are interwoven, in the latter half of the middle section, with
lines from the *Sermo*; (3) a self-contained passage on the Trinity
which appears as a conclusion to Ælfric's *Interrogationes Sigewulfi*
in two of the five manuscripts of that work (R and S) and appears
here also as a conclusion, lines 197–234.

The combination of the first two members is what provides the
structure of the discourse. The liturgically inspired passage from
the *Sermo* serves as a reminder of Christ's life on earth, his passion,
resurrection, and ascension, and his sending of the Holy Spirit to
the apostles. The passage from the *Letter to Wulfgeat* is a freely
elaborated statement of the creed, expatiating on the nature and
operations of the Trinity, touching on the emergence of evil in
Satan, then outlining God's dealings with man from creation to
judgement. The passage thus gives the whole sweep of universal
history before the nativity and after the sending of the Holy Spirit;
and in the middle, as it mentions the nativity and then moves at
once to the crucifixion, it overlaps the passage from the *Sermo*,
varying the account of the passion, resurrection, and ascension,
adding details of the harrowing of hell, and, like the creed, bringing in the last judgement as a conclusion immediately after the
scene of Christ sitting in heaven at his Father's right hand. It is
in the overlapping section that the compiler's ingenuity is most
clearly displayed, for he interweaves the two accounts so deftly as
to include all that each of them has to offer, word for word, in one
continuous fabric.

But there are three passages, of twenty, five, and twenty-six
lines respectively, that have been introduced to supplement the
two known passages just described. I have not found these three
passages anywhere else. The first, which has been substituted
for the brief mention of the nativity in the *Letter to Wulfgeat*

(61*b*–64), begins with God's plan for man's redemption, mentions the prophecies, then describes the annunciation and at last the birth. These twenty lines (54*b*–74) usher in Christmas, the first of the festivals of the *Sermo*. After six familiar lines, however, five other strange ones appear (81–85), this time to mention the twelve days of Christmas and reiterate the theme of man's redemption. Now follows (86–101), from the *Sermo*, the account of Epiphany and Candlemasday, ending with the blessing and prophecy of Simeon and Anna; whereupon the most impressive of the unfamiliar passages is introduced, twenty-six lines (102–27) celebrating the many miracles by which Christ revealed his divinity.

These three unfamiliar passages have precisely the character one would expect of Ælfric's own compositions on familiar themes: they not only exhibit his rhythmic prose under easy control but they echo his words and phrases in other treatments of the same themes without repeating any long passage from any one of them. That is, they have the air of free compositions built on the author's own store of formulaic expressions and regulated by his normal alliterative links and his habitual rhythms. For the first two passages, at lines 54*b*–74 and 81–85, the parallels quoted in the apparatus, though not exhaustive, may be enough to establish the point. The third passage, 102–27, is more complex than the others and has a brilliancy of organization that bespeaks such a master as Ælfric himself. Moreover, it stands in an interesting relation to several other passages on Christ's miracles that appear in Ælfric's writings from the beginning to the end of his career. In order to exhibit the significant structure of these passages I have quoted them in the note on 102–27 instead of breaking them up into lists of parallels in the apparatus.

Although Ælfric almost certainly composed the three passages, I do not think he intended them for the places here assigned to them. The first passage, on the Incarnation, proceeds smoothly as an expansion of the *Letter to Wulfgeat*, but the phrasing rather awkwardly anticipates the lines from the *Sermo* that follow. Ælfric would hardly have been satisfied with so crude a transition. It is almost the same with the second passage, the five-line sentence about the twelve days of Christmas. At first this looks like an inevitable part of the sequence, but again, as the parallels show, it rather clumsily echoes expressions in the lines from the *Sermo* that have become its neighbours. The passage on miracles avoids this fault and has great strength in itself, but although it extends the celebration of Christ in accord with the central purpose of the compilation it makes a surprising entrance into the sequence of feast-days. The point of entrance, immediately after the account of Candlemas and the mention of Simeon's prophecy, has a certain validity according to Ælfric himself, for in his homily on that festival, *CH* I. 144/34 sqq., he quotes a portion of Simeon's speech, 'To tacne com Crist, and þam is wiðcweden' (*Luc*. ii. 34), and explains that Christ's miracles were among the signs denied by the unfaithful, believed by the faithful. But in spite of this the shift from Candlemas to the miracles and back to the temptation in the wilderness at the beginning of Lent produces a degree of incoherence.

A very different impression is created if we read the three passages, 54*b*–74, 81–85, 102–27, as a consecutive series. They fit together surprisingly well, with no disturbing repetitions at the joints, and with one consistent theme: the glorification of Christ the redeemer. Passage 1 sets forth in order the Father's plan to send him, its proclamation by the prophets, the annunciation and the birth; passage 2, its twelve-day celebration; passage 3, the miracles by which he revealed his divinity during his life on earth. Consecutive or not, they probably belonged to the same composition, from which the compiler merely selected what he could best combine with the excerpts from the *Letter to Wulfgeat* and the *Sermo*. Like the other two passages, this unknown composition seems addressed to a comparatively uninstructed person or audience. It expounds elementary matters of the faith in a graciously persuasive, popular form, touching on the liturgy like the *Sermo* but dealing primarily with a portion of the divine action that is broadly set forth in the *Letter to Wulfgeat*. I am inclined to believe that we have here part of a similar letter, otherwise lost, from Ælfric to an interested layman.

The final passage, 197–234, is merely added, not interwoven with the other passages. It has been generally accepted as Ælfric's ever since 1883, when MacLean's edition of the *Interrogationes* made it generally available, and there is no reason to doubt the attribution. But recently the question has been raised whether it was originally intended as a conclusion for the *Interrogationes*. This abridged and otherwise modified version of Alcuin's exegetical treatise on *Genesis* has a short preface in rhythmic prose containing

remarks on Alcuin's career and the occasion of his writing this
particular work, followed by the long (though selective) series of
questions and answers, in which alliteration and other ornaments
appear but the rhythms are prevailingly those of ordinary prose.
In three manuscripts, C, P, and W, the piece ends abruptly with
the sentence, 'Nelle we na swiðor embe þis sprecan, for þan þe
we habbað þa nydbehefestan axunga nu awritene', without so much
as an *Amen*. In two others, the closely related R and S, the sentence continues with a co-ordinate clause beginning, 'ac we secgað
nu be þam soðan Gode', thus introducing the rhythmic passage
on the Trinity as a conclusion. MacLean, pointing to the abruptness of the conclusion in CPW, argued that the conclusion in RS
had been composed at the same time as the rest and had merely
been omitted by some impatient person from an ancestor of CPW.
Alternatively one might suppose that Ælfric had intended to add a
conclusion but did not have it ready when he first issued the *Lives
of Saints* and so allowed the piece to circulate for a time in an
unfinished state. But Dr. Clemoes (*Chronology*, 230) has suggested
that the passage on the Trinity was composed, not for the *Interrogationes*, but for the compilation here presented as XI*a*, and was
only later transferred to the *Interrogationes*, not necessarily by
Ælfric. Dr. Clemoes points to a line near the end (231 in this
edition), where we read in all three copies,

> Ðæs we him ðanciað on urum þeowdome.

Ælfric's mention of the liturgy, he suggests, is much more appropriate to XI*a* than to the *Interrogationes*; and it is true that the
liturgy is mentioned many times in XI*a* and only this once in the
Interrogationes. Yet I think this argument is not strong enough to
withstand the evidence on the other side.

I must begin by rejecting outright the notion that Ælfric could
have composed the passage for XI*a*; for if, as I have maintained,
he was not responsible for the compilation, this part of Dr.
Clemoes's argument collapses. But it is conceivable that the passage
formed a conclusion to some other composition, possibly the same
one that furnished the compiler with the three unique passages
already described. The second of these passages refers to the
liturgy, and the praise of Christ in all three might well be followed
(though probably not directly) by a celebration of the Trinity in
which the Second Person was singled out at the end.

Even this hypothesis, however, seems to me unlikely in view of the reasons for accepting the passage as Ælfric's conclusion to the *Interrogationes*. (1) MacLean's argument regarding the abruptness of the conclusion in MSS. C, P, and W is strong, for it is certainly not a characteristic way for Ælfric to end a discourse, whereas the announcement that he has said enough about one subject but will say something of another occurs elsewhere, notably in XI. 92 sq. Sooner or later one would expect such a continuation and conclusion as we find in R and S. (2) The rhythmic introduction to the *Interrogationes* is well balanced by this rhythmic conclusion. (3) The questions about *Genesis* produce answers that have much to do with God as creator of the universe and his earliest dealings with man; but *Genesis* itself yields a Trinitarian view of the deity only after subtle exegesis. It is therefore natural that Ælfric, whose chief authorities lay such heavy stress on the Trinity, should wish to supplement the account of God in the body of the *Interrogationes* with this explicit presentation of his triune being. Even the special notice of the Second Person at the end is easy to understand, for it is characteristic of Trinitarian doctrine to make the Second Person a participant in the creation as well as the agent of man's redemption. Thus the passage effectively offsets the emphasis on the First Person that appears naturally enough in the discussion of *Genesis*. As for the reference to the liturgy, I find it natural enough in its context to need no support from an earlier mention of the theme. (4) The evidence of R and S, the manuscripts containing the passage as a conclusion to the *Interrogationes*, points to its authenticity as such; for the author of the colophon in R (the compiler, apparently, of the ancestral manuscript from which both R and S are descended) does not admit having added anything to the *Interrogationes*, as he does to *De Auguriis* and *De Octo Vitiis*, and thus asks us to believe that he found the *Interrogationes* with the conclusion on the Trinity in his authoritative exemplar. (See the description of R in the Introduction, pp. 62–65.)

Consequently I find it probable that four different compositions of Ælfric are here combined: parts of the *Letter to Wulfgeat*, the *Sermo in Octavis Pentecosten*, the *Interrogationes*, and three passages, possibly consecutive in their original form, from another composition otherwise unknown. Everything except a few scattered words and phrases can safely be attributed to Ælfric, but the compilation as such appears to be the work of an editor. Conceivably this editor was also the scribe of the augmented codex, but since there are indications of scribal error it is probably advisable to think of the two as separate. The editor, then, wanting an introductory sermon for his volume, assembled three or four different works of Ælfric's and chose passages from each that were relevant to his basic themes. One passage, from the *Interrogationes*, he left intact as a conclusion. The others he wove together with considerable skill. Granted that he thought it his business to join together pieces already written by another, not to venture upon the role of author himself, he did a remarkably good job. But it was not such a job as Ælfric himself would have done. The various themes can easily be related to one another but there is incoherence, or repetition, or both at the joints. In addition to the examples already noticed, mention should be made of the interweaving of *Letter* and *Sermo* at 135–41. Line 137, with ingredients from both sources at once, has become overloaded, and line 141 (from the *Sermo*) repeats the phrases of 135*a* and 136*b* (from the *Letter*). Similarly, when the *Letter* is drawn upon for the next two lines (142 sq.), there is a repetition, both conspicuous and awkward, of the greater part of line 140, from the *Sermo*. Perhaps the incomplete line 191, which puts an unauthorized *geleafan* just ahead of its occurrence as a proper part of Ælfric's original in 193, should be blamed on the editor, but here there may be as much as a line and a half missing by mere scribal error, for two lines of the *Sermo* that are needed to complete the sense have been left out. A surer and more favourable view of the editor's quality may be gained at 162–70, where a passage from the *Letter* has been inserted into a sequence from the *Sermo*. Here the ease of transition is remarkable. The Ascension has been described, and the mind travels easily, by the path made familiar in the Creed, to contemplate Christ reigning with his Father in heaven and to dwell for a moment on the Last Judgement. But here again, as with the passage on miracles, though less violently, the natural development of the series of feasts has been interrupted. The scope has been increased, with a real gain for the sermon as an introduction to the faith, but at the cost of local coherence.

A few minor details remain to be mentioned. For the *Letter to Wulfgeat* the editor seems to have had a good though not wholly correct exemplar. Most of the small departures from Assmann's manuscripts can be understood as deliberate adaptations or attempted improvements. At line 44, for instance, it was proper editing to omit the personal address to Wulfgeat and the reference to earlier writings sent to him, although Ælfric himself would probably not have reduced two lines to a line and a half. At a few points, however, what I take to be errors suggest a faulty exemplar, one closer to Z than to P. Thus at line 26 the word *halgan* of P, useful for balance and alliteration, is omitted by Z and H, and at 39 the *manfulle gastas* of P, which completes the line and sums up the sentence, is replaced by the meaningless *manfulne gast* of Z and altogether omitted in H. The omission from H may be independent, but it may have been prompted by such a misreading as we find in Z. At line 164 there is a suspicious resemblance between the confused though fairly common spelling *demende* (for *demenne*) in H and the wholly incorrect *demde* of Z. At line 166 the inclusion of *menn* by Z and H as opposed to P is probably, though not certainly, unauthorized. The possibility that at one point all three manuscripts have inherited an error is discussed in the note on line 12.

The editor's exemplars for the *Sermo in Octavis Pentecosten* and the *Interrogationes* seem to have been very good. There are, however, two points in the text of the *Sermo*, lines 131 (an intrusive *he*) and 183 (*lofsange* for *sange*), where there are indications of an ancestor shared by R (which had *he*, later erased, and has, with T, *lofsangum*). In the text of the passage from the *Interrogationes* there is only one probable error, the omission of a line (by homoeoteleuton) after *nan*, 223. The omission is shared by R, whereas S has what I take to be the correct reading. At three other points H agrees, probably rightly, with R against S (199 *þæt he* for *se þe*; 213 *ac*; 220 *se* before *suna, -u*), and at several others it agrees, probably rightly, with S against R (202, 204, 206, 213 *he*, 229, 233). The one error shared with R and the absence of R's other errors point to a common ancestor for H and R not shared by S, though certainly the evidence is too slight to be counted on.[1] Such as it is, it seems to confirm the notion that the passage on the Trinity was excerpted by the editor from the *Interrogationes*.

[1] This relationship seems a little surprising, though not impossible, because R and the part of S here considered (as explained in the Introduction) appear to be descended from a manuscript containing the original of the colophon in R and all twenty-four of its full sermons. It now appears that there was a manuscript intermediate between this archetype and R, so that there were once at least three manuscripts with the same general content and the same colophon.

The only bits of composition I would attribute to the editor, apart from single transitional words and the little readjustments already mentioned, are the not very felicitous revision at lines 159 sq. and the necessary, rather skilful one that begins at 188 and runs into trouble (perhaps scribal) at 191.

The chief aids in reading the damaged text of MS. H are the well-preserved copies of the *Letter to Wulfgeat*, the *Sermo in Octavis Pentecosten*, and the *Interrogationes*; and it is fortunate that the unique passages (54*b*–74, 81–85, 102–27) have very few lacunae. For lines 1–177 there is a further aid. At some time before the foliation of H reported by Wanley (*Catalogus*, p. 208) someone undertook to make a copy of the homily and covered three sides of two folios with a painstaking though not entirely faithful transcript in a late medieval, or early modern, archaizing script. N. R. Ker dates this copy tentatively in the sixteenth century, rather than the fourteenth or fifteenth as suggested earlier at the British Museum, and he may well be right, though it seems to me odd that a scholar of that era would substitute levelled endings, *e* or *æ*, for OE -*um*. At any rate it is clear that the copyist was familiar with late ME spellings and that, on the other hand, he was ordinarily making a faithful copy, in an antiquarian spirit, of the Old English words. Occasionally he misread the old letters and produced nonsense. When he came to the bottom of the third page, having copied a little more than three pages of the original (to the middle of line 177), he stopped, leaving the verso blank. The two leaves seem to have been inserted in the volume between two leaves of the original version, for although Wanley does not mention them, his report of the foliation implies their presence. The original version began on f. 1ᵛ and finished on 5ᵛ. Somewhere between were the two leaves of the copy. At present, now that the fire-damaged leaves have been inserted in paper and rebound, the original version stands on f. 1ʳ (since this has been reversed by mistake), and on ff. 4ʳ–5ᵛ. The copy is on ff. 2ʳ–3ʳ. Untrustworthy though it is, it has some value in confirming readings no longer clearly visible (and sometimes altogether missing) in the original version, for sometimes the copy is legible where the original is not.

Because of the textual complications just outlined I have divided the apparatus into two main parts. In Apparatus I are the readings of the late secondary copy in H, ff. 2–3ʳ, marked Hᶜ, besides a few at beginning and end from Wanley's *Catalogus*. The readings of H^c are useless except as confirming the original readings of H for lines 1–177. In Apparatus II are collations with the texts of the excerpted passages as they stand in the three known works of Ælfric.

Apparatus III is of a different character. It contains parallels from Ælfric's other writings for the first two of the unique passages, lines 54*b*–74 and 81–85.

I have not attempted to supply sources for this compilation. Most of the passages of which it is composed seem to me to have been written freely by Ælfric without a source in front of him, though with many sources in his head. MacLean has printed an approximate source from Isidore for the concluding passage, but I question whether, for this familiar theme, Ælfric derived more than a few suggestions from it, if indeed he used it at all.

DE S*ANCTA* TRINITATE
ET DE FESTIS DIEBUS (PER ANNUM)

Se ælmihtiga Wealdend, ðe (ne on)gann næfre,
7 se ðe ana is soð God, gesceop 'ealle' ðing,
gesewenlice 7 ungesewenlice, ðurh his soðan Wisdom;
7 se Wisdom is witodlice his Sunu,
ure Hælend Crist, se ðe us alysde;   5
7 se ðridda had on (ðære halgan Ðryn)ny(sse)
is se halga Froforgast þe us 'ge'frefrað mid his gy(fe)
7 ure mod onliht æfre to góódnysse;
7 he ealra manna synna þurh his mihte forgyfð,
þam ðe mid dædbote doð geswicenyss(e).   10
Se is soðlice lufu ðæs (s)oðfæstan (Fæder),

This text as a whole occurs only in H (Cotton Vitellius C. v), ff. 1ʳ and 4–5ᵛ.
Lines 1–177 occur a second time on three pages of the same codex, ff. 2–3ʳ.
They are a late medieval or early modern copy of H, called Hᶜ in the apparatus
below. On this copy, and on the division of the apparatus, see the introductory
remarks just above. Thanks partly to Hᶜ but mainly to the well-preserved
contributory texts cited in Apparatus II, the lacunae in the fire-damaged H,
here designated by round brackets, can usually be filled with confidence.
Because of the uncertainties that nevertheless remain the ampersand of the
manuscript has been preserved and the expansions of the other abbreviations
are indicated by italics.

Apparatus I: H compared with Wanley (Catalogus, p. 208) and Hᶜ.—Title]
Barely distinguishable in H by aid of Wanley; not in Hᶜ. DIEBUS] *sic*; diuinis
in table, f. 1ᵛ, and Ker's Catalogue, p. 286.   1 Se] *sic*; Sæ *Wanley*.   (on) gann]
sic; ongan *Wanley*.   2 ealle] *on line Hᶜ*.   3 ungesewenlice] *sic*; -sewend-
Wanley.   5 alysde] alusde *Hᶜ*.   6 (ðære)] ðæne *Wanley, Hᶜ*.   halgan
ðrynnysse *Wanley*; ha(l)gan ðrinnysse *Hᶜ*.   *Wanley stops here. Hereafter all
unmarked variants are readings of Hᶜ.*   7 gefrefrað. gyfe.   8 goodnisse.
10 geswicenysse.   11 soð-.   fæder.

Apparatus II: H compared with texts from which it was compiled.—Lines 1–54a
correspond to Ælfric's *Letter to Wulfgeat*, Assmann I. 8–61a. (Lines 65–84 of
the letter are used later.) The two manuscript authorities for this part of the
letter are P (Hatton 115, formerly Junius 23), ff. 95–96, and Z (Laud Misc. 509),
ff. 115ᵛ–17. Assmann's printed text is designated by Am. Variations of spelling
are not ordinarily given.   1 Se] hu se, *continuing a sentence, PZ.* wealdend]
god *PZ.*   ðe] se ðe *PZ.*   2 and] *not in PZ.*   3 gesewenlice] *Am
prints at end of preceding line.*   5 ure hælend crist] *Am prints at end of
preceding line. His lineation differs to the end of line 12 below.*   6, 7 *In PZ*
is (7) *directly follows* had (6).   7 ge-] *not in PZ.*

7 his Suna lufu,

7 heora begra willa, for ðan ðe hi wyllað an.

7 ðurh ðone Gast syndon soðlice geliffæste

ealle ða gesceafta ðe se Fæder gesceop　　　　　　　　15

þurh his ancennedan Suna, swa swa us secgað béc.

Ðeos is seo halige Ðry[n]nyss þe ealle þing gesceop,

an anre Godcundnysse æfre wuniende,

on anum mægenðrymme, 7 on anum gecynde.

Englas he gesceop on ænlicre fægernysse,　　　　　　　20

manega ðusenda, on micelre strengðe,

þæt hi mihton geseon Godes mærða mid him,

7 mid him wunian on his ecum wuldre.

Hi nabbað nanne (licha)man, ac hi libbað on gaste,

ungesewenlice (u)s þe on synnum libbað.　　　　　　25

(An)d þa [halgan] englas, þe on heofenum wuniað,

ne worhton (næ)fre nane (synne, ne hi) syngian ne magon,

buton ða(m) anum ðe þanon af(eoll)on

for heora mo(dignysse) ongean ðone ælmihtigan Gód.

And hi wurdon ða awende to (awyr)gedum deoflum,　　30

for ðan ðe hi noldon habban h(eora) Scyppend he(om to)

　　hlaforde,

ac wolde se fyrmesta him sylf beon God.

(Ða) ne mihte he (ge)wunian on ðære micclan mærðe,

ne eac his gegadan butan Gode(s) mihte,

ac wurdon ða asyndrode fram ðam soðan Gode,　　　　35

for ðam ðe hi forleton his hlafordscipe ealle,

swiðe unwislice, fram him a(scir)ode,

mid (and)an afyllede 7 mid orwennysse

ælcere mildsu(nge), [manfulle gastas.]

And (ælc þæra yfela ðe) on ðissere worulde becymð,　　40

App I: Readings of H^c:　12 lufe.　　　14 gost.　　　16 ancennedæ sunæ.
17 ðrimnysse.　　　18 an] *no reading.*　　　19 ane mægenðrimme.　　ane
gecynde.　　24 licham(an).　　　27 næfre.　　synne.　　28 ðam. afeollon.
29 modignysse *PZ*; *perhaps simply* mo(de) *in H, H^c.*　　　gód] *no accent.*
31 heom to.　　　33 Ða.　　　37 asciro(de).　　　39 mildsunge.
40 ælc . . . ðe] *no reading*

App. II:　13 begra] agen *PZ.*　　　16 secgað bec] *sic AmP*; bec seccað *Z.*
17 þrynnys *AmP*; ðrinnisse *Z*; ðrymnyss *H.*　　18 an] on *PZ.*　　26 halgan]
sic AmP; *om. ZH.*　　27 næfre] *not in PZ.*　　30 ða] *not in PZ.*　　35 soðum
AmP.　　36 ealle] *followed by point H*; *preceded by point P*; *Am prints at head
of next line.*　　37 ascyrede *AmP.*　　39 manfulle gastas] *sic AmP*; manfulne gast *Z*; *om. H.*　　40 on . . . becymð] oð ðis becom *PZ.*

eall hit gewyrð æ(fre þurh) þa awyrgedan gastas,
7 ðurh ða yfelan menn þe hi magun (forlæran)
to ðam yfelan willan þe hi on wuniað.

Witodlice on angynne (se ælmihtiga) God ealle ðing gesceop,
heofonas 7 eorðan, 7 ealne (middaneard,   45
þone wid)gillan garsecg, 7 þa wundorlican niwelnyssa,
7 (syððan þa twegen men *on sawle) 7 on lichaman,   * f. 4
Adam 7 Euan, to his anlicnysse;
7 se d(eo)fol be(swac) syððan eft þa menn,
þæt hi godes bebod tobræcon ðurh his lare,   50
7 wur(don þa) deadlice 7 fordemde to helle,
7 eall heora ofspring, to ðam ecan wite.
(Ac se mild)heorta Fæder, ðe ús to mannum gesceop
þurh his ancennedan Suna, wolde e(f)t alysan
ðurh ðone ylcan Suna eall manncynn   55
of deofle 7 fram ðam ecan deaðe,
7 he cydde þæt ðurh witegana cyðnysse
on manegum wis(um) ær ðan ðe hit gewurde,
þæt se heofonlica Æðeling her on worulde sceolde
to menn beon acenned of anum mædene.   60

App. I. Readings of Hᶜ: 41 æfre þurh.   42 magun.   45 heofanas.
44 se ælmihtiga] no reading. Both copies of H have indefinite space at end of line.
45–46 middaneard . . . wid-] middane. . . .   46 garseig.   47 syððan
. . . sawle] (sy)ððan . . . on sawle.   48 onlic-.   49 -swac. men.
51 wurdon ða.   53 ac se mildheorta.   54 ef(t).   57 witegana] sic.
58 manegun.   60 men.

App. II. 44 Witodlice . . . god] replaces a line and a half in Am, Nu sæde ic
(ic sæde Z) ðe ær þis on þam ærrum gewritum, hu se ælmihtiga drihten (god P).
45–47 The large gaps filled from Am except for traces in Hᶜ noted above.   49
and se] and hu se PZ.   52 ecan wite] ecum witum PZ.   54 suna]
sunu PZ. At this point correspondence with the Letter to Wulfgeat ceases, to be
resumed intermittently from line 135 on.

App. III. Parallels for 54b–74. 54b, 55: God Fæder geworhte mancynn and
ealle gesceafta þurh ðone Sunu, and eft . . . asende he ðone ylcan Sunu to ure
alysednesse. (CH I. 24, 31 sqq.)   56: þæt he us alysde . . . fram ðam
ecan deaðe. (LS XVI. 111–12.)   59: þone heofenlican Æþeling. (CH I. 82,
31–32.) 59, 60 (71,72): On middes wintres mæsse-dæge acende þæt halige mæden
Maria þone heofenlican Æðeling. (CH I. 356, 8–9. Cf. also line 97 below, Ser.
23.) 60: he wearð acenned of anum clænan mædene . . . and mann wearð gesewen. (LS XVI. 108–9.)   60, 61, 63: Se ylca Hælend syððan on þære syxtan
ylde/ þyssere worulde wearð to men geboren/ of Marian þam mædene for mancynnes alysednysse. (Assmann III. 60–62.) Crist com to mannum of Marian
ðam mædene . . . on þære sixtan ylde þissere worulde. (Old and New Test.
891 sqq.)

Ða on þær(e) syxtan ylde þyssere worulde
asende se halga Fæder his heahengel Gabriel
to Marian þam mædene, þe wæs Cristes modor,
7 het hyre cyðan þæt heo cennan sceolde
þæ(s) heofonlican Godes Sunu on hyre halgum innoðe;   65
7 heo ða gelyfde ðære liflican bodunge
7 cwæð him to andsware, Ic eom Godes þinen,
getimie me æfter þinum worde.

Heo wearð ða mid cilde æfter þære segene,
7 heo eo(de) mid þam cilde æfter gewunan   70
nigon monðas fullice oð middewintres (ti)man,
7 heo ða acende Crist urne Hælend
butan earfoðnysse, þæs ælm(ih)tigan Godes Sunu,
on soðre menniscnysse, middan(eardes Aly)send.

Ð(onne) we wyrðiað on Midde[wintre]s Dæge   75
ures Hælendes acenn(ed)nysse,
hu he to man(num) cóm on soðre menniscnysse,
mid flæsce b(e)fangen, for ure alysedny(sse),
of ðam halgan mædene Maria gehaten,
seo ðe ana is ægðer ge mæden (ge) moder.   80
Twelf dagas we wurðiað to wyrðmynte þam Hælende

App. I. Readings of H^c: 61 þissere.   63 moder.   65 þæs.
66 gelufde.   67 þinen] þiien (?).   70 eode.   71 timan.   74 men-
nysse (!).   alysent.   75 Ðonne. wirðiað. middes (*as in H*).   76 acen-
næonysse (!).   77 mannum] manne. mennysc-.   81 wirðmynte.

App. II. 75 *Here begins correspondence with Hom. XI, Sermo ad Populum*
(*Ser*), 6 sqq. *Variations in spelling not recorded.*   75 Ðonne] Ærest *Ser.*
middewintres *Ser.*   77 mannum *Ser.*   81–85 *Not in Ser.*

App. III. Parallels for 54b–74, cont. 62–65: Þa asende he his engel Gabrihel
to anum mædene . . . seo wæs Maria gehaten. þa com se engel to hire . . . and
cydde hire þæt Godes Sunu sceolde beon acenned of hire. (*CH* I. 24, 21 sqq.)
God sende hyre ða to Gabrihel his heahengel/ þæt he hyre cydde Cristes acen-
nednysse/ þurh hyre innoð. (Assmann III. 192–4.)   65: þæs heofonlican
Godes Sunu. (*LS* XVI. 106.)   66: And heo gelyfde þæs engles bodunge.
(*CH* I. 200, 27.)   66, 69: And heo þa gelyfde his wordum, and wearð mid
cilde. (*CH* I. 24, 25–26.)   67, 68: Ða cwæð Maria to ðam engle, Ic eom
Godes ðinen; getimige me æfter ðinum worde. (*CH* I. 200, 10.)   71, 72,
74: Heo . . . onfeng God on hyre innoð, and hine bær oð middewintres mæsse-
dæg, and hine ða acende mid soðre menniscnysse. (*Ibid.* 27 sqq.)   74:
middaneardes Alysend. (*Old and New Test.* 892.)
   Parallels for 81–85. 81, 82a: Cf. lines 128–9 below; less closely, 87, 172,
183, 192. (All these from 'Sermo ad Populum'.)

mid (urum) lofsangum for his micclan lufe
on his acennednysse timan, for (ðan) ðe he cóm to ús þa
[us] to alysenne of ðam laðan ðeowte
hellewítes, (gyf we) hine lufiað.   85
On ðam twelftan dæge þære tíde ymbganges
we (wurðiað) mid lofsangum hu ða geleaffullan cyningas
of eastdæle (comon, þe) Criste lac brohton,
7 hu he wearð gefullod fram ðam fulluhte(re Iohanne)
on ðære ea Iordane on ðam ylcan dæge,   90
þeah ðe he unsynnig (wære), ac he wolde sylf swa
gehalgian úre fulluht mid his halg(u)m licham(an),
7 ealle wæterstreamas mid his ingange.
On ð(am feowerteogoðan dæge) fram his acennednysse,
þe we cweðað on Englisc Ca(ndelmæssedæg,   95
bær) þæt halige mæden his modor Maria
þone heofonlican Æðeli(ng to þam hal)gan temple
mid þam ǽlicum lácum, swa swa se ælmihtiga G(od
ær Moysen) bebead, þam mæran heretogan,
7 se ealda Simeon him sealde (þær blet)sunge,   100
7 be him witegode, 7 eac seo wuduwe Anna.
He worhte on ðissere (worulde) wundra wel fela,
to geswutelienne þæt he soð God is:
blinde (he ge)*hælde 7 þa beddridan,   * f. 4ᵛ
healt(e) 7 hreoflige to fulre hæle,   105
þa wod(an 7 þa ge)wittleasan he gebrohte on gewitte,

App. I. Readings of H^c: 82 urum. micela*n*.   83 ðan.   85 gyf we.
87 wurðiað.   88 comon þe.   89 fulluhtere ioha*nne*.   91 wære.
92 halgum lichama*n*.   94 . . . teogoðan dæge.   95 cwæðað.   (c)andel-
mæss(e)dæg.   96 þær *for* bær (*no reading H*).   moder.   97 þane.
æðeling to ðam (halg)æ.   98 god] *no reading*.   99 ær moysen.
100 eald.   þær blet-] *no reading*.   102 worulde] *no reading*.   104 he ge-.
106 wodan 7 þa ge-.

App. II. 84 us] *not in H; supplied by conjecture*.   Lines *86–101 correspond*
to Ser. 12–27.   86 ymbeganges *Ser*.   92 halgan *Ser*.   96 bær]
sic Ser.   102–27 *Not in Ser. For parallels and sources see commentary*.

App. III. Parallels for 81–85, cont. 82*b* (81–84): Ure Hælend . . . cydde his
mycclan lufe þe he to us mannum hæfde, swa þæt he wearð acenned . . . to
ðy þæt he us alysde. (*LS* XVI. 106–11.)   84 and he us alysde of þam laðan
ðeowte (*Letter to Wulfgeat*, 65; cf. line 135 below.) se þe us alisde of urum
ðeowte syððan (*Old and New Test*. 38–39.)   84, 85 wolde us alysan fram
helle wite. (*LS* XVI. 87.)

7 þa deofla áfligde þe hi gedrehton (ær.

Up)pan s(a)e he eode, 7 þa sælican yða
hi(n)e abæron; 7 he þone blawendan wind
(mid) his h(æ)se gestilde, þæt he ætstod sóna, 110
7 þa scipmenn sædon þæt he soð Godes (Sunu) wære.
Wæter he awende to wynsuman wine,
7 ealle untrumnyssa he eaðe(lic)e gehælde,
7 ða deadan arærde þurh his drihtenlican mihte,
þæt hi lange leofodon on ðisum life syððan, 115
7 ælc gód he tæhte, swa swa þæt godspell ús segð,
7 ælc yfel he forbead 7 unrihtwisnysse,
7 we hine wurðiað on his weorcum 7 lare.
On sumne sæl he afedde fif þusend manna,
butan wifum 7 cildum, 7 hi wel gereordode, 120
mid fif berenum hlafum 7 twam lytlum fixum,
7 þær (wæron) to lafe twelf wilian fulle.
On oðrum sæle he afedde feower ðusend manna
mid seofon hlafum 7 feawum fixum,
7 hi læfdon þæs metes seofon spyrtan fulle, 125
7 þa wifmenn næron mid heora winclum getealde.
Ðyllice wundra wurðiað hine.
    On Lenctenes anginne we eac swylce wyrðiað
mid urum (l)ofsangum hu se leofa Hælend
on ðam westene fæste feowertig daga tosom(ne 130
7 hu he hine) ð(ær) costnode se hetola deofol,
ac he wearð oferswiðed þurh (þon)e so(ða)n Hælend.
    (Eft) we wurðiað on ufeweardan Lenctene
on halgum (ræ)dingum þæs Hælendes ðrowunge,
hu he us álysde of þam laðan ðeowte, 135
(7 fram) ðæs deofles anwealde mid his ag(enu)m deaðe,

App. I. Readings of Hᶜ: 107 ær. 108 Uppan sæ] no reading. 109 hine.
blawendon. 110 mid, hæse] no readings. 111 -men. sunu] sune.
113 eaðelice. | 115 lyfe. 116 tæhte] cæhte (!). 122 wæron. lo(fe).
wile. 123 oðre. 125 seofun. 126 wifmen. 128 wirðiað.
129 lof-. 130 westene] wesce(ne). tosomne. 131 7 hu he hine ðær
(H has tops of ascenders of hu he hine). 132 þone soðan. 133 Eft.
134 halige rædinge. 136 7 fram. agenum.

App. II. Lines 128–34 correspond to Ser 28–34. 131 he] written and
erased R; not in other MSS. of Ser. ðær] sic Ser and Hᶜ; an apparent ða in
H is probably a mutilated ðær. 135 sq.] Letter to Wulfgeat, Am. 65 sq.,
with hu for And.

on rode ahangen for uru*m* (synnum), unsynnig h(im) sylf,
gefæstnod mid feower nægelum 7 mid spere ge(wundo)d
on his swiðran sidan syþþan he gewiten wæs,
7 hu he wæs bebyrged (on ðam) ylcan dæge   140
7 us swa alysde mid his agenum deaðe.

He wearð þa bebyr(ged on) ðam ylcan dæge,
7 he aras of deaðe on ðam þriddan dæge,
mid ðam (ylcan) lichaman ðe he ǽr on ðrowode
to ecum ðingum awend, mid undead(licnysse),   145
gewunnenu*m* sige of þam w(æ)lhreowan deofle,
7 he him of anam his (agen) handgeweorc,
Adam 7 Euan, 7 eall þæt he wolde
of heora cynne þe him ge(cwem)e wæron.

And we wurðiað þa tíd wurðlice mid sangu*m*   150
seofon niht on (an), swyl(ce hit an dæg sy),
for ðære micclan mærðe manncynnes alysedny(sse.

On ða)m feowerteogeðan dæge þæs ðe he of deaðe aras
he astah to heo(fonum to his hal)gan Fæder,
ætforan his ap*ostolu*m, ðe him folgodon on life,   155
mid þ(ære menniscnys)se þe he of Marian genam,
7 mid þam ylcan lichaman þe he of d(eaðe) arær(de).

And we eac wurðiað wurðlice ðone dæg
on þære Gangwucan, for ðan þe he geopenode ús
on ðam foresædan dæge infær to heofonum   160
mid hi(s) agenum upstige, gif we hit 'ge'earnian wyllað.

And he sitt 'nu' on heofonu*m* (soþlice) *án Crist   * f. 5

App. I. Readings of H^c: 137 ure sinne. him.   138 gewundod.   140 on
ðam.   142 bebyrged on.   144 ylcan.   145 undead(lic)nysse.
146 wæl-.   147 a(gen).   149 gec(weme).   151 on an.   on dæg si.
152 -nysse.   153 On ð(am).   154 heofonu*m* to . . .   155 lyfe.
156 þare men . . .   157 deaþe . . .   158 we eac] wetac (!).   159
-ofenode (!).   160 forescedan (!).   161 his. gyf. geearum (!).
162 sit nu. soð. . . .

App. II. 137–9] *Revision of Ser 35–37:* hu he wæs gefæstnod for urum synnum on rode/ on Langgan Frigedæge mid feower næglum,/ and gewundod mid
spere syððan he gewiten wæs. *Line 137 is modelled primarily on Letter, Am 67:*
on rode ahangen, unsynnig for us; *hence the overloading.*   140 sq.] *Ser 38 sq.*
142 sq.] *Letter, Am 68 sq., replacing Ser 40.*   144 *sq.*] *Ser 41 sq.*
146–9] *Letter, Am 70–73.*   146 of] on *PZ.*   150–4] *Ser 43–47. Line
154 is also in Letter, Am 74.*   155] *Ser 49 (out of order).*   156] *Letter,
Am 75.*   157] *Ser 48 (lacks 7).*   158] *Ser 50.*   159 sq.] *altered
from Ser 51 sq.:* on Ðunresdæg on ðære Gangwucan,/ for ðam ðe he geopenode
us infær to heofonum.   161] *Ser 53.*   162–70] *Letter, Am 76–84.*
162 he] *not in Am.*

æt his Fæder swiðran, 7 ealra gesceafta gewylt,
7 cymð eft to demende on ðam micclan dæge
eallum manncynne, ælcum be his dædum,   165
7 we ealle menn cumað cuce him togeanes
of urum deaðe aræred ðurh his drihtenlican mihte,
ælc mann ðe ær cucu wæs on his moder innoðe,
þæt ure ælc ðær onfo edlean æt Gode,
swa gód swa yfel, be ðam ðe we geearnodon.   170
Eft ðæs embe tyn niht on urum ðeowdome
we mærsiað þone dæg mid mærlicum wyrðmynte
þe we hatað Pentecosten, on ðam cóm se Halga Gast
of heofonum swegende ofer (ða h)algan apostolas
on fyres gelicnysse, 7 afylde þæt hús   175
þær þær hi inne sæton, 7 sealde heora ælcum
swa micele mihte þæt hi mihton sprecan
mid eallum gereordum þe on eorðan syndon,
7 hi eac gebylde to ðære godspellican bodunge,
swa þæt hi unforhte ferdon geond þas woruld,   180
7 þa hæðenan gebigdon to þæs Hælendes geleafan,
7 fela wundra worhton, 7 gefullodon manncynn.
Seofon dagas we wurðiað mid urum lofsange on cyrcan
þone halgan tocyme þæs Halgan Gastes,
for ðære seofonfealdan gife þe he gifð mannum.   185
He todælð his gifa on geleaffullum mannum
be ðam ðe he sylf wyle, for ðan ðe he soð God is.
On ðære Pentecosten wucan we wurðiað þa tíd,
7 on ðam Sunnandæge ðe syððan bið þæræfter
we heriað mid lofsangum þa halgan þrynnysse   190
mid soðum geleafa(n),
7 we belucað swa mid urum lofsangum
þone halgan geleafan þe we habbað to Gode,

App. I. Readings of H^c: 165 ealle. dæde.   168 modor.   174 ða
halgan.   177 micele] mice. . . . H^c, bottom of f. 3. The verso is blank; no
more was copied.

App. II. 164 demende] demenne AmP; demde Z.   166 menn] not in
AmP; men Z.   167 aræred] arærde AmP.   171–85] Ser 54–68.
183 lofsange] sange Ser (lofsangum RT).   186 sq.] Ser 70 sq. (69 was
omitted, and hu at beginning of 70.)   188–90] Revision of Ser 72 sq.: On
ðyssere wucan we wurðodon ðas tid,/ and nu todæg we heriað þa halgan
þrynnysse.   191] not in Ser: a reference to the week following the octave of
Pentecost, Ser 74–75, is lacking.   192–6] Ser 76–80: end of excerpt.

for þan ðe we gelyfað on þone lyfigendan God,
on ða halgan Ðrynnysse þe heofonas gewylt   195
7 ealle gesceafta, an ælmihtig Scyppend.

We secgað nu be ðam soðan Gode
(þe eal)le ðing gesceop, se ðe ana is God,
þæt he is wunigende, swa swa ða witegan secgað,
æ(fre) on ðrim hadum, butan anginne 7 ende.   200
Se ælmihtiga Fæder nis of nanum oðrum;
se ges(trynde) ænne Sunu of him anum acennedne,
7 se wæs æfre wunigende ær anginne mid him
(on) his halgum bosme, 7 ðurh hine he gesceop
ealle þa gesceafta þe gesceapene syndon,   205
(for) ðan ðe he is se wisdom of þam wisan Fæder,
7 seo micele miht of ðam mihtigan (Fæder,
ðurh) ðone þe he gedihte ðone deopan cræft,
7 he ealle þing geliffæste þurh (ðone lyfigen)dan Gast,
se ðe is witodlice heora Willa 7 Lufu,   210
him bam gemæne on anre G(odcundnysse,
7) on anum mægenðrymme anes gecyndes.
He nis na acenned, ac he (cymð of him bam)
swa swa lufu 7 willa, for ðan þe hi wyllað an,
se Fæder 7 se Suna 7 se foresæda (Halga Gast).   215
Hi synd þry on namum on Ðrynnysse wunigende,
ac seo an Godcundnyss þe him eallum (is gemæne)
nele geþafian þæt hi þry godas syndon,
ac an ælmihtig God on soðre annysse.
N(u is se Fæder) Fæder 7 se Suna Sunu,   220
7 heora begra Willa, þæt is witodlice seo Lufu
heora (micclan mægenþrym)mes, æfre swa wunigende,
þæt heora nan nis læssa (ne lat)or þonne oðer,

App. II. 197–234] *The conclusion appended to the Interrogationes Sigewulfi, ed.*
MacLean, 511–45. Only two MSS. have this conclusion: R (CCCC 178), in a
section misplaced in CCCC 162, pp. 159–60, and S (Hatton 116), pp. 327–9.
MacLean's text is a diplomatic transcript of R, with proposed emendations and
variants in the apparatus. Except as indicated, I have taken the readings enclosed in
round brackets, signifying gaps in H, from R. Variations of spelling are not recorded.
197 *In RS not a new sentence but a clause introduced by* ac.   199 þæt he] se
þe *S.*   202 se] *om. R.*   acennedne] *sic MSS.* ; *MacLean* acennede.
204 he] *om. R.*   206 se] *om. R.*   213 ac he] ac *R*; 7 he *S.*   216 naman
RS.   220 Nu is se fæder fæder *S*; *second* fæder *erased R.*   se suna sunu]
sunu sunu *S*; se sunu (sunu) *R.*   223 *Between* nan *and* nis *S has* ne awent
of þam þe he wes æror ne heora nan. *MacLean's report of this reading is inac-*
curate and he does not recommend its acceptance but it looks authentic.

for ð(an ðe seo Godcund)nyss ne gæð næfre on twá,
ne heo nateshwon (ne underfehð nane lytlunge.   225
Se Sunu ana) is soðlice acenned
ærest of þam Fæder buton (ælcere meder,
7 eft of Marian butan eorðlicum Fæder),
þæt he us alysde 7 ús lif forgeafe
on his heo(fenlican wuldre mid his halgum) *englum.   * f. 5ᵛ
Ðæs we him ðanciað on urum þeowdome,   231
7 his halgan Fæder þe hine asende to ús,
þam is an wyrðmynt mid þam Halgan Gaste
on ealra worulda woruld; we cweðað, Amen.

App. II. 225 -fehð] -fohð *R*; -fæhð *S*.   228 eorðlican *S*.   229 *second*
us] *om. R*.   231–4 *Quoted by Wanley and still legible*.   233 an] *sic HS,*
not on *as in Wanley*; a *R*.

NOTES

1. The substitution of *Wealdend* for *God* sacrifices alliteration, and *ðe*
for *se ðe* spoils the parallel with *se ðe* in the next line, where even the addition of *and* seems infelicitous. Perhaps the added weight of *Wealdend*
seemed desirable when the subordinate clause of the *Letter to Wulfgeat*
was converted into the main clause of this first sentence, but I think
Ælfric would have revised more adroitly.

12. *and his Suna lufu.* Although this line is incomplete in Assmann's
two manuscripts, as well as in H, and might be regarded as a third member
of the preceding line because of the alliterative link, I suspect that a
balancing half-line dropped out of a very early copy. A likely candidate
in this formulaic passage is *of him bam gelice*, as at vi. 235; for the *begra*
in the next line in H is unlikely to be the original reading, being opposed
by the *agen* of Assmann's two manuscripts. *Agen* has the advantage of
alliterating with *an*, and its inferiority in logical exactitude is better understood if Ælfric had already used *bam* in the preceding line. If line 12 is
indeed defective, there is all the more reason to believe that the compiler
of xia was not Ælfric; for although he might have overlooked the mistake
in a fair copy, he would surely have noticed and corrected it while he was
in the act of revising for the compilation.

56. *of deofle.* The phrase is unusually short for one of Ælfric's half-lines,
but the mere addition of a definite article before *deofle* would not be an
incontestable improvement, since it would reduce the contrast with the
next phrase, *and fram ðam ecan deaðe.* Ælfric generally has the definite
article with *deofol* but by no means always (cf. *CH*. I. 12/18, 20, 22;
16/19; 18/31; 20/2; 22/27). When he omits the article, *deofol* perhaps
approaches the status of a proper name like *Satan*.

57–60. Prophecies of Christ are assembled in the second nativity sermon, *CH* II. 1; and the prophecies of the Virgin Birth are segregated in the sermon on the Annunciation, *CH* I. xiii (Thorpe 192, 194). Parallels to the phrasing of 57 and 58 have not caught my attention.

84. *us.* I have supplied this word because the grammar is defective without it. The preceding *us* may well have misled a not very attentive scribe into leaving it out.

102–27. The earliest of Ælfric's passages on the miracles is that which appears in *De Initio Creaturæ*, *CH* I. 26/7–20. The whole sermon is one of the few for which Max Förster was unable to find an exact source, and this passage is no exception, although it is obviously derived from the Gospels. After the three specific miracles mentioned at the beginning, the details and the organization are governed by *Luke* vii. 21 and 22, but other passages are in view as suggested below:

Ða worhte he fela wundra, þæt men mihton gelyfan þæt he wæs Godes Bearn (cf. *Ioan.* ii. 23). He awende wæter to wine (*Ioan.* ii. 1–11), and eode ofer sæ mid drium fotum (*Matth.* xiv. 25; *Marc.* vi. 48; *Ioan.* vi. 19), and he gestilde windas mid his hæse (*Matth.* viii. 26; *Marc.* iv. 39; *Luc.* viii. 24), and he forgeaf blindum mannum gesihðe (*Luc.* vii. 21, 22), and healtum and lamum rihtne gang, and hreoflium smeðnysse, and hælu heora lichaman; dumbum he forgeat getingnysse, and deafum heorcnunge (*Luc.* vii. 22; *Ioan.* v. 9; *Matth.* viii. 3; *Marc.* vii. 35); deofolseocum and wodum he sealde gewitt, and þa deoflu todræfde (*Luc.* vii. 21; viii, 26–40 etc.), and ælce untrumnysse he gehælde (*Luc.* vii. 21); deade men he arærde of heora byrgenum to life (*Luc.* vii. 22; *Ioan.* xi. 44); and lærde þæt folc þe he to com mid micclum wisdome (this and what follows elaborated from *Luc.* vii. 22); and cwæð þæt nan man ne mæg beon gehealden, buton he rihtlice on God gelyfe, and he beo gefullod (*Marc.* xvi. 16), and his geleafan mid godum weorcum geglenge (cf. *Matth.* vii. 21); he onscunode ælc unriht and ealle leasunga, and tæhte rihtwisnysse and soðfæstnysse (cf. *Ephes.* v. 9–11.)

If we compare this passage with the one under discussion (lines 102–27), it appears that the two are closely similar at several points. Both begin with the idea that Jesus performed the miracles in order to reveal his divine nature. The order of the list of miracles is considerably changed, partly no doubt because of the difficulties posed by alliteration, and partly to secure a different emphasis; but the items in the list are nearly all the same. Only the 'bedridan' have replaced the 'lamum', perhaps mainly for alliteration, the 'deofolseocan' have become 'gewittleasan' for the same reason, the deaf and dumb have been omitted. At the close of the list both passages, following the lead of *Luke* vii. 22, mention Christ's teaching. But the second passage, after doing this more succinctly than the first, adds a summarizing line (118): 'and we hine wurðiað on his weorcum and lare,' after which it mentions two additional miracles, devoting four lines to each with several specific details, and bringing the whole passage to a close with another summarizing line that gives a new turn to the verb in the one

I have just quoted: 'Ðyllice wundra wurðiað hine.' Further, we may observe that the added miracles, the feeding of the five thousand and the feeding of the four thousand, are drawn from *Matthew* xiv and xv, and that a change not yet mentioned in the earlier list involves the same part of the Gospel. For the successive clauses, 'eode ofer sæ mid drium fotum, and he gestilde windas mid his hæse', which refer to two different miracles as indicated above, have been expanded into four lines in such a way as to suggest a single occasion (lines 108–11), and the last of these, 'and þa scipmenn sædon þæt he soð Godes Sunu wære', takes us specifically to *Matthew* xiv. 33, for only in this account of the walking on the water is there any mention of those who were in the ship and their conviction that this was the Son of God. There is some justification for attaching to this occasion the stilling of the tempest, for it is stated that when Jesus entered the ship the wind ceased; but the explicit command to the wind belongs to the other story. It looks as if Ælfric had deliberately revised his earlier treatment of the miracles in an effort not simply to adapt it to the alliterative style now habitual with him but with additional stress on the spectacular miracles as evidence of divine power. In achieving this stress he had vividly in mind and made significant use of the miracles recorded in the fourteenth and fifteenth chapters of *Matthew*. There is even a list of those healed, different from Luke's but evocative, at *Matthew* xv. 30 and 31, just before the feeding of the four thousand.

Three other passages in which Ælfric enumerates Christ's miracles deserve mention here. One of them, though much abridged, is close enough to the two passages already discussed to be quoted. It occurs in one of the latest of Ælfric's compositions, *On the Old and New Testament*, 910 sqq. I have arranged the lines metrically:

He wunode þa mid mannum on þisum middanearde
þreo and þrittig geara and sumne eacan þærto,
and Cristendom arærde and kydde mid wundrum,
swa swa his godspell secgað, þæt he Godes Sunu ys,
þa þa he þa deadan menn þurh his mihte arærde,
and ælce untrumnysse eaðelice gehælde,
and he wæter awende to winlicum drence,
and ofer sæ eode eall drium fotum,
and windas gestilde mid his wordes hæse,
and deofla adræfde of gedrehtum wodum,
and forgeaf gewitt æfter wodnysse.

This passage echoes both *De Initio Creaturæ* and the passage under discussion, but it rearranges the order, leaves out the enumeration of specific physical infirmities, alludes to the teaching in a single phrase near the beginning, and ends rather quietly with the restoration of sanity after madness.

The two remaining passages, closely similar to one another but more limited in range than those already presented, are to be found in *De Memoria Sanctorum*, LS XVI. 134–41, and in the present collection, XVII. 8–17. These passages take their form and their limitation from *Matthew* iv, 23 and 24 instead of *Luke* vii. 21 and 22. Such echoes as they contain are more or less inevitable in view of the overlapping of themes, but they have some interest for us here because they include the 'bedridan' among those healed.

119–26. The miracle of the five thousand is related in all four gospels, that of the four thousand in *Matthew* and *Mark*. Ælfric's mention of the women and children at lines 120 and 126 is derived from *Matth*. xiv. 21 and xv. 38. The adjective *berene*, 'of barley', on the other hand, applied to the loaves in line 121, is derived from the *panes hordeaceos* of *Ioan*. vi. 9. Following the Vulgate, Ælfric has made a verbal distinction between the baskets of one miracle and those of the other. The *cophini* of the first miracle (as they are called in all four versions) are here called *wilian*; the *sportæ* of the second miracle (in both versions) are here called *spyrtan*. Precisely the same distinction occurs in Ælfric's earlier homily for the fifth Sunday after Pentecost, *CH* II. 396, where he is contrasting the two miracles: in the miracle of the five thousand the remnants fill 'twelf wylian'; in the other, 'seofan spyrtan'. In contrast, the West Saxon Gospels use *wilian* for both miracles.

126. *winclum*. Bosworth–Toller cites *wencel* three times from OE texts with the meaning 'child', once (in the Supplement) with the meaning 'slave' or 'servant'. One of the three citations with the meaning 'child' is from Ælfric's version of Basil's *Admonitio ad Filium Spiritualem*, ed. H. W. Norman (in *The Anglo-Saxon Version of the Hexameron of St. Basil*, etc. London, 1848), p. 34. This ancestor of *wench* was probably much commoner colloquially than its rare appearance in OE texts would suggest.

162. *an Crist*. The exact sense of the *an* is explained by a passage in Ælfric's homily on the purification of Mary, *CH* I. 150/21 sq.: '[He] wunað nu æfre on godcundnysse and on menniscnysse, an Crist, ægðer ge God ge mann.' Cf. also *CH* I. 40/19–22.

164. *demende*. The proper form, no doubt, is *demenne*, as in MS. P and Assmann, but there was probably some confusion between the inflected infinitive and the participle. Cf. Ælfric's *Old and New Testament*, 920 sq.: 'and cymð to demende eallum mancynne/ on þam micclan dæge, ælcum be his dædum.'

XII[1]

DOMINICA I POST PENTECOSTEN

Ioan. iii. 1–15

THIS homily, like VIII, has already been printed in the late disguise of MS. B in Belfour's *Twelfth Century Homilies*, where it is the first, pp. 2–12. With the aid of M and U, two of the most reliable of the Ælfric manuscripts of the mid-eleventh century, a text much closer to the author's can be presented.

Here, as in the four homilies numbered VII–X, I have chosen M as the basis of the text, partly because it represents an earlier issue of the five homilies than that which appears in U. In this homily, however, there are no signs of revision. Such differences as we find are more easily attributed to error, several times in M, less often in U. B, as in homily VIII, shows greater affinity with U than with M, but is not a direct descendant of U, for it sometimes supports readings in M against U.[2]

I have preferred the readings of M against BU at 6, 52, 78, 117, 202, and 218, though perhaps only the omission of *þam* at 218 (where it is needed for alliteration) can be charged against BU as an outright error. At 32 and its repetition at 186 I have allowed the word-order of M to stand simply because it is not obviously inferior to that of BU. M's *þam* in 224, though allowed to stand, may well be wrong. At 156, however, M's syncopated *singð* is clearly the right form for Ælfric rather than the *singeð* of BU.[3]

On the other hand I have preferred the readings of BU against M at 14, 41, 96, 167, 216, and 219, and especially at 125, 137, 151, and 157, where M is significantly inferior. (B deviates from U in minor ways at 125 and 137 but is in substantial agreement against M.)

---

[1] On matters relating generally to homilies VII–X and XII, see VII, introduction, pp. 333–7 above.

[2] Thus U has minor deviations in opposition to M and B at 27, 39, 100, 134, 179, and 225, besides a plain error at 228.

[3] See the introduction to VIII, p. 355.

Since Belfour has presented the text of B in full, I have limited
the variants cited from it to differences of word or phrase, omitting
mere differences of spelling unless it seemed desirable to compare
them with the spellings of U. The distinction between the two
forms of *g*, which Belfour properly records, is here ignored.[1]

In composing the homily Ælfric appears to have been guided
mainly by two earlier treatments of his text: one by Bede, Homily
II. 18 in Hurst's edition, the other by Haymo, Homily CVIII. More
often than not I have found Bede somewhat closer than Haymo.
This homily of Bede's was included in the collection of Paulus
Diaconus and also (slightly abridged) in that of Smaragdus. It was
also incorporated from beginning to end in Alcuin's *Commentaria
in Ioannis Evangelium*, which in this section is duplicated by the
pseudo-Bede commentary on *John*. Thus we cannot be sure where
Ælfric found it.

Haymo's homily consists almost entirely of a restatement, with
some elaboration, of Bede's. It resembles Ælfric's as opposed to
Bede's in one respect: it stops with verse 15 of the gospel instead
of verse 16. But the chief evidence that Ælfric consulted it is in his
explanation for Nicodemus's coming to seek out Jesus by night.
Ælfric's statement (at line 50) that Nicodemus dared not come
by day for fear the Jews would outlaw him is supported by Haymo,
not by Bede, who emphasizes only the allegorical implication of
night as ignorance. In a few other places, especially near the
beginning of the homily, Haymo seems a little closer than Bede,
but there is nothing else so striking.

Apparently Ælfric turned also to Augustine's commentary on
John. In Tractates XI and XII of this work Augustine covers a
slightly larger portion of the gospel and develops at length the
major ideas that Bede's homily in turn sets forth. Yet the language
and the elaborations are usually very different. Ordinarily it is
obvious that Bede (or Haymo) is much closer to Ælfric than
Augustine. If Ælfric consulted Augustine, as I think he did, he
must have decided that, at most points, the compression of Bede

---

[1] I have collated Belfour's text with the manuscript and noted the following
very minor inaccuracies: p. 2/22 Israela] Israele MS.   p. 2/31 him] hine
MS.   p. 4/6 ðe] de MS.   p. 4/34 hæðene] hædene MS.   p. 6/3 michte]
mihte MS.   p. 8/10 þæs] ðæs MS.   p. 8/17 andswerde] andswærde MS.
p. 8/23 ðat] ðæt MS.   p. 10/3 heofon-] heofen- MS.   p. 10/3 sæcgæn] sæc-
gen MS.   p. 10/30 naddræn] næddræn MS.

would better serve his purpose. But at one point his attention was caught by Augustine. At lines 156–8 of his homily, when he explains how it is that one can hear the voice of the Holy Spirit, the starting-point of his illustration and the rhetorical development of it are clearly inspired by a peculiarly arresting sentence in the twelfth tractate, in which a threefold repetition gives emotional force and a sense of progression to three successive aspects of Christian worship: the sounding of the psalms, of the gospel, of the divine word itself. Ælfric's partly original sequence is discussed in relation to Augustine's in the note on the passage. There is nothing comparable in Bede or Haymo.

The probability that Augustine's twelfth tractate was familiar to Ælfric is increased by the fact that he had certainly made use of another passage in the same tractate some years earlier, when he composed his first exposition of Jesus's words about the brazen serpent on which he comments for the third time (as is made clear by his allusion) in lines 224–38 below. The first exposition was in *Dominica V Quadragesime*, *CH* II. 238, 240; the second, in our XX. 333–52. The history of the three successive expositions and the sources of the first one are set forth in some detail in the note on XX. 333–52.

At another of the places where Ælfric deviates from his chief guides (98–105) he makes use of an interpretation of *Genesis* i. 2 that occurs in Bede's commentary on the Pentateuch. Perhaps it is something he remembered from his earlier study of *Genesis*, for he alludes to the same idea in the preface to his translation. For further details see the note on the passage.

DOMINICA *PRIMA* POST PENTECOSTEN

*Erat homo ex Phariseis, et reliq*ua

Sum Phariseisc mann was geháten Nichodémus,
an þæra ealdra Iudeisces folces:
se cóm hwilon nihtes to þam Hælende, and cwæð,
We witon, leof lareow, þæt ðu fram Gode cóme:
ne mæg nán mann soðlice swylce tácna wyrcan   5
swilce swa ðu wyrcst, buton God beo mid him.
Se Hælend andwyrde and þus him cwæð tó:
Soð soð ic þe secge, þæt nán mann ne gesyhþ
Godes ríce æfre, buton he beo eft acenned.
Him cwæð Nichodémus to, *swiðe þæs ofwundrod,   * f. 283
Hu mæg se ealda mann eft beon acenned?   11
Mæg he, lá, inn faran to his modor innoðe eft,
and swá béon geedcenn'e'd? Ac him cwæð se Hælend tó,

Text based on M (ULC Ii. 4. 6), ff. 282ᵛ–9ᵛ. Collated with U (Trinity B. 15.
34), pp. 281–95, and B (Bodley 343), ff. 4ᵛ–6ᵛ. The text of the latter has been
printed by Belfour, *Twelfth Century Homilies*, No. 1, pp. 2–12.
U's variants are given in full except for those mentioned at 1, 73, 107, 113.
On B's, see above, p. 477. Sentence-capitals accord with M's except at 209.
At 49–50 and 88–89 U's punctuation (after *swa* and *eft*) is disregarded.

Sup.: *No title B*. pharisseis *U* (e *superimposed on second* s) phariseis nichodemus nomine, princeps iudeor*um B*.
1 man *U* (*and frequently hereafter*); mon *B* (*and regularly hereafter*).
5 swilce *U*.   6 swylce *BU*.   swa] *om. BU* (*cf. 58*)   butan *U*.   7 him
cwæð to] sæde to hi*m B*.   8 gesihð *U*; sihð *B*.   9 butan *U*.
10 nichodemus to] *transposed B*.   12 in *BU*.

SOURCES. 1–6 [*Ioan. iii. 1*] Erat autem homo ex Pharisæis, Nicodemus nomine,
princeps Iudæorum.
[*2*] Hic venit ad Iesum nocte, et dixit ei: Rabbi, scimus quia a Deo venisti
magister, nemo enim potest hæc signa facere, quæ tu facis, nisi fuerit Deus
cum eo.
7–17 [*3*] Respondit Iesus, et dixit ei: Amen, amen dico tibi, nisi quis renatus
fuerit denuo, non potest videre regnum Dei.
[*4*] Dicit ad eum Nicodemus: Quomodo potest homo nasci, cum sit senex?
numquid potest in ventrem matris suæ iterato introire, et renasci?
[*5*] Respondit Iesus: Amen, amen dico tibi, nisi quis renatus fuerit ex aqua,
et Spiritu sancto, non potest introire in regnum Dei.
[*6*] Quod natum est ex carne, caro est: et quod natum est ex spiritu, spiritus
est.

Soð soð ic [þe] secge, swa hwá swa ne bið geedcenned
of wætere and of ðam Halgan Gáste, ne mæg he inn to Godes
ríce.   15
Ðæt þe of flæsce byð acenned, þæt bið witodlice flæsc,
and þæt þe of gáste bið acenned, þæt bið gást úntwylice.
Ne wundra ðu nateshwón þæt ic ðe nú sǽde,
þæt eow gebyrað þæt ge beon eft acennede.
Se gást orðaþ soðlice þær ðær he orðian wile,   20
and þu his stemne gehyrst, ac ðu swaðeah nást
hwanon se gást cume, oþþe hwider he fare;
þus bið ælc þæra manna þe of ðam gáste bið acenned.
Nichodemus him cwæð tó, Hu magon þas þing gewurðan?
Se Hælend *him andwyrde eft, þus him secgende: * f. 283ᵛ
þu eart æðele lareow on Israhela þeode,   26
and ðu þas þing nást? And he eft him tó cwæð,
Soð, soð ic þe secge, þæt we soðlice sprecað
þæt þæt we geare witon, and we éac seðað
þæt þæt we gesáwon, and ge ure gecyðnysse   30
nellað underfón nateshwon mid eow.
Gif ic eorðlice þing openlice eow secge,
and ge þæra ne gelýfað, hu gelýfe ge þonne
gif ic þa heofenlican ðing eow secgan wylle?
And nán mann ne astihþ nateshwón to heofenum,   35
buton se ðe of heofonum hider nyðer astáh,

---

14 þe] *sic BU*; eow *M.*   sæcge *BU.*   15 in *U*; cumen in *B.*   16 byð]
bið *BU.*   17 acænned *U.*   19 gebyreð *U*; bureð *B.* (*Cf. 141.*)
20 wyle *U*; wule *B.*   22 hwanan *U.*   25 sæcgende *BU.*   27 to
cwæð] cwæð to *U.*   28 sæcge *BU.*   29–30 and we ... gesawon *added
in margin by contemporary scribe U.*   32 openlice eow] eow openlice *BU*
(*perhaps rightly*; *cf. 186*).   sæcge *BU.*   33 þæra] heom *B.*   34 heofon- *U.*
wille *U*   35 heofonum *U.*   36 niðer *BU.*

18–27a [7] Non mireris quia dixi tibi: oportet vos nasci denuo.
[8] Spiritus ubi vult spirat: et vocem eius audis, sed nescis unde veniat, aut
quo vadat: sic est omnis, qui natus est ex spiritu.
[9] Respondit Nicodemus, et dixit ei: Quomodo possunt hæc fieri?
[10] Respondit Iesus, et dixit ei: Tu es magister in Israel, et hæc ignoras?
27b–37 [11] Amen, amen dico tibi, quia quod scimus loquimur, et quod vidimus testamur, et testimonium nostrum non accipitis.
[12] Si terrena dixi vobis, et non creditis: quomodo, si dixero vobis cælestia,
creditis?
[13] Et nemo ascendit in cælum, nisi qui descendit de cælo, Filius hominis,
qui est in cælo.

þæt is mannes Sunu, se ðe is on heofonum.

And swa swa Moyses on þam micclan westene
þa næddran up ahóf to healicum tácne,
swa gedafenað to ahebbenne on sumere héahnesse   40
[þone] mannes Sunu, þæt þa men *ne losion   * f. 284
þe on hine gelyfað, ac habban heom þæt éce líf.

Ðis halige godspell þe ge gehyrdon nú
hæfð micele getacnunge, ac we moton eow secgan
be eowrum andgite, þæt ge ealles ne beon   45
þære láre bedælede, ne ure Drihtnes wórda.

Se Sunderhalga wæs gehaten Nichodémus,
þe on nihtlicre tíde genealæhte to Criste:
wolde gehyran his halgan láre,
swá huru digollice nihtes, for ðan þe he ne dorste dæges,   50
for ðan þe þa Iudeiscan mid dyrstigum anginne
ælcne geútlagodon þe on hine gelyfde.

He wæs án þæra ealdra of ðam yldostum witum
Iudeisces folces, and he férde nihtes
to þæs Hælendes spréce, and him ðus cwæð þa tó: 55
'We witon, leof láreow, þæt ðu fram Gode cóme:
ne mæg nán mann soðlice swilce tácna wyrcan
swilce *swa ðu wyrcst, buton God beo mid him.'   * f. 284ᵛ

Wíslice he understód þæs Hælendes wundra,
and þa micclan mihte þe he on mannum gefremode,   60
for ðan þe he gehǽlde ælcne þe him tó cóm

---

37 is on heofonum] on heofone is *B.*   39 ahof] hof *U.*   41 þone] *sic*
BU; om. M. (Cf. 222.)   42 hine] him *B.*   heom] him *altered to* hym *U.*
45 *andgyte U.*   46 ures *U.*   48 -licere *U;* -lice *B.*   49 and
wolde *B.*   52 hine] him *B.*   gelyfdon *U;* ilyfdon *B.*   55 cwæð þa] þa
cwæð *BU*   57 swylce *BU.*   wyrcean *U;* wurcen *B.*   58 swylce *U;*
om. B.   butan *U.*   61 him to com] to him com *B.*

38–42 [*14*] Et sicut Moyses exaltavit serpentem in deserto; ita exaltari oportet
Filium hominis:
[*15*] ut omnis, qui credit in ipsum, non pereat, sed habeat vitam æternam.
49–54a [*Haymo, Hom. CVIII*] Nicodemus, . . . cupiens plenius instrui, ut
secretius eius allocutione perfrui posset, nocte ad eum venit. . . . Vel certe, quia
princeps Iudæorum erat, nocte ad Iesum venit, metuens sibi imminere aliquod
periculum. . . . Iam enim conspiraverant Iudæi, ut si quis eum palam confite-
retur Christum, extra Synagogam fieret.
59–62a [*Haymo*] Nam, ut supra evangelica lectio retulit, prædicante Domino
Hierosolymis in die festo, multi Iudæorum crediderunt in nomine eius, videntes
signa quæ faciebat. . . . Ex eis ergo qui crediderant, unus erat iste Nicodemus.
[*Bede, Hom. II. 18*] . . . prudenter ea quæ ab illo fieri videbat intellegere curavit.

fram eallum únhælþum; and he cwæð þa him tó
þæt he fram Gode cóme, and þæt God him mid wære,
and wolde his láre leornian æt him
digollice nihtes, þa ða he dæges ne dorste.   65
'Se Hælend andwyrde and þus him cwæð tó:
Soð, soð ic þe secge, þæt nán mann ne gesihþ
Godes rice æfre, buton he beo eft acenned.'
He cóm nihtes to Criste, and seo niht getácnode
his ágene nytennysse, þæt he nyste þa gýt   70
þæt seo oðer acennednys þe Crist embe þa spræc
wæs þæt halige fulluht þe he sylf astéalde,
on þam þe ealle menn beoð fram synnum aðwogene;
and Nichodémus þa on his nytennysse cwæð,
'*Hu mæg se ealda mann eft beon acenned?   * f. 285
Maeg he, la, inn faran to his modor innoðe eft,   76
and swa beon geedcenned?'
Ðas wórd þe he gecwæð to Criste mid nytennysse,
be þære acennednysse þe fulcuð is ús eallum,
þæt heo eft ne mæg beon geedlæht on lífe,   80
þæt man oþre siðe of his meder beo acenned,
þa habbað getácnunge, swa swa ðes traht us segð,
þære gástlican acennednysse on Godes gelaþunge,
þæt heo ne mót na beon geedlæht on þam menn,
þæt he tuwa underfó fulluhtes on lífe.   85
þeah þe se mæssepreost mánfull beo on lífe,
and he cild fullie on þam soðan geleafan

---

70 nytenysse *BU.*   71 -nys] -nysse *BU.*   embe] ymbe *U.*   embe
þa] þa embe *B.*   73 men *BU (and often hereafter).*   74 nyte'n'nysse
U; nytenysse *B.*   76 in *BU.*   moder *BU.*   78 þe] *om. BU.*
80 on] to *B.*   82 sægð *BU.*   86 þe se] ðe *B.*   87 fullige *BU.*

69–73 [*Bede*] Quis . . . sine lavacro regenerationis remissionem peccatorum
consequi, et regnum valet intrare cælorum? Sed Nicodemus, qui nocte venit
ad Iesum, necdum lucis mysteria capere noverat. Nam et nox in qua venit, ipsam
eius qua premebatur ignorantiam designat.
78–90 [*Bede*] Quia enim secundæ nativitatis adhuc nescius perseverabat, . . .
necessario de una quam noverat nativitate . . . quærebat. . . . Notandum autem
quia quod de carnali dixit, hoc etiam de spiritali est generatione sentiendum,
nequaquam videlicet eam postquam semel expleta fuerit, posse repeti. Sive enim
hæreticus, sive schismaticus, sive facinorosus quisque in confessione sanctæ
Trinitatis baptizet, non valet ille qui ita baptizatus est a bonis catholicis re-
baptizari, ne confessio vel invocatio tanti nominis videatur annullari.

þære halgan þrynnysse, ne sceal þæt cild
eft syððan beon gefullod æt beterum láreowe,
þæt seo halige þrynnyss ne beo swa geúnwurðod;   90
ne se yfela preost ne mæg þurh his *agene synna   * f. 285ᵛ
Godes þenunga befylan þe of Gode sylfum cymð,
for ðan þe se Halga Gast aþwyhð þone hæþenan
fram eallum his synnum on þam soðan fulluhte.
    'Ac him cwæð se Hælend tó,   95
Soð, soð ic þe secge, swa hwá swa ne bið [ge]edcenned
of wætere and of ðam Halgan Gaste, ne mæg hé inn to Godes
ríce.'
Ðis wæs geswutelod sona on anginne,
þa þa God ærest gesceop gesceafta þurh his mihte:
þa wæs Godes sylfes Gást, swa swa seo bóc ús secgð,   100
gefered ofer wæterum, þæt ure fulluht wære
ða íu getácnod mid toweardre mihte,
and þæs wæteres gecynd wurde gehalgod
þurh þone Halgan Gást, þe gehalgað ure fulluht,
and þa sawle wiðinnan fram eallum synnum aþwyhð.   105
Nú ne scyle ge healdan eowre cild to plihte
to lange hæþene, for ðan þe hi nabbað
*innfær to heofonum, gif hi hæþene acwelað.   * f. 286
Hi ne beoð na cíld soðlice on Domes-dæg,
ac beoð swa micele menn swa swa hi mihton beon,   110
gif hi fulweoxon on gewunelicre ylde.
And þa hæþenan cild on helle á wuniað,

---

88 ðrymnysse B.   90 þrynnys U; ðrymnysse B.   92 þenunge B.
93 þe se] ðe B.   aþwyhcð U; aþwæchð B.   95 se hælend tó] to þe hælend B.   96 geedcenned] sic BU; edcenned M (cf. 14).   97 in BU.
98 geswutelod] om. B.   99 gesceapta U; alle gesceaftæ B.   100 swa swa]
swa U.   seo] om. B.   sægð BU.   105 aþwehcð U; aþwæchð B.
106 sceole BU.   107 hy U (and eight times hereafter); heo B (and regularly
hereafter).   108 infær BU.   acwelað] dægeð B.   111 full- U.
-licere U.   112 on helle a] a on helle B.

91–94 [Haymo, after repeating much of Bede as above] Hoc autem sacramentum
nec malus peius, nec bonus melius implere potest. Quia qualiscunque sit minister
exterior, Spiritus sanctus operator est interior. . . . Aqua igitur exterius significat
quod Spiritus sanctus interius operatur, id est, mundationem peccatorum.
    98–105 [Not in Bede's or Haymo's homilies. Cf. Bede, In Pentateuchum, PL
XCI. 193:] Hoc quoque quod dicit, Spiritus Dei superferebatur super aquas
(Gen. i. 2), figurat Spiritum sanctum descensurum super Christum de aqua
baptismi in specie columbæ.
    106–15 [Not in Bede or Haymo.]

and þa gefulledon faraðto heofenum,
on lichaman and on sawle, and libbaðá syððan,
ge þa áne ge þa oðre, butan geéndunge.   115
'þæt þe of flæsce byðacenned, þæt byðwitodlice flæsc,
and þæt þe of gaste byðacenned, þæt byðgást untwýlice.'
Seo gástlice acennednyss byðungesewenlic,
and þæs lichaman acennednyss is gesewenlic eall,
þonne þæt cild wyxt, and gewyrðeft cnapa,   120
and eft syððan cniht, oþþæt he swá becymð
to þære ylde þe him geann his Scyppend.
Seo gástlice acennednys, þæt man Gode beo acenned
on þam halgan fulluhte, þurh þone *Halgan Gást,   * f. 286ᵛ
is us unge[sewen]lic, for ðan þe wé geséon ne magon   125
hwæt ðær bið gefremed on þam gefullodan menn.
Ðu gesyxt hine bedyppan on þam scíran wætere,
and eft up atéon mid þam ylcan híwe
þe he hæfde æror, ær ðan þe he dúfe;
ac seo halige modor, þe is Godes Gelaþung,   130
wát þæt þæt cild bið synnfull bedýped
innto þam fánte, and bið up abróden
fram synnum aðwogen, þurh þæt halige fulluht.
Þurh Adames forgægednesse, þe godes bebod tobræc,

113 gefullodan U; ifullode B.   heofonum U (and regularly hereafter).
114 on lichaman] mid lichame B.   115 ge . . . ge] ge . . . and B.
116 of flæsce] oflæse U.   bið U (twice); bid B (twice).   117 and] om.
BU.   bið (twice) BU (and 118).   119 and] om. B.   -nys U; -nysse B.
120 wyxð U; weaxæð B.   gewurð U; wurð B.   122 geann] on B.
123 gode beo] beo gode B.   125 ungesewenlic] sic U; unsegenlic B,
ungewunelic M.   127 gesihst U; isihst B.   bedypan U; biduppen B.
sciran] om. B.   128 ilcan U; ylcæ B.   131 synfull U; synful B.
132 in BU.   133 aþwægen U.   134 -nysse BU.   abræc U.

118–29 [Bede] Natura spiritus invisibilis, carnis est visibilis : atque ideo carnalis
generatio visibiliter administratur visibilibus incrementis : qui in carne nascitur,
per ætatum momenta proficit ; spiritalis autem generatio tota invisibiliter agitur.
Nam videtur quidem qui baptizatur in fontem descendere, videtur aquis intingui,
videtur de aquis ascendere ; quid autem in illo regenerationis lavacro (v. l.
lavacrum regenerationis) egerit, minime potest videri.
130–8 [Bede] Sola autem fidelium pietas novit quia peccator in fontem
descendit, sed purificatus ascendit : filius mortis descendit, sed filius resurrectionis ascendit : filius prævaricationis descendit, sed filius reconciliationis ascendit ;
filius iræ descendit, sed filius misericordiæ ascendit ; filius diaboli descendit, sed
filius Dei ascendit. Sola hæc Ecclesia mater quæ generat novit. . . . Qui ex aqua
et Spiritu regeneratur, . . . de carnali efficitur spiritalis. . . . Is qui per gratiam
Dei renovatur invisibiliter, fit spiritalis et Dei filius.

beoð þa cild synfulle; ac þurh Godes sylfes gyfe   135
heora synna beoð adylegode, þæt hi Godes menn beoð,
an[d] of ðam flæsclicum [hywe w]urðað gástlice,
and Godes bearn gehátene, swa swa ús béc secgað.
Se Hælend cwæð syððan to Nichodéme þus:
'Ne wundra ðu nateshwón þæt ic ðe nú sæde,   140
*þæt eow gebyrað þæt ge béon eft acennede.'   * f. 287
He wolde þæt he cuðe þa gástlican acennednysse,
butan þære þe he ne mihte his folgere beon,
and he hine þa tihte to ðære acennednysse
mid his diglum wórdum, þe he onwréah ús syððan.   145
'Se gást orðað soðlice þær þær he orðian wile,
and þu his stemne gehýrst, ac ðu swaðeah nást
hwánon se gást cume, oþþe hwyder he fare.
þus byð ælc þæra manna þe of ðam gáste bið acenned.'
Se Halga Gást orðað þær ðær he orðian wyle,   150
þonne he [hæfð þa mihte þæt he] mæg onlihtan
þæs mannes mód þe he wyle, and awéndan hit to góde,
fram dysige to wísdome, fram gedwýlde to geleafan,
fram synna fremminge to soðre dǽdbote,
and fram eallum wóhnyssum awéndan to rihte.   155
Ðær man Godes lof singð, þær swegð þæs Gástes stemn,

135 gife *BU*.   136 adilgode *BU*.   137 and] sic *BU*; and hí *M*.
hywe wurðað] sic *U*; heo wurðæþ *B*; gewurðað *M* (*evidently taking* hiwe wurðað
as hi gewurðað *and transposing* hi).   141 buræð *B*.   146 wyle *U*;
wule *B*.   147 stæmne *U*; stæfne *B*.   148 hwanan *U*; hwider *BU*.
149 bið *BU*.   ðara *U*; ðare *B*.   151 hæfð þa mihte þæt he] sic *BU*;
om. *M*.   155 awændan *U*; awend *B*.   156 singeð *BU*.   stæmn *U*;
stæfne *B*.

142–5 [*Not precisely in Bede or Haymo; but cf. Bede, earlier*:] Et quia Nicodemus ad primam Domini responsionem sollicitus, quomodo sit intellegenda
diligenter inquirit, meretur iam planius instrui, et quia secunda nativitas non
carnalis sed spiritalis audire. [*Haymo on this verse*:] Cuius mentem Dominus ab
admiratione removens, sacramentum secundæ nativitatis manifestius declaravit.
150–2a [*Bede*] Spiritus ubi vult spirat, quia ipse habet in potestate cuius cor
gratia suæ visitationis illustret. [*Haymo*] . . . quia cuiuscunque mentem vult
illuminat.
152b–5 [*The enumeration not in Bede or Haymo.*]
156–8 [*Bede*] Et vocem eius audis, cum te præsente loquituris qui Spiritu
sancto repletur. [*Haymo*] . . . cum is quem repleverit, te præsente, Deum confitetur. [*Aug. Tract. XII.* 5] Sonat Psalmus, vox est Spiritus; sonat Evangelium,
vox est Spiritus; sonat sermo divinus, vox est Spiritus. [*See note.*]

[þær man Godes lare segð, þær swegð þæs Gastes stemn,]
*and þær man embe God sméað, þær bið þæs Gástes gifu; * f. 287ᵛ
ac þu ne miht na geséon hu se sylfa Gást cymð
innto þam gódan menn þe Godes Gást underfehþ,   160
þeah ðe þu him on lócige and his láre gehyre,
for ðan þe se Gást is ungesewenlices gecýndes;
and se mann bið oþer, fram his yfele abróden
to beterum willan þurh ðæs Gastes gife.
'Nichodemus him cwæð tó, Hu magon þas þing gewurðan?
Se Hælend him andwyrde eft, þus him secgende: 166
Ðu eart láreow on Israhe[l], and ðu þas þing nást?'
Ne séde se Hælend þas wórd him to tále,
þæt he láreow wære and nyste þas gerýnu,
ac he wolde swiðor þa soðan éadmodnysse   170
him on gebringan to his beterunge,
butan þære ne mæg nán mann geðéon Gode.
'And he eft him tó cwæð,' swa swa ús cyð þis godspell,
'Soð, soð *ic þe secge, þæt we soðlice sprecað   * f. 288
þæt þæt we géaru witon, and we éac seðað   175
þæt þæt we gesáwon, and ge ure gecyðnysse
nellað underfón nateshwón mid eow.'
Se Hælend him sæde þæt þæt he sylf wiste,
and þæt þæt he geseah he gesoðode éac

157 þær mon godes lare sægð, þær swegð ðæs gastes stæmn BU(swægð, stæfne
B); om. M. (The spelling in the text normalized to accord with M.)   158
ymbe U.   160 into BU.   165 cwæð to] to cwæð B.   þas] þa(n)
B?   167 israhel] sic U; israel B; israhela þeodum M (see note).   171 him
on] on him B.   173 eft . . . cwæð] cwæð eft to him B.   175 geare BU.
179 þæt þæt] þæt U.

159–64 [Bede] Sed non scis unde veniat, et quo vadat: quia etiamsi te præsente
quempiam Spiritu ad horam impleverit, non potes videre quomodo eum intra-
verit, vel quomodo redierit, qui natura est invisibilis. Sic est omnis qui natus est ex
Spiritu. Et ipse enim invisibiliter agente Spiritu incipit esse quod non erat, . . .
quia gratia regenerationis venit in adoptionem filiorum Dei, et vadit in per-
ceptionem regni cælestis.
168–72 [Bede] Non quasi insultare volens ei qui magister vocetur, cum sit
ignarus sacramentorum cælestium, sed ad humilitatis illum viam provocans, sine
qua ianua cælestis non potest inveniri. [Haymo almost the same, but has tanti
mysterii for sacramentorum cælestium.]
178–85 [Augustine and Bede do not comment on verse 11; Haymo takes the first
person plural as signifying the Trinity, then adds:] Testimonium eius non acceperunt, quia sicut ipse dixit: Ego veni in nomine Patris mei, et non suscepistis me
(Ioan. v. 43).

þurh his geseðnysse, þeah ðe hi sume noldon   180
of ðam Iudeiscum his láre underfón,
ne his geseðnysse, him sylfum to rihtinge;
ac manega underfengon on eallum middanearde
þæs Hælendes geleafan and his láre geornlice,
and swa doð gýt æfre, oþ énde þissere worulde.   185
'Gif ic eorðlice þing openlice eow secge,
and ge þæra ne gelyfað, hu gelyfe ge þonne
gyf ic þa heofenlican þing eow secgan wylle?'
Embe eorðlice þing he sæde þam Iudeiscum,
þa ða he him sæde be his sylfes ðrówunge,   190
and be þam æriste his agenes lichaman,
þe he *of eorðan genam of eorðlicre meder;   * f. 288ᵛ
and be heofenlicum he spræc hér be þam fulluhte,
and þa ða he eft spræc be his upstige to heofonum
to þam écan lífe, þe is heofonlic gewiss;   195
and þa ungesæligan his segene ne gelyfdon.
'And nán mann ne astihð nateshwón to heofenum,
buton se ðe of heofenum hider nyðer astáh,
þæt is mannes Sunu, se ðe is on heofenum.'
Se Hælend is soðlice anes mannes sunu,   200

---

180 *after* geseðnysse] *B inconsequently repeats lines 128b–138. See Belfour,
p. 8, n. (which should read, 'After line 25').*   182 him *altered to* hym *U*;
heom *B*.   185 get *U*.   ænde *U*.   186 openlice eow] eow openlice *BU* (*cf. 32*).   187 þæra] ðeo *B*.   188 gif *BU*.   heofon- *U*;
heofen- *B* (*Belfour* heofon-).   wille *U*.   190 him *altered to* hym *U*;
heom *B*.   sylfes] agene *B*.   191 þam . . . lichaman] his agene lichames
ariste *B*.   192 -licere *BU*.   193 heofon- *U*.   196 sægene *U*;
sæge *B*.   198 niðer *U*.

189–96 [*Bede*] Terrena illis dixit, ut in superiori lectione invenimus, cum de
passione ac resurrectione sui corporis, quod de terra assumpserat, loqueretur
dicens: *Solvite templum hoc, et in tribus diebus excitabo illud* (*Ioan. ii. 19*). Non
tamen credebant. . . . Qui ergo terrena audientes non capiebant, quanto minus
ad cælestia, id est, divinæ generationis capienda mysteria sufficiunt! Addit autem
adhuc Dominus et de cælestibus sacramentis, et de terrenis instruere eum. . . .
Cælestis namque est ascensio eius ad vitam sempiternam, terrena vero exaltatio
eius ad mortem temporalem. [*Ælfric passes over the last part of this sentence,
which looks ahead to verse 14*.]
200–11 [*Ælfric substitutes simple assurance for Bede's questions, but takes some
hints from the passage quoted below for 212–18 and also from the following:*] Sed
et hoc quærendum quomodo dictum sit: *Et nemo ascendit in cælum, nisi qui
descendit de cælo*, cum omnes electi se veraciter confidant ascensuros in cælum,
promittente sibi Domino quia *ubi sum ego, illic et minister meus erit* (*Ioan. xii. 26*).
. . . Iesus electorum omnium caput est: itemque omnes electi eiusdem capitis

swa swa nan oþer nis, and he is ure Héafod,
and he astáh of heofenum ús to alýsenne,
and he eft up astáh æfter his ðrówunge,
and he behét his halgum þæt hi him folgian moston,
and mid him wunian þær ðær he sylf wunað.   205
He astáh þa ána, ac him æfter fyligdon
his agene lima, up to ðam Héafde,
and ǽfre folgiað, oþ énde þissere worulde;
*for ðan þe his halgan heonon faraö to him,   * f. 289
of þisum lǽnan lífe to heora leofan Drihtne,   210
oþþæt hi ealle beon to þam Heafde gegaderode.
Seo menniscnys ne cóm ná mid Criste of heofenum,
ne heo on heofenum næs þa þa he þis gecwæð;
ac se án Hǽlend on ægðrum gecýnde,
Godes and mannes, mihte swa wel sprecan   215
swa [swa] ge gehýrdon on þissere rǽdinge,
þæt he of heofenum astáh, and on heofenum wǽre,
þa þa he þus gespræc to þam Nichodéme.
'And swa [swa] Moyses on þam micclan westene
þa næddran up ahóf to héalicum tácne,   220
swa gedafenað to ahebbenne on sumere héahnysse
þone mannes Sunu, þæt þa menn ne losion
þe on hine gelyfað, ac habbon heom þæt éce líf.'
Ðis andgit we sǽdon on þam twam oþrum spellum

---

201 nis] is *B.*   202 and] *om. BU.*   207 heafode *U.*   209 for] *cap. M.*
heonan *BU.*   212 -nyss *U*; nysse *B.*   215 wæl swa *B.*   216 swa swa]
sic BU; swa *M.*   218 þam] *om. BU.*   219 swa swa] *sic BU*; swa *M*
(*cf. 38*). on] in *B.*   220 neddran *U.*   223 habban *BU.*   heom]
him *altered to* hym *U.*   224 andgyt *U.*   þam] *om. BU.*

---

membra sunt (*Ephes. i. 22; I Cor. xii. 27*). . . . Nemo ascendit in cælum, nisi
Christus in corpore suo, quod est Ecclesia, qui in seipso quidem primum,
cernentibus apostolis eminentioribus nimirum membris suis, ascendit, et exinde
in membris suis quotidie ascendens se colligit in cælum.

212–18 [*Bede*] Merito autem quæritur, quomodo dicatur Filius hominis vel
descendisse de cælo, vel eo quo hæc in terra loquebatur iam fuisse in cælo. Nota
est namque confessio fidei catholicæ, quia descendens de cælo Filius Dei,
Filium hominis in utero virginali suscepit, eumque completa dispensatione suæ
passionis resuscitavit a mortuis et assumpsit in cælum. Non ergo caro Christi
descendit de cælo, neque ante tempus ascensionis erat in cælo. Et qua ratione
dicitur, *nisi qui descendit de cælo, Filius hominis, qui est in cælo*, nisi quia una
Christi persona est in duabus existens naturis? Atque ideo Filius hominis recte
dicitur et descendisse de cælo, et ante passionem fuisse in cælo, quia quod in sua
natura habere non potuit, hoc in Filio Dei a quo assumptus est, habuit.

swiðe gewislice, *ac we wyllað swaðeah   * f. 289ᵛ
sceortlice secgan þas geéndunge eow.   226
Moyses se heretoga on þam micclum wéstene
worhte be Godes hǽse ane ǽrene nǽddran,
þa þa þæt folc wæs fram ðam næddrum tosliten,
and he þa up arǽrde þa ǽrenan nǽddran   230
swilce to tácne, and hi besawon þærtó
þe ðær toslitene wæron, and heom sóna wæs bet.
Seo ærene nǽddre, þe búton attre wæs,
getacnode Cristes deaþ, þe unsynnig þrówode,
up ahafen on róde; and we to him beseoð   235
mid fullum geleafan, þæt we fram urum synnum
þurh hine beon alýsde, and líf habban mid him
á on écnysse, swa swa he ús behét;
þam is á wurðmynt and wuldor on écnysse,
mid his heofenlican Fæder, and þam Halgan Gáste,   240
on ánre godcundnysse; we cweðað, AMEN.

225 swiðe] om. U.   226 þas geendunge eow] eow þas endunge B.
228 worhte] om. U.   neddran U; neddræn B.   229 neddrum U; næddræn B.   231 swylce BU.   232 heom] him altered to hym U.
233 butan U.   237 alysede BU.   habbon U.   239 on] á on U.
240 heofon- U.

227–32 [Num. xxi. 4–9] Et tædere coepit populum itineris ac laboris. . . .
Quamobrem misit Dominus in populum ignitos serpentes. . . . Oravitque Moyses
pro populo, et locutus est Dominus ad eum: Fac serpentem æneum, et pone eum
pro signo; qui percussus aspexerit eum, vivet. Fecit ergo Moyses serpentem
æneum, et posuit eum pro signo; quem cum percussi aspicerent, sanabantur.
[Bede's summary seems no closer.]
    233–8 [Bede] Recte per serpentem æneum Dominus ostenditur, qui venit in
similitudine carnis peccati, quia sicut æneus serpens effigiem quidem ignitis
serpentibus similem, sed nullum prorsus in suis membris habuit ardorem veneni
nocentis, quin potius percussos a serpentibus sua exaltatione sanabat: sic
nimirum, sic redemptor humani generis non carnem peccati, sed similitudinem
induit carnis peccati, in qua mortem crucis patiendo credentes in se ab omni
peccato, et ab ipsa etiam morte liberaret.

NOTES

55. to þæs Hælendes sprǽce, 'to speak with the Saviour'. This idiom
seems to be of Latin origin, as is suggested by Haymo's partially similar
expression, eius allocutione, in the passage quoted as a source. A closer
parallel is Bede's account of Ethelred's reception of Augustine: rex . . .
iussit Augustinum . . . ad suum ibidem aduenire colloquium (Hist. Eccl. I,
cap. xxv, Plummer p. 45), which is translated in the Old English Bede,

se cyning . . . het Agustinum . . . þider to his spræce cuman (ed. Miller, I.
58/18–20; quoted by BT, 'spræc', VIII). Ælfric uses the expression also
at XXI. 380, *cuman to his spræce*, and at *LS* IV. 356 sq., *Bæde þu . . . þinre
modor spræce*, which Skeat translates, 'Thou didst ask for a conversation
with thy mother'. (Cited by BT.)

72–138. This section dealing with baptism has parallels in the *Sermo in
Æpiphania Domini, CH* II. 36–52, esp. 48, 50. With line 73, cf. Thorpe
48/29, ' þæt fulluht us aþwehð fram eallum synnum'. With the injunction
in 82–94 against being twice baptized, cf. Thorpe 48/13–25. With the
warning against delaying the baptism of children, 106–15, cf. Thorpe
50/15–25, and also the homely advice of *De Infantibus*, printed by Napier
in *Anglia*, X (1888), 154 sq. (On Ælfric's possible authorship of this piece,
see Introduction, pp. 55–56 above. Lines 98–105 and 118–38 are not anticipated in the earlier homily.

98–105. The prefiguration of baptism in *Genesis* i. 2 is not mentioned
elsewhere by Ælfric, so far as I have observed, except in his preface to
Genesis, *O.E. Hept.* 78/55 sqq.,

> Eft stynt on þære bec on þam forman ferse: *Et spiritus Dei ferebatur
> super aquas*; þæt is on Englisc, 'and Godes gast wæs geferod ofer
> wæteru.' Godes gast ys se Halga Gast, þurh þone geliffæste se Fæder
> ealle þa gesceafta þe he gesceop þurh þone Sunu, and se Halga Gast
> færþ geond manna heortan and sylð us synna forgyfnysse ærest ðurh
> wæter on ðam fulluhte. . . . .

Probably this passage, like the one under consideration, is derived from
Bede's commentary on the Pentateuch. There is no such explanation in
Bede's *Hexameron*, in Augustine's commentaries on *Genesis*, or in Alcuin's
Interrogationes.

101. *gefered ofer wæterum*. All three manuscripts have the dative
wæterum, but in Ælfric's preface to *Genesis*, quoted in the previous note,
and in his translation of *Genesis* (*O.E. Hept.*, p. 81), the accusative
wæteru is used, corresponding to Latin *aquas*.

111. *fulweoxon*. I have treated this, with hesitation, as one word, like
the past participle, *fulweaxen*, because the special sense seems to be best
conveyed if *ful-* is treated as a prefix with no more than secondary stress.
Ælfric's use of *w* for alliteration tends to support this. Cf. XI. 310 and
note.

137. *hywe*. This reading of MS. U (whose reading I have adopted for
the entire line) must be correct. Perhaps B's *heo* is intended as merely
another spelling of the same word, but it is easily mistaken for the nominative plural of the personal pronoun and was so understood by Belfour.

156–8. It is clear from the threefold sentence of Augustine that B and
U preserve the correct reading and M's has been accidentally shortened
by homoeoteleuton; but the relation of Ælfric's clauses to Augustine's is

interesting. Augustine, by his invariant *vox est Spiritus*, accents the progression, *Psalmus, Evangelium, sermo divinus*. Ælfric's *Godes lof* corresponds well to *Psalmus*, but his *Godes lare* appears to combine *Evangelium* and *sermo divinus*. Hence he completes Augustine's idea in a progression of two stages instead of three, and this is confirmed by his use of exact repetition, *þær swegð þæs Gastes stemn*, for the second stage only. He now creates a third stage of his own, where there is variation in both members, for *meditation* replaces song or speech and requires that *stemn* be replaced by such a purely spiritual term as *gifu* and *swegð* by a mere *bið*.

167. The reading of B and U is supported by several considerations. At first sight M seems to be repeating the text as it was given earlier and as we expect; but the adjective *æðele* of line 26 has dropped out. Omission of the adjective shortens the line, but retention of *þeode* (now altered to *þeodum*) prevents it from being reduced to a mere half. In B and U, on the other hand, a purposeful alteration may be seen: the whole line has become a half by omission of *æðele* and by reduction of *Israhela þeode* to *Israhel*. Now the next half-line, which would otherwise be left dangling at the close of the speech, completes a new whole. Proof that this was Ælfric's intention seems to be provided by the fact that the matching half-line (originally 27b, *And he eft him to cwæð*), when repeated at line 173, is supplied with a second half to complete it. There is no similar provision, however, for the splitting of line 13 at 77 and 95.

180. The word *geseðnyss*, 'affirmation', though it seems to have survived only in this passage, was cited by Napier from U in his 'Contributions to Old English Lexicography' and has been printed by Belfour, p. 8/25–27, with the late spellings *gesæþnysse* and *sæþnysse*.

224. *þam twam oþrum spellum*. One of these is the homily for the fifth Sunday in Lent, *CH* II. 224–40, primarily an exposition of *John* viii. 46–59, but introducing at the end (pp. 238–240) a careful exposition of the verses here under consideration, *John* iii. 14, 15. The other is evidently *De Populo Israhel*, our xx, for it not only gives the story of the brazen serpent (lines 304–32) as it is presented in *Numbers* xxi. 4–9, but interprets it (333–52) in accordance with the gospel, with an explicit reference to a previous treatment of the text in 'sumum oðrum spelle' (335). Thus the present homily, with its reference to *two* previous treatments of the subject, must have been composed after *De Populo Israhel*. On the three passages and their sources, see the note on xx. 333–52. The function of the demonstrative *þam* in M's reading is not clear to me. Ælfric could hardly have expected anyone else to know which two sermons he had in mind. I have allowed the reading to stand on the chance that we are dealing with an illogical colloquialism, but the reading of B and U may well be correct.